HANDBOOK OF HUMAN RESO
IN THE MIDDLE EAST

[redacted]

In memory of my nephew, Joginder Malik, and my parents, Major Abhe Ram and Daya Kaur. To Laxmi and Gaurav for their continuous support and love (PB).

In memory of my father. To my children, Ismail, Hamza and Leila, who never cease to amaze me (KM).

To those who have an interest in the management of human resources in the Middle East region.

Handbook of Human Resource Management in the Middle East

Edited by

Pawan S. Budhwar

Professor of International Human Resource Management, Aston Business School, Aston University, UK

Kamel Mellahi

Professor of Strategic Management, Warwick Business School, University of Warwick, UK

Edward Elgar
PUBLISHING

Cheltenham, UK • Northampton, MA, USA

Published by
Edward Elgar Publishing Limited
The Lypiatts
15 Lansdown Road
Cheltenham
Glos GL50 2JA
UK

Edward Elgar Publishing, Inc.
William Pratt House
9 Dewey Court
Northampton
Massachusetts 01060
USA

Paperback edition 2017

A catalogue record for this book
is available from the British Library

Library of Congress Control Number: 2016942185

This book is available electronically in the **Elgar**online
Business subject collection
DOI 10.4337/9781784719524

MIX
Paper from
responsible sources
FSC® C013056

ISBN 978 1 78471 951 7 (cased)
ISBN 978 1 78471 952 4 (eBook)
ISBN 978 1 78471 972 2 (paperback)

Typeset by Servis Filmsetting Ltd, Stockport, Cheshire
Printed and bound in Great Britain by TJ International Ltd, Padstow

Contents

Section C Human Resource Management in North Africa

Contributors

Fida Afiouni is an Associate Professor of HRM at the Olayan School of Business, American University of Beirut, Lebanon.

Khaled Essa Al-Ajmi is a Recruitment Consultant in Kuwait.

Sara Essa Al-Ajmi is Adjunct Faculty in the Mass Communication Department, College of Arts and Sciences, Gulf University for Science and Technilogy, Kuwait.

Rayya Al Amri is a Doctoral Researcher at the School of Management, University of Bradford, UK.

Fawaz Baddar ALHussan is an Assistant Professor in International Negotiations and Sales Management, IESEG School of Management, Lille Catholic University, France.

Faten Baddar AL-Husan is a Lecturer in International Human Resource Management, Newcastle University London, UK.

Misida Al-Jahwari is a Lecturer in Human Resource Management, Department of Management, College of Economics and Political Science, Sultan Qaboos University, Oman and also a Doctoral Researcher at Aston Business School, Birmingham, UK.

Rob E. Bateman is Director of Graduate and Executive Programs, School of Business and Management, American University of Sharjah, UAE.

Pawan S. Budhwar is a Professor of International HRM at Aston Business School, Birmingham, UK.

Nelarine Cornelius is Professor of Organisation Studies, Queen Mary, University of London, UK.

Abdallah Elamin is an Associate Professor, College of Industrial Management, King Fahd University of Petroleum and Minerals, Saudi Arabia.

Ali El Dirani is an Assistant Dean, Faculty of Business Administration, Al-Maaref University, Beirut, Lebanon.

Ghada El-Kot is a Professor in Human Resources and Organizational Behavior, Graduate School of Business and Deputy President for Strategic Affairs, Arab Academy for Science and Technology and Maritime Transport, Egypt.

Antonio Giangreco is Professor in HRM and OB at IESEG School of Management, Lille, France.

Alison J. Glaister is a Lecturer in Strategic Human Resource Management, The York Management School, University of York, York, UK.

Cherif Guermat is Professor at the Centre for Global Finance, Bristol Business School, University of the West of England, Bristol, UK.

Edelweiss C. Harrison is an Adjunct Faculty member at Business Bethany Global University, Bloomington, MN, USA.

Wes Harry is Knowledge and Development Advisor, GCC Foundation; Visiting Professor, University of Chester, UK and Honorary Fellow, Cass Business School, UK.

Arno Haslberger is Senior Research Fellow, Middlesex University Business School, UK.

Abderrahman Hassi is a Lecturer of Management School of Business Administration, Al Akhawayn University, Morocco.

Manjusha Hirekhan is a Doctoral Researcher at Aston Business School, Birmingham, UK.

Dima Jamali is a Professor of Management, Kamal Shair Endowed Chair in Leadership, American University of Beirut, Olayan School of Business, Beirut, Lebanon.

Ramin Mahmoudi is Faculty, Université d'Orléans, France.

Kamel Mellahi is a Professor of Strategic Management at Warwick Business School, UK.

Dima Ramez Murtada is Faculty at Université Paris Ouest Nanterre La Défense, Paris, France.

Sinine Nakhle is the Career Services Officer of the Faculty of Arts and Sciences and an Instructor of Psychology, American University of Beirut, Lebanon.

Pari Namazie is a Managing Partner, Atieh International, Vienna, Austria.

Yassir Abdulaziz Nasief is a Research Associate at Birkbeck College, University of London, UK.

Amir Mohammad Pahlavnejad is a Managing Director, Atieh Roshan Consulting, Vienna, Austria.

Eric Pezet is a Professor at Université Paris Ouest Nanterre La Défense, France.

Salma Raheem is a Doctoral Researcher at the London School of Economic and Political Science, London, UK.

Boumediene Ramdani is a Lecturer in Strategy, University of Exeter Business School, Exeter, UK.

Susan Sayce is Faculty at Norwich Business School, University of East Anglia, Norwich, UK.

Sneha Singh is a Lecturer in Maharani Kishori Devi College, Rohtak, India.

David P. Spicer is Associate Dean, Academic Management and Planning, School of Management and School of Law, University of Bradford, UK.

Mohammad Ta'Amnha is Faculty at German-Jordanian University, Jordan.

Hayfaa A. Tlaiss is Associate Professor, College of Business, Alfaisai University, Saudi Arabia.

Olga Tregaskis is a Professor of International HRM at Norwich Business School, University of East Anglia, Norwich, UK.

Jacob Vakkayil is an Assistant Professor OB and HRM at IESEG School of Management, Lille Campus, Lille, France.

Barbara Covarrubias Venegas is a Researcher and Lecturer, University of Applied Sciences for Management and Communication, Vienna, Austria.

Marie F. Waxin is an Associate Professor, School of Business Administration, American University of Sharjah, UAE.

Preface

Since we edited an initial volume on human resource management (HRM) in the Middle East a decade ago (see Pawan S. Budhwar and Kamel Mellahi 2006. *Managing Human Resources in the Middle East*. London: Routledge), a number of significant socio-political-, economic- and security-related developments have taken place in the region, some of which are still unfolding. In particular, the changes from late 2010 (i.e., from the initiation of the Arab Spring, forcing down of dictators and rulers from power and the proclamation of the world caliphate by ISIS – Islamic State of Iraq and Syria, which have led to major upheavals) have been phenomenal, resulting in both regional and global disturbances in the form of hundreds of thousands dead and mass migration from the region. Such developments have implications for the management of human resources in firms operating in the region.

Indeed, there is a growing body of literature now emerging related to the management of human resources in the region. Some attempt has been made to put together a collection of works to provide a more conclusive picture of the scene (e.g., see special issue of *International Journal of Human Resource Management*, 2014, vol. 25, issue 2, guest edited by Fida Afiouni, Huub Ruël and Randall Schuler). Nevertheless, there is no single volume which provides a comprehensive picture regarding the context-specific nature of HRM issues for the region. An attempt has been made in this volume to highlight the contextual and human resource (HR) functional issues, country-/region-specific forces determining HRM systems in eight countries, and a large number of emerging themes central to HRM and proposals for ways forward highly relevant for the region.

The shock created by the fall in oil prices in the late 1980s, a rapidly growing population and over-reliance on foreign workers and talent in order to run many economies in the region (amongst other factors), forced many countries of the region to think about reducing their dependency on the oil industry and diversify into other sectors via the development of their human resources. This is highly pressing in the present context (marked not only by the above-mentioned changes but also by the present crash in oil prices). Indeed, many countries in the region have been aggressively pursuing such a strategy, but it has created high levels of unemployment and other HRM related issues, which are examined in this volume. We hope this volume will provide useful information to both policy makers and researchers to enable them to deal with challenges faced by the HR function in the region in their respective ways. It will also help business students to gain an understanding of the different issues relating to HRM in the region. Thus, the objective of this book is to provide the reader with an understanding about the dynamics of HRM in the Middle East. It should also enable the reader to better understand the 'context-specific' nature of HRM in the region.

To achieve our objective, we invited all the contributions to be written around a set framework. It included an introduction and background information on a given topic/country; core issues pertinent to the given topic/country; factors influencing the core topic(s) of a given chapter; conceptual, theoretical and empirical development; the present scenario; emerging key challenges and recommendations; and the way forward. Accordingly, we believe this handbook consolidates in a single volume the dynamics of management of human resources in the Middle East, and in particular questions pertaining to the '*what*', '*why*' and '*how*' of HRM in the region. All the chapters in this volume are original contributions to the field and were specially commissioned for the handbook.

We would like to thank all those who have in various ways helped to make this project a success. Our special thanks to all the contributors and staff at Edward Elgar – Fran O'Sullivan, Emily Neukomm, Katy Roper, Benedict Hill and Aisha Bushby – for their enthusiasm and promptness, which helped us to complete this work.

Pawan Budhwar
Aston Business School
Kamel Mellahi
Warwick Business School

PART I

CONTEXTUAL AND FUNCTIONAL ISSUES

1. The Middle East context: an introduction

Pawan S. Budhwar and Kamel Mellahi

This handbook provides an in-depth input on a variety of topics related to human resource management (HRM) in the Middle East. It is divided into three parts: contextual and functional issues, country and regional perspectives, and emerging themes and the future of HRM in the Middle East. This introductory chapter has three main aims. First, to highlight the dynamic context of Middle East within which this handbook has been developed. Second, to analyse the key developments in the field of HRM in the region and the need for this volume. And third, to provide a summary of each chapter.

THE MIDDLE EAST CONTEXT

The term Middle East defines a cultural area, so it does not have precise borders, and a variety of terminologies have been used to denote the region. These vary from 'Middle East', 'Near East', 'Middle East–North Africa (MENA)', 'Southwest Asia', 'Greater Middle East', 'Levant', 'Arabian peninsula' or the 'Arab World' in a very general sense, terms used by both academics and policy makers (see Encyclopaedia Britannica, 2015). The most limited version of the region includes Gulf State countries, namely Kuwait, Saudi Arabia, Bahrain, Qatar, United Arab Emirates and Oman, as well as Iran, Iraq and the Levant region, while in some cases the region extends to countries in North Africa with a clear connection to Islam and that use the Arabic language, like Libya, Tunisia, Algeria, Morocco and Mauritania to the west and Sudan, Eritrea, Djibouti and Somalia to the south-east. For this handbook, the latter interpretation of the Middle East is used.

Despite some commonalities between the countries in the region, each nation has its own historical developments, an independent (and at times unique) set of socio-economic components, arising inevitably from the interplay of socio-cultural institutions, historical developments, demographic variables and political relations, and systems unique to themselves. This is further complicated by the different stages of industrialisation and economic and political development of each nation in the region. Such contextual complexities should be kept in mind while analysing HRM systems of the region.

The Middle East is the birthplace of three main religions: Islam (followed by approximately 95 per cent of the total population out of which 85 per cent are Sunnis and the remaining Shias), Judaism and Christianity. It is also home of some of the oldest civilisations of the world such as the Phoenicians, Babylonians and Egyptians. The population of the Middle East is over 380 million, representing about 6 per cent of the total world population. The region also hosts around 65 per cent of the world's known oil reserves. However, until the discovery of oil in 1960s and 1970s, the region had the lowest levels of economic development in the world. The economic growth of majority of the countries in the region has been flat. The sharp fall in oil prices by about 60 per cent between 2014 and 2015 is a specific challenge for many of the oil-exporting countries of the region. It is estimated that oil exporting countries in the Middle East may lose around $300 billion in oil revenues in 2016 (Knowledge@Wharton, 2016).

The slow economic growth in the region can be attributed to a combination of factors such as the so-called curse of natural-resource abundance (over-dominance of the oil sector in oil-rich countries); structural imbalances; deficient political systems and political reforms; underdeveloped financial markets; slow integration into the global economy; dominant, inefficient public sectors; growing unemployment; lack of creation of employable skills; strong inclination of many locals in Gulf State countries to work only in public sector firms, and, similarly, in managerial positions; under-utilisation of skilled women; dated and inefficient government systems in the region; and the conditions of war and conflict and mass migration (see Abdalla, 2015; Budhwar and Mellahi, 2006; Iles et al., 2012; Matherly and Al Nahyan, 2015; Sidani et al., 2015).

Further, developments since late 2010 (i.e., the beginning of the Arab Spring, the toppling down of governments in many countries in the region and the proclamation of the world caliphate by ISIS – Islamic State of Iraq and Syria – amongst others) have resulted in regional (and to some extent global) disturbances in the form of hundreds of thousands of dead and mass migration from the region – mainly from Syria, both into adjoining countries and into Europe (for details see Wikipedia, 2015). Such developments have serious implications for foreign direct investment (FDI) in the region, and due to serious concerns for security, a large number of multinationals have pulled out of the disturbed parts of the Middle East, leaving a significant vacuum for economic growth. Such developments have many socio-economic and human resource (HR) implications, such as dealing with increasing unemployment and human capital management (e.g., Goby et al., 2015; Matherly and Al Nahyan, 2015; Singh and Sharma, 2015).

Emerging evidence suggests that most countries in the Middle East are now focusing on both HR and organisational development (see Kolachi and Akan, 2014; Singh and Sharma, 2015). In particular, the oil-rich countries have been making serious efforts to reduce their dependence on oil and develop other sectors, which need skilled human resources (e.g., Manafi and Subramaniam, 2015; Obeidat et al., 2014). Similarly, many countries in the region have been concentrating on the development of 'locals' and reducing the number of 'foreigners' due to the pressure of rapidly growing populations, and to provide jobs to their natives (see Goby et al., 2015; Matherly and Al Nahyan, 2015). In this regard, many countries, such as Saudi Arabia, Oman and the United Arab Emirates (UAE), have been pursuing 'nationalisation programmes' (i.e., to reserve jobs for locals). However, there are serious concerns related to employable skills and the mind-set of the locals who prefer not to work in the private sector and on lower-level positions. Such developments have serious implications for the HR function in the region and in particular in relation to its role towards improving organisational performance (Waal and Sultan, 2012; Iles et al., 2012; Mellahi and Budhwar, 2006; Mohamed et al., 2015; Zaitouni et al., 2011).

Further, the globalisation of business and management education and training continues to progress in the Middle East, where West-based, reputed business schools have opened and/or plan to open branches in the region. The University of Qatar, for instance, was ranked as the world's most international university in 2016 by the Times Higher Education's ranking. These and other related institutions tend to adopt West-based curriculum and texts to teach and train local students, the majority of whom end up working in the region. Such skills are appropriate to work in large and multinational companies, which are run professionally, but less so in local and small firms. This creates a mismatch between educational and vocational training programmes and the creation of employable and suitable skills for the Middle East context. Such dynamics demand the need to develop context-specific HR programmes.

To summarise, the Middle East region is now continuously in the news and is of interest to most nations of the world for a variety of reasons including economic, political and demographic challenges, migration, the supply of oil, ongoing conflicts and security issues. Along with the above-reported developments, we can also see developments in the field of HRM with the establishment of HR departments and formalisation of HR functions in the region. Further, we are witnessing that most countries in the Middle East are placing a large emphasis on the development of their human resources. There is also a drive by most countries in the region to further assimilate into the global economy. Nevertheless, a number of macro-level phenomena unique to the region (discussed above) are creating challenges in this regard. Such developments have serious implications for the HRM function in the region, especially when HRM is known to play a significant role in the economic development of nations (e.g., Debrah et al., 2000). The next section provides an overview of developments in the field of HRM in the Middle East as reported in the literature.

DEVELOPMENTS IN MIDDLE EAST HRM

A review of the literature presents variations between the countries regarding both the kind of research conducted on HRM in the region and the nature and status of the HRM function. It also highlights the absence of systematic analysis, which can present an overview regarding the dynamics of HRM in the Middle East (for an exception see Budhwar and Mellahi, 2006). Nevertheless, we can see an increasing number of publications emerging related to various aspects of HRM in the Middle East (e.g., see the special issue 'HRM in the Middle East: toward a greater understanding' of the *International Journal of Human Resource Management* – Afiouni et al., 2014). Below we summarise the main HR-related works for the region and later highlight the key messages emerging from the same.

Perhaps the majority of the research work on HRM in the Middle East has focused on providing a country-specific overview. Our first book, a decade ago, provided an overview of HRM in 14 countries in the region (for details, see Budhwar and Mellahi, 2006). Here we report literature published in the field mainly after 2006 to avoid the duplication of information. In this regard, see the works of Al-Hamadi et al. (2007), Khan (2011), Katou et al. (2010) and Khan et al. (2015) on Oman; Tlaiss and Elamin (2015) on Saudi Arabia; Namazie and Frame (2007), Soltani and Liao (2010) and Manafi and Subramaniam (2015) on Iran; Omair (2010) and Singh and Sharma (2015) on the UAE; Altarawneh and Aldehayyat (2011) and Syed et al. (2014) on Jordan; Tzafair et al. (2007) on Israel; Leat and Al-Kot (2007) and Mostafa and Gould-Williams (2014) on Egypt; Ramdani et al. (2014) on Algeria; and Zaitouni et al. (2011) on Kuwait. The focus of the above-mentioned works has been to highlight the emerging patterns of HRM and related systems along with their key determinants in respective countries.

Other themes emerging from the literature include the effects of regulations on HRM in the Saudi Arabia private sector (Mellahi, 2007) and on employment policy in Kuwait (Al-Enizi, 2002), the impact of HRM on organisational commitment in the banking sector in Kuwait (Zaitouni et al., 2011), the efficacy of high-performance work practices in Algerian firms (Ramdani et al., 2014), the impact of HRM practices and corporate entrepreneurship on firm performance in Turkish firms (Kaya, 2006), talent management strategies in the UAE (Singh and Sharma, 2015), the impact of cultural value orientations on preferences for HRM (Aycan et al., 2007), HRM and labour productivity in Libyan oil companies (Mohamed et al., 2015), HRM and innovation in the Iranian electronics industry (Manafi and Subramaniam, 2015) and career development in Oman (Khan et al., 2015).

Over the past quarter of a century or so, there has been a consistent emergence of gender-based studies (in particular dedicated towards women in management-related issues) in Middle East countries. In this regard, see the works of Tlaiss (2015) and Abdalla (2015) for career success/facilitators and barriers for women in an Arab context, Sidani et al. (2015) for female leadership advantage and leadership deficit, Marmenout and Lirio (2014) for female talent retention in the Gulf, Metcalfe (2008) for women in management in the Middle East generally, and in particular for Bahrain, Jordan and Oman, Aycan (2004) for Turkey, Metle (2002) for Kuwait, and Izraeli (1987) for Israel.

Along with gender, another theme along which we have regular contributions is that of the influence of Arab culture and values on its management systems (e.g., Ali, 2004, 2010; Mellahi, 2003). A related focus of research has been to examine the impact of Islamic values, Islamic work ethics and Islamic principles on the management of human resources in the region (see Branine and Pollard, 2010; Mellahi and Budhwar, 2006; 2010). As expected, due to socio-cultural similarities, a number of countries (such as Egypt, Morocco, Turkey, Kuwait and Qatar) tend to be similar on various aspects of cultural value orientations, such as strong on group orientation, hierarchical structures, masculinity and following Arab traditions and weak on future orientation (see Kabasakal and Bodur, 2002). Mellahi and Budhwar (2006) reveal the influence of high power distance on managers' perception towards the delegation of authority to lower levels of employees and interaction with employees in countries like Morocco, Kuwait, Saudi Arabia and Egypt. They also highlight that in such contexts and socio-cultural and traditional set-ups, loyalty to one's family and friends is expected to override loyalty to organisational procedures and this often results in the use of inequitable criteria in recruitment, promotion and compensation. Ali (2004) and Mellahi (2006) further highlight that the influence of Islamic values and the principle of '*Shura*', that is, consultation, social harmony and respect, is manifested in consensus based decision-making styles, respect for authority and age, and concern for the well-being of employees and society at large in countries like Kuwait and Saudi Arabia. On the contrary, Ali and Al-Kazemi (2006) reveal that several ideal Islamic values such as equity and fairness are often not adhered to in practice. This explains the widespread adoption of some HRM practices in the Middle East that are not compatible with Islamic values, such as the use of nepotism in recruitment and compensation, known as '*Wasta*' in Gulf Cooperation Council (GCC) countries and '*Piston*', '*M'aarifa*' and '*K'tef*' in North African countries. Similarly, Iles et al. (2012) highlight the challenges for effective management of human resources in the public sector in Middle East where the impact of *wasta* is strong.

A review of the literature also reveals some publications related to the transfer of

HRM from overseas to the region (e.g., Al-Husan and James, 2009; Mellahi and Frynas, 2003). Nevertheless, due to significant differences (sociological, economic, legal, political, etc.) between the region and other parts of the world (the West, in particular), on the one hand, and the context-specific nature of HRM, on the other, it is recommended that a foreign element is, at best, not conducive to the development of sound management practices in the region (also see Neal and Finlay, 2008; Khan, 2011). Research by Saleh and Kleiner (2005) reiterates the above point for American companies stating that if they want to be successful in the Middle East then they should develop an understanding of the local culture, politics and people of the region. Along similar lines, Goby et al. (2015) highlight the usefulness of the creation of a positive diversity climate based on Arab cultural traditions in managing the diverse workforce (comprising both locals and expatriates) in the region.

A further rapidly emerging HR research and practice theme in the Middle East is related to 'human resource development', which not only focuses on the development of locals, and helps put them in jobs, but also focuses on issues related to the impact of Arab management styles on the effectiveness of cross-cultural negotiations and organisational development activities in the region (see Kolachi and Akan, 2014). In this regard, Matherly and Al Nahyan (2015) propose the need for effective governance of national–expatriate knowledge transfer to build competitiveness, whereas Goby et al. (2015) highlight the need for the development and practice of an interpersonal communication and diversity climate framework in order to facilitate workforce localisation in countries which mostly have an expatriate workforce such as the UAE. Al-Rajhi et al. (2006) reveal the challenges for HRM in the region regarding the adjustment of impatriates. The research by Rodriquez and Scurry (2014) further confirms the need for foreign firms and employees to be highly responsive/adaptive to the local requirements in order to be successful in the Middle East context.

As indicated above, a number of countries in the region have also been actively pursuing nationalisation programmes (i.e., bringing more locals into jobs and reducing the dependence on foreign nationals). Such policies have major implications for the management of workplace quotas (Matherly and Al Nahyan, 2015), talent management (Singh and Sharma, 2015), interpersonal communication and diversity management (Goby et al., 2015), and for making such nationalisation programmes successful (e.g., Al-Waqfi and Forstenlechner, 2014).

There is also evidence that the names and nature of traditional personnel departments are being changed in the Middle East to emphasise the development of effective HRM systems to help firms compete at home and abroad. However, due to the scarcity of skilled HR professionals in most Middle Eastern countries, HR managers often rely on 'trial and error' to cope with the impact of macro-level changes taking place in the region including severe international competition. In order to cover such skill gaps, Middle Eastern countries are heavily investing in the development of their human resources. However, several factors (such as a lack of emphasis on developing analytical thinking in schools, a lack of a vocation-based education system, a negative perception about the participation of women in the main workforce, amongst others), in combination, are proving to be the main bottlenecks (see Mellahi, 2006; Abdalla, 2015; Sidani et al., 2015).

Based on the above analysis, it can be concluded that certainly there has been a rapid increase in the emergence of literature regarding different aspects of HRM in the Middle

East. Though, at present it is patchy, as a result of which it is difficult to draw a conclusive and comprehensive picture of the scene. Such evidence also does not allow us to assume the existence of a 'Middle Eastern HRM model', that is, a single HRM model with distinct Middle Eastern characteristics (Khan, 2011). This can also be attributed to the diversity between nations in the region, the lack of a key role played by different institutions such as trade unions, the absence of an effective labour legislation framework and so on. As a result, it seems that organisations in the Middle East use a whole range of different HRM policies and practices, and that the professionalisation of HRM functions is at different stages in different countries. Nevertheless, we can see an emerging and reliable trend towards an increasing interest of both practitioners and researchers in finding out about the HRM systems relevant to the Middle East region. Also, it is evident that information regarding the use of local and indigenous constructs is now emerging (as highlighted in a few chapters in this volume). Research on such constructs is much needed as it will provide insights into the underlying processes relevant for effective management of human resources in the region and contribute to theory development. A possible way forward is to conduct a systematic analysis starting from the basics and leading to an advanced analysis before assessing forthcoming key issues. This can help to provide a comprehensive analysis and a more reliable picture of the scene. An attempt is made in this regard in this handbook.

PLAN OF THE HANDBOOK

The 23 chapters in this volume cover three broad themes: contextual and functional issues; country and regional perspectives; and emerging themes and the future of HRM in the Middle East. In order to achieve consistency and a comprehensive picture of the scene, we asked all the contributors to write along specific themes. These included background information; core issues pertinent to a given topic/country; factors influencing the core topic(s); conceptual, theoretical and empirical developments; the present scenario; emerging key challenges and recommendations; and the way forward. Most of the contributors are either natives of the Middle East or have worked, and/or are still working and researching in HRM in the region for a significant period of time. Hopefully, this has enabled the authors to present a more realistic picture about various aspects of HRM.

In Chapter 2, Namazie and Venegas explore the implications of culture on HRM in the MENA region. Initially they provide an overview on the impact of globalisation on HRM and the developments in HRM across cultures. Then they examine the MENA context with an overview of the region, followed by a discussion on the national culture and related socio-cultural factors affecting HRM in the region. In particular, they discuss the cultural perspectives and their link to HR practices. The chapter closes with the implications of linkages between culture and HRM for both practitioners and researchers.

Building on Chapter 2, Harry presents in Chapter 3, a critical perspective on the rapidly changing societies and regional situations which are driving the way HRM is practised in many organisations in the Middle East. He propagates the idea that the way HRM, or management in general, treats existing and potential employees plays into the manner in which society-level changes become positive or negative in their impact. Utilising information about the demographic changes taking place in the Middle East, the level of the education system dominating the region and the prevalence of a complex mix of societal-level factors, Harry highlights the challenges faced by principal HRM activities such as resourcing, learning, rewards, retention, and performance management. He concludes his chapter by indicating the positive developments taking place in the field of HRM in Middle East.

In Chapter 4, Giangreco and Vakkayil explore the nature and patterns of performance appraisal systems (PAS) emerging in the Middle East. In particular, they focus on the issues surrounding performance appraisals. They first summarise the logics embedded in the use of PAS in Western contexts and discuss their potential limitations when applied to the Middle East context. They then highlight the emerging logics important for PAS in the region and conclude their chapter by identifying key challenges and related recommendations, which could lead to successful results from PAS implemented in the Middle East set-up.

In Chapter 5, Raheem presents a thorough analysis of the past and present scenarios of talent management in GCC countries. Initially she presents her conceptual stance about the construct of talent management by defining it, and then she highlights the complex mix of institutional forces which affect talent management in the GCC nations. She also covers the topics of work ethics and the attitudes of locals and the challenges they create for the management of talent in the region. Raheem further highlights the organisational-level barriers to talent management and concludes her presentation by suggesting ways forward for effective talent management and future research avenues on the topic in the Middle East context.

The handbook provides in-depth information on the scenarios of HRM in eight countries in the region. In Chapter 6, Al-Jahwari and Budhwar present an overview regarding the nature of HRM in Oman, focusing on four main HR functions: recruitment, selection, training and compensation. To set the context for the analysis, information on Omani societal culture and its current political structure, economy, education and research is provided. They also discuss the issue of workforce localisation and HRM practices, the current challenges faced by HR managers and make recommendations regarding how best to handle the same. The latter part of the chapter looks at the emerging HRM model in Oman and sets an agenda for the future research direction.

In Chapter 7, Waxin and Bateman analyse the scenario of HRM in the UAE. They first examine the core issues and factors influencing HRM (such as the cultural and labour market characteristics, the evolving UAE education system and the Emiratisation process) in the country and then analyse the literature on HRM in the UAE. They also highlight the key HRM challenges in the UAE and make a number of recommendations for practitioners and researchers to tackle these by developing relevant systems and via research outcomes.

Chapter 8 is dedicated to HRM in Saudi Arabia. Tlaiss and Elamin first provide an overview of the major factors that impact the overall status of the workforce in Saudi Arabia, including various governmental reforms. Next, they summarise the key developments pertaining to research on HRM in the country. They also highlight the challenges faced by the HR departments and functions in Saudi Arabia and discuss the way forward. In addition, they discuss key findings from an empirical study that examined a set of traditional core HRM topics, such as selection and recruitment, performance appraisal and promotion, as well as the status of women, style of management, and business ethics.

In Chapter 9, Namazie and Pahlavnejad explore the nature and emerging patterns of HRM in Iran. They begin by examining the Iranian context and analysing the role of factors such as history, economy, demography, national culture and socio-economic developments, religion, management and leadership in Iran on HRM. Next they discuss HR developments in Iran and support their presentation with research findings on HRM in ten companies to highlight the nature of the HR function. Later, this chapter presents the key challenges faced by HRM and its future in Iran.

Chapter 10 deals with HRM in Lebanon. Afiouni and Nakhle present a systematic review of HRM and highlight the nature of national factors that might be shaping HRM practices. They further reflect upon current HRM practices and the challenges faced in light of cultural and institutional realities by HR functions in Lebanon. Lastly, the chapter covers areas of research that HR scholars and practitioners should focus on to push the field forward in the country.

El-Kot, in Chapter 11, highlights the critical need for an effective HRM function that can enable Egyptian organisations to compete internationally in the global economy. She begins the chapter with a description of the Egyptian business context by highlighting the importance of understanding the socio-culture and religion, which effect the implementation of HRM in organisations in Egypt. Next she provides an analysis of the core HR practices in Egypt such as recruitment and selection, training and development, performance appraisal, and rewards and benefits. Finally, El-Kot covers the key challenges and opportunities for future developments in human resources in Egypt.

In Chapter 12, Ramdani, Mellahi and Guermat focus on HRM in Algeria. They initially discuss how the recent changes in the socio-political and economic environment coupled with changes in the cultural and institutional environment are affecting HRM policies and practices in Algeria. They further discuss the status and role of the HR department in Algerian firms, with a specific focus on high performance work practices (HPWP). They utilise an empirical study to support their presentation and arguments. The chapter concludes with a summary of results, a brief discussion of the main challenges facing the HR function in Algeria, and suggestions for future research.

Chapter 13 highlights the state of HRM in Morocco. Hassi presents a portrait of HRM practices, focusing on Moroccan small and medium businesses. He uses data from semi-structured interviews with HR managers to highlight the nature and pattern of HRM practices. In order to set things in context, he provides a historical account of development in HRM. His discussion also covers challenges facing the HRM function and the future of HRM in Morocco.

The remaining ten chapters in the handbook are dedicated to emerging topics and ways forward for HRM in the Middle East. In Chapter 14, Al-Ajmi, Hirekhan, Budhwar, Al-Ajmi and Singh focus on the topic of employment relations in the context of domestic workers in Kuwait. Their analysis is based on the findings of an empirical study and from the perspective of employers. Initially they provide an overview on the scenario of domestic workers in the Middle East. This is followed by a presentation on the findings of their empirical research investigation. A variety of issues related to relevant legislation; sponsorship of domestic workers for jobs, their recruitment and the role played by the recruitment agencies in the same; and other issues surrounding the employment relations of domestic workers are highlighted. The chapter closes with a number of recommendations for different stakeholders.

Chapter 15 covers the topic of labour localisation and HRM practices in the Gulf countries. Waxin and Bateman first examine the literature on core issues pertinent to this theme such as demographic and labour-market characteristics in the GCC. They then discuss the objectives of localisation programmes and the major components of localisation policies. Next they analyse the literature on HRM practices that facilitate the implementation of localisation programmes and highlight the multiple challenges related to this. Finally, they make recommendations that can enhance the impact of localisation efforts.

In Chapter 16, Harrison and Haslberger focus on the topic of expatriate management across the MENA region. The authors aim to provide an understanding of the work developed to date on expatriate management in the region. In order to achieve this, they have analysed the literature on expatriate management across the MENA region, which has helped them to identify and discuss the key themes addressed in the field to date, discuss gaps in the literature and suggest a research agenda for future consideration.

Al Amri, Glaister and Spicer, in Chapter 17, examine the topic of talent management practice in Oman from an institutional perspective. Information from both private and public sectors is used to examine the role of institutional factors in shaping talent management systems in Omani companies. To set things in context, the analysis begins with a discussion of Oman's business environment and the impact of the nationalisation policy (Omanisation) on its industrial sectors. The concept of talent management is then introduced in the context of Oman's institutional environment, and, thereafter, the multiple perspectives of institutional theory are examined. Each of the perspectives is then related to the authors' empirical findings and these are used to critically evaluate the impacts of the institutional environment on talent management programmes and the challenges that lay ahead.

In Chapter 18, AL-Husan and ALHussan focus on HRM in foreign firms operating in the Middle East. In order to put things in context, the topics of privatisation and investments in the region are also discussed. They begin their chapter by providing an overview of FDI and privatisation in the Middle East. This is followed by a discussion on the factors that influence MNCs' transfer of HRM practices, the mechanisms used in the transfer process and the enablers of and constraints on this transfer. Evidence from three empirical case studies is used to examine the transfer of HRM practices from Western MNCs to state-owned enterprises (SOEs) that were privatised under the auspices of the Jordanian government's privatisation programme. The chapter concludes by covering the key challenges in the region and the way forward.

Chapter 19 is dedicated to the emerging topic of the role of HRM in corporate social responsibility (CSR) in the Middle East. Jamali and El Dirani examine the increasing affinities between CSR and HRM. They make the case that HRM's capabilities, expertise and knowledge in executing organisational strategies can potentially help in ensuring the integration of CSR within an organisation's culture and fabric and significantly help to advance the CSR agenda. The authors compile the CSR–HRM blueprint, outlining how the CSR and HRM functions can be better integrated, and provide evidence from two successful cases from the Middle East where companies have made significant strides in terms of enacting the necessary alignment and reaping the desired benefits from the synergies of CSR and HRM. They conclude the chapter by highlighting the implications and suggesting the way forward in relation to how organisations can create a better alignment between CSR and HRM and benefit from it.

In Chapter 20, Cornelius, Pezet, Mahmoudi and Murtada examine the scenario of HRM in public sector firms in the Middle East. They review the literature on public sector policy developments across the Middle East and then highlight the characteristics of HRM in the public sector. Later on, they point out the main challenges for the practice of HRM in the public sector in the Middle East and present implications for future research.

Chapter 21 is dedicated to an in-depth analysis of the topic of '*wasta*' in the Jordanian context. Ta'Amnha, Sayce and Tregaskis address the void in our understanding of the meaning and impact of *wasta* in contemporary Jordanian society. They draw on the available literature and empirical research to clarify the realities of *wasta* as experienced by those working in a Jordanian context, and to identify the cultural and institutional factors shaping the meaning of *wasta* and its impact. The authors also discuss the implications of the practice of *wasta* for the effectiveness of HRM and organisational performance.

In Chapter 22, Nasief proposes a framework for the analysis of HR localisation practices in GCC countries. Initially his presentation focuses on localisation within the GCC in general and Saudi Arabia in particular. Then he introduces work on institutional HRM and presents a framework for labour localisation, focusing on a case study conducted by him in order to provide research evidence for examining the framework. It is important to note that while this framework was applied to a case study in Saudi Arabia, the framework can be applied in other GCC countries with little adaptation. Finally, the chapter proposes ways in which to employ and develop the framework further.

In the last chapter, Mellahi and Budhwar summarise the emerging scenario of HRM in the Middle East. They also provide an overview of the current state of HRM research and highlight the emerging challenges for HRM in the region. It is believed that these issues are expected to be the focus of future research and will help to further enhance our understanding of HRM in the Middle East.

USEFUL WEBSITES

Fact Sheet: http://www.doingbusiness.org/~/media/GIAWB/Doing%20Business/Documents/Fact-Sheets/DB15/DB15MENAFactSheetEnglish.pdf
World Bank: http://www.worldbank.org/en/region/mena
GCC: http://www.worldbank.org/en/country/gcc
Arab League: http://www.arableagueonline.org
Middle East Media Research Institute: http://www.memri.org
Middle East Institute: http://www.mei.edu

REFERENCES

Abdalla, I.A. 2015. Career facilitators and barriers of Arab women senior executives. *International Journal of Business and Management*, **10**(8): 218–232.

Afiouni, F., Ruël, H. and Schuler, R. 2014. HRM in the Middle East: toward a greater understanding. *International Journal of Human Resource Management*, Special Issue, **25**(2): 133–143.

Al-Enzi, A. 2002. Kuwait's employment policy: its formulation, implications, and challenges. *International Journal of Public Administration*, **25**(7): 885–900.

Al-Hamadi, A.B., Budhwar, P. and Shipton, H. 2007. Managing human resources in the Sultanate of Oman. *International Journal of Human Resource Management*, **18**(1): 100–113.

Al-Husan, F.B. and James, P. 2009. Multinationals and the process of post-entry HRM reform: evidence from three Jordanian case studies. *European Management Journal*, **27**(2): 142–153.

Al-Rajhi, I., Altman, Y., Metcalfe, B. and Roussel, J. 2006. Managing impatriate adjustment as a core HRM challenge. *Human Resource Planning*, **29**(4): 15–24.

Al-Waqfi, M.A. and Forstenlechner, I. 2014. Barriers to Emiratization: the role of policy design and institutional environment in determining the effectiveness of Emiratization. *International Journal of Human Resource Management*, **25**(2): 167–189.

Ali, A. 2004. *Islamic Perspectives on Management and Organization*. Cheltenham, UK and Northampton, MA: Edward Elgar.

Ali, A. 2010. Islamic challenges to HR in modern organizations. *Personnel Review*, **39**(6): 692–711.

Ali, A. and Al-Kazemi, A. 2006. Human resource management in Kuwait. In P. Budhwar and K. Mellahi (eds), *Managing Human Resources in the Middle East*. London: Routledge, pp. 79–96.

Altarawneh, I. and Aldehayyat, J.S. 2011. Strategic human resources management (SHRM) in Jordanian hotels. *International Journal of Business and Management*, **6**(10): 242–255.

Aycan, Z. 2004. Key success factors for women in management in Turkey. *Applied Psychology*, **53**(3): 453–471.

Aycan, Z., Al-Hamadi, A.B., Davis, A. and Budhwar, P. 2007. Cultural orientations and preference for HRM policies and practices: the case of Oman. *International Journal of Human Resource Management*, **18**(1): 11–32.

Branine, M. and Pollard, D. 2010. Human resource management with Islamic management principles: a dialectic for a reverse diffusion in management. *Personnel Review*, **39**(6): 712–727.

Budhwar, P. and Mellahi, K. 2006. Introduction: managing human resources in the Middle East. In P. Budhwar and K. Mellahi (eds), *Managing Human Resources in the Middle East*. London: Routledge, pp. 1–19.

Budhwar, P. and Mellahi, K. 2010. Human resource management in the Middle East. In C. Brewster and M. Wolfgang (eds), *Handbook of Research in Comparative Human Resource Management*. Cheltenham, UK and Northampton, MA: Edward Elgar, pp. 512–527.

Debrah, Y., McGovern, I. and Budhwar, P. 2000. Complementarity or competition: the development of human resources in a growth triangle. *International Journal of Human Resource Management*, **11**(2): 314–335.

Waal, A. de and Sultan, S. 2012. Applicability of the high performance organization framework in the Middle East. *Education, Business and Society: Contemporary Middle Eastern Issues*, **5**(3): 213–223.

Encyclopaedia Britannica 2015. Middle East. https://www.britannica.com/place/ancient-Middle-East (accessed 18 July 2016).

Goby, V.P., Nickerson, C. and David, E. 2015. Interpersonal communication and diversity climate: promoting workforce localization in the UAE. *International Journal of Organizational Analysis*, **23**(3): 364–377.

Iles, P., Almhedie, A. and Baruch, Y. 2012. Managing HR in the Middle East: challenges in the public sector. *Public Personnel Management*, **41**(3): 465–492.

Izraeli, D.N. 1987. Women's movement into management in Israel. *International Studies of Management and Organization*, **16**(3–4): 76–108.

Kabasakal, H. and Bodur, M. 2002. Arabic cluster: a bridge between east and west. *Journal of World Business*, **37**(1): 40–54.

Katou, A., Budhwar, P., Woldu, H. and Al-Hamadi, A.B. 2010. Influence of ethical beliefs, national culture and institutions on preferences for HRM in Oman. *Personnel Review*, **39**(6): 728–745.

Kaya, N. 2006. The impact of HRM practices and corporate entrepreneurship on firm performance: evidence from Turkish firms. *International Journal of Human Resource Management*, **17**(12): 2074–2092.

Khan, S.A. 2011. Convergence, divergence or middle of the path: HRM model for Oman. *Journal of Management Policy and Practice*, **12**(1): 76–87.

Khan, S.A., Rajasekar, J. and Al-Asfour, A. 2015. Organizational career development practices: learning from an Oman company. *International Journal of Business and Management*, **10**(9): 88–98.

Knowledge@Wharton 2016. How low oil prices are battering the MENA region, January. http://knowledge.wharton.upenn.edu/article/how-low-oil-prices-are-battering-the-mena-region/ (accessed 9 February 2016).

Kolachi, N. and Akan, O. 2014. HRD role in organizational development (a case of corporate thinking at ETISALT, UAE). *International Business Research*, **7**(8): 160–167.

Leat, M. and Al-Kot, G. 2007. HRM practices in Egypt: the influence of national context. *International Journal of Human Resource Management*, **18**(1): 147–158.

Manafi, M. and Subramaniam, I.D. 2015. Relationship between human resources management practices, transformational leadership and knowledge sharing on innovation in Iranian electronic industry. *Asian Social Science*, **11**(10): 358–385.

Marmenout, K. and Lirio, P. 2014. Local female talent retention in the Gulf: Emirati women bending with the wind. *International Journal of Human Resource Management*, **25**(2): 144–166.

Matherly, L. and Al Nahyan, S.S. 2015. Workplace quotas: building competitiveness through effective governance of national–expatriate knowledge transfer and development of sustainable human capital. *International Journal of Organizational Analysis*, **23**(3): 456–471.

Mellahi, K. 2003. National culture and management practices: the case of GCCs. In M. Tayeb (ed.), *International Management: Theory and Practices*. London: Prentice Hall, pp. 87–105.
Mellahi, K. 2006. Human resource management in Saudi Arabia. In P. Budhwar and K. Mellahi (eds), *Managing Human Resources in the Middle East*. London: Routledge, pp. 97–120.
Mellahi, K. 2007. The effect of regulations on HRM: private sector firms in Saudi Arabia. *International Journal of Human Resource Management*, **18**(1): 85–99.
Mellahi, K. and Budhwar, P. 2006. HRM challenges in the Middle East: agenda for future research and policy. In P. Budhwar and K. Mellahi (eds), *Managing Human Resources in the Middle East*. London: Routledge, pp. 291–301.
Mellahi, K. and Frynas, J.G. 2003. An exploratory study into the applicability of Western HRM practices in developing countries: an Algerian case study. *International Journal of Commerce and Management*, **13**(1): 61–73.
Metcalfe, B.D. 2008. Women, management and globalization in the Middle East. *Journal of Business Ethics*, **83**(1): 85–100.
Metle, M.K. 2002. The influence of traditional culture on attitudes towards work among Kuwati women employees in the public sector. *Women in Management Review*, **17**(5–6): 245–262.
Mohamed, M.I., Multalib, M.A., Abdulaziz, A.M., Ibrahim, M. and Habtoor, N.A.S. 2015. A review of HRM practices and labor productivity: evidence from Libyan oil companies. *Asian Social Science*, **11**(9): 215–225.
Mostafa, A.M.S. and Gould-Williams, J.S. 2014. Testing the mediation effect of person–organization fit on the relationship between high performance HR practices and employee outcomes in the Egyptian public sector. *International Journal of Human Resource Management*, **25**(2): 276–292.
Namazie, P. and Frame, P. 2007. Development in human resource management in Iran. *International Journal of Human Resource Management*, **18**(1): 159–171.
Neal, M. and Finlay, J.L. 2008. American hegemony and business education in the Arab world. *Journal of Management Education*, **32**(1): 38–49.
Obeidat, B.Y., Masa'deh, R., Moh'd, T. and Abdallah, A.B. 2014. The relationships among human resource management practices, organizational commitment, and knowledge management processes: a structural equation modeling approach. *Journal of Business and Management*, **9**(3): 9–26.
Omair, K. 2010. Typology of career development for Arab women managers in the United Arab Emirates. *Career Development International*, **15**(2): 121–143.
Ramdani, B., Mellahi, K., Guermat, C. and Kechad, R. 2014. The efficacy of high performance work practices in the Middle East: evidence from Algerian firms. *International Journal of Human Resource Management*, **25**(2): 252–275.
Rodriquez, J.K. and Scurry, T. 2014. Career capital development of self-initiated expatriates in Qatar: cosmopolitan globetrotters, experts and outsiders. *International Journal of Human Resource Management*, **25**(2): 190–211.
Saleh, S. and Kleiner, B.H. 2005. Issues and concerns facing American companies in the Middle East. *Management Research News*, **28**(2/3): 56–62.
Sidani, Y.M., Konard, A. and Karam, C.M. 2015. From female leadership advantage to female leadership deficit: a developing country perspective. *Career Development International*, **20**(3): 273–292.
Singh, A. and Sharma, J. 2015. Strategies for talent management: a study of select organizations in the UAE. *International Journal of Organizational Analysis*, **23**(3): 337–347.
Soltani, E. and Liao, Y.-Y. 2010. Training interventions: fulfilling managerial ends or proliferating invaluable means for employees? Some evidence from Iran. *European Business Review*, **22**(2): 128–152.
Syed, J., Hazboun, N.G. and Murray, P.A. 2014. What locals want: Jordanian employees' views on expatriate managers. *International Journal of Human Resource Management*, **25**(2): 212–233.
Tlaiss, H. 2015. Neither-nor: career success of women in an Arab Middle Eastern context. *Employee Relations*, **37**(5): 525–546.
Tlaiss, H.A. and Elamin, A.M. 2015. Exploring organizational trust and organizational justice among junior and middle managers in Saudi Arabia: trust in immediate supervisor as a mediator. *Journal of Management Development*, **34**(9): 1042–1060.
Tzafair, S.S., Meshoulam, I. and Baruch, Y. 2007. HRM in Israel: new challenges. *International Journal of Human Resource Management*, **18**(1): 114–131.
Waal, A. de and Sultan, S. 2012. Applicability of the high performance organization framework in the Middle East. *Education, Business and Society: Contemporary Middle Eastern Issues*, **5**(3): 213–223.
Wikipedia 2015. Arab Spring. https://en.wikipedia.org/wiki/Arab_Spring (accessed 10 October 2015).
Zaitouni, M., Sawalha, N.N. and Al Sharif, A. 2011. The impact of human resource management practices on organizational commitment in the banking sector in Kuwait. *International Journal of Business and Management*, **6**(6): 108–123.

2. Cultural perspectives in human resource management in the Middle East and North Africa

Pari Namazie and Barbara Covarrubias Venegas

INTRODUCTION

As economic activity becomes more global, organisations and countries increase cross-border connections. International trade and foreign direct investment primarily influence the linkages between countries. The most important drivers of globalisation are multinational corporations (MNCs). Furthermore, greater mobility in the global labour market in general, as well as globalisation and the internationalisation of businesses, has resulted in more and more organisations being confronted with the challenge of managing an increasingly diverse workforce (Andreassi et al., 2014; Banutu-Gomez, 2002; Budhwar and Debrah, 2001a; Hofstede, 2009; Kundu and Malhan, 2009; Michailova et al., 2009; Ruona and Gibson, 2004).

The complexities of international business are no longer confined to large MNCs but now affect small to medium-sized enterprises (SMEs), international joint ventures (IJVs) and public and private sector and not-for-profit organisations (Brewster et al., 2005). These organisations may find themselves managing people with a range of different work values, attitudes and behaviour patterns. There is growing recognition in the literature that the success or failure of IJVs and international mergers and acquisitions depends on the way in which human resource issues are managed (Evans et al., 2011; Gooderham et al., 2004). Global competition leads to globalised business and thus begs the question of how human resources (HR) can best support business in the face of global integration and coordination, while maintaining local flexibility. This implies that the role of HR in global business ventures is crucial when it comes to implementing organisational strategies with sensitivity to cultural influences (Pucik, 1996).

Rosenzweig and Nohria (1994) describe this as the pressure for international consistency (the convergence debate) or the pressure for local isomorphism (the divergence debate). They suggest the degree of resemblance to local practices is significantly influenced by how foreign-based MNCs were founded, the presence of expatriates and the extent of communication with the parent company. Scholars in favour of the international consistency argument believe that a consistent approach to compensation and benefits is needed as employees may move to other subsidiaries. Although, without employee mobility, the argument is about internal equity and the adoption of consistent human resource management (HRM) practices globally. Nonetheless, it has to be considered that HRM practices in particular are shaped by local regulations, socio-cultural milieu making local amendments indispensable.

The purpose of this chapter is to explore the cultural implications on HRM in the Middle East and North Africa (MENA) region. It is divided into six sections, beginning with a brief review of the current literature regarding the impact of globalisation on

HRM. The second section presents literature on the development of HRM across cultures. The third section examines the MENA context with an overview of the region and then a discussion on the national culture and socio-cultural factors that influence HRM. The fourth section discusses factors affecting HRM in the MENA region, followed by the fifth section which looks at cultural perspectives in HR practices in the region. The final section brings the chapter to a conclusion by examining future implications both for practitioners and researchers.

IMPACT OF GLOBALISATION ON HRM

Some authors argue that the globalisation of business has resulted in the increasing recognition of the importance of a well-managed workforce. Furthermore, a paradigm shift from HR being an administrative or support function to one having strategic importance seems to be in progress (Karoliny et al., 2009). It can also be argued that due to globalisation, HR practices from more developed countries have been transferred to developing countries, forcing the latter to adopt HR practices that put an emphasis on people. However, Pucik (1996) draws our attention to the fact that although there are multiple value-adding opportunities for HR in the process of business globalisation, the positioning or recognition within companies does not display this assumption yet and the HR function is not seen as a full partner in the globalisation process.

Along with being performed differently, HRM is also conceptualised differently in different countries (Lazarova et al., 2008). Global business, and in particular international human resource management (IHRM), becomes even more complex when MNCs are operating in countries with different ethical standards of (business) practice, where issues like corruption, discrimination or unsafe working conditions are a daily occurrence (Chitakornkijsil, 2010).

Effective management of cross-border alliances can be particularly problematic, especially where the cross-border merger, acquisition or joint venture involves Western MNCs in developing countries, due to the different management traditions and work cultures involved (Napier and Vu, 1998; Al-Husan et al., 2009). The definitions and major models of HRM have certain underlying values, assumptions and priorities, which are highly culture specific rather than reflecting universally accepted norms. Different cultural assumptions regarding, for example, organisations as systems of tasks versus relationships, the role of the individual and the collective and the importance of being versus doing (achievement versus ascription) show HRM practices to be culture bound (Schneider and Barsoux, 1997).

Although firms tend to converge towards similar organisational structures, there are many factors which differ considerably between countries. Differences in the business systems in particular encourage distinct HR strategies, structures and practices (Dickmann, 2003). Lazarova et al. (2008) add different developmental trends and stakeholder preferences and relationships as factors influencing the way HRM is being performed and conceptualised in different countries. Tayeb (1995) maintains that the 'what' question in HRM might be universal (such as employee selection) but the 'how' question is more culture specific (such as relying on in-group networks or standardised tests). The need for a deeper understanding of this matter is highly relevant for researchers and practitioners of MNCs, as a conclusion, or an approach to a conclusion, would help to understand the transferability of HRM practices within MNCs (Nikandrou et al., 2005). These authors strengthen the evidence of the value of the contextual approach to IHRM. The literature suggests that differences in HRM practices persist, at least for now, and that differences in institutional and cultural environment are important explanatory factors (Lazarova et al., 2008).

DEVELOPMENT IN HRM ACROSS CULTURES

Just as the size of the organisation and the sector(s) in which the organisation operates have a considerable impact on how organisations manage their people, so does the fact of operating internationally (Schuler and Tarique, 2007). Cross-cultural management, which is considered to be a sub-discipline of international management (Aycan, 2005), focuses specifically on how and to what extent culture influences HRM practices vis-à-vis other institutional and structural forces (e.g., size, industry, ownership status, workforce characteristics, unionisation, labour laws). Many authors state that national culture and external factors such as socio-political and economic aspects, the role of the state, education, and religion all affect the competitive advantage of nations and influence the development and establishment of the HR base in countries (e.g., Budhwar and Debrah, 2001b; Budhwar and Sparrow, 2002). The definition of the socio-cultural context includes values, belief systems, assumptions and behavioural patterns that differentiate one group of people from another (Aycan, 2005).

When bearing in mind what impacts HRM transfer, it is important to take into consideration factors originating from both the cultural and institutional framework of the host country. The cultural and institutional frameworks of host countries are especially important when considering transitional, emerging and developing markets (Myloni et al., 2004; Aycan, 2005). Cross-cultural differences pose crucial problems when an MNC wants to transfer HR policies and practices to different countries and subsidiaries (Bae et al., 1998; Hofstede, 1980; Rosenzweig and Nohria, 1994), especially when some practices do not conform to the host country culture. Failure to adapt HRM practices to a host country's culture can result in negative consequences and may inhibit the performance of the subsidiary. Research shows that MNCs at least partly adapt their HRM policies and practices to the host country in which they operate (Beechler and Yang, 1994; Myloni et al., 2004; Schuler and Rogovsky, 1998; Tayeb, 1998). Indeed, subsidiaries that have been managed in line with headquarters' expectations have been found to perform better than subsidiaries managed otherwise (Newman and Nollen, 1996).

With regard to the development of HRM in the Middle East, Afiouni et al. (2013) undertook a thorough literature analysis, based on the HR value proposition model introduced by Ulrich and Brockbank (2005). Although exploratory, their findings indicate similarities between HRM within the Arab countries of the Middle East (not the whole Middle East), describing HR as a practice-oriented function in particular, with an internal focus, meaning taking care of employees and guaranteeing effective people flow, rather than being involved in designing business strategies. HR activities are centrally organised with a mostly inward rather than an outward orientation. Tayeb (1998) notes that some HRM practices are transferable across cultures and countries and others are culture specific, and Afiouni et al. (2013) note that most companies have corporation-wide HRM policies but find it more difficult to apply them in the form of country-specific HRM practices. Corporation-wide HRM policies involve high-level decision making, whereas their application to other countries requires changes in behaviour. As mentioned earlier, different HRM practices often have different levels of MNC standardisation and localisation, and the possibility of combining MNC and host country elements may vary among different HRM practices (Rosenzweig and Nohria, 1994).

Specific factors affecting HRM in the MENA region will be addressed below in the fourth section of this chapter.

THE MIDDLE EAST AND NORTH AFRICAN CONTEXT

Although the countries in the MENA region share important similarities, there are also many differences between them, not only in terms of religion, language and ethnicity, but also in terms of political, legal and economic development and governmental structures. The MENA is a wide region encompassing some 20 countries; however, for the context of this chapter only Arab-speaking countries and Iran are included. The demographic trends in the region, especially the rapidly growing youth population, put pressure on the region to adapt to social change and economic challenges. It is a region of great political and economic significance and also of great concern. There are significant differences in the sizes of populations across MENA countries. Egypt boasts a population of over 80 million, whereas Bahrain only has around 1 million inhabitants. Qatar has a gross domestic product (GDP) per capita of US$76,168, one of the highest in the world, while Yemen ranks among the world's poorer countries with a GDP per capita of only US$1,282 (Rogmans, 2012). One consequence of the region's recent demographic trends is an increasingly notable youth bulge. One in every three people living in the region is between 10 and 24 years of age. In addition, citizens must compete with foreigners for jobs in some Persian Gulf countries, where one-half or more of the labour force consists of foreign workers. All countries in the Persian Gulf region have introduced localisation policies to develop local talent and reduce the workforce dependency on foreign labour.

Religious Context

Three of the world's major religions originated from the region – Judaism, Christianity and Islam. Although the region is dominated mainly by Sunni Muslims, there are a number of different Sunni sects, as well as Shiite and other religions such as Christianity and Judaism practised in MENA.

Political Context

Politically, the countries in the region have different governmental systems, ranging from republics (most North African countries) to constitutional monarchies (Gulf States, Jordan and Morocco) (Kabasakal and Bodur, 2002). The laws governing the countries range from civil code to strict Islamic jurisprudence, Sharia law. Many countries have a combination of the two.

Globalisation Context

There are apparent signs of globalisation throughout the MENA region, more so in the Arab world, but there are also mixed perceptions towards it (e.g., Branine and Pollard, 2010). On the one hand, globalisation is seen as a vehicle for technological development and as a display of modernity and industrial and commercial competitiveness, for example in Qatar and the United Arab Emirates (UAE). On the other hand, it is also seen as a threat to Islamic values and national culture (Zineldin, 2002). Some of the consequences of the free-market economy are accumulation of wealth, excessive consumer spending, the introduction of overambitious projects, an overemphasis on training and development, and a presence of citizens who consume much more than they produce (Branine and Pollard, 2010). Some phenomena, such as accumulation of wealth and excessive consumer spending, clash with Islamic and traditional values. Most of the Middle Eastern countries have become major consumer markets for world-market producers. Branine and Pollard (2010) continue that despite the wealth of most of the Arab countries, these countries remain economically, socially and industrially underdeveloped. There are problems of unemployment, poverty, health and education, as well as high levels of social and political unrest. Other causes of economic stagnation are lagging political reforms, dominant public sectors, underdeveloped financial markets, high trade restrictiveness, lack of integration into the global economy, closed economy, overdependence on oil wealth and lack of privatisation initiatives (e.g., Budhwar and Mellahi, 2006).

The MENA is not only a large and rapidly growing market, but it is strategically located at the crossroads between Asia, Europe and Africa. Additionally, it is noteworthy that, immediately adjacent to the Arab Middle East, Turkey, India, and Iran are other huge emerging markets which, given their size and unique characteristics, provide great opportunities for the MENA as a supplier and hub for the wider region. It is also noteworthy that, gradually, a number of Middle Eastern MNCs (companies such as Aramex, Emaar, Emirates Airlines and Sabic), originating from the MENA region, are taking advantage of the opportunities in the region and entering emerging and developing markets.

Although each country in the region has its own specific characteristics, major trends in the Middle Eastern business environment can be summarised as follows: politically instable and (in some cases) improving business regulations, energy rich, the rise of women, turning eastward, regional integration, value-based consumption and a youth bulge (Rogmans, 2012).

A prevalent concern for foreign MNCs operating in this region is related to the political and market stability. It is expected that political risk will remain at relatively high levels for the foreseeable future. Within these dimensions, MNCs operating in the region will need to maintain a standardised, localised and sometimes hybrid strategy to operate effectively within the different countries in the region.

FACTORS AFFECTING HRM IN THE MENA REGION

To be effective, HRM practices must be aligned with social and organisational contexts (Aycan, 2005). As an attempt to explicate the role of culture in HRM practices, the model of culture fit (MCF) was proposed by Kanungo and his associates (Kanungo and Jaeger,

1990; Mendonca and Kanungo, 1994) and tested in several countries (cf. Aycan et al., 1999). The MCF assessed culture at two levels: societal (i.e., the socio-cultural context) and organisational (i.e., internal work culture).

The model asserts that the internal work culture consists of managerial beliefs and assumptions about two fundamental organisational elements: the task and the employees. Managerial assumptions which relate to the task deal with its nature and how it must best be accomplished. Those pertaining to employees deal with the nature and behaviour of employees. Managers implement HRM practices based on their perceptions on the nature of the task and the employees. Both the socio-cultural and institutional environment, in turn, shapes the internal work culture. On the one hand, task-driven perceptions are influenced by the characteristics of the institutional environment, such as size, ownership status, industry, market competitiveness and resource availability. On the other hand, employee-related perceptions are influenced by the characteristics of the socio-cultural context.

While studies using the MCF establish the link between culture and HRM by using culturally embedded assumptions held by managers, Aycan et al. (2007) applied the cultural-orientations framework according to Kluckhohn and Strodtbeck (1961), using employees' cultural orientations and preferences to study the extent to which cultural orientations influenced preferences for HRM policies and practices in Oman. The majority of the hypothesised relationships between cultural orientations and HRM preferences were confirmed. Aycan et al. (2007) illustrate that age in particular plays an important role when it comes to preferences regarding HRM policies or practices, thus pointing out that there might be large differences also within one country (cultural context). Sound evidence was found that group-oriented HRM practices, such as group-based performance evaluation and reward allocation, are preferred by employees who score high on collectivism, in comparison to those stressing the importance of individual accomplishment and rational decision making. Regarding hierarchy-oriented HRM practices (e.g., personnel decisions based on loyalty and seniority; top-down decision making concerning performance evaluations and training needs; and keeping critical information to the top-level executives), a clear preference was given by those who believed in the need of preserving a status hierarchy in society and organisations.

Meanwhile, a recent study conducted in the Maghreb (Morocco, Algeria, Tunisia, Libya and Mauritania) (Frimousse et al., 2012) supports the argument that subsidiaries that have been managed in line with headquarters' expectations, have been found to perform better than subsidiaries managed otherwise (Newman and Nollen, 1996). Frimousse et al. (2012) investigated whether the direct application of an imported HRM model works in the Maghreb. According to them, hybridisation of HRM practices increases employee commitment, meaning that in order to gain legitimacy, elements of contingency (culture, religion, etc.) must be included in HRM practices. Namazie and Frame (2007) found that the development of HRM in Iran depended on the stability of the environment, the influence of national factors and the role of organisational strategies and practices. Additionally, they found the MNCs studied in this research amended their HR policies and practices to take account of the local environment (localisation) and to obtain the best results from their staff throughout different subsidiaries. Evans and Lorange (1990) pointed out that those HRM practices closely associated with technical/product operation are expected to be more compatible than those which are influenced by socio-cultural diversity. Recruitment and training are assumed to have a high compatibility between countries as they are characterised by similar technical experiences. Other HRM practices, such as promotion, performance appraisal and compensation are more distinctive from one country to another because they are induced by socio-cultural factors (Hofstede and Bond, 1984). Bonache et al. (2012) showed that in countries with a higher performance-orientation culture, high-performing HR systems are likely to work better than in countries with a lower performance-orientation culture.

As discussed above, socio-contextual factors play a very important role in the transferability of HRM. Although the countries of the MENA region are similar in some ways, they are also very different. The third section, above, addressed some of the socio-economic issues in the MENA region; the section below examines specific factors such as national culture, the role of Islam and management, and how this effects HRM policies and practices.

NATIONAL CULTURE OF MENA

Several studies on national culture and value orientations focus on the Arab Middle East and in some cases make distinctions for individual countries in the region. Hofstede (1980) included Egypt, Iraq, Kuwait, Lebanon, Libya, Morocco, Turkey, Qatar, Saudi Arabia, Iran and the UAE in his Arab cluster. In turn, the GLOBE study (House et al., 2004) was conducted in the mid-1990s. Five countries related to this chapter were included in the study. Egypt, Kuwait, Morocco and Qatar were placed in the Middle Eastern cluster. Interestingly, Iran was placed in the South Asian cluster, along with India, Indonesia, the Philippines, Malaysia and Thailand, due to 'the rich interaction and balance between spirituality, psychology, philosophy, morality, politics, economics and society' (House et al., 2004, p. 188); however, the South Asian cluster and Iran in particular share significant and sustained interactions with the Arab cluster (House et al., 2004). For lack of inclusion of all MENA countries, the GLOBE study's Middle Eastern cluster and Hofstede's Arab cluster are used to generalise the behaviours and observable trends in the greater MENA region. Although other scholars have also contributed to national culture and values orientations, for the purpose of this chapter, the authors use Hofstede and the GLOBE study.

Hofstede (1991) studied the national culture of several Arab countries and referred to them as the 'Arab Group'. He characterised Arab countries as having a large power distance, relatively high uncertainty avoidance, higher collectivism than individualism, and a slightly more feminine than masculine preference. Uncertainty avoidance is the only dimension in which religion plays an important role (Obeidat et al., 2012). Countries with high power distance tend to be more collectivist. The loyalty of employees is to individuals, tribes and networks and not to the organisation itself. This manifests itself where people rather than the actual needs of the organisation take precedence (Al-Rasheed, 2001; Obeidat et al., 2012). Shaista et al. (2003) discuss the possibility that firms from countries with high uncertainty avoidance are more likely to transfer HR practices from headquarters to local subsidiaries than firms from countries with low uncertainty avoidance because the direct transfer of practices reduces uncertainty and risks. Similarly, one might expect that firms from countries with a high power distance may centralise control and therefore would be less likely to cede control of HR practices to local subsidiaries (i.e., low local adaptation). Hofstede (2001) also noted the positive relationship between power distance and paternalism. The Arab cluster showed more preference towards the feminine continuum, which focuses on relationships and working conditions or a 'work to live' culture (Hofstede, 2001). In these cultures, practices that damage relationships and working conditions are avoided and attempts to differentiate one employee from another, tie compensation to performance, or give negative feedback are regarded as potentially threatening to workplace harmony (Sale, 2004). Some management scholars believe that the feminine culture may affect managerial attitudes and behaviours about performance appraisal, compensation, and labour relations (Tayfur, 2013).

Additionally, results of the Middle Eastern cluster in the GLOBE study (House et al., 2004) include countries that are predominantly Muslim. This cluster showed a high score on in-group collectivism and lower score on future orientation, gender egalitarianism and uncertainty avoidance (House et al., 2004). This represents societies that are fatalistic, believe in the will of Allah and that the family forms the basis for insurance against future contingencies, and look towards male members of society for primary protection and support (House et al., 2004, p. 200). Findings from the GLOBE study reflect the importance of family and the network of interdependent relationships, which can reduce the importance of performance and future orientation in these societies (Kabasakal and Bodur, 2002).

It is noteworthy that Hofstede's dimensions show the Arab cluster to be low on uncertainty avoidance and the GLOBE study shows the Middle Eastern cluster to be high on uncertainty avoidance. Venaik and Brewer (2010) argue that these contradictory explanations are due to the fact that the studies measure different components of the uncertainty avoidance construct. Although Hofstede and GLOBE both incorporate a common cultural dimension labelled as 'uncertainty avoidance', there is disagreement on how it should be measured. Hofstede (2001, p. 146) describes uncertainty avoidance as follows: 'On the national cultural level, tendencies toward prejudice, rigidity and dogmatism, intolerance of different opinions, traditionalism, superstition, racism, and ethnocentrism all relate to a norm for intolerance of ambiguity that I have measured and expressed in a national Uncertainty Avoidance Index.' He emphasises that uncertainty avoidance is different from risk avoidance. GLOBE (House et al., 2004, p. 603) defines uncertainty avoidance as 'the extent to which members of collectives seek orderliness, consistency, structure, formalized procedures and laws to cover situations in their daily lives'. The GLOBE study adds that there is a positive and significant correlation between uncertainty avoidance and intolerance of ambiguity. Both Hofstede and GLOBE use the term 'uncertainty avoidance', but it appears to reflect different and perhaps contradictory characteristics of national culture (Venaik and Brewer, 2008). A further critique and discussion of the uncertainty avoidance dimension is beyond the scope of this chapter; however, the authors will continue to use the uncertainty avoidance dimensions as stipulated by Hofstede and GLOBE and interpret the implications on international business and management for the MENA regions.

ISLAM AND MANAGEMENT IN MENA

Even though over 80 per cent of people worldwide report that religion plays a significant role in their daily lives (Sedikides, 2010), research on the relationship between management and religion has only recently been examined. However, in what has recently been referred to as a religious re-awakening, religion has come to the forefront of management and organisational research (Mellahi and Budhwar, 2010). Since 2007 a growing body of research has examined HRM, management and Islam. Islam and its different sects promote a set of moral values and behaviours in society (Kabasakal and Bodur, 2002). Islam has, since its inception, placed great emphasis on work and views it as a necessary means to achieve equilibrium in one's social and individual life (Ali, 1988, 2010). By giving work a religious, social and economic dimension, Islam has promoted labour and those involved in economic activities to a noble position (Ali, 2010).

In addition, Islam places great emphasis on work ethics, management and leadership. The Holy Quran speaks about justice and honesty in trade and fairness in employment relationships, and encourages new skills to be learnt, cooperation in work, consultation in decision making and work that benefits the individual and the community (Branine and Pollard, 2010; Abuznaid, 2006). Due to the strong influence that Islam has on day-to-day lives, it is expected to also have a strong influence on how human resources are managed in organisations, work-related values, the expectations of employees, and the behaviour and approach of management (Aycan et al., 2007; Leat and El-Kot, 2007). Scholars outline different Islamic principles of Islam and their implications on HRM and management (Branine and Pollard, 2010; Mellahi and Budhwar, 2010):

1. *Being mindful of Almighty God (Taqwa)*. This enables one to behave in a just and steadfast manner.
2. *Kindness (Ehsan)* in terms of doing good deeds and forgiveness. Managers with a high level of Ehsan promote the training and development of their employees and encourage employment involvement and participation in decision making.
3. *Justice (Adl)*. Justice leads to equality and enables a sense of humility. In organisations where justice prevails this translates to employees being treated and rewarded equally and fairly and that laws and regulations, policies and procedures are followed and implemented.
4. *Trust (Al-Amanah)*. The concept of trust is a core value governing social relationships, as every person is held accountable for his/her doings in the community.
5. *Truthfulness (Al-Sedq)*. The concept of Sedq (or Sedak) implies doing and saying what is right to the best of one's knowledge. It is forbidden in Islam to lie or to cheat under any circumstances. Honesty and trustworthiness are central to effective management.
6. *Self-improvement (Etqan)*, which provides the basis for one's striving for self-betterment in order to do better work. In HRM this would translate to do better, work harder and improve the quality of ones products and services through the learning of new knowledge and skills.
7. *Consultation (Shura)*. It is a requirement that people seek advice and consult others before making decisions. Consultation is one of the main leadership values in Islam.

Islam may influence workplace behaviour with values such as respect for age and seniority, loyalty, obedience towards leaders and looking to seniors for direction, consultative decision making, and trustfulness between both superiors and subordinates (Namazie and Tayeb, 2006). Leat and El-Kot (2007) add that the Islamic work ethic is consistent with Hofstede's (1980) findings of low individualism, emphasising relationships and cooperation, and the desire to avoid uncertainty, which can be seen through hard work, living by the rules and consultation as a means of avoiding mistakes.

The main sects in Islam are Sunni and Shiite. Differences are observed between the sects in practices and cultural beliefs. Although interpretations of Islamic practices differ from one sect or country to another, overall, Islam promotes collectivism and power distance by emphasising religious brotherhood and accepting those in leadership positions of authority (Kabasakal and Bodur, 2002). According to some scholars (e.g., Kabasakal and Bodur, 2002), there are observable differences between the Sunni and Shiite doctrines, whereby Sunni is the more orthodox and traditionalist branch of Islam where a significant body of the law is complete and unchangeable, whereas, according to Kabasakal and Bodur (2002), Shi'ísm is generally more flexible in the practice of religion and is able to interpret and account for the new and different.

Kanungo and Jaeger (1990) argued that fatalism is seen as a characteristic of Islam. However, Acevedo (2008) suggests that fatalism in the Islamic world is a largely misunderstood phenomenon as Christians living in Muslim countries are also fatalistic. Acevedo (2008) continues that fatalism in the Muslim world may best be understood in light of the region's historical, economic, socio-political and cultural processes. Islamic fatalism assumes that Muslims accept a higher level of belief that the divine decree of God – Al Qadar – controls the outcome of one's life. In the workforce, this could broadly translate to employees feeling they are not in control of their actions and future development.

Islam emphasises the role of the family as well as the patriarchal relationship, expecting family members to respect and obey the leader of the family or society. As Tayeb (1997) points out, it is very difficult to disentangle the effects of Islam on HRM from the other deeply embedded social, economic and political factors, which make up the character of a society. It is noteworthy that some Islamic practices take on local features in the countries where they are practised and therefore there are clear variations among countries in their interpretation of some of the Islamic values (Tayeb, 1997).

Aycan et al. (2000) reported a high level of paternalism in Turkish organisations and show how supervisors take on a parental role by providing support and care. Subordinates, in turn, take on a child's role and show loyalty, deference and compliance towards the parent. Latifi (1997) found that Iranian employees consider their managers as sympathetic brothers and sisters or compassionate fathers and mothers who are seen to be involved in their employees' private lives and family matters. In a study on IJVs in Iran, Namazie (2007) found the selection of the managing director followed by the ownership structure of the IJV, management style of the local partner, and national culture were seen as crucial factors in the transferability of HR policies and practices to the IJVs, stressing the importance of paternalism in the Iranian context.

However, there appears to be a mismatch between some Islamic core values and what is practised in the workplace (Abuznaid, 2006; Ali, 2010; Branine and Pollard, 2010; Mellahi and Budhwar, 2010), partly due to management in the MENA region being influenced not only by Islam but also traditional and non-Islamic norms and values.

A clear example is seen in the importance paid to in-group collectivism where loyalty to family and personal relationships take precedence over organisational needs. This translates to nepotism in recruitment and compensation, which is not compatible with Islamic values of justice, equity and fairness. In this regard, it is important to examine and understand management processes and the cultural context of individual countries and to differentiate between them (Branine and Pollard, 2010).

Kanungo and Jaeger (1990) point out that, in response to the unpredictable nature of the environment in developing countries, organisations adopt coping strategies such as lack of long-term planning, lack of a long-term vision and goal, lack of time management, moderate risk taking and lack of trust in the system with a concomitant lack of trust in people and staff, both managers and workers. Although each country must be considered in its own right, studies of management in the MENA region show the significance of cultural and political influences on managerial behaviour and have recognised the importance of Islam, tribalism, state control and Western influence (Ali, 1990, 1998; Dadfar, 1993; Weir, 2000, 2001; Budhwar and Mellahi, 2006; Namazie and Tayeb, 2006). Studies have generally agreed that most Arab managers are authoritarian in dealing with their subordinates (Branine and Pollard, 2010). Decision making is greatly influenced by status, hierarchy and level of seniority (Al-Faleh, 1987). Namazie and Tayeb (2006) remarked that after the 1979 Islamic revolution in Iran, the need for a loyal workforce was greater than a skilled workforce and the value of merits was placed, therefore, not on actions and competencies but on loyalties and relationships. In a region with high political and social unrest, it is common to see swift changes in power; therefore, it is important to maintain good relationships both within your independent networks and with people with influence. Whether '*wasta*', '*piston*' or '*partybazi*', emphasising power, collectivism and the importance of relationships, 'how much you know' is not as important as 'who you are and who you know'.

Ali (1998) contends that the problem in Arab countries is due to the complex interaction between dominant social values, technology and the level of development achieved, such as too much centralisation and bureaucracy, poor communication, lack of management skills, and unrealistic performance measures (such as the importance of personal factors over the needs of the organisation) (Ali, 1998; Weir, 2000; Assad, 2002).

Allinson and Hayes (2000) argue that the state of economic development of the country is also a significant contextual issue. In this respect, Rahwar and Al-Buraey (1992) claim that Western organisational theory sits uneasily in Arab cultures because of its concentration on individualistic and performance-related and economic-measure-based approaches. They suggest, for example, that many important individual spiritual needs are ignored in Western management thought. Western theories of work motivation and work values may also be inappropriate for Islamic countries.

It seems, therefore, that there is ample evidence from the above-mentioned studies of a gap between what is practised in the MENA countries and what is really needed. It appears from the above discussion that there is a clear difference between theory and practice, and between what is expected, according to the Islamic principles explained above, and what is actually practised (Branine and Pollard, 2010). This creates the discrepancy between global integration and local responsiveness (Budhwar and Mellahi, 2010) and emphasises that each context needs to be studied individually. It is noteworthy that the MENA societies are in transition, and work-related changes may result, albeit very slowly. The issues for HRM lie in designing work practices that provide adequate motivation and appropriate sets of guidelines which incorporate local value systems and yet meet the needs of the enterprise in a globally competitive environment.

A number of scholars have also examined inter-generational cultural differences in emerging and developing countries (Aycan, 2005; Egri and Ralston, 2004; Ralston et al., 1999; Mellahi and Guermat, 2004). Bearing in mind the young population and youth bulge in the MENA region, it is possible that cultural values and preferences in transitioning societies will undergo change. In a study conducted in Oman, Aycan (2005) found that employees below the age of 40 years would be more likely to adopt values of egalitarianism, individualism and risk tolerance, which emphasises a shift from traditional (typically collectivist and conservative) values towards greater support for individualism, universalism and an openness to change. At the same time it is noteworthy that generational changes in culture are likely to be relatively small, and while generational differences in orientation might be expected, younger Omanis would still be expected to appear more Omani than Western in their cultural orientations. This study supported Mellahi and Guermat's (2004) view that, in developing economies, the younger generation moves away from traditional values. This is relevant for the MENA region, which has a young population. It will be interesting to see how the youth will challenge and change cultural norms and how each country will respond to the demands of globalisation and economic development.

CULTURAL PERCEPTIONS OF HR IN MENA

It is clear that national culture has a significant impact on HRM (Budhwar and Mellahi, 2006). The role, perception and applications of HRM are different in MENA countries. The remainder of this section addresses the general cultural perspectives of HR practices in the MENA region, namely recruitment and selection, performance appraisal, training and development, and compensation and reward management. However, as mentioned in Lu and Björkman's (1997) study, each HRM practice must be studied individually across geographical settings, MNC home countries, different industries and ownership structures (see also Schuler et al., 1993; Taylor et al., 1996). Therefore, for a more thorough understanding of the cultural implication of the mentioned HR practices, we advocate that each country must be examined individually taking the cultural and institutional factors of the country into account.

Recruitment and Selection

Recruitment and selection criteria are culture bound (Aycan, 2005). The MENA region being a collectivistic and high power distance region, personal and professional relationships, social and interpersonal skills, social class and age are often more important than merit and competencies (Namazie and Tayeb, 2006). Internal recruitment and promotion may be preferred to ensure stability in the work environment and loyalty to the organisation. Additionally, although the MENA region has a young population, most companies complain of a skills gap, and there is in fact a scarcity of qualified personnel (Branine and Pollard, 2010). Although many MNCs might adopt systematic selection processes, in local companies, it would not be uncommon for the method of selection to be based on face-to-face interviews, loyalty and connections, rather than more formal assessment and competency evaluation measures. Namazie and Pahlavnejad, in Chapter 9 of this handbook, found many Iranian companies preferred to recruit staff through word of mouth and more informal channels. Even though companies were adopting more systematic recruitment and selection practices, Namazie and Pahlavnejad found nepotism was too deep-rooted in the Iranian culture to be removed entirely. This was especially seen for higher managerial positions and in family-run businesses. Humility is a preferred behaviour in the MENA region, and an interview setting where one needs to talk highly of one's achievements is seen as culturally inappropriate. Having the right connections provides an indirect way for someone to be praised and recognised without seeming arrogant.

Recruitment channels are informal and network based, especially for mid- to high-level managerial positions. In some cases, especially with middle and senior management, candidates have already been preselected. The type of industry, nature of the job and ownership structure of the company also has an impact on recruitment and selection factors. In industries which require specific products, technologies and innovation and/or large organisations, recruitment and selection would be based on more formal, job-related skills and competencies. However, in smaller organisations and information-based industries such as the service sector, recruitment and selection would be based on social and interpersonal skills and related factors (Aycan, 2005).

Performance Appraisal

Performance appraisal is the most culture-bound practice and has been one of the most difficult HR practices to be transferred across cultures. In most MNCs this practice remains standardised. The question across cultures is what constitutes good performance? Good performance is seen and indeed measured differently across cultures. In an individualistic culture, performance criteria are more objective and quantifiable, with an emphasis on the individual, work outcomes and productivity (Harris and Moran, 1996; Aycan, 2005). In a collectivist culture, loyalty is valued more than productivity; in turn, mediocre performers are tolerated and protected as long as they have good relationships and are loyal staff (Kovach, 1995; Tung, 1984). Although work outcomes are important, social and relational criteria, such as trustworthiness, humility, respectful attitude, loyalty and harmony in interpersonal relations, have more weight. Namazie and Pahlavnejad (Chapter 9) found staff had a great deal of distrust towards their managers' objectivity and the outcome of the performance appraisal system. A common belief among local staff in Iran was that relationships were rewarded more than actions.

The way in which performance is evaluated also has cross-cultural variations. In collectivistic, high power distance cultures, performance evaluation would be more unsystematic, involving a top-down approach where superiors evaluate staff based on sometimes subjective factors (Aycan, 2005). It is possible that feedback tools such as 360-feedback could be more difficult as self-appraisal is not common in the MENA context.

Furthermore, in collectivistic cultures, the notion of giving feedback is not common. General feedback would be indirect, non-confrontational and private (Fletcher and Perry, 2001). Negative feedback is perceived as attacking someone personally. Additionally, who gives the feedback is important: it would be better accepted if feedback were initiated by a superior who is respected for his/her wisdom and expertise. In collectivistic cultures, giving feedback to the group instead of the individual is preferred.

Training and Development

Training and development is vital to organisational survival and growth (Aycan, 2005). However, organisations see this differently; in cultures which emphasise performance and excellence, there is a large budgetary allocation for training and development. On the other hand, in fatalistic cultures, there is the perception that staff may not be highly motivated to learn and improve, hence training budgets are managed in an informal and ad hoc way (Aycan et al., 2000). Outcomes of training and development are seen differently: in a high performance culture, training is conducted to improve individual and team performance and productivity; in collectivistic cultures, it is also seen as a method to motivate employees, and increase loyalty and commitment to the company (Tsang, 1994). In addition, it creates a sense of gratitude and loyalty to the employer (Wong et al., 2001).

The content and method of training also has cross-cultural variations. Earley (1994) examined the impact of individualism and collectivism during the process of training. He found that for collectivistic cultures, group-focused training was more effective, and that individual-focused training that emphasised personal capability and private self was more effective for individualistic cultures. Taking into account the cognitive style of cultures can also help with the design and delivery of training across cultures. For example, an analytical style (such as that found in developing countries) typically seeks certainty, while an intuitive style (such as that found in Anglo, Northern and Latin Europeans) might question the norms and assumptions and hence undermine the power distance between the trainer and the trainee (Aycan, 2005; Hayes and Allison, 1998). Analytical thinkers in high uncertainty avoidance and high power distance cultures expect one-way lecturing, rather than participative discussions (Parnell and Hatem, 1999). Indeed, in this cultural context the instructor is perceived as the 'expert' who must provide definitive answers and guidelines (Laurent, 1986; Thornhill, 1993).

The MENA region has made a very substantial investment in education, training and development. However, despite the abundance of educational programmes, the formal education system is unable to prepare the workforce for the future of the country. Additionally, education and learning in the MENA region is done more by rote memorisation and focuses on a strong theoretical base. Salehi Esfahani (2005) suggests the main task will be to shift unproductive skills, such as rote memorisation and test-taking skills, to productive but hard-to-test skills ranging from a specific skill, such as writing, to more general skills, such as creativity and ability to work in teams. Although there is a young and educated workforce, there is still a scarcity of talent, hence organisations try to attract the best candidates by offering high-quality training and development opportunities (Grossman, 1997).

Compensation and Rewards Management

Geringer and Frayne (1990) define compensation to include monetary and non-monetary, direct or indirect rewards, which an organisation exchanges for the contributions of its employees, both job-performance-related and personal contributions. Compensation is not only culture specific, it is also very much dependent on institutional factors, such as inflation, economic development, availability and quality of human resources, and labour laws pertaining to each country. In terms of transferability of HR practices, compensation is generally more localised as companies must conform to local norms; however, companies vary in the allocation of rewards and the understanding of financial and non-financial equity.

In high power distance cultures, the allocation of rewards is based on criteria other than performance, such as seniority or being on good terms with the management (see Hui and Luk, 1997; Leung, 1997). Schuler and Rogovsky (1998) found that countries with high levels of uncertainty avoidance preferred a seniority-based compensation as it emphasised predictability and certainty, whereas low uncertainty avoidance countries preferred performance- and skill-based compensation systems. Additionally, individualistic countries preferred pay-for-performance and individual performance in compensation practice and collectivistic cultures preferred group-based rewards (Schuler and Rogovsky, 1998; Gluskinos, 1988). Huo and Von Glinow (1995) found a strong positive correlation between collectivism and flexible benefit plans, workplace child-care practices, maternity leave programmes, career-break schemes and welfare programmes such as housing and contribution to the education of children (e.g., Quinn and Rivoli, 1991; Sparrow and Budhwar, 1997). This could also possibly be similar in feminine cultures.

In collectivistic and high power distance cultures like the MENA region, non-economic rewards are also important as they emphasise affiliation to an organisation as well as recognition (Mendonca and Kanungo, 1994). Intrinsic rewards, such as the feeling of respect and belonging and opportunity for growth and learning are more valued in small and family-run organisations compared to large ones (MacDermid et al., 2001). Additionally, organisations include housing or bonuses when there is a scarcity of a talented and high-quality workforce (Grossman, 1997).

CONCLUSIONS AND FUTURE RESEARCH

In the last few years the amount of literature and number of studies on HRM in the Middle East has increased significantly. There are different factors to consider within the MENA region, including culture, institutions and the environment while analysing the nature of its HRM. On the one hand, the young population is in need of economic development, but at a sustainable pace and one which needs to be aligned with the cultural norms and values of each society. On the other hand, in order to understand the role and impact of the MNC and transferability of HR practices, whether standardised or localised, each practice and country must be studied individually. As mentioned in the previous section, although the MENA region shares many commonalities, there are also huge differences. But differences cannot only be found between two countries: they may even appear within a single country. Azolukwam and Perkins (2009, p. 78), based on a study in Nigeria, point out that parts of the population are socialised to Western norms, and other parts are not, in particular suggesting that between perceptions of senior managers and 'average' employees, enormous differences might exist. Furthermore, it is important to bear in mind that it is not only Islamic core values, but also traditional and non-Islamic values and norms, which influence management in the MENA region.

The presence of MNCs in developing countries has a large impact on the development of HRM, such as is the case in the MENA region. Ali (1998) points out that MNCs should be culturally aware and identify the areas that might cause friction and misunderstanding (e.g., religious or political issues), have the appropriate intercultural and interpersonal skills necessary to modify their behaviours to appreciate Arab and Middle Eastern values, such as respect for elderly, religion and the importance of relationships.

The overall impression is that HRM in the MENA is developing towards a more strategic approach, and starting to implement HRM practices in a systematic manner in order to contribute to business success. In particular, we want to point out again that the role of HRM is also highly influenced by the status of HRM within organisations in a country. While in many developing countries HRM is still not one of the core functions within an organisation, the process of turning HRM into a core function appears to be currently under way in the MENA. In particular, significant (sometimes foreign) competition might stimulate the focus organisations put on their human resources and, consequently, their HRM practices.

As HRM continues to be developed in the MENA region, the literature and findings in this chapter suggest there is a growing need to examine each country individually and take into account its cultural and institutional contexts. Due to the many social, political, economic and demographic challenges the region is facing, it is undergoing a fast change. There is a possibility that the young generation moves away from traditional values and challenges cultural norms as suggested by Mellahi and Guermat (2004); but even so, as the cultural, environmental and institutional dynamics of each country in the region differs, so too will their response to the demands of globalisation and economic development. This chapter will help MNCs and local companies to understand how to differentiate HRM in each country and what cultural factors to bear in mind when deciding between standardising and localising HR practices in each country in the MENA region. It goes without saying that the region has a great deal of opportunity as well as risk, and companies must apply international consistency and local isomorphism in their policies and practices towards the MENA, on the one hand be able to make long-term plans, on the other be able to show flexibility in dealing with the uncertainty of the environment. As is commonly said in the Middle East, companies must have a great deal of patience.

USEFUL WEBSITES

CIA World Fact book statistics on MENA: https://www.cia.gov/library/publications/the-world-factbook/wfbExt/region_mde.html.

International Labour Organisation on global employment trends for youth in MENA/youth/women (2013): http://www.ilo.org/wcmsp5/groups/public/---dgreports/---dcomm/documents/publication/wcms_212899.pdf.

International Monetary Fund, MENA External Publications: https://www.imf.org/external/pubs/ft/reo/2014/mcd/eng/pdf/menacca0514.pdf.

Population Reference Bureau for research and statistics on MENA: http://www.prb.org/.

The International Bank for Reconstruction and Development, The World Bank, Doing Business in MENA 2014 Report: http://www.doingbusiness.org/Reports/~/media/GIAWB/Doing%20Business/Documents/Profiles/Regional/DB2014/DB14-Middle-East-North-Africa.pdf.

Trading Economics website for useful population statistics on the MENA region: http://www.tradingeconomics.com/middle-east-and-north-africa/population-total-wb-data.html.

Woodrow Wilson Center, Middle East Program, for good resources on Middle East region, women, politics, social trends: http://www.wilsoncenter.org/.

World Bank MENA region: http://www.worldbank.org/en/region/mena.

REFERENCES

Abuznaid, S. 2006. Islam and management: what can be learned? *Thunderbird International Business Review*, **24**(1): 125–139.

Acevedo, G.A. 2008. Islamic fatalism and the clash of civilizations: an appraisal of a contentious and dubious theory. *Social Forces*, **86**(4): 1711–1752.

Afiouni, F., Karam, C.M. and El-Hajj, H. 2013. The HR value proposition model in the Arab Middle East: Identifying the contours of an Arab Middle Eastern HR model. *International Journal of Human Resource Management*, **24**(10): 1895–1932.

Al-Faleh, M. 1987. Culture influence on Arab management development: a case study of Jordan. *Journal of Management Development*, **6**(3): 19–34.

Al-Husan, F.B., Brennan, R. and James, P. 2009. Transferring western HRM practices to developing countries: The case of a privatized utility in Jordan. *Personnel Review*, **38**(2): 104–123.

Al-Rasheed, A.M. 2001. Feature of traditional Arab management and organization in the Jordan business environment. *Journal of Transnational Management Development*, **6**(1/2): 27–39.

Ali, A. 1988. Scaling an Islamic work ethic. *Journal of Social Psychology*, **128**(5): 575–583.

Ali, A.J. 1990. Management theory in a transitional society: the Arabs' experience. *International Studies of Management and Organization*, **19**(2): 22–37.

Ali, A.J. 1998. The typology of the Arab individual: implications for management and business organizations. *International Journal of Sociology and Social Policy*, **18**(11/12): 1–19.

Ali, A.J. 2008. Islamic work ethic: a critical review. *Cross Cultural Management: An International Journal*, **18**(1): 5–19.

Ali, A.J. 2010. Islamic challenges to HR in modern organizations. *Personnel Review*, **39**(6): 692–711.

Allinson, C. and Hayes, J. 2000. Cross-national differences in cognitive style: implications for management. *International Journal of Human Resource Management*, **11**(1): 161–170.

Andreassi, J.K., Lawter, L., Brockerhoff, M. and Rutigliano, P.J. 2014. Cultural impact of human resource practices on job satisfaction. *Cross Cultural Management: An International Journal*, **21**(1): 55–77.

Assad, S. 2002. Sociological analysis of the administrative system of Saudi Arabia: in search of a culturally capable model for reform. *International Journal of Commerce and Management*, **12**(3/4): 51–82.

Aycan, Z. 2005. The interplay between cultural and institutional/structural contingencies in human resource management practices. *International Journal of Human Resource Management*, **16**(7): 1083–1119.

Aycan, Z., Al-Hamadi, A.B., Davis, A. and Budhwar, P. 2007. Cultural orientations and preferences for HRM policies and practices: the case of Oman. *International Journal of Human Resource Management*, **18**(1): 11–32.

Aycan, Z., Kanungo, R.N., Mendonca, M., Yu, K., Deller, J., Stahl, G. and Kurshid, A. 2000. Impact of culture on human resource management practices: a 10-country comparison. *Applied Psychology*, **49**(1): 192–222.

Aycan, Z., Kanungo, R.N. and Sinha, J.B.P. 1999. Organizational culture and human resource management practices: the model of culture fit. *Journal of Cross-Cultural Psychology*, **30**(4): 501–526.

Azolukwam, V.A. and Perkins, S.J. 2009. Managerial perspectives on HRM in Nigeria: evolving hybridization? *Cross Cultural Management: An International Journal*, **16**(1): 62–82.

Bae, J., Chen, S. and Lawler, J.J. 1998. Variations in human resource management in Asian countries: MNC home country and host country effects. *International Journal of Human Resource Management*, **9**(4): 653–670.

Banutu-Gomez, M.B. 2002. Leading and managing in developing countries: challenge, growth and opportunities for twenty-first century organisations. *Cross Cultural Management: An International Journal*, **9**(4): 29–41.

Beechler, S. and Yang, J.Z. 1994. The transfer of Japanese style management to American subsidiaries: contingencies, constraints and competencies. *Journal of International Business Studies*, **25**: 467–492.

Bonache, J., Trullen, J. and Sanchez, J.I. 2012. Managing cross-cultural differences: testing human resource models in Latin America. *Journal of Business Research*, **65**(12): 1773–1781.

Branine, M. and Pollard, D. 2010. Human resource management with Islamic management principles: a dialectic for a reverse diffusion in management. *Personnel Review*, **9**(6): 712–727.

Brewster, C., Sparrow, P. and Harris, H. 2005. Towards a new model of globalising HRM. *International Journal of Human Resource Management*, **16**(6): 949–970.

Budhwar, P.S. and Debrah, Y.A. 2001a. Rethinking comparative and cross-national human resource management research. *International Journal of Human Resource Management*, **12**(3): 497–515.

Budhwar, P.S. and Debrah, Y.A. 2001b. Introduction. In P.S. Budhwar and Y.A. Debrah (eds), *Human Resource Management in Developing Countries*. New York: Routledge, pp. 1–15.

Budhwar, P. and Mellahi, K. 2006. Introduction: managing human resources in the Middle East. In P. Budhwar, P. and K. Mellahi (eds), *Managing Human Resources in the Middle East*, London: Routledge, pp. 1–19.

Budhwar, P. and Mellahi, K. 2010. Human resource management in the Middle East. In C. Brewster and M. Wolfgang (eds), *Handbook of Research in Comparative Human Resource Management*. Cheltenham, UK and Northampton, MA: Edward Elgar, pp. 512–527.

Budhwar, P.S. and Sparrow, P. 2002. An integrative framework for understanding cross-national human resource management practices. *Human Resource Management Review*, **12**: 377–403.

Chitakornkijsil, P. 2010. The internationalization of human resource management in the host nation context and strategic approach of IHRM. *International Journal of Organizational Innovation*, **3**(2): 379–401.

Dadfar, H. 1993. In search of Arab management, direction and identity. *Proceedings of the First Arab Management Conference*, University of Bradford Management Centre.

Dickmann, M. 2003. Implementing German HRM abroad: desired, feasible. *International Journal of Human Resource Management*, **14**(2): 265–283.

Earley, P.C. 1994. Self or group? Cultural effects of training on self-efficacy and performance. *Administrative Science Quarterly*, **39**(1): 89–117.

Egri, A.P. and Ralston, D.A. 2004. Generation cohorts and personal values: a comparison of China and the United States. *Organization Science*, **15**(2): 210–220.

Evans, P. and Lorange, P. 1990. The two logics behind human resource management. In P. Evans, Y. Doz and A. Laurent (eds), *Human Resource Management in International Firms*, New York: St. Martin's Press, pp. 144–161.

Evans, P., Pucik, V. and Björkman, I. 2011. *The Global Challenge: Frameworks for International Human Resource Management*. New York: McGraw-Hill/Irwin.

Fletcher, C. and Perry, E.L. 2001. Performance appraisal and feedback: a consideration of national culture and a review of contemporary research and future trends. In N. Anderson, D.S. Ones, H. Kepir-Sinangil and C. Viswesvaran (eds), *Handbook of Industrial, Work and Organizational Psychology*, London: Sage, pp. 127–145.

Frimousse, S., Swalhi, A. and Wahidi, M.E.A. 2012. The hybridization and internationalization of HRM in the Maghreb: examining the case of commitment and intention to quit amongst employees of multinational companies. *Cross Cultural Management: An International Journal*, **19**(2): 257–270.

Geringer, J.M. and Frayne, C.A. 1990. Human resource management and international joint venture control: a parent company perspective. *Management International Review*, Special Issue, **30**: 103–120.

Gluskinos, U.M. 1988. Cultural and political considerations in the introduction of Western technologies: the Mekorot project. *Journal of Management Development*, **6**: 34–46.

Gooderham, P., Morley, M., Brewster, C. and Mayrhofer, W. 2004. Human resource management: a universal concept? In C. Brewster, M. Morley and W. Mayrhofer (eds), *Human Resource Management in Europe: Evidence of Convergence?* London and New York: Routledge, pp. 1–27.

Grossman, R.J. 1997. HR in Asia. *HR Magazine*, **42**(7): 104–110.

Harris, P.R. and Moran, R.T. 1996. *Managing Cultural Differences*. Houston, TX: Gulf.

Hayes, J. and Allison, C.W. 1998. Cognitive style and the theory and practice of individual and collective learning in organisations. *Human Relations*, **51**: 847–871.

Hofstede, G. 1980. Motivation, leadership and organization: do American theories apply abroad? *Organizational Dynamics*, **8**(3): 42–63.

Hofstede, G. 1991. *Cultures and Organisations: Software of the Mind, Intercultural Cooperation and Its Importance for Survival*. London: McGraw-Hill.

Hofstede, G. 2001. *Culture's Consequences*. Thousand Oaks, CA: Sage.

Hofstede, G.J. 2009. Research on cultures: how to use it in training? *European Journal of Cross-Cultural Competence and Management*, **1**(1): 14–21.

Hofstede, G. and Bond, M.H. 1984. Hofstede's culture dimensions: an independent validation using Rockeach's value survey. *Journal of Cross-Cultural Psychology*, **15**: 417–433.

House, R.J., Hanges, P.J., Javidan, M., Dorfman, P.W. and Gupta, V. 2004. *Culture, Leadership, and Organisations: The GLOBE Study of 62 Societies*. Thousand Oaks, CA: Sage.

Hui, C.H. and Luk, C.L. 1997. Industrial/organizational psychology. In J.W. Berry, Y.H. Poortinga and J. Randey (eds), *Handbook of Cross-Cultural Psychology*. Boston, MA: Allyn & Bacon.

Huo, Y.P. and Von Glinow, M.A. 1995. On transplanting human resource practices to China: a culture-driven approach. *International Journal of Manpower*, **16**(9): 3–11.

Kabasakal, H. and Bodur, M. 2002. Arabic cluster: a bridge between east and west. *Journal of World Business*, **37**: 40–54.

Kanungo, R.N. and Jaeger, A.M. (eds) 1990. *Management in Developing Countries*. London: Routledge.

Karoliny, Z., Farkas, F. and Poór, J. 2009. In focus: Hungarian and Central Eastern European characteristics of human resource management: an international comparative survey. *Journal of East European Management Studies*, **1**: 9–48.

Keitsch, M. 2012. Sustainable architecture: design and housing. *Sustainable Development*, **20**(3): 141–145.

Kluckhohn, F.R. and Strodtbeck, F.L. 1961. *Variations in Value Orientations*. Evanston, IL: Row, Peterson.

Kovach, R.C. Jr 1995. Matching assumptions to environment in the transfer of management practices. *International Studies of Management and Organization*, **24**(4): 83–100.

Kundu, S.C. and Malhan, D. 2009. HRM practices in insurance companies: a study of Indian and multinational companies. *Managing Global Transitions*, **7**(2): 191–215.

Latifi, F. 1997. Management learning in national context. PhD thesis, Henley Management College, UK.

Laurent, A. 1986. The cross-cultural puzzle of international human resource management. *Human Resource Management*, **25**(1): 91–103.

Lazarova, M., Morley, M. and Tyson, S. 2008. International comparative studies in HRM and performance: the Cranet data. *International Journal of Human Resource Management*, **19**(11): 1995–2003.

Leat, M. and El-Kot, G. 2007. HRM practices in Egypt: the influence of national context? *International Journal of Human Resource Management*, **18**(1): 147–159.

Leung, K. 1997. Negotiation and reward allocations across cultures. In P.C. Earley and M. Erez (eds), *New Perspectives on International Industrial/Organizational Psychology*. San Francisco, CA: The New Lexington Press, pp. 640–675.

Lu, Y. and Björkman, I. 1997. HRM practices in China–Western joint ventures: MNC standardisation versus localisation. *International Journal of Human Resource Management*, **8**(5): 614–628.

MacDermid, S.M., Lee, M.D., Buck, M. and Williams, M.L. 2001. Alternative work arrangements among professionals and managers: rethinking career development and success. *Journal of Management Development*, **20**(4): 305–317.

Mellahi, K. and Budhwar, P. 2010. Introduction: Islam and human resource management. *Personnel Review*, **39**(6): 685–691.

Mellahi, K. and Guermat, C. 2004. Does age matter? An empirical examination of the effect of age on managerial values and practices in India. *Journal of World Business*, **39**: 199–215.

Mendonca, M. and Kanungo, R.N. 1994. Managing human resources: the issue of cultural fit. *Journal of Management Inquiry*, **3**(2): 189–205.

Michailova, S., Heraty, N. and Morley, M.J. 2009. Studying human resource management in the international context: the case of central and Eastern Europe. In M.J. Morley, N. Heraty and S. Michailova (eds), *Managing Human Resources in Central and Eastern Europe*, New York: Routledge, pp. 1–24.

Myloni, B., Harzing, A.W.K. and Mirza, H. 2004. Host country specific factors and the transfer of human resource management practices in multinational companies. *International Journal of Manpower*, **25**(6): 518–534.

Namazie, P. 2007. Factors affecting the transferability of HR policies and practices in Iranian IJVs. Unpublished PhD thesis, Middlesex University Business School, London, UK.

Namazie, P. and Frame, P. 2007. Developments in human resource management in Iran. *International Journal of Human Resource Management*, **18**(1): 159–171.

Namazie, P. and Tayeb, M.H. 2006. Human resource management in Iran. In P.S. Budhwar and K. Mellahi (eds), *Managing HRM in the Middle East*. London: Routledge, pp. 1–39.

Napier, N.K. and Vu, V.T. 1998. International human resource management in developing and transitional economy countries: a breed apart? *Human Resource Management Review*, **8**(1): 39–77.

Newman, K.L. and Nollen, S.D. 1996. Culture and congruence: the fit between management practices and national culture. *Journal of International Business Studies*, **27**(4): 753–779.

Nikandrou, I., Apospori, E. and Papalexandris, N. 2005. Changes in HRM in Europe: a longitudinal comparative study among 18 European countries. *Journal of European Industrial Training*, **29**(7): 541–600.

Obeidat, B.Y., Shannak, R.O., Masa'deh, R. and Al-Jarrah, I.M. 2012. Toward better understanding for Arabian culture: implications based on Hofstede's cultural model. *European Journal of Social Sciences*, **28**(4): 512–522.

Parnell, J.A. and Hatem, T. 1999. Cultural antecedents of behavioural differences between American and Egyptian managers. *Journal of Management Studies*, **36**(3): 399–419.

Pucik, V. 1996. Human resources in the future: an obstacle or a champion of globalization? CAHRS Working Paper, no. 96–11. Ithaca, NY: Cornell University, School of Industrial and Labor Relations, Center for Advanced Human Resource Studies. http://digitalcommons.ilr.cornell.edu/cahrswp/181 (accessed 26 January 2016).

Quinn, D.P. and Rivoli, P. 1991. The effect of American and Japanese-style employment and compensation practices on innovation. *Organization Science*, **2**(4): 323–341.

Rahwar, M. and Al-Buraey, M. 1992. An Islamic perspective of organizational controls and evaluation. *American Journal of Islamic Social Sciences*, **9**(4): 499–514.

Ralston, D.A., Egri, C.P., Stewart, S., Terpstra, R.H. and Yu, K.C. 1999. Doing business in the 21st century with the new generation of Chinese managers: a study of generational shifts in work values in China. *Journal of International Business Studies*, **30**(2): 415–428.

Ridley, D. 2012. *The Literature Review: A Step-by-Step Guide for Students.* London: Sage.

Rogmans, T. 2012. *The Emerging Markets of the Middle East: Strategies for Entry and Growth*. Business Expert Press.

Rosenzweig, P.M. and Nohria, N. 1994. Influences on human resource management practices in multinational corporations. *Journal of International Business Studies*, **25**(2): 229–251.

Ruona, W.E.A. and Gibson, S.K. 2004. The making of twenty-first-century HR: an analysis of the convergence of HRM, HRD and OD. *Human Resource Management*, **43**(1): 49–66.

Sale, M.L. 2004. Performance appraisal along cultural dimensions: truth or consequences. *International Journal of Strategic Cost Management*, **2**: 3–9.

Salehi Esfahani, D. 2005. Human resources in Iran: potentials and challenges. *Iranian Studies*, **38**(1): 117–147.

Sedikides, C. 2010. Why does religiosity persist? *Personality and Social Psychology Review*, **14**(1): 3–6.

Schneider, S. and Barsoux, J.P. 1997. *Managing across Cultures*. Harlow, UK: Prentice Hall Europe.

Schuler, R.S., Dowling, P.J. and De Cieri, H. 1993. An integrative framework of strategic international human resource management. *International Journal Human Resource Management*, **4**: 717–764.

Schuler, R.S. and Rogovsky, N. 1998. Understanding compensation practice variations across firms: the impact of national culture. *Journal of International Business Studies*, **29**(1): 159–177.

Schuler, R.S. and Tarique, I. 2007. International HRM: a North America perspective, a thematic update and suggestions for future research. *International Journal of Human Resource Management*, **18**: 15–43.

Shaista, E., Rodriguez, J.K., Gomez, C.F. and Puck, J. 2003. Transferring human resource practices from the United Kingdom to China: the limits and potential for convergence. *International Journal of Human Resource Management*, **9**(4): 1995–2003.

Sparrow, P.R. and Budhwar, P.S. 1997. Competition and change: mapping the Indian HRM recipe against world-wide patterns. *Journal of World Business*, **32**(3): 224–243.

Tayeb, M. 1995. The comparative advantage of nations: the role of HRM and its sociocultural context. *International Journal of Human Resource Management*, **6**(3): 588–606.

Tayeb, M. 1997. Islamic revival in Asia and human resource management. *Employee Relations*, **19**(4): 352–364.

Tayeb, M. 1998. Transfer of HRM practices across cultures: an American company in Scotland. *International Journal of Human Resource Management*, **9**(2): 332–358.

Tayfur, O. 2013. Convergence or divergence? Evaluation of human resource practices in Turkey. *Journal of Economics and Behavioural Studies*, **5**(9): 625–638.

Taylor, S., Beechler, S. and Napier, N. 1996. Toward an integrative model of strategic international human resource management. *Academy of Management Review*, **21**(4): 959–985.

Thornhill, A.R. 1993. Management training across cultures: the challenge for trainers. *Journal of European Industrial Training*, **17**(10): 43–51.

Tsang, E.W.K. 1994. Human resource management problems in sino-foreign joint ventures. *International Journal of Manpower*, **15**(9): 4–22.

Tung, R.L. 1984. Human resource planning in Japanese multinationals: a model for US firms? *Journal of International Business Studies*, **15**(2): 139–149.

Ulrich, D. and Brockbank, W. 2005. *The HR Value Proposition*. Boston, MA: Harvard Business School Publishing.

Venaik, S. and Brewer, P. 2008. Contradictions in national culture: Hofstede vs GLOBE. Competitive paper presentation at the AIB Conference 2008, Track 8: International Human Resource Management, Cross-Cultural Management and Qualitative Research Methods, Milan, Italy.

Venaik, S. and Brewer, P. 2010. Avoiding uncertainty in Hofstede and GLOBE. *Journal of International Business Studies*, **41**: 1294–1315.

Weir, D. 2000. Management in the Arab Middle East. In M. Tayeb (ed.), *International Business, Theories, Policies and Practices*. Upper Saddle River, NJ: Pearson Education, pp. 501–510.

Weir, D. 2001. Management in the Arab world: a fourth paradigm? Paper presented at EURAM Conference, Sophia Antipolis, 2 December.

Wong, C.S., Hui, C., Wong, Y.T. and Law, K.S. 2001. The significant role of Chinese employees' organizational commitment: implications for managing employees in Chinese societies. *Journal of World Business*, **26**(3): 326–341.

Zineldin, M. 2002. Globalisation, strategic co-operation and economic integration among Islamic/Arab countries. *Management Research News*, **25**(4): 35–61.

3. Society-level factors impacting human resource management in the Middle East

Wes Harry

INTRODUCTION

This chapter presents information on the rapidly changing society and regional situations which drive the way that human resource management (HRM) is practised in many organisations in the Middle East. In turn, the way that HRM, or management in general, treats existing and potential employees plays into the manner in which society-level changes become positive or negative in their impact. The chapter does not aim to provide a study of conceptual, theoretical or empirical research, yet it provides the needed evidence to support or challenge everyday HRM activities.

When engaged in the regular work of HRM, it is often difficult to be aware of the major factors playing out in societies which have, or soon will have, an impact on the organisation, the individuals and those engaged in management functions. In Europe and North America, changes in legislation may give rise to discussion in HRM publications or even workshops for professionals to explain what these changes could mean for HRM practice. Yet, if there are far reaching macro factors such as massive changes in the demographic profiles of the society and mismatches between young people leaving education and employment opportunities, or major calamities such as civil strife, war and great movements of people, these are rarely thought about by those managing resourcing, retention, reward, managing performance and other aspects of HRM.

Intentionally there might be provocative elements to this chapter, but these elements and statements are intended to encourage the reader to think of situations which may be very different from those in their own experience. The discussion in this chapter highlights situations which are not often considered by those dealing with operational problems in HRM, but knowledge of these society-level matters will improve the performance of those engaged in managing people in the workplace. The chapter supports the country-focused debate in other parts of the book.

The macro factors of demography, lack of access to quality education (indeed any education in some places) and reduced employment prospects, particularly for the young, have consequences for HRM, for employees and for the employers. Seemingly enlightened developments in the management of human resources supported by professional managers are not always seen by others in such a positive way. For example, the move to increase access to the workplace for youths and females is resisted by those who already have jobs. The endeavours by governments in richer Arab countries to increase host-country nationals' (HCNs) participation in public and especially in private sectors is seriously resisted by employers who claim that they cannot afford the extra costs compared to the employment of temporary workers from Asia or from poorer parts of the Arab region.

Ten years ago, the major seismic forces building in the Middle East, discussed by Harry (2007) might have seemed remote from those involved in HRM. These major forces were predicted to lead to massive changes in the workplace as well as to the possibility of violence and social disruption. Now these factors impact on the day-to-day workings of HRM.

Some countries, including Libya, Syria and Yemen, have broken down into civil strife and conflict, where the result has been possibly the world's largest involuntary migration (UNHCR, 2015). In countries such as Jordan and Lebanon, many millions of displaced people from Syria seeking work undercut the host population in wages and conditions of employment as the desperate enter virtual slavery. The better educated, or better connected, seek employment in the apparently rich Arab countries of the Gulf Cooperation Council (GCC), yet these states are increasingly reluctant to welcome fellow Arabs from collapsing or struggling Arab nations (GulfTalent, 2015; BBC, 2015). The riches of the GCC are increasingly spent on citizens through job creation in the public sector (via the Host Country Employment Nationalisation programmes), which in a time of declining revenue from hydrocarbons places great strains on government budgets (Financial Times, 2015).

DEMOGRAPHIC CHANGES

The changes taking place in the demographic structure of the Middle East are massive and in some cases disastrous for communities. The region has, at 60 per cent, probably the highest percentage of young in the world (Youthpolicy.org, 2015). This should provide a significant boost to economic performance and consequently prosperity for employers and employees. More youngsters usually mean more productive workers in ratio to the 'non-productive' elderly, children and caregivers. Yet in the region a substantial proportion of the young are 'non-productive' in that they have no work. Many have no work because the state in which they were raised is experiencing conflict and civil strife (Iraq, Syria, Libya and Yemen in particular) and they have no access to wage-earning jobs. In search of safety and work, millions have migrated to neighbouring countries where employers might be expected to offer jobs. Lebanon now has Syrian refugees making up 25 per cent or more of the population, but when walking around the streets of Beirut it is clear that employers still bring in workers from Sudan, Bangladesh and Sri Lanka rather than employ fellow Arabs (Al Monitor, 2015). The host population, especially those displaced from low-skilled work by cheaper migrant labour, resent the newcomers, although they are happy to have the cheaper services provided by these incomers.

In the wealthy countries of the GCC, where non-Arabs make up more than half of the expatriate workers (and in the case of Qatar and the United Arab Emirates (UAE) more than half of the total population), there have been increased restrictions on employing nationals of Arab countries, which are experiencing such destruction (BBC, 2015). Rather than welcome the Arab diaspora, they are feared for the possibility that those displaced from such states will extend conflict to the host communities. Further reasons for their reluctance to employ Arabs will be discussed in the section on performance near the end of this chapter.

Where jobs are offered to young people, these are increasingly of the temporary contract or agency work type found in the USA, East Asia and Southern Europe. Older workers and those with *wasta* (see Ta'Amnha et al., Chapter 21 in this volume) hold permanent roles. This is particularly the situation in the public sector and quasi-government agencies, where governments previously created employment, but not necessarily productive jobs, to keep the population from challenging existing political systems. Governments, including the wealthiest of the Arab states, have experienced a vast increase in the cost of public sector employment (The Economist, 2015) at the same time as the numbers of young people reaching the age at which they seek work is rapidly increasing. No government can afford to keep creating jobs in the public sector, hence the drive to encourage (or force) the private sector to offer more jobs to citizens in employment localisation initiatives (discussed in the chapters on the UAE, Oman and Saudi Arabia) and as a condition of getting government contracts (Forstenlechner and Rutledge, 2010).

When recruitment was based on fitting numbers onto the payroll or appointing those with *wasta*, with little attention to productive work, then the role of HRM, especially in the public sector, was/is to process and pay recruits with not much thought about selection. In private sector and semi-government agencies, including national oil companies, HRM seems to have played more of a role as 'gatekeeper' to reduce access to jobs, so selection systems were geared to rejecting candidates or delaying decisions. With the main public sector routes to employment becoming less accessible, the increase in candidates elsewhere has caused HRM in most organisations in the region to be an obstacle to job-seekers. This will be discussed later in the section on resourcing.

A further major demographic shift we must consider is the swift urbanisation that has been a feature of Middle East societies in recent decades. The proportion of Arabs living in cities has increased from 1970 to 2010 at a rate of 400 per cent so that now 56 per cent of the population live in cities and the Middle East is one of the most urbanised regions in the world (Schafer, 2013); micro and small enterprises (MSE) have been increasingly marginalised in relation to major family-owned conglomerates (such as Olayan of Saudi Arabia, Egypt's Wadi or Jordan's Nuqul) or state-owned corporations (such as Kuwait Petroleum Corporation, Saudi Aramco or Mabadala of the UAE). When most citizens' lives were based on village and small town communities, where employment was in family businesses and/or MSEs where professional and specialist management functions were superfluous. When employment is given to family or friends there is no need to have skilled interviewers. When loyalty is based on kinship and relationships there is no need for sophisticated retention and reward strategies. With the rapid growth in urbanisation and large-scale organisations there comes a need for ways of being sure of the abilities, personal characteristics and motivation of recruits and staff, so HRM becomes one of the necessary management functions which help organisations survive in this setting.

No discussion of demographic changes can neglect the migration of Arabs away from their homelands and the arrival of others, especially from South Asia, to seek employment in richer Arab countries. Although reports of boatloads of refugees seeking security or a better life in Europe capture the imagination, the reality is that many Arabs, especially well-educated ones, move away to create a new life elsewhere in North America, Europe, South America and Australasia. These people take education, abilities and entrepreneur skills to their host countries and are a loss to their homelands and to organisations, which would value their contribution. The migration into the region tends not to be a replacement of highly skilled people but poor people with few attractions to employers apart from being cheap and capable of undertaking physically arduous or socially unacceptable work. In such circumstances, there is little added value in the selection or retention systems offered by HRM specialists. Dealing with large numbers of low-paid and low-skilled workers, the majority of employers, even highly respected international corporations, subcontract to outsource agencies or labour supply companies. These agents provide millions of cheap domestic service and unskilled or semiskilled workers from places where people are desperate for work, even if these jobs are for meagre wages and entail demanding tasks and living conditions which, no matter how bad, have the prospect of being better than 'at home'. The 'use and throw away' attitude towards expatriate workers (especially the low paid ones from South Asia) which was prevalent in the days when there were not enough host-country workers to provide needed services in many Arab countries has continued in many organisations even when there are potentially many Arabs willing to work in their home or neighbouring countries.

The availability of cheap labour (from poor Arab countries and even poorer African and South Asian countries including Afghanistan and Nepal which are challenging India and Pakistan as sources of manual labour and unskilled service sector workers) forms the basis of a lack of a systematic approach to HRM. We rarely find the type of HRM found in richer regions of the world where limited availability, or costs, of potential recruits encourages systematic and costly processes of finding and keeping those most likely to be of long-term value to the employer. The value of human capital is rarely recognised in a region where a plentiful supply of low-added-value employees and a short time orientation means that organisations are not too concerned with professionalising the HRM function.

EDUCATION

The low value placed on human resources in the Middle East-based organisations is one consequence of low education levels within the region. Even before the Arab Awakening events and civil strife, from 2010/11 the quality of education offered to most Arabs was of very poor quality (UNDP, 2003). Since 2011 education standards, if any education is available at all, often have been of a poor quality (World Bank, 2014). Undoubtedly there are oases of international standards of education in places such as Al Azhar University of Cairo (which is over a thousand years old), King Fahd University of Petroleum and Minerals in Saudi Arabia and the American University of Beirut. These places attract the very best students, but the majority of Arabs have very low quality tertiary education institutions available (Daib, 2015).

Even when in education, it is likely that students are taught by rote subjects which have little relevance in the world of employment. Knowledge of career paths and employers' requirements are gained by informal (and maybe misinformed) conversations. So young people usually leave education without the knowledge, skills and attitudes required by employers.

This lack of education might not matter if the destination for employment were the MSE or informal workplace. But such opportunities are increasingly limited due to the increasing competition for even such low-value-added work. It is relevant that the incident that became the catalyst for the Arab Spring or Arab Awakening was the death of Mohamed Bouazizi, a poorly educated Tunisian street vendor who aspired to a better life but was harassed by officials as he aimed to support his family. Mohamed Bouazizi had hoped to go to university but dropped out of school to try to earn a living, then finding that few opportunities exist for a young Arab with no qualifications and no *wasta* in a place where youth unemployment was more than 30 per cent (CIPE, 2013).

Even qualifications are not of much help as the standards are not trusted by employers who know that, apart from the few quality institutions, the certificates issued rarely signify the capability of the student. In one example of short-term expediency leading to the swift devaluation of supposed qualifications, in 2014 the Lebanese Minister of Education announced that all students who sat for qualifications had passed (Al Akhbar, 2014). No student failed!

The curriculums of most Arab educational schools, colleges and universities have not been revised for decades and are mostly concerned with concepts and subjects of increasing irrelevance in the internet age (Daib, 2015; Financial Times, 2013). So children who are familiar with the social media using smart devices are taught in classrooms where the teacher gives lessons, for example, about music playing on record players to a generation whose parents might just remember hearing a record being played. The world outside the classroom might not exist as far as the curriculum and lesson plans are concerned. Innovation and creativity are resisted, and the students are not expected to have any knowledge or views to be used by the teacher in a debate or conversation. The students are there to listen and repeat what they are told. And what they are taught is not often the STEM (Science, Technology, Engineering and Mathematics) subjects which employers increasingly need workers to understand.

Not only are the subjects of less relevance but also the teaching style is not suited to modern economic, social or individual needs. Individual teachers might wish to encourage learning but most have been trained to impart lessons rather than enable learning. Teaching in many parts of the world is a 'profession', but often Arab teachers feel that they are only one level above that of agricultural workers or domestic helpers (Elbaz, 2005). Parents of the children do not expect to be involved in the children's education except to complain about the teachers if the student does not do as well as the parents had planned. Bullying and harassment by parents and school management is a feature of the teachers' lives (Korany, 2014). In turn, this causes many people with the potential to be excellent teachers to seek other career choices.

Only the wealthy elites can avoid the poor quality education and go to expensive private schools and universities in the region or in Europe and North America. When the elites do not have to educate their children in the government or low-cost private schools there is little interest in reforming the ways of teaching or the subjects taught. Some reform is occurring, for example in the UAE, where the government has an initiative to reform education starting with STEM subjects to make up 50 per cent of study time in secondary schools from September 2015 (Gulf News, 2015).

CONSEQUENCES FOR HRM OF THE SOCIETY-LEVEL FACTORS

The discussion of macro-level social changes might not seem to be relevant to the daily tasks of the HRM staff dealing with employment matters, but the big issues within the region do impact upon the way that HRM works and what the function aims to achieve. If an organisation might not exist in a few weeks, due to conflict or strife, then ten-year marketing plans would be useless. If one hundred unskilled labourers are required for a construction site and there are a hundred thousand poor young men desperate for an income, then using sophisticated selection methods will be pointless. Expecting a High School Diploma in a candidate specification when every person leaving school has been issued with a certificate is more than naïve.

With employment prospects throughout most of the region being poor, attitudes and expectations are rapidly changing. Where once government jobs were the aspiration of most young people, these are now seen as of little worth in poorer countries. Arab governments previously created work to keep the youngsters leaving education occupied (World Bank, 2010). This work was mostly routine, low paid but offered long-term security. In recent years, governments in the GCC have substantially increased pay and benefits for citizens in government service so that such employment is now high paid and secure but still very often routine administrative work which can be undertaken by fewer staff with information and communication technology (ICT) skills. Outside the GCC, the public sector now offers lower security and lower pay with inflation and reducing subsidies (virtually every government is reducing subsidies on food and fuel to try to balance budgets even at the risk of civil unrest) making it difficult to live on public sector wages (Alaa Abdel-Moneim, 2016). Even in the apparently wealthy GCC states, the proportion of government income spent on wages is devastating national financial resources (Arabian Business, 2015). To help place these major issues in the HRM context we will now consider elements of HRM responsibilities and examine their impact.

Strategy and Long-term Planning

Instability in communities, societies and regions discourages long-term planning and resource allocation. If there might be a revolution or even a large change in the marketplace, important stakeholders in organisations will become risk averse. Major investments will be postponed and resources, financial ones especially, will be hoarded or sent away to more stable locations. Capital resources in the form of plant, machinery and property are usually fairly fixed in the short term but human capital is often a variable which can be dispensed with or shifted from regular to irregular employment.

These factors have caused HRM and other organisational functions in the region to be very short term in their orientation. For HRM there has been the added historical factor (mentioned in the earlier discussion on demographic changes) that with a large supply of candidates for low-skilled work, what is now known as HRM was an unimportant administrative service just dealing with routine processing services.

The legacy of that lack of importance is that there is not often HRM involvement in organisational strategy and planning. If a business plan needs human resources, there is the assumption that low skills are on tap at a cheap price and any high skills can be found among those with *wasta* or be bought from among the ranks of available expatriates. In neither case is it likely that much forward thinking will be necessary.

Rather than despair at the lack of long-term planning, or even long-term thinking, it is up to those in HRM who believe that they and their profession can be of value to present evidence to top management demonstrating how HRM can make a difference. If operational managers think in the short term and do not bother to motivate or develop staff, the organisation may not survive when competitors make better use of human resources. In even the direst situations, preparing for the future can benefit individuals, employers and societies. In less troubled parts of the region there are still serious social problems resulting from unemployment and underemployment. By placing emphasis on short-term solutions (such as creating public sector jobs, using skilled and qualified foreigners to make up for shortfalls in the education systems, and overpaying citizens in employment), governments and employers solve current challenges by creating future problems.

Resourcing

Often the assumption of a pool of available workers to meet immediate needs is correct. In much of the region youth employment levels of 30 per cent or 50 per cent or higher are common. Even in the rich GCC states very high levels of unemployment (or under-employment – filling jobs of no or little worth) among citizens exist in parallel with imported workers occupying up to 90 per cent of jobs in the private sector and sizable proportions of public sector jobs, albeit in outsourced or subcontracted work. This situation is discussed in detail in the chapter by Waxin and Bateman on localisation in this volume (Chapter 7).

The availability of large numbers of HCNs, fellow Arabs and non-Arab expatriates looking for employment gives great power to the gatekeepers in HRM and other positions able to decide who does and does not get a place. Not only *wasta* but also outright corruption is a feature of dealing with access to paid employment (Farooqui, 2011). The most obvious actors with power and influence in the situation are Labour Agents, who while getting a fee for supplying staff will (despite often having to sign a declaration that they do not engage in the practice) demand sizable payments from successful candidates or even potential candidates (Human Rights Watch, 2014).

It might be thought that the Labour Agents could be cut out from the resourcing process by using advertisements. While job advertisements to attract candidates are a feature of employment in most parts of the world, these are virtually absent in many places in the Middle East. Part of the reason is that the sheer number of potential candidates will soon overwhelm a typical recruitment section. In a spectacular instance a few years ago, a large national oil company in a GCC country advertised for graduate trainees and swiftly had more than 10,000 young men queuing to hand over their applications. The advertisements, which are seen online or in the newspapers, are invariably placed by recruitment or Labour Agents trawling for CVs and usually requiring a fee to be put on file for possible jobs. Quite sophisticated scams exist to part job-seekers from their cash including fake interviews, sometimes even taking place in reputable companies' offices with meetings conducted by genuine HRM staff who are paid to conduct interviews for non-existent vacancies (Farooqui, 2011).

Without objective (and transparent) systems for workforce planning, selection and recruitment, it is extremely difficult to identify the use of *wasta* and payments for places in the workforce. Even in situations of hundreds of potential candidates for each vacancy, it still makes sense to attempt to make sifting candidates and recruiting more closely related to the job needs. To return to the example of thousands of labourers needed for a construction site, simple physical capability tests can make sure that candidates are able to work outdoors carrying material or following safe work practices. To rely on random selections of workers by supervisors or Labour Agents risks wasted time by incapable workers, high staff turnover and serious accidents. Evidence of such risks must be presented by HRM as a reason for more organised resourcing practices.

It is probably no coincidence that among the foremost practitioners of systematic resourcing are the large family businesses, some of which are vast conglomerates spanning many industries and many countries. These businesses might have relied on family connections in their earliest days and might still have a predominance of core family members at senior levels, but in selection and recruitment major Arab family businesses use the best international standards including psychometric assessment (using Arabic language material and Arab norm groups), structured and focused interview techniques and job-based criteria for appointment.

For most organisations, examples of best practices are rarely followed. More often the 'problems' or workforce resourcing is shifted to labour supply companies (often linked to Labour Agents), who provide a set number of people for specific periods of time or on a contingent basis with no period of work guaranteed. The basis of the relationship between the service supplier and the service acquirer is rarely anything but financial, with the cheapest supplier getting the work and the workers getting the lower pay (Human Rights Watch, 2014). It is in this environment that abuse of workers and human rights abuses occur. While much media attention is focused on the principal organisation or host country (such as the regular reports on the situation in Qatar within the construction industry preparing stadia for the 2022 Football World Cup), virtually no publicity is given to the Labour Agents and labour supply companies that are the origin of much of the harm.

Retention

The ready supply of job-seekers and a legacy of undervaluing human capital has diverted many in senior levels of management, including HRM, from paying attention to staff retention. Where loyalty is considered as the primary requirement of staff (not only in MSEs and family-owned businesses), it is assumed that everyone will remain no matter how they are treated. In addition, having gone through the maze of opaque recruitment processes to get a job it is unthinkable to voluntarily decide to leave.

The expectation of everyone staying on as long as they can might apply to older and less-well-educated employees. For the younger ones with expertise in demand, and with innovative and creative thinking skills, to stay and wait for an improved situation is still common. These young, well-educated Arabs, even in wealthy countries, are inculcated by supervisors and traditional family values to patiently stay where they are.

This leads to two parallel tracks in many organisations. For the mass of workers little positive attempt is made to encourage retention, it being assumed that they will stay. For a small minority, with expertise or *wasta*, moving or threatening to move can bring rapid improvements in benefits and swift rises in the hierarchy. It can be taken for granted that foreigners (Arab or non-Arab) will be in the former category. Most in the latter category will be citizens, with a small number of other Arabs.

Expecting staff to stay and put up with however they are treated has a damaging effect on morale and motivation. Gossiping, poor customer service, lethargy, high absence rates and minor sabotage are all symptoms of neglecting to positively manage the retention of staff. These affects are amplified at supervisory and junior-management levels when problems of capability, or abuse of workers, are hidden often until crises erupt in the workplace.

The lack of understanding of the benefits of actively encouraging retention has implications for learning and development, performance management and reward policies, which will be discussed below.

Learning

Sadly, there is a worry about increasing capability through learning and development within many organisations in the Middle East region. This holds back the chances of change and improvement. There is a concern about the consequences that learning and changing produces, which is similar to the inertia that is seen in the teaching syllabus and teaching practices discussed above. The reliance on learning at work from others, who have years of experience but not necessarily expertise, is thought to be 'good enough' for the young and newly appointed.

Again, in many organisations, not just in the Arab region, learning and development budgets are seen as 'costs', which are difficult or impossible to justify in the short term. More successful organisations see these budgets as 'investments' with short-, medium- and, particularly, long-term returns to the organisation and society as well as to the individual.

With a mass of others seeking work, employers think that there must be some already trained who can do higher levels of work without higher pay. If necessary they will buy in expertise by paying just a little more than the previous employer, and it is thought that having saved the costs of training they will be able to afford to pay a little extra. Having this mentality, the employers think that their rivals would do the same to entice their trained employees to the competition. In such a way a downward spiral of lack of investment in learning can occur.

A further related concern is that learning and development of employees will lead staff to claim for increased pay and benefits based on their increased value to the existing or potential employers. Once a few are given increases in pay or benefits other staff will ask for increases, either because of *wasta* or because they will undertake self-improvement through learning. Hence a fear of creating an upward spiral of increasing payroll cost can be created.

These short-sighted views do not take into account the increased flexibility, innovation and productivity which comes with higher levels of expertise. Not only do benefits accrue when learning is completed and valued qualifications awarded, but also improvements in performance occur during the learning.

Owners, managers and, especially, front-line supervisors in traditional organisations worry that they will not be able to control staff who have been through learning and development. It is a feature of those with power in traditional organisations that they are tempted to use and abuse that power. The subordinate staff with no power, fearful of losing their jobs and with little in the way of necessary education, will put up with a great deal of abuse by employers and employers' agents.

Reward

The mismatch between education and employment along with the large numbers of low-skilled workers in the Middle East has led to increasing inequality especially at lower levels where many applicants are available and at higher levels where there are fewer potential recruits with education or relevant in-depth experience. This inequality is not restricted to the region and is a cause for concern even in the heartland of capitalism in the USA. Within the typical organisation in the Middle East it is not just the substantial multiple of average wages which is paid to the CEO, but from mid-level management upwards there is a disconnect between pay and benefits given at these levels and at lower levels. At the lower level, the increasing reliance on temporary and daily paid workers is partly driven by owners' and directors' uncertainty for the future; it is also driven by the massive number of young people desperate for work and income, like Mohamed Bouazizi.

Growing shifts in HRM policies and practices to reward employees based on contribution or on performance introduces uncertainty and shifts in power (further discussed below) compared to the traditional methods of rewarding based on loyalty and length of service. Even a few years ago there were major employers in the Middle East which had no pay structures, with reward at all levels determined by entirely subjective means by the owner or top management. It was not unknown for employees to have no increase in pay during decades of service. Such practices survive in times of stability and no inflation but cannot last when rapid changes occur.

Performance

When pay depends on loyalty or length of service, there is little point in managing performance. Only personal commitment and the march of time are important. In such circumstances virtually all the power is in the hands of the employer or at senior levels within the organisation.

The issue of power and abuse of power is regularly discussed in the work environment (and especially outside work by those affected) but not so often discussed in the academic literature. Yet Abubakr and Mohamed (2005), in their study of managers in the Arabian Peninsula, found that managers spend up to 20 per cent of their time dealing with conflicts in the workplace. Managing performance could make a positive contribution to success (Abutayeh and Al-Qatawneh, 2012). In practice, a lack of trust in performance management systems and in the supervisors doing the assessing leads to misalignment and, perhaps, worse performance. Western rule-based cultures, in which much of the drive for active performance management systems was developed, come to challenge the more communal cultures of the Middle East in which the individual and their relationships is of far more importance than the person's role or contribution. Hutchings and Weir (2006) show how relationship and emotional trust is of far greater importance than rules and procedures. Hayajneh et al. (1994) demonstrated (in the context of Lebanon, Jordan, Palestine and Egypt) that nepotism or favouritism is encouraged by the sociocultural structure originating from tribal and kinship relationships. This crucial importance of relationships challenges systematic HRM and its expectation of standardised rules being paramount.

As relationships are so important, Arab managers will seek to avoid direct conflict and spend a lot of time dealing in an indirect way, taking up a substantial amount of the working week (Abubakr and Mohamed, 2005). With the rapid demographic changes, the relationships between individuals become much more complex than in the rural tribal societies in which connections were so important. So in order to keep in line with rule-based systems and relationship-based practice, the typical manager, understandably, will look for ways to keep everyone happy, not least because in fluid situations of domestic and international conflict the person currently lacking power might be very powerful in the future.

This need to try to keep everyone happy (or at least avoid too much open conflict) only applies to citizens or, maybe, fellow Arabs. For foreigners, and particularly poor foreigners from poor countries, there is no need to avoid conflict. They can be bullied and abused with little consequence. These attitudes to others is creeping into the previously paternalistic organisations in the Middle East so that Arab refugees and migrants from rural areas or conflict zones are treated in the same way as powerless workers from poor parts of South Asia.

However, many of these Arab migrants, particularly co-religious Sunni Muslims, feel that as part of the wider Arab community (*ummah*) they have rights denied to non-Arabs and non-Muslims. It is a challenge for Arab supervisors to manage the performance of fellow Arabs in a way which Asian workers will accept (or at least are powerless to resist) when these Arabs believe that they have the same rights as the host-country citizens. The potential problems in the supervisor/supervised performance assessment/management relationship is one of several reasons for employers preferring to recruit Asian rather than Arab workers.

CONCLUDING REMARKS – SOME OPTIMISM

Five thousand years ago the Middle East was a major centre for human development with the use of arable agriculture in the Levant, Mesopotamia and Egypt. For almost a millennium, from the sixth to the sixteenth centuries CE, the region was the major centre for learning and innovation and had the highest levels of human achievement, far surpassing Europe in systems and development. Arab organisational ability enabled trading enterprises to link East Asia, Africa and Europe in ways which Gulf airlines, trading companies and sovereign wealth funds are now emulating. Young Arabs, using the highest standards of education, which they have attained often with government scholarships and family support, are demonstrating world-class management skills.

After the rebuilding of the societies which have been destroyed or severely damaged since the Arab Spring or earlier, there is likely to be a greater emphasis on the value of human beings and making the best use of their potential. That was the experience in Western Europe after the Second World War. It was in this experience of war and destruction that the UK and USA developed the beginnings of what has now come to be known as HRM. Many of the selection methods used every day in HRM were developed in conflict and its aftermath. Psychometric testing was first used to help assess millions of recruits and place them in roles to which they were likely to be well suited. Japan's system of learning within organisations and developing the skills of workers was the result of needing to nurture and support the survivors of the Sino/Pacific/Second World War.

In turn the experience of the 'great leap forward' and later 'cultural revolution' caused Chinese society to make the most of human capability (including the mass of unskilled and poorly educated migrants from rural to coastal cities) to rapidly develop its economy and society.

Due to the breakdown of close extended family and community relationships (with urbanisation and demographic changes), there will be increased tension within organisations and within wider societies between being 'rule following' or being 'context driven' in managing people. To the Western educated reader, it might seem a positive development to be more systematic in HRM. Yet such a move will be to the advantage of the better educated with more relevant work experience. Those with little education and not much work experience will not welcome ever more standardisation and systematic ways of making choices at work. For the disadvantaged, the strong bonds offered by family, community, nationalism and religion will be a means to cope with rapid change and uncertainty. Their concerns should not be dismissed as 'out of date' or irrelevant in a globalised world.

The HRM function has opportunities with larger numbers of capable Arabs of being better organised, more long term in its orientation and more receptive to the supportive aspects of Middle Eastern cultures so making significant contributions to employer success and community sustainability.

It may be expected that the experiences of recent rapid change, some positive as well as much which has been harmfully negative, along with a long Arab history of overcoming difficulties through the ability to apply knowledge and learning, will lead to improved methods of managing human endeavours and communities. The people of the region can overcome extreme challenges in demographic change, educational attainment and lack of added value work opportunities for young people. In the same way that post-war Europe and Japan recognised the contribution of human capital along with financial capital and technical resources to bring prosperity to their populations, there is every expectation that the region will improve the learning and work chances of people.

Young people in the region are making use of social media and ICT to share experiences and develop capabilities which traditional education methods have not enabled. The hopelessness which leads some to *Daesh* (known in the West as Islamic State) leads far more youngsters to Khan Academy, Massive Open Online Courses (MOOCs) and Technology, Entertainment, Design (TED) talks on the internet. Young people (Millennial kids and Generation Z) are taking more responsibility for their careers and their future in just the same way as Generation X and Y did before them but within a less secure and comfortable environment.

The HRM function, when supporting the long-term survival and success of organisations and societies, can make a substantial contribution to these young people (as well as more mature individuals) by encouraging independent learning and providing facilities for self-study to make up for shortcomings in the education systems. HRM leaders can work more closely with community leaders to understand the interaction between organisational cultures and host-community cultures – each can have much to learn from the other. Being only focused on short-term matters and expedient solutions will rarely lead to success in society, organisation, group or individual terms.

Academics and HRM professionals have wonderful opportunities to study the interaction of a variety of HRM techniques for managing people within societies, communities, organisations and workplaces experiencing rapid, complex and exceedingly challenging circumstances. In the Middle East all are living in anxious times – for the sake of future generations, let us make the most of this experience.

USEFUL WEBSITES

Middle East Association: http://the-mea.co.uk.
Middle East Investor Relations Society: http://the-mea.co.uk.
Centre for Middle East Policy: http://the-mea.co.uk.
London Middle East Institute: https://www.soas.ac.uk/lmei/.

RECOMMENDED READING

The Economist – a UK weekly newspaper available in print and digital formats.
Foreign Affairs – a US bimonthly magazine with a range of respected contributors available in print and digital formats.
Arabic newspapers such as *Al Hayat* (published in a number of locations) provide non-Western viewpoints but mostly in the Arabic language with those readers lacking Arabic literacy having to rely on translation software or reprints in other languages.

REFERENCES

Abubakr, M.S and Mohamed, H.A. 2005. Towards a high-performance workplace: managing corporate climate and conflict. *Management Decision*, **43**(5): 720–733.
Abutayeh, B. and Al-Qatawneh, M. 2012. The effect of human resource management practices on job involvement in selected private companies in Jordan. *Canadian Social Science*, **8**(2): 50–57.
Al Akhbar 2014. Lebanon: education minister passes all students in bid to undermine the UCC. http://english.al-akhbar.com/node/21064 (accessed 14 September 2015).
Al Monitor 2015. Lebanese domestic workers to unionize. http://www.al-monitor.com/pulse/originals/2015/03/lebanon-domestic-workers-union-rights-fenasol-ilo-kafala.html# (accessed 2 February 2016).
Alaa Abdel-Moneim, M. 2016. *A Political Economy of Arab Education: Policies and Comparative Perspectives*. Abingdon, UK: Routledge.
Arabian Business 2015. Kuwait slashes spending, projects big budget deficit, Reuters, 27 January. http://www.arabianbusiness.com/kuwait-slashes-spending-projects-big-budget-deficit-580049.html (accessed 2 February 2016).
BBC 2015. Migrant crisis: why Syrians do not flee to Gulf states. http://www.bbc.com/news/world-middle-east-34132308 (accessed 14 September 2015).
CIPE 2013. The youth unemployment crisis in Tunisia. http://www.cipe.org/blog/2013/11/18/the-youth-unemployment-crisis-in-tunisia/#.VfbKcJf051Y (accessed 14 September 2015).
Daib, H. 2015. The answer to our problems lies in educating our youth. *University World News Global Edition*, issue 369, 29 May.
Elbaz, F. 2005. *Teachers' Voices: Storytelling and Possibility*. Charlotte, NC: Information Age Publishing.
Farooqui, M. 2011. Job scam: the interview that never was. *XPRESS*, 24 February, p. 1.
Financial Times 2013. Arab school textbooks rewritten after regime changes, 20 October. http://www.ft.com/intl/cms/s/0/313bc0f4-1ba1-11e3-b678-00144feab7de.html#axzz3liegIlSZ (accessed 2 February 2016).
Financial Times 2015. Gulf states face 'double whammy' of lower oil prices and rate rise, 8 September, p. 12.
Forstenlechner, I. and Rutledge, E.J. 2010. Growing levels of unemployment in the Gulf: time to update the social contract. *Middle East Policy*, **XVII**(2): 38–51.
Gulf News 2015. Curriculum reform to develop graduates for UAE workforce, 25 March. http://gulfnews.com/news/uae/education/curriculum-reform-to-develop-graduates-for-uae-workforce-1.1478845 (accessed 15 October 2015).
GulfTalent 2015. *Employment and Salary Trends in the Gulf*. GulfTalent: Dubai.

Harry, W.E. 2007. Employment creation and localization: the crucial human resource issues for the GCC. *International Journal of Human Resource Management*, **18**(1): 132–146.
Hayajneh, A.F., Dwairi, M.A. and Udeh, I.E. 1994. Nepotism as a dilemma for managing human resources overseas. *Journal of Transnational Management Development*, **1**(1): 51–73.
Human Rights Watch 2014. *I Already Bought You*. New York: HRW.
Hutchings, K. and Weir, D. 2006. Understanding networking in China and the Arab world: lessons for international managers. *Journal of European Industrial Training*, **30**(4): 272–290.
Korany, B. (ed.) 2014. *Arab Human Development in the Twenty-First Century: The Primacy of Empowerment*. Cairo: AUC Press.
Schafer, K. 2013. *Urbanization and Urban Risks in the Arab Region*. 1st Arab Region Conference for Disaster Risk reduction, UN Habitat, Aqaba 19–21 March.
The Economist 2015. A day of reckoning for fuel prices in the Gulf. 5 August, p. 46.
UNDP 2003. *Arab Human Development Report*. New York: United Nations Development Programme.
UNHCR 2015. 2015 UNHCR regional operations profile – Middle East and North Africa (MENA). http://www.unhcr.org/pages/4a02db416.html (accessed 14 September 2015).
World Bank 2010. Young people in Arab countries: promoting opportunities and participation. Marseille workshop, April 28–30.
World Bank 2014. Education in the Middle East and North Africa, 27 January. http://www.worldbank.org/en/region/mena/brief/education-in-mena (accessed 19 July 2016).
Youthpolicy.org 2015. Middle East and North Africa: youth facts. http://www.youthpolicy.org/mappings/regionalyouthscenes/mena/facts/ (accessed 17 September 2015).

4. Performance appraisal systems in the Middle East[1]

Antonio Giangreco and Jacob Vakkayil

INTRODUCTION

The field of human resource management (HRM) has witnessed a growing interest in the value of a contextualized understanding of human resource (HR) processes and practices. This is especially true for HR performance appraisal in the light of increasing focus on measurement of outcomes in business organizations worldwide (Bourne et al., 2013). Although companies with international operations have the tendency to harmonize appraisal practices across borders, the local context might play an important role in the way performance measurement is experienced. In fact, interpreting and influencing human behaviours and associated practices in organizations require a serious consideration of organizational, economic and socio-cultural factors that form the context of such practices (Newman and Nollen, 1996; Saini and Budhwar, 2008). However, context is a multilayered and multidimensional concept and often it needs to be unpacked in more specific ways to be applied in a useful manner in studies that seek to incorporate context as a central consideration. More specifically, there is an increased focus on how geopolitical, societal and cultural features form part of the context of action influencing organizational outcomes. In this context, it has been observed that HRM is very likely to be deeply affected by national and cultural differences (Rosenzweig and Nohria, 1994; Aycan et al., 2000; Budhwar and Sparrow, 2002; Pudelko, 2006; Vaiman and Brewster, 2015). Here, the transplantation of HR practices that have evolved from and are rooted in a predominantly Western context has received much attention. Forces of globalisation have resulted in an increased expansion of the operations of multinational companies to emerging economic centres and the adoption of predominantly Western practices through isomorphic influences. The resultant directions and the emergence of new themes and practices is a fascinating area of research for scholars of HRM (Björkman and Lervik, 2007; Al-Husan, Brennan and James, 2009; Ramdani et al., 2014).

The Middle East (ME) represents one such context which has generated considerable interest among HR scholars not only because of conspicuous differences in cultural dimensions with the West, but also because of the emergence of the region as economically and geopolitically significant (Budhwar and Mellahi, 2007; Afiouni, Ruël and Schuler, 2014). Resultantly, there is a great deal of activity by global corporations operating with considerable differences within the context in which these companies are rooted. A number of scholars have explored the impact of these differences on various aspects of HRM (e.g., Al-Husan, Al-Hussan and Perkins, 2014) and leadership style (Bealer and Bhanugopan, 2014). Most often such work has focused on Gulf Cooperation Council (GCC) countries and more specifically the United Arab Emirates (UAE), which is a centre of commerce with a considerable presence of global corporations (e.g., Bealer and Bhanugopan, 2014). Though other countries such as Syria, Yemen, Palestine, Iraq or countries in the Maghreb area have received lesser attention in the past, this has recently begun to change with a number of studies focusing on multiple countries in the region (Afiouni, Karam and El-Hajj, 2013; Ramdani et al., 2014; Mostafa and Gould-Williams, 2014). This broader focus is likely to be useful as the ME is characterized by a great deal of diversity in terms of ethnicities, languages, political systems, economic resources, political (in)stability, etc. (Al-Hamadi, Budhwar and Shipton, 2007; Budhwar and Mellahi, 2007; Hutchings, Metcalfe and Cooper, 2010; Mellahi, Demirbag and Riddle, 2011). This focus on differences within the region is also likely to result in a more nuanced understanding of HRM issues in companies operating across various countries and a greater awareness of the multiplicities and complexities involved. In this chapter, we look closely at the issue of performance appraisal in the ME context. For this, we first focus on the logics embedded in the use of performance appraisal systems (PAS) in Western contexts. After that, we discuss the potential limitations in Western-driven PAS when applied to the context of the ME. We highlight then new emerging logics that might be important for PAS in the ME. We conclude by identifying key challenges and related recommendations which could lead to successful results from PAS implemented in the ME region.

PERFORMANCE APPRAISAL SYSTEMS: LOGICS AND ISSUES

The notion of performance is central to HRM, and performance management has been considered essential in efforts to achieve well-integrated and strategically aligned HRM. Within this context, the process of performance appraisal aims at driving individual efforts towards organizational goals and objectives (West et al., 2002). PAS form the backbone of this integrated approach to develop and deploy HR in the context of the challenging competitive environments that companies operate in. Generally, they are designed to meet the twin objectives of serving as inputs for HR decisions and assessing the developmental needs of employees (Brumback, 1988). The benefits of well-designed and implemented PAS can work at multiple levels, serving both the achievement of corporate performance (Delery and Doty, 1996; DeNisi and Smith, 2014) and the creation of positive attitudes and behaviours in individuals (Brown, Hyatt and Benson, 2010).

The issue of customization of PAS to suit local conditions by multinational companies has been researched in many contexts (Harvey, 1997; Claus, 2008; Claus and Briscoe, 2008; Varma, Budhwar and DeNisi, 2008). Researching in the East European context, Claus and Hand (2009) assert that local transferability of a Western PAS is problematic in cultures with high power distance where gender roles are specific. They found that often in those situations, upstream elements such as performance criteria for executives, appraisal instruments and so on tend to be standardized, while downstream elements such as appraisal interviews, feedback and so on might become localized.

Giangreco et al. (2010) uses the notion of *logics* to understand how PAS has been approached. They identify five key logics that have emerged from a review of literature on PAS (Table 4.1). This study reviewed Western organizations in most cases, and as such the philosophy, orientations and priorities of Western companies have been reflected in the logics. Resultantly, these logics can serve as a good tool to assess commonalities and differences influencing PAS in the West and other contexts.

The first logic is referred to as the logic of control. PAS is often used by managers to control and regulate employees (Klaas and DeNisi, 1989; DeNisi and Smith, 2014) and

Table 4.1 *Logics of performance appraisal*

Logic	Objective
Control	Obtaining predictability of behaviours and results through planning and accurate measurement of performances
Continuity	Ensuring that behaviours and results are linked across time to ensure development and future objectives
Formality	Guaranteeing fairness through formal processes and guidelines
Information	Facilitating upward and downward flow of information to connect individual and collective objectives
Motivation	Achieving higher motivation level through participation in goals setting and recognition of achieved results

to ensure that desired behaviours are displayed in a consistent manner. Precise quantitative measures often make it impossible for employees to deviate from prescriptive task behaviours to the exercise of discretionary control over own tasks. Though there has been a shift towards a focus on objectives and achieving results without undue prescription, the idea of accuracy is inherent in the planning, design and implementation of PAS (Lam and Schaubroeck, 1999; Iqbal, Akbar and Budhwar, 2015).

The second identified logic is referred to as the logic of continuity. PAS connects past performance to future objectives. Periodic measurements facilitate setting goals at the appropriate level of difficulty while considering the overall objectives to be achieved by the unit or the organization. There is also the essential linkage between developmental efforts in the past and new competencies acquired with responsibilities for the future. The appraisal process facilitates the identification of areas for improvement and provides essential inputs to developmental efforts, which in turn are further assessed in the next iteration. The results serve in fixing new responsibilities and objectives for future assignments. Such a continuous unbroken chain in the implementation of PAS also establishes and transmits an organizational culture where measurement of performance is considered important (Price, 2007).

The third logic is referred to as the logic of formality. PAS responds to the need to establish fairness and reduce arbitrariness through formal processes. For the employee, this involves a clear articulation of goals and objectives, while for the manager formality represents efforts to avoid subjectivity and bias in measurements of performance (Woehr, 1992; Bol et al., 2014). This is particularly true for large organizations where formality ensures a degree of consistency and uniformity across units, locations and so on. It sends the etic-oriented message that *the same rules apply for everyone* thus ensuring a perception of fairness and justice.

The logic of information is the fourth identified logic that drives PAS. The appraisal process involves exchange of key information (Baruch, 1996; Dessler, 2015) in both upward and downward directions. For the employee being appraised, it provides information about the priorities of the organization at a given point in time and what specific areas are being addressed in response to external challenges. For middle managers and executives, it provides information not only about individual levels of performance, but also about challenges on the ground level and patterns observed across units, enabling a strategic perspective. This information also serves as inputs for HR departments and subsequent HRM actions.

The last of the identified logics is called the logic of motivation. PAS ensure the clarification of objectives and goals as well as formalized and structured feedback, both of which can contribute to the motivation levels of employees. Clear, achievable, precise and time-bound goals have been linked to higher motivation levels (Tubbs, 1986; Pinder, 2008). It has also been noted that employee participation in goals setting can lead to higher motivation (Spector, 1986; Kim and Holzer, 2016). Further, as Cawley, Keeping and Levy (1998) and Kim and Holzer (2016) demonstrate, participative PAS results in higher satisfaction concerning the appraisal process itself. The structure feedback in the appraisal process ensures both adequate recognition of achieved results and clarification of the factors leading to that particular level of performance. These contribute to the nurturing of the virtuous cycle of motivation in employees.

The appraisal process ensures that goals and objectives have essential characteristics to enhance motivation and can facilitate employee involvement to ensure better commitment. Feedback also triggers the process of self-evaluation and has the potential to motivate corrective behaviour initiated by the employees themselves (Ivancevich and McMahon, 1982; Rasheed et al., 2015). Thus an ideal PAS is firmly rooted in the logic of motivation and the individual components of the system work towards ensuring and enhancing employee motivation (Kuvaas, 2006).

The five logics of PAS (Table 4.1) provide us with key dimensions along which PAS can be evaluated in other contexts such as the ME. It serves as a tool to assess areas of convergence and divergence and to see what new elements can be observed in novel situations.

PERFORMANCE APPRAISAL SYSTEMS IN THE MIDDLE EAST: COMPLEXITIES OF THE CONTEXT

Much like other concepts associated with HRM, the notion of performance needs to be approached in a contextualized manner (Claus and Briscoe, 2008). The focus on individual performance in the effort to realize annual objectives successfully draws from a philosophy of HRM that is mostly based in Western Europe and North America. Many of the assumptions inherent in this philosophy of HR practice may not hold in contexts in the ME, where collectivistic social norms place greater importance on collective performance as opposed to individual performance (Zaharna, 1996; Aladwan, Bhanugopan and Fish, 2014). This can also be influenced by the well-known concept of '*wasta*' in the ME (Hutchings and Weir, 2006) that refers to the use of reciprocal favours in a web of relationships. Tlaiss and Kauser (2011) consider the widespread presence of actions and behaviours rooted in *wasta* as an obstacle for HR professionalism in the region. Another factor that influences organizations strongly in many countries of the ME is the importance of religion in the socio-economic sphere (Mellahi and Budhwar, 2010). Al-Hamadi and Budhwar (2006) found that in Oman there is a triple influence of Islam, tribe and family, with the first being the factor of most importance. In studies that explore the link of Islam and the workplace, the importance of the relationship between employers and employees and the resultant mutuality of interests have been highlighted (Ali, 2010). This probably explains the importance attached to processes of consultation and information in these relationships in the ME (Tayeb, 1997). In addition, a key factor that cannot be ignored since it influences business and organizations in the ME is the level of political instability and existence of ongoing conflicts that characterize a few parts of the region.

Because of these particular contextual factors, the implementation and usage of PAS is likely to be driven by other factors rather than the five Western logics. Resultantly, practices of PAS based on these logics might face dissonance with other aspects of organizational life. All in all, there seems to be a gap between these ideals driving PAS and the reality of practice (Branine and Pollard, 2010), leading to situations of ambiguity. In view of this likely dissonance, we examine below particular factors that might change the influence of each of the five Western-driven PAS logics in organizations in the ME.

With regard to the first logic of control, it is likely to hold true equally strongly in the ME. For example, in filling HR requirements within companies operating in the region, there seems to be a clear preference for internal recruitment and promotion from within the organization (Afiouni, Karam and El-Hajj, 2013). Moreover, efforts at localization of the workforce in many countries of the ME also might result in better control of the workforce within the organization in terms of better cultural fit and alignment in ways of working. These efforts clearly focus on predictability, consistency and uniformity of expected behaviours in alignment with the logic of control.

The second logic of continuity is dominant in the literature on performance appraisal in the ME.

The emphasis on loyalty to the organization as a cultural feature of the ME is also likely to contribute to the logic of continuity. However, in practice this orientation might experience problems primarily because of the large number of expatriates working in the ME. Many of these employees work on short-term contracts of one to two years' duration (Khan, 2011). Though renewed often, the uncertainty associated with such contracts might drive a short-term orientation for employees in setting objectives and goals, leading to a dissonance with the logic of continuity.

The logic of formalization is also likely to show some amount of variance in the ME. On the one hand, organizations in the region are generally characterized by bureaucratic work structures and rigid rules (Afiouni, Karam and El-Hajj, 2013), and formalized procedures are considered desirable (Khoury and Analoui, 2004). On the other hand, in practice this does not always hold true. There seems to be an important difference in the way formalization is perceived in the ME. Unlike the Western contexts where formalization is associated with precision and uniformity, in the ME it is associated with respect for processes including certain organizational rituals of symbolic value (Zaharna, 1996). The combination of high power distance and low individualism might result in employees expecting to be directed by the managers' authority and loyalty rather than merely by bureaucratic systems and processes (Leat and El-Kot, 2007). Finally, relationships and loyalty to one's own group are highly valued in the ME, and this is often privileged over task achievement, resulting in nepotism (Parnell and Hatem, 1999). This again is likely to detract from the perception of fairness associated with formalized procedures of PAS. In view of these arguments, it is likely that the logic of formalization might not be perceived as an important driver for PAS in the ME.

There is reason to believe that the logic of information also may not be universally applicable for PAS in the ME. There seems to be a widespread prevalence of authoritarian management in many parts of the region (Bakhtari, 1995). It has been reported that in the area of performance appraisal, subordinate inputs are not often systematically considered by many managers (Abu-Doleh and Weir, 2007). This might be due to the cultural feature of high power distance operating at the workplace in the ME. In addition, the presence of high numbers of foreign employees with fixed-term contracts might act as a barrier in the free flow of information between managers and employees. As result of these particularities, the logic of information inherent in the Western model of PAS may not apply in organizations in the ME.

The fifth logic of motivation includes aspects of goal setting and feedback, and these can be important for settings in the ME (Chakrabarti et al., 2014). However, regarding the capability of these systems to enhance motivation and thus serve the fifth logic, there seems to be reason to expect divergence from Western settings. A number of studies in the ME point to the general reluctance of managers to encourage the involvement of employees. Many organizations still seem to function with an image of the employee as someone who dislikes work, justifying the use of external force rather than internal motivation (Suliman, 2001). Resultantly, managers may not come across as participative (Badaway, 1980; Bakhtari, 1995) and seeking participation might be regarded as a sign of weak management (Parnell and Hatem, 1999). Consequently, the application of the logic of motivation as perceived in the Western model of PAS might face serious difficulties in organizations in the ME.

NEW EMERGING LOGICS IN THE USE OF PAS IN THE MIDDLE EAST

As seen above, the concept of context is highly complex with multiple dimensions. In the ME, though there are striking commonalities that influence the deployment of PAS, we cannot have a comprehensive understanding by considering these commonalities alone. The results and changes implicated with the use of PAS are influenced both by these common features and by the particularities unique to the situation in question. It becomes imperative that these also become important elements of context in our quest to fully situate the use of PAS in ME settings.

The results of the study by Giangreco et al. (2012) about PAS implementation in a hospital in the West Bank operating during the second *intifada* illustrates the importance of such a nuanced understanding of context in the ME. They point to how a crisis-like situation outside the organization can change the way in which the logics of PAS function within the organization. Even the rationale used for evaluating the success of a PAS can be different in the ME. Often it depends on factors that seem external to the system itself and rooted in the social environment. Resultantly, outcomes that could be considered failures by Western notions of success might often be considered successful in this setting. Giangreco and colleagues observe that the logics of control, continuity, formality, information and motivation were utilized for the justification of the PAS in the initial design and planning stages (see Table 4.2). However, they argue that changes emerged during the actual implementation and use of the system.

First, the control logic lost importance during the conflict situation as measures such as severe sanctions or lay-offs could not be considered as options during this period. The

Table 4.2 Causes of dissonance for PAS logics

Logic	Causes of dissonance
Control	Shortage of employees, increasing demand, expectations from society
Continuity	Uncertainty about future, irregular living and working conditions
Formality	Different standard of formality (presence at the workplace), appraisal based on status
Information	Dubious and unverified information under critical conditions
Motivation	High uncertainty leading to difficulty in both goal setting and accurate assessment of performance

acute shortage of skilled employees and the large number of cases to be served made it imperative to keep every employee in the organization and continue to try to meet the expectations placed on it by the society. Resultantly, employees did not perceive the PAS as functioning from the logic of control. Second, the logic of continuity was also challenged as a long-term view could not be implemented in the critical conditions within which the hospital was operating. More long-term orientation is generally perceived as a priority when conditions resemble what is considered as *normal* and continuous. Lack or normality thus contributed towards lesser importance being attached to continuity. The logic of formality also seemed to suffer under the critical conditions. The idea of *fairness* inherent within this logic took a beating as substitutes were employed for performance. Often, mere presence at the workplace was considered a relevant measure of performance. At other times, status was equated to performance resulting, in persons of higher status in the organization, such as doctors, receiving higher scores than others such as nurses. The logic of information also decreased in importance as dubious and unverified information began to be entered in to the system. This resulted in a vicious cycle of further decreased importance given to the information in the system, thus aggravating further levels of dubious and wrong information. Finally, the motivation logic also suffered with the decreased importance accorded to the system as a fair process with reliable information reflecting true performance of the past. Similarly, accurate information regarding goals and objectives of the future were also missing from the system.

However, though these Western-oriented traditional logics began to decrease in importance, the use of the system was not discontinued. They remained in place as *official* logics providing espoused rationality for the initiative. In spite of this, interestingly, newer logics more in tune with the critical context within which the organization existed began to emerge. The authors name the first of these new logics as *dominance logic*, which seeks to maintain status quo instead of driving changes. Over the years, the average scores in PAS consistently increased across all the professional groups, thereby reassuring employees about the value of the status quo. The second newly observed logic was the *peacefulness logic*. In a context characterized by high levels of conflict outside the organization, PAS was understandably used to ensure somehow relational peace inside the organization, aiming therefore at a better organizational climate rather than a way to promote a more performance-oriented work culture and context.

The authors attribute the emergence of these two new logics to a tendency to depend more strongly on cultural factors in critical situations. The idea of *wasta* is reflected in both these logics, and it could be assumed that *wasta* can form a safe refuge when a situation becomes uncertain. The incorporation of familiar cultural elements into an organizational process thus illustrates the complex interplay of culture with organizational practices.

The presence of societal and political conflict outside the organization often leads to crisis-like situations and adds an important layer of complexity within organizations. This needs to be carefully considered while studying HR in conflict-driven or politically instable situations. A contextual view of PAS recognizes that this forms an integral part of the setting within which employees function and HR processes are planned and deployed.

Another layer of complexity can arise because of apparent changes in society attributed to Westernization. Behery and Paton (2008) report a study aimed at examining the impact of culture on performance appraisal in the UAE. Managers were asked how they perceived the appraisal processes, approaches and outcomes. While managers asserted that fit between culture and appraisal process was important for satisfaction, it was found that essentially Western approaches engrained within the appraisal process were perceived positively and welcomed as desirable by the managers. This pointed to the possibility that elements of the appraisal process were perceived as being aligned to their own culture. However, the authors highlight that these results might have been influenced by the particular features of the workplace setting they analysed. The sample of managers consisted of relatively affluent social groups exposed to external influences in an outward-looking region that is one of the biggest commercial hubs in the ME where Westernization was evident. Whiteoak, Crawford and Mapstone (2006) also point to the influence of change, especially in areas such as individualism, in the UAE. In spite of this, in other areas such as Islamic ethics at the workplace, the use of *wasta* in organizations and so on, there seemed to be greater stability and uniformity.

Another dimension of complexity of context in the ME points to the type of organization, public or private. One relevant study in this context was reported by Abu-Doleh and Weir (2007) concerning attitudes of HR managers towards PAS in Jordanian companies. Drawing from Cleveland, Tziner and Murphy (1989) they focused on the perceived functions of PAS such as between-individuals comparisons (promotion, salary administration etc.), within-individuals comparisons (training needs, feedback etc.), systems maintenance (personnel planning, goal achievement etc.) and documentation (noting decisions, meeting legal requirements etc.). The authors aimed at comparing public and private organizations in Jordan to see differences in the application of PAS functions. They found that PAS had far greater impact on the first two functions, influencing promotions, lay-offs, training needs identification, transfers and so on. Moreover, this influence seemed to be much stronger in private organizations than in public ones. This is significant in the context of the ME with large state-owned public organizations, which are popular employment destinations for the local population of many countries in the region (Ibrahim, Al Sejini and Al Qassimi, 2004).

Table 4.3 Challenges and recommendations for the use of PAS in the ME

Challenges	Recommendations
Equal opportunities for women	Ensuring fairness through PAS
Localization of employees	Increasing emphasis on development and use of PAS for this purpose
Management of foreign employees	Setting high standards beyond the legal requirements through innovative PAS

KEY CHALLENGES IN THE USE OF PAS IN THE MIDDLE EAST

Like any other contexts with their characteristic features, the context of the ME also poses challenges for HRM practitioners in many areas including the smooth implementation of PAS adopted (see Table 4.3). Issues associated with gender, including equal opportunities for women, have been prominently highlighted by researchers and observers of HRM practices (Al-Kharouf and Weir, 2008; Hutchings, Lirio and Metcalfe, 2012). There exist social and cultural features that prevent women from participating in the workplace and achieving their full potential in organizations (Gallant and Pounder, 2008; Marmenout and Lirio, 2014). Resultantly, this is an area that is particularly challenging for HRM practitioners. Metcalfe (2007) points out, for example, that equal opportunities are not emphasized in the implementation of HRM practices in Bahrain. Lack of organizational support and the prevailing business culture are cited as important reasons for the absence of equal representation. Drawing from various works that highlight the perceptions regarding women in employment, similar observations can also be made regarding other countries in the ME region (e.g., Marmenout and Lirio, 2014). HRM systems in general and PAS in particular must be planned, taking into account this important issue.

The second challenge relates to efforts of localization of the corporate workforce through regulation. In many countries of the ME, expatriate employees outnumber local employees in most sectors and are mainly concentrated in the public sector (Al-Waqfia and Forstenlechner, 2014). For example, expatriates account for approximately one-third of the workforce in Oman, three-quarters in Kuwait and almost four-fifths in Qatar and the UAE (www.dubaifaqs.com). To ensure the increased participation of local people in corporations, governments have called for localization efforts and stipulated that a fixed percentage of the employees in every company must be local. Researchers have examined the impact of such policies for organizations in various countries in the region (Al-Enzi, 2002; Mellahi, 2007; Rees, Mamman and Braik, 2007; Al-Ali, 2008; Williams, Bhanugopan and Fish, 2011; Al-Waqfia and Forstenlechner, 2014) and have highlighted a number of problems in the implementation of these policies (e.g., Syed, Hazboun and Murray, 2014 for expatriate–local relationship issues). Often, restrictions placed on companies and the adverse impacts they have on competitiveness are highlighted. Moreover, it has also been pointed out that companies often do not invest in the development of their local employees, leading to an aggravation of dissatisfaction with the impacts of this policy and the restrictions it places on HRM personnel (Khan, 2007). Since PAS is at the centre of HR efforts for employee management, the lack of emphasis on training and career development has a direct impact on the extent and the depth of PAS administration.

A third challenge relates to expatriate employees at the lower levels, such as construction workers, who function without minimum levels of protection in terms of legislation and collective rights (Connell and Burgess, 2013). Such a lightly regulated labour market seems to have encouraged the entry of many multinational companies into booming economic centres such as Dubai (Al-Ali, 2008). In such a situation, global companies need to be proactive in ensuring high standards of employee management and development measures by going beyond the minimum legal requirements. PAS usually play a critical role in the advancement of the human capital of organizations, as well as in ensuring fairness and just treatment of employees. This raises a very critical issue in terms of ethics and social responsibility for (Western and local) companies operating in the ME region.

All in all, HR policies and practices should always have a role in ensuring the successful adjustment, well-being, productivity and ethical treatment of employees. This is increasingly being recognized by business leaders in the region (Moideenkutty, Al-Lamki and Murthy, 2011; Al-Rajhi et al., 2012).

RECOMMENDATIONS FOR THE USE OF PAS IN THE MIDDLE EAST

In the light of the above discussions, it might be possible to put forth certain recommendations concerning the implementation of PAS in the ME context. These could serve towards ensuring that the use of this key HR practice is responsive to the needs of organizations and individuals.

First, it is important that context must be considered in all its richness. In the ME, a rich understanding of context would indicate consideration for culture, political uncertainties, segregated labour markets and so on. As illustrated above, PAS in companies must respond to the challenges arising from a combination of these factors in situations in which corporations operate. Second, HR personnel have to be aware of the logics that are driving PAS. Blind implementations of practices originating elsewhere can have a detrimental effect. However, systems based on Western and other logics, though used in ways that are unpredictable, need not always have negative impacts. These might pave ways for innovation and change within organizations not previously exposed to such systems. Third, there must be an increased emphasis on PAS in public institutions. It was pointed out above that, in public organizations, PAS were less closely tied to various HR decisions, functions and activities (Abu-Doleh and Weir, 2007). This is also important as organizations in the public sector are placed in a position of strength in terms of resources and comparative stability. This is affirmed in the context of Bahrain by Metcalfe (2007), who points out that innovative HRM practices are likely to develop and spread more readily from public organizations rather than from multinational companies. This is also likely to hold true for other countries in the region with large and important public organizations.

Finally, HRM in general and PAS in particular must aim to respond to the special challenges of the region pointed out above. The assumptions of fairness and equality associated with these systems might be put into question with regard to the incorporation and development of women or expatriate workers. Special emphasis on development as an outcome of PAS might work towards achieving these objectives. In addition, PAS systems must percolate to all levels of the organization to ensure performance coupled with fairness and organizational justice. Global companies not only need to adhere to local legal requirements, but also need to ensure that their practices are in line with global standards. In the context of the well-recognized strategic role of HR, the blackout of any particular segment of employees from the standard practices of PAS and the resultant development efforts are likely to be counterproductive in the long run.

NOTE

1. The authors contributed equally in the preparation of this chapter.

FURTHER READING

Abu-Doleh, J. and Weir, D. 2007. Dimensions of performance appraisal systems in Jordanian private and public organizations. *International Journal of Human Resource Management*, **18**(1): 75–84.

Behery, M.H. and Paton, R.A. 2008. Performance appraisal–cultural fit: organizational outcomes within the UAE. *Education, Business and Society: Contemporary Middle Eastern Issues*, **1**(1): 34–49.

Giangreco, A., Carugati, A., Pilati, M. and Sebastiano, A. 2010. Performance appraisal systems in the Middle East: moving beyond Western logics. *European Management Review*, **7**(4): 241–251.

Giangreco, A., Carugati, A., Sebastiano, A. and Altamimi, H. 2012. War outside, ceasefire inside: an analysis of the performance appraisal system of a public hospital in a zone of conflict. *Evaluation and Program Planning*, **35**(1): 161–170.

Khoury, G.C. and Analoui, F. 2004. Innovative management model for performance appraisal: the case of the Palestinian public universities. *Management Research News*, **27**(1/2): 56–73.

Suliman, A. 2001. Work performance: is it one thing or many things? The multidimensionality of performance in a Middle Eastern context. *International Journal of Human Resource Management*, **12**(6): 1049–1061.

USEFUL WEBSITES

www.dubaifaqs.com.
http://gulfbusiness.com/2015/02/hr-practices-gcc-compare-global-peers/#.VQwg1Y6G9Jg.
http://www.personneltoday.com/hr/challenges-facing-hr-professionals-moving-to-the-middle-east/.
http://www.shrm.org/hrdisciplines/global/articles/pages/practicing-hr-middle-east.aspx.
http://thehrreview.com/index.php?option=com_content&view=article&id=369%3Atalent-is-the-new-oil-of-economy&catid=45%3Aprevious-free-content&Itemid=147&lang=en.

REFERENCES

Abu-Doleh, J. and Weir, D. 2007. Dimensions of performance appraisal systems in Jordanian private and public organizations. *International Journal of Human Resource Management*, **18**(1): 75–84.

Afiouni, F., Karam, C.M. and El-Hajj, H. 2013. The HR value proposition model in the Arab Middle East: identifying the contours of an Arab Middle Eastern HR model. *International Journal of Human Resource Management*, **24**(10): 1–38.

Afiouni, F., Ruël, H. and Schuler, R. 2014. HRM in the Middle East: toward a greater understanding. *International Journal of Human Resource Management*, **25**(2): 133–143.

Al-Ali, J. 2008. Emiratisation: drawing UAE nationals into their surging economy. *International Journal of Sociology and Social Policy*, **28**(9/10): 365–379.

Al-Enzi, A. 2002. Kuwait's employment policy: its formulation, implications, and challenges. *International Journal of Public Administration*, **25**(7): 885–900.

Al-Hamadi, A.B. and Budhwar, P. 2006. Human resource management in Oman. In P. Budhwar and K. Mellahi (eds), *Managing Human Resources in the Middle East*. London: Routledge, pp. 40–58.

Al-Hamadi, A.B., Budhwar, P.S. and Shipton, H. 2007. Management of human resources in Oman. *International Journal of Human Resources Management*, **18**(1): 100–113.

Al-Husan, F.B., Al-Hussan, F.B. and Perkins, S.J. 2014. Multilevel HRM systems and intermediating variables in MNCs: longitudinal case study research in Middle Eastern settings. *International Journal of Human Resource Management*, **25**(2): 234–251.

Al-Husan, F.Z.B., Brennan, R. and James, P. 2009. Transferring Western HR practices to developing countries: the case of a privatized utility in Jordan. *Personnel Review*, **38**(2): 104–123.

Al-Kharouf, A. and Weir, D. 2008. Women and work in a Jordanian context: beyond neo patriarchy. *Critical Perspectives on International Business*, **4**(2/3): 307–319.

Al-Rajhi, A., AlSalamah, A., Malik, M. and Wilson, R. 2012. *Economic Development in Saudi Arabia*. Saudi Arabia: Routledge.

Al-Waqfi, M. and Forstenlechner, I. 2014. Barriers to emiratization: the role of policy design and institutional environment in determining the effectiveness of Emiratization. *International Journal of Human Resource Management*, **25**(2): 167–189.

Aladwan, K., Bhanugopan, R. and Fish, A. 2014. Managing human resources in Jordanian organizations: challenges and prospects. *International Journal of Islamic and Middle Eastern Finance and Management*, **7**(1): 126–138.

Ali, A.J. 2010. Islamic challenges to HR in modern organizations. *Personnel Review*, **39**(6): 692–711.

Aycan, Z., Kanungo, R.N., Mendonca, M., Yu, K., Deller, J., Stahl, G. and Kurshid, A. 2000. Impact of culture on HRM practices: a 10 country comparison. *Applied Psychology: An International Review*, **4**(1): 192–221.

Badawy, M.K. 1980. Styles of mid-eastern managers. *California Management Review*, **22**(2): 51–58.

Bakhtari, H. 1995. Cultural effects on management style: a comparative study of American and Middle Eastern management styles. *International Studies of Management and Organization*, **25**(3): 97–118.

Baruch, Y. 1996. Self-performance appraisal vs. direct manager appraisal: a case of congruency. *Journal of Managerial Psychology*, **11**: 50–65.

Bealer, D. and Bhanugopan, R. 2014. Transactional and transformational leadership behaviour of expatriate and national managers in the UAE: a cross-cultural comparative analysis. *International Journal of Human Resource Management*, **25**(2): 293–316.

Behery, M. and Paton, R.A. 2008. Performance appraisal–cultural fit: organizational outcomes within the UAE. *Education, Business and Society: Contemporary Middle Eastern Issues*, **1**(1): 34–49.

Björkman, I. and Lervik, J.E. 2007. Transferring HR practices within multinational corporations. *Human Resource Management Journal*, **17**(4): 320–335.

Bol, J.C., Kramer, S., Maas, V.S., Richtermeyer, S.B. 2014. 'Managers' incentives in the performance evaluation process: the role of information accuracy and bonus transparency. AAA 2014 Management Accounting Section (MAS) Meeting Paper.

Bourne, M., Pavlov, A., Franco-Santos, M., Lucianetti, L. and Mura, M. 2013. Generating organisational performance: the contributing effects of performance measurement and human resource management practices. *International Journal of Operations and Production Management*, **33**(11/12): 1599–1622.

Branine, M. and Pollard, D. 2010. Human resource management with Islamic management principles: a dialectic for a reverse diffusion in management. *Personnel Review*, **39**(6): 712–727.

Brown, M., Hyatt, D. and Benson, J. 2010. Consequences of the performance appraisal experience. *Personnel Review*, **39**(3): 375–396.

Brumback, G. 1988. Some ideas, issues and predictions about performance management. *Public Personnel Management*, **17**: 387–402.

Budhwar, P.S. and Mellahi, K. 2007. Introduction: human resource management in the Middle East. *International Human Resource Management*, **18**(1): 2–10.

Budhwar, P.S. and Sparrow, P.R. 2002. Strategic HRM through the cultural looking glass: mapping the cognition of British and Indian managers. *Organization Studies*, **23**(4): 599–638.

Cawley, B.D., Keeping L.M. and Levy, P.E. 1998. Participation in the performance appraisal process and employee reactions: a meta-analytic review of field investigations. *Journal of Applied Psychology*, **83**: 615–633.

Chakrabarti, R., Barnes, B., Berthon, P., Pitt, L. and Monkhouse, L. 2014. Goal orientation effects on behavior and performance: evidence from international sales agents in the Middle East. *International Journal of Human Resource Management*, **25**(2): 317–340.

Claus, L. 2008. Employee performance management in MNCs: reconciling the need for global integration and local responsiveness. *European Journal of Management*, **2**(2): 132–153.

Claus, L. and Briscoe, D. 2008. Introduction: special issue on global performance management in the European context. *European Journal of Management*, **2**(2): 128–231.

Claus, L. and Hand, M.L. 2009. Customization decisions regarding performance management systems of multinational companies: an empirical view of Eastern European firms. *International Journal of Cross Cultural Management*, **9**(2): 237–258.
Cleveland, J.N., Tziner, A. and Murphy, K.R. 1989. Does conscientiousness moderate the relationship between attitudes and beliefs regarding performance appraisal and rating behaviour. *International Journal of Selection and Assessment*, **10**(3): 218–224.
Connell, J. and Burgess, J. 2013. Vulnerable workers in an emerging Middle Eastern economy: what are the implications for HRM? *International Journal of Human Resource Management*, **24**(22): 4166–4184.
Delery, J. and Doty, H. 1996. Models of theorizing in strategic human resource management: tests of universalistic, contingency, and configurational performance predictions. *Academy of Management Journal*, **39**: 802–883.
DeNisi, A. and Smith, C.E. 2014. Performance appraisal, performance management, and firm-level performance: a review, a proposed model, and new directions for future research. *Academy of Management Annals*, **8**(1): 127–179.
Dessler, G. 2015. *Human Resource Management*. Upper Saddle River, NJ: Prentice Hall.
Gallant, M. and Pounder, J.S. 2008. The employment of female nationals in the United Arab Emirates (UAE): an analysis of opportunities and barriers. *Education, Business and Society: Contemporary Middle Eastern Issues*, **1**(1): 26–33.
Giangreco, A., Carugati, A., Pilati, M. and Sebastiano, A. 2010. Performance appraisal systems in the Middle East: moving beyond Western logics. *European Management Review*, **7**(4): 241–251.
Giangreco, A., Carugati, A., Sebastiano, A. and Altamimi, H. 2012. War outside, ceasefire inside: an analysis of the performance appraisal system of a public hospital in a zone of conflict. *Evaluation and Program Planning*, **35**(1): 161–170.
Harvey, M. 1997. Focusing the international personnel performance appraisal process. *Human Resource Development Quarterly*, **8**(1): 41–62.
Hutchings, K., Lirio, P. and Metcalfe, B.D. 2012. Gender, globalization and career development: a re-evaluation of the nature of women's global work. *International Journal of Human Resource Management*, **23**(9): 1763–1787.
Hutchings, K., Metcalfe, B. and Cooper, B. 2010. Exploring Middle Eastern women's perceptions of barriers to, and facilitators of, international management opportunities. *International Journal of Human Resource Management*, **21**(1): 61–83.
Hutchings, K. and Weir, D.T.H. 2006. Understanding networking in China and the Arab world: lessons for international managers. *Journal of European Industrial Training*, **30**: 272–290.
Ibrahim, M.E., Al Sejini, S. and Al Qassimi, O.A.A. 2004. Job satisfaction and performance of government employees in UAE. *Journal of Management Research*, **4**(1): 1–12.
Iqbal, M.J., Akbar, S. and Budhwar, P. 2015. Effectiveness of performance appraisal: an integrated framework. *International Journal of Management Reviews*, **17**: 510–533.
Ivancevich, J.M. and McMahon, J.T. 1982. The effects of goal setting, external feedback, and self-generated feedback on outcome variables: a field experiment. *Academy of Management Journal*, **25**(2): 359–372.
Khan, S.A. 2007. Emerging roles and challenges for the HR managers in Oman. *Proceedings of 10th International Conference on Creativity and Innovation: Imperatives for Global Business and Development*, Society of Global Business and Economic Development at Ryukoku University, Kyoto, Japan, 8–11 August.
Khan, S.A. 2011. Convergence, divergence or middle of the path: HRM model for Oman. *Journal of Management Policy and Practice*, **12**(1): 76–87.
Khoury, G.C. and Analoui, F. 2004. Innovative management model for performance appraisal: the case of the Palestinian public universities. *Management Research News*, **27**(1/2): 56–73.
Kim, T. and Holzer, M. 2016. Public employees and performance appraisal: a study of antecedents to employees' perception of the process. *Review of Public Personnel Administration*, **36**(1): 31–56.
Klaas, B.S. and DeNisi, A.S. 1989. Managerial reactions to employee dissent: the impact of grievance activity on performance ratings. *Academy of Management Journal*, **32**: 705–717.
Kuvaas, B. 2006. Performance appraisal satisfaction and employee outcomes: mediating and moderating roles of work motivation. *International Journal of Human Resource Management*, **17**: 504–522.
Lam, S.K. and Schaubroeck, J. 1999. Total quality management and performance appraisal: an experimental study of process versus results and group versus individual approaches. *Journal of Organizational Behavior*, **20**: 445–457.
Leat, M. and El-Kot, G. 2007. HRM practices in Egypt: the influence of national context? *International Journal of Human Resource Management*, **18**(1): 147–158.
Marmenout, K. and Lirio, P. 2014. Local female talent retention in the Gulf: Emirati women bending with the wind. *International Journal of Human Resource Management*, **25**(2): 144–166.
Mellahi, K. 2007. The effect of regulations on HRM: private sector firms in Saudi Arabia. *International Journal of Human Resource Management*, **18**(1): 85–99.

Mellahi, K. and Budhwar, P.S. 2010. Introduction: Islam and human resource management. *Personnel Review*, **39**(6): 685–691.

Mellahi, K., Demirbag, M. and Riddle, L. 2011. Multinationals in the Middle East: challenges and opportunities. *Journal of World Business*, **46**: 406–410.

Metcalfe, B.D. 2007. Gender and human resource management in the Middle East. *International Journal of Human Resource Management*, **18**(1): 54–74.

Moideenkutty, U., Al-Lamki, A. and Murthy, Y.S.R. 2011. HRM practices and organizational performance in Oman. *Personnel Review*, **40**(2): 239–251.

Mostafa, A.M.S. and Gould-Williams, J. 2014. Testing the mediation effect of person–organization fit on the relationship between high performance HR practices and employee outcomes in the Egyptian public sector. *International Journal of Human Resource Management*, **25**(2): 276–292.

Newman, K.L. and Nollen, S.D. 1996. Culture and congruence: the fit between management practices and national culture. *Journal of International Business Studies*, **27**(4): 753–779.

Parnell, J.A. and Hatem, T. 1999. Cultural antecedents of behavioral differences between American and Egyptian managers. *Journal of Management Studies*, **36**: 399–418.

Pinder, C.C. 2008. *Work Motivation in Organizational Behaviour*. Upper Saddle River, NJ: Prentice Hall.

Price, A. 2007. *Human Resources Management in a Business Context*. London: Thomson Learning.

Pudelko, M. 2006. A comparison of HRM systems in the USA, Japan and Germany in their socio-economic context. *Human Resource Management Journal*, **16**(2): 123–153.

Ramdani, B., Mellahi, K., Guermat, C. and Kechad, R. 2014. The efficacy of high performance work practices in the Middle East: evidence from Algerian firms. *International Journal of Human Resource Management*, **25**(2): 252–275.

Rasheed, A., Khan, S.U.R., Rasheed, M.F. and Munir, Y. 2015. The impact of feedback orientation and the effect of satisfaction with feedback on in-role job performance. *Human Resource Development Quarterly*, **26**(1): 31–51.

Rees, C.J., Mamman, A. and Braik, A.B. 2007. Emiratization as a strategic HRM change initiative: case study evidence from a UAE petroleum company. *International Journal of Human Resource Management*, **18**(1): 33–53.

Rosenzweig, P.M. and Nohria, N. 1994. Influences on human resource management in multinational corporations. *Journal of International Business Studies*, **20**(2): 229–251.

Saini, D.S. and Budhwar, P.S. 2008. Managing the human resource in Indian SMEs: the role of indigenous realities. *Journal of World Business*, **43**: 417–434.

Spector, P. 1986. Perceived control by employees: a meta-analysis of studies concerning autonomy and participation at work. *Human Relations*, **39**: 1005–1016.

Suliman, A. 2001. Work performance: is it one thing or many things? The multidimensionality of performance in a Middle Eastern context. *International Journal of Human Resource Management*, **12**(6): 1049–1106.

Syed, J., Hazboun, N. and Murray, P. 2014. What locals want: Jordanian employees' views on expatriate managers. *International Journal of Human Resource Management*, **25**(2): 212–233.

Tayeb, M. 1997. Islamic revival in Asia and human resource management. *Employee Relations*, **19**: 352–364.

Tlaiss, H. and Kauser, S. 2011. The importance of Wasta in the career success of Middle Eastern managers. *Journal of European Industrial Training*, **35**(5): 467–486.

Tubbs, M.E. 1986. Goal setting: a meta-analytic examination of the empirical evidence. *Journal of Applied Psychology*, **71**: 474–483.

Vaiman, V. and Brewster, C. 2015. How far do cultural differences explain the differences between nations? Implications for HRM. *International Journal of Human Resource Management*, **26**(2): 151–164.

Varma, A., Budhwar, P.S. and DeNisi, A. 2008. *Performance Management Systems: A Global Perspective*. London: Routledge.

West, M.A., Borrill, C., Dawson, J., Scully, J., Carter, M., Anelay, S., Petterson, M. and Waring, J. 2002. The link between the management of employees and patient mortality in acute hospitals. *International Journal of Human Resources Management*, **13**: 1299–1310.

Whiteoak, J.W., Crawford, N.G. and Mapstone, R.H. 2006. Impact of gender and generational differences in work values and attitudes in an Arab culture. *Thunderbird International Business Review*, **48**(1): 77–91.

Williams, J., Bhanugopan, R. and Fish, A. 2011. Localization of human resources in the state of Qatar: emerging issues and research agenda. *Education, Business and Society: Contemporary Middle Eastern Issues*, **4**(3): 193–206.

Woehr, D.J. 1992. Performance dimension accessibility: implications for rating accuracy. *Journal of Organizational Behavior*, **13**: 357–367.

Zaharna, R.S. 1996. Managing cross-cultural challenges: a pre-K lesson for training in the Gaza strip. *Journal of Management Development*, **15**(5): 75–87.

5. Talent management in the Middle East

Salma Raheem

Organizations around the world have begun to recognize the increasingly important value of managing talent well for organizational competitiveness and sustainability. Talent management (TM) issues – the identification, development and retention of talent – have become central for organizations as talent becomes more scarce, expensive and hard to retain (Dewhurst et al., 2012). The increasing difficulty of managing talent is a result of the varying dynamics of talent shortages, the strategic location and relocation of talent and the increasing compensation levels for key talent (Schuler et al., 2011). Additionally, as organizations become increasingly global, there is a further need to find talent that is equipped with cross-cultural skills (Scullion et al., 2007), is willing to share knowledge and is well coordinated across boundaries and is able to work effectively in multicultural workspaces. For many organizations, the criticality of managing talent well has propelled TM challenges beyond the purview of human resource (HR) managers alone, to include those involved in the leadership of the organization.

The conceptual boundary of what constitutes 'talent management' has been debated and discussed, with several definitions provided by scholars over the years (this is discussed in greater detail in the following section). For the purpose of this chapter, I use the well accepted definition provided by Collings and Mellahi (2009, p. 304), which describes TM as:

> Activities and processes that involve the systematic identification of key positions that differentially contribute to the organization's sustainable competitive advantage, the development of a talent pool of high-potential and high-performing incumbents to fill these roles, and the development of a differentiated human resource architecture to facilitate filling these positions with competent incumbents, and to ensure their continued commitment to the organization.

As is evidenced from this comprehensive definition, there are several organizational components to effective TM. For organizations based in the Middle East (ME), the consequences of these organizational TM challenges have increased in importance. In a 2010 survey, nearly 50 per cent of CEOs from the ME rated TM issues as the organization's current critical priority, with 95 per cent of them expecting increased competition for key talent over the next 3–5 years and the admission that TM challenges are ones that they are increasingly unprepared for (Mercer, 2010). Issues such as the availability of talent, succession planning, employee engagement, the development of talent pools and cost of talent all factor in areas of concern for organizations in the ME. In addition to exploring these organizational challenges, this chapter highlights how organizations operating in the ME have an added component of institutional factors, unique to the ME, that greatly influence an organization's ability to build TM systems and talent-development-based competitive advantages. These institutional factors are typically external to the organization's span of control, and range from historical contexts to strong demographic changes. These factors will, nevertheless, continue to significantly impact organizational TM practices, and they will need to be within the purview of all ME focused organizations as the region continues to grow economically, globalize and develop as a society.

This chapter draws on recent conceptual and empirical developments in the field as well as non-academic reports, with a view to informing organizational TM practices and approaches in the ME. It is to be noted that there is a significant paucity of academic literature in the field of TM in the ME. This chapter contributes to the limited research in the field of TM. It is divided into four main sections: the first section delves into the definition of TM, providing a conceptual framework by which TM issues are explored further in the chapter. The second section looks into the core TM issues faced by firms due to institutional factors, while the third section explores the impact of these unique contextual factors on the organizational challenges for TM in the ME. The concluding section suggests recommendations and the way forward before concluding with useful resources for further reading.

Before proceeding, it is important to highlight the fact that the ME is not a homogenous region in terms of its historical, political, socioeconomic or even cultural components (as reported in Chapter 1 as well). As will be evidenced by subsequent chapters in this book, although there are some common themes which run through each of the countries of this region, there are, more often than not, significant differences. For example, the World Bank (2008) categorizes countries of the broader ME region into three groups based on their availability of natural resources and labour. Countries such as Egypt and Jordan are resource-poor, labour-abundant countries while the Gulf Cooperation Council (GCC) countries are resource-rich and labour-poor, according to this classification. The wide-ranging differences across the region also manifest in national and organizational HR development approaches (Mellahi and Budhwar, 2006) and these influence organizational approaches to the management of talent as well. It is these differences that make this region a fascinating area of importance and study with regards to TM.

This chapter focuses on the TM issues around the GCC group of countries. The GCC consists of Saudi Arabia, Kuwait, Bahrain, Oman, Qatar and the United Arab Emirates (UAE). The GCC nations have several key components in common such as the abundance of oil (resource-rich) and the limited supply of a skilled indigenous workforce (labour-poor). Similarly, after the discovery of oil, most of these nations have followed similar patterns of economic development. These countries share similar historical, cultural and geographical links (Secretariat of the Gulf Cooperation Council, 2013). They also show relative political stability in comparison to other nations of the ME, sustained growth rates and have a robust history of investment by a variety of organizations, both regional and international in outlook. There is a certain level of development and homogeneity between organizational HR models across organizations in this region, and, thus, the region forms the focus in this chapter.

DEFINITIONS AND THEORETICAL BACKGROUND FOR THE STUDY OF TM IN THE GCC

Ever since the 'war for talent' (Michaels et al., 2001) and its importance for organizational performance began to be recognized, scholars have attempted to define the conceptual boundaries of what constitutes 'talent'. For the most part, TM theories have revolved around the assumption that organizations gain a sustained competitive advantage by maximizing the talents of their employees (Scullion et al., 2010). 'Talent', in this respect, is therefore viewed as the accumulated knowledge, skills and expertise embedded in the individuals of the organization such that they are able to contribute to an organization's superior performance, or, in other words, it refers to the accumulated human capital of the firm (Farndale et al., 2010). In this way, TM is strongly linked to human resource management (HRM) practices (Farndale et al., 2010).

However, there are other ways of viewing the 'talent' paradigm (see Al Ariss et al., 2014; Nijs et al., 2014 for reviews). Lewis and Heckman (2006) identify three key streams of TM research. The first involves using TM as a proxy for HRM, thereby limiting the focus to specific HRM activities of recruitment, development and succession planning. A second stream focuses on the importance of developing talent pools and the development of members of this pool through positions in the organizations. A third stream focuses on the identification and management of individuals who are recognized as key talent in organization and the importance of nurturing these 'A' players while mitigating the presence of the less talented 'C' players (Michaels et al., 2001). Meanwhile, there exists a fourth stream of TM research which distinguishes key positions in the organization as positions that have the potential to impact the competitive advantage of the firm and the strategic management of how these positions are manned (Collings and Mellahi, 2009; Huselid et al., 2005).

One of the most common definitions of TM, and the one used in this chapter, is by Collings and Mellahi (2009). Their comprehensive definition addresses several aspects of the TM scope including the identification of strategic positions, ensuring the development of the talent pool amongst employees to ensure high-calibre individuals are available to man these roles and the development of TM systems, distinct to HRM, to ensure the configuration of talent throughout the organization.

It is important to understand that organizational TM systems do not exist in a vacuum. Using an institutional theory framework, Tarique and Schuler (2010) identify certain 'exogenous factors' which influence the development, effectiveness and implementation of TM practices in organizations. Exogenous factors include aspects such as the national cultures, economic conditions, political and legal environments and workforce characteristics. These influential drivers impact organizations' operations significantly. However, organizations are limited in their abilities to contest these influences. Tarique and Schuler (2010) highlight three exogenous drivers which directly impact TM in organizations, namely, the global migration of talent, changing (workforce) demographics and demand–supply talent gaps.

Similarly, there are factors internal to the organizations that need to be in place for effective development of TM systems. A critical component of this is the maturity of and the efficiency in the functioning of the HR department. Efficiencies in the HR functions that directly impact the efficacy of TM systems include HR effectiveness in all activities related to attracting, developing and retaining talent (Tarique and Schuler, 2010, pp. 127–128).

For researchers studying TM in the ME, there is nascent acknowledgement that the scope of TM is affected by several other factors beyond those traditionally studied such as those mentioned above (see Biygautane and Al Yahya, 2014; Sidani and Al Ariss, 2014 as examples). These additional factors arise from a unique combination of the region's historical, cultural and socioeconomic contexts as well as the governance approaches found in the region. In this chapter I identify these unique factors as institutional factors and describe them and their impact on TM in detail in the next section.

INSTITUTIONAL FACTORS AFFECTING TM IN THE GCC

Historical Background

To begin to understand the institutional factors that affect TM, one needs an understanding of how the region has developed. The GCC countries, up until the 1950s, were characterized by smaller populations which were primarily nomadic and/or rooted in traditional occupations such as fishing, agriculture, pearl cultivation and processing, crafts (such as pottery and metalwork), trade and seamanship. The discovery of 'black gold' – oil – in 1932 in Bahrain and 1938 in Saudi Arabia, and subsequently in other Arab nations, changed the landscape of the regions dramatically. The relatively young governments of these states knew very well the significance of this new and abundant resource, and with the oil boom of the 1970s visionary plans were chalked out for rapid urbanization and economic development.

1. Early dependence on expatriate[1] talent

The ruling monarchies soon realized that their people did not have the required skills; nor did the countries have the required quantity of manpower to tap into this resource to facilitate economic development at the desired rate (Fasano and Goyal, 2004; Forstenlechner, 2010; Al-Kibsi et al., 2007). Governments of these countries, therefore, chose to import foreign talent, at all levels of education, as 'temporary workers', to achieve this rapid level of development (Al-Dosary and Rahman, 2005; Baldwin-Edwards, 2011; Kapiszewski, 2006). The decision was clearly to import talent on a 'short-term' basis in lieu of the long-term development of the native workforce (Baldwin-Edwards, 2011; Winckler, 2010; Kapiszewski, 2006). Meanwhile, some efforts were made to address the issue of national manpower development and training in many of these countries. But it was clear that for the sustained rapid pace of industrialization and modernization, national efforts to meet the skill and labour requirement would be insufficient and the need for imported skills persisted (Al-Dosary and Rahman, 2005; Baldwin-Edwards, 2011). From the period of the oil boom onwards, the expatriate inflow into the GCC continued to rise consistently to the extent that by 2008 expatriates in the GCC countries numbered 10.6 million compared to 8.5 million in 2005 (Winckler, 2010). Currently, the predominance of the expatriate labour force is such that they now constitute between 50 and 94 per cent of the labour force in the GCC (Kapiszewski, 2006; Baldwin-Edwards, 2011). With some estimates, and in certain years, this figure has been as high as 99 per cent (Al-Kibsi et al., 2007). This has resulted in expatriates constituting almost 41 per cent of the total population (Baldwin-Edwards, 2011), as per latest available figures (see Figure 5.1 and Table 5.1).

2. Employment preferences amongst local[2] talent

Essentially, the oil wealth and the fruits of the rapid economic development of the oil boom were distributed to the relatively smaller local population of the time. A primary

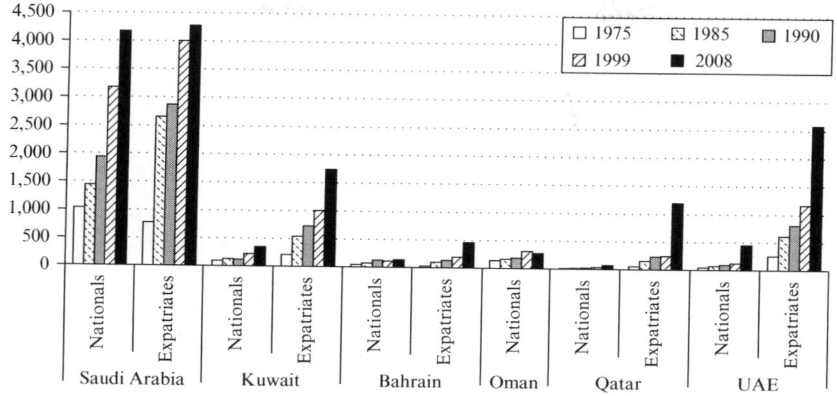

Figure 5.1 *National and expatriate elements of the GCC labour force (1975–2008) (000s) adapted from Baldwin-Edwards (2011) (data from Table 5.1)*

avenue for distribution of this wealth was through the employment of the local population through public sector employment – employment that came with generous salaries, benefits, pension plans and a relatively relaxed work environment (Winckler, 2010; Baldwin-Edwards, 2011; Al-Kibsi et al., 2007). Promotion was based on seniority, with less emphasis on performance, and there was a high level of job security supported by a favourable legal system (Baldwin-Edwards, 2011; Fasano and Goyal, 2004). Culturally speaking, for this region, one's job role and the social interactions within it affect the social status of the employee, and thus the type of work and the industry of employment are of importance beyond the organizational setting (Mellahi, 2007). The drive to obtain the prestige and comfort of a public sector job essentially created a 'rentier mentality', where income is a result of the situation and not proportionate to the efforts exerted (Winckler, 2010; Shaham, 2009), ultimately creating a strong preference amongst locals for public sector jobs over private sector employment (Harry, 2007; Al-Kibsi et al., 2007; Forstenlechner, 2010; Mellahi, 2007; Forstenlechner and Mellahi, 2011; Hertog, 2013). The desire for public sector employment was so strong that nationals were willing to be unemployed and wait several years for a job in the public sector, rather than join private organizations (Baldwin-Edwards, 2011). As can be imagined, this also led to persistent situations of rampant underemployment in the region (World Bank, 2008; Shaham, 2009).

3. Resulting structural inequalities affecting the availability and ability to attract and develop talent pools and retain talent

Expatriates, meanwhile, were largely employed in the private sector. They came primarily from Asian and other Arab nations which were resource-poor but labour-rich (World Bank, 2008), with the majority of imported labour arriving from South Asian countries such as India, Pakistan and the Philippines (The Economist Intelligence Unit, 2009; Kapiszewski, 2006; Girgis, 2002; International Labour Organization, 2009). Much of the imported labour were employed in low-wage, blue-collar occupations such as those related to construction and domestic services, and such as restaurant workers, taxi drivers and wholesale and retail workers (International Labour Organization, 2009; Shaham, 2009).

Table 5.1 National and expatriate elements of the GCC labour force (1975–2008) (000s)

		1975	1985	1990	1999	2008
Saudi Arabia						
	Nationals	1,027	1,440	1,934	3,173	4,173
	Expatriates	773	2,662	2,878	4,003	4,282
	Total	1,800	4,102	4,812	7,176	8,455
	% Expatriates	42.9	64.9	59.8	55.8	50.6
Kuwait						
	Nationals	92	126	118	221	351
	Expatriates	213	544	731	1,005	1,742
	Total	305	670	849	1,226	2,093
	% Expatriates	69.8	81.2	86.1	82.0	83.2
Bahrain						
	Nationals	46	73	127	113	139
	Expatriates	30	101	132	194	458
	Total	76	174	259	307	597
	% Expatriates	39.5	58.0	51.0	63.2	76.7
Oman						
	Nationals	137	167	189	312	276
	Expatriates	71	300	442	503	809
	Total	208	467	631	815	1,085
	% Expatriates	34.1	64.2	70.0	61.7	74.6
Qatar						
	Nationals	13	18	21	36	72
	Expatriates	54	156	230	244	1,193
	Total	67	174	251	280	1,265
	% Expatriates	80.6	89.7	91.6	87.1	94.3
UAE						
	Nationals	45	72	96	124	455
	Expatriates	252	612	805	1,165	2,588
	Total	297	684	901	1,289	3,043
	% Expatriates	84.8	89.5	89.3	90.4	85.0

Source: Baldwin-Edwards (2011).

Organizations in the private sectors exhibited rent-seeking behaviour where the cheapest labour was employed, driving wages downwards and making employment in the private sector even less attractive to nationals (Hertog, 2013; Shaham, 2009; Baldwin-Edwards, 2011). For professional or highly skilled jobs, pay structures reflect the cost of repatriation to the countries of origin, including aspects such as standard of living, perquisites and higher levels of basic pay. Hence, pay packets vary by nationality in the ME. For example, an American can potentially receive a higher pay package than an Indian for the same job, with the local Arab national sometimes earning more than the Western expatriate (Mellahi and Al-Hinai, 2000). Labour laws are mostly silent on these anomalies.

Further, labour laws protecting the rights of expatriates, especially low-skilled labour, were extremely lax or non-existent, allowing private sector industries to fire their employees as and when they deemed fit (Shaham, 2009; World Bank, 2008; International Labour Organization, 2009; Fasano and Goyal, 2004), further adding to the locals viewing themselves as a 'natural middle class' (Forstenlechner, 2010) entitled to the benefits of public sector employment.

Structurally, this has resulted in a dual market system where the public sector is the preferred employment sector for nationals, who therefore traditionally enjoy higher salaries, job security and benefits. Meanwhile, expatriates are generally employed in the private sector, which exhibits rent-seeking behaviour, with salaries, job security and benefits at much lower levels, especially for those in unskilled or semi-skilled levels of employment. This structural imbalance is further exacerbated with nationals avoiding job roles that involve physical labour such as domestic services, maintenance, construction, food industry and so on. Lastly, due to rentier model of development adopted in the early stages of economic development, the lack of planned investment in developing national human resources for the job market has resulted in many nationals lacking the required skills appropriate to organizational needs and expectations.

As a result of these historical events and resulting structural inequalities, I identify three significant institutional factors that impact TM practices in the ME, namely, (1) the attitude and approach of locals towards employment, (2) demographic and governmental pressures, and (3) the increasing importance of women in the labour force influencing the process of identifying, attracting and nurturing talent. These are detailed in the next section.

Institutional Factors

1. Work ethics and attitudes of locals

For organizations developing their TM systems, possibly the most telling concern which aggravates the structural imbalance, is the differences in the approach to work between locals and expatriates. The fixation on securing public sector employment for the majority of locals leaves them with little interest in career planning, including basic awareness on subjects of relevance to professional work environments. For example, 70 per cent of graduates earn degrees in the humanities or social sciences – fields that do not traditionally lend themselves to skill sets required for competitive organizations (Biygautane and Al Yahya, 2014). Thus, with limited opportunities and interest for exposure to competitive educational and work requirements, information regarding work life is gleaned from social and familial connections. With many of the nationals employed in a public sector characterized by severe underemployment and a rewards culture not necessarily bound by performance, the information thus gleaned about work practices does not come from the best of examples. With a focus on easier public sector employment, from a TM perspective it therefore becomes extremely challenging for private sector organizations to attract high-potential graduates or local talent from public sector employment, as private sector organizations can neither offer salaries in line with public sector units, nor promise benefits or promotions at equivalent levels. Conversely, for public sector units, attempting to change the entrenched 'rentier' culture to reward talent proves a significant challenge. Further, due to the dearth of qualifications amongst graduates, industry leaders in the

Gulf indicate only an abysmal 37 per cent satisfaction rating with the supply of qualified graduates (Lootah and Simon, 2009).

Moreover, traditional cultural norms view occupations heavily dependent on physical labour as 'low status', and this has resulted in social undesirability towards low-skilled jobs as a strong part of the mental make-up of nationals (Mellahi and Al-Hinai, 2000; Mellahi, 2007). This results in unrealistic evaluations of self-worth and value to organizations, poor understanding and knowledge in fulfilling job requirements, and misunderstandings of performance evaluation, promotion processes and organizational dynamics in general. Hence, nationals' lack of knowledge, skills (including soft skills and language skills), willingness to work in low- or semi-skilled occupations and exposure to professional, competitive work environments, including working in multicultural work environments (Mellahi, 2007), makes the management of nationals challenging for organizations (Al-Lamki, 1998; Al-Waqfi and Forstenlechner, 2014; Forstenlechner, 2010; Kapiszewski, 2006; Mellahi and Al-Hinai, 2000). The United Nations Development Programme (UNDP) refers to this situation of the local labour force as characterized by 'the poverty of capability and poverty of opportunity' (UNDP, 2000).

Employers' perceptions of the national labour force perpetuate this general stereotype, making local recruits a less desirable choice for organizations (Rees et al., 2007). Regional employers claim that a quarter of national employees have irregular attendance while some quit within six to nine months after being recruited claiming boredom or a lack of interest (Al-Kibsi et al., 2007). In many cases, once hired, locals are also difficult to fire. Employment of the national workforce is claimed to require significantly more investment in recruitment, training, salaries and benefits, with the added liability of absenteeism, low productivity and job engagement, general indiscipline and low organizational citizenship behaviours (Al-Waqfi and Forstenlechner, 2014; Harry, 2007; Hertog, 2013). Added to this is the difficulty of some locals to integrate with the multicultural workforce, including having to accept a foreign supervisor (Kapiszewski, 2006; Mellahi, 2007). Thus, employers wonder, what is the incentive to hire someone 'who won't show up, won't care and can't be fired?' (Mellahi, 2007, p. 90). Overall, the relationship between private sector employers and nationals has not been one of mutual trustworthiness. In the World Competitiveness Report of 2010 (World Bank, 2011), organizations across the GCC rated the poor work ethics of the national labour force as one of the key obstacles to doing business in the GCC (see Table 5.2 below).

However, those locals who are highly qualified and have the needed skills enjoy multiple job offers and find employment with greater ease (Alzalabani, 2002). For organizations in the ME, considerable investment will have to be made in finding and attracting high-performance individuals from this limited pool. Additionally, an organization will have to develop retention strategies, such as well-defined proposals for professional growth and career progression, to ensure the continued commitment of these employees to the organization. Further, TM systems will have to incorporate a significant investment in training – both on the job as well as soft skills training – along with long-term career planning to ensure a continued talent pipeline in the organization.

2. Demographic trends and government pressures

Unlike many other parts of the world facing falling population rates and large ageing populations, the ME is facing the opposite demographic trend – a booming youth popu-

Table 5.2 *Ranking of 'poor work ethic in the national labour force' amongst 15 obstacles to doing business in the GCC*

Country	Ranking
Bahrain	2
Kuwait	7
Oman	4
Qatar	10
Saudi Arabia	6
UAE	7

Source: Hertog (2013).

Table 5.3 *GCC population by country*

	2000	2005	2010	2015	2020
Total (millions)	29.63	35.08	41.45	47.52	53.41
Average annual change over previous five years	2.80	3.44	3.40	2.80	2.40
Bahrain	20.47	23.12	26.18	29.59	33.34
Kuwait	2.23	2.99	3.58	4.40	5.20
Oman	3.24	4.61	5.57	6.44	7.06
Qatar	0.64	0.89	1.18	1.45	1.66
Saudi Arabia	2.40	2.51	3.11	3.32	3.53
UAE	0.64	0.97	1.82	2.33	2.79

Source: The Economist Intelligence Unit (2009).

lation and a growing total population. The total population for the GCC is expected to increase to 53.4 million by 2020 – a 30 per cent increase from 2007 (The Economist Intelligence Unit, 2009 – see Table 5.3). According to the Arab Human Development Report (AHDR) 2010 (Mirkin, 2013), the region is now seeing an all-time high in its youth population, with the 15–24 age group providing a 'youth bulge'. This has resulted in 60 per cent of the population being under the age of 30. Additionally, the working population (25–59 age group) is also at an all-time high, resulting in immense pressures on labour markets (World Bank, 2008; The Economist Intelligence Unit, 2009) and exacerbating issues of unemployment.

The issues of youth unemployment and underemployment have become politically charged issues for many of the GCC governments, especially in the backdrop of the 'Arab Awakening'. Governmental response to these demographic pressures has been to compel private sector organizations to absorb the surplus labour and nationalize their workforces while simultaneously making it difficult for private sector organizations to hold on to their foreign employees. Recent governmental policies in Saudi Arabia, for example, have seen punitive measures meted out on private sector organizations such as the cancellation of licences to operate, refusal to grant visas for foreign recruitment, blacklisting of companies on the basis of poor nationalization levels and so on. In countries such as the UAE, these policies work as a form of positive discrimination to support the minority local population. Governmental dictates on nationalization may occur in a variety of forms (see Chapter 7 in this volume for a detailed discussion on the topic), but from a TM standpoint they all result in difficulties for ME organizations to efficiently manage their TM approaches without interference. The pressure to appease changing legal requirements on this issue forces organizations to relegate TM to the back of other more strategic priorities, such as ensuring continued licensing permission to operate in the country, ensuring supportive governmental relations, reputational issues, added financial burdens and so on. Further, the implementation of many of these nationalization policies is irregular, forcing organizations to at times take very reactive, rather than proactive, approaches to their HRM in general, let alone any strategic approach to TM.

3. The increasing importance of the female labour force and an employee differentiated value proposition for women

Another key demographic that has been gaining in importance is the availability and utilization of the female workforce. Women's participation in the workforce has been historically low in the region and continues to be low in comparison to other regions as well as the world average (see Figure 5.2). However, with the region's governments providing increasing support to this demographic the overall regional participation of women has increased significantly to become one of the fastest growing in the world. For example, in Saudi Arabia, labour force participation by women jumped from 5 to 15 per cent between 2000 to 2010 (International Labour Organization, 2010 as quoted in Aon Hewitt, 2010).

Similarly, regional female literacy rates have shown the greatest improvements worldwide (World Bank, 2008), and with increasing opportunities for higher education, Arab women now outnumber men in many universities in the GCC (The Economist Intelligence

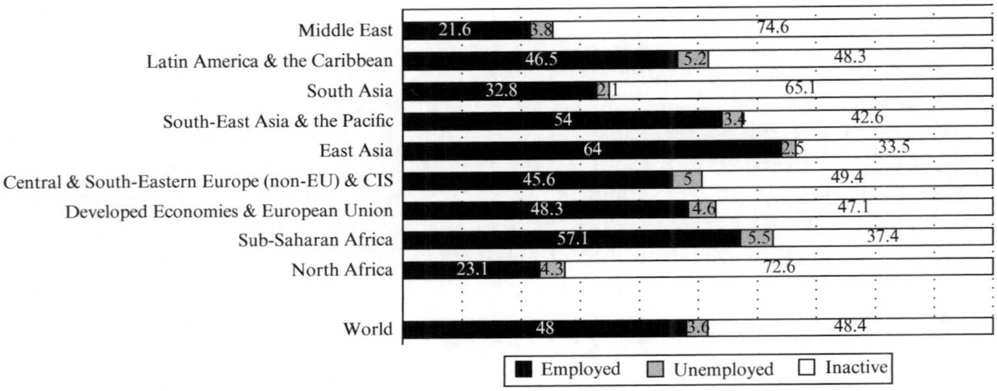

Note: CIS = Community of Independent States.

Source: United Nations (2010).

Figure 5.2 Percentage of women's participation in labour force by region (women above 15 years of age)

Unit, 2009). Further, women who participate in the labour force in the region tend to be those with higher educational qualifications rather than those with lower educational qualifications (World Bank, 2008), reflecting a trend for women to choose non-traditional subjects such as finance, engineering, IT and journalism rather than be confined to traditional occupations such as teaching or medicine (The Economist Intelligence Unit, 2009). Additionally, Arab women are reported to be more comfortable about working in multicultural work contexts than their male counterparts (Aon Hewitt, 2010), reflecting better adjustment to the changing dynamics of the ME. Work attitude amongst women show interesting trends as well. A recent youth survey found that 73 per cent of Arab women and 58 per cent of Arab men believe that women should have equal opportunities for professional advancement (ASDA'A Burson-Marsteller, 2014). Women are increasingly taking up leadership positions in both private and public sectors and at increasingly senior positions such as those related to governance, policy decisions, media, business, law, politics and so on (Dubai Women Establishment and PwC, 2009), including holding ministerial positions in some of the GCC countries (Kapiszewski, 2006).

In this respect, women present an untapped pool of talent for organizations in the ME. However, organizations need to understand that the approach and reasons which inspire and motivate women to work in the ME are strongly influenced by Islamic values and are very different from the West (Wagner, 2012; Metcalfe, 2008). Additionally, it is important for organizations to understand and adapt their work environments to the unique work-life challenges women in the ME face (Marmenout and Lirio, 2014), especially with those challenges rooted in cultural traditions of the region (Syed, 2010). Hence, although the trend of more women entering the workforce will continue, organizations need to be cognizant of this caveat and will need to be creative in developing unique employee propositions in order to attract, develop and retain this talent pool. For example, an interesting recent finding shows that Arab women feel the least engaged at the workplace compared to both male nationals and expatriates in general (Aon Hewitt, 2010). This may be due to the fact that success for women in this part of the world may not be solely tied to financial security but instead Arab women are more likely to find self-satisfaction, opportunities for growth, a sense of achievement and happiness as greater motivators to work than financial gains alone (Omair, 2011).

In the next section, the chapter focuses on the organizational TM challenges faced by firms in the ME.

ORGANIZATIONAL TM ISSUES IN THE ME

At the organizational level, there are several barriers to effective TM outlined in the academic literature. Schuler et al. (2011) synthesize them as (1) insufficient time spent on TM by senior managers, (2) organizational structures which constrain the collaborative efforts and the sharing of resources needed for TM, (3) lack of knowledge about, and commitment to, TM responsibilities by middle and front-line managers, (4) inability or unwillingness of managers to acknowledge differences in performance levels amongst employees, (5) insufficient involvement and ownership of managers at all levels in the development of the organization's TM strategy, (6) HR department's lack of TM competencies and inability to ensure senior management is committed to TM implementation,

Table 5.4 GCC countries GDP percentage change 2007–2013

							Projected	
		2007	2008	2009	2010	2011	2012	2013
				(percentage change)				
National accounts and prices								
Real GDP								
	Bahrain	8.4	6.3	3.2	4.7	2.1	4.8	4.4
	Kuwait	6.0	2.5	−7.1	−2.4	6.3	6.2	0.8
	Oman	6.7	13.2	3.3	5.6	4.5	5.0	5.1
	Qatar	18.0	17.7	12.0	16.7	13.0	6.2	5.1
	Saudi Arabia	6.0	8.4	1.8	7.4	5.6	5.1	3.6
	UAE	3.2	3.2	−4.8	1.7	3.9	4.4	4.0
	GCC countries	6.5	7.8	0.9	6.4	7.7	5.2	3.7

Source: IMF (2013).

and (7) a 'knowledge–doing' gap that impedes the implementation of TM by managers even after a commitment to TM is established. These hold true for organizations in the ME as well. However, there are organizational TM issues specific to the ME and these are highlighted in this section.

The organizational TM issues in the ME include (1) an intense sustained competition for talent, (2) TM in its infancy in the region, and (3) providing differentiating employee value propositions and changing the current social/psychological contract in the backdrop of existing structural imbalances. These are detailed below.

1. Intense Competition for Talent: Regional Economic Growth and Investment Plans

With sustained economic growth, diversification and plans for further investment, the GCC countries continue to be areas of strong investment opportunities for organizations worldwide. The region has weathered the recent economic crises better than other parts of the world and an overall GDP growth rate is expected at just over 4 per cent for the region (IMF, 2013) (see Table 5.4). In comparison, the worldwide economic growth rate from 2007 to 2010 was 1.87 per cent (Saddi et al., 2010). Although economic growth in the GCC was initially fuelled by progress in the energy sector, governments of the ME are clearly diversifying into non-oil related industries such as media and entertainment, renewable energy, retail, education, technology and entrepreneurship, and this trend will continue (SAMBA, 2012). Additionally, governments in the region have been investing strongly into infrastructure projects (IMF, 2013) such as Dubai's investments for World Expo 2020 and Qatar's preparations for the FIFA World Cup in 2022.

As organizations develop their plans to invest and grow in these markets, there will be an amplified need for a continuous pool of well-qualified talent to tap into for competitiveness and sustainability. In fact, senior HR managers in the ME indicate that the demand for new employees alone is expected to increase by 13 per cent between 2012 and 2017 (Oxford Economics, 2012). In a separate survey comparing talent challenges on account of sustained growth between organizations based in the ME and African regions and Europe, 53 per cent of the respondents from ME-/Africa-based organizations anticipated a significant increase in competition for key talent over the period of 2015–2020 compared to 46 per cent for respondents from Europe (Mercer, 2010). However, there already exists a shortage of talent in the region and the talent landscape has not been positive. It is also a region where an environment to nurture and find the right quality of talent is difficult as outlined earlier. For example, in the 2011 Global Talent Index, Saudi Arabia fell in the bottom 15 countries out of 60 in terms of a conducive talent environment, and in the bottom 5 in terms of quality of the labour force (Hendrick & Struggles, 2011). This difficult situation is clearly reflected in GCC CEO's outlooks regarding the talent crunch. In a survey conducted by PricewaterhouseCoopers (PwC), only 20 per cent of GCC CEOs felt that there was a sufficient supply of qualified national workers available, with 91 per cent of them stating the need to depend on the recruitment of expatriates to fill key positions (Lootah and Simon, 2009). Given the limited availability of required expertise and skills, the sustained growing demand and existing intuitional pressures outlined earlier, there will be an unrelenting battle for the best talent in the ME. Due to this mounting intensity, HR managers and those in charge of TM have recognized the demand for talent to be one of the most critical TM issues they are currently faced with and will continue to face in the near future (Mercer, 2010).

2. TM in its Infancy in the Region

The HRM function in the ME has been primarily a transactional department concerned with managing employment visa issues (with respect to expatriates) and legal compliance (with regard to local employees). As a 'low status' function, HR managers do not necessarily have the required training or expertise to address the more strategic roles that the HR function should play in organizations (Mellahi and Budhwar, 2006), such as those required for the identification or development of TM systems. Possibly, this low status can be attributed to the manner in which decisions regarding employee treatment were made in the past. Traditionally, HRM activities in the ME, especially those related to recruitment, treatment of employees and rewards, have been strongly influenced by the concept of '*wasta*'– the use of networks/social connections to seek favours (Harry, 2007; Mellahi and Budhwar, 2006; Sidani and Al Ariss, 2014). This results in a top-down, relationship-based approach of managing human capital rather than those based on actual merit, talent and measurable performance. This also has a negative effect on TM aspects as basic as identifying key talent in an organization, to more strategic TM activities such as succession planning for key positions. Further, due to the lack of professionalism and expertise in the field, many key TM activities, such as recruitment of key individuals, are outsourced to recruitment agencies. This results in delays, waste of resources and recruitment that doesn't support strategic TM objectives of the firm. Lastly, HR managers lack technical know-how in planning, monitoring and analysing any TM decisions, which are critical for TM systems to be effective. For example, only 19 per cent of HR professionals surveyed amongst ME- and Africa-based organizations are confident about their abilities to measure the effectiveness of their TM investments, with 34 per cent of them clearly admitting that they have no confidence in their current abilities to effectively measure TM investments and the remaining 47 per cent indicating some levels of confidence (Mercer, 2010).

Thus, many HRM professionals in the ME lack the expertise and a strategic perspective of their role in leading effective TM in organizations. These result in reactive TM measures, leaving very little room for organizations to be flexible or spend adequate time in developing robust TM systems. Often key TM activities are either lost to inefficacy or forgotten altogether.

Another interesting aspect of a traditional feature of managing talent in the ME is the common practice of 'stereotyping talent by nationality' (Sidani and Al Ariss, 2014). In this regard, certain nationalities are equated with specific skill sets, such as Indians being good accountants, or Filipinos being good nursing professionals and Egyptians being skilled as medical representatives. Organizations tend to seek out 'talent' by using nationality as a proxy rather than any measurable rubric. This skews the organizations' approach to talent attraction and development and is further reflective of the infancy of TM in the region.

3. Providing Differentiating Employee Value Propositions and Changing the Current Social/Psychological Contract in the Backdrop of Structural Imbalances

At the organizational level, given the structural inequalities and the demographic trends, one of the most disconcerting TM issues for organizations will be the difficulty in providing unique employee value propositions for their talented employees across the spectrum of local, expatriate and female workers. In itself, this is a challenging task given the fact that each of these employee segments has distinctively different motivators. Attempting to do this while maintaining fairness and equity and an organizational climate that is conducive to employee engagement and talent retention will be an even greater challenge.

With the current trends (e.g., push for nationalization, pressure of increased working population), attempting to differentiate on pay and benefits is not a long-term, financially viable solution for organizations. Therefore, private sector organizations will have to be creative in developing a different value proposition when it seeks to find and retain the best talent. For both expatriates and nationals, financial security has been traditionally a key motivational driver. However, this is not the case anymore (Aon Hewitt, 2010; Festing and Schäfer, 2014). For expatriates, family support and spousal influence play a key role in their decision to continue on expatriate assignments (Tung, 1988; Bhaskar-Shrinivas et al., 2005). Recent research on self-initiated expatriates in the ME also indicates the critical importance of organizational career support, which will be challenging given the institutional TM challenges of the region (Rodriguez and Scurry, 2014). Family considerations, such as schooling, quality of life and access to higher education opportunities, are also key motivators for expatriates in the ME (Schoepp and Forstenlechner, 2010). Further, expatriate employees as well as nationals are looking for opportunities for career growth and professional development, including training, higher education and opportunities to work in foreign locations. Longevity and stability in employment are also key drivers for both groups of employees in the backdrop for the battle for talent and economic and political changes (Manpower, 2008). Hence, in terms of being the employer of choice, TM leadership in organizations needs to develop more meaningful employee value propositions that address these issues. In turn, in order to retain their current talent, TM responsible functions/leaders need to chalk out the specifics of the talent deal they presently offer in terms of sustained employment, training and development, career progressions plans, increased engagement opportunities and so on. As the aspirations and desires of both expatriates and locals converge towards a common platform, HR leadership needs to accept that a dual HR system catering to these different employee segments is going to be unsustainable. Similarly, high-performance female employees may need their own unique employee value propositions considering work–life balance issues that are central to their employment in this region. In the end, talented employees will move to those organizations that show progressive TM leadership reflected in policies and procedures which demonstrate respect for talent and a nurturing environment for the growth of talent. These in turn will result in greater employee engagement, a positive psychological contract and better talent retention.

CONCLUSIONS AND AVENUES FOR FUTURE RESEARCH

As talent becomes scarce, expensive and harder to retain, the importance of TM for organizational competitiveness and sustainability has become well recognized by practitioners and researchers alike. Unlike organizations located elsewhere, organizations operating in the ME face unique challenges that greatly influence an organization's ability to build TM systems. However, research regarding TM in the ME is extremely limited. Additionally, the limited research in the field has taken a more macro-perspective to TM issues (e.g., see Singh et al., 2012), with the focus on issues of TM at the national level. In this chapter, we contribute to the nascent literature by outlining the unique institutional and organizational challenges in the specific context of TM in the region. This helps advance the field of TM in the ME by moving the discussion from a macro-perspective of TM issues to the organizational- and individual-level TM perspective.

As discussed earlier in this chapter, recent trends in the demographics of the local population, intensified demand for talent, the changing aspirations of the youth and women and the limited application of sound TM practices, all make TM issues even more challenging for organizations in the ME than in other parts of the world. As previously outlined, historical precedents of TM in the region have further hampered the sustenance of equitable working environments for both locals and expatriates. This combination of institutional and organizational factors has, in turn, put immense pressures on the criticality, development and implementation of TM systems for organizations operating in this region. Further, organizations will need to find creative employee value propositions, specific to the region and specific to the various employee segments, to understand how best they may attempt to attract and develop talent. Organizations will also have to work aggressively to move away from traditional approaches to TM to more innovative and sustainable models in order to retain the scarce talent in the region.

As is evidenced from this chapter, the field of TM is in its infancy in this region. Similarly, the field of TM in the ME is a severely under-researched area with a focus on broader TM macro-perspective issues such as the quality of the educational systems, unemployment issues and the challenges of managing nationalization in the region. Meanwhile, related HRM research has extensively focused on gender issues, nationalization concerns, and expatriate and local employee attitudes and work conditions.

In their work, Biygautane and Al Yahya (2014) argue that without significant changes at the national policy level, there will continue to be significant challenges to progressing on TM issues. They outline that governments of the region must first invest in employment generation, enabling knowledge transfer from expatriates to locals and the reformation of the educational systems, in order to pursue TM objectives.

Sidani and Al Ariss (2014) propose a framework for TM practices adapted to the GCC context with a view to institutionalizing the TM process. Their work emphasizes the challenges that companies face as they attempt to strike a balance between the local adaptation and the global assimilation of their TM processes. The authors focus on the issue of nationalization where they find that companies are challenged to sustain their 'legal' legitimacy through nationalization while simultaneously attempting to improve their economic sustainability. The authors find that organizations have adopted HR practices such as 'decoupling', where, as a matter of policy, legal compliance for nationalization is disassociated with strategic objectives of TM. The authors conclude that such approaches provide mixed results and that further research needs to assess the actual impact on TM in these organizations.

The paucity of research in this area leaves many avenues rich for future exploration. Some broad themes for future research are outlined below.

To begin with, given the institutional TM challenges organizations face in the ME, it is important that research looks into the current TM practices being employed in organizations in order to explore what kinds of TM systems and practices are presently used in this region. Further, it will be important to understand whether there are differences between TM systems employed in the private and public sectors, what these differences are, if any, and what their different impacts are. Researchers could also consider exploring whether there are different TM practices and approaches employed by organizations when TM leadership is led by expatriates or by locals and whether this has any impact on TM outcomes and employee engagement. Researchers could further explore the impact of differential TM practices on perceptions of fairness and justice between expatriate employees and locals. An interesting study that begins to touch on this area is one done by Fernandes and Awamleh (2006). Fernandes and Awamleh (2006) explored the perceptions of organizational justice amongst the two groups of employees – nationals and expatriates – in a UAE-based organization on (self-assessed) performance. Interestingly, they find that expatriates' performances are not affected by their perceptions of organizational justice, although job satisfaction was correlated to organizational justice for both groups and perceptions of organizational justice did have an impact on job performance for locals. Further research needs to explore whether organizational justice issues, considering the differences between expatriates and locals work regulations in the ME, impact actual performance and the development and retention of talent.

Similarly, given the institutional challenges, future research could explore how organizations in the ME currently attempt to support an organizational climate that nurtures talent. For example, as already discussed, in many ME organizations expatriate employee value propositions have not been well developed. However, in spite of having short-term contracts, many expatriates continue to renew their employment contracts and reside in the country over several decades (Baldwin-Edwards 2011). Employees who remain with organizations over such long periods of time potentially represent individuals with entrenched organizational, industry-specific and/or local knowledge and skills. Assuming that such employees are considered 'talent' in their respective organizations, researchers could explore why such expatriate employees continue to remain in organizations, when the value proposition for expatriates to stay on in long-term employment is not clear. Further, what kind of organizational climate and employee value propositions do such organizations offer in order to retain talent over this prolonged period of time? Similarly, what are the value propositions that would really be meaningful for locals? Researchers may find that organizations employ unique retention strategies not normally seen in the Western context.

For example, in a case study done in the University of Oman, Neal (2010) finds that in spite of several factors of alterity, local and expatriate faculty members used humour and shared long-term organizational goals to counter the imbalances of some of the institutional factors that affect local and expatriate employment. In this manner, there was a greater emphasis on employee (in this case, faculty) development and value for talented employees, allowing for a well-respected talent development programme for young local faculty members. This also led to a culture of mutual respect and cooperation. Neal (2010) also notes that this university has lower turnover rates compared to similar universities in Oman. Interestingly, the talent development programme at the university was led by an Omani who was the Dean.

In a similar vein, there may be different engagement and retention strategies that organizations in the ME develop in order to take advantage of the mostly untapped pool of talent represented by the women of the region. In a recent paper based on qualitative interview data on how Emirati women navigate workforce participation, Marmenout and Lirio (2014) find that several factors, distinct to the region, play into women's ability to join organizations, such as issues of modesty. Based on their findings, they suggest several strategies which are meaningful for the retention of female talent, including the need for flexible work arrangements. They also find that the Emirati women in their study had a strong desire for entrepreneurship. Future research in this area needs to be extended to other parts of the ME and also needs to include expatriate women.

A further area of research could explore whether the adoption of practices such as internships and campus recruitment, which are used in other regional contexts, impact TM pressures in the ME as well. Again, as the need for TM grows in importance and organizations transition from traditional approaches to more strategic ones, it may become critical to understand the different ways in which TM systems will evolve in the GCC region. To this effect, it may be interesting to understand whether who is even defined as 'talent' changes during this transition.

These are just a few areas in which the topic of TM in the ME can be furthered studied. It is to be noted that research in the ME, in general, tends to be more descriptive, anecdotal, case based, normative and/or conceptual (Zahhra, 2011). In this regard, along with a broader spectrum of TM themes for research, there is also a need for more empirical studies and longitudinal research designs. Further, a mix of both qualitative and quantitative approaches will undoubtedly provide richer findings which could incorporate both the nuances of practices unique to the region and their impact and effectiveness in dealing with the challenges that organizations face in this region. With the use of more rigorous methods, the focus should be to move from research that describes TM in the ME towards an understanding of the dynamics of how TM is uniquely crafted to bring about strategic impacts for organizational sustainability and competitiveness in the ME.

With the limited research that is currently available, TM in the ME is an exceptionally rich avenue for significantly impactful research. The field is ripe for exploration.

NOTES

1. The terms 'expatriate', 'foreign workers' and 'foreigners' are used interchangeably in this chapter to indicate individuals who have come to work in the region, either by their own volition or as an organizational assignee from another country.
2. The terms 'locals' and 'nationals' are used interchangeably in this chapter in reference to the indigenous population.

REFERENCES'

Al Ariss, A., Cascio, W.F. and Paauwe, J. 2014. Talent management: current theories and future research directions. *Journal of World Business*, **49**(2): 173–179.

Al-Dosary, A. and Rahman, S. 2005. Saudization (localization) – a critical review. *Human Resource Development*, **8**(4): 495–502.

Al-Kibsi, G., Benkert, C. and Schubert, J. 2007. Getting labor policy to work in the Gulf. *McKinsey Quarterly – Special Edition: Reappraising the Gulf States*, pp. 19–29.

Al-Lamki, S.M. 1998. Barriers to Omanization in the private sector: the perceptions of Omani graduates. *International Journal of Human Resource Management*, **9**(2): 377–400.

Al-Waqfi, M.A. and Forstenlechner, I. 2014. Barriers to Emiratization: the role of policy design and institutional environment in determining the effectiveness of Emiratization. *International Journal of Human Resource Management*, **25**(2): 167–189.

Alzalabani, A.H. 2002. International briefing 11: training and development in Saudi Arabia. *International Journal of Training and Development*, **6**(2): 125–140.

Aon Hewitt, 2010. *Qudurat: A Pioneering Research Study*. Dubai, UAE.

ASDA'A Burson-Marsteller, 2014. *Arab Youth Survey 2014: We Want to Embrace Modern Values*. http://arabyouthsurvey.com/wp-content/themes/arabyouth-english/downloads/AYS-Whitepaper-en.pdf (accessed 14 August 2015).

Baldwin-Edwards, M. 2011. Labour immigration and labour markets in the GCC countries: national patterns and trends. Kuwait Programme on Development, Governance and Globalisation in the Gulf States. Research Paper No. 15. London School of Economics, UK.

Bhaskar-Shrinivas, P., Harrison, D.A., Shaffer, M.A. and Luk, D.M, 2005. Input-based and time-based models of international adjustment: meta-analytic evidence and theoretical extensions. *Academy of Management Journal*, **48**(2): 257–281.

Biygautane, M. and Al Yahya, K.O. 2014. Talent management in the MENA and GCC regions: challenges and opportunities. In A. Al Ariss (ed.), *Global Talent Management: Challenges, Strategies, and Opportunities*. Cham. Switzerland: Springer International Publishing, pp. 197–215.

Collings, D. and Mellahi, K., 2009. Strategic talent management: a review and research agenda. *Human Resource Management Review*, **19**(4): 304–313.

Dewhurst, M., Pettigrew, M. and Srinivasan, R. 2012. How multinationals can attract the talent they need. *McKinsey Quarterly*, June.

Dubai Women Establishment and PwC 2009. *Arab Women Leadership Outlook 2009–2011*. Dubai, UAE.

Farndale, E., Scullion, H. and Sparrow, P. 2010. The role of the corporate HR function in global talent management. *Journal of World Business*, **45**(2): 161–168.

Fasano, U. and Goyal, R. 2004. Emerging strains in GCC labor markets. IMF Working Papers, 04(71): 1.

Fernandes, C. and Awamleh, R. 2006. Impact of organisational justice in an expatriate work environment. *Management Research News*, **29**(11): 701–712.

Festing, M. and Schäfer, L. 2014. Generational challenges to talent management: a framework for talent retention based on the psychological-contract perspective. *Journal of World Business*, **49**(2): 262–271.

Forstenlechner, I. 2010. Expats and citizens: managing diverse teams in the Middle East. *Team Performance Management: An International Journal*, **16**(5/6): 237–241.

Forstenlechner, I. and Mellahi, K. 2011. Gaining legitimacy through hiring local workforce at a premium: the case of MNEs in the United Arab Emirates. *Journal of World Business*, **46**(4): 455–461.

Girgis, M. 2002. Will nationals and Asians replace Arab workers in the GCC? Paper presented at the Fourth Mediterranean Development Forum, Amman, 2 October.

Harry, W. 2007. Employment creation and localization: the crucial human resource issues for the GCC. *International Journal of Human Resource Management*, **18**(1): 132–146.

Hendrick & Struggles 2011. Global Talent Index. http://www.globaltalentindex.com/Resources/gti-map.aspx (accessed 14 August 2015).
Hertog, S. 2013. The private sector and reform in the Gulf Cooperation Council. Kuwait Programme on Development, Governance and Globalisation in the Gulf States. Research Paper No. 30. London School of Economics, UK.
Huselid, M.A., Beatty, R.W. and Becker, B.E. 2005. 'A players' or 'A positions'? The strategic logic of workforce management. *Harvard Business Review*, December, pp. 110–117.
International Labour Organization 2009. *International Labour Migration and Employment in the Arab Region: Origins, Consequences and the Way Forward*. Beirut.
International Monetary Fund (IMF) 2013. *Economic Prospects and Policy Challenges for the GCC Countries*. Riyadh, Saudi Arabia.
Kapiszewski, A. 2006. *Arab versus Asian Migrant Workers in the GCC Countries*. United Nations Expert Group Meeting on International Migration and Development in the Arab Region, Population Division, Department of Economic and Social Affairs, Beirut.
Lewis, R.E. and Heckman, R.J. 2006. Talent management: a critical review. *Human Resource Management Review*, **16**(2): 139–154.
Lootah, S. and Simon, A. 2009. *Arab Human Capital Challenge*. PriceWaterHouseCoopers.
Marmenout, K. and Lirio, P. 2014. Local female talent retention in the Gulf : Emirati women bending with the wind. *International Journal of Human Resource Management*, **25**(2): 144–166.
Mellahi, K. 2007. The effect of regulations on HRM: private sector firms in Saudi Arabia. *International Journal of Human Resource Management*, **18**(1): 85–99.
Mellahi, K. and Al-Hinai, S. 2000. Local workers in Gulf Co-operation countries: assets or liabilities? *Middle Eastern Studies*, **36**(3): 177–190.
Mellahi, K. and Budhwar, P. 2006. Human resource management in the Middle East: emerging HRM models and future challenges for research and policy. In P. Budhwar and K. Mellahi (eds), *Managing Human Resources in the Middle East*. London: Routledge, pp. 291–301.
Mercer 2010. *EMEA Employers Plan to Reshape Talent Programmes as the Economy Shifts towards Growth*. Mercer's Future of Talent Management Survey. http://cl.exct.net/?qs=e3637ddcc50b3ee6f354d1b904c6c311 9e21490c0056b92ebb73d9b6e54ea342 (mercer.com) (accessed 14 August 2015).
Metcalfe, B.D. 2008. Women, management and globalization in the Middle East. *Journal of Business Ethics*, **83**(1): 85–100.
Michaels, E., Handfield-Jones, H. and Axelrod, B. 2001. *The War for Talent*. Boston, MA: Harvard Business School Press.
Mirkin, B. 2013. Arab Human Development Report. UNDP Arab Human Development Report Research Paper Series, 2013, New York: UNDP.
Neal, M. 2010. When Arab–expatriate relations work well: diversity and discourse in the Gulf Arab workplace. *Team Performance Management: An International Journal*, **16**(5/6): 242–266.
Nijs, S., Gallardo-Gallardo, E., Dries, N. and Sels, L. 2014. A multidisciplinary review into the definition, operationalization, and measurement of talent. *Journal of World Business*, **49**(2): 180–191.
Omair, K. 2011. Women in management in the Middle East. In L. Husu et al. (eds), *Women, Management and Leadership*. Helsinki: Women, Management and Leadership, pp. 149–159.
Oxford Economics 2012. *Global Talent 2021: How the New Geography of Talent Will Transform Human Resource Strategies*. Oxford: Corporate Headquarters, Abbey House.
Rees, C.J., Mamman, A. and Braik, A.B. 2007. Emiratization as a strategic HRM change initiative: case study evidence from a UAE petroleum company. *International Journal of Human Resource Management*, **18**(1): 33–53.
Rodriguez, J.K. and Scurry, T. 2014. Career capital development of self-initiated expatriates in Qatar: cosmopolitan globetrotters, experts and outsiders. *International Journal of Human Resource Management*, **25**(7): 1046–1067.
Saddi, J., Sabbagh, K. and Shediac, R. 2010. Measures of leadership. *Strategy+Business*, Summer, issue 59. http://www.strategy-business.com/article/10203?gko=64f7f (accessed 14 August 2015).
SAMBA 2012. *Saudi and GCC Opportunities 2012–16*. Riyadh, Saudi Arabia: Economics Department, Samba Financial Group. http://www.gulfinthemedia.com/files/article_en/608373.pdf (accessed 14 August 2016).
Schoepp, K. and Forstenlechner, I. 2010. The role of family considerations in an expatriate majority environment. *Team Performance Management: An International Journal*, **32**(5/6): 309–323.
Schuler, R.S., Jackson, S.E. and Tarique, I. 2011. Global talent management and global talent challenges: strategic opportunities for IHRM. *Journal of World Business*, **46**(4): 506–516.
Scullion, H., Collings, D.G. and Caligiuri, P. 2010. Global talent management. *Journal of World Business*, **45**(2): 105–108.
Scullion, H., Collings, D. and Gunnigle, P., 2007. International human resource management in the 21st century: emerging themes and contemporary debates. *Human Resource Management Journal*, **17**(4), pp.309–319.

Secretariat of the Gulf Cooperation Council 2013. GCC. http://sites.gcc-sg.org/ (accessed 14 August 2015).
Shaham, D. 2009. Foreign labor in the Arab Gulf: challenges to nationalization nationals and expatriates: segmented labor markets. *Al-Nakhlah*, Fall, pp. 1–14.
Sidani, Y. and Al Ariss, A. 2014. Institutional and corporate drivers of global talent management: evidence from the Arab Gulf region. *Journal of World Business*, **49**(2): 215–224.
Singh, A., Jones, D.B. and Hall, N. 2012. Talent management: a research based case study in the GCC region. *International Journal of Business and Management*, **7**(24): 94–107.
Syed, J. 2010. An historical perspective on Islamic modesty and its implications for female employment. *Equality, Diversity and Inclusion: An International Journal*, **29**(2): 150–166.
Tarique, I. and Schuler, R.S. 2010. Global talent management: literature review, integrative framework, and suggestions for further research. *Journal of World Business*, **45**(2): 122–133.
The Economist Intelligence Unit 2009. *The GCC in 2020: The Gulf and Its People*. http://graphics.eiu.com/upload/eb/Gulf2020part2.pdf (accessed 14 August 2016).
Tung, R.L. 1988. American expatriates abroad: from neophytes to cosmopolitans. *Journal of World Business*, **33**(2): 124–144.
United Nations 2010. *The World's Women 2010 Trends and Statistics*. New York: UN Department of Economic and Social Affairs.
United Nations Development Programme (UNDP) 2000. *Human Development Report*. Oxford: Oxford University Press.
Wagner, R. 2012. Islamic feminism in the Middle East. *International Policy Digest*, 2 February. http://intpolicydigest.org/2012/02/02/islamic-feminism-in-the-middle-east/ (accessed 22 June 2016).
Winckler, O. 2010. Can the GCC weather the economic meltdown? *Middle East Quarterly*, **17**(3): 51–61.
World Bank 2008. *MENA Development Report: The Road Not Traveled – Education Reform in the Middle East and North Africa*, Washington, DC.
World Bank 2011. *Middle East and North Africa Region Economic Developments and Prospects*. Washington, DC: IBRD.
Zahhra, S.A. 2011. Doing research in the (new) Middle East: sailing with the wind. *Academy of Management Perspective*, Symposium, November, pp. 6–21.

PART II

COUNTRY AND REGIONAL PERSPECTIVES

Section A

Human Resource Management in the Gulf Cooperation Council Countries

6. Human resource management in Oman

Misida Al-Jahwari and Pawan S. Budhwar

INTRODUCTION

This chapter presents an overview regarding the nature of human resource management (HRM) in Oman, focusing on the four main human resource (HR) functions of recruitment, selection, training and compensation. It also discusses the current challenges faced by the HR manager, offers recommendations and suggests future research directions. It starts with a background on Oman's location and population and aspects of its societal culture, current political structure, economy, education and research. After setting the context, the chapter offers a discussion on HRM practices in Oman with a focus on workforce localisation – the top HR priority for the government and the private sector. The later part of the chapter looks at the emerging HRM model in Oman and offers a conclusion. Information to develop this chapter was gathered from relevant literature, current media documents, government websites and practical insights from 16 Omani HR professionals and non-managerial employees.

OMAN: A STRATEGIC LOCATION AND GROWING POPULATION

Oman is an ancient country that lies in the south-east corner of the Arabian Peninsula, sharing land borders with Saudi Arabia, Yemen and the United Arab Emirates. The country is the third largest in the Arabian Peninsula after Saudi Arabia and Yemen with an area of 309,500 sq. km. Oman has a long coastline that stretches 3,165 km along the Gulf of Oman, Indian Ocean and a small area touching the Arabian Gulf waters. Sitting in the Indian Ocean and facing the East has made Oman more outward looking rather than inward towards the deserts. In fact, since olden days, Oman has been a gateway to Asian, Arab and African markets. 'This combination of being geographically outside the gulf and being strategically essential to it gives Oman a unique place in the regional setting of the Gulf Cooperation Council and the industrial nations of the west as well' (Al-Barwani and Albeely, 2007: 120).

Oman is made up of governorates and regions and each region is further subdivided into states called '*wilayaat*'. Locals in each state share a common culture, dialect and traditional clothing. Muscat, the capital, is the only city in Oman that is dominated by expatriates. Omanis make up only 39 per cent of the population in the capital while expatriates make up 61 per cent. Oman's population reached 4.27 million in October 2015 (NCSI, 2015a). There are 2.369 million Omanis making up 55.5 per cent of the total population and 1.9 million expatriates who make up the remaining 44.5 per cent. The Omani population has been growing at a fast rate, with youth representing the majority. According to a forecast for Oman, between 2015 and 2040 the population will increase by 2.4 million

(NCSI, 2015a). The two biggest challenges for Oman today are diversifying away from oil and providing jobs for the growing number of young Omani job-seekers.

THE SULTAN AND THE POLITICAL STRUCTURE: TOWARDS A PARTICIPATORY GOVERNMENT

Oman has been a self-governing country since 1650 after defeating the Portuguese in Omani coastal cities. Besides a ten-year Persian invasion between 1737 and 1747, Oman was never colonised by any foreign power nor was it legally part of the British Empire.[1] In fact, between the seventeenth and nineteenth centuries Oman built a remarkable empire of its own, crossing the Gulf of Oman and the Indian Ocean and covering parts of East Africa. Today, Oman is a single geographical entity and an absolute monarchy ruled by Sultan Qaboos bin Said since July 1970, a direct descendant of the royal Al-Busaidi dynasty founded in 1744.

There can be no fair discussion of the modern Oman without shedding light on the role of the Sultan's 45 years of rule, which is referred to as the 'renaissance era' because he managed to convert a country that was shut off from the world for decades and struggling with debts and tribal conflicts, to a growing, peaceful and tolerant nation that has preserved its culture and heritage in the face of rapid modernisation. Sultan Qaboos is a visionary leader who is highly esteemed by his followers. Since the beginning of his rule, the Sultan had a vision for Oman, which he has been clearly and consistently communicating in his speeches to the nation over the decades. The continuous and consistent communication to the people of Oman has helped to create commitment and a sense of unity towards an aspired future. The Sultan is also a renowned peacemaker and a mediator in various world affairs. He has managed to 'maintain security and stability with all nations through cooperation and peace rather than conflict' (Ministry of Foreign Affairs, 2015). Due to his foreign policy, the country has not been involved in any regional or international conflict for the last 45 years.

It is obvious in the current political structure of the country that a 'participatory, representative government is establishing its roots in Oman, grounded firmly in the Islamic traditions' (Cecil, 2006: 67). Historically, the democratic framework of Oman is a by-product of the tribal traditions that is considered the oldest form of political arrangement (Almoharby, 2010: 12). The Sultan rules by decree and is supported by the Council of Ministers and special advisers. There is also the Council of Oman, which consists of *Majlis Al Shura* (The Shura Council) and *Majlis Al Dawla* (The State Council). This council's main role is to raise issues of concern from various *wilayaat* (states), debate policy, suggest revisions to laws, submit proposals to the Council of Ministers and even call ministers and discuss issues of concern with them. In October 2011, the Sultan offered some legislative powers to the two bodies and announced the establishment of *Majlis Al Baladi* (The Municipal Council) in all governorates with elected members to represent all the *wilayaat* in each governorate. Each municipal council is expected to make recommendations to the government on development projects in its respective state.

Although Oman is an absolute monarchy, the Sultan has been regularly meeting the general public, listening to their concerns and suggestions and consulting them on various issues via different channels. Besides the councils, the Sultan has since 1975 conducted annual 'Meet-the-People Tours' along with his ministers and advisers. Meetings with the general public take place in special camps set up for the tours and some occur spontaneously whenever citizens get the chance to chat with the Sultan. Many of the Sultan's decisions and decrees have been formulated after the annual Meet-the-People Tours. This participative approach has its roots in Islam and has been the Omani way of leadership and governance for centuries (Almoharby, 2010). In a magazine interview, the Sultan said: 'These meetings with my people are of paramount importance to me. The tradition of our country is that each Omani should be able to meet his sultan directly' (Figaro Magazine, 30 April 1994 in Plekhanov, 2004).

OMANI SOCIETAL CULTURE

The Omani societal culture has a strong Islamic and Arab identity. It has great similarities with the cultures of its neighbours in the Arabian Peninsula due to a common ancestry, language, religion, intermarriages and centuries of economic, social and political interactions. Mellahi and Wood (2001) found that people in the Arab Gulf countries are highly collectivist within the in-group (tribe or extended family) and highly individualist with the out-group (non-kin and guest workers). According to Kabasakal and Bodur (2002: 47), Islam creates this highly collectivist culture by promoting and maintaining family and kinship relationships. We believe that besides Islam, Arab tribalism in the Arabian Peninsula is also a main cause of the common cultural value of collectivism within the in-groups.

Further, centuries of seafaring and international trade exposed Oman to waves of ancient migrations to and from Arabia, Persia, South Asia and East Africa. This made Omanis interact with people from different races, languages, religions and cultures for centuries. 'The Omanis have thus been globalised for centuries, and this has contributed to the development of a widely shared, open-minded and outward-looking cultural disposition' (Neal, 2010: 255). Cecil (2006: 66) also described Omanis as having 'a deeper tradition of tolerance for differing ideas'. Moreover, according to Jones and Ridout (2013), the people of Oman are believed to have a strong commitment to anti-sectarianism, the practice of '*Shura*' (consultation) and a preference to avoid open expression of differences. It is interesting to see that these descriptions of Omanis are consistent with the values and principles of the '*Ibadhi*' thought. The Ibadhi state was first established in Oman in the mid-eighth century (Peterson, 1978) and *Ibadhism* is still one of the main sects of Islam in Oman besides *Sunnism* and *Shiasm*. 'Ibadism is known for its conservatism and tolerance . . . aversion to political violence [and] agreeable disagreement with friends and peaceful compromise with enemies . . .' (Lefebvre, 2010).

The Omani society 'exhibits a wealth of diversity in ethnic groups and native languages' (Peterson, 2004: 31). In today's modern Oman, one can find the dominant Omani culture with its strong Arab-Islamic identity, the Bedouin and Dhofari cultures and aspects of the East African, Baluchi, Persian and South Asian cultures. Arabic is Oman's dominant and official language and English is widely used as the country's business language. Almost all signs and writings in Oman appear in both Arabic and English. English is widely demanded in the job market and is the only second language taught as a requirement in Oman from nursery to high school and in many higher education institutions. Omanis speak Arabic in different dialects, and it is common to find locals who use a second language at home besides Arabic. For example, several Omanis speak Swahili and Baluchi due to Oman's long historical rule in East Africa and Gwadar of Baluchistan that currently lies between Pakistan and Iran. The geographical proximity of Oman to the Indo-Pak subcontinent and Iran led to the existence of the Luwati language and other South Asian languages, the Persian language and Kumzari, a South Western Persian language. In addition to these, the tribal people in Dhofar speak a variety of South Arabian Semitic languages. Hence, Oman, with its multi-languages and subcultures, exercises what Barth (1983) called 'cultural pluralism', which had existed before the European colonial intrusions in the Indian Ocean. This cultural pluralism developed over a long period and is believed to have formed a distinctive culture.

As briefed above, the main distinguishing characteristics of the Omani culture are its geographical location, its exposure to ancient migrations, its long-time political independence, history of seafaring, and years of interaction with its overseas dominions outside Arabia, the influence of Ibadhism on managing its affairs, and the rich ethnic diversity in its society. Several researchers pointed out that these factors make Oman different (Pridham, 1987; Cecil, 2006; Al-Barwani and Albeely, 2007; Jones and Ridout, 2013), and more in-depth knowledge of the Omani culture can help advance our understanding of organisational behaviour, people management and leadership in Omani workplaces.

THE PRACTICE OF SHURA IN OMAN

Among all other aspects of the Omani culture, '*Shura*' stands out as an influential component in the lives of Omanis. Shura is a participative approach to decision-making that was practised by Islam more than 14 centuries ago. The Omanis have maintained and developed Shura in managing their affairs over centuries, and among other countries in the Islamic world, Oman is known to be ahead in practising Shura in decision-making (Almoharby, 2010: 15). In fact, even today, Shura is central to Oman's way of managing its affairs and dealing with others internally and externally. This we believe is largely due to the dominant values in the Omani societal culture and the influence of the Ibadhi thought. The followers of Ibadism call themselves 'the people of Shura (consultation)' because Shura is one of the main principles that distinguish them from other sects of Islam when it comes to electing a leader and decision-making (Al-Barwani and Albeely, 2007).

Today, the prevalence of this participative approach is obvious in both the Omani society and the political structure of the country. At the individual and group levels, Shura is practised on a day-to-day basis within and between tribes, in villages and among family members and friends. There is also an emphasis on practising Shura among the young emerging society of educated Omanis, in particular via social media tools.

At the government level, the practice of Shura is obvious in Oman's political structure. Omanis participate in Majlis Al Shura (Shura Council), Majlis Al Dawla (State Council) and Majlis Al Baladi (Municipal Councils) to raise issues, suggest proposals and influence government decisions that concern their present and future lives. According to researchers, consultation in the Middle East and North Africa region '. . . is not used as a power sharing mechanism as in the western cultures, but as a way to show that the leader cares about the subordinates and values their opinions' (Kabasakal et al., 2012: 528). In Oman, however, both purposes of consultation apply. The evidence for this lies in the various changes that the Sultan makes after listening to people's concerns in the Shura Council and the annual Meet-the-People Tours. The recent establishment of the first college department of political science in Oman is also a clear indication of the Sultan's intention to gradually prepare Omanis for more participation in decision-making. In fact, Sultan Qaboos said two decades ago: 'I have every intention of ensuring that this popular participation is further developed to the benefit of my people and country' (Middle East Insight, Nov–Dec 1995 in Plekhanov, 2004).

THE TRIANGLE OF ISLAM, TRIBES AND FAMILIES IN OMAN

Islam plays a central role in the lives of Omanis, while the tribe and the family are the second top authorities after Islam in formulating the culture of the country. The people of Oman adopted Islam in AD 630, and the country has been Islamic ever since. Islam is viewed as a code of life that covers all spheres of the past, present and future. 'The Omani government follows Islamic law for civic cases and modern civic law for criminal cases' (Al-Hammadi and Budhwar, 2006: 41). According to Naser (1993), the *Sharia Law* in Oman does not interfere in government affairs but the government consults the Sharia and scholars. Researchers have found Islam to be very influential in Oman and Omani employees give high priority to Islam and their socialisation process (Al-Hammadi and Budhwar, 2006). In fact, several authors have asserted that Islamic beliefs and values provide a core basis for understanding organisational behaviour and leadership in Arab countries (Smith, Achoui and Harb, 2007).

Apart from Islam, the tribe has continued to play a fundamental role in the lives of Omani people. The majority of the locals in the Arab Gulf States bear a tribal name rather than a family name. 'Conceptually, a tribe is defined to be a clan or a group of clans that are organised around a common ancestor' (Al-Barwani and Albeely, 2007: 122). Omanis are grouped into hundreds of tribes across the country and vary on the basis of their origin, geographical location and dispersion, size, cohesiveness and power. Tribes are a kind of identity; a tribal name tells you which part of the country a person originates from and, in some cases, where their ancestors migrated from. Each tribe in Oman has a sheikh elected by members of the tribe and is known and approved by the government. Tribal sheikhs have specific roles to perform towards the tribe, and '. . . legitimacy to continue [with the position] is conferred upon continued tribal satisfaction with duties performed' (Al-Barwani and Albeely, 2007: 123). The claim that 'the status of the individual is determined by his/her tribal or group affiliation and rarely by individual merits' (Kazan, 1993: 190) is no longer fully applicable in Oman. There are many exceptions to this statement because since the 1970s several Omani men and women from various tribes have managed to create high social and economic status for themselves from their personal successes in education, work and business.

Along with both Islam and the tribe, the family occupies a central place in both individual and social life in Oman. Islam, the tribal system, Oman's history and the influence of its overseas dominions and monarchical system have contributed to the formation of the character of the Omani person and the Omani family (Al-Barwani and Albeely, 2007).

The researchers said that the Omani family fits well with the general definition of an Islamic/Arab family. It is based on a detailed set of rules about interpersonal relationships, rights and obligations. In Islam, a family is 'a special kind of structure whose principal members are related to one another through blood ties and/or marital relationships, and whose relatedness is of such a nature as to entail mutual expectations that are prescribed by religion, reinforced by the law and internalised by the individual' (Abd al 'Ati, 1997:1). Islam determines all issues like inheritance, custody, marriage and divorce. 'The mutual expectations of the family members are not established only by familial relationships, but also by the membership in a larger social system which derives from a common religious brotherhood . . . [that] reinforces family ties, complements them and prevents their abuse' (Al-Barwani and Albeely, 2007: 131).

'The extended family is still very strong in Oman and the support of the members of the extended family in ensuring their well-being is the prime duty and responsibility of all members' (Al-Barwani and Albeely, 2007: 138). Further, 'even though the younger generation seems to generally prefer to live independently after marriage, they normally do not opt to live far from their parents' (Al-Barwani and Albeely, 2007: 138). In fact, Omani sons and daughters see it as their religious and cultural obligation to be close to their parents and to look after them when they grow old. Special arrangements are made, usually in the house of the eldest son or daughter, to accommodate for the elderly, who could be parents, grandparents or even elderly uncles and aunts who have no one to look after them.

THE ECONOMIC CONTEXT

'Omanis had for centuries been trading with the east coast of Africa, with India and even China . . .' (Cecil, 2006: 61). The country prospered for centuries, and in particular from 1650 until 'during World War I when its trade and economy started to deteriorate' (Gonzales et al., 2008). The country then gradually stagnated for decades in debt and poverty. It lacked infrastructure and was shut off from the rest of the world until 1970. In July 1970, the new Sultan 'found himself in charge of a stagnant, conflict-ridden country in which there there were less than ten miles of paved road and only one 12-bed hospital' (Cecil, 2006: 61). Since then, Sultan Qaboos has been modernising the country, educating its people and building relationships with other nations.

Oman, under Sultan Qaboos, has accomplished great achievements. It was named the most improved nation in terms of development and education in the 2010 UN Human Development Report. Today, Oman is a middle-income economy that is transitioning from an efficiency-driven economy to an innovation-driven economy (World Economic Forum, 2015). It is the 22nd largest oil producing country in the world (EIA, 2013) and, like its Arab Gulf neighbours, it heavily relies on oil and gas revenues. According to the Central Bank of Oman (CBO) Annual Report 2014 (CBO, 2014), oil and gas revenues stood around 40 per cent and 37.8 per cent of Oman's gross domestic product (GDP) in the years 2013 and 2014. Also, the oil and gas sectors, as a share of GDP, stood around 47.2 per cent in 2014, and their combined contribution to government revenues stood at around 85 per cent and 65.5 per cent of total merchandise exports.

Other major industries that contribute to the GDP include construction, cement, copper, steel, chemicals, optic fibre, banking and finance, agriculture and fisheries, travel and tourism. The tourism sector's contribution to GDP is expected to increase from 6.4 per cent in 2013 to 8.2 per cent by 2024 (OBG, 2015).

In comparison to its neighbours, Oman is considered a small oil exporter but also 'the most prolific Middle Eastern producer that is not a member of OPEC' (The Oil and Gas Year, 2015: 16). With oil reserves estimated by various sources to deplete in 2022, Oman had to plan early on how to diversify its economy and reduce its reliance on oil revenues.[2] Since 1995, the government has been committed to its strategic plan and vision. It has been actively pursuing privatisation, industrialisation, diversification, education reforms and the creation of more private sector jobs for locals to reduce Oman's vulnerability to uncertainty in the global oil market and help create private sector jobs. The end objective is to reduce the oil sector's contribution to the GDP to 9 per cent by 2020. So far, oil contribution to the overall GDP reduced from 50.6 per cent in 2013 to 47.2 per cent in 2014 (CBO, 2014). Also, the non-oil sector contribution reached to 19.5 per cent of the overall real GDP in 2014. The small and gradual decreases in the oil sector's contribution to the GDP associated with an increasing contribution of the non-oil sectors indicate steady progress in Oman's diversification programme.

In terms of economic performance and growth, Oman's GDP grew by an estimated 4.4 per cent in 2014 (Ministry of Finance, 2015). According to The Economist Intelligence Unit (EIU, 2013), experts had agreed that Oman would experience an economic growth averaging 4 per cent in the period 2014–2018 due to strong domestic demand, expansionary fiscal policy and gains in the non-oil economy. However, declining oil prices and increased oil and gas cooperation with Iran have changed the economic outlook for Oman. If oil prices continue to fall, the government's ability to effectively balance its budget will be greatly challenged. As per expectations, oil prices remained low in 2015 and beyond. A further drop in oil prices would worsen the fiscal and economic outlook (IMF, 2015). Oman so far has managed to make up for the drop in oil prices by heavily investing in a variety of enhanced oil recovery techniques that have increased production in recent years. All in all, 'the future prospects of the Omani economy in general remains promising, taking into account the pace of economic diversification, large expenditure planned by the government and the role of the private sector in the development process' (CBO, 2014: 11).

EDUCATION AND RESEARCH IN OMAN

Oman has witnessed a remarkable improvement in education since the 1970s when there were only three boys' schools, with less than 1,000 students and 30 male teachers in the country. Major reforms took place during the 1970s to mid-1990s, and the country witnessed a remarkable increase in the quantity and quality of education. By the year 2012–2013 there were over 1,000 schools with a total of 594,049 students and 53,195 teachers throughout Oman (NCSI, 2015a; Ministry of Education, 2015). Oman has also witnessed an extraordinary rapid increase in formal education for girls from 0 per cent in 1970 to 12.7 per cent in 1971–1972 and to over 49 per cent in 2008–2009 and the following years. By 2012–2013, there were a total of 258,671 boys and 255,996 girls in government schools (Ministry of Education, 2015).

Oman now has 59 higher education institutions, 27 of which are privately owned. These institutions include 8 universities, 38 colleges and 13 institutes (NCSI, 2015a).

Student enrolment in these institutions reached 33,980 during 2015. In order to further ensure quality, the Oman Academic Accreditation Authority (OAAA) was established in 2010 'to provide confidence to the public that the quality of higher education in Oman meets international standards, and to encourage continuous improvement in the quality of higher education' (OAAA, 2015).

One of the biggest challenges facing the higher education sector in Oman is further aligning its curricula to industry needs so that graduates can be better qualified for more private sector jobs. The situation is aggravated by the fact that the yearly number of graduates in Oman exceeds the number of jobs available (Al-Barwani, Chapman and Ameen, 2009) and the country has acute skill shortages among locals in the areas of Science, Technology, Engineering and Mathematics. In addition, private employers continue to prefer expatriates to local graduates in various jobs. Employers blame schools and higher education for not adequately preparing graduates for the workplace (Ernst and Young, 2015). The government has been giving great attention to education and research in Oman. In 2015, about 21.3 per cent of the overall government expenditure was allocated to education (OBG, 2015). Also, to help support research and innovation and move towards a knowledge-based economy, The Research Council was established in 2005. The council serves as a policy-making body and a funding agency. In the current five-year plan (2011–2015), 1 per cent of Oman's GDP will be spent on research, and the government aims to spend 2 per cent of GDP on research and development by 2020. This is a huge investment that should help Oman achieve its vision of building the largest research capacity in the region, excel in fields of national importance, become a regional hub for innovation, and have a world-class infrastructure for evidence-based policy making (The Research Council, 2015). Besides focusing on education and research, both the 8th and 9th five-year development plans of Oman (2011–2015 and 2016–2020) focus on creating job opportunities for Omanis. With these efforts, it is hoped that education and research will improve and the number of youth job-seekers and level of skill shortages will gradually reduce.

'Despite the very late start, education participation levels in Oman are now equal to or above other countries in the Middle East and North Africa region' (Muscat Daily, 2013). According to the article, Oman's success story was described in a 2001 World Bank Report as 'massive', 'unprecedented' and 'unparalleled by any other country'. Massive changes have been implemented and several reforms are underway. The whole education system is being reviewed in response to the directives of the Sultan to satisfy community and labour-market needs and align education with the future directions and vision of Oman. Several improvements influenced by best practices from advanced nations are underway. The reforms cover areas like curricula design, teaching methods, enhancing research capabilities, inspections, evaluations, quality assurance and accreditation. Also, the higher education institutions and large organisations have begun to cooperate in various ways to narrow the gap between what is taught and what industries need.

TOWARDS A COMPREHENSIVE APPROACH TO WORKFORCE DEVELOPMENT

Oman has largely followed a traditional workforce development model where most of the training occurs in higher education institutes before employment. However, with

Omanisation on the top of Oman's HR agenda and the misalignments between higher education, student preferences and industry requirements being increasingly recognised, workforce development in Oman has been moving towards a more comprehensive approach. This is evident in the government's support for self-employment via entrepreneurship and the recent entrance of the private sector in workforce development. Due to workforce localisation, a growing number of private organisations in Oman have been adding new forms of training programmes specially designed for Omani graduates and new employees. These programmes are conducted both on the job and off the job in special training centres owned by private companies. The training is further supported by personal development plans and career advancement. The automotive industry has taken the lead and established the first industry-driven educational institute in Oman, the National Automotive Higher Institute. With private employers entering the workforce development arena, better and faster results are expected in terms of the numbers of Omanis qualified for private sector jobs and the numbers hired and retained.

It seems that the emerging workforce development paradigm in Oman is combining the traditional workforce development model, entrepreneurship and aspects of employee-centred learning. In this, students are formally trained and certified by higher education institutions and then employers take charge to give them the needed job-specific knowledge and skills via special on-the-job training and development programmes or industry-owned institutes. This is a useful start, and in higher education we suggest fostering employer engagement in curricula design and delivery, encouraging employers' interaction with student bodies and facilitating the establishment of more industry-owned higher education institutes. Also, higher education institutes need to move towards more hands-on practice and skill development rather than information sharing.

HRM IN OMAN

People management in Oman has been influenced and regulated by a combination of the above-discussed forces over years. Researchers found that Islam, the government, the societal culture, a variety of ideologies brought by the earliest foreign consultants, and senior managers and social elites in both the government and private sectors influence HRM in Oman (Weir, 2001; Budhwar and Mellahi, 2006). Cultural orientations are also found to influence the preferences for HRM practices in the Omani context (Aycan et al., 2007). In addition to these, the increasing participation of new generations of young, educated Omanis in the private sector, who like their Arab counterparts in the region have an 'increased awareness of their collective power' (Sidani and Thornberry, 2013), is another influential factor. Also, pressures from international bodies like the World Bank, International Management Fund (IMF) and International Labour Organization (ILO) are also changing the way people are managed (Harrigan and Wang, 2006). In addition, the labour requirements of some international agreements like the free-trade agreement between Oman and the United States also caused changes. The key institutions that formally regulate HR practices in Oman are the Ministry of Civil Service, Ministry of Manpower, Ministry of Education, Ministry of Higher Education, Ministry of National Economy, Council of the Civil Service and the Institute of Public Administration (Al-Hamadi, Budhwar and Shipton, 2007), along with the Council of Ministers.

Besides the shapers and regulators of people management practices in Oman, many modern HR practices are diffused into organisations in the Omani context through multinational corporations, international business partners, international consulting firms, formal management training, Omani managers and staff with Western education, and industry stories. With multinational companies and industry leaders adopting modern HRM and winning the war for talent, Omani organisations feel the pressure to modernise their HR systems in order to improve their image and performance.

HRM, as a distinct and new approach to managing people at work, has been growing steadily in Oman since the late 1980s and early 1990s. Traditionally, the department in charge of making decisions, taking action and doing the paperwork for the employment relationship in Oman is called 'Personnel Affairs or Administration' (PA). The first organisations that have changed their people management function from PA to HRM in Oman are the large industry leaders in different sectors, the multinational organisations and other local companies with international business partners. According to some HR managers, Petroleum Development Oman LLC in the oil industry was the first Omani organisation to move from traditional PA to HRM in the late 1980s and early 1990s. Today, the majority of the organisations in Oman have adopted HRM or are in the process of adopting its name and roles. An increasing number of private organisations are resorting to international HRM consultants and implementing modern HR information systems. Today, the name 'Personnel Affairs' or 'Personnel Administration' is almost unheard of in Oman's private sector, but many organisations in the government sector still use PA. Also, there are organisations in both sectors that have adopted the name 'HRM' but still function with the traditional administrative mindset of PA.

There are several differences between HR practices in the private and government sectors of Oman. These are mainly due to the various institutions that govern and influence employment in each sector and various internal and external forces. The Civil Service Council is responsible for developing policies that affect the civil service and the Ministry of Manpower is responsible for developing and enforcing policies that affect employment in the private sector. HRM practices in Oman's private sector are to a large extent similar to Western HRM practices (at least when they are designed) mainly due to the influence of multinational corporations, international business partners, foreign employees and management teams, modern training, reliance on international HRM consultants and the urge to continuously improve. In the government sector, people management is still to a very large extent an administrative function mainly due to the lack of links with organisational strategies, a focus on routine work, the absence of competition and the resulting lack of a sense of urgency. But the differences in people management practices between Oman's private and government sectors are expected to reduce as the government has been gradually harmonising various employment aspects between the two sectors to make them equally attractive to job-seekers. For example, prior to April 2013, there were differences between the two sectors in terms of weekend days and working hours. Private sector employees had a 40–48 hours working week depending on company policy, with Friday as the official weekend, while those in the government sector had a 40 hours working week with both Thursday and Friday as the weekend. The national holidays were also longer for the government sector. But starting from 1 May 2013, employees of both sectors had Friday and Saturday as their official weekend thereby unifying the working week and working hours. This was done 'to reduce the gap between benefits given to employees in the government sector and those in the private sector and to strengthen family and social ties because of their positive effect on the psychological stability of all employees in the state' (Times of Oman, 2013). More areas are expected to be unified by the government, with the most recent ones being salaries and benefits and public holidays between the two sectors. The aim is to make both sectors equally attractive to the young Omani job-seekers who have been showing a clear preference for government jobs for many years now.

HR departments in Oman are well represented, and most of the HR managers report directly to the CEOs. This direct-reporting relationship to the CEO shows that organisational leaders in Oman believe in the importance of HR departments and the value they can add. In fact, 'there seems to be an increasing awareness of Omani managers regarding the role of HR in organisations – the dynamics of HR policies and practices' (Muncherji, Gopalakrishnan and Dhar, 2009: 229). One HR planner interviewed from a large organisation said:

> Managers and company owners today are more aware that people and people issues can greatly affect us . . . After 2011–2012, HRM in Oman is taken seriously in companies and even at the top government levels. See how most if not all CEOs have special advisors who were former HR managers . . . what does that tell you?

According to Mamman and Al-Kulaiby (2014), HR practitioners in Oman perform all the five roles of Ulrich's model with strategic partner being the least performed one. This does not mean that HR departments in Oman are lagging behind but rather indicates the nature of their orientation. It is still not known what percentage of organisations in Oman have strategic HR departments, but the unanimous answer from all the interviewed HR professionals and employees offers support to Mamman and Al-Kulaiby's (2014) findings. When asked if the HR departments in Oman are strategic or not, all the eight HR professionals and eight employees unanimously agreed on the function being reactive.

> Our work is to support the business strategies in terms of staffing, training, motivating and so forth . . . So it's fair to say that we are strategic in the sense that we try to align what we do to support the business strategies. But, we still don't participate in designing these strategies. (HR manager in a medium-sized private organisation)

> . . . most of what we do is responding to demands of our internal clients . . . many times the different HR activities have no interdependencies . . . people can't see the links . . . so from within we find HR professionals working in silos . . . which is wrong . . . I mean if we were clearly connected to business strategies, that would have given us one direction. (HR manager in a large private organisation)

> No, we do not design business strategies . . . we are a support function. The HR manager has consultative power on this matter. (HR planner in a large private organisation)

The above comments support the findings of Khan (2011), who concluded for a large Omani company that 'organisations [in Oman] have reactive HR strategies'. However, 'what remains unclear is whether this lack of strategic focus is because HR practitioners lack the competencies seen as necessary to be a business partner, or because they have them but are not required to use them, or because there is a lack of clarity on the strategic competencies needed' (Lo, Macky and Pio, 2015: 2311). It is also obvious from the interviewed HR managers in Oman that they would like their departments to become strategic partners, because they believe that strategic HRM leads to better organisational performance. This expected HRM–performance relationship is an important area to shed light on because it directly addresses the view of Omani HR professionals and touches the credibility and value of HRM as a function in Oman's organisations.

It is now well known that HRM practices not only affect the attitudes, behaviours and skills of employees but also their motivation and commitment to behave in ways that benefit the firm and increase its performance (e.g., Purcell and Hutchinson, 2007). In the Omani context, there is only one study that has investigated the HR–organisational performance relationship. Moideenkutty, Al-Lamky and Murthi investigated 87 companies and found that 'organizations that implement highly selective staffing, extensive training, performance management practices and employee empowerment are likely to have higher performance' (2011: 246). The researchers believe that 'even in labour markets supportive of traditional HRM practices, high-involvement HRM practices make a difference in organizational performance'.

Changing from a reactive, transaction-oriented HR function to a strategic partner will most likely require a lot of changes. First, organisations will need leaders who understand and believe in the strategic role of HRM and its requirements. Second, the HR leaders and practitioners themselves will need to acquire strategic HR competencies besides their functional HR competencies. The strategic competencies will enable them to understand the whole business as an open system with interdependent parts, use financial language and make sound strategic decisions. Nevertheless, despite the available evidence, we still haven't reached to the level of confidence in the HR–organisational performance quest to argue that a strategic HR role in all organisations in Oman will always lead to better organisational performance (see Guest, 2011; Lo, Macky and Pio, 2015). The intent here is not to reject or downplay the potential benefits of strategic HR roles but rather to emphasise that becoming a strategic partner has many requirements which current HR departments in Oman might not be aware of or might not be ready to satisfy. Also, research findings on the HR–performance relationship are still debatable and inconclusive.

HRM PRACTICES IN OMAN

Recruitment: Challenges and Solutions

Organisations in Oman rely on both internal and external sources of recruitment and a combination of methods to reach out to and attract the right candidates. One of the biggest recruitment challenges in Oman is attracting the right Omani applicants for various jobs, in particular in the private sector, and making them stay. This challenge has emerged as organisations have been trying to meet their workforce localisation quotas. It is further aggravated by the current lack of qualified locals for professional jobs in the fields of science, technology, engineering and mathematics. Also, the different preferences and perceptions of private sector employers and young Omani job-seekers towards each other further hinder the recruitment of locals. Moreover, the current reactive recruitment strategies in Oman are also to be blamed. Organisations lack proactive recruitment strategies and employer branding that can help ensure a continuous flow of the right applicants whenever needed.

Organisations in Oman use internal and external recruitment, either sequentially or simultaneously, and a variety of methods. Job posting, job bidding and employee referrals are used for internal recruitment. Despite the fact that employee referrals are a highly effective recruitment method, organisations don't use them formally. This could be out of caution to avoid perceptions and accusations of nepotism or to avoid behaviours that could reinforce them. The most common recruitment methods used to reach to external recruits in Oman are job advertisements, online recruitment, recruitment agencies, executive search firms and internships. Organisations also have to refer to the Ministry of Manpower pool of registered job-seekers. Others also directly contact local colleges and universities for graduates and participate in job fairs. Online recruitment is widely used in Oman, and many organisations no longer accept walk-ins and hand-to-hand paper applications. Even government job vacancies are advertised simultaneously in local newspapers and on government websites. For both sectors, the two main requirements of this stage are filling out job application forms and submitting CVs/résumés. As for the job-seekers, the top three methods that young Omanis use to find a job opportunity are applying in the Ministry of Manpower, responding to job advertisements and asking family and friends for job vacancies and referral opportunities (NCSI, 2015c).

Organisations in Oman have been competing for local talent mainly due to workforce localisation quotas and shortage of talent. They use various methods, but their recruitment efforts are reactive and insufficient to build a desired organisational identity and maintain organisational attraction. For example, organisations do not have the habit of promoting themselves as good places to work (i.e., employer branding) beyond the channels of job fairs and job advertisements. In fact, many employers believe that word of mouth, job advertisements and attractive company websites are sufficient to attract job-seekers. But the fact is that advertisements alone are not sufficient to create a desirable identity and attract applicants (Collins and Stevens, 2002). Large organisations in Oman can afford to use other means to build a positive image and increase their attractiveness. Many of them advertise competitive compensation packages, have modern open-plan work areas with various in-house facilities, and sponsor countrywide events. But to build and maintain attraction, organisations need to continuously work on creating a positive and desirable identity along with a good reputation (Cable and Turban, 2003) even if they don't have job vacancies. This means that they should continuously try to communicate and portray an image of a unique and desirable workplace for the targeted Omani job-seekers.

To attract the targeted job-seekers, organisations in Oman need to find out what they should add, reduce and/or remove from their work environments, careers and employment packages so that they can meet the needs and expectations of their ideal job-seekers. They can only do this if they find out what the priorities of these job-seekers are and include these aspects in their workplaces and branding efforts. Omanis have '. . . a strong social norm around commitment to family more so than an organisation . . .' (Swailes, Al-Said and Al-Fahdi, 2012: 362), and the two top priorities in a job for Omani youth are job security and good salary and incentives (NCSI, 2015c). Also, according to a National Centre for Statistics and Information (NCSI) opinion poll, the two top causes of work dissatisfaction for Omani youth are bad pay and bad working conditions. In terms of work–life balance concerns, the increasing numbers of young Omanis who move to Muscat for work but who still have to perform their social obligations towards the extended family living in other regions and the increasing numbers of working Omani women with dependent children are all an indication that family-friendly practices could also attract more Omanis to work in the private sector. Examples of family-friendly practices that organisations could consider in Oman are flexible working hours, more emphasis on completing the work rather than just being at work (presenteeism), on-site childcare and company events that involve families.

Recruiting locals in Oman is also challenged by the conflicting preferences and perceptions of private employers and young Omani job-seekers. The private sector has for many years shown a preference for hiring foreigners. Foreigners are a more attractive option because they come qualified and are easier to control and get rid of due to the two-year work contracts. Foreigners with working visas and under the sponsorship system are also unlikely to be demanding or show dysfunctional behaviours due to their concern to remain in their jobs. The two-year visa ban has also intensified this concern. 'Expatriates are vulnerable since both their in-country families and, often, their extended families are economically dependent on them' (Schmidt, Moideenkutty and Al-Busaidi, 2013: 243). The researchers also found that expatriates have a greater incentive to work hard in extra-role behaviours and organisational citizenship behaviours directed towards supervisors in order to maintain their employment at a time when the national pressure to replace them is increasing. The preference for foreign workers is also driven by a general lack of trust in the calibre of graduates and the widespread negative stereotypes towards young Omani job-seekers. For some sectors and jobs, foreigners are a more cost-effective alternative. They are relatively inexpensive compared to locals in entry-level and lower-level jobs due to the minimum wage and due to their readiness and willingness to accept low-level jobs without conditions. Also, the project-based nature of some sectors entails hiring temporary workers rather than permanent employees. For example, the construction industry prefers hiring expatriates to work for the duration of their projects only rather than hire permanent locals. Hence, for such organisations, hiring locals for the long term is relatively more challenging.

As for the Omani job-seekers (predominantly those who qualify for entry level and other lower-level jobs), a well-paid government job in relatively better working conditions is almost always preferred over a comparable job opportunity in the private sector. According to a 2015 opinion poll on youth work trends in Oman, young Omanis still show a very high preference for government work, and the preference has increased among Omani students in higher education (NCSI, 2015c). This preference is mainly due to job security, better compensation for entry level and other lower-level jobs, better working conditions and, at times, the associated prestige of working with a significant government organisation. The better compensation is highly valued as it gives youth access to bank loans thus enabling marriage and building or buying a property. Moreover, other factors include the existence of relatively more Omani managers and non-managers in government workplaces, the use of Arabic language and the prevalence of a more familiar work culture in which all members share its dominant values, norms and beliefs. All these factors give government workplaces the identity of a more familiar and desirable place of work.

Based on interviewee responses, many first time job-seekers also dislike the working hours of the private sector, and those with low self-efficacy and low need for achievement also do not like the connection between individual performance, pay and career growth in private organisations. They prefer the group and equality-based pay system of the government sector. In addition, the existence of a high number of expatriates in the sector is also one of the main factors that discourage Omani youth from private sector work. The dominance of expatriates creates many uncertainties in the minds of the young Omani job-seekers. One of two newly hired Omani graduates in the government sector said, 'When we [my friend and I] were applying for jobs in private companies, many questions were a concern for us . . . Will the selection process be fair? Will I perform well in the job? Will I get real support to grow?' These uncertainties were ignited by various expectations of injustice and widespread negative assumptions towards Omanis in the private sector. Interviewees also mentioned areas like the management style used in the private sector, the expected work ethics and opportunities to learn and grow. As a result, many young Omanis who qualify for entry level and lower-level jobs prefer to wait for the ideal government job rather than seize opportunities in the private sector and face uncertainties. Others even leave their low-paid private sector jobs for government work whenever an opportunity arises. However, the preference for government work has slightly reduced among job-seekers and employed Omanis (NCSI, 2015c). In fact, there is evidence that some competent Omanis resign from the government sector to take private sector jobs (Swailes and Al-Fahdi, 2011). According to the researchers, the main reasons for this turnover are dissatisfaction with the management style, reward practices and promotion opportunities in the government sector.

Based on the available evidence, we can conclude that the young Omani job-seekers generally prefer government jobs because they have a higher a level of certainty and identification with the government as an employer than the private sector. The current government efforts in unifying and harmonising practices between the two sectors are helpful because they are reducing some of the uncertainties by making the two sectors similar. Further investigations in this area could help give answers on how private employers can reduce these uncertainties and make themselves familiar and equally attractive to the young Omani job-seeker. Strategies could include getting closer to the young Omanis in schools and higher education institutions, giving them a realistic preview of what it is like to work in the private sector, and reducing their uncertainties and negative perceptions through regular collaborations and sponsorships with higher education institutions and student bodies.

As the pressure to hire more Omanis will only increase, private employers need to convince themselves that Omanisation is a necessity for the well-being of the Omani society and for the future performance of their organisations. Unlike the current reactive recruitment practices where organisations advertise themselves only when there are immediate job vacancies, private organisations in Oman should take into consideration the priorities of Omani youth in job design, compensation and recruitment and pursue corporate advertising and employer branding regularly. These will help allow the targeted Omani job-seekers to identify with private employers, reduce their uncertainties, like them and want to work for them.

Employee Selection: Few Competencies and Many Stereotypes

Reviewing CVs and face-to-face interviews are the two widely used steps in employee selection in Oman. Several large organisations also rely on a variety of achievement and aptitude tests, assessment centres and background investigations. A medical test is also required at this stage. According to HR professionals, two main concerns arise from the current employee selection processes in Oman: lack of well-trained and competent selection experts within organisations and the strong influence of negative stereotypes towards Omani job applicants. The selection process and decision in Oman is usually left to the department in need, which often creates a panel to reach the final decision. But a major concern around this process is the lack of competent interviewers and selection experts. As one former HR manager – and current senior adviser to the CEO – with 32 years of work experience in the Omani private sector said:

> Selection is a very complex process and not any HR officer or department manager can do it . . . This process is left to user departments with little assistance from HR. End users are not trained for the required competencies and little training is given to HR personnel as well. Success requires a lot of training, exposure and long experience.

There are three possible solutions to this problem. One is to rely on external selection experts or permanently hire such experts to work in HR departments. The second solution is to offer regular training to all managers and staff involved in selection processes. Third, in order to ensure effectiveness, organisations should structure their selection processes, link them to objective, job-related criteria and make decision makers accountable.

The second concern facing employee selection in Oman is the prevalence of negative perceptions and stereotypes towards Omani youth. Studies have shown that Omanis (like the other Gulf nationals) are negatively stereotyped by managers and co-workers (e.g., Mellahi and Al-Hinai, 2000) and are perceived by a significant number of private sector firms to be unskilled, more expensive to employ compared to expatriates and lacking the required work ethics. The first concern is not true as Omanis perform jobs in all skill levels. However, there is an acute shortage of Omanis in the mid-skill and high-skill jobs of science, technology, engineering and mathematics. In addition, the claim that Omanis are generally more expensive to employ is also not true. Omanis are more expensive than expatriates only in entry-level and other low-level positions that are tied to the minimum wage. In fact, many Omanis believe that white-collar expatriates are paid a lot higher than locals in comparable jobs. This issue was recently raised by the Shura Council, who urged that Omanis who have the same or similar qualifications and certificates to their foreign counterparts should receive the same salaries and benefits (Times of Oman, 2015a). Last, the assumption that Omanis lack work ethics is a widespread stereotype that has become a cliché, although it has not been supported by any research up to now.

Stereotypes can make selection processes subjective and encourage managers to silently resist workforce localisation via various practices. In the absence of clearly structured selection processes that rely on job-related criteria, managers could give ratings to job candidates based on their undeclared discriminatory criteria, that is, stereotypes. Also, when managers view workforce localisation as a forced process, and do it just to meet the quotas, they (could) lower their standards and employ locals who cannot succeed on the job, thereby reinforcing their stereotypes (Al-Waqfi and Forstenlechner, 2010), that is, confirming bias. According to the interviewed Omani employees, some private sector managers resist Omanisation using this approach. They intentionally select Omanis who will not be able to succeed on the job and later convince the Ministry of Manpower that Omanis are not qualified, lack motivation and do not stay on the job. In this way, they justify their need for expatriates for the positions they see as instrumental to them. Also, negative stereotypes towards Omani youth have made employers believe that Omanisation could reduce their competitive ability. This belief leads to disliking and resisting Omanisation through undesirable practices. For example, employers have resorted to 'employing ghost workers' (Moideenkutty, in press) and hiring expatriates for jobs under different work visas (Daily Mail, 2015).

Even when a qualified Omani is hired, some employers resort to giving the most important tasks of the jobs to the desired expatriates thereby limiting the learning and growth of the locals in these jobs. But the expectation that private organisations could lose their competitive ability as a result of hiring unqualified individuals is debatable. New research on workforce localisation in Oman offers evidence that a set of systematic HR practices that focus on effective Omanisation is positively related to financial performance (Moideenkutty, in press). The research found that it is the quality rather than the quantity of local employees that has a stronger relationship to financial performance, and only those organisations that have a set of HR practices designed for Omanisation will have qualified locals who can contribute to financial performance. Hence, winning the commitment of private sector managers to workforce localisation is 'a key antecedent of success' (Al-Waqfi and Forstenlechner, 2010: 377). Managerial commitment can help overcome problems faced in the selection of Omani youth for work in the private sector.

On the applicants' side, stereotyping can reduce their motivation (Page, 2007) and affect their willingness and readiness to apply for jobs, to compete with other job candidates and even to work harder after they get hired. In fact, when a job-seeker believes that a dominant group in an organisation or a sector negatively stereotypes them, their expectations and perceptions of justice are negatively influenced, too. These negative perceptions of justice influence job-seekers' relational certainty (Walker et al., 2013) and in turn could make them dislike the employer or decide to withdraw psychologically or physically. These negative stereotypes and perceptions could prove to be one of the major silent and invisible obstacles towards hiring locals and Omanisation efforts in general.

Besides stereotypes, employee selection processes could also become subjective due to '. . . personalised relationships, kinship and regional favouritism as well as the presence of a large number of guest workers and employers' (Ali, 2010: 700). Maintaining good relationships and facilitating processes for members of the in-group or those with personal power are common aspects of social life in Oman. This predisposition to help members of the in-group 'stems from the high in-group orientation of collectivist Arabs in the Middle East' (Kabasakal et al., 2012). In fact, according to the local culture, it could be a shame to refuse helping members of the in-group. An individual could be stigmatised as selfish, greedy, envious or even disloyal to the in-group if they don't make things easier for members of that group. However, in recent years, the private sector has managed to combat the influence of personal relationships in selection decisions to a large extent via rules, policies and procedures. Nevertheless, personal relationships, kinship and favouritism still influence decisions at work to some extent in the private sector but to a larger degree in the government sector.

On the expatriate side, there is evidence that some expatriate groups show regional favouritism in selection decisions. Twelve of the interviewed HR managers and Omani employees reported that some expatriate groups have a cultural tendency to practice nepotism and others simply prefer job candidates from their social groups for cultural and linguistic reasons. Studies have shown that decision makers prefer hiring job candidates from their own social groups (e.g., Whitely and Kite, 2009). However, latest research has shown that managers in selection teams discriminate in favour of candidates that are seen as more instrumental to their personal goals and avoid candidates that are stereotyped as more capable for the job because they could be competitors and harmful to the decision makers' personal outcomes later on (Lee et al., 2015). This means that nationality and regional favouritism are not as influential in selection and workplace relationships as many assume. In fact, a recent study by Schmidt, Moideenkutty and Al-Busaidi (2013) in Oman found that nationality of supervisor/subordinate does not necessarily determine workplace relationships and performance. The researchers urged that 'we need to reassess the assumption that the same nationality between supervisors and their subordinates will result in quality workplace relationships and ultimately enhanced individual performance' (Schmidt, Moideenkutty and Al-Busaidi, 2013: 245).

To address the identified concerns in employee selection, organisations in Oman are recommended to rely on recruitment and selection experts, offer regular training to all managers (new and established ones) involved in selection processes and reduce the reliance on stereotypes and other biases. The latter can be achieved through diversity training, self-awareness training and by adding more structure to selection processes (OPP, 2013), and also by relying on an objective clear list of the selection criteria derived from up-to-date job analyses and using selection methods that have high predictive validity. In addition to these, not rushing decision makers, building their intent and commitment to being unbiased both orally and in writing via contracts, using standardised scoring, selecting candidates into the process rather than out, relying on multiple assessments, multiple decision makers and aggregate scores can all help (Shire Professional Chartered Psychologists, 2010). Organisations should also carefully handpick members of the selection panels. First, to avoid job candidates' perceptions of injustice, any social group should not dominate selection teams. Second, employers need to find ways to identify the cognitive biases of decision makers. For example, administering bias tests on all members of the selection panels can help identify and measure their biases and the likelihood that these biases can unintentionally affect their choices and behaviours (Shire Professional Chartered Psychologists, 2010). Such tests will send out a strong message to managers, job candidates and external stakeholders like the Ministry of Manpower that the organisation is serious about ensuring fairness. Last but not least, when choosing members of a selection panel, organisations need to be aware that potential interdependencies between decision makers, job candidates and stereotyping tendencies can lead to discrimination.

Employee Training and the Need for Knowledge Management

Employee training is one of the top priorities of both government and medium to large private organisations in Oman. According to HR managers, the Omani government is trying to create learning environments in its workplaces and private organisations invest a good amount of their yearly budgets in training managerial and non-managerial employees. Many large organisations have begun to refer to this activity as Learning and Development. Several have their own training centres and academies which offer both on- and off-the-job training. In the private sector, organisations rely on both in-house trainers and international experts. There are also local training firms and higher education institutions that organisations deal with. The majority of organisations in both sectors still rely on traditional training methods and in particular face-to-face lecture-based training. Few organisations offer online, self-paced training. This simply indicates that most training and development departments and experts in Oman have not yet moved towards skill development, hands-on methods and employee-centred learning. Also, they have not kept up with the preferences of the new generations in using the Internet and other training technologies.

Organisational training processes in Oman have many weaknesses and lack links with organisational strategies, trainees' jobs and other HR processes. Despite the government's attempt to create learning-oriented work environments, training in the Omani government sector lacks a defined strategy, management support and coordination (Rajasekar and Khan, 2013). In some private sector organisations, the learning opportunities offered are strictly job related and based on actual needs. But, in the government sector, training has no linkages with the job and performance reviews (Swailes and Al-Fahdi, 2011). In general, employee training in Oman is still generic and often not related to organisational strategies, jobs, performance appraisals and career growth.

Evaluating training from the individual level up to the organisational level is still in its infancy stage in Oman. There is an absence of follow-up, continuity and evaluation in the government sector (Swailes and Al-Fahdi, 2011). Also, it is extremely rare to hear about levels of training evaluation or the return on training investment in Oman's private organisations. In fact, the focus of training evaluation in Oman is more administrative. Many organisations in both sectors consider positive reactions on the trainers and the training as sufficient indicators for the effectiveness of training even if there are few work results. Due to the absence of evidence on how organisational training contributes to the overall performance of organisations, training is generally not believed to be a real value-adding process, and its budget is always one of the first to be reduced when organisations pursue cost cutting.

The effectiveness of training in Oman is also hindered by wrong perceptions of training, lack of commitment to training, lack of transfer of training and lack of knowledge sharing. For a long time, training has been viewed as a reward for the lucky ones, time away from work and a ticket to promotion rather than a learning opportunity to improve performance. Many managers and their subordinates in both sectors share this attitude. According to Rajasekar and Khan (2013: 48), 'this attitude is a major impediment to the transference of knowledge and learning at the workplace. It kills any enthusiasm for the real learning of new skills and seriously reduces the competence of the government sector employees in Oman'. The researchers believe that the low interest in learning and transferring knowledge is also caused by the bureaucratic approach used in the government sector to assign employees to training and the design of training programmes. We also believe that they are the results of a lack of management accountability and the narrow administrative focus of training. Unlike the case in the government sector, where training is not clearly linked to performance appraisals, salary increases and promotions, employees in the private sector are relatively more motivated to learn because training and improved performance will more likely lead to promotions and/or financial rewards. But for those trainees who learn and are motivated to transfer their training, the work environment often doesn't provide sufficient support. One former HR manager in a large private sector organisation clearly explained this situation: 'Lots of training is given to individuals but when they return to their daily work, they often get tied up with frustrating work procedures that limit their creativity and innovation.'

Barriers to knowledge sharing and transfer also influence the effectiveness of training in Oman.[3] Researchers identified some evidence of barriers to knowledge transfer between experienced expatriates and locals in Oman (Swailes, Al-Said and Al-Fahdi, 2012). One of the known barriers is the fear that knowledge sharing could lead to 'the loss of certain advantages like a position of privilege, power, superiority, promotions and recognitions' (Chang, Gong and Peng, 2012). A study on physicians in a hospital in Oman found that some of the barriers to knowledge transfer are lack of trust, busy schedules, overtime work and secrecy in doing one's work (Jabr, 2007). In addition to these, we believe that the limited socialisation between expatriates and locals also hinders the exchange of knowledge between the two groups. Other barriers are linguistic and cultural, that is, different languages and differences in social beliefs, values and norms and in occupational cultures between expatriates and locals.

At a time when the Omani government is focusing on hiring more youth across industries, organisations are facing the risk of losing valuable knowledge more than ever before. This knowledge resides with long-standing and highly qualified locals and expatriates. The private sector, in particular, should embark on knowledge-management initiatives. They should seek ways to foster learning and encourage the transfer of training from learning environments to the real job. Also, facilitating knowledge sharing and knowledge transfer can help reduce the chances of losing firm-specific knowledge that is with retiring locals and leaving expatriates and enable both new recruits and other local employees to get qualified at a faster pace.

Further, the challenges facing organisations in the area of employee learning are many. The training function needs many changes in order to be effective in Oman. Organisations need to define their training strategies and establish links and coordination between training, actual jobs of trainees, business strategies and HR processes. Linking training to actual and expected needs, performance appraisals and compensation will help give training a purpose and create a sense of responsibility. Making managers accountable for identifying training needs, assigning employees to training with job-related justifications and offering post-training results can help encourage both managers and employees to take training more seriously. These requirements will ensure that training is always done for a need, trainees will be given the support needed to apply what they learn on the job (i.e., transfer of training) and the improved behaviours and results will be measured. Adding accountability will also help rectify the wrong perceptions towards training because then training will be seen as a responsibility that comes with accountability for both managers and their subordinates. Moreover, linking the learning and performance of subordinates to the performance appraisals of direct supervisors and senior managers can increase managers' concern and commitment to subordinate learning, which in turn will increase knowledge sharing and transfer from the more competent and experienced staff (including the managers) to others in need. Training processes in Oman also need 'a greater level of coordination between supervisors, HR managers, training managers and senior managers' (Rajasekar and Khan, 2013). In addition, the training administrators and trainers should turn their attention to the design of programmes and reduce their reliance on traditional training methods. Utilising modern training methods will not only prove to be cost-effective and more engaging but also more suitable for building skills. Investing in digital learning platforms will also meet the preferences of the current generation of employees.

Using the Internet and intranets can make learning a routine, self-initiated exercise where employees are given the responsibility to search for knowledge and share knowledge with others rather than wait to be assigned to a formal learning programme. Also, creating learning cultures by continuously motivating and supporting employees to learn will help build the needed talents.

Encouraging trainees to transfer their knowledge and skills from the training environment to the real workplace and fostering an environment of knowledge sharing will help disseminate and speed up learning. Long-standing and highly qualified locals and expatriates should be seen as a source of knowledge, and the right arrangements should be made to increase their motivation and willingness to transfer their knowledge successfully to locals. Organisations should also ensure that their staff has the required ability to absorb and apply the transferred knowledge (Chang, Gong and Peng, 2012).

Performance Appraisals and the Challenge of Performance Improvement

Generally, organisations in Oman evaluate employees' performance once a year using traditional methods and generic appraisal forms that require inputs from the manager and, more recently, the subordinate, too. The process is mainly backward looking, judgemental and done for narrow administrative purposes. Employees are evaluated against a combination of traits, behaviours and results. Many organisations use standardised generic appraisal forms rather than job-specific appraisal forms. Most of them use traditional methods like graphic rating scales, forced-choice method, forced distribution, grading, essays and confidential reports, while others use methods like Management by Objectives and 360-degree appraisals. A growing number of organisations have started to ask employees to evaluate themselves and comment on their development needs and the results of the appraisal. It is a norm in both sectors to have all appraisals reviewed by a higher authority (i.e., a senior manager) and give employees who disagree with their appraisal the right to appeal.

The process of evaluating employees' performance in Oman is seen as routine paperwork that focuses on past performance and only needed to make administrative HR decisions on matters like bonus allocation, salary increases, training and promotion. Due to this backward-looking focus, the exercise is perceived as more judgemental rather than developmental. The process puts managers in the uncomfortable position of a judge who criticises people about their past mistakes and, in the worst cases, decides on a salary cut, or disqualifies the employee for a reward or even recommends an undesired career move. This often arouses negative emotions that can easily spoil relationships with the supervisor and the organisation. This judgemental feature of performance appraisals partially explains why most managers and employees in Oman are uncomfortable with the process. Being judgemental in a culture where people dislike confrontations and criticism can be emotionally draining for managers. In general, Omanis, like many other

Arabs, 'consider criticism as personal and harmful' (Al-Kandari and Gaither, 2011). Hence, when a manager directly criticises his/her subordinate, the whole process will most likely be perceived as a bad experience. Research has proven that a low-quality experience in a judgemental administrative performance appraisal process is likely to generate stronger reactions among employees than in a more developmentally focused performance appraisal process (Youngcourt et al., 2007 in Brown, Hyatt and Benson, 2010). Consequently, many managers in Oman have an aversion to face-to-face confrontation and an inclination to avoid any source of conflict (Khan, 2010).

The end-of-year feature of this assessment coupled with the narrow administrative purposes and a preference to avoid conflicts could lead managers to many biases in their evaluations. For example, managers could give inflated ratings to employees in order to avoid conflicts and bad relationships. The problem is this 'leniency makes performance appraisals unreliable' (Bernardin, Cooke and Villanova, 2000). To avoid badly inflated ratings in a relationship-oriented and collectivist context, several organisations in Oman use forced distribution. This is a popular performance appraisal method in Oman, but it also has its problems. Forced distribution often leads to perceptions of discrimination and employee dissatisfaction. One reason is that most managers use their own reasoning especially when there is no clear and common rationale shared by the appraisers (Risher, 2014).

There are differences in how employees' performance is evaluated in the government and private sectors of Oman. In the government sector, the process, for a long time, had a secretive nature, and the employee was usually not involved. The secretive nature of performance appraisals coupled with other features of work in the government sector like nepotism, groupism, and distance between managers and their subordinates created perceptions of unfairness. The situation has begun to change now as more government workplaces offer employees the chance to view their appraisal reports. But the current processes still lack a shared purpose and do not have links with other HR processes. According to research, performance appraisals based on a fair assessment of performance are absent in the Omani government sector (Swailes and Al-Fahdi, 2011). These aspects are expected to change because '. . . there is now a sense of urgency to design, develop and implement a performance measurement process which is fair and transparent and drives a high-performance culture in addition to rationalizing the increase in payroll cost' (Kapoor, 2014: 7).

In the private sector, evaluating employees' performance is often a relatively transparent process that involves the concerned employees and is linked to assigning learning opportunities, financial rewards and promotions. But the overriding purpose of the process is administrative even in this sector. Although performance appraisals are relatively transparent in the Omani private sector, there is evidence that the process is still not as fair as it should be. One former HR manager in a large private organisation said:

> [The process] is still not fair as it is often based on poorly set objectives and done for the purpose of fulfilling the procedure and meeting targets. It cannot be fair as long as it is done by individuals not fully capable of the task due to the little preparation given before moving them to managerial positions.

HR managers reported that employees often have negative emotions attached to the process and build perceptions of unfairness because of its pure judgemental nature and their lack of trust in managers' ability to evaluate objectively. This should be a concern for organisations because 'when employees have low quality performance appraisal experiences, organisations will likely face lower job satisfaction and organisational commitment and higher intentions to quit' (Brown, Hyatt and Benson, 2010: 390).

One of the current performance challenges facing organisations in Oman is handling Omanis who do not perform well. The Omani employment law makes no distinction between Omanis and non-Omanis, but there is a level of reluctance among private sector managers to handle underperforming Omanis (Swailes, Al-Said and Al-Fahdi, 2012: 364). Managers often get trapped between two costly options: to keep the underperforming Omani in the same job, train them or transfer them to another job just to satisfy the Omanisation quotas or to get rid of the employee and seek a suitable replacement. The latter option is neither easy nor desirable because it doesn't guarantee a quick or better replacement and it puts the organisation in an awkward situation in front of the Ministry of Manpower. Terminating a local at a time when the government expects organisations to hire more locals and meet quotas is not the preferred alternative. As a response, organisations have resorted to 'a tightening of recruitment and selection practices in relation to hiring Omanis followed by better training' (Swailes, Al-Said and Al-Fahdi, 2012: 364). Also, underperforming Omanis are not entitled to the mandatory 3 per cent annual increase in their salaries (Gulf News Oman, 2012). These are effective methods because implementing highly job-related recruitment and selection processes can ensure that the Omani hired will be able to perform at least the minimum requirements (i.e., job fit) and 'dramatic changes in performance often occur when pay is made more contingent on performance' (Rynes, Gerhart and Minette, 2004). But ensuring person–job fit alone is not sufficient for effective staffing. Organisations also need to ensure that the job candidate will be able to survive and thrive in the organisation's culture (i.e., organisation fit).

The most widely assumed reasons for the poor performance of some Omanis in the private sector are lack of ability and bad work ethics. In reality, poor performance is not always and only caused by lack of ability and/or bad work ethics. The causes could be due to low motivation and lack of opportunities for learning and development within organisations. For example, a recent study on 51 randomly selected manufacturing organisations in Oman found that poor people management practices is the biggest obstacle towards productivity improvement programmes followed by employee job dissatisfaction and poor HR management (Bashir, Alzebdeh and Al-Riyami, 2014). The researchers identified the existence of improper planning, supervisors who lack an understanding of productivity, poor employee relations and poor coordination as causes of poor performance and barriers to productivity improvement. Therefore, the problem of underperforming Omani workers cannot be addressed by blaming the workers' ethics and abilities only. Organisations need to review their performance management systems and question, themselves, 'what is it that keeps these workers unqualified and show undesirable behaviours even years after they join their organisations?' In short, the solution will depend on the cause of poor performance.

The current status of evaluating employees' performance in Oman indicates that there is a need for more modern, job-related and forward-looking performance appraisals that are clearly linked to organisational strategies and other HR processes like rewarding, learning and career development. Top managers should support the process and make its uses clear to all appraisers and appraisees. The users should jointly set goals that are linked to organisational strategies and plan and discuss performance more often than once a year. Regular training is needed for all managers (new and established ones) to understand the purposes of performance appraisals and handle the process in a more effective way. Making managers accountable for how well they conduct performance appraisals and using measures of how results are achieved can help increase effectiveness (Lawler III and Benson, 2012). HR professionals should be the advisers in the process and work closely with managers to guide them on various people management issues not only when the appraisals are conducted but throughout the year.

Compensation Issues in Oman

Compensating employees remains to be one of the most useful practices for recruiting the right people, controlling their behaviour and motivating them. In fact, unlike what many employee self-reports and articles in practitioner journals suggest, money is a very important motivator for most people, but it is also not the only motivator and nor the most important one for everyone (Rynes, Gerhat and Minette, 2004). This is true for Omani youth whose top priorities when applying for jobs are job security and a good salary (NCSI, 2015c). Also, poor pay and poor working conditions are the main causes of job dissatisfaction among these youth (NCSI, 2015c). These causes of job dissatisfaction could be related to job-seekers' intentions to apply for jobs and employees' intentions to quit.

The government of Oman is aware of the role of compensation in enhancing recruitment, behaviour control and motivation. Sincere attempts are made to make sure that people are paid well in Oman. This is evident in the country's recent pay increases, which resulted in the region's highest average pay increase in the private sector (GulfTalent, 2014). Pay decisions in Oman are highly centralised and salaries are mainly job and market based. Variable pay and performance-based pay are rare, and salary growth usually relies on seniority and increased qualifications, which also often go hand in hand with promotions. Some of the contemporary compensation issues in Oman are addressing the long-time perceived pay gaps between government and private sector jobs and between Omanis and expatriates. A current compensation trend is attracting more Omanis to the private sector by improving compensation, among other incremental HR reforms.

Differences exist between compensation in Oman's government and private sectors. In the government sector, salaries are mainly job and seniority based whereas the private sector relies more on market pay levels besides job evaluation to make pay decisions. Salaries are generally higher in the government sector for entry-level and other lower-level jobs, and this is one of the reasons why the first-time Omani job-seekers who qualify for these jobs prefer to join the government sector. On the other hand, salaries are more competitive in the private sector especially for mid-career jobs and professional high-skilled technical and managerial jobs, which are mainly filled by expatriates, who are a majority in the Omani private sector. Salary growth and promotions in the private sector are relatively faster and based more on the individual's actual performance, the skills they gain and their qualifications rather than seniority, personal relationships and group promotion strategies. In Islam, rewards must be linked to performance and behaviour and reinforce good deeds (Ali, 2010), among other guidelines. This feature of rewarding exists in the private sector and is one of the reasons why competent Omanis, both fresh graduates and government sector employees, who qualify for middle-skilled and managerial jobs, prefer to join the private sector. In fact, people with a high need for achievement find organisations that base their pay raises on individual performance more attractive than those that rely on seniority-based raises (Turban and Keon, 1993). Salary growth in the government sector is still slow and not related to actual performance but rather to seniority and on 'collective promotion strategies where batches of employees are promoted to a higher salary grade (not a higher position) every four or five years' (Swailes and Al-Fahdi, 2011). According to research, when people receive similar salary increases regardless of individual performance, such increases will do little to motivate their performance (Rynes, Gerhart and Minette, 2004). Perhaps this is one of the reasons why there is a general feeling of low motivation among employees in the government sector. Also, promotions to higher grades and positions in the government sector are based on seniority, qualifications, directions from top management, and other undeclared criteria like the personal power of the employee and personal relationships.

There has been a long-time perceived pay gap between locals and foreigners in middle-skill and high-skill professional jobs in Oman. According to the NCSI April 2015 Monthly Bulletin Statistics (NCSI, 2015b), the majority of the Omanis who work in the private sector are in the minimum wage category, and among the 204,591 Omanis who work in the private sector, only 6,924 of them receive a salary of more than 2,000 Omani Riyals (i.e., USD 5,195). There are no published statistics on the salaries of expatriate workers in Oman, making it impossible to identify the magnitude of the pay gap in different job groups and at different levels. But, the existence of a considerably large gap is evident in the Shura Council members' proposal to the government on matching the salaries of professional Omanis to expatriates who have comparable or the same qualifications and educational certificates. This gap is mainly caused by the high demand for qualified expatriates not only in Oman but also in the neighbouring countries. Omani employees are also sensitive to the high pay gap between managers and non-mangers in both sectors regardless of nationality. One of the guidelines of compensation in Islam is 'rewards should not generate ill feelings among subordinates . . . [they] should be based on objective measures and given to those who deserve [them]' (Ali, 2010: 702). However, ill feelings are expressed in Oman when the rewards of top managers in both sectors are discussed in social media. The social media conversations clearly reflect perceptions of unfairness and inequity. During the 2011–2012 small-scale demonstrations in Oman, and in the following work strikes in some of Oman's largest private organisations, one of the demands was to increase the salaries of Omani workers and oppose the practice of overpaying others. According to the equity theory, the feeling of being underpaid caused this reaction. In response to the demands, the government raised salaries and the Omani minimum wage twice, increasing it by over 60 per cent to 325 Omani Riyals (i.e., USD 844).

Better compensation, among other factors like Omanisation quotas, the two year visa ban on expatriates and the reduction of illegal foreign workers in the private sector, has helped increase the number of Omanis employed in the private sector. According to the NCSI April 2015 Monthly Bulletin Statistics, the numbers of Omanis working in the private sector and earning basic salaries in the categories of 600–700, 1,000–2,000 and 2,000 Omani Riyals or more have all increased (NCSI, 2015b). The statistics indicate that the government and private sector efforts have been effective in increasing the number of Omanis in various jobs. Better compensation, among other incremental reforms, is arguably one of the main factors that have been facilitating workforce localisation in Oman after 2011–2012.

In the midst of increased workforce localisation pressures and salary increases for Omani nationals, it has been pointed out that expatriate workers in Oman do not have a minimum wage (Times of Oman, 2015b). Some argue that it is not fair that a minimum wage does not exist for the massive numbers of blue-collar foreign workers and those in low-skill jobs. Others argue that setting a minimum wage for expatriate workers will help increase the employability of locals by making expatriates equally expensive. The expectations are that a minimum wage for expatriate workers will address perceptions of unfairness and hopefully increase the employability of nationals. But in the current unusual labour structure of Oman, a minimum wage for expatriates will not necessarily increase the employment of nationals in these sectors. Omanis are currently a majority in three sectors – finance, utilities and minerals – but their numbers are very small in the largest labour sectors of construction, wholesale, retail and manufacturing (Ennis and Al-Jamali, 2014; NCSI, 2015b). In fact, a large number of the expatriate workforce in Oman is employed in low-pay and low-skill positions in the service and construction industries. It is these large sectors that also have the highest number of jobs and the highest numbers of non-nationals. A proof that young Omani job-seekers do not shy away from strenuous manual work can be seen in the oil and gas industry, the second leading sector in Omanisation after banks. This industry has more than 20,000 Omani workers and attracts and hires many young Omani job-seekers every year for low-skill, middle-skill and high-skill jobs. Several Omanis in this sector perform tough manual work in the fields in tough working conditions. The sector's ability to attract job-seekers lies in its familiar and desirable identity among Omani youth. Oil and gas companies in Oman pay special attention to providing safe work environments, adhering to high professional standards and offering good salaries and incentives, regular job-related training, personal development plans and clear career-growth opportunities. If the largest labour sectors in Oman (construction, wholesale, retail and manufacturing), or at least the largest organisations in these sectors, follow the example set by the oil and gas industry, employment of nationals in blue-collar jobs is very likely to increase with or without a minimum wage for expatriates. Therefore, merely setting a minimum wage for expatriates will not necessarily increase the employment of Omanis in the largest labour sectors, because it will not necessarily encourage Omanis to apply for the unattractive, low-paid blue-collar jobs, nor will it encourage employers to hire them. These sectors need to reform their HR practices and create a familiar and desirable identity among the youth if they are committed to Omanisation.

HRM Model of Oman: Islamic, Arab Middle-Eastern, Western or Mixed?

Based on the description of various people management practices offered above, it is still not known if Oman has a distinct HRM model of its own or not. What is known is that the current policies and practices are influenced and shaped by several forces. Also, it is clear that there is a gap between what is aspired in HRM in Oman and what actually exists. As researchers indicated, while the HR rules and policies are designed with a

Western framework in mind, the practices that reside are still to a large extent determined and influenced by the societal culture (Mellahi, 2003; Al-Hamadi, Budhwar and Shipton, 2007). But, due to the increasing number of Omanis receiving modern training inside and outside Oman and the high presence of foreign managers and international HR consultants, among other external pressures, it is expected that 'HR practitioners will operate under increasing liberalisation, diversity and global influence that can challenge their cultural orientations towards their roles' (Mamman and Al-Kulaiby, 2014: 2823).

Although Islam greatly influences all facets of life in Oman, it is not clear so far if HRM in Oman is closer to the Arab-Islamic principles or Western HRM principles or somewhere in the middle path. Khan (2011) was the first to raise this question on HRM in Oman. He evaluated various HRM models in 'Convergence, divergence or middle of the path: HRM model for Oman' and concluded that 'There is a need to adopt a middle of the path approach which can integrate the qualities of both [convergence and divergence] approaches . . . rather than trying to ascertain one more valid than the other' (Khan, 2011: 83). Currently, there is a gentle push and pull between preferences for more culturally fit practices and more international best practices. Although research has found many contradictions between Western HRM and Islamic principles (Ali, 2010), there is also a clear gap identified between what is being practised in Arab workplaces and what Islam teaches. This is mainly due to the overriding effect of the complex and multi-dimensional Arab culture. As Roland K. Yeo explained, 'the cultural dynamics of human interaction [in the Arabian Gulf region and the Middle East at large] are multi-layered and until one is immersed in the culture in one way or another, one cannot fully appreciate the complexity (and mystery) of the social dynamics here' (2014: 7). Despite the contradictions between some work practices and Islamic principles, 'researchers have found that features of the Arab culture are different from those in western communities and the western managerial theories and practices should not be applied without adapting them to fit the norms and traditions popular in Arab countries' (Obeidat et al., 2012: 519).

Although some Islamic principles are not applied and others are contradicted in workplaces, Islam remains to have a great influence on the lives of people in Oman. It is true that 'Arabs have been changing but they resent imposed changes that they perceive to be not indigenous' (Sidani and Thornberry, 2010: 49). This resentment can be explained by Arabs' commitment to religion, attachment to history/resistance to change, and sense of pride (Al-Kandari and Gaither, 2011). Hence, when attempting to transform their HR functions, organisations might want to consider grounding and justifying their existing or new policies and practices using Islamic principles. For example, researchers have reported '. . . a level of variance between the teachings of Islam and workplace practices' in Oman (Swailes and Al-Fahdi, 2009). Practices like '*Wasta*'[4] and nepotism are against the principles of equality and justice in Islam, but the overriding effect of the culture has made people see this as the right thing to do towards one's group. In societies where *Wasta* is a norm, 'It is almost considered unethical if people do not use their influence and position power to benefit their in-circles' (Sidani and Thornberry, 2013: 76). According to the researchers, *Wasta* from a business perspective is close to using one's network to get things done. But the Omani private sector has greatly challenged both practices through various HR policies and by adding structure and multiple decision makers to processes. This change against *Wasta* and nepotism could not be resisted as the ethics of the new HR practices were clearly aligned to Islamic values. Hence, change in people management practices and behaviour via a well-designed Islamic discourse is more likely to gain the acceptance, commitment and support needed due to the strong influence of Islam and the high trust Muslims have in verses and stories from the Quran and Sunnah (Al-Kandari and Gaither, 2011; Sidani and Thornberry, 2013). In other words, if organisations adopt the habit of aligning the ethicality of their HR practices with Islamic values, then locals are more likely to be committed to them even if the practices conflict with popular Arab cultural norms like *Wasta* for the in-group. If 'aligning the ethicality of HR practices to Islamic values' (Yeo, 2014: 7) becomes a trend, 'then just like how Islamic banking developed as a distinct financial system, HRM practices could also be motivated and governed by Islamic management principles and lead to the emergence of a distinct typology of HRM theory of the Middle East' (Yeo, 2014).

Do HR practices in Oman fit with the Arab Middle Eastern (AME) HR model, whose contours were identified by Afiouni, Karam and El-Hajj (2013)? Several features of the AME HR model seem to be more applicable to the Omani government sector than the private sector. For example, the existence of highly formalised work environments, lack of employee empowerment, weak strategic focus and an inward orientation with limited attention to external business realities seem to apply more to the government sector. Also, several widely used people management practices in Oman do not fit with the model. For example, online recruitment along with newspaper advertising are the main recruitment methods used by government organisations in Oman. The majority, if not all, of the large private organisations use these methods too. In addition, the use of open-space work arrangements is very popular in Oman. Moreover, unlike the AME HR model, there are known cases of workforce reductions in Oman's large organisations. Furthermore, performance-management tools like key performance indicators (KPIs), benchmarks and balance scorecards are widely used in middle and large organisations in Oman. These discrepancies cannot be ignored, and they may be pointing to three facts. First, people management practices in Oman differ in government and private sectors and there are variations within these two sectors based on company size, ownership and performance. For example, large, high-performing organisations and industry leaders have advanced HR systems, processes and practices, and many characteristics of the AME HR model do not apply to them. Some of these organisations have even won regional awards for their exemplary HR practices. Second, the perceptions of nine Omani HR managers in nine banks on the most and least common HR practices may not be representative of the diverse people management practices in Oman. Several points support this argument. The banking sector in Oman is more Omanised than any other sector in the Omani private sector, and the dominance of Omanis influences the kind of HR practices designed at the strategic level and the way these practices are actually implemented and perceived. Also, it is not clear if whether the Omani HR managers reported their perceptions of the 'intended HR practices' in their banks, or their perceptions of what is actually implemented, or what they and their colleagues perceive as employees. There are clear differences between these that can lead to different findings (Vandenberg, Richardson and Eastman, 1999; Wright and Boswell, 2002).

An interesting question to ask is if HRM in Oman should follow best practices or seek a best-fit model. The answer is not yet available, but as Boxall and Purcell (2003) argued, 'best practice' and 'best fit' HRM might be right in their own way. This is true because some practices could be universally successful but the success of other practices will always depend on the specifics of the organisational contexts. From this standpoint, one finds truth in what Pieper (1990: 18) said: 'HRM seems to be more of a theoretical construct than an applied reality.' This is because the actual HRM practices in Oman or elsewhere are choices made under specific conditions and surrounded by specific constraints, which can be in many cases quite far from the ideal theoretical HRM models.

To sum up, what HR model currently exists in Oman? Despite the available information on the strong influence of Islam and the Omani societal culture, we do not have sufficient empirical evidence to talk about a model or argue for a distinct regional or Islamic or even a context-specific HRM model in Oman. The bits of evidence that we have on the nature of HRM practices in Oman indicate the widespread existence of a traditional, administrative and reactive form of HRM with loosely connected processes. However, we have found that HRM in Oman also manifests itself quiet differently in different sectors and within different groups of organisations. Overall, we expect to see the emergence of a mixed HRM model that will continue to adopt and adapt practices to fit with the valued principles of Islam and the Omani culture, the demands of new generations of employees, international bodies and other essential aspects that govern work in Oman. As such, what we can advocate for at this stage on 'HRM in Oman' is the need for more research that can help us explore, describe and explain people management practices in the Omani context. To discover what HRM is really like in Oman, we need to cover different groups of companies in different sectors, 'all employee groups' (Paauwe and Boselie, 2005) and the external stakeholders as well (Boxall and Purcell, 2003; Afiouni, Karam and El-Hajj, 2013).

Overall, HRM in Oman manifests itself very differently in different groups of employees and organisations, and the function, as a whole, is still undergoing change and has not yet taken any specific form to be able to include it under any model. More research will help us identify the form(s) of HRM that exist. All in all, what HRM in Oman needs now is the '. . . designing [of] work practices that provide adequate motivation and appropriate working practices which incorporate local value systems and yet meet the needs of the enterprise in a globally competitive environment' (Branine and Pollard, 2010: 722). Table 6.1 summarises the main challenges faced by the HR function in Oman and also proposes the way forward.

CONCLUSIONS

Oman is a country undergoing steady transformation guided by long-term strategies and a visionary leader. The major challenges facing the country are diversifying away from oil and securing jobs for the increasing numbers of young local job-seekers. Islam is central to the Omani culture and the family and tribe play significant roles in shaping Oman. The practice of Shura (consultation) is a unique cultural component of Oman and is obvious in the socio-political nature of the country.

HRM is a growing phenomenon in Oman, but its practices are still largely traditional and reactive. The various HR processes are often designed with Western practices in mind. But, when carried out, the practices are often not well aligned to business strategies, they are implemented for narrow administrative purposes and remain loosely connected to each other. Due to the urgent need to localise jobs and the demands of the new

Table 6.1 Challenges for HR function in Oman and the way forward

HRM challenges in the Omani private sector	Recommendations for the Omani context
Recruitment	
1. Attracting and retaining the right Omanis. 2. Different preferences and perceptions of private sector employers and young Omani job-seekers towards each other. 3. Current recruitment strategies are reactive and insufficient to create organisational attraction and a desirable identity.	1. Take into consideration the priorities of Omani youth (job security, good salaries, good working conditions and family-friendly practices) in job design, compensation and recruitment and pursue corporate advertising and employer branding regularly. Continuously try to communicate and portray an image of a unique and desirable workplace for the targeted Omani job-seekers. 2. Get closer to the young Omanis in schools and higher education institutions, give them a realistic preview of what it is like to work in the private sector, and reduce their uncertainties and negative perceptions through regular collaborations and sponsorships with higher education institutions and student bodies. 3. Implement proactive recruitment strategies and employer branding.
Selection	
1. Lack of competent interviewers and selection experts. 2. The prevalence of negative perceptions and stereotypes towards Omani youth.	1. Rely on recruitment and selection experts, offer regular training to all managers (new and established ones) involved in selection processes. 2. Reduce the reliance on stereotypes and other biases by carefully handpicking members of the selection team, offering diversity and self-awareness training, administering bias tests and building intent and commitment to being unbiased. Also, adding more structure to selection processes, using selection methods that have high predictive validity, using standardised scoring, relying on multiple assessments, multiple decision makers and aggregate scores, and not rushing decision makers.
Training and Knowledge Management	
1. Training processes have narrow administrative purposes and lack links with organisational strategies, trainees' jobs and other HR processes. 2. Lack of management accountability, commitment, follow-up, evaluation and transfer of training to the real work. 3. Wide use of traditional training methods 4. Risk of losing valuable, firm-specific knowledge with retiring locals and leaving expatriates and lack of knowledge sharing.	1. Link training to actual and expected needs and HR processes, especially performance appraisals and rewards. 2. Increase managers' commitment to training and their concern for transfer of training by linking subordinates' learning and improved performance to the performance appraisals of direct supervisors and their rewards. 3. Invest in digital learning platforms, skill-building methods and employee-centred learning where learning becomes a routine, self-initiated exercise. 4. Build learning cultures, embark on knowledge management initiatives and motivate employees to seek and share knowledge.

Table 6.1 (continued)

Performance Appraisal	
1. Performance is evaluated once a year using traditional methods and generic appraisal forms. 2. Process seen as routine paperwork that focuses on past performance (backward-looking and judgemental) and only needed to make administrative HR decisions such as bonus allocation, salary increases, training and promotion. 3. Process done with poorly set objectives and lack of management training and preparation leading to biases and bad experiences. 4. The dilemma of handling poor performers among local employees.	1. Use more modern, job-related performance appraisals that are clearly linked to organisational strategies and HR processes and conducted more often than once a year. 2. Introduce forward-looking and developmentally focused performance appraisals and train all persons involved on the purposes, process and uses. 3. Top managers should support the process, users should jointly set objectives and regular training is needed for all managers (new and established ones). To increase effectiveness, make managers accountable for how well they conduct performance appraisals and use measures of how results are achieved. 4. Address the issue of poor performers by implementing job-related recruitment and selection to ensure person–job and person–organisation fit, offering regular job-related training and making pay more contingent on performance.
Compensation	
1. A long-time perceived pay gap between government and private sector jobs. 2. The felt pay gap between Omanis and expatriates in comparable jobs.	1. Make pay for entry-level and other lower-level positions in both sectors similar. Link pay and pay increases to individual performance more so than to seniority and group promotion strategies. 2. Work on narrowing the felt pay gap between locals and expatriates in comparable jobs by hiring more Omanis into high-paid jobs and senior management teams and commit to internally developing Omanis and moving them up the organisational ladder.

generations of employees, incremental reforms in people management practices have begun to emerge, and these are expected to diffuse to a wider scale across industries. Despite the incremental reforms and the discontent of Omani HR professionals with the current reactive role of HR, we do not expect to see a proactive strategic HR role emerging very soon nor any major reforms to occur in the area of HRM in Oman. This is partly because of the long-time administrative focus and the sticky bureaucratic approach to management, which is evident in the tall hierarchies and highly formalised work environments. As Bordeau and Lawler III (2014: 232) said, 'the more organizations pursue a bureaucratic and low-cost-operator approach to management, the less their HR organization engages in advanced strategic activities, is satisfied with its HR skills, plays a strong strategic role, implements an HR decision science, and adds value to the organization'.

It is still not clear if HRM in Oman is closer to Islamic principles or Western practices or has a distinct model of its own. This is partly because 'on the one hand, there is an increased emphasis on Omanisation and adherence to Islamic principles yet, on the other hand, globalization imposes pressures to adopt global standardised HRM practices and policies' (Aycan et al., 2007: 30). What currently exists indicates a more traditional and reactive form of HRM that is slowly developing into a kind of a mixed HRM model that will continue to adopt and adapt practices to fit with the valued principles of Islam, demands of the new generation of workers and other essential aspects that govern work in Oman.

The social and political trends in Oman have proved that HRM practices in the private sector have profound impacts on the social and political contexts of the country. 'Given this powerful role, which is more likely to increase in the future, HR activities require serious consideration' (Greenwood, 2013). Hence, there is a great need for more studies that can explore, describe and explain HRM in Oman. The current studies are fragmented and insufficient for giving a comprehensive description of HRM practices in Oman or for making generalisations and offering practical solutions. As Budhwar and Mellahi (2007) pointed out, each country in the Middle East might have their own HR practices, and a better approach is to examine these practices within their contexts and investigate how culture and other contextual forces influence people, their thinking, preferences and behaviours in organisations. Hence, future research should set out to explore, describe and explain the common HRM practices in Oman. Researchers should also investigate the success and failure of various practices in the Omani context. In addition, more research is needed on the beliefs, values and norms of Omanis and how these influence and shape behaviours in both the private and government sectors. Useful practical recommendations cannot be offered without having a clear understanding of the context, the current status of HRM, its challenges and future directions.

ACKNOWLEDGEMENTS

We would like to extend our appreciation to all the HR professionals, senior consultants to the CEOs, and employees in Oman for sharing their knowledge and views on people management practices. These include Mr Munther Al-Manthari, Ms Sara Al-Raisi, Mr Rashid Al-Nasri, Ms Aysha Al-Kalbani, Mr Masoud Al-Musallami and Ms Kawthar Al-Mahrooqi along with another ten who preferred to remain anonymous. We would also like to thank Mr Salim Al-Jahwari and Mr Ibrahim A. Said for their constructive comments on an earlier version of this chapter.

NOTES

1. The Sultanate of Oman: A forgotten empire, http://www.britishempire.co.uk/maproom/oman/sultanate.htm.
2. Oman was the first among its Arab Gulf neighbours in 1995 to craft a vision and a strategic plan that would take the country 25 years into the future.
3. We are aware that there are no clear distinctions between knowledge transfer and knowledge sharing in the literature (Paulin and Suneson, 2012). For the purpose of this chapter, we view knowledge sharing as the willingness and readiness of a party to impart their knowledge and the actual sharing of that knowledge excluding any guarantees that the knowledge will be successfully transferred/transmitted, absorbed and used by the receiver(s). We consider knowledge transfer as the transmission of knowledge from one side to another excluding any assumptions that the knowledge was shared willingly and accurately, and that it will be absorbed and used appropriately by the receiver(s). Knowledge barriers are all the environmental, individual, surface and deep-level factors that can hinder the overall process of sharing, transferring, absorbing and using knowledge.

4. 'Wasta is more far-reaching (Izrael, 1997) [than nepotism]. Wasta means "an intermediary" (Al-Ramahi 2008), and it means "using one's connections to reach to a certain desired end"' (Sidani and Thornberry, 2013: 75).

KEY WEBSITES

Central Bank of Oman: http://www.cbo-oman.org.
Ministry of Education: www.moe.gov.om.
Ministry of Finance: www.mof.gov.om/english.
Ministry of Foreign Affairs: www.mofa.go.om.
Ministry of Higher Education: www.mohe.gov.om.
National Centre for Statistics and Information: www.ncsi.gov.om.
Oxford Business Group: www.oxfordbusinessgroup.com/oman-2015.
Times of Oman: http://www.timesofoman.com.

REFERENCES

Abd al 'Ati, H. 1997. *The Family Structure in Islam*. Indianapolis, IN: American Trust Publications.

Afiouni, F., Karam, C. and El-Hajj, H. 2013. The HR value proposition in the Middle East: identifying the contours of an Arab Middle Eastern HR model. *International Journal of Human Resource Management*, **24**(10): 1895–1932.

Al-Barwani, T.A. and Albeely, T.S. 2007. The Omani family: strengths and challenges. In J. DeFrain and S. Asay (eds), *Strong Families around the World: Strengths-Based Research and Perspectives*. New York: The Haworth Press, Inc., pp. 119–142.

Al-Barwani, T., Chapman, D.W. and Ameen, H. 2009. Strategic brain drain: implications for higher education in Oman. *Higher Education Policy*, **22**(4): 415–432.

Al-Hammadi, A.B. and Budhwar, P.S. 2006. Human resource management in Oman. in P.S. Budhwar and K. Mellahi (eds), *Managing Human Resource in the Middle East*. Oxford: Routledge, pp. 40–58.

Al-Hamadi, A.B., Budhwar, P.S. and Shipton, H. 2007. Management of human resources in Oman. *International Journal of Human Resource Management*, **18**(1): 100–113.

Al-Kandari, A. and Gaither, T.K. 2011. Arabs, the West and public relations: a critical/cultural study of Arab cultural values. *Public Relations Review*, **37**: 266–273.

Al-Waqfi, M. and Forstenlechner, I. 2010. Stereotyping of citizens in an expatriate-dominated labour market: implications for workforce localisation policy. *Employee Relations*, **32**(4): 364–381.

Ali, A.J. 2010. Islamic challenges to HR in modern organisations. *Personnel Review*, **39**(6): 692–711.

Almoharby, D. 2010. Shuratic decision-making practice: a case of the Sultanate of Oman. *Humanomics*, **26**(1): 4–17.

Aycan, Z., Al-Hamadi, A.B., Davis, A. and Budhwar, P. 2007. Cultural orientations and preferences for HRM policies and practices: the case of Oman. *International Journal of Human Resource Management*, **18**(1): 11–32.

Barth, F. 1983. *Sohar: Culture and Society in an Omani Town*. Baltimore, MD: John Hopkins University Press.

Bashir, H.A., Alzebdeh, K. and Al-Riyami, A.M. 2014. Factor analysis of obstacles restraining productivity improvement programs in manufacturing enterprises in Oman. *Journal of Industrial Engineering*, 1–7.

Bernardin, H.J., Cooke, D.K. and Villanova, P. 2000. Conscientiousness and agreeableness as predictors of rating leniency. *Journal of Applied Psychology*, **85**(2): 232–234.

Bordeau, J. and Lawler III, E.E. 2014. Stubborn traditionalism in HRM: causes and consequences. *Human Resource Management Review*, **24**(3): 232–244.

Boxall, P. and Purcell, J. 2003. *Strategy and Human Resource Management*. London: Palgrave Macmillan.

Branine, M. and Pollard, D. 2010. Human resource management with Islamic principles: a dialectic for a reverse diffusion of management. *Personnel Review*, **39**(6): 712–727.

Brown, M., Hyatt, D. and Benson, J. 2010. Consequences of the performance appraisal experience. *Personnel Review*, **39**(3): 375–396.

Budhwar, P.S. and Mellahi, K. (eds) 2006. *Managing Human Resources in the Middle East*. London: Routledge.

Budhwar, P.S. and Mellahi, K. 2007. Introduction: human resource management in the Middle East. *International Journal of Human Resource Management*, **18**(1): 1–10.

Cable, D.M. and Turban, D.B. 2003. The value of organisational image in the recruitment context: a brand equity perspective. *Journal of Applied Social Psychology*, **33**: 2244–2266.

Cecil, C.O. 2006. Oman's progress toward participatory government. *Middle East Policy*, **13**(1): 60–68.

Central Bank of Oman (CBO) 2014. *Central Bank of Oman Annual Report 2014*, Economics Research and Statistics Department, June 2015. http://www.cbo-oman.org/annual/CBOAnnualReport2014ENG.pdf.

Chang, Y.-Y., Gong, Y. and Peng, M.W. 2012. Expatriate knowledge transfer, subsidiary absorptive capacity, and subsidiary performance. *Academy of Management Journal*, **55**(4): 927–948.

Collins, C.J. and Stevens, C.K. 2002. The relationship between early recruitment-related activities and the application decisions of new labour-market entrants: a brand equity approach to recruitment. *Journal of Applied Psychology*, **87**: 1121–1133.

Daily Mail 2015. Oman to deport over 1,000 foreign workers at airport project, 27 May. http://www.dailymail.co.uk/wires/reuters/article-3099265/Oman-deport-1-000-foreign-workers-airport-project.html#ixzz3sbYUTQOC.

Economist Intelligence Unit (EIU) 2013. Oman. http://country.eiu.com/oman.

EIA 2013. US Energy Information Administration: Oman 2013. http://www.eia.gov/countries/cab.cfm?fips=mu.

Ennis, C.A. and Al-Jamali, R.A. 2014. Elusive employment development planning and labour market trends in Oman. London: Chatham House.

Ernst and Young 2015. How will the GCC close the skills gap? http://www.ey.com/Publication/vwLUAssets/EY-gcc-education-report-how-will-the-gcc-close-the-skills-gap/$FILE/GCC%20Education%20report%20FINAL%20AU3093.pdf.

Gonzales, G., Karoly, L.A., Salem, L.C. and Goldman, C.A. 2008. *Facing Human Capital Challenges of the 21st Century: Education and Labour Market Initiatives in Lebanon, Oman, Qatar and the United Arab Emirates*. Monograph, Santa Monica, CA: RAND Corporation.

Greenwood, M. 2013. Ethical analyses of HRM: a review and research agenda. *Journal of Business Ethics*, **14**: 355–366.

Guest, D.E. 2011. Human resource management and performance: still searching for some answers. *Human Resource Management Journal*, **21**: 3–13.

Gulf News Oman 2012. Annual salary increase for Omanis mandatory in private sector: Manpower Ministry makes it mandatory for employers in private sector to give Omani staff annual salary increase, 14 February 2012. http://gulfnews.com/news/gulf/oman/annual-salary-increase-for-omanis-mandatory-in-private-sector-1.980657.

GulfTalent 2014. *Employment and Salary Trends in the Gulf*. http://www.gulftalent.com/repository/int/Employment%20and%20Salary%20Trends%20in%20the%20Gulf%202014.pdf.

Harrigan, J. and Wang, C. 2006. The economic and political determinants of IMF and World Bank lending in the Middle East and North Africa. *World Development*, **34**: 247–270.

International Monetary Fund (IMF) 2015. Press Release No. 15/189: IMF executive board concludes 2015 Article IV consultation with Oman, 5 May. https://www.imf.org/external/np/sec/pr/2015/pr15189.htm.

Jabr, N.H. 2007. Physicians' attitudes towards knowledge transfer and sharing. *Competitiveness Review: An International Business Journal*, **17**(4): 248–260.

Jones, J. and Ridout, N. 2013. *Oman, Culture and Diplomacy*. Edinburgh: Edinburgh University Press.

Kabasakal, H. and Bodur, M. 2002. Arabic cluster: a bridge between East and West. *Journal of World Business*, **37**(1): 40–54.

Kabasakal, H., Dastmalchian, A., Karacay, G. and Bayraktar, S. 2012. Leadership and culture in the MENA region: an analysis of the GLOBE project. *Journal of World Business*, **47**: 519–529.

Kapoor, G. 2014. Changing times: reward practices in the GCC countries. *Hay Group*, pp. 1–9. https://www.haygroup.com/downloads/uae/2013%20-%2010%20%20changing%20times%20reward%20practices%20in%20the%20gcc%20countries%20-%20final.pdf.

Kazan, F. 1993. *Mass Media, Modernity, and Development: Arab States in the Gulf*. Westport, CT: Praeger Publishers.

Khan, S. 2010. Managing performance: the case of an Omani oil company. *Journal of Business Perspective*, **14**(4): 285–293.

Khan, S. 2011. Convergence, divergence or middle of the path: HRM model for Oman. *Journal of Management Policy and Practice*, **12**(1): 76–87.

Lawler III, E. and Benson, G.S. 2012. What makes performance appraisals effective? *Compensation Benefits Review*, **44**(4): 191–200.

Lee, S.Y., Pitesa, M., Thau, S. and Pillutla, M.M. 2015. Discrimination in selection decisions: integrating stereotypes fit and interdependence theories. *Academy of Management Journal*, **58**(3): 789–812.

Lefebvre, J.A. 2010. Oman's foreign policy in the twenty-first century. *Middle East Policy*, **17**(1): 99–114.

Lo, K., Macky, K. and Pio, E. 2015. The HR competency requirements for strategic and functional HR practitioners. *International Journal of Human Resource Management*, **26**(18): 2308–2328.

Mamman, A. and Al-Kulaiby, K.Z. 2014. Is Ulrich's model useful in understanding HR practitioners' roles in

non-Western developing countries? An exploratory investigation across private and public sector organizations in the Sultanate Kingdom of Oman. *International Journal of Human Resource Management*, **25**(20): 2811–2836.
Mellahi, K. 2003. National culture and management practices: the case of GCCs. In M. Tayeb (ed.), *International Management: Theory and Practices*. London: Prentice Hall, pp. 87–105.
Mellahi, K. and Al-Hinai, S. 2000. Local workers in Gulf co-operation countries: assets or liabilities? *Middle Eastern Studies*, **36**(3): 177–190.
Mellahi, K. and Wood, G. 2001. Human resource management in Saudi Arabia. In P.S. Budhwar and Y. Debrah (eds), *Human Resource Management in Developing Countries*. London: Routledge, pp. 135–150.
Ministry of Education 2015. Report July 2013. www.moe.gov.om.
Ministry of Finance 2015. Oman. www.mof.gov.om/english.
Ministry of Foreign Affairs 2015. Oman. www.mofa.go.om.
Moideenkutty, U. in press. Localization HRM practices and financial performance: evidence from the Sultanate of Oman. *International Journal of Commerce and Management*.
Moideenkutty, U., Al-Lamky, A. and Murthi Y.S. 2011. HRM practices and organisational performance in Oman. *Personnel Review*, **40**(2): 239–251.
Muncherji, N., Gopalakrishnan, C. and Dhar, U. 2009. *Partners in Success: Strategic HR and Entrepreneurship*. Institute of Management, Nirma University of Science and Technology, Ahmedabad, New Delhi: Excel Books.
Muscat Daily 2013. From access to success: the story of Oman's school education system, 18 November. http://www.muscatdaily.com/Archive/Oman/From-access-to-success-The-story-of-Oman-s-school-education-system-2pri#ixzz3slDoIVzm.
Naser, S.H. 1993. *A Young Muslim's Guide to the Modern World*. Chicago, IL: Kazi Publications.
NCSI 2015a. National Centre for Statistics and Information, Oman. www.ncsi.gov.om.
NCSI 2015b. *Monthly Bulletin Statistics April 2015*, National Centre for Statistics and Information, Oman. https://www.ncsi.gov.om/Elibrary/Pages/LibraryContentDetails.aspx?ItemID=l0KNk21fo4bdRER6JkTePw%3D%3D.
NCSI 2015c. Opinion poll on trends of Omani youth toward work: third session. National Centre for Statistics and Information, Oman. www.ncsi.gov.om.
Neal, M. 2010. When Arab–expatriate relations work well: diversity and discourse in the Gulf Arab workplace. *Team Performance Management*, **16**(5/6): 242–266.
OAAA 2015. Oman Academic Accreditation Authority. www.oaaa.gov.om.
Obeidat, B.D., Shannak, R.O., Masa'deh, R. and Al-Jarrah, I.M. 2012. Toward better understanding for Arabian culture: implications based on Hofstede's cultural model. *European Journal of Social Sciences*, **28**(4): 512–522.
OBG 2015. *The Report: Oman 2015*. Oxford Business Group. www.oxfordbusinessgroup.com/oman-2015.
OPP 2013. *Combating Bias in Hiring Decisions: How a Structured Hiring Process Can Help Companies Select the Best Candidate*, OPP Ltd. https://www.opp.com/~/media/Files/PDFs/White_papers/Combating_bias_in_hiring_decisions.pdf.
Paauwe, J. and Boselie, P. 2005. HRM and performance: what's next? *Human Resource Management Journal*, **15**(4): 68–83.
Page, S.E. 2007. Making the difference: applying a logic of diversity. *Academy of Management Perspectives*, **21**(4): 6–20.
Paulin, D. and Suneson, K. 2012. Knowledge transfer, knowledge sharing and knowledge barriers – three blurry terms in KM. *Electronic Journal of Knowledge Management*, **10**(1): 81–91. www.ejkm.com.
Peterson, J.E. 1978. *Oman in the Twentieth Century: Political Foundations of an Emerging State*. London: Croom Helm.
Peterson, J.E. 2004. Oman's diverse society: northern Oman. *Middle East Journal*, **58**(1): 31–51.
Pieper, R. 1990. *Human Resource Management: An International Comparison*. New York: Walter de Gruyter.
Plekhanov, Sergey 2004. *A Reformer on a Throne: Sultan Qaboos bin Said Al Said*. London: Trident Press.
Pridham, B.R. 1987. *Oman: Economic, Social and Strategic Developments*. London: Croom Helm.
Purcell, J. and Hutchinson, S. 2007. Front-line managers as agents in the HRM-performance causal chain: theory, analysis and evidence. *Human Resource Management Journal*, **17**(1): 3–20.
Rajasekar, J. and Khan, S. 2013. Training and development function in Omani public sector organizations: a critical evaluation. *Journal of Applied Business and Economics*, **14**(2): 36–52.
Risher, H. 2014. Performance management needs to be fixed. *Compensation and Benefits Review*, **46**(4): 191–194.
Rynes, S.L., Gerhart, B. and Minette, K.A. 2004. The importance of pay in employee motivation: discrepancies between what people say and what they do. *Human Resource Management Special Issue: The Contributions of Psychological Research to Human Resource Management*, **43**(4): 381–394.
Schmidt, S.M., Moideenkutty, U. and Al-Busaidi, A. 2013. Expatriate and Omani workplace relationships and individual performance. In J. Rajasekar and L.-S. Beh (eds), *Culture and Gender in Leadership: Perspectives from the Middle East and Asia*. Palgrave Macmillan, pp. 228–250.

Shire Professional Chartered Psychologists 2010. Unconscious bias. http://www.cipd.co.uk/NR/rdonlyres/666D7059-8516-4F1A-863F-7FE9ABD76ECC/0/Reducingunconsciousbiasorganisationalresponses.pdf.
Sidani, Y. and Thornberry, J. 2010. The current Arab work ethic: antecedents, implications and potential remedies. *Journal of Business Ethics*, **91**: 35–49.
Sidani, Y. and Thornberry, J. 2013. Nepotism in the Arab world: an institutional theory perspective. *Business Ethics Quarterly*, **23**(1): 69–96.
Smith, P.B., Achoui, M. and Harb, C. 2007. Unity and diversity in Arab managerial styles. *International Journal of Cross Cultural Management*, **7**(3): 275–289.
Swailes, S. and Al-Fahdi, S. 2009. Barriers to human resource development in the public sector of the Sultanate of Oman. University of Hull. http://www.ufhrd.co.uk/wordpress/wp-content/uploads/2009/07/2-19-refereed-paper.pdf.
Swailes, S. and Al-Fahdi, S. 2011. Voluntary turnover in the Omani public sector: an Islamic values perspective. *International Journal of Public Administration*, **34**(10): 682–692.
Swailes, S., Al-Said, L.G. and Al-Fahdi, S. 2012. Localisation policy in Oman: a psychological contracting interpretation. *International Journal of Public Sector Management*, **25**(5): 357–372.
The Oil and Gas Year 2015. *The Oil and Gas Year Oman 2015: The Who's Who of the Global Energy Industry*. www.theoilandgasyear.com.
The Research Council 2015. Oman. https://home.trc.gov.om.
Times of Oman 2013. Friday–Saturday to be weekend holidays now, 7 April. http://timesofoman.com/article/13259/Oman/Friday-Saturday-to-be-weekend-holidays-now.
Times of Oman 2015a. Replace expats in all top jobs with Omanis: Majlis Al Shura, 3 May. http://www.timesofoman.com/article/51522/Oman/Replace-expats-in-all-top-jobs-with-Omanis:-Majlis-Al-Shura.
Times of Oman 2015b. Expat workers should get minimum wage in Oman, 16 June. http://timesofoman.com/article/58493/Oman/Call-for-expat-workers-in-Oman-to-get-a-guaranteed-minimum-wage-under-revised-labour-laws.
Turban, D.B. and Keon, T.L. 1993. Organizational attractiveness: an interactionist perspective. *Journal of Applied Psychology*, **78**(2): 184–193.
Vandenberg, R.J., Richardson, H.A. and Eastman, L.J. 1999. The impact of high involvement work processes on organizational effectiveness. *Group and Organisation Management*, **24**(3): 300–339.
Walker, J., Bauer, T.N., Cole, M.S., Bernerth, J.B., Field, H.S., and Short, J.C. 2013. Is this how I will be treated? Reducing uncertainty through recruitment interactions. *Academy of Management Journal*, **56**(5): 1325–1313.
Weir, D. 2001. Management in the Arab world: a fourth paradigm. Paper presented at the first European Academy of Management conference, Barcelona, April.
Whitely, B.E. and Kite, M.E. 2009. *The Psychology of Prejudice and Discrimination*. Belmont, CA: Wadsworth.
World Economic Forum 2015. *World Economic Forum Global Competitiveness Report 2014–2015*. www.reports.weforum.org/global-competitiveness-report-2014-2015/economies/#economy=OMN.
Wright, P.M. and Boswell, W.R. 2002. Desegregating HRM: a review and synthesis of micro and macro human resource management research. *Journal of Management*, **28**(3): 247–276.
Yeo, R.K. 2014. Looking beyond the shores: emerging HRM and HRD trends in the Middle East. *International Journal of Human Resources Management and Development*, **14**(1/2/3): 1–16.

7. Human resource management in the United Arab Emirates

Marie F. Waxin and Rob E. Bateman

INTRODUCTION AND BACKGROUND

As British forces withdrew from the Middle East, seven sheikhdoms on the north-east horn of the Arabian Peninsula agreed to join a loose confederation giving each emirate substantial autonomy, except in a few policy areas reserved in their constitution for federal control (e.g., defence, education and foreign policy). Abu Dhabi, Dubai, Sharjah, Ajman, Um Al Quwain, Ras Al Khaimah and Fujairah came together in 1971 and 1972 to form the United Arab Emirates (UAE).

The UAE is one of the most developed economies in the Middle East region and is classified as a high-income developing economy by the IMF (International Monetary Fund) (IMF, 2011). With a per capita gross domestic product (GDP) ranked 15th in the world ($36,500) by 2011 IMF estimates, the leadership of the UAE aims to create a sophisticated knowledge-based economy. The oil and gas resources of the new nation, primarily located in Abu Dhabi, fuelled a rapid expansion of public infrastructure and services throughout the country (Suliman, 2006). To the north, Dubai was able to build on its traditional role as a trading hub by investing heavily in world-class ports and airports, but it went on to leverage these assets to become a tourist destination and emerging centre of financial services as well. A decision to create free zones allowing 100 per cent foreign ownership has boosted the re-export of products from the UAE and has helped the country to become a business hub for the region. Dubai has also positioned itself as a pioneer of e-government services in the Arab World (Zhao, Scavarda and Waxin, 2012). Neighbouring Sharjah focused on cultural and educational initiatives, providing a more traditional counterpoint to Dubai's constantly changing skyline.

Human resources (HR) are the 'organizationally relevant capabilities of groups and individuals' (Scott-Jackson et al., 2014a), and strategic human resource management (HRM) is 'a pattern of planned deployments and activities intended to enable an organization to achieve its goals' (Wright and McMahan, 1992).

Article 20 of the UAE Constitution specifically commits the national government to 'endeavour to ensure that employment is available for citizens and to train them so that they are prepared for it'. Indeed, 'UAE Vision 2021' lists 'skilled human capital' as the first of seven strategic enablers, consistent with the role of HR in 'building strategic capabilities' to achieve strategic goals (Wright and McMahan, 1992; Scott-Jackson et al., 2011). HRM clearly has a key role to play in the economic and social achievement of national and organisational goals in the UAE, and indeed in the wider Gulf Cooperation Council (GCC) (Scott-Jackson et al., 2014a).

However, there is a lack of academic research on HRM in the Arab world in general (Rees, Mamman and Bin Braik, 2007; Forstenlechner, 2010) and in the Gulf countries in particular. The difficulty of finding reliable data and conducting research in the region may be contributing factors to this deficit (Forstenlechner and Rutledge, 2010; Harry, 2007).

This chapter reviews the current state of the research literature on HRM in the UAE, in part because more work has been published on 'HRM in the UAE' than on any other country in the GCC or even the Middle East (Afiouni, Karam and El-Hajj, 2013) and also to provide an up to date picture of the scene. We searched the ABI/INFORM and EMERALD databases for published, peer-reviewed academic articles using the keywords human resource management (HRM), personnel, HR practices, HR policies, HR strategies, human resources roles, HR planning, job analysis, recruitment, selection, training, development, performance management, rewards, compensation, talent management, in combination with United Arab Emirates or UAE, without limiting the time frame. We excluded from this review any studies dealing primarily with HRM practices related to Emiratisation, as this topic is covered in Chapter 15 of this volume on labour localisation and HRM practices in the Gulf countries.

The chapter is organised as follows. First, we examine the core issues and factors influencing HRM in the country, such as the cultural and labour market characteristics of the UAE, the evolving UAE education system and briefly the Emiratisation process. We then review the literature on HRM in the UAE and on the key HRM challenges in the UAE. Finally, we conclude with recommendations for practitioners and researchers.

CORE ISSUES AND FACTORS INFLUENCING HRM

In this section, we will describe the core issues and factors that influence HRM practices in the UAE. These are related to the UAE national culture, the labour market, its evolving education system and the drive towards workforce localisation.

Cultural Characteristics of the UAE

Emirati culture is based on traditional tribal mores and is strongly influenced by Islam (Zhao, Scavarda and Waxin, 2012). It shares many aspects of a common Gulf culture emphasising the importance of religion, family, education and success (Abdalla and Al-Homoud, 1995; Al Bahar, Peterson and Taylor, 1996; Klein, Waxin and Radnell, 2009). Below we present the characteristics of the Arab cultures using the frameworks of Hofstede (1980) and Trompenaars and Hampden-Turner (1998).

Hofstede's (1980) research was based on a comparative analysis of 53 countries from five continents. He proposed four universal national culture dimensions that are said to capture the universality of social behaviour within the work context. The Arab sample included Egypt, Iraq, Kuwait, Lebanon, Libya, Saudi Arabia and the UAE. The following results are for the Arab sample as a whole.

Power Distance: The Arab countries have a high power distance score of 80 on this dimension, and a ranking of 7th highest score out of 53 countries, indicating a high level of acceptance for inequality of power and wealth within the society.

Uncertainty Avoidance: The Arab world scores 68 on this dimension, indicating the Arab society's low level of tolerance for uncertainty.

Masculinity: The results for the Arab world on this dimension show a masculinity score of 52, only slightly higher than the 50.2 average for all the countries and the 23rd highest score out of 53 countries/regions. This indicates that while women in the Arab world are limited in their rights, it may be due more to religious mores than a cultural paradigm.

Individualism: The result of the Arab world on this dimension is a score of 38, compared to a world average ranking of 64. This translates into a collectivist society as compared to an individualist culture, as manifested in a close, long-term commitment to the member group, that being a family, extended family, or tribe.

Trompenaars and Hampden-Turner (1998) administered a research questionnaire to over 15,000 managers from 28 countries over a period of ten years. They proposed seven dimensions of value orientation: (1) universalism versus particularism (rules versus relationships), (2) communitarianism versus individualism (the group versus the individual), (3) neutral versus affective (the range of feelings expressed), (4) diffuse versus specific (the range of involvement), (5) achievement versus ascription (how status is accorded), (6) attitudes to time, that can be synchronic or sequential, and (7) attitudes to the environment, that can be internally or externally controlled. The authors considered six Arabic-speaking countries, including five Gulf countries (Bahrain, Egypt, Kuwait, Oman, Saudi Arabia and the UAE) in their research, but did not consistently refer to them in their results, making comparisons across value orientations and countries difficult. According to their study, Arabic cultures are rather universalistic, communitarianist, affective, have a diffuse view of life, are rather ascriptive, have a synchronic time orientation and appreciate internal control.

Characteristics of the UAE Labour Market

Probably the most unusual characteristics of the UAE labour market are its extensive reliance on expatriates and its dual labour market. As the country began its rapid development, the existing skill and education levels of the local populace was no match for the needs of a quickly expanding economy, resulting in a high demand for imported labour (Fasano-Filho and Goyal, 2004). Expatriates from the UK, Europe, the US and Australia were hired to bring management skills and technical expertise. Workers from low-wage countries were eager to fill jobs in construction, services and other unskilled or semi-skilled occupations. Workers from India and Pakistan make up 36.5 and 12.7 per cent of the population, respectively (Al Bayan, 2008). When workers from Bangladesh, Nepal and Sri Lanka are included, more than 60 per cent of the inhabitants hail from the Indian subcontinent. Other Arab nationalities represent 12.7 per cent of the UAE population. Taken together, these and other expatriate labourers make up the larger side of a two-part labour market. Foreign workers are contracted for a fixed period and sponsored for a work visa by their employer. The employee may only change employers with a letter of 'no objection' from the prior sponsor, effectively limiting the mobility of expatriate labour. The UAE's extensive reliance on expatriates from all over the world requires the HR function to provide efficient administration processes, and efficient expatriation management, diversity management and workforce integration strategies and practices.

Emirati nationals make up the other, smaller segment of the labour market. By 2010, native citizens made up only 11.6 per cent of the total population and only 4.2 per cent of the total workforce (Forstenlechner and Rutledge, 2011). Although the overwhelming majority of these nationals prefer the higher wage levels, shorter working hours and better fringe benefits that go with government employment in the UAE, local employees also benefit from a number of rules that increase their pay and provide guaranteed job security in the private sector. Emirati workers and expatriate workers are not substitutes for each other in many cases, so the two market segments may be considered complementary. At the low-skill end, many jobs are not socially acceptable for Emiratis. For high-skilled jobs, there may not be a sufficient number of Emiratis with the requisite education or training.

Unemployment and UAE Nationals

Rapid growth in the expatriate population and employment has unfortunately been accompanied by high and rising unemployment among Emiratis. It is estimated that in the next ten years, 200,000 young Emirati nationals will be entering the labour force (Toledo, 2013). In 2011, the unemployment rate among all UAE nationals was 13.8 per cent, with about 2 per cent being unemployed national males and 12 per cent unemployed national females (Rutledge et al., 2011). However, based on the 2009 UAE Labour Force Survey only 54 per cent of UAE citizens are participating in the workforce. Among these, 85 per cent work in the public sector, and of these, 23 per cent serve in the police or the military. Low participation rates of UAE nationals in the private sector are often a result of voluntary unemployment (Vazquez-Alvarez, 2010), typically young graduates waiting for an appealing government job to open up.

Women's education and their active participation in the UAE workforce are well supported by UAE leaders. Women (UAE citizens + expatriates) represent only 30 per cent of the total UAE population (UAE National Bureau of Statistics, 2010). The participation rate in the workforce of all females (nationals + expatriates) was 42 per cent (Shehadi et al., 2011). Even though 77 per cent of Emirati women go to university (Madsen, 2010) and form over two-thirds of the UAE's university graduates (Abdulla and Ridge, 2011), the participation rate of UAE women in the labour force was only 28 per cent in the UAE. Women form an interesting and growing talent pool, but one that is still underutilised. The strategic recruitment, development, integration and retention of UAE nationals and women in the workforce require HR managers to design and implement efficient talent, diversity and change management processes.

UAE Education System

As explained further in chapter 15 of this volume on workforce localisation in the GCC, governments in the UAE and other GCC nations have recognised the importance of education and talent development, directing extensive public investment towards education. Increasing numbers of higher education institutions and, more limited, technical schools have contributed significantly to increasing the talent pools of skilled and professional personnel, both national and expatriate.

However, much remains to be done to reform the education sector in the UAE, especially with respect to the education of UAE nationals at the primary and secondary levels. The available literature suggests that graduating Emiratis often have inadequate preparation for work life. Specifically, graduates often lack market-oriented skills (Randeree, 2009), language skills in English (Al-Ali, 2008; Randeree, 2009), relevant work experience (Al-Ali, 2008), and vocational motivation (Rees, Mamman and Bin Braik, 2007; Forstenlechner et al., 2012).

The educational attainment of UAE nationals is generally lower than that of expatriates, and the school system suffers from dramatic variability in quality. Vazquez-Alvarez (2010) finds that UAE nationals that participate in employment typically enter the market with 11–12 years of schooling, an average that is 1–2 years more than that of expatriates from developing economies and 1–2 years below the average obtained by other Arabs from the Middle East and North Africa (MENA) region (excluding GCC economies). However, this is about 6 years less than the average obtained by Western expatriates.

Although education for Emiratis is free up to the university level, this is not always the advantage that it seems. The rigour of public secondary school programmes remains low, often leaving students unprepared for university studies (Fox, 2008). Forstenlechner and Rutledge (2010) quoted a UAE government reform agenda, 'Strategy 2010–2020', with a statistic indicating that 94 per cent of students entering one of the country's national universities require at least one remedial course. This situation has resulted in the development of a two-track educational system at the primary and secondary levels. In part due to the dramatic influx of expatriates, many private schools have sprung up, mostly for-profit enterprises following an American or British curriculum taught in English. They position themselves based on their ability to meet world standards, such as with the International Baccalaureate programme. Many Emirati and expatriate parents who want their children to secure a good education have opted for these 'international' schools at significant expense to the family budget.

National universities have been fast at improving educational quality than have public secondary schools, in part due to an emphasis on curricular reform and international accreditation (Gonzalez et al., 2008), but here again many other options are available, including local branch campuses of universities based in the US, UK, France and other developed nations. Similar conditions prevail to varying degrees in other GCC countries, with good intentions often hampered by resistance to abandoning established practice.

An important challenge for the future of economies in the UAE, and in the GCC, is the relative disinterest among nationals for so-called STEM (science, technology, engineering and maths) subjects. Although schools in the GCC have moved away from their traditional emphasis on Islamic studies and culture, religious instruction still consumes more than 10 per cent of class time for grades 7–9. No time is devoted to vocational skills, at least at this level (Farah and Ridge, 2009). University instructors in the region often point to weak quantitative skills as one reason for limited interest in the physical sciences and engineering, though the UAE's implementation in 2009 of a new proficiency assessment in maths was intended to give secondary schools an incentive to rectify this problem.

Emiratisation Policies

As a response to the growing need to find employment for Emiratis, the UAE government has identified the hiring and development of talented nationals as a key policy objective. So-called Emiratisation requirements have been implemented in an attempt to help more Emiratis benefit from the economic expansion and to reduce their demand for employment in the public sector. The National Human Resource Development and Employment Authority (TANMIA) was established in 1999 to facilitate the implementation and monitoring of the government's Emiratisation policies.

Three pillars form the basis of the Emiratisation emphasis: education enhancement, economic diversification away from reliance on petroleum, and regulation of the labour market (Forstenlechner and Rutledge, 2010). Regulatory approaches are operationalised using a variety of elements, the most visible of which are quotas for hiring of nationals in companies with more than 50 employees. From 1998 onwards, all banks in the UAE were required to employ UAE nationals at the rate of 4 per cent annually. Equivalent annual occupational quotas for insurance (in 2003) and trade (in 2004) were 5 per cent and 2 per cent, respectively. Another regulatory element is the use of mandates that prohibit the hiring of non-national workers in certain job categories. For example, in September 2005, the Ministry of Labour issued a decree with regards to the employment of Public Relations Officers (PROs), a title somewhat misleadingly used for employees responsible for coordinating visas and work permits with the various government offices. Thus, starting from January 2006, companies with 100 or more employees were mandated to employ an Emirati when the company needed new PROs or replaced existing ones. As a way to make sure that this mandate was observed, the Ministry of Labour would not accept any labour transaction unless submitted by a PRO who is a UAE national. Saudi Arabia has a similar requirement for nationals to staff positions in purchasing departments.

Neither the UAE Ministry of Labour nor the Ministry of Social Affairs stipulates a wage premium in favour of Emirati employees. The exception seems to be in banking, where banks were required to offer minimum wages to nationals and provide them with other benefits such as insurance (Kapiszewski, 2000) and more flexible working hours (Rees, Mamman and Bin Braik, 2007). However, empirical evidence shows the clear existence of a premium mainly due to the overrepresentation of locals in the public sector, where the wage rate is above the equilibrium wage in the private sector and nationals are often eligible for large, across-the-board pay increases.

The Ministry of Labour does involve itself with the job security of Emiratis. As a result of a ministry order, which underlined existing legislation, private companies are only able to dismiss UAE nationals for serious misconduct, including absenteeism, theft or drunkenness. Economic conditions are not considered a sufficient reason to make Emirati staff redundant. Employers seeking to dismiss locals must apply to the Labour Ministry 30 days in advance of any termination order (Kerr and England, 2009).

These policies have been relatively successful in the governmental sector, with some agencies reaching almost 100 per cent local employment (e.g., the Ministry of Labour and Foreign Affairs were at 98 per cent local employees at the end of 2010), and other departments were making significant progress towards their planned objectives. Overall, the Emiratisation rates in the federal government and federal ministries reached 57 and 67 per cent respectively at the end of 2010 (The Federal Authority for Government Human Resources, 2010).

Success in the private sector has been harder to document. One of the main goals of the Emiratisation programme was to gradually increase the participation of Emiratis in private sector employment. Analysis of the 2009 UAE Labour Force Survey shows that only 54 per cent were actively employed, and only 9 per cent of those who were employed worked fully outside the public domain. This low contribution to the private workforce is ironic, given the demand for labour. For example, 2008 figures from TANMIA showed a total of 26,000 unemployed Emiratis even as the local labour market showed about 100,000 vacancies. There is clearly a tendency for the private sector to hire non-nationals even in the face of government-imposed quotas for the hiring of Emiratis. Indeed, the quota policy had little effect in the trade sector until the government introduced a penalty system (Randeree, 2012). By 2014, the average rate of Emiratisation for national banks was 34 per cent, but the rate for non-national financial institutions was only 21 per cent (Duncan, 2014).

Emiratisation policy in the UAE has changed the HR landscape, so it has become increasingly unlikely for a large organisation to establish itself in the UAE without some plan to address the issue of localisation of HR (Randeree, 2009). The importance of the localisation process provides HR managers with an opportunity to make a significant contribution by designing, implementing and monitoring efficient local talent management processes.

HRM PRACTICES IN THE UAE

In this section, we review the literature on HRM in the UAE. Since available articles were not comprehensive enough to sufficiently inform readers about all HRM practices in the UAE, we extended our review to include relevant reports and also included a few observations based on our own experience working with businesses and government offices. We organised the review content into the following sections: (1) work values, organisational commitment, job satisfaction and HRM practices, (2) staffing practices, (3) training and development, (4) performance management and rewards, and (5) self-initiated expatriation.

Work Values, Organisational Commitment, Job Satisfaction and HRM Practices

Wils et al. (2011) examined work value differences across several generations among respondents in Quebec and Arab respondents in the UAE. This quantitative study used an abridged version of the Wils, Luncasu and Waxin (2007) work value inventory, including 28 work values arranged on four poles: self-enhancement, self-transcendence, openness-to-change and conservation. In the Quebec sample, there were no significant differences between generations on the four work value poles. In the UAE sample, the younger generation attached less importance to self-enhancement, but more importance to self-transcendence than the older generation, with a small effect size. Culture had only a small impact on the average of the four work value poles, which supports Gerhart and Fang's (2005) findings that the impact of culture of origin is often exaggerated in international management research. Conversely, the diversity in work values among generations and cultures found in their samples confirms the importance of selective hiring within high performance work systems (HPWS), because each country and each generation had respondents with a wide variety of work value preferences. These findings suggest that it is possible to recruit selectively in order to achieve the best fit between the work values of employees and the philosophical principles underlying HPWS. Although job appointments in Gulf countries often depend on '*wasta*', or personal connections, this study supports the idea that selective hiring may be just as effective in emerging as in developed countries.

Using a sample of middle managers working in diverse industries in Dubai, Behery and Paton (2008) confirmed that fitting the performance appraisal to organisational culture had a positive impact on job satisfaction and commitment, and a negative impact on turnover intention. Citizenship (local or expatriate) had an impact on job satisfaction, but gender did not have any impact.

Later, Behery (2011) also examined the impact of high involvement work practices (HIWPs) upon trust and commitment in service organisations within the UAE. The results showed that training opportunities, objective appraisal methods, employment security, profit sharing and internal consistency between HRM practices were valid predictors of trust, whereas internal career opportunities, employment security and the consistency of HRM practices were significant predictors of commitment. The authors controlled for work status (casual versus permanent workers) and citizenship (local versus non-local worker), and found that these did not affect the relationship between HIWPs and trust and commitment. They conclude that managers should realise that implementing and benefiting from high-involvement policies is not as simple as instituting a single practice. An organisational culture that cultivates HIWPs does appear to be essential.

Finally, Abdulla, Djebarni and Mellahi (2011) studied the determinants of job satisfaction among employees of the Dubai Police. They found that salary and incentives had the highest impact on job satisfaction, followed by the positive perception of work aspects (e.g., variety, autonomy), favourable public perception of the job, clear organisational policy and strategy, clear supervision, positive relationship with co-workers and promotion opportunities.

Staffing Practices

Published academic research on HR planning, recruitment and selection practices in the UAE is limited. Sarabdeen, El-Rakhawy and Khan (2011) studied the impact of employer branding, Siddique (2004) focused on job analysis, and Ababneh and Chhinzer (2014) examined applicant reactions to different selection methods in the UAE. Academic literature on staffing practices used in the public sector is noticeably absent.

Sarabdeen, El-Rakhawy and Khan's (2011) description of employer branding initiatives at three well-established companies in the UAE (Nestlé Middle East, Gulf Food Trade, Emirates Airlines Group) showed the existence of such practices and their importance for attracting new employees. The visibility and status of the employer clearly had an impact on its ability to attract good applicants. Siddique (2004) examined the impact of proactive job analysis on four measures of organisational performance (administrative efficiency, quality of organisational climate, financial performance and relative performance in the industry). This study also considered the moderating effect of sophisticated HR information systems, HR involvement in strategic planning and a competency-based job analysis approach on the job analysis–performance relationship. The author controlled for four variables: company size, company age, ownership status, and training and development resources, using quantitative data from CEOs, general managers and heads of department in governmental, semi-governmental and private organisations in Dubai and Sharjah. The results revealed a strong positive association between proactive job analysis practice and organisational performance. The moderating variables' direct effects on organisational performance were nearly as strong as their interaction effects.

These findings extended work on the HR–performance research pursued in Western countries to a GCC context and suggest that a company-wide policy of job analysis is an important source of competitive advantage, which merits due attention from HR professionals, line managers and executives.

Based on quantitative surveys from Emirati students, university educators and employers, Scott-Jackson et al. (2014b) report interesting insights into preferred recruitment methods in the UAE. The three most popular ways for Emirati university students to look for job opportunities were applying online (31 per cent), seeking recommendations from personal contacts in the organisation (32 per cent) and attending recruitment fairs (32 per cent). However, employers in the UAE were most likely to attend recruitment fairs (52 per cent), commission a recruitment agency (52 per cent) and seek recommendations from senior business colleagues (44 per cent). There appears to be a disparity between the preferred job-search practices of potential local employees and the venues selected by potential employers.

Ababneh and Chhinzer (2014) studied applicants' perceptions of fairness across 12 personnel selection concepts in the UAE. Based on a quantitative survey completed by senior undergraduate business students of different nationalities, the results show that interviews, résumés, personal references and ethnicity/nationality are the most common selection methods in the UAE, while graphology and honesty tests are least common. Interviews, résumés and work-sample tests showed the highest rates in terms of favourability perceptions; face validity, extent of use, employer's right to obtain information and opportunity to perform showed the strongest correlations with process favourability perceptions. These are also the strongest predictors of organisational attractiveness and applicant intentions to apply or to recommend the organisation to others. The authors concluded that despite different cultural, social and economic, and political contexts, the patterns of applicant reactions towards selection methods are similar across countries.

We observe that organisations in the UAE use a variety of online selection tests for language skills, cognitive ability, personality and achievement. Assessment centres are also common, integrating individual and team exercises such as case study analyses, in-basket exercises, presentations, leaderless group discussions and interviews. Selection interviews range from unstructured interviews to structured, competency, behavioural, situational, and sequential and panel variants. Our experience is that big local and foreign organisations have a tendency to use best practices, whereas many smaller employers struggle to use more than unstructured interviews. Best practices coexist with significant deviations in such key decisions as choice of selection criteria, selection testing and interviewing techniques.

We did not find any research with a specific focus on staffing practices in the UAE public sector. Based on our own conversations and experience, public sector recruiting and selection practices vary, but exhibit a strong preference for nationals. Posting of positions on the organisational website, online advertising and use of both formal and informal networks of current employees are among the most common means of attracting interested applicants. There is not a presumption that all public positions must be advertised, but most public organisations do have internal policies that define the selection process, even if these are often truncated to expedite the hiring of an appealing Emirati candidate.

Training and Development

The Arab region is one of the largest consumers of corporate training worldwide (Jones, 2007), but the number of academic articles related to training in the UAE is quite limited. Wilkins (2001) focused on training and development strategies among top companies in Dubai, whereas Scott-Jackson et al. (2014b) offered insights into the use of the different training and development methods in the UAE generally. Jones (2007) highlighted the cultural challenge of using Western-style training methods. Work by Ibrahim (2004) and by Yaseen and Khanfar (2009) examined the evaluation of training effectiveness.

Wilkins (2001) explored training and development strategies along with their implementation in large, successful business organisations in the UAE. The findings showed that top companies were very aware of best training and development practices used by their foreign counterparts, and found that they generally tried to adopt similar methods and strategies. This research is based on quantitative data collected from 22 of the 100 'Top Companies in Dubai', in 1998. Using measurements such as the proportion which have a director of HR, a training manager or a training centre, or the proportion of organisations with a formal training and development strategy, the author concluded that the best companies in the UAE actually compared favourably with European countries. Companies in the UAE spent less on training than those in most West European countries as percentage of payroll costs, but it should be remembered that in some European countries there are legal, political or cultural reasons why expenditure on training might be higher. Although the study results looked positive, the sample size is admittedly limited to a small sample of organisations in the UAE that were willing to share their best training practices. These may be those enterprises that are most progressive in their approach to HR, so the possibility of a self-selection bias cannot be ignored.

Research by Scott-Jackson et al. (2014b) provides interesting insights into training and development methods used in the UAE. These authors show that most organisations use the least effective methods of developing local talent (e.g., classroom instruction) most often, and use the most effective methods (e.g., structured on-job learning, coaching) least. Also, employers in the UAE often fail to use developmental schemes to retain their local talent.

Of course, local culture can present challenges for training efforts intended to improve efficiency, profitability and productivity. Jones (2007) monitored a bank-sponsored training programme that was designed to enhance the customer interaction skills of 70 Emirati participants. Although the literature suggests that collaborative and competitive styles were most positively correlated with performance, the participants' preference for compromising and avoiding styles had a significant negative influence on the expected training outcomes. As evident in the UAE, cultural preferences can present a substantial risk for using Western-style training programmes. The author went on to discuss how current approaches to training in the region might be modified to improve results.

Ibrahim (2004) examined the effectiveness of one training programme, considering both the reactions of trainees and the degree to which they gained desired levels of knowledge and skills. Yaseen and Khanfar (2009) examined the effectiveness evaluation practices of sales training programmes in the UAE, based on a quantitative survey answered by managers involved in the planning and delivery. These authors suggested that the HR function should be more involved in training-needs assessment, design and effectiveness evaluation of training programmes, and the linking of training to other HRM practices.

We did not find any published research on training and development in the public sector. However, based on our experience working with government organisations, training and development in the public sector is improving. Some government-controlled businesses and governmental agencies follow many accepted best practices in managerial and executive development, including thorough assessments using competency models and 360 feedback, individual development plans, education, on-going mentoring or coaching, and rotational assignments in both domestic and international positions. The progress of participants is monitored carefully as the programme progresses, and their career trajectory is a source of much interest. The programme itself may be subjected to external review by an independent accrediting organisation. In contrast, other government offices take a more haphazard approach in which a certain amount of money is budgeted for each employee to receive training, but the training selected may depend on a variety of factors unrelated to employee development requirements. However, there is a growing demand for the assessment of training effectiveness. Dubai has a school of government that provides a variety of educational opportunities. Continuing education courses often bring in instructors from some of the top universities around the world, which lends these programmes a certain amount of credibility. However, there is a strong preference within the government for instruction in the Arabic language, usually delivered by current or former officials. Demand for custom courses is also relatively high.

Nationals working in the public sector particularly benefit from generous support for training and development. Emiratis are often hired into positions and then supported in their education, training and development needs to meet the necessary qualifications, obtaining full or partial tuition payments or release time to participate in programmes deemed to contribute to their career development.

Performance Management and Rewards

No published academic research so far has systematically studied all components of the performance management process in any of the GCC countries. However, two studies have addressed performance management issues specifically in the UAE (Behery, Jabeen and Parakandi, 2014; Suliman, 2003), and another focused on preferred rewards among Emiratis (Younies, Barhem and Younis, 2008). Behery, Jabeen and Parakandi (2014) examined the transition of a small UAE organisation from the traditional to a modern performance management system (PMS), based on a balanced scorecard (BSC) and organisational strategy map. This research appears to be the first to study contemporary PMS within a middle-eastern context. Using a qualitative case-study analysis, the authors found that different BSC components already existed in the company, but that these components were not properly integrated into one 'whole organisation' system. Such components, if integrated together and aligned with organisational objectives and strategies, can facilitate comprehensive adoption of the BSC system and enhance the measurement and management of organisational performance. This study suggested that many of the roles played by traditional performance management in the Middle East can be substituted by, or supported by, other mechanisms at the corporate level (BSC and a strategy map for the company, for instance).

Suliman (2003) examined the relationship between self- and supervisor-rated performance evaluations in the UAE. Based on quantitative data collected from employees and managers in private and public organisations, the results showed a clear gap between employees' perception of their performance and their managers' observations. Married, older, longer tenured and more educated employees all reported higher levels of self-rated performance. Supervisors with these same characteristics also evaluated their subordinates more positively. Gender, sector and nationality had no impact on either rating, whether self or supervisory.

Younies, Barhem and Younis (2008) examined the preferred rewards of employees working in the UAE health sector. Based on a quantitative analysis, the results showed that monetary rewards were most attractive to employees, with cash, paid vacation and health insurance leading the list of desirable material rewards. The most desirable non-material rewards were recognition, training and educational opportunities, access to new technologies, flexibility of working hours, and more control in the organisation.

Self-Initiated Expatriation

Due to the heavy reliance of the UAE on foreign labour, expatriation is an important consideration. Five academic articles have focused on self-initiated expatriation in the UAE. Two focus on Western women (Stalker and Mavin, 2011; Harrison and Michailova, 2012); two on academics (Bashir, 2012; Isakovic and Whitman, 2013); and the fifth examines expatriation from the point of view of Emirati co-workers (Al Ariss, 2014).

Harrison and Michailova (2012) studied the experiences of Western females (self-initiated expatriates, trailing spouses and assigned expatriates) in the UAE, using both surveys and interviews. They found that Western women successfully adjusted to life and work in the UAE despite significant cultural differences between their home countries and their new location. Stalker and Mavin (2011) describe the experiences of 12 self-initiated expatriate women in the UAE using semi-structured interviews. Their findings pointed to four key themes: vulnerability in being a foreigner; gendered workplaces; informal learning; and women's own agency in their learning and development. These women had little access to formal organisational support for learning and development. Networking through professional associations, businesswomen's groups or personal contacts for both personal and professional development and support seemed to be more common. Both of these studies found that the large Western expatriate community was the primary source of social ties and support for the respondents, whereas interacting with UAE nationals was more often an exception and did not provide essential ties or support. These experiences could help HR managers to (1) refine their selection processes to ensure women are not automatically overlooked when positions in the Middle East need to be filled, (2) develop appropriate training offerings for those posted to the region, and (3) consider seriously the large and well-elaborated expatriate communities as a source of social ties and support.

Using quantitative analysis, Bashir (2012) found that perceived organisational support positively impacted the three facets of intercultural adjustment (work, interaction and general adjustment) of self-expatriated academics and supervisory staff in the UAE. Isakovic and Whitman (2013) also examined these aspects of intercultural adjustment among self-expatriated academics in the UAE, using a quantitative survey. They found that the degree of satisfaction with previous overseas work experience but not the length of that experience was positively correlated with the three adjustment facets. Conversely, the degree of culture novelty was negatively correlated to the three facets of intercultural adjustment, but foreign language ability was not. Gender and length of employment in current job also had an impact on the sociocultural experiences of self-expatriated academics.

Finally, Al Ariss (2014) studied expatriation from the point of view of local UAE managers who worked with expatriates. This research is based on interviews with Emirati managers and two case study analyses (NBK Capital and Strata). He found that, on the one hand, UAE respondents felt privileged by the Emiratisation practices of their organisations and tended to classify the expatriates based on their nationality. On the other hand, UAE respondents felt themselves to be a minority in their own country, perceived expatriates as a threat to their career opportunities, and felt negatively stereotyped by those same expatriates. The authors concluded that the HRM function should (1) play a more aggressive role in diversity management, (2) design better expatriate management practices (recruitment, selection, career management and retention processes), and (3) support more fully collaboration and knowledge sharing between locals and expatriates.

KEY HRM CHALLENGES IN THE UAE

The HRM function faces at least four challenges in the UAE that are common to each of the other GCC countries. The first test is to effectively align HR strategies and practices with organisational strategic goals. Scott-Jackson et al. (2014a) found that while 80 per cent of GCC business leaders recognise that HR is crucially important for the success of their enterprise, their country and the GCC as a whole, only 25 per cent of HR leaders rated the practice of their discipline in the GCC region as excellent compared to global best practice. We found a single article focusing on the strategic role of HRM in the UAE. Yaseen (2013) studied the role of HR managers in UAE educational institutions, finding that the two immediate priorities for HR departments in these organisations were building leadership capabilities through cultural and behavioural adaptation. However, most HR activities actually focused on the routine administrative aspects of HR management, leading the author to conclude that HR's role in UAE educational institutions is not that of a strategic partner. Moreover, we observe that the role of HR as a contributor to corporate strategy is acknowledged at an executive level, but many organisations in both the public and private sectors struggle to operationalise key strategic HRM concepts. One government department had more than 10 per cent of its staff devoted specifically to strategy, but no human capital goals were explicitly included in its list of more than a dozen objectives.

A second challenge is to improve the effectiveness of HR processes particularly in key areas identified as most important by business. HRM departments in the UAE are struggling to establish objective and efficient HR systems (Suliman, 2006; Yaseen and Khanfar, 2009; Yaseen, 2013; Al Ariss, 2014). Scott-Jackson et al. (2014a) found that business leaders and HR leaders disagree on organisational priorities for HR and also differ on their evaluations of the performance of HR activities. When both HR leaders and business leaders were asked to rate the degree to which they thought HR was performing on a range of different competencies, HR leaders gave higher performance ratings for almost all HR practices than their business executives. HR is perceived as underperforming in key areas essential to supporting the rest of the enterprise. Although this finding also appears in other global surveys, the disparity is somewhat greater in the GCC (Scott-Jackson et al., 2014a).

The third challenge is to improve the professionalism of HR practitioners. HR professionals in the GCC lack relevant experience and education (Scott-Jackson et al., 2014a): on average, respondents report four years of experience working in HR roles, but much of this experience was administrative and sometimes barely related to HRM. Moreover, too few HR professionals received specific HR training and education. In some cases, individuals are moved into HR roles from other disciplines and trained after the fact. HR training is least often available in smaller organisations where the job function is likely to be self-reliant. Finally, too few HR practitioners benefit from membership in any professional body that could help to advance their HR skills. Even though 90 per cent of respondents mentioned that they would value a professional association for HR in the GCC, only 10 per cent were members of existing professional bodies such as the Society for Human Resource Management (SHRM), the Chartered Institute of Personnel and Development (CIPD) or the Arabian Society for Human Resource Management (Scott-Jackson et al., 2014a). We also observe that many university graduates in business and management in the UAE have not taken any introductory coursework in HRM, and that graduate programmes related to HRM in the UAE are very limited. However, we also observe that the country is very active in hosting international, regional and national conferences on HRM and talent management. Dubai is also the home of The Human Resources Forum (THRF), founded in the mid-1970s by a group of enthusiastic HR managers who were interested in networking, sharing experiences and seeking continuous professional development. This group currently counts over 300 members, representing more than 150 companies from most business sectors across the Emirates.

A fourth significant challenge is related to the development of HRM processes that are relevant for the UAE and which meet the specific needs of national or organisational cultures and management models in the country. As for the GCC nations generally, these requirements are usually related to local talent management processes, including recruitment, development, engagement and retention of local citizens (Scott-Jackson et al., 2014a). Management of expatriates and diversity management are critical topics in this context (Al Ariss, 2014). In a transient environment with high turnover and the lack of a corporate culture that provides expatriate employees with training or defined career paths (Al-Ali, 2008), the long-term engagement and retention of these workers is a key consideration as well. Finally, both local and expatriate women form an educated talent pool that has yet to be fully engaged.

RECOMMENDATIONS AND WAY FORWARD

The UAE is the GCC country with the highest number of published articles on HRM, and the growing number of both academic and professional publications is a sign that HRM is attracting more attention from both researchers and business leaders. The growth of large domestic companies and the establishment of multinationals in the UAE have been crucial in introducing modern and innovative HRM practices. The multiple foreign and local universities that now enrol students in the UAE have also brought experienced HRM researchers.

However, so far the HRM function in the UAE has not demonstrated its value, nor effectively contributed to the achievements of the organisational strategic goals. Many generally accepted HR practices have yet to be implemented fully. There are significant variations in the ways in which HRM strategies and practices are formulated and implemented in the UAE.

Managerial Recommendations

The HR environment in the UAE is very complex, due to the evolving educational system, the existence of a dual labour market, the extensive reliance on an expatriate workforce, the diverse and multicultural labour pool, the challenges of engaging and retaining employees, the increasing pressures for Emiratisation, and evolving UAE governmental regulations. In this context, HR managers require expertise in administration, strategic management, expatriation, diversity, change, talent, engagement and retention management. Clearly, the HRM function is presented with important challenges, but these also represent opportunities to inform, teach and train. HR managers have an opportunity to develop and implement strategic HRM systems that help organisations achieve their strategic and tactical objectives. HR managers have an opportunity to develop effective HRM strategies and practices that can support business leaders and managers in their organisational challenges. HR professional who are lacking experience and expected competencies have an opportunity to seek specialised education and training with HR certificate programmes, presumably with the goal to design and implement world-class HRM practices for their organisations. Education in HR would add value, not only for HR managers but also for functional and line managers, who could lead their teams and departments more effectively. Finally, HR managers have the opportunity to contribute to the design and implementation of a unique, UAE-specific model of HRM, taking into account the UAE culture and labour market specificities, to effectively manage workforce localisation, expatriation management and workforce diversity.

Future Research Avenues

Our analysis allowed us to identify several specific research gaps. More quantitative and qualitative research is needed on all HRM functions in the UAE, but especially on strategic HRM, on HRM in the public sector and on strategic talent management. Three points stand out. First, very few academic empirical articles have been published on strategic HRM in the UAE, as in the GCC. Given the critical importance of human capital development for the future of the local economy, research focused on defining and mitigating barriers to efficient, strategic HRM will be essential. Second, there is a need to understand how HR management systems have been designed and implemented in the public sector. In light of the important leading role given to the public sector, as evidenced by Dubai's ranking as the top eCity in the Arab world (Zhao, Scavarda and Waxin, 2012), and its position as an important employer, little research seems to have been done on the design and evolution of public HR systems. Third, strategic talent management may be defined as:

> activities and processes that involve the systematic identification of key positions which differentially contribute to the organisation's sustainable competitive advantage, the development

> of a talent pool of high potential and high performing incumbents to fill these roles, and the development of a differentiated human resource architecture to facilitate filling these positions with competent incumbents and to ensure their continued commitment to the organisation. (Collings and Mellahi, 2009, p. 304)

Scholars from different theoretical perspectives have investigated strategic talent management, but there is a lack of empirical research in talent management practices and strategies in emerging markets, in general, and in GCC countries in particular. It would be interesting to research how UAE organisations define talent and talent management, the roles and impact of various stakeholders in the talent management process, how key positions are identified, and the talent acquisition, development and retention strategies used. Talent management is a topic that is recognised as important and relevant in the UAE, particularly by private companies and the more progressive government-controlled enterprises, but no published article has examined talent management practices in the UAE.

To summarise, in this chapter, we reviewed the literature on HRM in the UAE and the key HRM challenges in this country. Further, we identified some precise managerial implications, research gaps and avenues of future research. In doing so, we hope to draw needed attention to unique aspects of HRM in the UAE which are not yet fully addressed in international academic journals or relevant professional literature.

USEFUL WEBSITES

Dubai Statistics Center: http://www.dsc.gov.ae.
The Arabian Society of Human Resource Management: http://www.ashrm.com.
The Human Resource Forum: http://thrf.ae.
The National Human Resources Development and Employment Authority, TANMIA: http://www.tanmia.ae/english/Pages/default.aspx.
United Arab Emirates National Bureau of statistics: http://www.uaestatistics.gov.ae/EnglishHome/CensusEN/tabid/202/Default.aspx.

REFERENCES

Ababneh, K.I. and Chhinzer, N. 2014. Job applicant reactions to selection methods in the United Arab Emirates. *International Management Review*, **10**(2): 32–72.

Abdulla, F. and Ridge, N. 2011. Where are all the men? Gender, participation and higher education in the United Arab Emirates. Working Paper Series No. 11–03, Dubai School of Government. http://www.dsg.ae/en/publication/Description.aspx?PubID=228&PrimenuID=11&mnu=Pri (accessed 30 August 2015).

Abdalla, I.A. and Al-Homoud, M. 1995. A survey of management training and development practices in the State of Kuwait. *Journal of Management Development*, **14**(3): 14–25.

Abdulla, J., Djebarni, R. and Mellahi, K. 2011. Determinants of job satisfaction in the UAE: a case study of the Dubai Police. *Personnel Review*, **40**(1): 126–146.

Afiouni, F., Karam, C.M. and El-Hajj, H. 2013. The HR value proposition model in the Arab Middle East: identifying the contours of an Arab Middle Eastern HR model. *International Journal of Human Resource Management*, **24**(10): 1895–1932.

Al-Ali, J. 2008. Emiratisation: drawing UAE nationals into their surging economy. *International Journal of Sociology and Social Policy*, **28**(9/10): 365–379.

Al Ariss, A. 2014. Voicing experiences and perceptions of local managers: expatriation in the Arab Gulf. *International Journal of Human Resource Management*, **25**(14): 1978–1994.

Al Bahar, A.A., Peterson, S.E. and Taylor, W.G.K. 1996. Managing training and development in Bahrain: the influence of culture. *Journal of Managerial Psychology*, **11**(5): 26–32.

Al Bayan 2008. عت تا. تاي فاقث ة سنجلا ي فلتخملا ة ف ر لودلا ابل ثؤي ى س ة لع ةيوهلا ينطولا. 29 October. http://www.albayan.ae/servlet/Satellite?c=Article&cid=1223993414930&pagename=Albayan/Article/FullDetail.

Bashir, S. 2012. Perceived organizational support and the cross-cultural adjustment of expatriates in the UAE. *Education, Business and Society: Contemporary Middle Eastern Issues*, **5**(1): 63–82.

Behery, M. 2011. High involvement work practices that really count: perspectives from the UAE. *International Journal of Commerce and Management*, **21**(1): 21–45.

Behery, M., Jabeen, F. and Parakandi, M. 2014. Adopting a contemporary performance management system. *International Journal of Productivity and Performance Management*, **63**(1): 22–43.

Behery, M.H. and Paton, R.A. 2008. Performance appraisal–cultural fit: organizational outcomes within the UAE. *Education, Business and Society: Contemporary Middle Eastern Issues*, **1**(1): 34–49.

Collings, D.G. and Mellahi. K. 2009. Strategic talent management: a review and research agenda. *Human Resource Management Review*, **19**(4): 304–313.

Duncan, G. 2014. Banks lead the way in Emiratisation. *The National*, 25 August. http://www.thenational.ae/business/banking/banks-lead-the-way-in-emiratisation (accessed 30 August 2015).

Farah, S. and Ridge, N. 2009. Challenges to curriculum development in the UAE. Dubai School of Government Policy Brief, no. 16.

Fasano-Filho, U. and Goyal. R. 2004. Emerging strains in GCC labor markets. International Monetary Fund, Working Paper No. WP/04/71.

Forstenlechner, I. 2010. Workforce localization in emerging Gulf economies: the need to fine-tune HRM. *Personnel Review*, **39**(1): 135–152.

Forstenlechner, I., Madi, M.T., Selim, H.M. and Rutledge, E.J. 2012. Emiratisation: determining the factors that influence the recruitment decisions of employers in the UAE. *International Journal of Human Resource Management*, **23**(2): 406–421.

Forstenlechner, I. and Rutledge, E. 2010. Unemployment in the Gulf: time to update the social contract. *Middle East Policy*, **17**(2): 38–51.

Forstenlechner, I. and Rutledge, E. 2011. The GCC's demographic imbalance perceptions, realities and policy options. *Middle East Policy*, **18**(4): 25–43.

Fox, W.H. 2008. The United Arab Emirates and policy priorities for higher education. In C. Davidson and P.M. Smith (eds), *Higher Education in the Gulf States: Shaping Economies, Politics and Culture*. London: Saqi, pp. 110–125.

Gerhart, B. and Fang M. 2005. National culture and human resource management: assumptions and evidence. *International Journal of Human Resource Management*, **16**(6): 971–986.

Gonzalez, G., Karoly, L., Constant, L., Salem, H. and Goldman, G. 2008. *Facing Human Capital Challenges of the 21st Century: Education and Labor Market Initiatives in Lebanon, Oman, Qatar and the United Arab Emirates*. RAND Corporation.

Harrison, E.C. and Michailova, S. 2012. Working in the Middle East: Western female expatriates' experiences in the United Arab Emirates. *International Journal of Human Resource Management*, **23**(4): 625–644.

Harry, W. 2007. Employment creation and localization: the crucial human resource issues for the GCC. *International Journal of Human Resource Management*, **18**(1): 132–146.

Hofstede, G. 1980. *Culture's Consequences: International Differences in Work-Related Values*. Beverly Hills, CA: Sage.

Ibrahim, M.E. 2004. Measuring training effectiveness. *Journal of Management Research*, **4**(3): 147–155.

International Monetary Fund 2011. *United Arab Emirates-2011 – Article IV Consultation Concluding Statement*. International Monetary Fund Country Report No. 11/111.

Isakovic, A.A. and Whitman, M.F. 2013. Self-initiated expatriate adjustment in the UAE: a study of academics. *Journal of Global Mobility*, **1**(2): 161–186.

Jones, S. 2007. Training and cultural context in the Arab Emirates: fighting a losing battle? *Employee Relations*, **30**(1): 48–62.

Kapiszewski, A. 2000. Population, labour and education dilemmas facing GCC states at the turn of the century. http://crm.hct.ac.ae/events/archive/tend/AndKP.html (accessed 30 August 2015).

Kerr, S. and England, A. 2009. UAE to safeguard jobs of nationals. *Financial Times*, 18 February. www.ft.com/cms/s/0/7dfbc81e-fe0d-11dd-932e-000077b07658.html#axzz3FRQ3oqYx (accessed 30 August 2015).

Klein, A., Waxin, M.-F. and Radnell, E. 2009. The impact of the Arab national culture on the perception of ideal organizational culture in the United Arab Emirates: an empirical study of 17 firms. *Education, Business and Society: Middle Eastern Issues*, **2**(1): 44–56.

Madsen, S.R. 2010. The experiences of UAE women leaders in developing leadership early in life. *Feminist Formations*, **22**(3): 75–95.

Randeree, K. 2009. Strategy, policy and practice in the nationalisation of human capital: 'project Emiratisation'. *Research and Practice in Human Resource Management*, **17**(1): 71–91.

Randeree, K. 2012. Workforce nationalization in the Gulf Cooperation Council states. Center for International and Regional Studies, Georgetown University, School of Foreign Service in Qatar. https://repository.library.georgetown.edu/bitstream/handle/10822/558218/CIRSOccasionalPaper9KasimRanderee2012.pdf?sequence=5 (accessed 30 August 2015).

Rees, C.J., Mamman, A. and Bin Braik, A. 2007. Emiratization as a strategic HRM change initiative: case study evidence from a UAE petroleum company. *International Journal of Human Resource Management*, **18**(1): 33–53.

Rutledge, E., Al Shamsi, F., Bassioni, Y. and Al Sheikh H. 2011. Women, labour market nationalisation policies and human resource development in the Arab Gulf States. *Human Resource Development International*, **14**(2): 183–193.

Sarabdeen, J., El-Rakhawy, N. and Khan, H.N. 2011. Employer branding in selected companies in United Arab Emirates. *Communications of the IBIMA*, **2011**(228533): 1–9. http://ro.uow.edu.au/cgi/view content.cgi?article=1501&context=dubaipapers (accessed 19 July 2016).

Scott-Jackson, W., Druck. S., Mortimer, T. and Viney, J. 2011. HR's global impact: building strategic differentiating capabilities. *Strategic HR Review*, **10**(4): 33–39.

Scott-Jackson, W., Owen, S., Whitaker, D., Owen, S., Kariem, R. and Druck, S. 2014a. HRM in the GCC: a new world HR for the new world economy. *Oxford Strategic Consulting, Research Series*.

Scott-Jackson, W., Owen, S., Whitaker, D., Cole, M, Druck, S., Kariem, R., Mogielnicki, R. and Shuaib, A. 2014b. Maximizing Emirati talent in engineering. *Oxford Strategic Consulting, Research Series*.

Shehadi, A., Hoteit, L.R., Lamaa, A. and Tarazi, K. 2011. *Educated, Ambitious, Essential Women Will Drive the GCC's Future*, Booz and Co. http://www.strategyand.pwc.com/media/uploads/Strategyand-Educated-Ambitious-Essential.pdf (accessed 30 August 2015).

Siddique, C.M. 2014. Job analysis: a strategic human resource management practice. *International Journal of Human Resource Management*. **15**(1): 219–244.

Stalker, B. and Mavin, S. 2011. Learning and development experiences of self- initiated expatriate women in the United Arab Emirates. *Human Resource Development International*, **14**(3): 273–290.

Suliman, A.M.T. 2003. Self and supervisor ratings of performance: evidence from an individualistic culture. *Employee Relations*, **25**(4): 371–388.

Suliman, A.M.T. 2006. Human resource management in the United Arab Emirates. In P. Budhwar and K. Mellahi (eds), *Managing Human Resources in the Middle East*. London: Routledge, pp. 59–78.

The Federal Authority for Government Human Resources 2010. Emiratization plan in federal government sector and mechanism for coordination and follow-up, 2010–2013. http://www.fahr.gov.ae/Portal/Userfiles/Assets/Documents/2ccd4cfe.pdf (accessed 30 August 2015).

Toledo, H. 2013. The political economy of Emiratization in the UAE. *Journal of Economic Studies*, **40**(1): 39–53.

Trompenaars, F. and Hampden-Turner, C. 1998. *Riding the Waves of Culture: Understanding Diversity in Global Business*. New York: McGraw-Hill.

UAE National Bureau of Statistics 2010. UAE women statistics. http://www.dwe.gov.ae/stat.aspx (accessed 19 July 2016).

Vazquez-Alvarez, R. 2010. *The Micro-Structure of Wages and Wage Determination in the UAE*. Dubai Economic Council.

Wilkins, S. 2001. International Briefing 9: training and development in the United Arab Emirates. *International Journal of Training and Development*, **5**(2): 153–165.

Wils, T., Luncasu, M. and Waxin, M.-F. 2007. Développement et validation d'un modèle de structuration des valeurs au travail. *Relations Industrielles/Industrial Relations*, **62**(2): 305–332.

Wils, T., Saba, T., Waxin, M.-F. and Labelle, C. 2011. Intergenerational and intercultural differences in work values in Quebec and the United Arab Emirates. *Relations Industrielles/Industrial Relations*, **66**(3): 445–469.

Wright, P. and McMahan, G. 1992. Theoretical perspectives for strategic HRM. *Journal of Management*, **18**: 295–320.

Yaseen, Z. and Khanfar, M. 2009. Sales training effectiveness: managers' perceptions in the United Arab Emirates organizations. *Business Review, Cambridge*, **13**(2): 120–128.

Yaseen, Z.K. 2013. Clarifying the strategic role of the HR managers in the UAE educational institutions. *Journal of Management and Sustainability*, **3**(2): 110–118.

Younies, H., Barhem, B. and Younis, M.Z. 2008. Ranking of priorities in employees' reward and recognition schemes from the perspective of UAE health care employees. *International Journal of Health Planning and Management*, **23**(4): 357–371.

Zhao, F., Scavarda, A.J. and Waxin, M.-F. 2012. Key issues and challenges in e-government development: an integrative case study of the number one ecity in the Arab world. *Information Technology and People*, **25**(4): 395–422.

8. Human resource management in Saudi Arabia

Hayfaa A. Tlaiss and Abdallah Elamin

INTRODUCTION

Ibn Sa'ud established the Kingdom of Saudi Arabia (KSA), the birthplace of Islam, as a monarchy in 1932. It is a large Arab country that has witnessed exponential economic growth since the discovery of oil in the 1930s and its commercialization in the 1970s. The rapidly growing economy attracted multinational corporations (MNCs) and created millions of jobs across the country (World Bank, 2004). However, this fast-paced development led to the marginalization of a local Saudi workforce lacking the education, skills and competencies needed to handle the newly created jobs. It also paved the way for an influx of cheap skilled and unskilled labour from the South Asian and Indian subcontinent and of experts from Western nations, thus creating a multicultural society.

Despite the cultural influences of expatriates and the country's spectacular transition to an urban society, KSA society and culture remains highly traditional and conservative. Traditions and customs, along with Islamic ideologies, continue to govern its legal, political, civil, societal and cultural spheres. Political and business life are strongly entrenched in patriarchal, tribal cultural values and are heavily influenced by a conservative religious society. These factors, along with high unemployment levels among Saudis, recent programmes of nationalization and the global attention that the status of women and human rights in KSA have received lately, created a complex business environment and numerous challenges for human resource management (HRM) in Saudi Arabia.

In this chapter, we first provide an overview of the major factors that impact the overall status of the workforce in Saudi Arabia, including various governmental reforms. Second, we will provide a brief overview pertaining to research on HRM in KSA, cover the challenges faced by the human resources (HR) departments and functions in KSA, and discuss the way forward. In our attempt to attend to the paucity of knowledge on various HRM practices in Saudi, we will discuss key findings from a larger study that looked at a set of traditional core HRM topics, such as selection and recruitment, performance appraisal and promotion, as well as the status of women, style of management and business ethics.

FACTORS INFLUENCING HR IN SAUDI ARABIA

Saudi Arabia is geographically the largest, economically the richest and demographically the most populated country among what is commonly known as the Gulf Cooperation Council (GCC) countries. The Saudi Arabian economy is dependent on oil and oil derivatives, which account for more than 90 per cent of the country's total exports, contribute around 75–80 per cent of government revenues and constitute around 55 per cent of the nation's gross domestic product (GDP) (Jadwa Investment, 2014). To minimize its reliance on oil, successive Saudi governments have exerted significant efforts to liberalize the economy by empowering the private sector and administering major reforms to speed up the country's integration into the world economy (Mellahi and Wood, 2001; Mellahi, 2006). Moreover, with a current population of 29.9 million, that is projected to grow to 46.3 million by 2030, local governments have also been actively trying to increase job creation for Saudis and better prepare the local workforce for employment using numerous educational and development initiatives (Al-Dosary and Rahman, 2005; Jadwa Investment, 2014).

As previously mentioned, the growing petroleum industry in Saudi Arabia and the development of major oil-related industries and projects created a huge demand for labour. The growing demand for labour could not be met locally as the majority of Saudis were Bedouins working as fishermen and lacking the skills needed. This labour shortage was further exacerbated by the Saudis' eagerness to secure jobs that local governments were providing in abundance in various sectors, including police stations, fire stations, local schools and other governmental facilities (Al-Asfour and Khan, 2014). The growing gap between labour demand and supply paved the way for a dramatic increase in the number of expatriates to cope with the booming oil industry and created a local private sector that is highly reliant on cheap foreign labour and labour-intensive occupations (Mellahi and Wood, 2001; Mellahi, 2006, 2007; Achoui, 2009; Al-Asfour and Khan, 2014). Although the influx of Western experts and South-East Asian and Indian skilled and unskilled labour reduced the labour shortage, they significantly impacted the landscape of the workforce in KSA.

Overview of Workforce Status

Despite the efforts of successive governments to increase the participation of Saudis in the local workforce, particularly in the private sector, high unemployment rates among Saudis continue to persevere for several demographic, cultural, economic and legal reasons. Demographically, the jobs created by successive governments have fallen short of attending closely to local needs as a result of high birth rates and the age of the local population. Accordingly, the youth unemployment rate in KSA stands at a record high rate of 30 per cent (Afiouni, Ruël and Schuler, 2014). KSA currently hosts one of the highest birth rates in the world, and its population is growing exponentially, at an estimated 2.15 per cent per year as reported in 2013 (Central Department of Statistics and Information, 2014; Jadwa Investment, 2014). With more than 60 per cent of the KSA population under the age of 21 (Mellahi, 2006), Saudi governments continue to face enormous difficulties in job creation and providing sustainable employment for young Saudis (Mellahi, 2007).

However, the problems in job creation are not only limited to high birth rates and population growth; they are also rooted in a number of cultural, societal and tradition-related factors. As previously noted, Saudi Arabian culture is patriarchal, masculine and high on power distance. Saudi society is highly stratified according to economic prosperity and access to power. Social status is also highly associated with both the type of work and sector of employment (Mellahi, 2007). Manual or technical work is often associated with lower social status. Therefore, Saudis are less likely to do similar work to avoid the social stigma associated with such jobs, having their pride hurt and to increase their social acceptance (Achoui, 2009). Moreover, nationals in KSA and other GCC countries are reluctant to 'apply' for jobs because the mere act of applying for a job is an indication of one's lack of power, connections (Harry, 2007), networks or *wasta* (Tlaiss, 2013), low social status and inability to land a job. Motivated by cultural values of high uncertainty avoidance, Saudis do not apply for jobs but rather contact their networks, connections and *wasta*, who provide them with access and help them land desired jobs in international banks and expanding Saudi firms. This posits a significant problem for HR departments that are swamped with unsolicited job applications and often forced to create unneeded positions and for Saudis to avoid upsetting powerful networks (Mellahi, 2006, 2007). In addition, recent studies suggest that young Saudis suffer from a high sense of entitlement, which creates further challenges for HR departments. In other words, supported by a strong cultural value of power distance and sense of pride, young Saudis feel entitled to higher salaries than those paid to foreign labour (Achoui, 2009). They prefer administrative or managerial jobs (Achoui, 2009) and expect to land middle to upper managerial positions as soon as they graduate from college (Al-Asfour and Khan, 2014). Such expectations often lead to the creation of two sets of HR practices in terms of recruitment and promotion: one for the local workforce and another for the expatriates. While the private sector and MNCs are less likely to provide such discriminatory practices, these preferential treatment practices continue to occur, are far from being ruled out and are a common practice in the public sector (Viviano, 2003; Al-Asfour and Khan, 2014). Hence, it does not come as a surprise that Saudis prefer working for government entities, which also offer job security, availability of educational and training opportunities, clear career paths, and the social status and power often associated with holding a managerial position in the public sector (Al-Asfour and Khan, 2014). Other compelling reasons underlining the oversaturation of Saudis in the public sector compared to the private sector include higher salaries, shorter working hours and more relaxed performance assessment procedures. Accordingly, while the local labour force accounts for 83.3 per cent and 79.8 per cent of the total labour force in the oil and gas sector which is government-owned/influenced and public sectors, respectively, it accounts for 38.9 per cent of total employment in the private sector (Achoui, 2009; Jadwa Investment, 2014).

High expectations among Saudis in terms of salaries and working conditions, along with a lack of needed skills and competencies in the local workforce, provide the private sector with ample reasons to continue to hire foreign workers who are less expensive to hire and who offer Western expertise that is easier to manage (Atiyyah, 1996; Mellahi and Wood, 2001). The perception that expatriates are easier to manage is further endorsed by virtue of the employment visas and work permits that allow the private sector to control expatriates, leaving them with minimal rights. In other words, work permits for expatriates in Saudi are granted under the sponsorship of a specific employer and for a specific job or occupation. Accordingly, foreign workers who cannot change jobs without the consent of their employers are left with little bargaining power (Viviano, 2003) and are more likely to tolerate the authoritative style of Arab management (Elamin, 2012) to maintain their jobs. While similar working conditions further support the widespread stereotype that foreign workers are more disciplined than their local counterparts (Mellahi, 2006, 2007), they have attracted the attention of international media and human rights groups calling for laws that protect foreign workers and grant them more rights and freedoms (Mellahi, 2006, 2007; Viviano, 2003).

The previously described issues illustrate the overall status of the workforce in Saudi Arabia and the various challenges that local governments face. Given the determination of KSA to reduce local unemployment and the dependency on and repercussions of a foreign labour force, the KSA government launched a series of reforms and human development initiatives which range from the enforcement of a nationalization strategy, through to the creation of King Abdallah's scholarship programme, the 'Vision' project, new laws granting foreign workers more rights, and further advancing the role of women in the kingdom.

REFORMS

Saudization: Objectives and Success

In an attempt to reduce the high levels of unemployment among Saudis, the oversaturation of the public sector by the local workforce, and as part of a bigger initiative to improve the HRM function in the private sector (Mellahi, 2007), the KSA government enforced a nationalization initiative in 1994 (Atiyyah, 1996; Al-Harbi, 1997). Saudi nationalization or Saudization is a development strategy that aims to facilitate the transfer of skills, knowledge and jobs from the foreign to the local workforce in a planned and phased way (Al-Harbi, 1997). It also obliges private companies to have a specific percentage of Saudi workers, which varies according to economic sectors. This created a quota system for private companies in terms of their local and international hires and ensured the increased employment of Saudis in the private sector.

To ensure the effectiveness of the Saudization process, local governments issued several subsequent laws to overcome the local unemployment dilemma. For example, in 2007, the government of Saudi Arabia issued a follow-up or an amendment to the original Saudization initiative that further explains the kingdom's strategic plan to ensure eventual full employment for Saudis through the initial control of unemployment, followed by its reduction, leading to the creation of a fully competent local labour force (Ministry of Labor, 2013). The follow-up also outlined quantifiable short-, mid- and long-term objectives that should serve as milestones guiding the efforts of the government to reduce local unemployment. Additionally, it illustrated new initiatives that the government is taking to further develop local human capital and improve the nation's overall productivity. Furthermore, motivated by the changing economic and demographic conditions and the need to increase the participation of Saudis in the local workforce, the Saudi government also launched the 'Vision' project (Saudi Government, 2002). The 'Vision' project focuses on economic diversification, development of HR, promoting the expansion of the private sector as an important partner and increasing the representation of the local workforce in the private sector.

In tandem with the Saudization strategy and its premise of human development, successive Saudi governments have invested heavily in the education of nationals to ensure their readiness to assume leadership roles in the future. These educational initiatives included the creation of national and international colleges, universities and centres for technical and vocational education. Today, the Kingdom hosts 24 universities, and a total of 508 national and international colleges are affiliated with these universities (Al-

Asfour and Khan, 2014). There are also 75 training institutes for vocational fields under the supervision of the General Organization for Technical Education and Vocational Training (GOTEVT) (Al-Dosary and Rahman, 2005). To enhance the exposure of Saudis to developed countries' education, sciences and business, King Abdullah launched the King Abdullah scholarship programme in 2005. This programme funds the educational pursuits of Saudi nationals around the world in countries including Canada, the United States and the United Kingdom for a period of five years. King Abdallah's scholarship is a major project that confirms the kingdom's commitment to the education and development of its locals, with 25 per cent of the country's budget spent on education in 2013 (Al-Asfour and Khan, 2014). In addition to its commitment to formal education, the Kingdom launched the 'Hafiz' initiative in 2011, which aims, through the creation of physical employment centres, job fairs, exhibitions and websites, to provide nationals under the age of 25 with instrumental support to help them gain employment.

The previously outlined educational and professional initiatives have been undertaken to further advance the Saudization process by creating infrastructure – a competent Saudi workforce that encourages private companies to hire locals. Nonetheless, the limited uptake by the private sector to Saudization (Mellahi, 2007) had resulted in a mere 13 per cent of Saudization at the end of 2012 (Al-Asfour and Khan, 2014). Despite relentless efforts, the local unemployment rate remains high (11.8 per cent) with more than 60 per cent of the Saudi workforce being expatriates (Jadwa Investment, 2014). Despite the private sector's realization that a serious long-term workforce management problem is lurking on the horizon and the necessity to attempt to lessen it (Al-Harbi, 1997), it continues to favour expatriates given their adequate qualifications, proficiency in English and cheap labour costs when compared to their Saudi counterparts (Ramady, 2010). Moreover, the resistance of Saudis to pursue certain types of careers that portray lower social status and the widespread stereotypes and perceptions among private employers that Saudis are less disciplined and more difficult to control than their foreign counterparts (Atiyyah, 1996; Ramady, 2010) discourages private employers from hiring Saudis and further questions the success of the Saudization initiative.

Another issue that questions the contribution of the Saudization initiative to increasing locals' employment levels in the private sector is that of the 'ghost workers' phenomenon. Despite the widespread negative stereotypes regarding performance levels of the local workforce, private employers are obliged to meet their quota of Saudi employees as outlined by the 'Nitaqat programme' in 2011. This obligation resulted in what is commonly known as the 'ghost workers' phenomenon, where private companies hire Saudi citizens, pay them a salary, but ask them not to come to work (Al-Asfour and Khan, 2014). This expensive phenomenon is commonly practised since it helps private companies to maintain high performance levels and avoid the low productivity levels associated with hiring locals. It also defies the objectives of the Saudization initiative as it creates the illusion that Saudi unemployment is decreasing. While this indeed might be the case in terms of Saudi employees listed on the payrolls of private companies, this practice draws attention to ethics in the Saudi Arabian workplace. It also highlights a significant gap in the psychological contracts between Saudis and private employers, and a lack of synchronization between government initiatives and HR-related practices in the private sector.

Accordingly, the success of the Saudization initiative in the private sector is questioned, particularly as the majority of progress has occurred in the public sector (Al-Dosary and

Rahman, 2005). To that end, Sadi (2013) argues that the Saudization process did not achieve its objectives because the government's focus was more on increasing the number of Saudis in the private sector and less on ensuring that they had the required education and skills. It has also reduced productivity given that some Saudis are not as qualified as foreign labour and are thus less productive and effective. Others argue that Saudization actually increased labour costs for private companies by forcing them to replace foreign workers with higher-paid Saudis (Sadi, 2013).

In the absence of concrete results or a reduction in the unemployment rate, there is no clear evidence to suggest that Saudization has been effective in reducing unemployment among young Saudis (Achoui, 2009). However, as previously mentioned, high unemployment among the local labour force is not the only workforce problem faced by KSA. The maltreatment of foreign labour, along with human rights violations and the subordination of women in the Kingdom, attracted global attention and resulted in the adoption of several relevant governmental reforms.

OTHER REFORMS

In an attempt to respond to external pressures from international organizations such as the World Trade Organization (WTO) and the International Labor Organization (ILO), and other external obligations, the Saudi government launched a set of laws and reforms in the private sector with the aim of meeting international standards related to the labour force. As part of an extensive framework to regulate the management of people in private organizations (Mellahi, 2007), these reforms included improvements in foreign labour laws and working conditions in private companies, as well as granting foreign workers social protection. New laws were also issued to grant and protect some basic legal rights of expatriates, including standardizing working hours, the right to annual leave, maternity leave, and health and safety measures. Laws relating to increasing minimum wages for Saudis were also revised in 2011 (Ministry of Labor, 2013) and wage increases were imposed to encourage young Saudis to join the private sector.

KSA has pursued several initiatives to improve the overall status of women in the country. These initiatives included campaigns to encourage the education of females and their participation in the labour force. Consequently, the number of females graduating from elementary, intermediate and secondary schools has been increasing since 2006. Females account for 30 per cent of Saudi students studying abroad and constitute more than 50 per cent of Saudi university graduates (Central Department of Statistics and Information, 2014). These advancements in women's education are confirmed by the Global Gender Gap Report (World Economic Forum, 2012) that highlights the significant improvement in education levels of women in the Middle East and North Africa (MENA) region and how the gender gap in education has closed by more than 90 per cent. They have also contributed to the increase in women's employment in the Kingdom and were further supported by the Nitaqat programme. According to the Ministry of Labor (2013), the number of women employed in the private sector has tripled since 2011, to reach a total of 180,000 by the end of 2012. In total, the number of Saudi women employees increased from 55,000 in 2010 to a staggering 398,538 in 2013. Moreover, the overall unemployment rate of Saudis fell from 12.1 per cent in 2012 to

11.7 per cent in 2013 as a result of the reduction in female unemployment from 35.7 per cent to 33.2 per cent between 2012 and 2013 (Jadwa Investment, 2014). These improvements have been attributed to the increase in women's education and the 'Saudization and Feminization of Industrial Jobs for Women' initiative that was launched in 2011 (Ministry of Labor, 2013). This initiative facilitated women's participation in the labour force and reduced the social and cultural pressures that working Saudi women face by providing them with various work options, such as working from home and job sharing.

Despite increased educational attainment levels and labour force participation, more than 33 per cent of Saudi females were unemployed in 2013. Saudi women represent a mere 20 per cent of the Saudi workforce (Central Department of Statistics and Information, 2014) and are mostly employed by the public sector (62 per cent). Despite the various governmental initiatives to reduce social and culture pressures, local women continue to struggle to find the right balance between their plans for career advancement and the expectations of a conservative Saudi society in terms of gender roles and stereotypes (Al-Asfour and Khan, 2014). According to Harry (2007), Saudi women are mainly employed in education, health services and the public sector because working for the government is less of a shame or '*aib*' than working for private companies. Despite its status as one of the most economically and commercially liberal Islamic countries, Saudi Arabia adopts a very conservative approach to social and gender matters as women continue to cluster in what are traditionally known as 'feminine' education and employment choices, such as the humanities, arts, teaching and healthcare. Accordingly, the limited presence of females in labour-intensive jobs (jobs that are often perceived as masculine) is not surprising and posits a serious question as to the impact of the Saudization initiative on the increased participation of women in the labour force (Harry, 2007). Furthermore, in a recent study that solicited the attitudes of more than 300 Saudi men to working women in Saudi Arabia, Elamin and Omair (2010) reported that Saudi men do not have a favourable attitude towards working women. This negative attitude is fuelled by widespread gender discrimination and stereotypes that limit the responsibilities of women to the private realm, which further hinders women's attempts to join the workforce and build careers. The researchers in this latter study also stressed the encumbering role that traditional interpretations of verses in the Quran that pertain to women's mobility and freedom (e.g., the non-mixing of men and women in several work environments) have on further tightening the grip of societal constraints on Saudi women's attempts to join the labour force. These societal, cultural and religious barriers are often reflected within organizational boundaries through structural and attitudinal barriers that hinder the advancement of working women through the ranks and create further challenges for HR departments trying to support women's careers and create women-friendly organizational cultures.

THE CURRENT STATE OF HRM IN GCC AND KSA

Amid this intertwined web of economic, legal, cultural and demographic factors impacting the overall status of the workforce in Saudi Arabia, one topic is largely absent, that is, the focus on HRM practices in organizations in Saudi Arabia, although there have been some exceptions (e.g., Elamin, 2012). To explore the current state of HRM in

Saudi Arabia, we used several strategies. As suggested by Afiouni, Karam and El-Hajj (2013), we searched Emerald and Scopus databases using a number of keywords, such as human resource management/policies/practices, personnel, and others in combination with Islam, culture, Saudi Arabia and GCC. We then repeated this keyword search within the databases of a number of journals such as *International Journal of Human Resources Management* (*IJHRM*) and *Personnel Review*. As reported by Afiouni, Karam and El-Hajj (2013), interest in HRM in the Arab world in general is minimal, with 23 articles published between the mid-1990s and 2006 that are related to HRM and the larger Arab world, including the GCC and several countries in the Levant area.

Nonetheless, things have been improving, and interest in HRM in the Arab world has been growing, slowly but surely. In 2007, Budhwar and Mellahi (2007) guest edited the first special issue on HRM in the Middle East in the *IJHRM*, noting the scarcity of research on HRM practices in the region, and urged scholars to undertake relevant research to attend to this lack of knowledge. This call, along with the major demographic, political and economic changes that the region has been witnessing, increased scholars' interest in conducting HRM-related research in the Arab world. Gradually, research on HRM in the Arab world gained momentum, and a more recent special issue on HRM in the Middle East was edited by Afiouni, Ruël and Schuler (2014) and published in the *IJHRM*. As the number of studies looking at various HRM issues in the Middle East started to increase, HRM researchers have gradually come to realize the importance of understanding the context-specific nature of HRM in this region (Budhwar and Mellahi, 2007). They have also come a long way in understanding how HRM practices are impacted by the uniqueness of the situation in almost every Arab country, albeit with widely perceived commonalities. In addition to the growing interest in HRM in the Middle East, interest in exploring the relationship between Islam and HR practices continues to grow, as illustrated in the recent special issue on 'Islam and HRM' edited by Mellahi and Budhwar and published in *Personnel Review* in 2010. Another area of research that has been attracting a significant amount of attention is the relationship between Islam, Arab culture and traditions, and gender; this has been reflected in the proliferation of related studies in various Arab countries (Tlaiss, 2013), including to a lesser extent, Saudi Arabia (Al-Ahmadi, 2011).

However, while research interest in HRM in several Arab countries, including Oman (Al-Hamadi, Budhwar and Shipton, 2007), Jordan (AL-Husan, AL-Hussan and Perkins, 2014) and the United Arab Emirates (UAE) (Harry, 2007; Al-Waqfi and Forstenlechner, 2014) continues to grow, the same cannot be claimed about Saudi Arabia. Moreover, currently available studies on HRM in the GCC are skewed towards the UAE, with minimal information on HRM and related topics in Saudi Arabia. For example, in the most recent special issue on HRM in the Middle East published by *IJHRM* (Afiouni, Ruël and Schuler, 2014), 50 per cent of the studies looked at HRM-related issues in the UAE while none looked at Saudi Arabia.

Present State of HRM in the KSA

Interest in HRM and human resources development (HRD) practices in Saudi Arabia is in its infancy, with relevant knowledge almost non-existent until early 2000. Despite the increase in recent studies that seek to understand the various factors that impact the management and development of HR in Saudi Arabia (e.g., Mellahi, 2006, 2007; Ramlall, Maimani and Diab, 2011; Elamin, 2012), our knowledge of how core HRM practices are executed within Saudi organizations remains minimal. If and when studies are available, these studies often deal with random isolated issues.

For example, Mellahi and Wood (2001) stressed the influence of national culture on HRM and the impact of Islam on managerial attitudes and practices. They also revealed how the emphasis Islam places on marriage and childbearing has been a major factor hindering the active participation of women in the workforce. Mellahi (2006) focused on highlighting the differences in HRM practices between the public and the private sectors in KSA. While the practice of HRM in public organizations continues to be hindered by cultural values and the salience of *wasta*, HR managers operate two sets of HRM practices: a lax one for Saudis that results in high salaries and low standards and a relatively standardized set of practices for expatriates. Private employers grant these luxuries to Saudis to encourage them to join the private sector and to meet the quotas imposed by Saudization (Mellahi, 2006). Ramlall, Maimani and Diab (2011) looked at compensation practices and plan effectiveness in Saudi Arabia and reported that employees in Saudi Arabia have little input into the design and implementation of compensation schemes. The HR managers solicited in this study stated that pay in Saudi Arabia is tied more to seniority than to performance and that the salaries of Saudis do not follow any scale and are case-specific. Other available studies are mostly interested in various organizational behaviour constructs, such as job satisfaction (Elamin, 2012), and their impact on HRM practices. For example, in this latter study, the author revealed that organizational justice has a significant impact on employees' commitment in Saudi Arabia. Consequently, he argues that by understanding the role that organizational justice plays in employee commitment, HR managers would be better able to find ways to distribute workloads, responsibilities and rewards among employees in a manner that improves their overall work-related attitudes.

Accordingly, to date, there is limited research exploring how the local context, its workforce situation, and employment regulations influence some of the HRM practices of private organizations in Saudi Arabia. There is also no clear understanding of how core HRM practices, such as selection and recruitment, promotions, and training and development, are actually carried out in the private sector.

HRM AND RESOURCING IN KSA: AN EMPIRICAL STUDY

In an attempt to attend to the paucity of knowledge regarding traditional topics related to HRM such as selection and recruitment, and training and development, the current study (conducted by the authors) supports a growing interest among international and regional scholars in further exploring HRM in developing countries and understanding its role in light of a dynamic and ever-changing business world. Unlike other studies in the region that have solely focused on understanding the impact of localization initiatives (e.g., Al-Waqfi and Forstenlechner, 2014), the current study is more interested in understanding HRM practices in Saudi Arabia, given various national and organizational influences. Its primary objective is to better understand how HRM practices of recruitment, selection, and training and development are carried out within existing private Saudi Arabian organizations and how do local national factors and institutional environments influence them.

Due to its exploratory nature, the study was conducted using a qualitative approach that capitalized on face-to-face, semi-structured interviews with HR managers. Access to HR managers was secured through snowball sampling and the personal networks and connections of the authors. The interviewees were promised complete anonymity throughout the process. The interviews were all tape-recorded and lasted between 50 and 90 minutes. Interviewees were asked questions about some traditional core HRM practices, such as selection, recruitment, compensation, performance appraisal, training and development, and promotion. Given that some of the interviews were conducted in Arabic or were a mix of Arabic and English, the manuscripts were translated and back-translated by the researchers and an independent bilingual researcher familiar with the area of research. The interviews were directly transcribed and coded using thematic analysis.

Our interviewees worked in medium to large organizations (with more than 100 employees), in various organizations across the private sector, including health services, education and financial services, in Riyadh, Jeddah and Mekka. All the interviewees had at least a tertiary level of education and at least five years of experience in their work domain. The interviewees were between the age of 31 and 57 years and were married with at least one child. A total of 11 interviews were conducted.

Recruitment and Selection: Expatriates versus Saudis

When asked about selection and recruitment practices, the Saudi nationalization movement seemed very relevant despite the lack of consensus on what Saudization really meant and the highly diverse definitions provided by HR managers. As the HR manager of a hospital in Riyadh said: 'Localization or Saudization is a very broad concept . . . and every company interprets it in the manner that it sees suitable.' Accordingly, it was unsurprising to find that the interviewees were split between perceiving it as: (a) a burden that HR managers have to meet in terms of quotas regarding the percentage of locals on the payroll, and (b) a significant government initiative to ensure the transfer of knowledge from expatriates to Saudis.

Concerning the actual recruitment and selection processes and the impact of Saudization on HRM practices, the majority of the interviewees confirmed the existence of one set of rules and standards for Saudis and another for expatriates. According to the HR managers interviewed, the recruitment of expatriates is usually through commonly used recruitment procedures, such as sending résumés to HR specialists, delivering résumés to HR departments or being recommended by professional recruitment companies. Although several factors, such as years of education and experience, proficiency in the English language, and skills and competencies, are considered during the selection process, the actual selection remains arbitrary as factors such as 'how well they would get along with their boss' are prioritized. Some of the responses were as follows:

> . . . I also ask the department managers to interview potential candidates because it is very important for the new employees to get along with their direct supervisors. In the past we

> hired individuals that had all the required skills but did not click with their boss. This impacted their performance and we had to let them go. So I pay attention to avoid similar situations. (HR Manager, Insurance Company, Riyadh)

When reflecting on the impact of Saudization on the recruitment and selection of expatriates, the interviewed HR managers stressed the negative consequences of the nationalization movement. They complained about the resulting difficulties in obtaining work visas for foreigners and the black market for visas, where ghost companies are willing to sell their quota of foreign workers to other companies for large amounts of money.

As for the recruitment and selection of Saudis, the HR managers described the difficulty in having a pool of potential local candidates as Saudis are less likely to submit their CVs online or to use a hiring company for vacant positions. To solve this problem, and meet the requirements of Saudization and quotas for hiring young locals, the interviewees had to find alternative approaches. These approaches included participating in local career and job fairs, contacting local colleges and universities to offer internships to Saudis with good academic standings and attending the graduation ceremonies of Saudi students studying abroad that are usually held at Saudi Arabian Cultural Bureaus. In terms of recruiting Saudis for more senior positions, the services of local headhunters and networks and connections for referrals were capitalized on. The HR managers for a training and development company in Mekka stated:

> Although the number of Saudi applications that we are receiving online has been increasing, it is rarely enough. So what I generally do is get in touch with the Deans of some local schools for some recommendations or contact some of my connections for nominations. (HR Manager, Training and Development Company, Mekka)

To attract young Saudis and meet the Saudization quota, HR managers offer locals higher salaries than those given to expatriates for doing the same job. The duality of standards also extends to selection criteria that are usually lowered when extending offers to locals. HR managers also emphasized the role that *wasta* plays in the selection process. Several interviewees described situations where the Saudi with the strongest *wasta* and not the strongest profile was selected.

> To be honest, it is very well known that the qualifications of the Saudi workforce are gradually improving, but for now, it is less than what the expatriates are bringing to the table. Therefore, to meet our Saudization quotas, we sometimes find ourselves hiring Saudis from unrelated majors, for example, and we train them and help them learn what our jobs require. (HR Manager, Hospital, Riyadh)

Training and Development: Expatriates versus Saudis

The HR managers interviewed stated that firms in the private sector rarely have a HR development strategy and referred to the absence of long-term development strategies emphasizing continuous education and learning. Training and development activities are rarely perceived as a priority or accounted for in budgets. If and when training actually occurs, it is done on an ad hoc basis without collecting any feedback from employees or conducting a needs assessment. Nonetheless, the interviewees stressed the organizational needs for various on- and off-the-job training, including decision making, time management and motivation, as well as providing new hires with mentors and coaches. The majority of the interviewees also seemed frustrated with their organizations as training and development continues to be perceived as an expense rather than an investment. To that effect, the HR manager of a hospital in Riyadh said:

> Despite the fact that we are in the health services industry, which is constantly improving and becoming highly technical and digitized, every year I have to fight to convince the senior managers of the need to allocate a bigger budget to the development of our staff in various means, including training.

When comparing the interest levels of Saudis and expatriates in training and development opportunities, the HR managers stated that expatriates are usually more eager to participate in training opportunities and are happy to attend development workshops. The Saudis were described as less enthusiastic or keen on taking any development opportunity because of their sense of entitlement and the Saudization initiative that guarantees them a secure job and a salary. According to the HR manager of an educational institute in Jeddah:

> The training opportunities offered are the same to all our employees. However, the way they are received is different. For example, we often offer our teachers the opportunity to attend workshops or seminars about new ways of teaching or instruments to be used in classroom teaching. However, our expatriate teachers are always the first to register their names. Sometimes, I find myself contacting Saudi teachers from different departments to encourage them to go to these workshops.

KEY CHALLENGES

In the absence of empirical studies on HRM practices in Saudi Arabia, we have attempted to explore both the current status of recruitment, selection, and training and development practices and the contextual factors that impact these practices. We also provide insights into what is actually happening and the resulting challenges for HRM in KSA.

Concerning recruitment and selection, the duality of standards between Saudi employees and expatriates posits serious concerns regarding corruption and discrimination and the challenge that HR departments face in their attempts to administer sound HRM practices. Lowering of standards in order to recruit Saudis and create a pool of candidates to meet nationalization requirements in Saudi Arabia is problematic and alarming for various reasons. First, it undermines billions of dollars that are being invested by the government to enhance the educational levels of young Saudis. Second, it questions the usefulness of governmental initiatives, such as the Hafiz programme, in changing the 'pride' mentality of young Saudis who consider applying for jobs to be a sign of lower social status. Third, it provides a disservice to Saudis and reduces any initiative to excel in educational pursuits with the express aim of securing a good job, since graduates with widely divergent grades are being hired to meet quotas. Even when academic qualifications are used as selection criteria, the influence of *wasta* outweighs them. Fourth, it provides further evidence of the failure of the Saudization initiative and the Nitaqat programme to achieve their objectives since HR departments seem more concerned with quantity rather than quality. Although the current study perceives the rationale for Saudization from economic, political and demographic perspectives to be a worthwhile endeavour that emphasizes the development of Saudi human capital, the strategy needs to be modified. In its current form and manner of execution, it seems to fall short of executing its objectives and lacks the commitment of HR managers. The empirical data collected highlighted the need for the development of a clear mechanism to enhance the execution of Saudization in a local context.

Moreover, by handing Saudis high salaries and fast career paths, the motivation to perform and excel is removed, leading to the salience of the stereotype that Saudi employees are ineffective and inefficient. *Wasta* and connections also play a role in determining salaries for Saudis and their recruitment and selection. As Saudi salaries continue to be determined on a case-by-case basis (Mellahi and Wood, 2001), the double standards used in the selection and recruitment processes for Saudis and expatriates result in feelings of inequity, run counter to Islamic teachings and reduce the productivity of employees, and the country, by extension, which again opposes the core objectives of the Saudization programme. These findings make us question the rationale underlining government regulations and excessive interference in local HRM, especially as the consequences of these regulations prove to be counterproductive to Saudis, government attempts to advance the local workforce, and the further development of the country.

Despite significant government investment in developing Saudi human capital, local organizations perceive the training and development of their human capital as an expense rather than an investment. Accordingly, we argue that rather than focusing on meeting quotas, the Saudi government should focus on regulations that compel private companies to allocate a certain percentage of their profits to various HRD activities, including training and development. If the Saudi government is indeed committed to improving the quality and development of local human capital, bringing the public and private sector on board for a national strategy that is committed to investing in the development of that human capital, in addition to providing formal education, is imperative. However, the efforts of government alone are insufficient. Although HR departments in Western countries have long been perceived as strategic partners affecting employee performance and organizational competitiveness, HR managers in Saudi Arabia seem constrained by an authoritative style of management and are hesitant to ask for money to execute training. This finding questions the perception of Saudi senior management to HR departments, their role and their contribution to the organizational decision-making process. The lack of power and decision-making authority that the HR managers in this study reported creates a further challenge for HR departments and managers to claim their role as strategic partners rather than merely responsible for hiring and payroll, as noted by Dirani (2006) in the context of HR managers in Lebanon.

RECOMMENDATIONS AND WAY FORWARD

Hindered by governmental regulations, the salience of cultural values and expectations, and the prevalence and importance of connections and *wasta*, current HRM practices in Saudi Arabia seem to promote a discriminatory model that is lax, supportive, tolerant, flexible and paternalistic for Saudis and strict, tough, competitive and authoritative for foreigners. As per the suggestions made by Mellahi (2006, 2007), we argue for the need to change current disruptive workplace practices that treat foreign workers unequally. Rather than using recruitment and selection practices that further enhance inter-group differences, HR managers should be focusing on embracing diversity and its potential contribution by facilitating communication and collaboration. Moreover, government regulations that are constantly changing and that do not portray a clear HRM strategy seem to further augment the resistance to Saudization. These findings suggest the urgent need for an upward flow in feedback to management, which has long been resisted in Saudi as noted by Mellahi (2007). To ensure that Saudization along with other government initiatives meet their intended objectives, the feedback of the private sector needs to be solicited and recognized, in an attempt to avoid adverse effects. Furthermore, to enhance the globalization of Saudi products and organizations, the Saudi government needs to take serious measures to eliminate all forms of discrimination, including those in recruitment requirements and salary differentials. As such, future studies should be concerned with developing frameworks to make government legislation more responsive to the experiences of the private sector. Future research should also consider ways to transform government legislation so that it meets local requirements and realities, particularly that pertaining to the quality of young Saudi human capital. Widespread cultural values that consider applying for a job to be demeaning to one's pride and the dependence on *wasta* and connections are, in principle, counter-intuitive to the government's efforts to educate the local workforce and provide Saudis with instrumental support to help them gain employment. If indeed Saudis continue to rely on *wasta* to access employment, KSA will not realize any return on the billions of dollars spent on educating the local workforce. Moreover, Saudis will not be able to take pride in their achievements as they have been handed to them.

Moving forward, our study has a number of implications for theory and practice. Our review and empirical findings clearly depict how macro-level factors impact HRM at the organizational level. They also highlight the difficulty in implementing Western-based HRM practices in Saudi Arabia given the idiosyncrasies of cultural values and nationalization regulations. Although this study is not specifically looking at the controversy of standardizing versus localizing HRM policies and practices in the Middle East, its findings further contribute to the debate on whether HRM in the Arab region needs a specific model that is capable of capturing the different levels or factors that impact HRM. To this extent, we argue that adopting a multilevel approach that integrates the cultural, socioeconomic, political and Islamic factors shaping HR factors and HRM practices seems pivotal. While calling for a more cultural-bound approach to HRM practices in Saudi Arabia, we support attempts by Afiouni, Karam and El-Hajj (2013) to identify the contours of an Arab Middle Eastern HR model. We also support the notion of developing professional HR functions that take the unique cultural and demographic factors of KSA into consideration, while focusing on developing better techniques for talent management. We argue that the road to the creation of a highly skilled labour force is lengthy in the absence of organizational HRD strategies that consider education and continuous learning as priorities. Moreover, bound by our scepticism towards the prevailing localization policies and how the structural and cultural barriers hinder their effective implementation, we argue for governmental intervention to facilitate the creation of a strategic fit between HR practices and business strategies in KSA. Accordingly, HR systems should not merely mimic HR systems in the West but rather be sensitive to the context and make adjustments accordingly. Legislative regulations against discrimination are strongly welcomed as they portray the commitment of the Kingdom to respecting human rights and further support the attempts of local organizations to partake in global opportunities. Nationalization efforts are also welcomed if they aim to find suitable employment options for young Saudis rather than handing them managerial positions. Nonetheless, for change to actually occur, Saudis need to have the desire to change and the commitment to persevere.

CONCLUSION

Despite the passing of King Abdallah, the turmoil that the Arab Middle East region is facing and declining oil prices, King Salman declared his commitment to pursuing the late King Abdallah's vision in terms of economic reforms, redistribution of wealth, enhancing the livelihood of Saudis, focusing on local workforce development, and education among others. Accordingly, education was the key focus area in 2015's expansionary budget. As evident in the recent cabinet changes, King Salman is interested in hearing from younger Saudis and involving them in decision-making processes. Now, more than ever, the Kingdom is devoted to its citizens and their well-being, with the aim of avoiding triggering any form of social unrest or increasing local unemployment. This commitment, along with the Kingdom's huge untapped foreign reserves and low debt to GDP ratio, did not impact the economic situation of the Kingdom and had no effect on the expansionary oil and gas projects mostly managed by MNCs.

Given the new Saudi leadership's commitment to better preparing the Kingdom for the challenges ahead, a major campaign to raise awareness among Saudis is essential. This campaign should aim to help Saudis take pride in their educational pursuits and their ability to land a job without the interference of external parties or *wasta*. It should also work on reducing the sense of entitlement that Saudis have and encourage Saudi employees to pursue training opportunities in order to enhance their human capital and market competiveness. The campaign can also capitalize on Islamic values that promote hard work and its value, by urging individuals to be productive and effective, reject unfairness, dishonesty and discrimination, uphold the equality of all human beings and consider any financial reward that was not lawfully earned as forbidden. However, to ensure the success of such a campaign and to help create a more responsible generation of young Saudis, the government needs to revisit the Saudization process and the Nitaqat programme. The focus should therefore shift away from quantity and meeting quotas and be more focused on ensuring that Saudis have the necessary education, training, skills and experience before being hired for a job. The government should also grant private companies more flexibility to punish the poor performance of Saudi employees; this will significantly reduce both the sense of entitlement and the relaxed approach to a job and performance that many Saudis display. It will also facilitate the process of eradicating all the duality that currently exists in HRM practices in the private sector. Accordingly, the same recruitment and selection standards should apply to all employees, in line with the Islamic standards of fairness, equality and justice. Saudis should be encouraged to trust themselves, apply for jobs through regular recruitment channels and refrain from using *wasta*. Corruption in all its forms, including the use of *wasta*, should be strictly punished. To conclude, we believe that young Saudis and future generations hold the key to success that will allow them to overcome future challenges.

USEFUL WEBSITES

http://www.sa.undp.org/.
https://data.un.org/CountryProfile.aspx?crName=Saudi%20Arabia.
http://www.mep.gov.sa/themes/Dashboard/index.jsp.

REFERENCES

Achoui, M.M. 2009. Human resource development in Gulf countries: an analysis of the trends and challenges facing Saudi Arabia. *Human Resource Development International*, **12**(1): 35–46.

Afiouni, F., Karam, C.M. and El-Hajj, H. 2013. The HR value proposition model in the Arab Middle East: identifying the contours of an Arab Middle Eastern HR model. *International Journal of Human Resource Management*, **24**(10): 1895–1932.

Afiouni, F., Ruël, H. and Schuler, R. 2014. HRM in the Middle East: toward a greater understanding, *International Journal of Human Resource Management*, **25**(2): 133–143.

Al-Ahmadi, H. 2011. Challenges facing women leaders in Saudi Arabia, *Human Resource Development International*, **14**(2): 149–166.

Al-Asfour, A. and Khan, S.A. 2014. Workforce localization in the Kingdom of Saudi Arabia: issues and challenges, *Human Resource Development International*, **17**(2): 243–253.

Al-Dosary, A.S. and Rahman, S.M. 2005. Saudization (localization) – a critical review. *Human Resource Development International*, **8**(4): 495–502.

Al-Hamadi, A.B., Budhwar, P. and Shipton, H. 2007. Managing human resources in the Sultanate of Oman. *International Journal of Human Resource Management*, **18**: 100–113.

Al-Harbi, K. 1997. Markov analysis of Saudization in engineering companies. *Journal of Management in Engineering*, **13**(2): 87–91.

AL-Husan, F.B., AL-Hussan, F.B. and Perkins, S.T. 2014. Multilevel HRM systems and intermediating variables in MNCs: longitudinal case study research in Middle Eastern settings. *International Journal of Human Resource Management*, **25**(2): 234–251.

Al-Waqfi, M.A. and Forstenlechner, I. 2014. Barriers to Emiratization: the role of policy design and institutional environment in determining the effectiveness of Emiratization. *International Journal of Human Resource Management*, **25**(2): 167–189.

Atiyyah, H.S. 1996. Expatriate acculturation in Arab Gulf countries. *Journal of Management Development*, **15**(5): 37–47.

Budhwar, P. and Mellahi, K. 2007. Introduction: human resources management in the Middle East. *International Journal of Human Resource Management*, **18**(1): 2–10.

Central Department of Statistics and Information 2014. The Kingdom of Saudi Arabia. http://www.cdsi.gov.sa/ (accessed 23 August 2014).

Dirani, K. 2006. Exploring socio-cultural factors that influence HRD practices in Lebanon. *Human Resource Development International*, **9**(1): 85–98.

Elamin, A.M. 2012. Perceived organizational justice and work-related attitudes: a study of Saudi employees. *World Journal of Entrepreneurship, Management and Sustainable Development*, **8**(1): 71–88.

Elamin, A.M. and Omair, K. 2010. Males' attitudes towards working females in Saudi Arabia. *Personnel Review*, **39**(6): 746–766.

Harry, W. 2007. Employment creation and localization: the crucial human resource issues for the GCC. *International Journal of Human Resource Management*, **18**(1): 132–146.

Jadwa Investment 2014. *Macroeconomic Update: Economic Projections for 2014*. Riyadh, KSA: Jadwa Investment.

Mellahi, K. 2006. Human resource management in Saudi Arabia. In P.S. Budhwar and K. Mellahi (eds), *Managing Human Resources in the Middle East*. London: Routledge, pp. 97–122.

Mellahi, K. 2007. The effect of regulations on HRM: private sector firms in Saudi Arabia. *International Journal of Human Resource Management*, **18**(1): 85–99.
Mellahi, K. and Wood, G. 2001. Human resource management in Saudi Arabia. In P.S. Budhwar and Y. Debrah (eds), *Human Resource Management in Developing Countries*. London: Routledge, pp. 135–152.
Ministry of Labor 2013. *The Annual Statistical Report*. Ministry of Labor, Government of the Kingdom of Saudi Arabia.
Ramady, M.A. 2010. Population and demographics: *Saudization* and the labor market. In *The Saudi Arabian Economy: Policies, Achievements, and Challenges*, 2nd edn. New York: Springer, pp. 351–393.
Ramlall, S., Maimani, K. and Diab, A. 2011. Compensation practices and plan effectiveness in Saudi Arabia. *Compensation and Benefits Review*, **43**(1): 52–60.
Sadi, M. 2013. The implementation process of nationalization of workforce in Saudi Arabian private sector: a review of 'Nitaqat Scheme'. *American Journal of Business and Management*, **2**(1): 37–45.
Saudi Government 2002. Vision symposium on Saudi economy 2020. Paper presented at a symposium organized by the Saudi government, 19–23 October 2002.
Tlaiss, H. 2013. Women managers in the United Arab Emirates: successful careers or what? *Equality, Diversity, and Inclusion: An International Journal*, **32**(8): 756–776.
Viviano, F. 2003. Kingdom on edge: Saudi Arabia. *National Geographic*. http://ngm.nationalgeographic.com/features/world/asia/saudi-arabia/saudi-arabia-text (accessed 5 March 2013).
World Bank 2004. *Unlocking the Employment Potential in the Middle East and North Africa: Toward a New Social Contract*. Washington, DC: World Bank.
World Economic Forum 2012. *The Global Gender Gap Report*. Switzerland: World Economic Forum.

Section B

Human Resource Management in Levant Countries

9. Human resource management in Iran

Pari Namazie and Amir Mohammad Pahlavnejad

INTRODUCTION AND BACKGROUND

Iran is a country rich in resources, both natural and human. It has the world's largest hydrocarbon reserve base, the third largest oil reserves and the largest gas reserves. Iran is also the third largest oil producer in the Organization of Petroleum Exporting Countries (OPEC) after Saudi Arabia and Iraq. Further, Iran has been the Middle East and North Africa (MENA) region's second largest economy, after Saudi Arabia, and has the second largest population, after Egypt.

Similar challenges face many countries in the MENA region, such as unequal wealth distribution, youth bulge, high unemployment, low female labour force participation rates, low levels of private sector development, weak public and corporate governance, large public sectors, limited competition and high levels of corruption (Cordesman et al., 2013). Iran has a young population, with approximately 40 per cent of Iran's 77 million population being between the ages of 15 and 40 (Atieh Bahar Consulting, 2014), thus putting great pressure on the country to provide education and employment opportunities in order to maintain social stability. Iran, similar to the MENA region nations, suffers high youth unemployment (ages 15–24), which currently stands at 18.6 per cent (Atieh Bahar Consulting, 2014). The Iranian population is highly literate – adult literacy (percentage of people ages 15 and above) was reported at 84 and youth literacy (percentage of people ages 15–24) reported at 98.66 (World Bank, 2016). Sixty-nine per cent of the population are urban dwellers (Trading Economics, 2011), one of the factors which has placed Iran on the Goldman Sachs (2007) list of the next 11 emerging economies after the BRIC (Brazil, Russia, India and China) nations.

Although the Iranian economy has developed and industrialised significantly over the past decades, the country faces a number of significant challenges, both internally and externally. Internally, although Iran has witnessed economic growth, it has been hampered by high inflation, elevated unemployment, underemployment and brain drain (Ilias, 2009; Khajehpour, 2009), in addition to economic mismanagement, widespread economic inefficiency, corruption, political instability and social and demographic issues. External challenges are due to continued and heightened sanctions against Iran, mainly because of Iran's nuclear ambitions. Various forms and measures of sanctions have been imposed on Iran since 1979, focused on isolating Iran from international financial and commercial systems. Recent sanctions not only target international companies operating in Iran, but also foreign and Iranian banks have been undermined by sanctions. Recent sanctions on Iran, effective since July 2012, include an oil embargo imposed by the European Union (EU), forcing countries to stop importing oil from Iran. At the time of finalising this chapter, a framework agreement was signed by Iran and the world powers (2 April 2015) which aims to significantly decrease Iran's nuclear ambitions in return for an ease in sanctions. Should this agreement stand, it will have a very positive impact on Iran's economic and international development.

This chapter explores human resources management (HRM) in Iran. It begins by examining the Iranian context and explores factors such as history, economy, demography, national culture and socio-economic developments, religion, management and leadership in Iran. The chapter further discusses HR developments in Iran and shares research findings on HRM in ten companies, consisting of both local private sector and multinational corporations (MNCs), to highlight the nature of the human resource (HR) function. Lastly, the chapter presents the key challenges faced by HRM and its future in Iran.

THE IRANIAN CONTEXT

The following section discusses the Iranian context and key points which have shaped and influenced Iran, both in the past and in the present day. This includes a review of Iran's main historic developments, the current Iranian economy, demography, women and socio-economic trends, national culture and the role of religion and management.

History

History has a role to play in how national culture is shaped and, in turn, how HRM develops in a given country. Table 9.1 highlights Iran's history and the influence of events on the Iranian psyche and culture.

As the table below shows, Iran and Iranians show a strong ability to survive and adapt. Throughout its history, the Iranian race has placed a great deal of importance on education and scientific and literary knowledge; however, there has been in many cases a gap in the level of understanding between educated legislators and the needs of the ordinary people. But Iran has survived by being individualistic and flexible, and by maintaining a strong in-group orientation, showing loyalty to friends and family and building strong networks. This shows the deep-rootedness of culture and how, as HRM takes shape in Iran, these factors will need to be heeded and developed in line with cultural realities.

Economy

Iran's economy is faced with a number of challenges including: high inflation, job creation, unemployment, subsidy reform, sanctions and lack of foreign investment (Atieh International, 2014). Through the years, Iran has suffered with an economy marked by statist policies and an inefficient state sector. Although rich in resources, the economy has relied on oil as a major source of government revenues. Table 9.2 shows some key economic indicators of Iran.

As the figures above show, Iran shows economic growth; however, it suffers with high inflation (over 30 per cent) and has an official unemployment rate of over 10 per cent (unofficial unemployment is over 18 per cent). The youth unemployment rate is 22.2 per cent.

The newly appointed moderate government of Mr Rohani (June 2013) announced its highest priority to be in the field of economic development, with the promise to pay greater attention to containing unemployment and providing incentives for job creation and new investments. Salehi Esfahani (2005) argues that perhaps the most important economic event of the last century in Iran has been the transition from high to low fertility.

Table 9.1 Historic developments and the influence on Iranian national culture

History	Impact on Culture
Ancient civilisation dating back 6,000 years	Sense of pride, good scientific and literary knowledge
	Values: humility, justice, community
	Strong sense of equality and fair treatment for all races, ethnic groups, religions
	Sense of survival
Islamisation in 7th century	Survival and adaptation
	Maintaining Persian as opposed to Arabic
	Shi'a Islam as opposed to Sunni
	Translating to a deep sense of survival and individualism
	Distrust towards power, gives rise to strong in-group orientation and reducing the radius of trust
	Importance of relationships and loyalty
20th century	2 revolutions: Constitutional 1906 and Islamic 1979
	1920–1930s saw period of rapid modernisation, new laws; universities and centres for higher education were established for men and women
	Iran's first administrative and employment law was written in 1922 based on a merit system, equal opportunity and fair play; revised in 1966
	1963 women's right to vote and run for office
	1965 first woman minister appointed
	1970s oil boom years, fast-paced economic growth
	Rapid modernisation which was not aligned with country's socio-economic realities
	1979 Islamic revolution replaced monarchy with an Islamic republic
	Major Iranian industries were nationalised, many industrialists left the country creating a major leadership and workforce skills gap
	Women forced into early retirement
	Management and leadership know-how was replaced with loyalty and trustworthiness
	1980s Iran–Iraq war dictated a war economy with lasting impact on HR, professionalism and development
	1990s onwards known as the era of reconstruction
	Attention to professionalism, skills over ideology, education
	Slow process of reconstruction, many obstacles such as nepotism, corruption and transparency

Source: Namazie (2007); recent observations and notes.

This implies that in 2020 there will be twice as many adults (parents and teachers) per child as there were as recently as 1995. This presents Iran with a tremendous opportunity for growth of human capital and economic growth in the next 25 years.

Additionally, in 2005, Iran produced a 20-Year Prospective Document (also known as Vision 2025) calling on the Iranian government to pave the way for Iran to become a knowledge-based economy and the region's top economic and technological power by 2025. Among some of the key policies presented in this document are the promotion of a knowledge-based economy through drafting and implementing a comprehensive scientific plan for the country and promoting innovation, with the ultimate goal of becoming the

Table 9.2 Economic indicators in Iran

Indicators	2014	2015
Economic growth	−2.2%	1.5%
GDP growth (real in Rial)	−2.4%	2.3%
GDP (nominal in US$ at median exchange rate)	$294.9 bn	$370.9 bn
GDP per capita (in US$)	$3,816	$4,731
GDP per capita growth	8%	24%
Inflation: official (unofficial)	34.8% (35.3%)	28.5% (30.9%)
Population (millions)	77.3	78.4
Active workforce (% of the total population)	36.7%	38.3%
Unemployment: official (unofficial)	10.4% (18.6%)	10.7% (18.2%)
Youth unemployment rate	21.2%	22.2%
Oil and gas exports	$65.9 bn	$79.5 bn
Non-petroleum exports (including services)	$34.5 bn	$48.2 bn
Imports	$56.2 bn	$61.0 bn
Trade surplus	$37.3 bn	$49.4 bn

Source: Iran Economics Magazine, August 2014.

number one knowledge-based economy of the region, and the improvement of Total Factor Productivity based on the empowerment of domestic HR through skills education.

The Iranian economy has the potential to move from its current below-average performance to becoming a developed economy. It has all the resources (natural, human and geostrategic) that an economy would need to play a much more significant role on the international stage. The missing links are in the areas of responsible and accountable policymaking, legal transparency and modern institutions. Should Iran improve its economy and work towards the Vision 2025 document, this will not only positively impact Iran's HR development, but also put better policymaking procedures into place.

Demography, Women and Socio-economic Trends

Similar to the MENA region, Iran also suffers with a youth bulge. Based on figures in the CIA World Factbook (CIA, 2014), approximately 40 per cent of Iran's 77 million population is between the ages of 15 and 40, thus putting great pressure on the country to provide education and employment opportunities in order to maintain social stability. Between 2012 and 2050, Iran's population is expected to grow from 79 million to 100 million (Population Reference Bureau, 2013). One of the noteworthy demographic developments in Iran has been the decline in fertility (World Bank, 2012a). Lower fertility not only helps reduce the future growth (and demands) of the workforce, but more importantly provides an opportunity for economic growth by allowing the ratio of adults to children to rise dramatically for the next 20 years (Salehi Esfahani, 2005). Due to the young population, there are some 800,000 entrants to the job market annually (Iran Economics, 2010). Youth unemployment (ages 15–24) currently stands at 22.2 per cent (Atieh Bahar Consulting, 2014). The emigration of young skilled and educated people continues to pose a problem for Iran. Iran Economics (2010) quoted that according to the International Monetary Fund (IMF), Iran has the highest 'brain drain' rate in the world, translating to 150,000–180,000 Iranian talents annually. An estimated 25 per cent of all Iranians with post-secondary education now live in 'developed' countries of the Organisation for Economic Co-operation and Development (OECD). The World Bank estimates the cost of brain drain on Iran's economy to be US$50 billion per year (Iran Economics, 2010) and suggests the reasons for brain drain are economic, political and social pressures, including a tight domestic job market.

Although the Western world sees Iranian women as oppressed, in reality they play an active role in Iranian society, are able to work in most fields and sectors and can run their own businesses. At the time of the Islamic revolution in 1979, professional women were forced into early retirement, creating a gender gap. However, interestingly, a consequence of the Islamic revolution was the re-emergence of women in society. In pre-revolutionary Iran, women members of the family would not be allowed into society because they were unprotected in an un-Islamic environment. However, through veiling, a safe environment has been created, whereby parents allow their daughters to study at university, live in student housing and work, such that today over 60 per cent of university entrants in Iran are women and 70 per cent of Iran's science and engineering students are women. Women's participation in the labour market in Iran amounts to almost 15 per cent (population ages 15–64) (International Labour Organization, 2008). However, it is noteworthy that some researchers claim this figure is higher because of the informal female labour force which is not recorded and suggest this figure is in fact 40 per cent of the active population (Moghadam, 2009). Based on World Bank (2012b) statistics, the female youth (15–24 year olds) literacy rate is 98 per cent in Iran. Interestingly, the results of the latest nationwide census (October 2011) shows that Iran has witnessed a socio-economic transformation in the past two decades. This transformation is not just seen in simple quantitative aspects (such as population growth), but also in some structural and value-based realities that will have an impact on future behaviours in the Iranian society.

The census results show that the average Iranian is moving away from traditional Islamic values. The prevalence of families headed by women, the increase in the number of divorce cases, the decision by young Iranians not to get married and to live single and the increasing age of marriage all clash with traditional Islamic beliefs. This transformation can be attributed to urbanisation, the emergence of international (mainly Western) norms as behaviour patterns in society, socio-economic realities and the fact that a young couple have to both work to make ends meet, as well as the negative outlook of the Iranian society's future and disenchantment with Islamic values that have been imposed on the Iranian society. Additionally, the growing new role of the mother and woman is shifting away from the paternalistic structures that existed in Iran. The new Iranian woman is not happy with the traditional role of being subordinated to men anymore (be it the father or the husband), and this will have a clear impact on the behaviour and thinking of future generations.

It is noteworthy that Iran's fertility rate currently stands at 1.7, which is 'below the replacement level' of 2.1 (Al-Monitor, 2014). One the one hand, lower fertility provides an opportunity for economic growth, but, on the other hand, if it falls to below the replacement level it could result in a population which is demographically unsustainable (Population Reference Bureau, 2001). Factors which contributed to Iran's declining birth rates include an increase in female participation in higher education and the workforce.

What influence does this have on HRM in Iran? The above factors show that the changing demography, role and active participation of women in society and emerging socio-economic trends clearly portray the demands of the Iranian society for education, jobs and equal opportunities and the transformation that has occurred in these areas. In turn, companies and institutions will have to transform in order to keep up with the needs of society.

INFLUENCE OF NATIONAL CULTURE AND RELIGION ON MANAGEMENT AND LEADERSHIP IN IRAN

Developing countries including those in the MENA region have similarities in their management systems, namely applying local cultural norms and restricted participation in decision making (Debrah and Budhwar, 2004). National culture is one of the factors to consider in understanding the Iranian socio-economic framework. This underlines factors which recognise management style, the meaning of work and values, the attitudes and manners of the workforce, the assumptions that shape managers' perceptions and insights and so forth. The major work-related values which are rooted in a country's culture include power and authority relationships, tolerance of ambiguity and uncertainty, individualism/collectivism, commitment and inter-personal trust, superior–subordinate relationship and role patterns, achievement orientation and feminine/masculine attitude to success (Hofstede, 1980; Tayeb, 1988). Iran stems from an ancient civilisation dating back to pre-Islamic days, yet one of the factors that influences the Iranian national culture is the role of Islam and, more importantly, Islamic values. Islamic values are based on the pillars of consultation, honesty, trust, justice and fairness in dealing with employees, teamwork and cooperation and perfection/excellence (Abuznaid, 2009; Ali, 2010); however, in practice there is a divergence in terms of which values are observed and to/by which social and religious strata. Bani-Asadi (1984) points out that religion should not be viewed as the only source of Iranian national character and suggests that the Iranian culture is a mixture of three different cultures which have coexisted for centuries: an Ancient Persian culture which has been in existence for over 6,000 years; an Islamic culture for 1,400 years; and the Western culture which has a history of over 200 years in Iran. These have all influenced the Iranian national culture and management style in Iran. The different styles of management can be seen in various organisations and throughout Iranian management history. The traditional style of management is very culture specific, based on cultural factors, family relationships, hierarchies and nepotism, in which relationships and networks are given a great deal of importance. The Islamic style of management adheres to Islamic values of equality, justice and protection and support for subordinates and workers. In terms of the Western style of management, this developed throughout the 19th and 20th centuries, both with the entry of foreign expatriates and with exchange programmes with foreign universities. Due to the close links with Europe and the US from pre-revolutionary Iran, the more accepted style of management and enterprise was imported from the 'West'. This is seen especially in second generation Iranian repatriates and indeed in many private sector enterprises. Today there are many different MBA courses offered in Iran, promoting Western and modern concepts of management. The young and educated entrants in the workforce are not only technologically savvy, but also aware of these modern management concepts.

Researchers (see Bani-Asadi, 1984; Mortazavi and Karimi, 1990; Mortazavi and Salehi, 1992) view Iranian managers as paternalistic figures. Latifi (1997) found that Iranian employees view their managers as sympathetic brothers and sisters or compassionate fathers and mothers who were frequently involved in their employees' private lives and family matters. Javidan and Dastmalchian (2003) also reinforce that Iranian managers value leaders who are charismatic, team oriented, and humane in their relationships with others. They do not put much value on participative leadership. Again, this is changing gradually, especially due to the young workforce that looks for opportunities to be empowered and involved.

House et al. (2004), in the GLOBE (Global Leadership and Organizational Behavior Effectiveness) project, showed interesting results for Iran. Using cluster analysis of countries, Iran ended up in the South Asian cluster along with India, Indonesia, the Philippines, Malaysia and Thailand, and not in the expected Arab country cluster. While Iran is geographically located in the Middle East and can be studied as a Middle Eastern country, its culture is similar to that of its eastern neighbours in South Asia. Javidan and Dastmalchian (2003) argued that the most distinguishing feature of Iranian culture is its family and in-group orientation, indicating a strong preference for sustaining a very high level of family loyalty. Compounded with high power distance, this translates to decisions based on personal relationships. Additionally, strong family orientation means trust in in-group members but lack of trust in outsiders. This also explains the high number of family-run businesses in Iran and also the region. What this means for HRM is that although Western management concepts are learnt, they are hard to adopt as they need to fit within the strong national culture values of Iran.

HR DEVELOPMENTS IN IRAN

HRM in Iran has been dependent on internal and external forces. Challenges such as demographic, social, economic, employment and brain drain have all been main concerns which have pushed Iran to develop her human resources. It is due to these factors that some management researchers believe Iran has embarked on a course of HRM (Namazie, 2007; Namazie and Frame, 2007; Namazie and Tayeb, 2006); others maintain that in the public sector there is still very much personnel management (Yeganeh and Su, 2008). In a study of international joint ventures (IJVs) in Iran, Namazie (2007) found that Iranian partners' perception of HRM, its strategic nature and the benefits of linking HRM to business realities was very different from that of their MNC partners. The development of HRM in Iran is, however, a slow process and dependent on the stability of the Iranian environment, overall business environment and organisational strategies (Namazie and Frame, 2007).

A review of the development of HRM in pre- and post-revolutionary Iran shows that before the Islamic revolution (pre-1979), Iran had some progressive labour policies and practices, as was discussed earlier in the chapter. From the beginning of the revolution until the end of the war (1979–1989), the country was coping on survival mode and strategies. However, from the Rafsanjani years (1989–1997) and the emergence of post-war reconstruction, Iran saw the re-emergence of foreign companies, opened its doors to foreign investment and had a significant number of Iranian diaspora returning to invest in Iran. HR continued to develop steadily during the Khatami (1997–2005) years, where Iran returned to a somewhat stable environment. During this period business confidence continued to grow, there was a significant amount of foreign investment and the socio-cultural environment was more relaxed, and together these factors influenced Iran's HR development at the time. In 2003 Iran hosted her first HR conference, organisations questioned ideology versus competency and a wave of assessment and development centres began, the position and role of the HR manager and HR business partner was discussed, and there was a surge of foreign and Iranian business schools that started introducing MBAs, executive MBAs and MAs in HRM.

This momentum of reform and development stagnated during the hard-line Ahmadinejad years (2005–2013). The government itself put great emphasis on loyalty instead of competency, thus significantly giving rise to corruption and nepotism and undoing much of Iran's progress in HRM. This begged the question: what happens to HRM in countries when they experience instability or crisis? In developed countries, HRM tightens its belt in a time of crisis, but what about in developing countries, where HRM is young and fragile? Would companies resort to traditional practices?

A number of researchers found companies adopted different HRM practices during economic crisis and recession (Roche, 2011; Rowley and Warner, 2004; Shen and D'Netto, 2012; Van Rooy et al., 2011). They found that good HR practice and the importance of fairness became more significant during the economic crisis, with a greater emphasis on face-to-face communication. Companies combined both hard and soft HR practices. Hard practices focused on cost reductions, productivity improvements and reduced working times and soft practices focused on maintaining staff motivation and commitment and included areas such as communications, employee engagement and talent management. The research showed that soft HR practices were preferred, especially in terms of increased communication between staff. Companies implemented programmes combining hard and soft practices, ensuring that payroll reductions should not be done at the expense of a severe loss of motivation and commitment.

In the case of Iran, Namazie (2014) conducted a study to examine how sanctions and other environmental factors (high inflation, unemployment, brain drain, inefficiency, political tensions, mismanagement, socio-economic hardship and also the indirect effects of the global economic crisis) affected HRM and development in Iran. The research supported the literature on HR trends in the global economic crisis and showed the importance of combining hard and soft HR practices in order to deal with the crisis. The added impact of sanctions was felt by all the companies, in addition to the pressures caused by high inflation, recession and low morale; however, some companies also saw the crisis as a market opportunity. Market opportunities were felt due to the absence of MNCs caused by sanctions, which gave rise to more Iranian private sector participation in large-scale projects, but also as private and public companies alike were forced to develop an export orientation, especially to neighbouring countries. Although the skilled talent pool looked for opportunities to leave Iran, due to the economic crisis, some found there were more opportunities inside Iran than outside.

The impact on HR caused by Iran's situation was similar to the literature on how companies dealt with the last global economic crisis, in terms of staff reductions and budget cuts, but at the same time practices such as employee engagement, improved communication and retention policies were also of greater significance. It was interesting to note the added loyalty and commitment staff felt towards their organisations, and indeed those organisations which spent more time communicating issues to staff were the ones which witnessed higher staff engagement, commitment and loyalty. The role of HR was varied; some companies felt the role of HR had become more important and others felt HR was taken less seriously or not at all due to the crisis and survival mode of operation of companies.

FACTORS INFLUENCING THE DEVELOPMENT OF HRM IN IRAN

The host country, with its cultural value system, has a significant influence on HRM. Budhwar and associates developed a framework for studying cross-national HRM (Budhwar and Debrah, 2001a, 2001b; Budhwar and Sparrow, 2002). They proposed four factors to be taken into consideration within the context of developing countries, namely national culture, institutions, dynamic business environment and industrial sector (outer context). What they describe as inner context refers to contingent variables such as life-cycle stages, level of technology, and presence of unions, HR strategies and different stakeholders' interests. They argue that because HRM is in its infancy in many developing countries, only the impact of national factors can be further addressed. Tayeb (2001), in agreement with Budhwar and associates (Budhwar and Debrah, 2001a, 2001b; Budhwar and Sparrow, 2002), adds that national culture, external factors such as socio-political, economic, the role of the state, education and religion all affect the competitive advantage of nations and influence the development and establishment of the HR base of countries.

Table 9.3 summarises the factors known to influence the development of HRM.

National culture, religion, socio-economic, political and management trends have been summarised in Table 9.3. In addition, the authors describe the following factors which have and are influencing the development of HRM in Iran:

1. Western MNCs definitely had an impact on developing HRM in Iran (Namazie and Frame, 2007; Namazie and Tayeb, 2006). However, the absence of MNCs has also played a role in continuing this development in HRM. Western MNCs in Iran have a positive reputation for being transparent, fair and, more importantly, providing good remuneration packages, career development opportunities and internationalisation possibilities for Iranian talents. Iranian talent prefer working in these environments not only because of the above factors but also to be in contact with expatriates, an international work environment and international practices. Until tight sanctions were imposed on Iran and MNCs working in Iran (1989–2009), MNCs provided a valuable learning and development ground in Western management practices for local staff. The first author remembers an example from one of the MNC General Managers in Tehran who in 2003 complained about the poor teamwork among Iranian staff. In 2010, the local Iranian project team in the same MNC was recognised globally as the most successful project team.
2. The impact of sanctions forced many Western companies to exit the Iranian market; consequently, the locally trained staff in MNCs introduced these concepts to their new employers, hence developing the field of HR and management development in

Table 9.3 Factors influencing HRM

Factors	Characteristics
National culture factors	National culture determines the management styles relevant for a given national context, the meaning of work and values, the attitudes and manners of the workforce, and the assumptions that shape managers' perceptions and insights.
National institutions and the role of the state	National institutions and the role of the state include national labour laws, politics, educational and vocational establishments, trade unions, government institutions, professional bodies and labour markets.
Industrial sector	The industrial sector concerns strategies, business logic and goals, regulations and standards, developments in business operations, and labour or skill requirements.
Dynamic business environment	The dynamic business environment relates to sub-components such as competition, business alliances, the changing composition of the workforce, restructuring, focus on the customer, technological change and the effects of the globalisation of business.
Religion	Religion also plays a significant role in portraying the national culture of nations and in influencing the cultural characteristics of their people and institutions.
	Islam has always encouraged its believers to engage in commerce and private enterprise. Among the values espoused by Islam are individual responsibility within a framework of cooperation with others and fatalism but also a recognition of personal choice, work ethic, patience, self-discipline and abstinence, resolve, sincerity, truthfulness and trust. Countries such as Indonesia and Malaysia may be the first Muslim countries to achieve industrialisation based on these beliefs and values without relying on oil and underground resources.

Sources: Summary of Budhwar and Debrah (2001a, 2001b); Budhwar and Sparrow (2002); Tayeb (2001); and Namazie (2007).

Iran. Additionally, the indirect impact of sanctions, brain drain and harsh economic realities also influenced the development of HRM in Iran. As Iran lost some of its best and brightest, companies struggled to recruit and retain talent. At the same time, the harsh economic realities, both inside and outside Iran, made the workforce more selective about where and for whom they wanted to work, in addition to more short-term oriented and demand driven on employment decisions, pay and career development. The indirect impact of sanctions provided some Iranian companies with new market opportunities. The urgency of developing new markets forced Iranian companies to attract, manage and retain qualified staff but also to professionalise and become more attractive employers.

3. Salehi Esfahani (2005) argues that the greatest obstacle to the development of Iran's human resources is the rigid labour market. Iran's labour law offers a high degree of protection to employed workers in the form of job security and fixed remuneration unrelated to productivity. Iran's labour law was re-written in 1989[1] shortly after the Iran–Iraq tussle. The law remains very pro-employee and gives reason for companies

to be very hesitant to employ people on permanent contracts, such that it is customary in the private sector to have short-term contracts usually for the duration of one year and sometimes for even shorter periods of time. With a market known for high unemployment, these short-term contracts do not offer employees much job security and, on the other hand, the rigid labour law does not invite employers to offer longer-term job security. The public sector has a different set of rules and regulations pertaining to contracts; however, although there is more job security in the public sector, there is much lower productivity as well. It is evident that institutional reform is needed in Iran's labour law and codes, and one way to begin this is by increasing competition between the employed and unemployed, which will allow for productivity to increase. It is evident that Iran's labour law needs to support the development of HRM in the country; at present it is too inflexible and outdated.

4. Based on Iran's priorities in the Vision 2025 document, Iran realises the need to create a knowledge-based economy and to improve education. Also, the significant changes in the Iranian demography, youth and role of women means Iran currently has around 3 million university students of which over 60 per cent are women. Iran has both state and privately run universities. In 1978 the number of state universities was 22; in 2000 this figure reached 98. Although there is such an abundance of education in Iran, only 15 per cent of the graduates in Iran have sufficient job skills to enter the market; the remaining 85 per cent of graduates are said to lack job skills (Atieh Bahar Consulting, 2014).
5. Latifi (1997) mentioned there is a gap between the professional and skills needs required by Iranian managers in order to operate successfully in the current Iranian economy and what is offered in universities and business schools. Almost 20 years later, the same challenge still exists. As Salehi Esfahani (2005) remarks, 'If education is not contributing to higher output why is more education being produced?' A phenomenon which is seen throughout the MENA region is the drive for more education, but consistently the same problem exists – the gap between education and workforce skills remains. A recent report called 'Talent 2021' by Oxford Economics (2012) identifies that over the next decade a critical 'reskilling' of labour will be required in order to meet the new demands of a highly digitised and interconnected world where higher skill sets will be required. The skills in demand will be digital and agile skills such as dealing with ambiguity and the ability to prepare multiple scenarios, interpersonal and communication skills and, finally, global operating skills such as the ability to manage diverse employees, understand international markets and speak foreign languages (Oxford Economics, 2012). In Iran, the main task will be to shift unproductive skills, such as rote memorisation and test-taking skills, to productive but hard-to-test skills ranging from a specific skill, such as writing, to more general skills, such as creativity and ability to work in teams (Salehi Esfahani, 2005). Iran is under a great deal of pressure with the demographic as well as economic challenges; it is already unable to produce jobs for its 800,000 annual entrants into the workforce, let alone equip them with the right skills. Interestingly, this is an area the private sector and MNCs have started to work on, gradually but consistently. A number of companies, in realising this gap, increasingly use management development and leadership training based on professional assessment and development centres to improve these competencies and skills in staff.[2] This will be elaborated in the section below.

HRM POLICIES AND PRACTICES IN IRAN

A qualitative research was conducted with HR managers and general managers in ten private sector and MNC companies, from the fast-moving consumer goods (FMCG), information and communication technology (ICT), pharma, banking and manufacturing industries. The discussions below are based on a combination of interview results with these ten companies and the authors' insight into the Iranian market, based on their consulting experience.

The Role of HRM

There was some dichotomy over the role of HRM. Respondents believed HRM was strategic and its role was to facilitate the achievement of organisational objectives, recruitment, employment, training and development. Most companies had HR Managers who were on the management team and/or involved in strategic decisions and the management supported the role of HRM through setting policies and clarifying objectives. However, only three research firms had a HR strategy. When asked how HRM was perceived in their company, most respondents answered that it is perceived positively throughout the organisation; however; two respondents mentioned that employees did not trust HR because they had incorrect expectations about the role of HR.

Recruitment and Selection

Bearing in mind that culturally Iran is a relationship-based country, with a strong family and in-group orientation (Javidan and Dastmalchian, 2003), it is expected that nepotism is a commonly observed practice in many Iranian companies which prefer to recruit staff through word of mouth and more informal channels. Previously (please see Namazie and Tayeb, 2006), MNCs took the lead in systematic recruitment and selection whereas Iranian companies tended to use more traditional selection factors such as seniority, level and location of education, work experience and prestige of the company previously worked in. Some public sector companies even went as far as applying clinical psychometric tests and ideological tests to assess the individual's knowledge of Islamic values and beliefs when selecting staff. From 2003 until 2007, Iran had several HR conferences and introduced a competency/meritocracy drive through assessment and development centres along with performance management systems. However, during the Ahmadinejad years (2007–2013), this process was not seen as prominently. Since 2013, systematic and objective recruitment and selection appears to be present once again.

All sample companies had a thorough and systematic process. The all had a competency framework, and mentioned the following core competencies most frequently: customer orientation, honesty, communication skills, flexibility, teamwork, creativity, innovation, conflict management, industriousness, outcome-orientation, responsibility, problem-solving, openness to change, accountability and professional ethics.

The respondents believed the Iranian workforce had shortcomings and needed to be developed in the following competencies: openness to change and teamwork, creativity, analytical thinking, organising, process-orientation, accountability, communication skills, customer-orientation, strategic thinking and professional ethics.

This is in line with Iran's cultural orientation. Coming from a strong family and high power distance society, being creative, accountable for one's own actions, sharing information with others and being part of a team are not common skills nurtured at home or developed in society. It can indeed be learnt if incorporated into primary, secondary and tertiary educational curricula over time and with consistency, as was the case of the local project team working in an MNC who were recognised globally for their team effort and initiatives (described above).

When hiring staff, all ten companies believed candidates' skills and competencies was the most important factor, followed by educational qualifications. One respondent mentioned behaviour and another mentioned honesty as the most important factors on hiring staff. Although the trend in recruitment and selection is increasingly moving towards selection based on competencies and potential in candidates, the authors believe that nepotism in Iranian companies will still remain a selection factor, as it is too deep-rooted in the Iranian culture. This will especially be seen for higher managerial positions and in family-run businesses. Companies should invest more time in culture-building initiatives, which are led by senior management, as staff look up to senior management for guidance and as role models.

Training and Development

Training and development is indeed significant for the development of the HR base in organisations; however, what is available on the market and what is the desired outcome are two very different matters. Companies mentioned that training was provided to everyone in the company, based on organisational needs and performance appraisal results. Training was conducted both inside and outside Iran and on a wide variety of technical/non-technical and skills-related courses.

In terms of availability, the more common training schools are rather theoretical in nature and lecture-type courses. There are a handful of training/HR consulting companies who provide management development, team development and leadership training, in addition to MBA and DBA courses. The academic courses, such as the MBA, DBA and Project Management are more preferred especially as they provide a certification. Some companies also bring in external trainers/academics with the aim of providing latest practices; however, companies have to be very careful with external trainers and ensure their training is localised for the Iranian market. Also language can be a barrier to understanding.

The importance of training and development is seriously felt, as companies realise the lack of critical skills, but if training is done for the sake of ticking a box, then it will be useless. It is important, as mentioned above, that education is provided with the aim of increasing productivity, hence it is necessary to understand the needs of the Iranian workforce, the present and future needs of industry, and also to link training and development to the HR cycle to ensure sustainability and increased productivity.

Performance Appraisal

Although companies mentioned they had a performance management system, the authors believe this is the weakest link in the HR process. Performance appraisal is normally used as a tool to set goals and expectations, measure outcomes and provide feedback to staff. This translates into identifying development needs, career-path growth and promotions, where appropriate. However, performance management in Iran is not seen as a means to develop staff; it is somehow a mechanism to assess the person's actions but not necessarily to develop them as resources to the company. Furthermore, there is normally much distrust between superiors and subordinates, and hence the staff feel that their managers are not being fair in the appraisal. One common belief among local staff in Iran is that relationships are rewarded more than actions, hence the distrust towards performance appraisal measures and methods.

Additionally, the increased economic challenges have caused a great deal of demotivation in staff. In this rather tense environment, it is critical that if performance appraisals are being done, they are clear, objective, help staff see their career development path, link to reward (both financial and non-financial) and also help improve morale and motivation.

Respondents understood performance management as the main key for employees to take major steps, a significant influence on the process of promotion, career, employee transfer, and employee privileges; helps to identify goals, reaching an agreement with manager on individuals' development plans, design of precise individual objectives (SMART) based on organisational objectives and priorities, receiving feedback from line manager.

On identifying what is being measured, respondents answered: competencies and employee performance. On the one hand, respondents perceived performance appraisals as honest but, on the other hand, unfair. However, it was obvious from the responses that performance appraisal was still not well implemented and quite subjective. The most important shortcoming is that it was not linked to the rest of the HR functions.

Compensation and Rewards

With inflation at 30 per cent, employers and employees alike are feeling the pressure. At the beginning of each Iranian new year (20 March), the government announces an annual minimum wage increase which is roughly between 5 and 7 per cent; however, many companies, if they can, increase this figure to be more in line with unofficial inflation figures and perhaps provide two salary adjustments in the year. MNCs have always been able to pay higher compensation packages; however, the private sector is also catching up in order to attract and retain talent. Originally, MNCs were the more flexible, not only due to providing a higher salary structure, but also through offering more attractive benefits including loans, additional medical services and recreational club benefits. However, today the private sector has also determined very good compensation and benefits packages. The private sector has been quite successful both due to the absence of MNCs but also because many of the leading private sector companies are becoming more and more international and require a highly skilled talent pool for international assignments. The public sector does not have a transparent compensation package, but it does provide a diverse and complex basket of benefits, sometimes even loans for the purchase of a house and life-long employment. The system is still rather bureaucratic and does not link benefits to performance. Young graduates are attracted to the public sector for these reasons; however, it is also known as an environment which does not encourage empowerment, creativity and participation.

One of the factors which has greatly helped companies develop a transparent culture of remuneration in Iran, is an annual compensation survey carried out by a local Iranian HR consulting firm.[3] This has had a great impact on equitable pay, developing compensation expertise, designing job grades, remuneration strategy, benefits, and financial and non-financial rewards. The survey, which began in 2002 with just 20 companies, has grown to over 100 companies at present. The growth has been slow, but more importantly it has been consistent and very evident in the market.

The sample companies understand the role of remuneration as being a transparent, objective and fair comparison, a tool to attract, motivate and retain professional, capable and experienced employees, the ability to maintain internal and external organisational justice, achieving competitive advantage through recruitment.

THE FUTURE OF HR IN IRAN

Respondents were asked how they believed HR has changed in Iran over the past ten years and where they see it in the next ten years? All respondents believed HR has improved during the last ten years and that it would improve much further in the next ten years, resulting in more professional HR managers. Comments include that companies see the budget spent on HR as an investment, not an expense, companies are realising that their employees are their main assets, HR is more and more seen as a strategic business partner, HR has a seat on the senior management team and has a growing influence in an organisation's strategic decision making.

However, HR can certainly be improved by educating senior managers and involving them more in HRM decisions, providing more practical training for all organisational levels on the role and function of HR, providing more support and buy-in from senior management and leadership, communicating the role of HR better, providing more transparency in HR's obligations and responsibilities, allowing more collaboration between Iranian companies and experienced foreign consultants, and enhancing the importance of HRM and its role in achieving strategic organisational objectives. Finally, when the market becomes more stable, this would indeed influence HR development in Iran.

KEY CHALLENGES FACING HRM AND THE WAY FORWARD

The HR function in Iran faces a number of challenges. These can be seen as educational, cultural, institutional and environmental.

From the educational perspective, the challenges to the development of HR are seen as a lack of proper understanding of HR in organisations and a lack of HR professionals. Although there are university programmes on HRM, these appear to be theoretical and lack applicability. This lack of appreciation translates to misplaced expectations from HR and then distrust. Management needs to support the role and function of HR more. They have to be more involved in how HR can add value to the organisation and benefit them.

Educationally, Iran also needs to create a better link between skills and industry. This is an area which the whole region suffers with. In addition, it will be important to have a medium- to long-term view of how to use education to improve economic output, with a focus also on the skills that are needed in the future. Education will be important to all countries in the region; perhaps a regional protocol might be in order. Suggestions could include joint programmes with foreign universities, giving Iranian students the opportunities to understand broader issues and develop international skills in the process. However, joint programmes can also be effective if they address local issues and challenges and help HR professionals and managers find solutions to local problems.

Culturally, Iran needs to shift from a relationship-based/nepotistic society to a culture of meritocracy. In creating a culture of meritocracy, objectivity, professional conduct and ethical behaviour are of value, as well as setting and abiding by regulations, policies and practices. This is a long-term cultural development which will need to be developed gradually and reinforced through different programmes throughout society and education. As mentioned earlier, socio-economic and demographic pressures are forcing the Iranian society and organisations to transform.

Iran cannot develop her HR base without addressing institutional reform to the labour law and codes, such as job classification and selection factors. But more importantly, if Iran really wants to work on building a robust economy, promote a knowledge-based economy and improve total factor productivity, there are a great deal of institutional and legal reforms which will be needed.

Finally, and perhaps the biggest challenge for HR to further professionalise is national environment. Challenges such as sanctions, inflation, brain drain, overall economic stagnation and an unstable economic scenario are damaging to Iran's HR development. At the same time, as seen above, these challenges have caused Iranian companies to become more resilient and self-reliant, but it is also obvious that there are more losses than gains. The sooner Iran reduces some of these tensions, the sooner will it see the market and HR flourish.

There are signs that Iran is continuing its development of HRM; it is a gradual but consistent process. The trends in the development of HRM in Iran can be summarised as follows:

1. The role of HR has become more strategic; HRM is seen in management teams and on board levels. HR is being given a voice in strategic organisational issues. However, this trend needs to be supported further by educating HR professionals and senior management but also through the creation of professional networks such as HR forums, conferences and seminars, which would come together to share best practices and learning.
2. Iran is developing a more systematic and objective approach to HRM, with procedures, and practices being created and implemented. HR functions are each becoming more professional and systematic. Surveys like the Iran Annual Compensation Survey have had a great impact on educating the market on professional reward strategies and structures. While there is a gap in terms of international HR companies, local, respected HR consulting firms have a role to play in developing the culture of HRM in Iran.
3. In light of the many challenges, economic, political, demographic and social, Iranian organisations have become more resilient and lean. On the one hand, the youth, demography and socio-economic pressures are signs of a dynamic society in demand of change. On the other hand, external factors such as the impact of sanctions and

economic mismanagement have taken its toll on society and organisations. However, as seen earlier, HRM is still developing. The question will be at what rate.
4. Iran has the added challenge of its Vision 2025 document. If it wishes to become a knowledge-based economy and achieve its objectives, it needs to undergo institutional, educational and economic reform.

Culturally, Iran and the MENA region need to work more towards reducing nepotism and increasing meritocracy and fairness. Although, Islam is a factor in the Iranian culture and management style, the values may be seen differently in each country. The pace of HRM development in each country in the region will be different. Continued longitudinal research programmes are valuable to analyse how each country develops its HR knowledge, expertise and practice, especially in light of the volatile and fast-changing environments in this region.

A final recommendation would be for the MENA countries to share experiences and learn from one another, and create synergies in developing talent pools and reducing the skills gap. The region will not be able to create enough jobs for all the youth; however, it might be able to take advantage of training and developing talents to work in talent-deficient markets.

NOTES

1. http://www.princeton.edu/irandataportal/laws/labor-law/.
2. Some leading private sector local consultancies in this regard are Atieh Borna Negar and Atieh Roshan Consulting, both part of the Atieh Group. Please see useful websites for links.
3. Atieh Roshan Consulting has been running the Iran Annual Compensation Survey (IACS); please visit www.atiehroshan.com for more information.

USEFUL WEBSITES

Atieh Group – leading consulting group covering economic, social, political, legal analysis, HR consulting services, produce multi-client and weekly reports: www.atiehgroup.com.

International Labour Organization – Key Indicators of the Labour Market (KILM) 7th Edition for all key labour, employment, indicators: http://ilo.org/empelm/pubs/WCMS_114060/lang--en/index.htm.

International Monetary Fund – economic and market indicators, analysis on Iran: http://www.imf.org/external/pubs/ft/scr/2014/cr1493.pdf.

Population Reference Bureau – population and demography reports: http://www.prb.org/. www.gooya.com – online resource to all Iranian media sources.

REFERENCES

Abuznaid, S. 2009. Business ethics in Islam: the glaring gap in practice. *International Journal of Islamic and Middle Eastern Finance and Management*, **2**(4): 278–288.

Ali, A.J. 2010. Islamic challenges to HR in modern organizations. *Personnel Review*, **39**(6): 692–711.

Al-Monitor 2014. Iran plans to eliminate free birth control. *Al-Monitor Iran Pulse*. http://www.al-monitor.com/pulse/originals/2014/04/iran-eliminate-family-planning-programs.html (accessed 26 January 2016).

Atieh Bahar Consulting 2014. *Iran Weekly Brief*, 15 September 2014. www.atiehbahar.com (accessed 26 January 2016).

Atieh International 2014. Re-engaging the Iranian market. *Multi-client Report*, January 2014. www.atiehinternational.com.
Bani-Asadi, H. 1984. Interactive planning on the eve of the Iranian revolution. PhD dissertation, University of Pennsylvania.
Budhwar, P.S. and Debrah, Y.A. 2001a. Rethinking comparative and cross-national human resource management research. *International Journal of Human Resource Management*, **12**(3): 497–515.
Budhwar, P.S. and Debrah, Y.A. 2001b. Introduction. In P.S. Budhwar and Y.A. Debrah (eds), *Human Resource Management in Developing Countries*. New York: Routledge, pp. 1–15.
Budhwar, P.S. and Sparrow, P. 2002. An integrative framework for understanding cross-national human resource management practices. *Human Resource Management Review*, **12**: 377–403.
CIA 2014. Iran. In *The World Fact Book 2014*. https://www.cia.gov/library/publications/resources/the-world-factbook/geos/ir.html (accessed 26 January 2016).
Cordesman, A.H., Coughlin-Schulte, C. and Yarosh, N.S. 2013, The underlying causes of the crises and upheavals in the Middle East and North Africa: an analytic survey. *Center for Strategic and International Studies*, 4th edn, 21 August 2013. www.csis.org (accessed 26 January 2016).
Debrah, Y.A. and Budhwar, P.S. 2004. Conclusion: international competitive pressures and the challenges for HRM in developing countries. In P. Budhwar and Y. Debrah (eds), *Human Resource Management in Developing Countries*. London: Routledge, pp. 238–253.
Goldman Sachs 2007. The N-11: more than an acronym. Goldman Sachs Economic Research, Global Economics Paper No. 153. http://www.chicagobooth.edu/~/media/E60BDCEB6C5245E59B7ADA7C6B1B6F2B.pdf (accessed 26 January 2016).
Hofstede, G. 1980. *Culture's Consequences*. Thousand Oaks, CA: Sage Publications.
House, R.J., Hanges, P.J., Javidan, M., Dorfman, P.W. and Gupta, V. 2004. *Culture, Leadership, and Organizations: The GLOBE Study of 62 Societies*. Thousand Oaks, CA: Sage Publications.
Ilias, S. 2009. *Iran's Economic Conditions: U.S. Policy Issues*. Congressional Research Service, CRS Report for Congress, 15 June 2009, pp. 4–5.
International Labour Organization 2008. *Key Indicators of the Labour Market (KILM)*, 7th edn. http://www.ilo.org/empelm/pubs/WCMS_114060/lang--en/index.htm (accessed 26 January 2016).
Iran Economics 2010. Falling IQ: brain drain in an insecure environment. February 2010, pp. 24–29 (in Persian).
Javidan, M. and Dastmalchian, A. 2003. Culture and leadership in Iran: the land of individual achievers, strong family ties and powerful elite. *Academy of Management Executive*, **17**(4): 127–142.
Khajehpour, B. 2009. An analysis of the Iranian economy. Presentation to Stiftung für Wissenschaft und Politik, Berlin, Germany, November 2009.
Latifi, F. 1997. Management learning in national context. PhD thesis, Henley Management College.
Moghadam, F.E. 2009. Undercounting women's work in Iran. *Iranian Studies*, **42**(1): 81–95.
Mortazavi, S. and Karimi, E. 1990. Cultural dimensions of paternalistic behaviour: a cross-cultural research in five countries. In S. Iwawaki, Y. Kashima and L. Kwok (eds), *Innovation in Cross-Cultural Psychology*. Amsterdam, Berwyn, PA: Swets & Zeitlinger, pp. 147–151.
Mortazavi, S. and Salehi, A. 1992. Organisational culture, paternalistic leadership and job satisfaction in Iran. Paper presented at the 22nd International Congress of Applied Psychology, Erlbaum, UK.
Namazie, P. 2007. Factors affecting the transferability of HR policies and practices in Iranian international joint ventures. Unpublished PhD thesis, Middlesex Business School, Middlesex University, London, UK.
Namazie, P. 2014. The effect of sanctions on human resources management in Iran. In M. Makinsky (ed.), *Léconomie Re'elle de l'Iran*. Paris: L'Harmattan, pp. 109–128.
Namazie, P. and Frame, P. 2007. Developments in human resource management in Iran. *International Journal of Human Resource Management*, **18**(1): 159–171.
Namazie, P. and Tayeb, M.H. 2006. Human resource management in Iran. In P.S. Budhwar and K. Mellahi (eds), *Managing HRM in the Middle East*. London: Routledge, pp. 1–39.
Oxford Economics 2012. Global talent 2021: how the new geography of talent will transform human resource strategies. https://www.oxfordeconomics.com/Media/Default/Thought%20Leadership/global-talent-2021.pdf (accessed 26 January 2016).
Population Reference Bureau 2001. Low fertility not politically sustainable. http://www.prb.org/Publications/Articles/2001/LowFertilityNotPoliticallySustainable.aspx (accessed 26 January 2016).
Population Reference Bureau 2013. Demographic trends in Muslim countries. http://www.prb.org/Publications/Articles/2013/demographics-muslims.aspx (accessed 26 January 2016).
Roche, W. 2011. Irish research throws light on HR's recession. *People Management*, July 2011, pp. 3–35.
Rowley, C. and Warner, M. 2004. The Asian financial crisis: the impact on human resource management. *International Studies of Management and Organisation*, **34**(1): 3–9.
Salehi Esfahani, D. 2005. Human resources in Iran: potentials and challenges. *Iranian Studies*, **38**(1): 117–147.
Shen, J. and D'Netto, B. 2012. Impact of the 2007–09 global economic crisis on human resource management among Chinese export-oriented enterprises. *Asia Pacific Business Review*, **18**(1): 45–64.

Tayeb, M.H. 1988. *Organizations and National Culture: A Comparative Analysis*. London: Sage Publications.
Tayeb, M.H. 2001. *International Business and Partnership: Issues and Concerns*. Basingstoke, UK: Palgrave.
Trading Economics 2011. Urban population in Iran. http://www.tradingeconomics.com/iran/urban-population-percent-of-total-wb-data.html (accessed 26 January 2016).
Van Rooy, D., Whitman, D.S., Hart, D. and Caleo, S. 2011. Measuring employee engagement during a financial downturn: business imperative or nuisance? *Journal of Business and Psychology*, **26**: 147–152.
World Bank 2012a. Fertility rate. http://data.worldbank.org/indicator/SP.DYN.TFRT.IN (accessed 26 January 2016).
World Bank 2012b. Youth female literacy rate. http://data.worldbank.org/indicator/SE.ADT.1524.LT.FE.ZS (accessed 26 January 2016).
World Bank 2016. Iran. http://www.worldbank.org/en/country/iran (accessed 19 July 2016).
Yeganeh, H. and Su, Z., 2008. An examination of human resource management practices in Iranian public sector. *Personnel Review*, **37**(2): 203–221.

10. Human resource management in Lebanon

Fida Afiouni and Sinine Nakhle

INTRODUCTION AND BACKGROUND

This chapter presents an overview regarding the scenario of human resource management (HRM) practices in Lebanon. It is the first attempt to review the body of knowledge produced around HRM practices in the country while reflecting upon the nature of national factors that might be shaping such practices. More specifically, this chapter aims to (1) present an overview of the current HRM literature in Lebanon, (2) reflect upon the current human resource (HR) practices and challenges faced in light of cultural and institutional realities, and (3) suggest areas of research that HR scholars and practitioners should focus on to push the field forward.

Unlike the vast majority of its neighbouring countries, Lebanon is a secular and democratic state with a service-based economy representing around 80 per cent of its gross domestic product (GDP), which is characterized by a strong banking (Habib, 2013) and healthcare sectors (El-Jardali et al., 2014). Moreover, Lebanon prides itself with an educated human capital (Nahas, 2011) that serves as a source of national competitive advantage. The Lebanese workforce is highly skilled, and is generally trilingual, familiar with Arabic, English and French. This pushes Lebanon to the top of the list among its neighbouring countries in the field of education (The Economist Intelligence Unit, 2007). In fact, according to 2007 estimates, the overall literacy in the Lebanese population (age 15 and above) reached 89.6 per cent, with 93.4 per cent literacy in males and 86.0 per cent in females (CIA World Factbook, 2014), reflecting the importance of education in the Lebanese society.

A service-based economy relies on its human capital to deliver high-quality services, which puts an effective HR function at the heart of the competitiveness of the Lebanese economy. A brief historical review of the development of the HR function in Lebanon clearly highlights the unfulfilled potential of this function. Until the year 2000, the HR function was merely a personnel department, responsible for handling payroll and social security, employee files and complaints, and basic administrative functions. Interestingly, because there is a prevalent belief that HR is a feminine position that essentially deals with employees and their problems, HR staff in Lebanon is mostly composed of women. Moreover, a common phenomenon in Lebanon is the hiring of superfluous employees based on '*wasta*' – which literally means 'intermediary' in Arabic, and designates the use of a personal connection to reach any certain goal (Sidani and Thornberry, 2013). These employees are often assigned to the HR department, where the damage they can bring to the company's operations is allegedly minimized, since the HR department is perceived as a non-productive function.

With the turn of the century, the appellation of the function changed from Personnel to HRM department, while its practices remained somewhat constant. This stagnating status of the HR function in Lebanon was perhaps due to the lack of any professional body governing the HR profession, and of any form of HR education, be it in terms of academic degrees or of professional certifications. In fact today, most HR managers in Lebanon do not hold any formal education or professional certification in HRM, which numbs the awareness that the HR function adds value to business.

Currently, the HRM function is at a turning point in Lebanon, with many companies taking an interest in topics such as strategic HRM, talent management, employee engagement, performance management and so on. HR has become a real buzzword in many universities and among early to mid-career individuals. This shift in perception of the HR function over the last few years was triggered by a variety of factors such as the establishment of undergraduate and graduate studies in HRM in leading universities; the possibility to study and sit for globally recognized HRM certifications; the proliferation of professional HR networks; and the organization of HR conferences and summits by different professional and academic bodies.

While recent years have witnessed a major shift in the perception of the HR function, the available literature on HRM in Lebanon still points to a variety of challenges specific to the Lebanese context that affect current HR practices as well as individual career choices. The next sections provide an overview of the field and its related challenges, as well as some recommendations for moving the field forward.

A REVIEW OF THE LITERATURE ON HRM IN LEBANON

A modest body of research is available on HRM in Lebanon but research in this area is clearly gaining momentum. The available research is multidisciplinary, drawing from the fields of health sciences, nursing and business. To identify articles written about HRM in Lebanon and capture their multidisciplinary nature, we browsed databases such as Scopus, Emerald, Elsevier, ProQuest and PsycINFO using the following keywords: Human Resources, Human Resource Management, Lebanon, Career, Women/Gender, and Employee. We did not include books, dissertations and theses, and conference papers and proceedings. Only academic journal articles were considered for the literature review. In total, 24 articles were identified and included in the review below.

Given the importance of the banking and healthcare sectors to Lebanon's economy, it is no surprise that most research on HRM in Lebanon consists of empirical investigations in these sectors. We were able to identify and review eight articles written on HRM in the healthcare industry in Lebanon. The majority of studies focus on issues related to healthcare professionals' satisfaction and retention (Alameddine et al., 2012; El-Jardali et al., 2009a; El-Jardali et al., 2010; El-Jardali et al., 2013; Maamari and Chaanine, 2013), and others focus on performance appraisals (Osman et al., 2011), HR challenges in this industry (El-Jardali, Tchaghchagian and Jamal, 2009b) and specific challenges that women managers working in healthcare face (Tlaiss, 2013). We were also able to identify and review six articles written about HRM practices in the banking sector. Similar to the healthcare industry, researchers in the banking sector focused on employee satisfaction and performance (Crossman and Abou-Zaki, 2003; Dirani, 2009; Dirani and Kuchinke, 2011; Jamali, Safieddine and Daouk, 2006; Tlaiss, 2013), and the strategic nature of HR practices (Afiouni, 2007). In addition to these sector-specific studies, we identified and reviewed ten articles that revolved around three major themes. Five articles specifically tackled the impact of macro-level factors on HRM/HR development (HRD) practices

Table 10.1 Research themes on HRM in Lebanon by sector

Healthcare sector	Banking sector	Other
Healthcare professionals' satisfaction and retention (5)*	Employee satisfaction and performance (5)	Employee satisfaction (2)
HR challenges in the industry (1)	Strategic nature of HR practices (1)	HR practices and the HR function (2)
Specific challenges for women managers (1)		The impact of macro-level factors on HRM/HRD practices (5 of which)
		The implications on diversity management (1)
		The implications on women's careers (3)
Performance appraisals (1)		

Note: * Numbers between brackets reflect the number of articles identified within each theme.

(Dirani, 2006), with some specifically addressing the implications on diversity management (Jamali, Abdallah and Hmaidan, 2010) and barriers to women's careers (Jamali, Sidani and Safieddine, 2005; Tlaiss and Kauser, 2010, 2011). Two articles tackled employee satisfaction (Ismail and El Nakkache, 2014; Tlaiss and Mendelson, 2014), and two others tackled HR practices and the HR function (Chami-Malaeb and Garavan, 2013; Ezzedeen and Swirecz, 2001).

Table 10.1 captures the key themes along which the literature on HRM exists in different sectors in Lebanon.

HRM in Healthcare

The healthcare industry in Lebanon provides attractive medical treatment to both Lebanese citizens and citizens of neighbouring countries that are attracted by its superior services, closeness and cheaper costs in comparison to Europe. According to an estimate by Banque Bemo (2013), health expenditure per capita in Lebanon is estimated at 622 USD, among the highest in the world. The rapid growth of this industry coupled with the universal shortage of healthcare professionals explains the multidisciplinary research interest in HRM in that sector. We depict below the key themes identified.

HRM challenges and strategies in the healthcare industry

El-Jardali et al. (2009b) investigated perceptions of HR managers in Lebanese hospitals concerning the challenges they face and the current strategies adopted to overcome these challenges. The most frequently reported challenges were poor employee retention (56.7 per cent), lack of qualified personnel (35.1 per cent) and lack of a system for performance evaluation (28.9 per cent). Additional challenges included a lack of a strategic HR plan, limited capacity of the HR department, competition with other hospitals, absenteeism, poor communication across departments and a lack of trust in hospital administration. Some of the strategies used by hospitals to mitigate the above challenges included offering continuing education and training for employees (19.6 per cent), improving salaries (14.4 per cent) and developing retention strategies (10.3 per cent). The authors also noted that most HR managers in Lebanese hospitals come from a non-HR background, getting promoted to HR management even though they lack the professional HR knowledge and competencies necessary to develop the best HR practices. The authors concluded that the HR function within Lebanese hospitals ought to be strengthened by delineating departmental responsibilities and correcting mismatches between challenges and strategies used.

Job satisfaction and retention of healthcare professionals

Job satisfaction and retention has been a heavily investigated topic in the healthcare industry in Lebanon. According to El-Jardali et al. (2009a), Lebanon is suffering from excessive nurse migration, low job satisfaction, poor retention and high turnover. They sought to determine nurses' intent to leave and examine the impact of job satisfaction on intent to leave. The study findings show that an alarming 67.5 per cent of nurses reported intent to leave within the next one to three years, many of whom disclosed intent to leave the country (36.7 per cent). Of the nurses who reported intent to leave the hospital but stay in Lebanon, 22.1 per cent planned to move to a different health organization, 29.4 per cent planned to leave the profession and 48.5 per cent had 'other' plans. Nurses reported being least satisfied with extrinsic rewards, which was a common predictor of intent to leave the hospital and the country. The authors recommend that healthcare managers and policy makers develop and institutionalize targeted nurse recruitment and retention strategies, while taking into consideration the predictors and outcomes of nurses' intent to leave both the hospital and the country.

Perhaps the reason behind nurses' intent to leave lies in the workplace characteristics that determine their job satisfaction. El-Jardali et al. (2010) systematically examined the various aspects of nurses' work environment in Lebanese hospitals and how they relate to nurses' intent to leave their jobs. Their findings indicated that Lebanese nurses believed they had little say in decisions about their own professional practice (e.g., scheduling), and that this heightened their intention to leave the workplace. Young nurses in the early stages of their careers perceived that their participation in the workplace did not count for much, and that they had little access to professional and career development opportunities, which also increased their intent to leave. According to El-Jardali et al. (2010), action on the part of the government, professional bodies, policy makers and health managers would help overcome the above-mentioned challenges that account for attrition.

In the same spirit, Alameddine et al. (2012) investigated Primary Healthcare Centers (PHC), looking at work characteristics, level of burnout and likelihood to quit. The results revealed that close to two-fifths of the respondents (39.4 per cent) indicated a likelihood of quitting their jobs (likely or very likely), and an additional 13.4 per cent were undecided. Surveyed providers gave a variety of reasons behind the compulsion to quit, the top five of which were poor salary (54.4 per cent), better job opportunities outside the country (35.1 per cent), lack of professional development (33.7 per cent), job instability (31.6 per cent) and the lack of support from the administration (31.2 per cent). The authors argue in favour of developing retention strategies, namely improved compensation and access to professional development opportunities. Moreover, targeted mentorship and support programmes should be dedicated to new graduates and younger recruits who are particularly prone to quitting their jobs. A year later, El-Jardali et al. (2013) examined nurses' job satisfaction in PHC and hospitals in underserved rural areas in Lebanon. The study showed that while nurses were satisfied with their relationship with co-workers, they were not content with the centres' or hospitals' extrinsic rewards, which is aligned with the findings of previous studies. Moreover, the authors found that married nurses and those married with children were twice as likely to indicate intention to stay in their current job as compared to their unmarried counterparts, which is worthy of further investigation.

Other studies have investigated drivers for improved nurses' satisfaction in the healthcare industry. For example, Maamari and Chaanine (2013) investigated the impact of healthcare information system usage on the job satisfaction of nurses in Lebanon and found a significant relationship between the level of information system use at work and job satisfaction. The authors further highlighted the role of training and user participation in the decision-making process, in enhancing the nurses' job satisfaction. In the same vein, Osman et al. (2011) proposed a data envelopment analysis (DEA) model for the appraisal and relative performance evaluation of nurses. The DEA model is shown to be an effective talent management and motivational tool, providing clear managerial input for promoting, training and development activities from the perspective of nurses, hence increasing their satisfaction, motivation and acceptance of appraisal results.

Barriers facing women managers in the healthcare industry

Shifting from a focus on healthcare professionals to a focus on women managers within the healthcare industry, Tlaiss (2013) conducted a study identifying both barriers and enablers that women managers face. Her findings portray the spillover effect of societal expectations and cultural gender stereotypes into the organizational realm. This spillover results in attitudinal and structural organizational barriers for women managers in the healthcare industry. The majority of the interviewees described the culture of their organizations as discriminatory and promoting gender stereotypes and prejudiced attitudes. The interplay between socio-cultural and organizational factors was evident when interviewees described the cultures of their employing organizations as a reflection of Lebanese society at large. For example, several women described their experience with hostile attitudes questioning their commitment to work. These women also highlighted how they were considered to be unsuitable for management and decision-making positions by virtue of their gender (Tlaiss, 2013).

In sum, despite the significant growth in the healthcare industry in Lebanon, excessive nurse migration poses a serious threat, which is augmented when coupled with low job satisfaction, poor retention and high turnover indicators. Moreover, there are problems related to the level of professionalism of the HR function, with a shortage of qualified HR professionals, and gendered organizational practices that limit females' career advancement. Some of the initiatives being put in place to tackle this include the provision of professional development opportunities and mentoring programmes, more flexible work arrangements, improved performance management and information systems, and more competitive compensation packages. Other challenges pertaining to the high migration of nurses and the shortage of nurses still need to be addressed at a governmental level.

In the following section, we turn our attention to the literature on HRM in the banking sector, and highlight some of the key areas of focus, identified challenges and suggested initiatives.

HRM in Banking

The Banking industry is a key player in the Lebanese economy, accounting for 35 per cent of GDP growth (Association of Banks in Lebanon, 2011). There are around 92 banks of different sizes, nature and ownership structure in Lebanon, all of which fall under the jurisdiction of the Bank of Lebanon (BDL), the country's central bank.

The banking sector in Lebanon has been one of the fastest growing and more profitable and liquid sectors, ensuring the relative stability of the Lebanese economy as a whole. Its growth has been driven by the banking secrecy law, a stable currency and a skilled workforce that is able to garner many foreign funds. According to the Association of Banks in Lebanon, the number of employees in the Lebanese banking sector at the end of 2012 amounted to 22,637. It is worth noting that 45.6 per cent of all bank employees are women, 57.8 per cent are below 40 years old and 72.2 per cent are university graduates. The Lebanese banking sector is said to constitute an exemplary model for other sectors when it comes to modernization and restructuring (Afiouni, 2007) and remains an employer of choice for many graduates due to its attractive financial benefits and its relative job security.

Research on HRM in the Lebanese banking industry constitutes the second most important stream of the literature, with a total of six identified articles tackling employee satisfaction and performance (Crossman and Abou-Zaki, 2003; Dirani, 2009; Dirani and Kuchinke, 2011; Jamali et al., 2006; Tlaiss, 2013) and an attempt to understand the strategic nature of HR practices (Afiouni, 2007).

Investigating the strategic nature of HRM practices

In one of the early studies on HRM in the banking sector, Afiouni (2007) investigated the strategic nature of HRM practices applied in the Lebanese banking sector and found no vertical fit between HRM practices and the bank's strategy in seven out of the ten cases under study. By examining the HR practices in those banks, Afiouni (2007) found that they often lacked a well-defined HRM plan. Even if they did have a charted plan, they had difficulty implementing it for reasons such as lack of line manager's buy in, and nepotism and favouritism that distort proper selection, training, promotion and compensation practices. This, in turn, creates a perception of internal inequity among employees, who subsequently lose faith in the partiality of HR practices. This leads to the loss of credibility of all HR initiatives, and ends up demeaning the HR function.

Job satisfaction and employee performance

Similarly to the literature on HRM in the healthcare industry, much work has been done to investigate job satisfaction and employee performance in the Lebanese banking sector. Crossman and Abou-Zaki (2003) conducted one of the first studies on job satisfaction and employee performance in the sector and found that respondents overall were satisfied with their jobs. A significant interaction was found, however, between gender and job satisfaction with regard to pay and supervision. Female employees were found to be more satisfied with pay than their male counterparts, whereas male employees were more satisfied with the quality of supervision. However, and contrary to trends found in the literature on HRM in healthcare, no significant relationships were observed between job satisfaction and performance. In other words, whether employees were satisfied with their jobs did not affect how well they performed at the workplace. Sidani, Konard and Karam's (2015) questions were similar to those of Crossman and Abou-Zaki (2003), and they found that females are more susceptible to organizational support than males. Interestingly, the more females perceived their organizations to be supportive, the fewer work–family conflicts they reported. Moreover, Sidani et al. (2015) found a notable disparity between the wages of single female and single male employees, irrespective of education level and position. When it came to managerial positions, females did receive similar salaries in comparison to males. Yet behind this gender parity is a back-story about organizational structure: it seems that the handful of women who are able to struggle their way through the glass ceiling and into top management positions do indeed receive fair salaries; but those who still lag behind in middle- or lower-management positions are not treated equally to their male counterparts. It is perhaps for this reason that females reported lower job satisfactions and higher intentions to leave their organization.

Other studies conducted by Dirani (2009) and Dirani and Kuchinke (2011) found that job satisfaction and organizational commitment were significantly correlated, and that satisfaction was a significant predictor of commitment. Dirani (2009) also found that employees were more committed when they were involved in setting, owning and implementing the vision of their bank with their management, and when their banks were more connected and linked to their communities. Such findings raise questions with regard to how employees' satisfaction and commitment are related. Dirani and Kuchinke (2011) showed that respondents were more committed than satisfied due to the high supply of qualified and educated human resources. The authors also identified a negative relationship between the number of female employees and rank distribution, which suggests that female employees face bigger challenges than male employees before reaching a managerial level in their banks. Tlaiss (2013) further probed demographic and work-related factors implicated in female employees' job satisfaction in the banking sector. Her findings showed that women were more satisfied with intrinsic rather than extrinsic factors. Moreover, women managers were dissatisfied with their promotions, salaries and benefits package, but were satisfied with their current position, their career progression and their personal self-development. Unlike tenure, or size of organization, which were unrelated to job satisfaction, managerial ranking and salary proved to be strong predictors of job satisfaction. The author concluded that in developing countries where social security systems are weak, extrinsic factors such as pay, job security and working conditions are strongly linked to job satisfaction.

In the same line of work, Jamali et al. (2006) explored the perceptions of Lebanese women managers regarding the impact of corporate culture and corporate practices on their career advancement. The authors found that most women in banking plateau at middle-management positions. Surprisingly, the findings suggest that the common precepts of the glass ceiling theory are not supported in the context of Lebanese banks, with Lebanese women managers having overall positive inferences and perceptions in relation to their work environment and daily work experiences.

Overall, research on HRM in the banking sector shows that the challenges faced by the HR departments in both the banking and healthcare industry present many similarities. They both suffer from lack of strategic focus, low employee satisfaction and gendered organizational practices that limit women's equal opportunities to progress to higher managerial positions. While research on the banking sector focuses on employee performance because of the highly competitive nature of the industry, research on the healthcare sector focuses on the retention of healthcare professionals because the global talent of nurses makes retention a crucial factor for the sustainability of healthcare centres. More striking, however, are the differences found between the healthcare and banking sectors. As the above review shows, banks offer better extrinsic rewards, better work conditions, more professional and career development opportunities, and better job stability than the healthcare sector. It could be that hospitals do not offer salaries and benefits that are as attractive to their employees. Moreover, hospital settings, especially with the shortage of nurses, usually bring about high burnout rates, making employees increasingly dissatisfied with their jobs, and more likely to quit. Thus, the level of employee satisfaction in the banking sector is much higher than that in the healthcare industry, which might constitute an interesting area for further investigation.

Other HRM Research on Lebanon

Other research on HRM in Lebanon addresses a variety of topics, predominantly, the effect of macro-level factors on both HRM policies and practices, and women's careers. Similar to the themes identified in the healthcare and banking industries, some studies tackled the nature of HR practices and the HR function, and employee satisfaction and performance. Most studies focused on the service sector, which represents the major pillar of Lebanon's economy.

Research on HRM practices and the HR function

Ezzedeen and Swiercz (2001) highlighted the shortcomings of the HR function in a company under transformation during the post-war privatization period in Lebanon. The authors found that while the company was growing considerably, the HR department remained small in size, and failed to exercise proper communication and control. The HR Unit reported to the administrative department, which prevented the unit from contributing to the business. Management had negative perceptions of the HR function, seeing it as operational and administrative as opposed to strategic. More recently, Chami-Malaeb and Garavan (2013) examined the relationship between investment in talent and leadership development practices in Lebanese organizations, and the behavioural outcomes of affective commitment and intention to stay. Affective commitment was found to be a particularly important mediating variable in explaining the impact of talent and leadership development practices on intention to stay. This shows that talent and leadership development initiatives pay off, with increased commitment and retention of high-potential employees.

Macro-level factors affecting HRM practices and individuals' careers in Lebanon

HRM practices are embedded in culture and are, naturally, tainted by the mores and norms of the society in which they operate. Dirani (2006) explored a list of external organizational factors and socio-cultural aspects that affect HRD practices in Lebanon, such as demographic factors, war, family and gender, religion and education. The author argued that much like other Arab countries, Lebanon experiences cultural dissonance, torn as it is between the influence of the East and that of the West. The perceived duality forms conflicting expectations from leaders in Lebanese society when it comes to relationships, performance and improvement. Lebanese organizations are affected by the culture's emphasis on family connections, gender and religion, which is reflected in the kind of bonds that form in the workplace. In other words, the norms of family and familiarity infiltrate the workplace, and the alleged professional relationship almost becomes a paternal one.

Tlaiss and Kauser (2010) explored the perceptions of Lebanese female managers with regard to career advancement barriers. The authors found that organizational culture and practices, as well as the lack of *wasta*, constitute a major obstacle to female career advancement. On the other hand, there was no evidence that the lack of mentoring and tokenism, and the lack of organizational networks and interpersonal relationships, negatively affected career progression. As such, the results highlighted the salience of discriminatory and gender-centred barriers in the organization, such as a discriminatory culture and discriminatory recruitment, professional development and promotion practices that the authors attribute to the prevailing patriarchal values and cultural norms in the region.

In the same spirit of demonstrating the impact of socio-demographic variables on women's career advancement, Tlaiss and Kauser (2011) examined the views of Lebanese women managers on gender, work and family-related responsibilities, and looked into whether these factors impact career progression. The authors found that the career advancement of Lebanese women managers has not kept pace with the increase in the number of working women. The fact that women face greater barriers than men within the workplace has more to do with tradition rather than women's skills or abilities. In fact, the women under study did not think of their gender and family responsibilities as a hindrance to their careers, and were overall career oriented. Similarly, Jamali et al. (2005) found that even though the constraints reported by Lebanese women managers were cultural, they were similar to those reported worldwide. The main differences revolve around the strongly felt salience of cultural values and expectations. More specially, the authors classified the constraints facing Lebanese women into three main types/categories. The first is related to the socio-cultural environment and its implications in terms of behavioural expectations. The second set of barriers stems from stereotypical attitudes perpetuated within corporate cultures. And the third is more structural in nature, relating to organizational policies and practices that impede women's development.

Perhaps the socio-cultural and political factors shaping HRD practices and the career progression of individuals, especially women, can be remedied through diversity management. Jamali et al. (2010) examined the peculiar interpretations of diversity management in the Lebanese context. Generally, the responses obtained from HR managers show that they support diversity management rhetorically, but not through concrete action. The authors attribute this resistance to equity and diversity management, to deeply entrenched patterns of power relations, dominance and past discrimination. The majority of the women interviewed expressed gratitude for employment and reported positive attitudes towards their institutions despite having given concrete examples of discrimination, exclusion, marginalization and lack of specific support in the face of felt pressure and frustration. The authors highlight thus a clear tendency to deny any need to address gender diversity issues, by both the women and HR managers.

Overall, it seems that organizations in Lebanon are as submerged as society in cultural mores. Family connections, gender and religion affect workplace relationships and more often than not result in favouritism. A person without personal connections or *wasta* cannot expect career advancement, especially if that person is a woman. Even though organizations advertise a pro-diversity management image as a means to attract partners, investors and sponsors, they engage in gender-based discrimination that affects recruitment, professional development and promotion practices. This implies that although Lebanese women's participation in the workforce is on the rise, their career advancement remains uncertain.

Employee satisfaction

Ismail and El Nakkache (2014) explored the effects of extrinsic and intrinsic job factors on motivation and satisfaction in Lebanon. Their results show that employees' expectations of basic salary and promotion were not adequately met in Lebanese firms. Moreover, in terms of intrinsic job factors, the results also show that employee recognition and a challenging work environment were hardly present in the organizations. The fact that many of the job factors were below expectations, which are likely to be translated to the low job satisfaction and motivation scores in this study. Similarly, Tlaiss and Mendelson (2014) found that women managers in the service industry in Lebanon were largely dissatisfied with the objective aspects of their careers, namely with their pay level, benefits and promotions.

The review of the literature on HRM in Lebanon has consistently alluded to a set of institutional and cultural factors that shape the development and implementation of HR practices and affect individual career choices. In an attempt to better understand the underlying factors behind some of the current HR practices in Lebanon, and in an effort to push the research agenda forward, we present an overview of these factors. We then go a step further in the last section by addressing scholars and practitioners on what could be done to move the field forward.

CULTURAL AND INSTITUTIONAL FACTORS SHAPING HRM IN LEBANON

The above analysis alludes to a myriad of cultural and institutional factors that shape HRM practices in the country. In this section, we draw on a broader literature stream to present an overview of such factors, namely family centrality; nepotism and patriarchy; sectarianism and *wasta*; political situation and the brain drain; rigid labor laws; weak labour movements; and lack of equal employment opportunities.

Family Centrality, Nepotism and Patriarchy

Family members in Lebanon live interdependently and generally provide each other financial and social support (Tlaiss, 2014). They possess norms demanding members' behaviour to fit cultural habits: loyalty, self-sacrifice and maintenance of family honour, for example, are given particular weight in the average Lebanese home. The Lebanese family also consists of a patriarchal structure, with the father as the centre piece, economic unit, property owner, and provider on whom the rest of the family relies (Moghadam, 2004). As is the case in other patriarchal societies, the remaining roles that the family assigns to different members rely mostly on gender, and the norms valuing family honour apply more stringently on female members (Latreille, 2008). Thus, women's access to career opportunities is affected by family roles: women are encouraged to seek safe jobs that facilitate work–family balance and that allegedly require feminine traits like patience, precision, organization, or care for others (Tlaiss and Kauser, 2010), which partially explains why few women make it to managerial positions, as shown in the literature review above.

Family centrality and patriarchy guide career choices: in Lebanon's interdependent cultures, parents act as career planners for their children by encouraging them to take over family businesses (Miller and Brown, 2005; Young, Leese and Sibbald, 2001). The life and career choices of one member then become extremely susceptible to the expectations of others in the family. In fact, the influence of family is so powerful that it transcends household norms and permeates the business sector: family-owned businesses comprise 90 per cent of the private sector in Lebanon (Charbaji, 2009). These family businesses are driven by motivations to improve social status rather than by motivations to increase wealth (Fahed-Sreih et al., 2009), and some family names are even influential within certain religious groups. This further closes up some business circles whose recruitment process relies on family recommendations alone. Another illustration of how family centrality guides individual career choices can be seen in Afiouni's (2014) work. She found that patriarchy and family centrality lead women to privilege flexible jobs over others to cater for their family responsibilities.

Family centrality, nepotism and patriarchy are intricately linked: children grow up with the idea that family is the centre, that the father is the economic unit, and that his business awaits their contribution. Young adults are very likely to feel guilt and shame if they do not take over the family-owned business. Because they value their family members and the harmony of their households, they often adhere to what is expected of them with regard to work, which reinforces the process of nepotism. A thorough analysis of the link between family centrality and nepotism is provided by Sidani and Thornberry (2013). They explain, through an institutional lens, how it was impossible for a rational-legal model of bureaucracy to hold in Arab states. That is because the practice of nepotism is institutionalized and is common practice. The rationale for using it is that it enhances communication, creates a friendly work environment, strengthens ties among members and is better accepted by some stakeholders (Sidani and Thornberry, 2013). However, nepotism relies on non-objective measures that are based on kinship rather than talent or professionalism, which undermines meritocracy from the recruitment process. Sidani and Thornberry (2013) warn that when an organization grows, nepotism becomes especially problematic. The authors call for the need of a transitional form of organization, and stress that it is through a manager's training that a company handles competitive pressures, not through undependable favouritism to family members.

Sectarianism and *Wasta*

One of the most distinguishing characteristics of Lebanon is its diverse population made up of 18 religious groups that are officially recognized by the government (Faour, 2007), rendering Lebanon the most religiously diverse country in the Middle East. As of 2014, the CIA World Factbook estimates the following: Muslim 54 per cent (27 per cent Shia Islam, 27 per cent Sunni Islam), Christian 40.5 per cent (includes 21 per cent Maronite Catholic, 8 per cent Greek Orthodox, 5 per cent Greek Catholic, 1 per cent Protestant,

5.5 per cent other Christian), Druze 5.6 per cent and very small numbers of Jews, Baha'is, Buddhists and Hindus. Unfortunately, what should have constituted Lebanon's cultural richness became the fuel of its civil war. When political outburst is group based, sectarian feelings among people ignite and filter through several institutional structures. Social psychologist Harb (2010) conducted a study on 1,200 Lebanese youth, with sectarian and geographic criteria mirroring the distribution of the country. First, the results showed that the Lebanese youth are highly educated, with over 41 per cent of the population with a university degree in hand. Harb then analysed inter-sectarian relations and found an off-putting profile, with significantly high levels of sectarian bias or in-group favouritism. The youth reported only mild acceptance of other sects, and low acceptance of inter-sectarian relationships. High urgency comes in par with these results, as they show the educated youth's willingness for sectarian strife, regardless of gender or sect. The results further showed that Lebanese youth strongly identify with their families and their sect. This is somewhat surprising, since youth usually identify more with their peers, valuing their independence and individualism. This is not the case in Lebanon according to Harb (2010).

Since sectarianism is so prevalent among the Lebanese population, it certainly affects career decisions and HRM practices. For example, job-seekers often apply for jobs within organizations dominated by the same sect or religion; and organizations often seek employees who belong to preferred sects. Moreover, political leaders who also happen to be business men and sect leaders in the country, often interfere in the form of *wasta* to place individuals in organizational jobs. As a result, job discrimination based on sect is common practice in Lebanon. Although scholars often conflate the terms, a *wasta* is different from nepotism in that it has a far reaching impact. *Wasta* has not only become common practice in Lebanon, but is often a necessary condition to work entry or upward mobility. Tlaiss and Kauser (2011) found that women managers perceived *wasta*, as opposed to education and achievements, to be the most essential catalyst of career progression. The authors even found *wasta* to override gender bias when it comes to career development.

In sum, the prevalence of sectarianism and the institutionalization of political and sectarian *wasta* in Lebanese organizations greatly affect recruitment, selection and promotion decisions – as evidenced by Tlaiss and Kauser in most of their studies reviewed above. It is worth noting that in Lebanon the public sector has installed religious quotas in recruiting applicants in public positions to guarantee that all sects are fairly represented in public office. In the private sector, however, such quotas are not the norm, and organizations often rely on an implicit recruitment code favouring, or not, specific sects. It is not unusual for HR managers to overlook talent simply because employees have a sect-based *wasta* giving them a way into prominent positions in the organization.

Political Factors and the Brain Drain

Instability and military conflict have plagued Lebanon ever since the civil war broke out in 1975. Nevertheless, despite 15 years of civil war, Lebanon's economic fabric did not rupture irreparably, considering the country's rate of growth (Makdisi and El-Khalil, 2013). Productive sectors and systems were also affected by the war (Fattouh and Kolb, 2006). One of the most significant repercussions of Lebanon's political and economic insecurity is the migration of the educated youth to Gulf Cooperation Council (GCC) countries, Europe and the United States, looking for better prospects. Lebanon thus witnessed a phenomenon known as brain drain, 'whereby professionals and skilled workers with international transfer prices (i.e., with skills that are easily transferable in the international market) emigrated, leaving semi-skilled or unskilled workers behind to fend for themselves' (Kubursi, 1999, p.72). Migration expands young Lebanese workers' social network and gives them more job opportunities (Hourani and Sensenig-Dabbous, 2007). According to a survey by Kasparian (2003, 2009) on Lebanese households, an estimated 990,000 Lebanese left the country from 1975 to 1990, leaving 40 per cent of the total population with the status of 'permanent emigrants'. Nearly three-quarters of migrants departing at that time travelled to Western Europe, North America or Australia. The survey suggested that over 70 per cent of migrants acquired a second nationality, and 64 per cent had no intention of returning to Lebanon whatsoever.

Long after the civil war in Lebanon was over, pervasive political instabilities lingered on, causing brain drain and international reluctance to invest in the country. Moreover, since 2011, Lebanon has been also dealing with the Syrian war spillover, with over one million Syrians fleeing to Lebanon in the past few years. This constant political instability, in addition to the flux of Syrian refugees, accentuated group differences among the Lebanese people, affecting their perceptions and attitudes towards out-group members.

The political instability and the resultant brain drain limit the talent pool of skilled labour, and leads to high employee turnover rates as well, since employees often quit to pursue better opportunities abroad. This particular challenge is also reflected in the literature on HRM in Lebanon, namely within the healthcare industry. The implications of this political instability and this brain drain on individuals' career choices and HRM practices are pervasive. For example, and due to the important wave of emigration that happened during the 15 years of civil war, most Lebanese citizens have cousins and relatives in various parts of the world. This, coupled with the high level of education of many and their ability to speak multiple languages, affords them many opportunities to go and work abroad whenever the political or economic situation becomes unbearable to them. Moreover, the labour market in Lebanon is characterized by a high level of talent mobility, whereby employees move from one company to another in the hope that the move offers them increased compensation or faster career prospects. All this has profound implications on prevalent HRM practices, whereby any investment in employees is considered a risky investment, given the high volatility of talent.

Moreover, the political instability greatly affects Lebanon's service-based economy. For example, the hospitality sector has suffered tremendously from its inability to accurately forecast occupancy rates, namely in high seasons. Many hotels prepare themselves for a busy summer only to find that their occupancy levels have not reached the projected figures due to unexpected political turmoil and occasional bombings. In response to this turmoil, hotels have opted to keep their headcounts to a minimum, leading thus to a slow-down in recruitment. One of the positive side effects of brain drain, however, is that the high levels of male immigration rates have opened up opportunities for women to join the workforce and increase their level of participation in many sectors such as health and social services, education and banking (Tlaiss, 2013). As noted earlier in the literature, and despite the higher levels of female labour force participation, women still face many barriers at work, namely the absence of legal protections as shown in the next section.

Rigid Labour Laws, Weak Labour Movements, and Lack of Equal Employment Opportunities

Lebanon is characterized by rigid labour laws and a weak labour movement crippled by sectarian discord. The labour movement in Lebanon can be traced back to the early 20th century. For almost 50 years, it remained stratified, mainly due to governmental policies aiming to undermine its unity and power, and thus encouraged the formation of multiple unions representing the same sectors (Baroudi, 1998). It wasn't until 1970 that the labour movement achieved unity, when all unions and federations agreed to join the General Confederation of Labor (GCL). Throughout the civil war years, and against all odds, the GCL remained unified and immune to sectarian divisions and was able to gain several demands, such as paid holidays, increased minimum wage, working hour reduction and increased employer contribution to the national social security fund (NSSF) (Clark and Salloukh, 2013). Unfortunately, in the post-war era, the GCL became entangled in Lebanese politics (Baroudi, 1998). Sectarian elites weakened the GCL's unity by creating their own labour unions and federations, which in 2010 amounted to 580 unions and 50 federations representing various sects and political parties. To this day, the labour movement remains weak, stratified and with a crippled collective bargaining power, unable to protect workers' interests (Clark and Salloukh, 2013).

As for the Lebanese labour law, it was put in effect on 23 September 1946 and is mostly modelled on the French labour law. Employment in Lebanon follows a due diligence process and is characterized by high levels of rigidity, difficulty in hiring foreign skilled labour, and a custom of entitlement binding employers' decisions. For example, all types of monetary bonuses will lead to employee entitlement if given regularly over a few years. Moreover, the labour law is very protective of employee rights, which could often backfire on them. For example, Article 52 of the labour law prohibits employers from issuing a warning or from firing a pregnant employee throughout the duration of her pregnancy. Moreover, females are entitled to seven weeks of fully paid maternity leave. Although on the onset, this article aims to protect women's interests, it is actually instigating discrimination against them as it pushes employers to view childbearing women as a liability, thus favouring male employees when recruiting. Moreover, the prevalent patriarchal norms often spill over to the organizational level, leading to unfair selection practices. To illustrate, it is very common in selection interviews to ask female candidates personal questions regarding their marriage or childbearing intentions, and when considering candidates for promotion, females are not considered in the pool due to stereotypical assumptions that they give priority to their families as opposed to work. Finally, the weak labour unions in Lebanon, coupled with an uncertain economic situation and a high unemployment rate among the youth, leads employers to offer very low entry-level packages, which accentuates employees' intention to leave and the prevalent brain drain.

THE WAY FORWARD

In the previous sections, we reviewed the existing literature on HRM in Lebanon and highlighted some of the challenges faced in light of the macro-level factors predominant in that country. In this section, we reflect upon the features of the needed HR practices in Lebanon that would improve organizational performance while being mindful to the country's cultural and institutional realties. This section will add theoretical depth to the existing bulk of research by shedding light on key areas that HR scholars and practitioners should focus on to better manage HR in Lebanon.

Elevating HR Standards through HR Education and Professional Certification

Both our academic readings and our professional exposure to HRM practices in Lebanon point towards an underdeveloped HR profession with a low strategic impact. This can be explained by several factors. First, in Lebanon, there are no professional HR bodies regulating the HR profession to ensure the standardization of practices and the dissemination of best practices. Moreover, certifications are not required for entry into the profession, and HR jobs are often occupied by employees who have never had any sort of formal HR education. Professional bodies similar to the Society of Human Resource Management (SHRM) in the United States and the Chartered Institute of Personnel and Development (CIPD) in the United Kingdom are non-existent in Lebanon, which accounts for the underdevelopment of the function. Moreover, HRM as a discipline has not entered the academic curriculum until recently, which implies that the majority of HR professionals have never been exposed to HR education. In our view, there is an urgent need to elevate the HR standards through a focus on HR education and professional development. Luckily, the American University of Beirut has recently launched a Master in HRM, rendering it the first in the country to offer such a graduate programme in English. The Saint-Joseph University offers a similar degree in French. Although this represents an important step forward, more efforts need to be exerted to bridge the academic/professional gap. For example, current academic research needs to be made available to professionals in simpler forms through local professional publications, and advancements in the field ought to be communicated through professional HR seminars and workshops. In parallel to establishing a professional HR body and further HR education, efforts need to be exerted at the organizational level to raise awareness about the potential contribution of HR to the business, as discussed next.

Raising Awareness Regarding the HR Function

Another challenge facing the HR function in Lebanon is the lack of credibility at the organizational level. Instead of being considered as a trusted business partner and being allocated important funds, the HR function is perceived as a purely administrative function with limited budgets and decision making, and lack of elaborated HR processes. HR managers would gain much by initiating awareness campaigns within their organizations; targeting CEOs and line managers, preaching the merits and value of a strategic HR function, and a cooperative HRM/line management partnership. This should be geared towards convincing the CEO of the long-term financial and strategic value of such a partnership and soothing the fears of the line managers by demonstrating how this can be a win/win situation for all. Moreover, it is very important for HR managers to meet, compare notes, learn from each other's experiences, exchange ideas and recommendations in seminars and conferences, and build up their professional profile as discussed above. Of course, the credibility of the HR function cannot be gained unless the HR manager's credentials are built up, and a professional body of knowledge is created to regulate the HR profession as noted above.

Moreover, the HR function in Lebanon is perceived as a highly feminine profession, and surveys conducted with HR managers in the country often come back with a 70 per cent rate of female respondents. This feminization of the HR profession can also be seen in the classroom, with around 70 per cent of participants in HR classes being female. The feminization of the HR profession in Lebanon can be one of the possible reasons for its underdevelopment. Given the patriarchal gender norms discussed above, a high concentration of females in the HR profession might explain why it is often looked down on, as it is considered a soft, feminine function aimed at playing the role of employee advocate as opposed to contributing to business performance. Moreover, women HR managers are not part of the boys' club, which might lead to their isolation from powerful organizational networks. Therefore, women need to play a more active role in asserting their position within the organization and in further working on their self-development on two fronts. The first is HR related: women should acquire proper credentials and certifications; and the second is related towards nurturing strong organizational and inter-organizational networks to assert their power and credibility among key organizational stakeholders.

Dancing with the Elephant: Dealing with Nepotism and *Wasta*

Nepotism and *wasta* are prevalent practices among the Lebanese population and are often observed at the national and organizational level. Such practices create negative vibes for underprivileged employees in the workplace and put into effect the glass ceiling phenomenon for non-family employees or for religious minorities. Eligible and talented employees see opportunities being swiped from under their feet, which might explain the low level of satisfaction, the high intentions to quit and the glass ceiling effect that some face within their organizations, which we explain in the literature review above. Theoretically speaking, one can preach, and rightfully so, for the need to eliminate these types of discriminatory practices from organizations and adopt more impartial and professional standards namely in selection and promotion. On the ground, however, these practices are well engrained in the Lebanese social fabric, and one must think of realistic and less radical ways to deal with sectarianism, nepotism and *wasta*. Hence, what we suggest here are ways of dancing with the elephant instead of preaching for a radical change that seems unlikely to occur anytime soon.

Perhaps the first step to deal with these realities is to acknowledge their existence and to develop policies that specifically address them. When it comes to nepotism, for example, the family-owned enterprises can limit the detrimental effects of indiscriminate family employment, which lies in what the Lebanese Transparency Association (LTA, 2009) calls a family constitution. The LTA recommends that family-owned enterprises draft a family constitution document that encompasses, among other things, the family's policy regarding the employment of family members. The family employment policy should include the required criteria for the recruitment of family members, such as education and experience. In addition, it should clearly state that family members should be hired only when they have the necessary skills and competencies and when there is an actual business need for their employment. Moreover, the policy can go one step further by opening up the selection process to non-family members whenever the required qualifications are not met by the family members. It should be made clear, however, that the evaluation, promotion and remuneration of family and non-family employees are based on the same criteria.

In the same spirit, specific organizational policies ought to be developed to address *wasta* and sectarianism. Perhaps a way to decrease the negative impact of *wasta* is to institutionalize it within organizational practices, and to subject it to a specific set of standards. For example, the way many banks in Lebanon have dealt with *wasta* is by subjecting all referred candidates to a set of psychometric tests. As a result, only those who meet the minimum level of qualifications can be considered among the pool of applicants. Moreover, we believe that dealing with *wasta* will be easier for HR professionals if the two points discussed above are met, namely if more professional HR practices are developed and implemented, and when top and line managers perceive the potential value added of the HR function to the business.

From Sectarianism to Diversity Management: Capitalizing on a Highly Diverse Workforce

Lebanon's religious diversity has once been the source of its demise, igniting the civil war that ravaged the country for over 15 years. Capitalizing on this religious diversity through adapted diversity policies and non-discriminatory HR practices can turn Lebanon's diversity into a key strength despite its political instability. For example, Lebanon has recently witnessed a series of bombings targeting various areas in Beirut, which led to road blockages that made it difficult for some residents to reach their work. Because the population is clustered in various geographical sect-based areas, religious diversity actually ensures the continuity of services when such a scenario unfolds. This would be especially true in the healthcare industry, where patient care needs to be continuously ensured, regardless of any political turmoil. The continuity of services can also be ensured during holidays whereby Christian employees can report to work on Islamic holidays and vice versa. Thus, religious diversity can sometimes facilitate HR practices imbedded in political turmoil.

The Association of Lebanese Banks, the Association of Lebanese Industrialists and the Beirut Traders Association, to name a few, seem to have overcome post-war sectarian imbalances by establishing religious quotas. A close examination of their Board of Directors' composition clearly reveals that different sects are represented, in an effort to rule out sectarian conflicts (Baroudi, 2000). While some might legitimately argue that sectarian balances and quotas based on religion in the workplace perpetuate the existing strife between the various sects, they are unavoidable at this stage. As long as the confessional system remains at the foundation of the political culture, and as long as sectarian loyalties dominate recruitment practices in some organizations, such measures are necessary to abolish sectarian discrimination in the workplace.

Neutralizing Patriarchy by De-gendering Organizational Practices

The analysis at the beginning of the chapter shows that gendered HR practices and policies are a direct reflection of the predominant patriarchal structures in the country. The literature evidenced many barriers facing female employment and career development that have resulted from these gendered practices. According to Kolb et al. (1998), the way in which companies implement work–life balance policies and practices depends on underlying gender ideologies. Similarly to dealing with nepotism and *wasta*, perhaps the best way to neutralize patriarchy is to first recognize its existence, embrace a clear gender ideology, and incorporate it into HR initiatives that support women's career development. To achieve gender parity, and instead of assuming that success is genderless, the first step would be to demolish gender-biased structures (Kolb et al., 1998). This would require companies to acknowledge that social differences between genders exist, and that they should therefore focus on eliminating structural barriers that block women's career advancement, by adopting, for example, a 'gender-neutral selection', or implementing family-friendly practices. From an economic perspective, both organizations and the Lebanese economy have much to gain if women are afforded equal opportunities in career advancement.

CONCLUSION

In this chapter, we have provided a comprehensive analysis on HRM in Lebanon, and have highlighted some of the salient national factors that are likely to affect people's career choices and HRM practices in the country. Following this, we suggested areas that HR scholars and practitioners should focus on to capitalize on the country's diverse and educated workforce while accounting for political risk, sectarianism, patriarchy, *wasta* and other relevant cultural and institutional factors. It is hoped that this chapter allows for a better understanding of HRM practices in Lebanon and contributes to an enhanced cultural understanding of the dynamics underlying the development (or not) of specific HRM practices in that country.

The reader should be aware, however, that conducting research on HRM in Lebanon is not without challenges. In what follows, we flesh out the main challenges facing HR researchers and put forward a few recommendations as to how to overcome these challenges in order to conduct effective research in Lebanon. Based on our experience, as well as on that of our colleagues, there are three major interrelated challenges facing academic researchers in Lebanon. These challenges are: (1) the absence of a research culture in the country, (2) the difficulty of access to human subjects, and (3) the unavailability of country-specific databases and statistics. We will explain each in turn and put forward a few suggestions to overcome these challenges.

Lebanon has around 40 operating business schools, the majority of which, however, are teaching institutions. Only a handful of business schools produce academic research, and within these research institutions, there are only a few professors investigating HR related issues. This absence of a critical mass of HR researchers in the country results in an absence of a research culture, which renders HR managers and other potential research participants suspicious of the motives of the researcher, and uncertain about how the collected data will be used and disseminated. What augments the suspicion of HR managers are the weak (and often non-existent) institutional review boards that play a key role in inspiring trust and in safeguarding the confidentiality and anonymity of the collected data. In that context, HR managers who are contacted to participate in a research study are often reluctant to be totally transparent. This renders problematic the ability to capture how nepotism, sectarianism and patriarchy, for example, come into play in Lebanese organizations. It is unlikely that HR managers will acknowledge the prevalence of such practices to project a positive image through fear of seeing their answers reported to the public. Moreover, and due to the lack of a research culture, there seems to be a big divide between academia and the profession, whereby HR professionals do not get exposed to the latest research findings, slowing thus the advancement in the field.

A second challenge pertaining to conducting research in Lebanon is the difficulty to access primary data. Access to research participants in Lebanon is challenging for many reasons, the absence of a research culture discussed above being one of them. Another factor that accounts for the difficulty of collecting data is the fact that HR practices in Lebanon are underdeveloped, lack strategic impact and are biased by nepotism, *wasta*, sectarianism and so on. As a result, organizations are often reluctant to participate in research studies that will make them look unprofessional, using below-par HR practices or policies. This is accentuated by the lack of ethical safeguards, as discussed above. The lack of access to research participants often compromises the methodological rigour of the research projects as research investigators often find themselves in need of relying on convenience sampling, snowballing techniques and single-source responses. Another possible explanation for the difficulty of access to research subjects is that organizations do not trust unknown researchers, who are often considered as outsiders or out-group members. They are deemed to reside outside of the trusted circle, which ruptures the possibility of pro-social behaviour even in the realm of research, because of the importance of groups, connections and trust in the country.

A third challenge pertaining to conducting research in Lebanon is the absence of national databases with reliable statistics on company profiles and practices, or even reliable statistics on employment and other relevant indicators that can be used to conduct large-scale quantitative research.

In light of these challenges, conducting effective research in HRM requires the research investigator to invest his/her time to build professional ties with the HR community, in order to inspire trust and credibility. Moreover, the affiliation of the researcher to a trusted higher education institution, with an effective institutional review board, will ease the access to research participants as it will inspire more trust. Moreover, we recommend HR scholars to work actively on bridging the gap between the academic and the professional worlds. For example, having HR scholars participate in professional HR events and disseminate their research findings in professional HR outlets and conferences might provide a wider acceptance and legitimacy of HR research.

In sum, the field of HRM in Lebanon provides a dynamic opportunity for further investigation as it has not yet reached its full potential. We hope that the reflections provided in this chapter will help the reader gain a better understanding of the field and its specific challenges, as well as insights on how to move both HR research and practice forward.

KEY WEBSITES

Career consulting services: http://www.careerslb.com/.

Human Resource Association, Lebanon: https://www.linkedin.com/groups?gid=2874299&trk=vsrp_groups_res_name&trkInfo=VSRPsearchId%3A4293883111426242484330%2CVSRPtargetId%3A2874299%2CVSRPcmpt%3Aprimary.

HR summit in Lebanon: http://www.forwardforum.com/attraction.shtml.

Human Resources and Social Committee, Association of Banks in Lebanon: http://www.abl.org.lb/commissions.aspx?pageid=149.
Master in HRM at the American University of Beirut: http://www.aub.edu.lb/osb/osb_home/program/MHRM/Pages/ProgramOverview.aspx.
Master in HRM at Université Saint-Joseph: http://www.usj.edu.lb/admission/dipl.htm?cursus=135.
Ministry of Labor: http://www.labor.gov.lb/_layouts/MOL_Application/default.aspx.
National Employment Office: http://www.neo.gov.lb/home.aspx.
The HR review magazine: http://www.thehrreview.com/.

REFERENCES

Afiouni, F. 2007. Human resource management and strategy in the Lebanese banking sector: is there a fit? *Journal of American Academy of Business*, **13**(1): 63–69.

Afiouni, F. 2014. Women's careers in the Arab Middle East: understanding institutional constraints to the boundaryless career view. *Career Development International*. **19**(3): 314–336.

Alameddine, M., Saleh, S., El-Jardali, F., Dimassi, H. and Mourad, Y. 2012. The retention of health human resources in primary healthcare centers in Lebanon: a national survey. *BMC Health Services Research*, **12**(1): 419.

Association of Banks in Lebanon 2011. Lebanese banking sector. http://www.abl.org.lb/landingpage.aspx?pageid=315 (accessed 16 February 2015).

Banque Bemo 2013. *Hospitals in Lebanon*. http://www.bemobank.com/files/Hospital%20Industry%20Report.%20June%202013.pdf (accessed 16 February 2015).

Baroudi, S. 1998. Economic conflict in postwar Lebanon: state-labor relations between 1992 and 1997 *Middle East Journal*, **52**(4): 531–551.

Baroudi, S. 2000. Sectarianism and business associations in postwar Lebanon. *Arab Studies Quarterly*, **20**(4): 81–108.

Central Intelligence Agency (CIA) 2014. Lebanon. In *The World Factbook*. https://www.cia.gov/library/publications/the-world-factbook/geos/le.html (accessed 16 February 2015).

Chami-Malaeb, R. and Garavan, T. 2013. Talent and leadership development practices as drivers of intention to stay in Lebanese organizations: the mediating role of affective commitment. *International Journal of Human Resource Management*, **24**(21): 4046–4062.

Charbaji, A. 2009. The effect of globalization on commitment to ethical corporate governance and corporate social responsibility in Lebanon. *Social Responsibility Journal*, **5**(3): 376–387.

Clark, J. and Salloukh, B. 2013. Elites strategies, civil society, and sectarian identities in postwar Lebanon. *International Journal of Middle Eastern Studies*, **45**(4): 731–749.

Crossman, A. and Abou-Zaki, B. 2003. Job satisfaction and employee performance of Lebanese banking staff. *Journal of Managerial Psychology*, **18**(4): 368–376.

Dirani, K. 2006. Exploring socio-cultural factors that influence HRD practices in Lebanon. *Human Resource Development International*, **9**(1): 85–98.

Dirani, K.M. 2009. Measuring the learning organization culture, organizational commitment and job satisfaction in the Lebanese banking sector. *Human Resource Development International*, **12**(2): 189–208.

Dirani, K.M. and Kuchinke, K.P. 2011. Job satisfaction and organizational commitment: validating the Arabic Satisfaction and Commitment Questionnaire (ASCQ). *International Journal of Human Resource Management*, **22**(5): 1180–1202.

El-Jardali, F., Alameddine, M., Dumit, N., Dimassi, H., Jamal, D. and Maalouf, S. 2010. Nurses' work environment and intent to leave in Lebanese hospitals: implications for policy and practice. *International Journal of Nursing Studies*, **2**(48): 204–214.

El-Jardali, F., Alameddine, M., Jamal, D., Dimassi, H., Dumit, N.Y., McEwen, M.K., Jaafar, M. and Murray, S.F. 2013. A national study on nurses' retention in healthcare facilities in underserved areas in Lebanon. *Human Resources for Health*, **11**(49). http://dx.doi.org/10.1186/1478-4491-11-49 (accessed 13 February 2015).

El-Jardali, F., Bou-Karroum, L., Ataya, N., El-Ghali, H.A. and Hammoud, R. 2014. A retrospective health policy analysis of the development and implementation of the voluntary health insurance system in Lebanon: learning from failure. *Social Science and Medicine*, **123**: 45–54.

El-Jardali, F., Dimassi, H., Dumit, N., Jamal, D. and Mouro, G. 2009a. A national cross-sectional study on nurses' intent to leave and job satisfaction in Lebanon: implications for policy and practice. *BMC Nursing*, **8**(3): 1–13.

El-Jardali, F., Tchaghchagian, V. and Jamal, D. 2009b. Assessment of human resources management practices in Lebanese hospitals. *Human Resources for Health*, **7**(84): 1–9.

Ezzedeen, S.R. and Swiercz, P.M. 2001. HR system effectiveness in the transformative organization: lessons from Libancell of Lebanon. *Competitiveness Review*, **11**(1): 25–39.
Fahed-Sreih, J., Pitsuri, D., Huang, W. and Welsch, H. 2009. Family contributions to entrepreneurial development in Lebanon. *International Journal of Organizational Analysis*, **17**(3): 248–261.
Faour, M.A. 2007. Religion, demography, and politics in Lebanon. *Middle Eastern Studies*, **43**(6): 909–921.
Fattouh, B. and Kolb, J. 2006. The outlook for economic reconstruction in Lebanon after the 2006 war. *MIT Electronic Journal of Middle East Studies*, **6**: 96–113.
Habib, O. 2013. Lebanese banking sector healthy, resilient despite regional and local crises. *McClatchy – Tribune Business News*. http://search.proquest.com/docview/1399413743?accountid=8555 (accessed 13 February 2015).
Harb, C. 2010. Describing the Lebanese youth: a national and psycho-social survey. Issam Fares Institute for Public Policy and International Affairs. Working Paper, Beirut.
Hourani, G.G. and Sensenig-Dabbous, E. 2007. *Insecurity, Migration and Return: The Case of Lebanon following the Summer 2006 War*. Robert Schuman Centre for Advanced Studies, San Domenico di Fieso le (FI): European University Institute.
Ismail, H. and El Nakkache, L. 2014. Extrinsic and intrinsic job factors: motivation and satisfaction in a developing Arab country – the case of Lebanon. *Journal of Applied Management and Entrepreneurship*, **19**(1): 66–82.
Jamali, D., Abdallah, H. and Hmaidan, S. 2010. The challenge of moving beyond rhetoric: paradoxes of diversity management in the Middle East. *Equality, Diversity and Inclusion: An International Journal*, **29**(2): 167–185.
Jamali, D., Safieddine, A. and Daouk, M. 2006. The glass ceiling: some positive trends from the Lebanese banking sector. *Women in Management Review*, **21**(8): 625–642.
Jamali, D., Sidani, Y. and Safieddine, A. 2005. Constraints facing working women in Lebanon: an insider view. *Women in Management Review*, **20**(8): 581–594.
Kasparian, C. 2003. *L'entrée des jeunes Libanais dans la vie active et l'émigration: L'insertion professionnelle des jeunes*. Beirut: Presses de l'Université Saint-Joseph.
Kasparian, C. 2009. Liban: La dimension démographique et économique des migrations. *Migrations Méditerranéennes*, Istanbul.
Kolb, D., Fletcher, J.K., Meyerson, D.E., Merrill-Sands, D. and Ely, R.J. 1998. Making change: a framework for gender equity in organizations. In R. Ely (ed.), *CGO Insights*. Boston, MA: Simmons School of Management, Center for Gender in Organizations.
Kubursi, A.A. 1999. Reconstructing the economy of Lebanon. *Arab Studies Quarterly*, **21**(1): 69–95.
Latreille, M. 2008. Honor, the gender division of labor, and the status of women in rural Tunisia – social organizational reading. *International Journal of Middle East Studies*, **40**(4): 599–621.
Lebanese Transparency Association (LTA) 2009. http://www.transparency-lebanon.org (accessed 19 July 2016).
Maamari, B.E. and Chaanine, J.C. 2013. Job satisfaction of the modern information-system-using nurse in Lebanon. *Journal of Technology Management in China*, **8**(2): 120–136.
Makdisi, S. and El-Khalil, Y. 2013. Lebanon: the legacy of sectarian consociationalism and the transition to a fully-fledged democracy. Research, Advocacy and Public Policy-Making and Institute of Financial Economics, Working Paper Series no. 14, pp. 30. http://oemmndcbldboiebfnladdacbdfmadadm/http://www.aub.edu.lb/fas/ife/Documents/downloads/IFE%20WP%20No.1,2013.pdf (accessed 13 February 2015).
Miller, M.J. and Brown, S.D. 2005. Counseling for career choice: implications for improving interventions and working with diverse populations. In S. Brown and R. Lent (eds), *Career Development and Counseling*. New York: Wiley, pp. 441–465.
Moghadam, V.M. 2004. Patriarchy in transition: women and the changing family in the Middle East. *Journal of Comparative Family Studies*, **35**(2): 137–162.
Nahas, C. 2011. Financing and political economy of higher education: the case of Lebanon. *Prospects*, **41**(1): 69–95.
Osman, I.H., Berbary, L.N., Sidani, Y., Al-Ayoubi, B. and Emrouznejad, A. 2011. Data envelopment analysis model for the appraisal and relative performance evaluation of nurses at an intensive care unit. *Journal of Medical Systems*, **35**(5): 1039–1062.
Sidani, Y.M., Konard, A. and Karam, C.M. 2015. From female leadership advantage to female leadership deficit: a developing country perspective. *Career Development International*, **20**(3): 273–292.
Sidani, Y.M. and Thornberry, J. 2013. Nepotism in the Arab world: an institutional theory perspective. *Business Ethics Quarterly*, **23**(1): 69–96.
The Economist Intelligence Unit 2007. *World Investment Prospects to 2011: Foreign Direct Investment and the Challenge of Political Risk*.
Tlaiss, H.A. 2013. Determinants of job satisfaction in the banking sector: the case of Lebanese managers. *Employee Relations*, **35**(4): 377–395.

Tlaiss, H.A. 2014. Conformers, fighters and rebels: the unfolding of the careers of women in the United Arab Emirates. *Human Resource Development International*, **17**(13): 339–357.
Tlaiss, H. and Kauser, S. 2010. Perceived organizational barriers to women's career advancement in Lebanon. *Gender in Management: An International Journal*, **25**(6): 462–496.
Tlaiss, H. and Kauser, S. 2011. The impact of gender, family, and work on the career advancement of Lebanese women managers. *Gender in Management: An International Journal*, **26**(1): 8–36.
Tlaiss, H.A. and Mendelson, M.B. 2014. Predicting women's job satisfaction with personal demographics: evidence from a Middle Eastern country. *International Journal of Human Resource Management*, **25**(3): 434–458.
World Bank 2005. *The Economic Advancement of Women in Jordan: A Country Gender Assessment*. Washington, DC: Social and Economic Development Group.
Young, R., Leese, B. and Sibbald, B. 2001. Imbalances in the GP labour market in the UK: evidence from a postal survey and interviews with GP leavers. *Work, Employment and Society*, **15**(4): 699–719.

Section C

Human Resource Management in North Africa

11. Human resource management in Egypt

Ghada El-Kot

INTRODUCTION

Recently, Afiouni, Ruël and Schuler (2014) noted that there is a growing interest in contextualization research in human resource management (HRM); however, little is known about HRM in Egypt (Burke and El-Kot, 2011), other Arab countries (Afiouni, Karam and El-Hajj, 2013) or in the Middle East (Budhwar and Mellahi, 2007) as there is less literature available on these parts of the world (Afiouni, Karam and El-Hajj, 2013). Accordingly, there is no clear picture about the current or best human resource (HR) practices in the Arab Middle East region, which adds some challenges to HR implementation in the region (Afiouni, Karam and El-Hajj, 2013). The HR role is one of the critical challenges for the Arab organizations that need attention to enhance competitive advantage in the global economy (Sabri and Rayyan, 2014).

The role of HR departments in Egypt, like in most Arab countries, mainly focuses on the administrative work in dealing with employees from the entry stage (recruitment) through to the leaving stage (retirement) (Budhwar and Mellahi, 2007). There are some challenges to the development of HR in Egypt, such as those related to employment, external competition, adoption of new technology, privatization, vulnerable groups (child labour and gender discrimination) and training. Egypt is also facing other challenges such as a lack of government transparency and disrespect for personal/human rights and dignity (World Bank, 2014). A high level of corruption and crony capitalism, along with a high level of favouritism, has probably added to Egyptians' sense of unfairness, Egypt also suffers from a high unemployment rate, high poverty rate, low foreign direct investment and low standards of living (Abdou and Zaazou, 2013; Ghanem, 2013). In addition to the absence of social justice (Mansour, 2012) and economic and political reforms in Egypt (Ghanem, 2013), all these challenges, and the resultant social inequality and political instability, led to the Egyptian revolution in January 2011.

The Egyptian revolution has played an important role in changing Egyptians' attitudes and behaviour towards their country (Kirby and Ibrahim, 2012). Its aim was to improve the well-being of Egyptians (A'aish) and increase freedom (Horraya) and social justice (Adalaa Egtemaia), which continue to pose a challenge to economic rejuvenation, employment creation, poverty alleviation and improvements in standards of living. For the Egyptian revolution to have any positive and lasting effect on the quality of life of Egyptians, there must be economic growth. This economic growth is likely to come from younger Egyptians who are interested in entrepreneurial activity and business start-ups and the upcoming generation of managers and professionals working in larger organizations (Burke and El-Kot, 2011).

These challenges could have an effect on the kind of jobs that may be created in the Egyptian context and raise the issue of the importance of the HRM policies that should be implemented (ILO, 2010; Burke and El-Kot, 2011). Seventy-five per cent of Egyptians are under the age of 25, with just 3 per cent over the age of 65; making Egypt one of the most youthful populations in the world. Therefore, focusing on the youth for Egypt's development and for attracting investment, improving the business environment, supporting large and medium size firms and promoting entrepreneurship are all needed to reduce unemployment by creating decent jobs for youth. According to an International Monetary Fund report (IMF, 2015), the Egyptian government has developed a plan centred on structural reform and investment promotion to raise growth and create jobs. Leat and El-Kot (2007) identify HR development as a critical factor in determining the ability of Egyptian organizations to effectively confront external competition and to make the best use of new technology. There is also a need to utilize the concept of talent management to encompass employee development, recruitment, selection and retention issues. Therefore, it is suggested that firms need to embrace new technologies to attract talent, and to embrace flexible working and contracts to enable more women to work. This would help in the creation of wealth and jobs.

This chapter aims to highlight the critical importance of effective HRM with an appropriate staff that needs to be recruited, trained and developed to implement new technologies, practices and ideas and enable Egyptian organizations to compete internationally in the global economy (Burke and El-Kot, 2011). The chapter is divided into three main parts. It begins with a description of the Egyptian business context by highlighting the importance of understanding the socio-culture and religion that affect HRM implementations in organizations. Core HR practices in Egypt, including recruitment and selection, training and development, performance appraisal, and rewards and benefits, are then reviewed and analysed. Finally, an overview of the key challenges and opportunities for future developments in HR in Egypt is provided.

EGYPTIAN BUSINESS CONTEXT

In a regional context, Egypt is especially important as it is the largest single market in the region, with a rapidly growing population, reaching almost 85 million in 2015 (Egypt Government Profile, 2015). The Egyptian economy is being transformed, with a growing contribution towards the gross domestic product (GDP) from the private sector. In 2013, the GDP growth for Egypt was 2.0 per cent, and this is expected to be 6.5 per cent by 2018 (Egypt Economic Statistics and Indicators, 2014). Egypt's economic growth depends mainly on the agriculture, media, petroleum exports, natural gas and tourism sectors. Unemployment remained high at 13.1 per cent in the third quarter of 2014, as reported by the IMF (2015). In 2015, Egypt witnessed major positive developments towards economic growth and political stability. Afiouni, Ruël and Schuler (2014) mention the important association between political reform and economic reform. The Egyptian government, after the revolution, is committed to boosting economic growth, attracting investment and paving the way for social justice (Egypt 2030 vision).

The World Factbook by the Central Intelligence Agency (CIA, 2015) highlights that Egypt, from 2004 to 2008, aggressively pursued economic reforms to attract foreign investment and facilitate growth. After the unrest erupted in January 2011, the Egyptian government backtracked on economic reforms, drastically increasing social spending to address public dissatisfaction, but political uncertainty at the same time caused economic growth to slow significantly, reducing the government's revenues. This report mentions that tourism, manufacturing and construction were among the hardest hit sectors of the Egyptian economy, pushing up unemployment levels, and economic growth remains slow amid political uncertainty, government transitions, unrest and cycles of violence. El Saady (2011) argues that the Egyptian economy should absorb the shocks generated from the recent political transformation by empowering the small and medium size enterprise (SME) sector, which is expected help the Egyptian economy grow. The government proposed 28 mega projects in the Economic Summit in March 2015 (Ministry of Investment, 2015). These projects include both the governmental and private sector and are considered as a cornerstone for Egypt's growth (IMF, 2015). They cover different sectors such as energy, tourism, housing, mining, agriculture, transportation and logistics, information and communication technology and manufacturing, with more focus on SMEs. Examples of these mega projects include the Suez Canal area development, agricultural land reclamation of one million acres, building one million social housing units, creating new development axes, the establishment of a number of storage and logistics centres in Damietta, and the development of the north-west coast.

Due to the Egyptian revolution in 2011, Egypt is suffering from political uncertainty and economic slowdown, hence its government has started to implement policies to raise growth, create jobs and restore economic stability (IMF, 2015). Egypt scores high on Hofstede's index of uncertainty avoidance (El-Kot and Leat, 2002), hence HRM practitioners needs to be aware that employees may resist developmental opportunities that involve learning new skills. Therefore, HRM needs to reduce ambiguity by preparing detailed plans and schedules, providing a structure for change, providing management with detailed returns on investment and reassuring employees that they will be equipped with the skills they need to adjust to the changes (Ismail, 2010). The focus should be on job creation for youth that would help them find decent jobs, with the aim of decreasing the unemployment rate in Egypt among educated youth, male and female (Saddi et al., 2012; IMF, 2015; Farid, 2014). Job creation is considered as the main priority to deal with the high percentage of unemployment among male and female youth in Egypt. This has implications for HRM in Egypt in focusing on recruiting and training the right employees for the new jobs; further attention can be given to youth education programmes, with more focus on vocational education and vocational training to fit with the many jobs that will be needed for the mega projects. Female participation in work in Egypt needs attention and requires more development. HR policies and practices concerning labour law should also be considered, especially with the foreign investment that the Egyptian government is trying to encourage. Training is one of the important HRM practices that needs more development, especially in regard to delivering soft and other skills needed for generating entrepreneurship in Egypt.

Socio-Cultural Context and Religion

Afiouni, Ruël and Schuler (2014) argue that the political reform in the Middle East region is unprecedented, and both political challenges and economic reforms are associated with each other. They also note that HRM practices in the Middle East region differ from country to country due to cultural factors, religion, employment policies, and their implications for employees. These factors have impacts on the implementation of HRM in any country. This section will focus on investigating some of these factors in Egypt to see their impact on HRM implementation.

The politics of Egypt are based on republicanism, with a semi-presidential system of government. Following the revolution of 2011, and the resignation of President Hosni Mubarak, executive power was assumed by the Supreme Council of the armed forces, which dissolved the parliament and suspended the constitution. In 2014, AlSisi was elected as Egypt's seventh president. The political system in Egypt is divided into the executive authority, the judiciary authority and the legislative authority, which includes the 'People's Assembly' – '*Maglis El-Shaab*' – and the 'Consultative Council' – '*Maglis El-Shura*'.

Egypt's new constitution of 2014 focuses on six chapters, which include 247 articles emphasizing Egyptians' welfare. Among these important articles, the constitution focuses on building a modern democratic state with a civil government. It also closes the door on any corruption, affirms that the principles of Islamic Sharia are the principal source of legislation, and that the reference for interpretation thereof is the relevant texts in the collected rulings of the Supreme Constitutional Court. The constitution is expected to achieve equality between Egyptians in terms of rights and duties, with no discrimination. It paves the way to a future for Egyptians which is in line with the Universal Declaration of Human Rights, maintains Egyptians' freedom and protects the nation against every threat to it.

According to the Egyptian constitution, political parties are allowed to exist. However, religious political parties are not allowed, as this would not respect the principle of non-interference of religion in politics and that religion has to remain in the private sphere to respect all beliefs. As of 2012, there were more than 40 registered political parties in Egypt, the largest among them being the Freedom and Justice Party, Al-Nour Party, New Wafd Party, Free Egyptians Party, Justice Party, Wasat Party, and the Egyptian Social Democratic Party. The variety of political parties provides diversity in the political life of Egypt. Political participation, including women's and youth's involvement in the political life of Egypt, is considered as an important factor for Egyptians' future. However, per the 2014 World Press Freedom Index, Egypt is ranked 159 out of 180 countries for freedom in participation and education of women (Kortam, 2014); and as per the World Economic Forum for 2013, it is ranked 125 out of 136 countries in discrimination between genders. According to these indicators, the Egyptian government should put in more efforts to improve Egypt's ranking in the level of participation and in education issues. One of the proposed approaches to doing this is increasing the female participation level by paying more attention to female participation in education. The government should focus on improving the education system and should introduce the concept of political participation in its curricula; this might be considered as an invitation to Egyptians to participate in political life.

Hatcher (2009) refers to the impact of politics in developing HR due to the changing nature of global societies, and perceives politics as one of the leading causes of sweeping economic globalization and changes in the workplace. Politics has an effect on organizations and on HR development in these organizations designed to deal with such factors. The HR role in organizations might include hiring qualified people, developing required skills and knowledge, training people to understand differences between groups of people and how to work in different groups rather than count on only one specific group on the basis of ethnicity, gender, age, economic status or political opinion. HR departments in organizations might also introduce certain practices in order to avoid causing conflict in the workplace due to differences in political opinions.

Egyptian culture is a blend of Arab and Middle Eastern influences (Parnell and Hatem, 1999), where the influence of the religion (Islam) may be significant in explaining dominant values, attitudes, behavioural expectations and behaviour at work (Leat and El-Kot, 2007). It is important to determine the principles of Islam on work-related issues in organizations and see if there is an implementation of these principles in reality. The Islamic principles refer to the performing of basic HR functions such as recruitment, selection, training, performance appraisal and compensation in accordance with guidelines prescribed in the holy book of the Qur'an and sayings (Hadith) by Prophet Mohamed (Hashim, 2010). In which employees will tell the truth about the jobs offered including job description, and compensation package. At the same time, according to Islamic values, the applicants are required to provide true and honest information about themselves as Islamic values expect people to behave with honesty and truth.

There is a direct effect of the Islamic perspective on HRM practices such as recruitment, selection, training and development, performance appraisal and compensation. From the Islamic perspective, the principle of justice should be implemented when selecting the right person for the job. Therefore, nepotism, favouritism, or egoism that reflects injustice is completely forbidden according to Islam (Ali, 1996; Hashim, 2010).

Selecting employees should also be based on employee's competencies. From the Islamic perspective, an employee is not being appointed to the job based on family relationships, friendship or any other criteria such as political power, age, gender or wealth (Hashim, 2010). With an Islamic view on HRM practices, honesty is important among managers to ensure that they make the right decisions in relation to their employees. Performance appraisal according to the Islamic point of view is recognized as a mechanism to ensure that every effort will be rewarded. Therefore, it is important to reward or at least acknowledge good performance and contribution of effort by individuals even if they do not meet their target as a motivational approach to do make more effort. Ali (2005) mentions that performance appraisal in Islam is based on the normative instructions and practice of prophet Mohamed. This means that each individual is responsible for his/her work and the responsibility associated with that work, and no one should be held responsible for the mistakes of others. Employees are expected to have the moral duty to monitor their performance without external supervision (Ali, 2005; Hashim, 2010). This means that employees should work hard, complete their duties with perfection and be responsible for what they do, irrespective of their positions in the hierarchy of the organization.

Training and development is important to increase employees' knowledge, skills and abilities at all levels and according to the Qur'an, man's basic qualification for being the representative of God on Earth is possession of knowledge (Hashim, 2010). This gives priority to training and development of all employees if HR functions are implemented from an Islamic perspective.

As for compensation, Islam emphasizes that employers should give employees an adequate and reasonable compensation package for their work based on the quality of their work outcomes, based on their needs and also based on the overall economic condition of the society (Ahmed, 1995).

Concerning investigating Islamic Work Ethics (IWE) in Egypt, El-Kot and Burke (2014) examined the relationship of IWE and individualism among a large sample of supervisors working in Egypt, replicating earlier work by Ali (2005, 1987). The comparison of the results of this research with those that have used IWE in a variety of other countries raises an interesting issue, i.e., managers and employees in all Middle Eastern countries that have completed IWE score very high on it. This means, managers and employees endorse IWE to a very high degree. Yet economic performance in these countries has lagged. This might be explained by more macro-level factors 'preventing' work-committed employees from being successful. These factors include badly trained supervisors, autocratic management styles, bureaucratic policies and structures and government regulations.

Burke and El-Kot (2011) argue for the importance of certain HRM practices in Egypt based on the examination of the Egyptian context to draw a number of tentative conclusions about the nature of HRM practices to be expected or which might be appropriate in Egyptian organizations. Given the influence of culture and Islam, it is expected that an Egyptian model or system of HRM will emphasize job descriptions which are implicit rather than explicit with long term employment, employee security and utilization of the internal labour market for filling vacancies. According to an ILO survey (ILO, 2010), it is expected that training will emphasize skills rather than general development, team working and a group or team focus to the organization of work and training and development. In addition, it is expected that compensation, pay and advancement will be based on seniority and an emphasis upon behaviour and relationships rather than task and individual performance, and perhaps skills acquisition rather than aspects of individual performance or outcome. It is also expected that organizations with a human resource strategy would have an impact on implementing HRM practices (Burke and El-Kot, 2011).

For Egypt's economic development, Egyptian organizations should focus on the development of their resources by creating a human resource department that is responsible not only for hiring and firing employees, but also for attracting, developing and retaining employees and focusing on increasing their motivation, commitment and loyalty towards their organizations. The future of Egypt doesn't need the traditional HR department that just focuses on the administrative work in dealing with employees from the entry stage (recruitment) through to the leaving stage (retirement) (Budhwar and Mellahi, 2007), it needs a strategic partner to foster competitive advantage and to give Egypt the stability to be able to compete globally. The mega projects proposed by the government need the cooperation between government, private sector and civil organizations to attract, train and develop the needed skills for the new jobs that will be created (IMF, 2015). Robbins et al. (2011) argue that HR is important for three reasons: (1) it could be a significant source of competitive advantage, (2) HRM is an important part of organizational strategies, and (3) the way organizations treat their people has significant effect on organizational performance. They argue for the importance of high-performance work practices for organizational effectiveness. In Arab countries, even if organizations do not use high-performance work practices, they should focus on some HR practices to ensure that they hire qualified people who are needed for the jobs; these HR practices should focus on: (1) selection function, which includes HR planning, recruitment and selection methods; (2) developing and updating employees' skills and knowledge through orientation and training; and (3) retaining qualified employees through performance management, compensation and benefits and career development.

Based upon the above, HRM practices play an important role in achieving success to improve the economic and political conditions and work towards an ambitious development plan to rebuild Egypt. As Leat and El-Kot (2007) identify human resource development as a critical factor in determining the ability of Egyptian organizations to effectively confront external competition and make the best use of new technology. Iles, Almhedie and Baruch (2012) note that there is a need for increasing management awareness of the key role that HRM can potentially play in enhancing organizational effectiveness in the Middle East region. Therefore, recruitment, selection, training, performance appraisal and evaluation and compensation are important HRM practices that should be improved. The following part of the chapter will focus on HRM in Egypt.

SUMMARY OF HRM IN EGYPT

The concept of HRM was introduced in Africa in the 1990s, when personnel departments were changed into HR functionary departments, but without any significant changes in people management practice (Issa, 2011). In 1952, Egypt witnessed ambitious attempts to transform its economy from an agricultural to an industrial one, The year 1974 witnessed the start of the 'open door' policy, which included many laws to encourage the private sector, with a focus on revitalizing the industrial revolution to cope with the foreign companies entering Egypt, which needed to adapt and implement new methods for managing the administrative work. In the 1990s, the private sector started to take part in developing the Egyptian economy by creating more employment opportunities due to the structural readjustment programme initiated by the government at that time. According to the Privatization Coordination Support Unit Report (PCSU, 2002), pre-privatization employment levels have been maintained at many privatized firms, and in a number of cases new job opportunities have been created. The total number of jobs lost due to privatization was estimated at 365,000 (assuming 10 per cent of the privatized labour force, and 167,000 early retirees), or about 36 per cent of the total labour force at the outset of the programme. However, at the same time, the Egyptian economy was creating 436,000 jobs each year between the years 1991 and 1999. These new jobs needed qualified employees to perform the jobs effectively. Therefore, training was one of the priorities the administrative ministry had to deal with at that time.

The implementation of HRM practices in organizations in Egypt has been affected by many factors; one of them is the management style. During the 1950s and 1960s, Egypt adopted an autocratic management style, therefore there was a big gap between managers and employees and there HRM was missing. In the 1970s, due to the increase in private organizations, the relationship between employees and managers changed. The role of HRM started to occur in organizations as a personnel role. Given the high level of political concern with employment and social stability in Egypt in the 1990s, while recognizing the level of overstaffing in state enterprises, the government gave high priority to these factors when preparing to implement privatization by creating a social safety net in order to minimize negative impacts of privatization (PCSU, 2002). One of the main issues that the government focused upon at that time was providing labour assistance programmes such as job retraining, job placement and entrepreneurship schemes to the employees, which raised the importance of HRM. The privatization made considerable positive contribution to the government's adjustment and restructuring at that time.

HR in government enterprises still plays a traditional role and is named the personnel or administrative department. The main focus is on payroll and the basic HR functions including hiring and less developmental performance appraisals. Budhwar and Mellahi (2006) note that job descriptions in Arab countries are produced as part of the personnel administration process, the same is the case in Egypt as there are missing job descriptions and, where they are in place, they are not updated and not properly implemented. Moreover, there is no clear link between job description and performance appraisal. On the contrary, the role of HRM in private and multinational organizations is implemented properly. Accordingly, the effect is clear in improving organizational satisfaction and employee satisfaction.

Although highly topical, not enough research has been conducted on HRM in Egypt, and HRM practices are still influenced by those of the West (Burke et al., 2011). Considering the changes taking place in Egyptian culture after the revolution, and the implementation of the new Civil Service Law, there is a need for introducing the new HR role in Egypt to its employees. Hence, training and orientation programmes play crucial roles in the success of the new Civil Service Law by increasing employees' awareness about the benefits that they might gain at their workplace (IMF, 2015).

Ramadan (2014) highlights some differences in the implementation role of HRM in Egypt before and after the Arab spring. He mentions that HR management suffered first from having to keep business operations running without any effects on employees' security. This was managed by decreasing the working hours and changing the work shifts for some organizations. Other organizations accepted the idea of flexible working hours and flexible system and allowed employees to work from home. This encourages HR management in Egypt to consider the opportunity of implementing the flexible work system not only at work but also in recruitment processes in the organizations when recruiting employees at that time. Ramadan (2014) also mentions that during the revolution period, permanent contracts, salary increases, developing retirement plans, incentives and profit shares were some of the HR issues raised by employees.

Due to the revolution, some differences in political belief were also found among employees in the workplace, which had some negative impacts on the work environment and work performance. Therefore, HR departments had to work to develop policies, encourage team building and link performance with incentives to encourage employees to focus on work and avoid any negative manners in their attitudes and behaviour at work due to these differences in political beliefs. Ramadan (2014) argues that there is no clear strategic planning in Egypt concerning its human resources, and he argues for the need to align the country strategy with the HR development strategy that should be delivered via specific HR initiatives. He also argues for the requirement for effective employee relations and work life balance. He further adds the necessity to develop the human resources who are capable of dealing with crises by focusing on risk management. Lastly, he highlights the need to change the labour law and adjust it to fit with the changes in the Egyptian context. To sum up and based upon the above presentation, HRM in Egypt focuses on the administrative role in the majority of cases and plays the HR functionary role on other occasions. There is no clear picture yet if it is playing the strategic role or not in Egyptian organizations. Next we highlight the core HR functions based on the available literature, which focuses on recruitment and selection, training, performance appraisal, and compensation.

Recruitment and selection: Aladwan, Bhanugopan and Fish (2014) argue for the importance of recruitment and selection for business competitive advantage and refer to the problems that recruitment and selection processes face in Arab countries, which is reflected in the absence of job descriptions for employees. They argue that the job description is produced just for the procedural work at the organizations as an administrative process.

El-Kot and Leat (2008) note that in Egypt, recruitment and selection is not subject to legislation encouraging equality of opportunity and seeking to prevent discrimination, though there are some restrictions upon the employment of foreign nationals, for example. The importance of relationships, loyalty to the group and friendship are considered as a cornerstone of Egyptian culture because nepotism has been common in recruitment and promotion practices.

In Arab countries, vacant positions are usually filled through connections and often friends and relatives are offered the jobs even if they are not qualified (Budhwar and Mellahi, 2006). Nepotism is also found in Egypt in the recruitment and selection process. El-Kot and Leat (2008) argue that in Egypt, there is widespread use of both internal and informal recruitment practices. They found informal mechanisms such as word-of-mouth have advantages in terms of maintaining a family dimension to organizations, with the importance of friendship and relationships providing a means through which effective peer pressure can be used to exert control, with preferences to fill vacancies internally. They conclude that Egyptian organizations continue to use traditional methods in recruitment and selection but when confronted with the need to be competitive, a poorly educated and relatively unskilled labour force, and labour and skill shortages, they are ready to adopt new methods and technologies and also to use a range of methods to get talent. They also found evidence of the use of the web based recruitment in some cases. El-Kot and Leat (2008) suggest that organizations in Egypt are using the same three traditional methods, which have been found to be popular in other parts of the world, i.e., interviews, application forms and references.

Concerning the responsibility for recruitment and selection, El-Kot and Leat (2008) and Darrag, Mohamed and Abdel Aziz (2010) refer to the shared responsibility between HRM professionals and line management with evidence of increasing devolution of this responsibility to line management, which is giving the upper hand to HRM departments in organizations. This is consistent with Western models of HRM arguing a more strategic role for HRM within organizations, the advantages claimed for the involvement of line management, and a desire on the part of line management to be involved in the decisions regarding the staff working directly for them.

Training and development: Aladwan, Bhanugopan and Fish (2014) refer to the important need for training and development in Arab countries to draw a future training and development map for HR practitioners. They argue that training and development is considered as the most important indicator of HR development as it increases and modifies the knowledge, skills and capabilities employees and managers have to perform their jobs more effectively to contribute to organizational success.

Training in Arab countries in the majority of cases is still not shown as a significant function that contributes to organizational success, but is considered as a leisure time activity, which is normally offered to relatives or friends of managers (Aladwan, Bhanugopan and Fish, 2014); this is the same in Egypt. Human capabilities are relatively fixed and limited and in consequence career planning and progression with supportive training within organizations tends to be extremely limited. However, where new skills are needed and there are shortages in the external labour market and where human resource development is a priority (Evans-Klock and Lim, 1998), employers have little option but to try and develop skills within. The focus upon job-specific training and specialized career paths demonstrated by these employers is explicable. The influence of Islam suggests that employees are likely to be receptive to the acquisition of new skills even though this may appear to be at odds with the strong desire to avoid uncertainty and ambiguity. The low individualism of Arab countries would support a team rather than an individual focus to training and development that is undertaken; therefore, self-training or self-development is given more importance than organizational development among qualified employees.

Performance appraisal: Aladwan, Bhanugopan and Fish (2014) argue that performance appraisal systems and performance management evaluations are critical topics within the HRM field, and further argue that performance appraisal has not received the appropriate attention in Jordanian organizations. This may be the same case in Egypt. Leat and El-Kot (2007), investigating performance appraisal in Egyptian organizations, found a preference for outcomes rather than process or behaviour as the criteria of performance appraisal. The performance appraisal system is conducted once a year by direct managers and not necessarily linked to promotion or training needs. They argue that the awareness of the sociocultural context in Egypt would encourage the conclusion that performance appraisal is an inappropriate activity in Egyptian organizations, even from a developmental perspective, unless it is group based and concerned with behaviours and relationships rather than task outcomes. It is also worth noting that Egyptian organizations have been exposed to Western influences and management practices, exhorted to improve efficiency and productivity, and in this context it is understandable that employers are practising outcome-based appraisal.

Compensation: Compensation in Egypt is implemented the same way as found in the majority of Arab countries, i.e., normally the government controls the minimum and maximum wages and salaries for all employees in all sectors. As mentioned by Budhwar and Mellahi (2006), the reward system is related to the employee's experience, age and position. The majority of employees receive a basic salary in addition to bonuses and incentives that are determined on the basis of an employee's position, age and type of work. Leat and El-Kot (2007) indicate that wage structures tend to be based on job evaluation rather than being skills based and pay increases are related to performance rather than seniority. The cultural profile of low individualism, strong desire to avoid uncertainty, moderate masculinity and strong power distance implies that appropriate compensation systems should be standardized, emphasize hierarchy and seniority, group rather than individual behaviour and the importance of relationships rather than performance. The influence of Islam is generally supportive of this in that while hard work is perceived to be a source of financial independence, this is accompanied by a strong ethical and moral stance and a belief in an equitable distribution of wealth in society. Moralism rather than materialism is likely to be the basis for measuring individual achievement (Kanungo and Jaeger, 1990).

HRM in SMEs

The Egyptian government is attempting to increase the size of the SME sector by making finances available, addressing corruption in the SME sector, and streamlining government bureaucracy. El-Kot and Burke (2014) found emerging evidence that the use of HRM practices can contribute to the effectiveness of SMEs. These HRM practices can contribute to improvements in employee attraction and selection, motivation, development, and retention. With such improvements, one can expect higher levels of SME performance. The findings showed the important role played by HRM practices in organizational performance. Genc (2014) found that there is a relationship between SME size and HRM activities. He found that the percentage of employees who face formal appraisal systems in small organizations is higher when compared with the large ones; with more focus on training programmes to keep talented employees. Concerning the potential job opportunities developed by SMEs in Egypt, Handoussa (2010) suggests that the National Micro, Small and Medium Enterprises (MSME) Development Strategy will lead to an expanding MSME sector in Egypt. A 30 per cent increase in the number of MSMEs by 2013 (i.e., the addition of close to one million) and an increase in the average size of MSMEs from 2.3 to 2.5 workers were projected to result in an additional 2.25 million MSME job opportunities over the following five years (an average of 450,000 per year). This highlights the importance of SMEs in the recovery of the Egyptian economy and of giving much more care to training programmes that need to be implemented. In addition, this links up with Egypt's 2030 developmental strategy, which proposes to focus on HR development through the new constitutional articles.

Factors Affecting HRM Implementation

Friedman (2013) refers to four important factors affecting HRM in any country: government regulations, economic conditions, technological advancements and workforce demographics.

Government regulations influence every process of the HR department, including hiring, training, compensation, termination, and much more. Without adhering to such regulations a company can be fined extensively, which if it were serious enough, could cause the company to shut down. In Egypt, according to the Egyptian constitution (2014), equality, children, women and the disabled are supported by delivering equal opportunity in hiring, and focus on training is based on the need analysis and fair performance appraisal. No discrimination in pay based on gender differences is expected when doing the same jobs; this is mentioned as one of the criterion for equal opportunity. Compensation is based on a 40 hours working week, the pay rate for overtime and the minimum wages mentioned protect employees' rights and also protect employees' investment in their pensions. A safe and secure workplace environment is also expected to be provided by employers to protect employees' health and safety. Organizations in Egypt should consider all these related issues in law and regulation for its HR functions to protect the employees' right in the workplace.

Economic conditions are considered as the biggest external influencer shaping an economy. Not only does it affect the talent pool, but it might also affect one's ability to hire. One of the main ways to prepare against economic conditions is to not only know what is happening in the world around you, but also to create a plan for when there is an economic downturn. All companies in the country can make do in a bad economy if they have a rainy day fund or plan to combat the harsh environment. According to Egyptian economic reform programmes, that is, attracting investments to help Egyptian economy to grow, HR should be seen as a source of competitive advantage and organizations should have efficient selection, training and development, performance appraisal, wages and salaries to retain talent in their organizations (Genc, 2014).

Technological advancements are considered as an external influence because when new technologies are introduced the HR department can start to look at how to downsize and how to save money. A job that used to take 2–4 people could be done by a single person. Technology is revolutionizing the way we do business and not just from a consumer standpoint, but also from that of internal cost-savings. Genc (2014) argues that organizational revenue will grow with more technology implemented in the business environment, which would improve wages and salaries of employees. Technology has its impact on the HRM practices such as recruitment and selection, training and development, performance appraisal and wages and salaries. With more technological advances, fewer employees might be needed to do the same job, which means more qualified employees will be needed. Organizations in Egypt should focus more on training and development programmes to keep its talent and to prepare other employees to fit the job requirement, especially when focusing on the new mega projects.

Workforce demographics covers issues related to an older generation retiring and a new generation entering the workforce where the human resources department must look for ways to attract a new set of candidates. This would affect the methods of hiring and the kind of offers that suit the younger generation. As mentioned above, 75 per cent of Egyptians are under the age of 25 with just 3 per cent over the age of 65, making Egypt one of the most youthful populations in the world. Therefore, focusing on the youth for Egyptian development and attracting investments, improving the business environment, supporting large and medium size firms and promoting entrepreneurship are needed to reduce unemployment by creating decent jobs. Organizations should bring into consideration the long-term contracts, retirement plans, and other compensation issues.

Socio-cultural context refers to analysing a situation from the viewpoint of relevant social and cultural attitudes and values, which are shaped by society and culture (https://publicprojects.mop.gov.eg). There are some differences between what is expected when implementing IWE and the reality. In Egypt, one might argue that there is a rapid emergence of many unique formations of youth subcultures, mainly driven by the transitory political scene. Subcultures have formed through the process of socio-cultural change. El-Kot and Leat (2007) suggest that the Egyptian culture is a blend of Arab and Middle Eastern influences and argue that the influence of Islam may be significant in explaining dominant values and attitudes, behavioural expectations and behaviour in the workplace. El-Kot and Burke (2014) argue that IWE emphasize and encourage hard work; engagement in economic activity is perceived as an obligation. It stresses honesty and justice and an equitable and fair distribution of wealth in society, and encourages the acquisition of skills and technology. IWE also emphasize cooperation and consultation in work, the latter being seen as a way of overcoming obstacles or avoiding mistakes. Social relations at work are also encouraged; it is important to have good relationships at work with both equals and superiors partly for the satisfaction this brings of itself and partly because links inside and outside work can be vital to survival and success. El-Kot and Burke (2014) raise the following question: why are levels of economic performance in Egypt relatively low despite very high levels of commitment to IWE from employees? They suggest that the answer might be in the inefficient use of Human Resources and the feeling that corruption is adversely affecting many organizations, which could affect employees' motivation level and performance.

Egyptian employment law – the Egyptian labour market is regulated by the unified Labour Law No. 12 for 2003, which includes regulations regarding the content of employment contracts which must include details concerning the job description and the contract period; restrictions upon probationary periods (which must not exceed 3 months) and fixed term contracts; the conditions under which employees may be dismissed; maximum hours and days of work per week; minimum paid holiday entitlements; minimum annual paid sick leave entitlements, minimum paid maternity leave; minimum annual percentage increments; and compulsory profit sharing.

Minimum and maximum wages – the government's official legislative gazette published the regulations for setting maximum wages, with no exemptions for the judicial system, police forces or banking sectors. The regulations also illustrate that maximum wages will be applied to administrative authorities that belong to the state, economic bodies and holding companies. These regulations indicate that maximum wages will be applied to the Central Bank of Egypt, Nasser Social Bank (NSB), National Investment Bank (NIB) and Principal Bank for Development and Agricultural Credit (PBDAC). Maximum wages will also be applied to general authorities and holding companies in the country. This includes the Egyptian Post Authority, the Egyptian General Petroleum Corporation (EGPC), the Egyptian Petrochemicals Holding Company (ECHEM) and the Food Industries Holding Company. The list also includes the Egyptian Radio and Television Union (ERTU), National Telecommunications Regulatory Authority (NTRA), Egyptian Competition Authority (ECA), Consumer Protection Agency (CPA) and Al-Azhar institutions. Not all employees in the Egyptian context are happy with these decisions concerning the minimum and the maximum wages level, which appear to increase the resignations from some managers in the top levels of these organizations.

HRM CHALLENGES AND OPPORTUNITIES

Due to the revolution in 2011, the political and economic factors remain uncertain, given the high level of corruption, high level of unemployment especially among educated youth, lack of transparency, low level of enterprise creation, low female employment or participation and high level of poverty in Egypt. According to the IMF (2015), there is a real need to encourage a teamwork concept and develop a sustainable development strategy that would involve the government, the private sector, the civil society and other international communities to rebuild a new Egypt. Currently, there are many challenges facing Egypt and HRM implementation; perhaps the biggest challenge for the government, given the young population of the country, is that of job creation (Oxford Business Group, 2013). Handoussa (2010) highlights that Egypt's challenges include long-standing challenges such as gender equity, political participation, transparency and public accountability, and strengthening respect for human rights. Muwanga (2011) argues that human rights emphasize that recruitment and promotion must be competency based and follow transparent and objective procedures to implement the equal opportunity concept in the workplace with a focus on continuous updates to employees' skills through training and development programmes that are related to performance. Also, fostering open discussion between managers and employees to enhance their involvement, which would improve their motivational level at work. Fair compensation, satisfactory reward and career paths based on fair performance appraisals should also be considered to deal with these challenges.

There are other important challenges and opportunities facing the Egyptian society, which would have impacts on the implementation of HRM in Egypt. Some of these challenges and opportunities include the following.

Unemployment rate: CAPMAS, Egypt (2014) reports that the unemployment rate in Egypt remains unchanged at 13.40 per cent in the first quarter of 2014 from 13.40 per cent in the fourth quarter of 2013. The unemployment rate in Egypt averaged 10.55 per cent between 1993 and 2014, reaching an all-time high of 13.40 per cent in the third quarter of 2013 and a record low of 8.10 per cent in the second quarter of 1999. According to the UNDP (2006), over the past few decades, women in Egypt have achieved remarkable gains in education, political participation and economic independence. However, despite these improvements gender inequalities continue to be a challenge. Today more than half of the women in Egypt remain illiterate in comparison to less than one third of males. Female rates of unemployment stand higher than those of males. The new projects proposed by the government will create new jobs for Egyptians, especially with the focus on the SMEs supported by the government and there are also new jobs to be offered in the new area at the New Suez Canal project. This would help in decreasing the unemployment rate in Egypt in the future.

Over-employment in the public sector: As reported by the ILO (2010), according to the 2006 Census almost 27 per cent of workers are employed in the government and public sectors. Despite the fact that the Egyptian government abolished the guaranteed employment scheme in the 1990s, public sector jobs are still attracting a large proportion of young graduates. This could be explained by the lack of entrepreneurship spirit, misconceptions regarding certain occupations, and a general mistrust in private sector practices. It has also been observed that public sector jobs remain of particular attraction as they provide high levels of protection in relation to the termination of contracts, social insurance, and comfortable working conditions. According to the new Civil Service Law, 2015, with the new HR system that will be implemented in the government sector, only competent employees will remain in jobs and this will help in solving the over-employment in government organizations.

Low productivity and wage levels: American Chamber of Commerce (2009) refers to the weak link between pay and productivity in Egypt. They argue that productivity problems in Egypt include most particularly a high labour turnover, lack of skills, and a significant degree of absenteeism. They also refer to job-matching procedures which often hinder vacancies being filled with the most qualified people. Senior positions are reported to be frequently filled by friends or relatives without regard for merit, which is not expected in an Islamic country implementing IWE at work. The new constitution and the new Civil Service Law argued for the right wages and treatment for all employees, with the offer of a guarantee of minimum and maximum wages. By implementing such a fair HR policy on compensation in the governmental sector, employees' productivity will increase due to feelings of satisfaction and trust in their government's decisions.

Child labour: In Egypt, child labour is still a widespread practice, especially in small towns and rural areas. Areas such as the Damietta region have the highest rate of child labour in the country. In this region, which is a major producer of wood furniture, some children are forced to labour all day in workshops (ILO, 2010). One of the challenges for the Egyptian government is to enable children to find their way back into school or receive vocational training. In Damietta province, child labour is a common practice that involves nearly 80 per cent of children. Many of them are forced to work between eight and nine hours a day. This is considered as child abuse and the Government should work on implementing child protection policies by encouraging the reduction of child labour. This is important to promote children's physical and psychological wellbeing in Egypt.

Mismatches between supply and demand: According to ILO (2009), the demand-supply mismatch refers to both the number of jobs available (quantity) as well as the skills required (quality). Although there are some improvements in the quantitative indicators for education in Egypt, the overall quality of education is still considered as inadequate, and the link between the education system and the labour market is often missing. Sectors such as manufacturing, tourism and construction lack workers with adequate skills. The stark mismatch between outputs of education and vocational training institutions and labour market demand is causing serious economic bottlenecks. It is generally observed that the large majority of firms do not provide their employees with any structured training, with the exception of very limited on-the-job training for basic production skills. Only a small number of large local firms and multinational corporations allocate some resources for training and use more diverse training methods than the traditional on the job training. According to the 2030 'sustainable strategy', with the real role of investing in human resources, there is a need to link the curricula offered in educational institutes at all educational levels with what is needed by society. Training and developing employees is as important as offering those educational certificates. Vocational education and vocational training is considered an important sector that the government in Egypt should focus on developing in the future. HR policies and procedures in organizations should focus on analysing the skills requirements for each job to allow a best fit between employees/candidates and the jobs. It might be suggested that there is a need to engage employers in the formulation of curricula and training and development policies and programmes.

Youth emigration: Some changes are observable in youth's attitude to migration due to the political and depressing economic situation since 2011. The International Organization for Migration (IOM) surveyed youth migration intentions (IOM, 2011) and revealed that the first few weeks after the Egyptian revolution on 2011 did not seem to have directly influenced the decision of Egyptian youth to emigrate. However, the job and income losses that were the direct result of the contraction of economic activity following the January 25 revolution may have acted as the primary push factor for youth who reported intentions to migrate. The survey findings revealed that unemployment, corruption, security, wages and constitutional reforms are the most important issues concerning young Egyptians after the events of 25 January. Egyptian youth is cautiously optimistic regarding the political situation, security, economy and household income security. In relation to employment, before 25 January, 50 per cent of the respondents were working, mainly in the service sector and industry. The open participation between the government and the youth in the coming years is considered as a key factor which might persuade the youth to stay in the country. The youth empowerment policy offered by the government at the beginning of 2015 is a new way to attract the youth to be part of the country.

Civil society role: Handoussa (2010) notes that civil society and its organizations have a significant role to play in national development, in partnership with the government and the private sector as a result of their experience in welfare and social development programmes, because they are home to important interest groups, and since they are able to give voice to those many segments of society that have been marginalized.

Syndicates role: Article 77 in Egyptian constitution 2014 states that:

> the law shall regulate the establishment and administration of professional syndicates on a democratic basis, guarantees their independence, and specify their resources and the way members are recorded and held accountable for their behaviour while performing their professional activities, according to ethical codes of moral and professional conduct. No profession may establish more than one syndicate. Receivership may not be imposed nor may administrative bodies intervene in the affairs of such syndicates, and a judicial ruling may only dissolve their boards of directors. All legislation pertaining to a given profession shall be submitted to the relevant syndicate for consultation.

This would have effects on the HR policies and procedures in organizations by requiring them to update their policies in relation to a union role towards employees' rights. This might also have an impact on the structure of the labour contracts by modifying the compensation to match with the minimum wage and in improving working conditions for workers.

The informal labour market: According to the ILO report (2014), the Egyptian economy is characterized by a large and growing informal sector that has been a major source of job creation for some time. However, the jobs created in this sector are not decent enough in terms of wage, sustainability and work conditions. The report added that a lot of jobs in the informal sector lack stability due to the absence of social security coverage and work contracts, as employers refuse to enter into binding work contracts and complain about the high cost of the social security system. According to ILO (2014), informal employment reached 10.8 million in 2008, representing 48.1 per cent of total employment. Approximately 20 per cent of informal employment was among females, representing 48 per cent of total female employment. Overall almost 23.7 per cent of employed Egyptians work in the government and 3.4 per cent in the public sector, while the private sector employs 22.9 per cent in the formal private sector and 48.1 per cent in the private sector outside establishments, which has been taken as a proxy for the informal sector.

Women's empowerment and gender equity: The Egyptian constitution guarantees the same respective rights to men and women. However, the culture now seems to be less accommodating in opening the doors for women, especially to enter the workforce and employment, with a regression in the female participation rate to under 20 per cent. Political and even judicial institutions also show slow movement forward, in contrast to other social indicators, especially on the education, health, and personal status fronts. The National Council for Childhood and Motherhood (NCCM) and the National Council for Women (NCW) have both provided an institutional framework to address gender issues and support women's participation in the development process. The NCW has spearheaded a number of institutional reforms for more participation of women in government bodies, legislative changes to enhance civic and marital status, and the mainstreaming of gender issues in the national planning process. One important reform has been the introduction of gender responsive budgeting (GRB) in ensuring gender parity. Nonetheless, there is still a long way to go in meeting the challenge of gender equity, not only in the economic and political spheres, but also in socio-cultural life.

According to an UNDP report (2010), the government of Egypt has shown a commitment to gender equality and the empowerment of women. The reports shows that the gender target in primary education is very likely to be achieved by 2015 while female enrolment rates in general secondary education is higher than those of boys and the gender gap in secondary education is expected to exceed the expected target in 2015. Concerning female literacy, the gender gap was expected to reach 0.4 per cent in 2015, but the share of women in waged employment in the non-agricultural sector is very low and it is not expected to change significantly in the next few years. According to Handoussa (2010), the female participation rate in the labour market in 2008 lagged far behind that of males (22.7 per cent for females compared to 75.5 per cent for males), and achieving gender equality is not expected by 2015. At the same time, the unemployment rate of women at the national level in 2009 reached 22.9 per cent (4.3 times the rate for men of 5.3 per cent). The share of women in wage employment in the non-agriculture sector is also very low and declined in the period 1990–2005. Female representation in both houses of parliament is still far below equality.

Industry diversity: Egypt is a relatively industrialized country, especially in textiles and garment manufacture, cement, metal works of various kinds, and armaments. Various makes of automobile are assembled in Egypt. In the second half of the twentieth century, many of these industries were government-owned. At the end of the twentieth century, they were in the process of being privatized. There are also many small private workshops producing shoes, doorframes, furniture, clothing, aluminium pots, and similar items for local consumption (www.everyculture.com). The government is trying to encourage SMEs to use its youth for improving the economic development as part of the economic reform programme that Egypt is implementing (Egypt vision 2030). However, Handoussa (2010) believes that the MSME sector in Egypt suffers from many constraints such as: (1) Demand constraints, such as the weak purchasing power of their low-income customers, and limited linkages to larger firms; (2) Input constraints, such as low utilization of technology, inadequate access to finance and to business development services; (3) Labour constraints, due to a scarce supply of skilled and trained workers and inability to pay high wages and cover high non-wage labour costs; and (4) Legal and regulatory constraints, which impose heavy compliance burdens and costs on the smallest enterprises, leading to the high level of informality. In Egypt, due to the sectorial or industrial diversity, HRM practices should differ to fit with each industry need. Organizations should be aware of the importance of training and compensation to keep talent.

CONCLUSION

This chapter started by highlighting the importance of the HRM role in Egypt with a description of the Egyptian business context and the effect of the socio-culture and religion on the implementation of HRM in Egypt. A summary of HRM in Egypt was provided with a focus on core HRM practices such as recruitment and selection, training and development, performance appraisal and compensation. The final part of this chapter focused on the factors affecting HRM implementation and highlighted the challenges and opportunities that HRM faces in Egypt.

Based on the above analysis, it can be concluded that HRM in Egypt has received little attention and there is still a long way to go towards changing the HRM role from the administrative role to the strategic role in Egyptian organizations. By investigating the socio-culture factors of Egypt and the economic and political reform programmes that are proposed to improve economic growth, it can be concluded that there is a need to focus on the important role of HRM as it plays a crucial role in organizational success.

As Egypt has a rapidly growing young population, training and development would be the key for success in the Egyptian context by investing in education, training to prepare the new generation to match the workplace requirements. There is a need to utilize the concepts of talent management to encompass employee development, recruitment, and selection and retention issues, therefore, it is suggested that companies need to embrace the new web based technologies to attract talent and embrace flexible working and contracts to enable more women to work.

Egypt suffers from many challenges such as a lack of government transparency and a disrespect for personal/human rights and dignity (The World Bank, 2014). A high level of corruption and crony capitalism has probably added to Egyptians' sense of unfairness with high levels of favouritism, high unemployment rates, high poverty rates, low foreign direct investment and low standards of living (Abdou and Zaazou, 2013; Ghanem, 2013). In addition to the absence of social justice (Mansour, 2012) and the absence of economic and political reform in Egypt (Ghanem, 2013); such challenges seem to have contributed to the Egyptian revolution in January 2011 which occurred as a result of both social inequality and political instability.

There are some proposals from the Egyptian government (over recent years) to deal with these problems which negatively affect the country's economic growth and political stability by introducing the Egyptian constitution 2014 that includes 247 articles for Egyptians' wellbeing. By implementing equal opportunities among employees and delivering fair compensation packages to them, offering employment contracts and focusing on the importance of the job description and the performance appraisal criteria as well as recruitment and selection being based on qualifications and not nepotism, proper HRM practices would help in creating trust among employees at the workplace.

It is important to update HRM policies and procedures in organizations to protect employees' rights in the workplace and to match with the new constitution articles. The HRM role is crucial in Egypt, not only in moving it from an administrative role to a strategic role but also in dealing with the new issues appearing since the revolution, such as diversity of beliefs and the effect of religion on employees' behaviour in the workplace. Focusing on gender equity and issues such as female participation in education, finding jobs and participation in political life are considered a real need for females in Egypt to feel equality in their society. The mega projects proposed by the Government in March 2015 have the potential for re-building the Egyptian economy. The role of HRM in improving Egyptian organizational performance by focusing on training and development programmes to retain talent, other HRM practices such as recruitment and selection, performance appraisal and wages and salaries should also be considered.

Buciuniene and Kazlauskaite (2012) argue for the critical role that HRM plays in promoting and enhancing corporate social responsibility (CSR) as HR contributes to the development of synchronicity between economic goals, social goals and organizational performance. This means that organizations should recruit and select employees with certain morals and values, and develop an appraisal system which would help to enhance employees' social performance. They should also focus on training and development to help employees understand these values and reward employees for the value attunement. This is important in creating a positive attitude and behaviour characteristics at the workplace. Zizek and Mulej (2013) suggest that CSR has positive impacts on organizational performance, organizational growth and development and employees' wellbeing through HRM in any organization.

There is also a need to make a deliberate effort towards empowering a professional HRM role as a strategy in Egyptian organizations to gain efficient and effective organizational performance. Egyptian organizations can contribute more effectively to Egyptian society if they give more attention to HRM practices and their implementations at an individual and organizational level of performance. Some advice to the policy makers would be to invest in the youth, create jobs, provide the right training, implement equal employment opportunity (EEO), encourage investments, empower women, work hand in hand with civil society, encourage participation in political life and build trust in government, as these are the key factors in re-building Egypt.

USEFUL WEBSITES

American Chamber of Commerce: http://www.amcham.org.eg.
Countries and their Cultures: http://www.everyculture.com/Cr-Ga/Egypt.html#ixzz38NpWML79.
Economy Watch: http://www.economywatch.com/economic-statistics/country/Egypt/2014.
Egypt Economic Statistics and Indicators 2014: http://www.tradingeconomics.com/egypt/gdp-per-capita.
Reuters Middle East. Sisi's economic vision for Egypt: back to the future, 22 May 2014: https://en-maktoob.news.yahoo.com/sisis-economic-vision-egypt-back-future-133555142.html.
The World Bank: http://www.worldbank.org/en/country/egypt/overview.

REFERENCES

Abdou, D.S. and Zaazou, Z. 2013. The Egyptian revolution and post socio-economic impact. *Middle Eastern and African Economies*, **15**: 92–115.

Afiouni, F., Karam, C.M. and El-Hajj, H. 2013. The HR value proposition model in the Arab Middle East: identifying the contours of an Arab Middle Eastern HR model. *International Journal of Human Resource Management*, **24**(10): 1895–1932.

Afiouni, F., Ruël, H. and Schuler, R. 2014. HRM in the Middle East: toward a greater understanding. *International Journal of Human Resource Management*, **25**(2): 133–143.

Ahmed, M. 1995. *Business Ethics in Islam*. The International Institute of Islamic Thought, Islamabad.

Aladwan, K., Bhanugopan, R. and Fish, A. 2014. Managing human resources in Jordanian organizations: challenges and prospects. *International Journal of Islamic and Middle Eastern Finance and Management*, **7**(1): 126–138.

Ali, A.J. 1987. Scaling an Islamic work ethic. *Journal of Social Psychology*, **128**: 575–583.

Ali, A.J. 2005. *Islamic Perspectives on Management and Organization*. Cheltenham, UK and Northampton, MA, USA: Edward Elgar.

American Chamber of Commerce 2009. Overall assessment of selected apparel manufacturing factories. Paper presented at conference on Improving labour productivity in Egypt's ready-made garment sector, Cairo, 5 April.

Buciuniene, I. and Kazlauskaite, R. 2012. The linkage between HRM, CSR and performance outcomes. *Baltic Journal of Management*, **7**(1): 5–24.

Budhwar, P. and Mellahi, K. 2006. *Managing Human Resources in the Middle East*, New York: Routledge.

Budhwar, P. and Mellahi, K. 2007. Introduction: human resource management in the Middle East. *International Journal of Human Resource Management*, **18**(1): 2–10.

Burke, R. and El-Kot, G. 2011. Human resource management research in Egypt. *Review of Management*, **1**(4): 1–6.

Burke, R., El-Kot, G., Fikskenbaum, L., Koyuncu, M. and Jeng, W. 2011. Potential antecedents and consequences of work family conflict: a three country study. Creating Balance?: International Perspectives on the Work–Life Integration of Professionals. In Stephan Kaiser and Cornelia Reindl (eds), *Creating Balance?: International Perspectives on the Work–Life Integration of Professionals*. Berlin: Springer.

CAPMAS 2014. Egypt. *Industrial Statistics Bulletin*.

CIA 2015. Egypt economy 2015. In *CIA World Factbook*. http://www.theodora.com/wfbcurrent/egypt/egypt_economy.html (accessed 22April 2015).

Darrag, M., Mohamed, A. and Abdel Aziz, H. 2010. Investigating recruitment practices and problems of multinational companies (MNCs) operating in Egypt. *Education, Business and Society Contemporary Middle Eastern Issues*, **3**(2): 99–116.

IOM 2011. *Egypt after January 25: Survey of Youth Migration Intentions*, IOM, May 2011.

Egypt Economic Statistics and Indicators 2014. GDP per capita. http://www.tradingeconomics.com/egypt/gdp-per-capita.

Egypt Government Profile 2015. http://www.indexmundi.com/egypt/government_profile.html (accessed 24April 2015).

Egyptian Constitution 2014. Generated at 11 March 2015. www. constituteproject.org.

El-Kot, G. and Leat, M. 2002. An exploratory investigation of some work related values among middle managers in Egypt. 2002 International Applied Business Research Conference, Puerto Vallarta, Mexico, 14–19 March.

El-Kot, G. and Burke, R. 2014. The Islamic work ethics among employees in Egypt. *International Journal of Islamic and Middle East Finance and Management*, **7**(2): 228–235.

El-Kot, G. and Leat, M. 2007. HRM practices in Egypt: do Egyptian and foreign owned organizations adopt similar HRM practices in an Egyptian context? *Arab Journal of Administration*, **27**(1): 175–199.

El-Kot, G. and Leat, M. 2008. A survey of recruitment and selection practices in Egypt. *Education, Business and Society: Contemporary Middle Eastern Issues*, **1**(3): 200–212.

El Saady, R. 2011. The role of SMEs in Mediterranean economies: the Egyptian experience. *Economy and Territory*, pp. 224–227.

Evans-Klock, C. and Lim, L.L. 1998. Options for human resource development in Egypt: the labour market context. ILO Employment and Training Paper 35.

Farid, D. 2014. Egypt's economy over three years of turmoil. *Daily News Egypt*. http://www.dailynewsegypt.com/2014/09/20/egypts-economy-three-years-turmoil/ (accessed 22April 2015).

Friedman, E. 2013. 4 external factors that affect human resource management. http://www.blogging4jobs.com/hr/4-external-factors-that-affect-human-resource-management/ (accessed 26April 2015).

Genc, K.Y. 2014. Environmental factors affecting human resources management activities of Turkish large firms. *International Journal of Business and Management*, **9**(11): 102–122.

Ghanem, H. 2013. The role of micro and small enterprises in Egypt's economic transition. Global Economy and Development, Working Papers 55.

Handoussa, H. 2010. *Situation Analysis: Key Development Challenges Facing Egypt*. Ministry of International Cooperation.

Hashim, J. 2010. Human resource management practices on organizational commitment: the Islamic Perspective. *Personnel Review*, **39**(6): 785–799.

Hatcher, T. 2009. Political issues in human resource development, Human Resources and Their Development, vol. 1, *Encyclopaedia of Life Support System EOLSS*.

Iles, P., Almhedie, A. and Baruch, Y. 2012. Managing HR in the Middle East: challenges in the public sector. *Public Personnel Management*, **41**(3): 465–483.

ILO 2009. *Country Level Rapid Employment Impact Assessment*. Geneva.

ILO 2010. Growth, economic policies and employment linkages in Mediterranean countries: the case of Egypt, Israel, Morocco and Turkey. By Gouda Abdel-Khalek. Employment Sector, Employment Working Paper No. 63.

ILO 2014. Labour market transitions of young women and men in Egypt. By Baesoum G, Ramadan, M. and Mostafa, M. Youth Employment Programme, Employment Policy Department, Work4Youth Publication Series No. 16.

IMF 2015. *IMF Country Report No. 15/33. Arab Republic of Egypt*. February 2015. http://www.imf.org/external/pubs/ft/scr/2015/cr1533.pdf.

Ismail, A.H. 2010. Cultural influences on human resources management practices: implications for Arab subsidiaries of multinational enterprises. Unpublished MSc thesis, University of Illinois at Urbana-Champaign.

Issa, F. 2011. Public sector human resource managers promoting professionalism and implementing the public service charter at the national level: facilitating and inhibiting factors and strategic actions. Discussion paper 2 at workshop on promoting professionalism in the public service: the strengthening the role of HRM managers in the public sector for the implementation in Africa public service charter, 14–18 March.

Kanungo, R.N. and Jaeger, A.M. 1990. Introduction: the need for indigenous management in developing countries. In R.N. Kanungo and A.M. Jaeger (eds), *Management in Developing Countries*. London: Routledge, pp. 1–19.

Kirby, D. and Ibrahim, N. 2012. An enterprise revolution for Egyptian universities. *Education, Business and Society: Contemporary Middle Eastern Issues*, **5**(2): 98–111.

Kortam, H. 2014. Egypt ranks 159th of 180 countries in 2014 World Press Freedom Index. *Daily News Egypt*. http://www.dailynewsegypt.com/2014/02/13/egypt-ranks-159th-180-countries-2014-world-press-freedom-index/ (accessed 26April 2015).

Leat, M. and El-Kot, G. 2007. HRM practices in Egypt: the influence of national context? *International Journal of Human Resource Management*, **18**(1): 147–158.

Mansour, E. 2012. The role of social networking sites (SNSs) in the January 25th revolution in Egypt. *Library Review*, **61**(2): 128–159.

Ministry of Investment 2015. http://www.investment.gov.eg/en/.

Muwanga, A.D. 2011. The role of human resource managers in the public service in promoting professionalism and implementing the charter role for public service in Africa. Discussion paper 3 at workshop on promoting professionalism in the public service: the strengthening the role of HRM managers in the public sector for the implementation in Africa public service charter, 14–18 March.

Oxford Business Group 2013. The Report: Egypt 2013. http://www.oxfordbusinessgroup.com/egypt-2013.

Parnell, J.A. and Hatem, T. 1999. Cultural antecedents of behavioral differences between American and Egyptian managers. *Journal of Management Studies*, **36**: 399–418.

PCSU 2002. *The Result and Impacts of Egypt's Privatization Program*. Privatization Coordination Support Unit, Special Study August 2002.

Ramadan, M. 2014. *HR Management and the Arab Spring*. CIPD.

Robbins, S.P., Coulter, M., Sidani, Y. and Jamali, D. 2011. *Management Arab World Edition*. Edinburgh: Pearson.

Sabri, H.A. and Rayyan, M. 2014. Managing human capital in Arab countries: the leadership and cultural challenges. *International Journal of Economics, Commerce and Management*, **2**(12): 1–9.

Saddi, J., Sabbagh, K., Shediac, R. and Jamjoum, M. 2012. Staying on the road to growth: why Middle East leaders must maintain their commitment to economic reform. Booz & Co White Paper. http://www.booz.com/global/home/what-we-think/reports-white-papers/article-display/staying-road-growth-middle-east.

The World Economic Forum 2013. *The Global Gender Gap Report 2013*.

UNDP 2006. Human Development Report 2006: Beyond Scarcity: Power, Poverty and the Global Water Crisis. http://hdr.undp.org/en/content/human-development-report-2006.

UNDP 2010. *Egypt Human Development Report 2010*: youth in Egypt: building our future. http://www.eg.undp.org/content/dam/egypt/docs/Publications/Docs%20HDRs/02_NHDR%202010%20english.pdf.

World Bank 2014. Forecast table. http://www.worldbank.org/en/publication/global-economic-prospects (accessed 16 April 2015).

Zizek, S. and Mulej, M. 2013. Social responsibility: a way of requisite holism of humans and their well-being. *Kybernetes*, **42**(2): 318–335.

12. Human resource management in Algeria

Boumediene Ramdani, Kamel Mellahi and Cherif Guermat

INTRODUCTION

The Global Competitiveness Report (2013–2014) classified Algeria as a transition economy at 'stage 2' of development. That is, Algeria is in the process of transiting from a 'factor' driven economy where it competes primarily on its 'factor endowments – primarily unskilled labour and natural resources' (Schwab and Sala-i-Martín, 2013, p. 10) to an efficiency driven one. To make the progression from a factor driven economy to an efficiency driven economy, Algeria needs to enhance its human capital capabilities by investing in higher education and training, achieving higher labour market efficiency and developing more efficient production processes (Schwab and Sala-i-Martín, 2013). This highlights two critical issues. First, the deeply institutionalised, but highly ineffective human resource management (HRM) practices of Algerian organisations need to be transformed. Second, organisations in Algeria need to take human resources (HR) seriously and develop a new paradigm of the management of people. This chapter addresses these issues by exploring the external and internal contexts within which HRM takes place to discover the forces driving the change, the role and the status of the HR department/function, and examining HRM policies and practices within Algerian organisations.

The chapter begins with a discussion on how the recent changes in the socio-political and economic environment coupled with changes in the cultural and institutional environment are affecting HRM policies and practices in Algeria. It then discusses the status and role of the HR department in Algerian firms, before looking at HRM policies and practices within Algerian organisations, focusing on High Performance Work Practices (HPWP). Because of the lack of published literature on HRM in Algeria, the discussions on the status and roles of the HR department and HRM policies and practices are based on an empirical study of a sample of Algerian firms. This chapter will conclude with a summary of results, a brief discussion of the main challenges facing the HR function in Algeria and suggestions for future research.

ECONOMIC AND POLITICAL CONTEXT

Despite Algeria's significant oil and gas resources and its position as the 48th largest economy globally and the 4th in Africa (IMF, 2014), it has been rated relatively low (93 out of 187 countries) on the Human Development Index (UNDP, 2014). The labour market is highly inefficient and was ranked last by the Global Competitiveness Index (Schwab and Sala-i-Martín, 2012). The Algerian economy is dominated by small and medium-sized enterprises (SMEs). There are about 750,000 SMEs in Algeria, 90 per cent of which are micro businesses (MIDIPI, 2013). The failure rate of SMEs is very high. About six thousand SMEs disappeared after their creation in 2008 due to the incompetence of SMEs' owners or managers, particularly in the management of HR (Tabet-Aouel and Bendiabdellah, 2010). This explains the high labour turnover and low job security within the Algerian SME sector.

According to the World Bank, unemployment has remained at 10 per cent since 2010, with youth unemployment as high as 24.8 per cent (World Bank, 2015). Although unemployment has been reduced, it remains a significant cause of social exclusion and unrest. The public sector has been and remains the main source of employment, while the private sector remains too small to continue absorbing the workforce that could not be employed by the public sector. This sector, like in most emerging and developing countries, suffers from ineffective HRM practices and poor recruitment policies due to the lack of training opportunities and weak transparency of recruiting public servants.

In order to contribute to job creation, since the 2000s, the Algerian government has encouraged the creation of private businesses by introducing a number of programmes including generous micro-credits, incentives for entrepreneurs to employ young people, and new education and training opportunities. Employee relations are not a priority for owners and managers of micro businesses because labour supply is greater than demand, and the culture of filing complaints and/or disputes is non-existent in Algeria (Tabet-Aouel and Bendiabdellah, 2010).

Since 2010, Algeria has been undergoing a number of ambitious programmes to improve the country's infrastructure and human development. In order to realise these development programmes, the Algerian authorities could not rely on local expertise as most companies are SMEs and do not possess the necessary capabilities to handle large projects. In their analysis of one of the major construction projects, Morana et al. (2014) show that the majority of employees were of Chinese origin. Their main conclusion regarding this large, and arguably typical, enterprise is the near complete lack of HR policies. Specifically, they found that the identification of skills was not formalised and that recruitment was chaotic.

The Development of the HR Function

The HR function has been shaped by the economic and political context within which it has operated. Generally, the development of the HR function in Algeria has gone through five major phases of development. The first phase followed the independence of the country in 1962. After more than 130 years, the country found itself with a poorly skilled and largely uneducated population. As a result, the HR function then focused on filling the gaps left by the departing French managers (Nellis, 1977). Understandably, inexperienced managers held top management positions during this early stage.

Recruitment was considered as the main answer to a social need to absorb high levels of unemployment (Branine, 2001). Under immense social pressure, the new state ordered companies to recruit even when they were overstaffed and even when those recruits were unskilled or unqualified.

The second phase saw the rise of the socialist enterprise in the 1970s, an ambitious industrial development programme which was initiated by building huge manufacturing sites (Branine, 1994; Branine, 2002). A self-management system was introduced whereby committees made up of elected worker representatives played a significant role in the day-to-day running of their organisations. Because of lack of experience in managing large-scale organisations, industrial complexes were not efficiently managed. The HR role focused on supporting national programmes by establishing training centres to address severe skill shortages.

The third and fourth phases saw restructuring reforms in the 1980s and 1990s, respectively. During these two phases, state-owned firms were given significant autonomy. This meant that HR departments took on the tasks of developing job descriptions and administering personnel tools. Managers with 'appropriate' political affiliation held top positions. The 1990s saw further restructuring by introducing the 90-11 Act, which marked a significant departure from the old employment regulation (Boutaleb, 2012). This act was in fact the official signal that Algeria intended to move away from a centrally controlled to a more liberal system of management. However, there were signs that the management of HRM needed rethinking, as a significant number of strikes took place because managers were not equipped with the necessary tools to manage effectively and take appropriate decisions on promotions, incentives and relocation. As a result, this era was dominated by a lack of trust between employees, who struggled to adjust to a more managed approach, and management, who lacked the necessary toolkit to manage effectively. Perceptions of distributive and procedural injustices were very high.

In the final (current) phase, the government focused mostly on renewing the country's out-dated infrastructure and partly relieving society from the severe housing crisis. Foreign expertise was called upon to carry out these projects, which led to an influx of multinational firms, particularly from Italy, China, France and Turkey. The vast majority of Algerian firms, which are limited in size and capabilities, are mostly involved in smaller-scale projects (Morana et al., 2014), or as subcontractors to multinational firms. These massive development programmes created new realities of HR needs and expectations. Some aspects of these needs and expectations will be explored later in the chapter.

CULTURAL CONTEXT

The Algerian society resembles many Arab and Islamic societies. Similar to these, Algerians are deeply religious, characterised by high fatalistic orientations, high power distance and collectivism (Tiliouine et al., 2009; Ramdani et al., 2014). As a religious society, people tend to explain 'outcomes' as divine providence. Also, there is a significant gap between values and attitudes and actual behaviours in the workplace (Mellahi and Budhwar, 2010). While Islamic core values such as the principles of honesty (*al-Sidq*), trust (*al-Amanah*), justice and fairness in dealing with employees (*al-'Adl*), teamwork and cooperation (*al-Ta'awun*; *al-Takaful*), and perfection/excellence (*al-Ikhlas*) (Mellahi and Budhwar, 2010) are prevalent in Algeria, they are not reflected in practice.

The implications of these cultural traits are twofold. Employee fatalistic orientations may induce employees to become passive and non-responsive to the HR department's policy or directives. Also, as a result of the incongruence between cultural and religious beliefs and actual behaviour there is a big gap between the rhetoric, which is often based on cultural and religious beliefs, and real practice.

Also, like other Middle Eastern countries, employee relations in Algeria are driven by high power distance and strong collectivist tendencies (Calza et al., 2010; Ralston et al., 2012). Algerian employees and managers have high uncertainty avoidance (Seghir, 2009), are highly risk averse and tend to have a low performance orientation. Seghir (2009) recognises that the culture of Algerian companies does not align with employees' expectations. Paradoxically, there is little obedience to authority in Algeria. Algerian employees tend to resist subordination and submissiveness even though the country is characterised as a high power culture. The often-reported high power distance in Algeria is a reflection of the *existence* of psychological and physical distances between managers and employees but not their *acceptance* by the latter group. The above realities point to potential difficulties faced by the HR department in Algerian firms in dealing with disciplining, rewarding and motivating their workforce.

TRAINING AND EDUCATION CONTEXT

The skill base of the country is weak. Despite more than 40 years of government investment in education and training, skilled labour remains scarce. This lack of trained personnel is generally attributed to inadequate, poor quality, education and training systems. It is also the result of the brain drain, particularly to the West and the Gulf, and especially during the political unrest of the 1990s (Kendel, 2008). The higher education sector does not seem to provide the business sector with appropriately qualified graduates. Despite the mushrooming of universities and technical colleges, and the consequent increase in the number of graduates in the recent decade, the quality of graduates has not improved. The Algerian media is replete with stories of poor quality graduates and mismatch between education output and labour market needs. Most of the managers we interviewed highlighted the lack of technical and general skills in new recruits as well as, what they believe as graduates' unreasonable expectations. As highlighted by one interviewed manager, new recruits tend to ask for high wages and are unwilling to start at the bottom of the ladder and get the necessary experience. These aspirations are often justified solely by the acquisition of degrees rather than the required skills. One manager from the service sector complained that almost all new recruits were unable to communicate, in writing or verbally, in French, which is the business language of Algeria. Another manager from the electronics industry complained that university engineering graduates have such poor general skills that it is extremely difficult to retrain them to acceptable levels.

Because of the strong influence of nepotism, commonly known as '*ma'arifa – connections*' or '*kta'f – knowing someone powerful*', historically the recruitment process in the government sector required an educational certificate as a *sine qua non* for obtaining a non-manual job. These practices led to the culture of 'get a degree – get a dream job', which, overtime, has become deeply rooted in Algeria. Although this culture is dominant in the government sector, it is also present in the private enterprise.

These deeply rooted problems complicate the recruitment and training tasks of the HR department. Because the majority of potential recruits have a low or irrelevant skill set, it is difficult to hire competent employees. Government pressure, on the one hand, and nepotism on the other, puts severe constraints on the HR department in recruitment. Further, the low skills of recruits would mean the firm needs to allocate a greater share of resources to the training department. For instance, it is common practice for firms in Algeria to train fresh graduates after they are appointed.

INSTITUTIONAL CONTEXT

We focus here on the industrial relations context. According to Branine et al. (2008), the current Algerian system of employee relations is the product of historical circumstances and institutional arrangements that has enabled the state to hold control over unions. In their historical analysis of employee relations in Algeria, they argue that by configuring and reconfiguring the employee relations system, the state developed iron-cage-like institutional arrangements that limit what unions and other labour representatives are able to do and even influence their actions. The landscape of employee relations in Algeria went through a number of changes from the one-union employment relations system dominated by the Union Générale des Travailleurs Algériens (UGTA) – a unitarist industrial relations model – to a pluralist employee relation system during the early 1990s. Since the 2000s, the state has continued to shape the system by favouring the UGTA over other independent unions.

During the colonial era, Algerian workers could not set up trade unions because of their inability to organise themselves into national organisations as well as the dominance of French trade unions, especially the Confédération Générale du Travail (CGT), to which some Algerian workers were affiliated. Algerian workers formed an independent trade union named 'Union Générale des Syndicalistes Algériens', which remained the national trade union until it was absorbed by the UGTA in 1956.

After independence, the UGTA maintained its autonomy and focused on helping the workers occupy the vacant jobs left by French managers. In 1963, the state intervened with legislation to organise the self-management enterprises and undermine the role of trade unions. Many local unions went on strike to protest against the party's control over the trade unions, the imposed UGTA leadership, the inadequate setting up of management committees, corruption and mismanagement, and the long delays in receiving wages and salaries.

By the end of 1968, trade unions were formally under state control. The UGTA became a state-controlled and sponsored organisation supporting the ruling party by opposing mass strikes and public demonstrations and supporting legislation to prohibit strikes in state-owned enterprises. The state created large firms managed by state-appointed directors and introduced a state-imposed system of workers' participation – Socialist Management of Enterprises, 'Gestion Socialiste des Entreprises' (GSE). This was rejected by local trade unions, while the UGTA had to welcome and accept the proposals for the GSE charter. After the introduction of the GSE, trade union membership went from 65 per cent to 85 per cent of the working population in 1973 (Saadi, 1982). This level of membership reflected the role of nationalised trade unions, with state employees having access to social and material privileges, rather than a sign of workers' unity and solidarity.

The situation continued relatively unchanged until 1990. In October 1988, riots and political unrest shook the country, and the government promised fundamental economic and political reforms. As a result, a new industrial relations law was introduced in 1990 laying the foundation for the development of trade union pluralism. The new law contained the formation of autonomous trade unions and the right to collective bargaining for all trade unions, and prohibited any kind of discrimination by employers against union members and leaders. Employees had the right to form and to be represented by trade unions of their choice for the first time. From 1991 to 2001, the country plunged into a civil war and subsequently 'organizing workers became a secondary concern, at best' (Alexander, 2000, p. 484). Successive governments introduced far-reaching reforms that radically changed employment relations in Algeria. They adopted a market economy strategy and encouraged market competition, as well as provided managers with great discretion to reform their organisations and their HRM systems. While the number of independent trade unions continued to rise in the 1990s, the state needed a well-established partner and backed the UGTA as the official union. Partnering with the UGTA, the state has been able to side-line independent unions and by-pass them by involving only the UGTA in its employment relations reforms.

From the early 2000s, the UGTA acquired another privileged status by becoming the only partner the government chose to work with. The UGTA was subsequently reinstated as the only state-sponsored and recognised national trade union. The culture of 'them and us' dominates the current employment relations landscape between the UGTA and independent unions. The approach of the UGTA is to influence employment relations by being a partner of, and working with, the state. Being sidestepped by the government, independent unions have little choice but to adopt a confrontational approach that opposes most of the UGTA's initiatives. Even though the landscape of employee relations in Algeria is different from the previous single-party union system, the government has been unable to transfer the system to a pluralist one.

HR ROLES AND HPWP

As noted earlier, because of lack of empirical data on HRM in Algeria, we collected both qualitative and quantitative information from a sample of Algerian managers. Qualitative data was obtained via a number of interviews. The quantitative data was mainly on HPWP, and was obtained from a survey of HRM managers in Algeria. We adopted a questionnaire design based on earlier work by Collings et al. (2010), Fey and Björkman (2001), Minbaeva et al. (2003) and Björkman et al. (2007). We also collected data on the status and role of the HR department in Algerian firms. Firm-level surveys are problematic in Algeria, and we faced a number of obstacles getting responses from HRM managers. Managers were not inclined to provide us with firm information despite assurances of confidentiality. Also, HR managers were unsure of their company's procedures as to whether it was possible for them to disclose firm details to outside parties. In addition, managers would not complete the questionnaire unless they had some personal, albeit indirect, connection with the researchers. Consequently, we used a snowballing approach starting with personal contacts to increase the response rate. This resulted in a total of 81 valid responses. Although the original questionnaire was written in English, it was translated and back-translated into and from Arabic and French.

The distribution of respondents is shown in Table 12.1. Nearly 80 per cent of the respondents were middle to upper HR managers. About 40 per cent of the firms were from manufacturing and the rest from the services sector. We matched our sample with the national survey carried out by the Algerian National Office of Statistics (ONS, 2012). Using only firms with ten or more employees in the ONS sample shows that our sample matches closely that of the ONS in terms of sectors' activities. The majority of HR managers are middle aged (30 to 49 years). However, there are a large proportion (30.9 per cent)

Table 12.1 Frequency statistics of respondents

		Respondents' characteristics (n = 81)			
Age	Category	21 to 29	30 to 39	40 to 49	50 or older
	%	8.6	22.2	38.3	30.9
Qualification	Category	Business/ Management	Humanities/ Soc. Sciences	Engineering	Other
	%	25.3	30.4	15.2	29.1
Managerial Level	Category	Upper-Level Management	Middle-Level Management	Lower-Level Management	
	%	43.2	35.8	21.0	
		Firm Characteristics			
Firm Size	Category	50 or less	51–200	201–1000	1001+
	%	25.9	16.0	27.2	30.9
Firm Age	Category	10 or less	11–20	21–30	31+
	%	24.4	24.4	24.4	26.9

of HR managers that are 50 or older. In contrast, the young generation of managers represents 8.6 per cent only. If our sample is representative of the Algerian population, then it would seem that the old generation of managers is not being replaced fully.[1] This attrition could ultimately lead to Algeria relying mostly on foreign management skills similar to most rentier economies of the Middle East. It also indicates that old HRM practices are still prevalent within Algerian firms. Only a quarter of the managers in our sample have business or management degrees, while the remaining three-quarters are dominated by managers holding humanities or social sciences degrees (30.4 per cent). Managers with engineering degrees represent around 15 per cent of the sample, and the remaining 29.1 per cent come from various other backgrounds such as law, arts or linguistics.

THE CURRENT STATUS OF THE HR FUNCTION

Table 12.2 shows that Algerian organisations tend to integrate the HR function with other managerial functions and align it with the strategy of the organisation. It is not yet, however, a full strategic partner. The results of the survey suggest that the HR department is less involved in providing adequate input to the organisation's long-term strategy and planning.

As argued by Bennett et al. (1998), the likelihood that the HR department has an impact on the organisation's strategic decisions is dependent on its early involvement in the strategic decision process. Thus, the organisation's strategy may not reflect some of the important HR issues faced by HR departments in Algeria if the HR managers do not actively contribute to the strategy formulation stage. Buyens and De Vos (2001, p. 74) noted that

> the stage of involvement can be considered as a relevant indicator of the integration and appreciation of the HR function within the organisation (p.74) . . . (and) strategic integration means more than simply matching HR policies with business strategy. The extent to which human resources are perceived to be of central importance for the business will determine the perceived added value of the function within the organisation.

Table 12.2 *Role and status of the HR department and function in Algeria*

Role	Mean	SD
The HR department provides input into our organisation's long-range strategic planning	2.94	1.528
The HR department meets regularly with the organisation's manager to discuss HR issues	3.13	1.529
The HR department's role is to implement rather than advise	2.81	1.558
The HR department adopts and modifies HR systems to implement firm's strategies	2.93	1.456
Our company makes an explicit effort to align business and HR/personnel strategies	3.31	1.329
HR/personnel managers are viewed as partners in the management of the business and agents for change	3.35	1.510
My firm's HRM policies and practices in the various HRM areas are closely integrated with each other	2.96	1.299

Note: Respondents were asked to rate their agreement with the above statements (from 1 for 'strongly disagree', to 5 for 'strongly agree'). The average response is an overall view of the respondents' perception of a particular statement.

Interestingly, HR managers believe that they are viewed as valuable partners in the management of the business and perceived as active agents for change (mean = 3.35).[2] This perhaps reflects the fact that compared with the past when the HR function was at the bottom of the managerial food chain; the status of the HR function has risen significantly (Yanat and Scouarnec, 2006). The results suggest that the HR function in surveyed Algerian organisations has evolved from being seen as a purely administrative function with disconnected responsibilities to the organisation's overall goals, to playing a significant role in the implementation of the organisation's strategy. This reflects our earlier discussion of the recent changes in the competitive landscape in Algeria. Borrowing Gratton et al.'s (1999) and Fombrun et al.'s (1984) terminology, the analysis suggests that Algerian organisations are applying the 'matching' or 'best fit' model whereby they are seeking to match their HR strategies to their business strategies. Overall, the HR function in Algeria appears to play a supporting role by aligning its practices to support the implementation of the organisation's strategy and operations.

HR CAPABILITY

Although managers of organisations in Algeria seem to realise, and appreciate, the importance of managerial-oriented models to the management of human resources, there appears to be a problem in equipping HR managers with the necessary tools to make full use of their human resources. A significant number of HR managers (mean = 2.84) reported that they lack the knowledge and skills to develop and carry out long-range integrated HRM programmes. This explains perhaps why top managers tend not to involve HR managers in strategy formulation. Interestingly, HR managers see their roles as 'routine administration instead of attempting to maximise the long-term benefits for the firm and its employees' (mean = 3.21). Furthermore, the analysis suggests that HR managers do not only believe that they lack the skills to make a strategic contribution to

Table 12.3 HR capabilities in Algerian organisations

HR capability	Mean	SD
Our HR staff lack the knowledge and skills to develop and carry out a long-range integrated HRM programme	2.84	1.42
My firm's HRM staff see their job as routine administration instead of attempting to maximise the long-term benefits for the firm and its employees	3.21	1.48
Our HRM staff lack the influence and credibility to gain the resources and management commitment to implement effective new policies and practices	3.02	1.41

Note: Respondents were asked to rate their agreement with the above statements (from 1 for 'strongly disagree', to 5 for 'strongly agree'). The average response is an overall view of the respondents' perception of a particular statement.

the firm, but they also lack the influence and credibility to obtain the necessary resources and management commitment to carry out their policies and practices effectively (see Table 12.3). This is surprising given that most organisations reported that their 'top managers view employees as a key factor to our success rather than a cost to be minimized' (mean = 3.28).

HPWP IN ALGERIA

Rather than identify and discuss the actual HRM practices in Algeria, we believe it is more important to focus on the extent to which HPWPs are practised in Algeria. In recent years, many Algerian firms have begun adopting global 'high-performance' practices, resulting in 'heavy borrowing' of fashionable Western HR practices, especially by newly established firms. Also, a number of foreign firms have flocked to Algeria, benefiting from the close proximity to Europe, low cost of labour and potential growth opportunities (Peretti and Slama, 2009), and bringing with them new global norms and practices. Moreover, a number of private business schools with European associations have been nudging local firms to adopt international best practices. Given the adoption of HPWP by firms in Algeria (Ramdani et al., 2014), it would be interesting to assess the extent to which they are practised by Algerian firms.

The dominant view that 'good US practices are good (anywhere)' (Newman and Nollen, 1996) has been challenged recently by many scholars (e.g. Fey et al., 2009). Cultural and institutional considerations often intervene in the practice-performance process (Hofstede, 1993; DiMaggio and Powell, 1983). Many scholars have doubted this implicit universality of HPWP and debated whether they are appropriate in emerging and developing countries (Horwitz et al., 2002; Sun et al. 2007; Collings et al., 2010). This has been substantiated by studies in Africa (e.g. Azolukwam and Perkins, 2009; Anakwe, 2002). In this section, we consider five HPWP, namely, employee training, employee empowerment, performance-based compensation, competence-based performance appraisal and merit-based promotion. These are based on Fey et al.'s (2009) list of HRM practices and have been used previously in many studies (cf. Minbaeva et al., 2003; Collings et al., 2010).

Employee Training

This is one of Pfeffer's (1998) most recommended practices. Training enhances the human capital of the firm (Becker, 1975) and improves firm performance (Delaney and Huselid, 1996; Koch and McGrath, 1996; Stavrou et al., 2010). For employees, training is a signal that the firm values them and cares about developing their careers (Noe, 1986; Keep, 1989). This in turn leads to greater employee commitment and attitudes (Lowry et al., 2002; Bartlett, 2001; Morris et al., 1993). However, training is expensive and open to abuse. Organisations, therefore, may see little return from training (Salas et al., 1999; Wright and Geroy, 2001; Caudron, 2002). In the West, there is clear evidence on the positive impact of training on firm performance (Black and Lynch, 1996; Garcia, 2005; Tharenou et al., 2007). Dysvik and Kuvaas (2008, pp.140–141) emphasise that high levels of training end up creating feelings of employee obligation, which, in turn, 'influences employees to benefit the organisation through behaviours that exceed minimal requirements of employment'.

Algeria is characterised by a low performance orientation (Calza et al., 2010) and strong collectivist tendencies (Ralston et al., 2012). These tend to undermine the level of investment in training and development (Aycan, 2005). Although training has been found to be a major concern for entrepreneurs, micro businesses do not establish appropriate training programmes, and carry out the necessary training in-house with cost as the only criterion (Tabet-Aouel and Bendiabdellah, 2010).

We measure training by three items as shown in Table 12.4. The first item is the number of days per year of formal training for managerial employees. The second item relates to non-managerial employees. The third item is a perceptive variable on whether the respondent's firm places a great deal of importance on training, and is measured on a 5-point Likert scale.

Employee Empowerment

Empowerment enhances firm performance through motivating harder and more flexible work (Hackman and Oldham, 1976), encouraging the use of initiative (Frese et al., 1996) and making employees more proactive (Parker et al., 2006). As Algeria is a high power distance society, there may be a greater emphasis for subordinates to show respect for their superiors. However, this view can be countered by two considerations. First, the long experience of 'self-management' that Algeria has had up to the 1970s (Branine, 2006; Branine et al., 2008) has left a legacy whereby employees continue to expect to be involved in the management of their organisations. The second consideration is cultural. The Algerian mentality is anti-class, and, although regionalism does exist, it does not lead to a feeling of superiority or entitlement, both of which Algerians despise. In addition, Islamic teachings, which emphasise equality and the process of consultation, '*Shura*', are deeply rooted in Algerian behaviour.

Empowerment was captured by two items (Table 12.5), namely the extent to which managers agree or disagreed with the statement that their employee input and suggestions are highly encouraged and often implemented (Collings et al., 2010). In the case of employee empowerment both sample means are below the neutral value of 3. The low standard deviations (1.40 and 1.28, respectively) suggest that respondents do not

Table 12.4 Training in Algerian organisations

	None	1–9 days	10–15 days	>15 days	Mean	SD
On average, how many days of formal training do managerial employees receive annually?	32.1%	23.5%	22.2%	22.2%	10.70	13.83
On average, how many days of formal training do non-managerial employees receive annually?	38.3%	35.8%	22.2%	3.7%	5.52	5.92
Our company places a great deal of importance on training	—	—	—	—	3.18	1.40

Note: Respondents were asked to rate their agreement with the above statements (from 1 for 'strongly disagree', to 5 for 'strongly agree'). The average response is an overall view of the respondents' perception of a particular statement.

Table 12.5 High performance work practices in Algeria

Practices	Survey items	Mean	SD
Employee empowerment	Employee input and suggestions are highly encouraged	2.95	1.40
	Employee input and suggestions are often implemented	2.59	1.28
Performance-based compensation	Our compensation system is closely connected with the financial results of the company	3.41	1.57
	Our company uses performance-based compensation	3.18	1.52
Competence-based appraisal	Formal appraisal exists for at least some occupations	3.21	1.42
	Appraisal is linked to pay	3.10	1.50
	Appraisal is conducted at least once a year	3.41	1.47
	Appraisals are used for a non-financial purpose (e.g. feedback, behaviour change)	3.07	1.46
Merit-based promotion	Qualified employees have the opportunity to be promoted to positions of greater pay and/or responsibility within the company	3.42	1.35
	Our company places a great deal of importance on the following factors when making promotion decisions:		
	A. Merit	3.66	1.34
	B. Seniority	3.47	1.16
	C. Good personal relationships	3.44	1.41

Note: Respondents were asked to rate their agreement with the above statements (from 1 for 'strongly disagree', to 5 for 'strongly agree'). The average response is an overall view of the respondents' perception of a particular statement.

diverge in their perception. Managers' perception on whether employee input is highly encouraged has a mean of 2.95, which means that some managers slightly disagree while others slightly agree. Still, overall this value does not show support for the statement and thus it is reasonable to assume that employee input and suggestions are not encouraged in Algerian enterprises. There is an even stronger disagreement with the suggestion that employee input and suggestions are often implemented. Here the mean is 2.59, which clearly reflects strong disagreement with the statement.

Performance-based Compensation

Performance-based reward has been identified as one of the best HRM practices (Pfeffer, 1998; Minbaeva et al., 2003; Fey et al., 2009; Collings et al., 2010). Compensation schemes motivate employees (Guest, 1997) and usually lead to better organisational performance (Gomez-Mejia and Wiseman, 1997; Becker and Huselid, 1998). While this might be the case for high-performance-oriented cultures, it may be a different case for cultures with high power distance (Aycan et al., 2000). Indeed, in collectivist societies, compensation schemes or reward programmes can sometimes be counterproductive by inducing resentment from those who were less lucky (Aycan, 2005). Evidence from developing countries, however, points to a positive link between performance-based compensation and individual and business performance (Mellahi et al., 2013; Gurbuz and Mert, 2011; Wang et al., 2011).

As illustrated in Table 12.5, compensation was measured by two items. These relate to whether the firm linked compensation to financial performance, and whether it uses performance-based compensation (Björkman et al., 2007). First, there seems to be a slight agreement that compensation depends on the financial results of the company. The average response of 3.41 suggests that there is more agreement than disagreement. However, the standard deviation is also high which suggests divergence of opinions amongst the surveyed managers regarding the relation between the company's financial performance and its compensation system. Second, there is less overall agreement that compensation is based on employee performance. The average of 3.18 tends towards the neutral (neither agree nor disagree) perception on this statement. We can therefore conclude that there is a general negative perception by managers regarding the reward system in their firms (although the high standard deviation suggests mixed views amongst the managers).

Competence-based Performance Appraisal

The aim of an effective performance appraisal system is to help identify employee performance as well as possible gaps that could be addressed through training (Locke et al., 1990). A good appraisal system would help distinguish good and poor performers (so that rewards are allocated equitably and effectively), convey to employees what is expected of them, motivate desired performance and identify training needs. In developed economies, it is generally recognised that performance appraisal leads to better firm performance (Katou and Budhwar, 2006). However, performance measurement is both system and culture bound (Aycan, 2005). For the former, performance measurement is usually based on quantifiable metrics such as productivity, timeliness and quantity of outputs. While individualist cultures adopt performance measures that are more objective, relatively accurate, and observable (Harris and Moran, 1996), firms in developing countries may not have the means or resources to obtain such objective and observable measures. For the latter, collectivist cultures value loyalty over productivity (Aycan, 2005). So even if performance was measurable, performing employees may be ostracised because 'standing out' may disturb group harmony and invoke resentment (Kovach, 1995; Vallance, 1999).

In a study of Algerian micro businesses, Tabet-Aouel and Bendiabdellah (2010) found that owners and/or managers did not carry out annual appraisals. As shown in Table 12.5, appraisal was measured by four items, based on Ramsay et al. (2000). The perception of appraisal by managers is generally negative. Of the four appraisal statements, two have average scores near the neutral value of 3, suggesting that appraisal is not linked to pay and that it is not conducted for non-financial purposes. However, there is some slight agreement with the presence of some formal appraisal, especially with the statement that appraisal is conducted at least once a year, where the average response is 3.41. If we put all items together, it is apparent that although appraisal does exist as a formality in more than half of the surveyed firms, managers do not see it as an effective tool (i.e. as a means that partly determines pay, or as a means that helps employee behaviour through feedback).

Merit-based Promotion

When a good promotion system is present within the firm, employees are likely to be strongly motivated (Pfeffer, 1994; Lepak and Snell, 1999). A promotion system encourages employees to remain with the firm, and signals the firm's commitment to its employees (Minbaeva et al., 2003). However, when employee promotion decisions are made on the basis of non-performance criteria, such as relationships, organisational tenure or employee age, their effect can be negative (Fey et al., 2009). Unlike high-performance cultures, promotion decisions are usually not based on merit in Algeria. Being a collectivistic culture, favouritism dominates as promotions are usually based on seniority, loyalty and good interpersonal relationships with other employees and superiors (Aycan, 2005). Merit-based promotion was measured by four items, based on Gardner (2011). The first item emphasises the opportunity for qualified employees to be promoted, whereas the second to fourth items focus on the importance of merit, seniority and good personal relationships in getting promotion.

In contradistinction to the previous practices, promotion seems to be viewed slightly positively by managers – average scores are above 3.40 with relatively small standard deviations (suggesting general agreement by managers). The weakest agreement is with the statement that qualified employees have the opportunity for promotion. The average response is 3.42, which indicates some level of agreement by managers. However, this agreement is only marginal, because for an average to be close to 3, many responses had to be negative or strongly negative.

The second to fourth items, which reflect the promotion decision, show strong agreement with the perception that promotions are influenced by merit, seniority and personal relationships. Although merit is the strongest factor (with an average of 3.66), seniority and personal relationships are not far behind and are almost as important as merit.

CONCLUSIONS

This chapter describes the current realities of HRM in Algeria and attempts to relate the past and future of HRM in Algeria. The chapter begins by highlighting the main hard and soft institutional features of Algeria within which individuals are employed and managed. The second part of the chapter discusses the role and importance of HRM in light of the social and economic challenges facing Algeria, and further explores the key dimensions behind HRM policies and practices, including various aspects of the HR department, a number of the most important HRM practices, and the perception of managers on HRM practices and policies.

The discussion of the HRM context in Algeria reveals that both formal institutional factors, such as education system and industrial relations framework, and social norms, such as work values, govern how firms behave, and in so doing have a strong influence on the management of people in Algeria. The discussion of the political and economic contexts reveals that while Algeria has undergone a radical transition from a centrally commanded economy to a mixed or market economy, the old economic and political system still exerts major influences on how employees are managed in Algeria. Although the Algerian government has continuously decentralised the decision-making process and, as a result, managers of public organisations have, at least officially, more discretion in the management of their plants, there is little evidence that public sector enterprises are no longer influenced by deeply entrenched, old ways of doing things. Also, the private sector is largely influenced by centrally adopted political and economic policies through government subsidies and creation, and through generous financial support of private SMEs. This is expected given the rentier nature of the Algerian economy where over 90 per cent of revenues come from natural resources, namely oil and gas. This said, the competitive landscape has changed significantly over the last decade, where firms are under increasing pressure to enhance their competitiveness through efficiency enhancing practices. The legal framework governing employee relations is still in the developmental stage, and employees' protection rights in the private sector, especially SMEs, are still relatively weak. In addition, the enforcement of labour laws is patchy across Algerian firms.

The education system has a strong influence on the HR function in Algeria. Algeria has made great leaps and strides in terms of building educational infrastructures such as new universities, 'grande écoles' and other specialised 'instituts'. Unfortunately, the education system continues to suffer from the old problem of mismatch between what the education institutions provide and what the job market needs. In addition to formal institutions, the religious and cultural fabric of Algeria exerts a strong influence on HRM.

The empirical evidence presented in this chapter suggests that the HR function is undergoing a paradigm shift within Algerian organisations. It is no longer perceived as the bottom of the pile in terms of prestige and contribution to the organisation's strategy. HR managers reported that they are valued by the top management and expected to contribute to the firm's overall strategic objectives by aligning HRM policies and practices with other managerial functions and, more importantly, with the firm's overall strategy and long-term objectives.

With regard to HPWP, Algerian HR managers do not feel that employee training is important for their companies, which implies low levels of training. Also, employee inputs are not encouraged or implemented, suggesting low levels of empowerment in Algerian firms. Although compensation was found to depend on an organisation's financial performance, there is generally a negative perception by HR managers regarding the reward system in Algerian companies. Moreover, appraisal seems to be a formality as HR managers do not see it as an effective tool. Finally, contrary to other HPWP, promotion is viewed slightly positively by managers.

CHALLENGES FOR HR AND WAY FORWARD

This chapter has explored the internal and external contexts within which HRM in Algeria takes place. In addition to the discussion of contemporary HRM practices within Algerian organisations, the chapter highlighted the key challenges facing HR managers. These include dealing with strong incongruence between stated values and attitudes, managing high levels of disdain and contempt for managerial authority, and coping with the ills of an ineffective education system.

For scholars, the chapter reveals significant avenues for future research. Future research looking at how Algerian values influence HRM within Algerian organisations and implications thereof on performance is highly warranted. Also, more research is needed on how the overall institutional milieu is shaping the practice of HRM in Algeria.

NOTES

1. One interviewed manager stated that he delayed his retirement because a proper replacement could not be found. Related to this point, it is common knowledge that 4 and 5 star hotels are now employing French and Lebanese middle- and upper-level managers.
2. Throughout the chapter, the mean response reflects the average perception of managers as measured on the Likert scale (1 = strongly disagree, to 5 = strong agree).

USEFUL WEBSITES

Ministère du Développement Industriel et de la Promotion de l'Investissement: http://www.mdipi.gov.dz.
Statut Général de la Fonction Publique: http://www.joradp.dz/hfr/Dgfp.htm.
Office Nationale des Statistiques: http://www.ons.dz.
UNDP Human Development Report: http://hdr.undp.org/en.

REFERENCES

ADP 2011. Dialogue note 2011–2012. African Development Bank Group, May. http://www.afdb.org/fileadmin/uploads/afdb/Documents/Project-and-Operations/Algeria-%20Dialogue%20Note%20%202011–2012%20(01%20juin%202011)%20Revised%20English%20final.pdf (accessed 27 July 2016).

Alexander, C. 2000. Opportunities, organizations, and ideas: Islamists and workers in Tunisia and Algeria. *International Journal of Middle East Studies*, **32**: 465–490.

Anakwe, U.P. 2002. Human resource management practices in Nigeria: challenges and insights. *International Journal of Human Resource Management*, **13**: 1042–1059.

Aycan, Z. 2005. The interplay between cultural and institutional/structural contingencies in human resource management practices. *International Journal of Human Resource Management*, **16**: 1083–1119.

Aycan, Z., Kanungo, R.N., Mendonca, M., Yu, K., Deller, J., Stahl, G. and Kurshid, A. 2000. Impact of culture on human resource management practices: a 10-country comparison. *Applied Psychology*, **49**: 192–222.

Azolukwam, V.A. and Perkins, S.J. 2009. Managerial perspectives on HRM in Nigeria: evolving hybridization? *Cross Cultural Management: An International Journal*, **16**: 62–82.

Bartlett, K.R. 2001. The relationship between training and organizational commitment: a study in the health care field. *Human Resource Development Quarterly*, **12**: 325–352.

Becker, E.B. and Huselid, M.A. 1998. High performance work system and firm performance: a synthesis of research and managerial implications. *Research in Personnel and Human Resource Management*, **16**: 53–101.

Becker, G.S. 1975. *Human Capital: A Theoretical and Empirical Analysis with Special Reference to Education*. New York: Colombia University Press.

Bennett, N., Ketchen Jr, D.J. and Shultz, E.B. 1998. An examination of factors associated with the integration of human resource management and strategic decision making. *Human Resource Management Journal*, **37**: 3–16.

Björkman, I., Fey, C.F. and Park, H.J. 2007. Institutional theory and MNC subsidiary HRM practices: evidence from a three country study. *Journal of International Business Studies*, **38**: 430–445.

Black, S.E. and Lynch, L.M. 1996. Human-capital investments and productivity. *American Economic Review*, **86**: 263–267.

Boutaleb, K. 2012. Les politiques des salaires poursuivies en Algérie: une quête contrariée d'efficience. Colloque International Algérie: cinquante ans d'expériences de développement Etat-Economie-Société, Alger, 8–9 Décembre. http://www.cread-dz.org/cinquante-ans/Communication_2012/BOUTALEB.pdf.

Branine, M. 1994. The rise and demise of participative management in Algeria. *Economic and Industrial Democracy*, **15**: 595–630.

Branine, M. 2001. Human resource management in Algeria. In P. Budhwar and Y.A. Debrah (eds), *Human Resource Management in Developing Countries*. Oxon: Routledge, pp. 155–173.

Branine, M. 2002. Algeria's employment policies and practice: an overview. *International Journal of Employment Studies*, **10**: 133–152.

Branine, M. 2006. Human resource management in Algeria. In P. Budhwar, and K. Mellahi (eds), *Human Resource Management in the Middle East*. New York: Routledge, pp. 250–272.

Branine, M., Fekkar, A.F., Fekkar, O. and Mellahi, K. 2008. Employee relations in Algeria: a historical appraisal. *Employee Relations*, **30**: 404–421.

Buyens, D. and De Vos, A. 2001. Perceptions of the value of the HR function. *Human Resource Management Journal*, **11**: 70–89.

Calza, F., Aliane, N. and Cannavale, C. 2010. Cross-cultural differences and Italian firms' internationalization in Algeria: exploring assertiveness and performance orientation. *European Business Review*, **22**: 246–272.

Caudron, C. 2002. Just say no to training fads. *Training and Development*, **56**: 40–43.

Collings, D., Demirbag, M., Mellahi, K. and Tatoglu, E. 2010. Strategic orientation, human resource management practices and organizational outcomes: evidence from Turkey. *International Journal of Human Resource Management*, **21**: 2589–2631.

Delaney, J.T. and Huselid, M. 1996. The impact of human resource management practices on perceptions of organizational performance. *Academy of Management Journal*, **39**: 949–969.

DiMaggio, P.J. and Powell, W.W. 1983. The iron cage revisited: institutional isomorphism and collective rationality in organizational fields. *American Sociological Review*, **48**: 147–160.

Dysvik, A. and Kuvaas, B. 2008. The relationship between perceived training opportunities, work motivation and employee outcomes. *International Journal of Training and Development*, **12**: 138–157.

Fey, C.F. and Björkman, I. 2001. The effect of human resource management practices on MNC subsidiary performance in Russia. *Journal of International Business Studies*, **32**: 59–75.

Fey, C.F., Morgoulis-Jakoushev, S., Park, H.J. and Björkman, I. 2009. Opening up the black box of the relationship between HRM practices and firm performance: a comparison of USA, Finland and Russia. *Journal of International Business Studies*, **40**: 690–712.

Fombrun, C., Tichy, N.M. and Devanna, M.A. 1984. *Strategic Human Resource Management*. New York: Wiley.

Frese, M., Kring, W., Soose, A. and Zempel, J. 1996. Personal initiative at work: differences between East and West Germany. *Academy of Management Journal*, **39**: 37–63.

IMF 2014. *Report for Selected Countries and Subjects*. World Economic Outlook, International Monetary Fund, April. http://www.imf.org/external/pubs/ft/weo/2014/01/weodata/index.aspx (accessed 27 July 2016).

Garcia, M. 2005. Training and business performance: the Spanish case. *International Journal of Human Resource Management*, **16**: 1691–1710.

Gardner, T.M., Wright, P.M. and Moynihan, L.M. 2011. The impact of motivation, empowerment, and skill enhancing practices on aggregate voluntary turnover: the mediating effect of collective affective commitment. *Personnel Psychology*, **64**: 315–350.

Gomez-Mejia, L.R. and Wiseman, R.M. 1997. Reframing executive compensation: an assessment and outlook. *Journal of Management*, **23**: 291–374.

Gratton, L., Hope-Hailey, V., Stiles, P. and Truss, C. 1999. *Strategic Human Resource Management*. Oxford: Oxford University Press.

Guest, D.E. 1997. Human resource management and performance: a review and research agenda. *International Journal of Human Resource Management*, **8**: 263–276.

Gurbuz, S. and Mert, I.S. 2011. Impact of the strategic human resource management on organizational performance: evidence from Turkey. *International Journal of Human Resource Management*, **22**: 1803–1822.

Hackman, J.R. and Oldham G.R. 1976. Motivation through the design of work: test of a theory. *Organizational Behavior and Human Performance*, **16**: 250–279.

Harris, P.R. and Moran, R.T. 1996. *Managing Cultural Differences*. Houston, TX: Gulf.

Hofstede, G. 1993. Cultural constraints in management theories. *Academy of Management Executive*, **7**: 81–94.

Horwitz, F.M., Kamoche, K. and Chew, I.K. 2002. Looking east: diffusing high performance work practices in the southern Afro-Asian context. *International Journal of Human Resource Management*, **13**: 1019–1041.

Katou, A.A. and Budhwar, P.S. 2006. Human resource management systems and organizational performance: a test of a mediating model in the Greek manufacturing context. *International Journal of Human Resource Management*, **17**: 1223–1253.

Keep, E. 1989. Corporate training: the vital component? In J. Storey (ed.), *New Perspectives on Human Resource Management*. London: Routledge, pp. 109–125.

Kendel, H. 2008. Mobilité des compétences et gestion des compétences en Algérie. http://isdm.univ-tln.fr/PDF/isdm33/isdm33_Hayat-Kendel.pdf (accessed 27 July 2016).

Koch, M.J. and McGrath, R.G. 1996. Improving labor productivity: human resource management policies do matter. *Strategic Management Journal*, **17**: 335–354.

Kovach, R.C. Jr 1995. Matching assumptions to environment in the transfer of management practices. *International Studies of Management and Organization*, **24**: 83–100.

Lepak, D.P. and Snell, S.A. 1999. The human resource architecture: towards a theory of human capital allocation and development. *Academy of Management Review*, **24**: 31–48.

Locke, E.A., Latham, G.P. and Smith, K.J. 1990. *A Theory of Goal Setting and Task Performance*. Englewood Cliffs, NJ: Prentice Hall.

Lowry, D.S., Simon, A. and Kimberley, N. 2002. Toward improved employment relations practices of casual employees in the New South Wales registered clubs industry. *Human Resource Development Quarterly*, **13**: 53–70.

Mellahi, K. and Budhwar, P.S. 2010. Introduction: Islam and human resource management. *Personnel Review*, **39**: 685–691.

Mellahi, K., Demirbag, M., Collings, D., Tatoglu, E. and Hughes, M. 2013. Similarly different: a comparison of HRM practices in MNE subsidiaries and local firms in Turkey. *International Journal of Human Resource Management*, **24**(12): 2339–2368.

MIDIPI 2013. Bulletin d'information de la PME. Ministère du Développement Industriel et de la Promotion de l'Investissement, No. 23, November 2013. http://www.mdipi.gov.dz/IMG/pdf/bulletin_PME_23_francais_vf_nov_2013.pdf (accessed 27 July 2016).

Minbaeva, D., Pedersen, T., Björkman, I., Fey, C.F. and Park, H.J. 2003. MNC knowledge transfer, subsidiary absorptive capacity, and HRM. *Journal of International Business Studies*, **34**: 586–599.

Morana, J., Brahimi, F., Bont-Fernandez, D. and Teulon, F. 2014. Compétences de la main-d'oeuvre locale en Algérie et management de projets nationaux: le cas de l'autoroute est-ouest. Ipag Business School, Working Paper 247. http://www.ipag.fr/wp-content/uploads/recherche/WP/IPAG_WP_2014_247.pdf (accessed 27 July 2016).

Morris, M., Lydka, H. and O'Creevy, M.F. 1993. Can commitment be managed? A longitudinal analysis of employee commitment and human resource policies. *Human Resource Management Journal*, **3**: 21–30.

Nellis, J.R. 1977. Socialist management in Algeria. *Journal of Modern African Studies*, **15**: 529–554.

Newman, K.L. and Nollen, S.D. 1996. Culture and congruence: the fit between management practices and national culture. *Journal of International Business Studies*, **27**: 753–779.

Noe, R.A. 1986. 'Trainees' attributes and attitudes: neglected influences on training effectiveness. *Academy of Management Review*, **11**: 736–749.

ONS 2012. Premier recensement economique, resultats definitifs de la premiere phase. Office Nationale des Statistiques, Collections Statistiques N 172, Algiers. http://www.ons.dz/img/pdf/resultats_definitifs_phase_i_re2011.pdf (accessed 27 July 2016).

Parker, S.K., Williams, H.M. and Turner, N. 2006. Modeling the antecedents of proactive behaviour at work. *Journal of Applied Psychology*, **91**: 636–652.

Peretti, J.-M. and Slama, Y. 2009. Mobilité iternationale: les expatriés dans les entreprises multinationales en Algérie. 11e Université de Printemps de l'Audit Social, Audit Social & Renouvellement de la GRH, Sidi Fredj, Algérie, Du 30 au 31 Mai. http://www.auditsocial.net/wp-content/uploads/2011/06/Actes-Ias-Alger.pdf (accessed 27 July 2016).

Pfeffer, J. 1994. *Competitive Advantage through People*. Boston, MA: Harvard Business School Press.

Pfeffer, J. 1998. *The Human Equation: Building Profits by Putting People First*. Boston, MA: Harvard Business School Press.

Ralston, D.A., Egri, C.P., Riddle, L., Butt, A., Dalgic, T. and Brock, D.M. 2012. Managerial values in the greater Middle East: similarities and differences across seven countries. *International Business Review*, **21**(3): 480–492.

Ramdani, B., Mellahi, K., Guermat, C. and Kechad, R. 2014. The efficacy of high performance work practices in the Middle East: evidence from Algerian firms. *International Journal of Human Resources Management*, **25**: 252–275.

Ramsay, H., Scholarios, D. and Harley, B. 2000. Employees and high-performance work systems: testing inside the black box. *British Journal of Industrial Relations*, **38**: 501–531.

Saadi, R.N. 1982. Syndicat et relations du travail dans les entreprises socialistes en Algerie. *Annuaire de l'Afrique du Nord*, **21**: 123–132.

Salas, E., Cannon–Bowers, J.A., Rhodenizer, L. and Bowers, C.A. 1999. Training in organizations. *Research in Personnel and Human Resources Management*, **17**: 123–161.

Schwab, K. and Sala-i-Martín, X. 2012. *The Global Competitiveness Report 2012–2013*. World Economic Forum. http://www3.weforum.org/docs/WEF_GlobalCompetitivenessReport_2012–13.pdf (accessed 27 July 2016).

Schwab, K. and Sala-i-Martín, X. 2013. *The Global Competitiveness Report 2013–2014*. World Economic Forum. http://www3.weforum.org/docs/WEF_GlobalCompetitivenessReport_2013–14.pdf (accessed 27 July 2016).

Seghir, S. 2009. Culture et management en Algérie: comment la culture des Algériens influence la gestion des ressources humaines. 11e Université de Printemps de l'Audit Social, Audit Social & Renouvellement de la GRH, Sidi Fredj, Algérie, Du 30 au 31 Mai. http://www.auditsocial.net/wp-content/uploads/2011/06/Actes-Ias-Alger.pdf (accessed 27 July 2016).

Stavrou, E., Brewster, C. and Charalambous, C. 2010. Human resource management and firm performance in Europe through the lens of business systems: best fit, best practice or both? *International Journal of Human Resource Management*, **21**: 933–962.

Sun, L.Y., Aryee S. and Law K.S. 2007. High performance human resource practices, citizenship behavior, and organizational performance: a relational perspective. *Academy of Management Journal*, **50**: 558–577.

Tabet-Aouel, W. and Bendiabdellah, A. 2010. Quelle GRH dans la TPE Algérienne? Colloque GRH, PME et Entrepreneuriat: Regards Croisés, 1er Avril 2010, Montpellier, France. http://colloquemontpellier.free.fr/grh_pme_entrepreneuriat_en/communications/TabetAouel_Bendiabdellah.pdf (accessed 27 July 2016).

Tharenou, P., Saks, A. and Moore, C. 2007. A review and critique of research on training and organizational level outcomes. *Human Resource Management Review*, **17**: 251–273.

Tiliouine, H. and Cummins, R.A. and Davern. M. 2009. Islamic religiosity, subjective wellbeing, and health. *Mental Health, Religion and Culture*, **12**: 55–74.

UNDP 2014. *Human Development Report 2014: Sustaining Human Progress: Reducing Vulnerabilities and Building Resilience*. United Nations Development Programme. http://hdr.undp.org/sites/default/files/hdr14-report-en–1.pdf (accessed 27 July 2016).

Vallance, S. 1999. Performance appraisal in Singapore, Thailand and the Philippines: a cultural perspective. *Australian Journal of Public Administration*, **58**: 78–86.

Wang, S., Yi, X., Lawler, J. and Zhang, M. 2011. Efficacy of high-performance work practices in Chinese companies. *International Journal of Human Resource Management*, **22**: 2419–2441.

World Bank 2015. Algeria overview. http://www.worldbank.org/en/country/algeria/overview#1 (accessed 27 July 2016).

Wright, C.P. and Geroy, D.G. 2001. Changing the mindset. *International Journal of Human Resource Management*, **12**: 586–600.

Yanat, Z. and Scouarnec, A. 2006. *Perspectives sur la GRH au Maghreb: Algérie-Maroc-Tunisie*. Paris: Vuibert.

13. Human resource management in Morocco

Abderrahman Hassi

INTRODUCTION

Settled in the western corner of North Africa across the Straits of Gibraltar, Morocco is a constitutional monarchy with an area of 710,850 square kilometres. A strategic location at the crossroads of the Mediterranean Sea and the Atlantic Ocean, proximity with several civilizations, a history under French and Spanish colonization and North African and Middle Eastern characteristics expose Morocco to a myriad of European, African and Arab influences.

These influences are reflected in several spheres of life in Morocco, including management practices. In this respect, human resource management (HRM) constitutes a blend of transplanted and local practices. HRM as a concept was first formally introduced into the Moroccan context during the colonial era. Ever since then, there has been growing interest in HRM in Morocco with HRM evolving from a mere focus on personnel administration to a strategic unit within organizations (Badri and Alami Lâaroussi, 2013).

The purpose of this chapter is to present a portrait of HRM practices focusing on Moroccan small and medium businesses (SMBs), which constitute 95 per cent of companies operating in the country. In order to do so, semi-structured interviews were conducted with human resource (HR) managers to gather insights about HRM practices. In addition to these first-hand insights, literature analysis is utilized to highlight the history of HRM, challenges facing HRM, and the future of HRM in Morocco. To set the stage for the chapter, background information about the country is presented next.

COUNTRY CONTEXT AND BACKGROUND

Demographic Context

The Moroccan population has experienced a significant increase in recent times, evolving from 20 million in 1980 to 32.6 million in 2012 (Haut-commissariat Au Plan, 2012). In 2012, the young population was recorded at 64.5 per cent under 35 years old and 47.7 per cent under 25. The active population aged 15 and above counts for 11.5 million, representing nearly half of this age group, with an activity rate of 48.4 per cent. Women account for 26.3 per cent of the active population and men 73.7 per cent. In 2012, the number of employed individuals was 10.54 million.

The unemployment rate is high in urban areas, among the youth and with educated individuals. While the rate at the national level is 9 per cent (8.7 per cent female and 9.9 per cent male), figures from 2012 place unemployment at 13.4 per cent in urban areas, and 26.3 per cent among those with a university degree. Lastly, 81 per cent of unemployed individuals are under 35 (Haut-commissariat au Plan, 2012). To tackle persistent youth unemployment, the government subsidizes internships through the Employment Action Program (*Action-Emploi*) by funding a portion of the remuneration attributed to trainees and tax cuts for employers.

Moreover, the population appears to be growing faster than the gross domestic product (GDP), hence the economy lags behind in terms of creating sufficient jobs to meet employment demands. According to Denoeux (2001), the Moroccan economy generates 200,000 jobs annually but 300,000 individuals enter the job market every year. It should be mentioned that unemployed workers do not benefit from any employment insurance or income support systems in Morocco. In sum, the job market can be subdivided in two segments: a formal segment consisting of public sector and organized private companies with established rules and regulations, and an informal segment operating without formal rules. The latter does not favour investment in human capital (Agénor and El Aynaoui, 2003). It employs about two million individuals representing roughly 20 per cent of the workforce and contributes 14.3 per cent to the GDP.

In terms of implications of the above presentation for HRM in Morocco, it should be noted that the low level of formal qualification of the active population hampers aspects of HRM related to availability of skills, recruitment and eventually performance efforts within organizations as 63.2 per cent of workers do not hold any academic degrees and only 11.6 per cent completed high school.

Economic Context

The Moroccan economy depends enormously on tourism, agri-industries, textiles, clothing and leather, and is the largest exporter of phosphates in the world. It is presently going through a period of modernization. Free-trade zones are being established, several public companies are being privatized and there is a move towards diversification, focusing on information technology. Despite these developments, Moroccan industry appears to be fragmented and lacking organization. Further, most of the economic activity is concentrated on the industrialized Casablanca–Rabat–Tangiers coastal axis, particularly the economic hub city of Casablanca.

Morocco's GDP was US$101.8 billion in 2012 and the GDP per capita was approximately US$5,400. The GDP composition by sector is 14 per cent for agriculture, 28 per cent for industry and 58 per cent for services. In terms of the percentage employment by economic sector, 42.2 per cent work in agriculture, 21 per cent in industry and 36.8 per cent in services. While the Moroccan economy has recently been improving, the public debt was 20.012 billion MAD (US$2.33 billion) in 2012, the inflation rate was 2.1 per cent and the deficit of public revenues represented 7.1 per cent of the GDP (Haut-commissariat Au Plan, 2012).

As mentioned above, the Moroccan economy is dominated by SMBs, but also has large public and private companies, holdings and consortia such as Ynna and Omnium Nord-Africain, and branches of multinational companies such as Sony, Philips and Microsoft. It is important to note that a substantial number of SMBs lack a formal organizational structure. In 2002, the National Agency for Small and Medium Businesses (*Agence nationale des petites et moyennes enterprises*) was established to assist in developing SMBs.

Given this context, managers running HRM departments within SMBs generally do not have adequate formal training (Benson and Al Arkoubi, 2006), and formal and modern practices are far from being implemented in these businesses. However, there are some large Moroccan companies that have integrated concerns for employees in their HRM values and practices such as Ynna Holding (Hassi and Storti, 2014). Overall, it is the branches of multinationals that seem to set exemplar models in respect of the adoption of innovative HRM practices in the country.

Cultural Context

Based on Hofstede's (2001) cultural dimensions, Moroccan national culture can be described as (1) marked by a high level of power distance as hierarchy and unequal distribution of power are socially acceptable; (2) collectivist as the group, rather than the individual, is considered the most crucial entity in society; (3) fairly masculine as it emphasizes more drive and competition, than caring and nurturing behaviours (feminine culture); and (4) uncertainty averse as it perceives unknown situations as threatening and its members tend to avoid them.

The HR system within Moroccan organizations mostly places a priority on seniority rather than performance. This constitutes an attribute of cultures with a high power distance, which assumes that wisdom resides in hierarchy and age. For instance, the area of training and development heavily depends on the knowledge and expertise of seniors and automatically places juniors in a position of knowledge receivers (Hassi and Storti, 2011). As a corollary, Moroccan junior employees perceive themselves as apprentices working under the direction and supervision of the 'master' until they become fully skilled. Along the same line, it has been documented in the context of training in Morocco that instructors are perceived as role models to follow, similar to the perceptions people have about leaders (Hassi, Storti and Azennoud, 2011).

Due to the high level of uncertainty avoidance embedded within the Moroccan national culture, Moroccan workers abhor commission-based compensation systems and prefer those with a fixed salary. Moroccan national culture also cherishes the values of loyalty and obedience of individuals in leading positions as long as they behave in a just way towards the followers (Allali, 2008). As a consequence, recruitment is oftentimes based on personalized relationships and kinship. The preference is accorded to those who are relatives or are recommended by friends, in some cases, irrespective of their qualifications. These practices render the selection process subjective and sometimes worthless. As Morocco was once under colonial rules, namely French and Spanish, accordingly its civil service laws were developed and have been implemented and they influence the HR practice.

Islam, which is the predominant religion in Morocco, does not separate between the sacred and secular spheres of life. This makes it mandatory for faithful individuals to observe Islamic principles in their daily business and management dealings such as justice and equity in all HRM aspects. Nonetheless, the application of these principles is limited and several religious guidelines are not always fully observed in the way that economic or business considerations are accorded priorities. It seems that the practice of HRM within Moroccan organizations is subject to cultural, religious and colonial influences.

HRM IN MOROCCO: HISTORICAL OVERVIEW

The HR function appeared within Moroccan organizations in the beginning of the 20th century with the advent of the French colonization and the introduction of new business management modes. The history of HRM can be divided into the following periods.

HRM Under the French Protectorate (1912–1956)

During this period, the foundations of the traditional economy experienced a drastic metamorphosis (Allali, 2008) yielding an abundant workforce due to the fact that peasants fled in great numbers their agricultural land to settle in larger cities. This massive exodus yielded an imbalance in workforce supply and demand as the colonial economy took advantage of cheap labour. Hence, the employers had large pools of workers to select from in order to staff their job vacancies, the workers were smoothly moved around depending on organizational needs, businesses did not worry about staff turnover, and higher levels of output were demanded through incentivizing workers. In addition, French employers were vehemently against the implementation of any labour legislation (Baayoud and Zouanat, 2011). It should be mentioned that personnel management of the local workers varied drastically from personnel management of the European workers. For instance, whenever employers had to deal with local workers, they would exercise strict control over them and bound them by tough rules, the working conditions lacked basic rights and amenities, and arbitrary measures were adopted in managing employees. Conversely, European workers benefited from more decent work conditions and better labour rules and regulations; a systematic management approach was consistently used and employees were equally treated.

HRM After Independence (1956) Until 1990

After the end of the French colonization in 1956, the HRM system within Moroccan organizations was similar to that under the Protectorate, insofar as HR practices continued to follow an autocratic and traditional approach marked by the absence of decent work conditions and tight control over workers. A high turnover and a precarious workforce marked it. HRM practices were part of the responsibility of the business owner, who solely decided on almost every aspect of the business in this regard. Getting around legal constraints such as the minimum wages and employee benefits was a common HRM practice. This practice is an integral part of HRM as it is concerned with employee compensation. Consequently, personnel administration was formalized and even stringent for businesses given that the Moroccan government imposed a culture of social dialogue to enhance cooperation and smoothen collective bargaining between unions and employers. Further, homogenous and consistent labour regulations were implemented. Personnel functions focused on establishing and maintaining good relationships with employees and their representatives due to the rise of the trade union militancy and its political connections (Baayoud and Zouanat, 2011). Key HRM roles were carried out by the business owner or by close individuals such as family members; however, employee training and development was not well perceived and was considered an unproductive investment.

HRM in the 1990s

At of the beginning of the 1990s, Morocco witnessed major political and economic changes that consequently impacted its business environment. Free-trade zones were created with the European Union to foster Morocco as an attractive destination for outsourcing. To do so, in the HRM area, Moroccan public authorities worked on improving employee relations within companies to live up to this internationalization challenge. On the private businesses end of the spectrum, human capital had to be taken into account in their strategic positioning to face growing international competition. In this respect, a more professional approach to managing human resources was gradually implemented with practices such as hiring highly qualified employees, resorting more to employee training, motivating the workforce with the pursuit of accreditations and certifications, and so forth. During this period, HRM experienced a drastic shift with some traditional HRM activities and beliefs (such as considering employee training as an expense rather than an investment and centralized HR-related decision making) fading away, while other matters that were historically neglected started to draw the attention of employers such as occupational health and employee training and development.

Requirements of efficiency of HRM techniques and methods paved the way for employers to lean towards information technology. However, this shift depended on contingency factors such as the size, industry, status of the organization and the strategic positioning vis-à-vis the internationalization. During this era, key HRM roles were carried out by a personnel manager with limited power and with by no means any strategic influence within the organization.

It is worth mentioning that up to the 1990s, issues regarding HRM were dealt by the personnel functions within companies. Since then, the HR function has replaced personnel management (Cox et al., 2005) as an indication of its readiness to adopt innovative HRM practices, apparently due to the influence of Western multinational companies operating in the country that have introduced modern managerial practices (Benson and Al Arkoubi, 2006).

HRM in the 21st Century

Strategic positioning vis-à-vis the internationalization of business activities has constituted an important contingency factor to HRM practices as it has led to both interest and urgency in implementing appropriate HR strategies and practices in the hopes of tackling constraints and seizing opportunities, particularly for medium and large companies that have the resources to expand their businesses internationally. In fact, with the advents of globalization, free trade and information technology, Moroccan companies can be divided into two categories pertaining to the nature of HRM practices they adopted while tackling these changes:

1. Companies that embraced the requirements of the new world economy in their strategic orientation, banking on the human factor to gain a competitive advantage. Some companies took this direction anticipating global competition. They opted for a large restructuring of their operations combined with modernizing their production systems and management approaches as a way to face the new global

competition. Conversely, there were other companies that drastically shifted their HRM approach as their shareholders, investors or business partners imposed it, such as in the case of French companies outsourcing to their Moroccan counterparts. In this regard, for a Moroccan company to benefit from an outsourcing contract with a French business, the former has to observe some HRM standards such as the legal age of workers and meet hygiene requirements.

2. Companies that resisted the adoption of the requirements of the internationalization mode. These companies had been used to the leniency of the control authorities and getting around labour regulations for decades. It was clearly evident that these companies faced a major challenge to shift overnight to a labour-law-abiding approach. Within these companies, HR divisions continue to focus on daily issues within organizations, and it is not unusual that the finance manager fulfils the responsibilities of the HR manager. In this respect, Denoeux (2001) contends that a lot of Moroccan firms are not familiar with modern HRM practices.

HRM PRACTICES IN MOROCCO: A TWO-TIER SYSTEM

There is a dearth of studies on HRM practices in Morocco. The majority of existing studies have been carried out lately by consulting firms and are a challenge to track (Benson and Al Arkoubi, 2006). However, none of them appear to be comprehensive, with many of them not even published. For these specific reasons, it is unfeasible to provide a complete portrait of existing literature on HRM practices in Morocco; hence, we conducted an exploratory study in order to present a general overview of HRM practices within Moroccan SMBs. To do so, 20 HRM managers within Moroccan SMBs were interviewed following a convenience sampling method, as they were selected based on their willingness to participate in the study.

This sampling method seems to be the most efficient one given the difficulty to gather data and conduct research in the Moroccan context. The main objective of the study was not to seek establishing causal relationships between contextual variables and HRM practices, but rather to look into evidence of HRM practices adopted by Moroccan SMBs.

The interview questions dealt with diverse HRM practices such as the description of the HR function, selection, recruitment and hiring practices, the systems of remuneration and compensation, performance appraisal practices, training and staff development practices and unionization. The results show that the HRM system is not homogenous within Moroccan SMBs as there is a two-tier HR system.

The HR Function

Most research companies have an HR function. All interviewees agree that people constitute a valuable resource for their company and are aware that the primary role of the HR department is to develop this resource. However, in terms of practice, the companies of the interviewees can be divided into two categories:

1. Companies where HR activities play a strategic role and which adopt a proactive HR management approach consisting of anticipating problems and identifying HR

opportunities while appropriately dealing with them in a timely manner; this is the case for several professionally managed businesses, where the HR function is significantly linked to the overall business strategies to the point that it is an inseparable part of the company. These companies declared the existence of a HRM strategic plan, indicating that they have established a 2–3 year period medium-term plan in the hopes of efficiently managing their personnel. The respondents contend that the management of human resources is a set of practices essential to the overall management of an organization and hence are not about minimizing cost, but rather about how to get the most output for the least amount of input while obtaining the most optimal results from the company's human capital.

2. Companies that adopt a reactive HR management approach marked by focusing on daily routines and short-term objectives. They lack HR planning and only respond reactively to HR issues and opportunities; this is the case mainly for family businesses. In these companies, one of the main goals of the HR team or department is to constantly reduce and minimize the cost of their labour force, which contributes to the overall cost of operations. There are no specialists who take care of the HR department and the latter is centralized if it ever even exists. There is an absence of collaboration between HR specialists and other managers within the organization. As a corollary, there is a lack of integration of HRM in the overall strategic business planning as well as a lack of basic HRM strategic planning.

It is worth pointing out that 7 companies out of 20 in the present study adopt a proactive HR approach, while the remaining espouse a reactive HR approach. Although HR activities and programmes of different companies vary, the HR departments or units within most research companies undertake the following common roles: job design and analysis, recruitment and selection, orientation, performance appraisal, training, compensation and labour relations.

HR Policies

HR policies are guidelines that define acceptable and unacceptable behaviours and practices; they establish an organizational position on issues such as recruitment, staffing, orientation, training, performance appraisal and compensation. HR policies assist in defining and reaching goals and managing a business in a consistent manner.

As the Moroccan national culture is risk averse and scores high on the uncertainty avoidance index of cross-cultural frameworks (see Hofstede, 2001), one would expect Moroccan companies to rely on HR written policies. However, this is not the case, as in our sample firms there is a lack of resorting to HR policies; this seems to be due to the verbal and informal tradition of the Moroccan culture. The companies that adopt a proactive HR management approach find HR policies important, but they do not use them in a regular and consistent way. The companies that adopt a reactive HR management approach do not find it important to have HR policies in place and do not make use of them in workplace settings.

Job Design and Analysis

The companies that adopt a proactive HR management approach carry out job design and analysis in order to identify the tasks, skills, abilities and qualifications required by each position. This task is part of the HR manager's responsibilities in collaboration with other managers. However, procedures and methods used in this regard are not clearly defined; hence, the challenge in drafting employee career plans, identifying qualitative and quantitative needs in terms of workforce, evaluating promotion opportunities and workload assignment. On the other hand, the companies that adopt a reactive HR management approach do not have a formal approach to job design and analysis. Respondents contend that it exists but it is carried out on an informal basis.

Recruitment

The companies that adopt a proactive HR management approach resort to recruitment and selection methods based on Western practices (e.g., resorting to professional recruiting firms), specifically the French tradition (such as according more importance to degrees and formal qualifications rather than to professional experience), due to Morocco's strong ties to Europe in general and France in particular (Kessels, 2002). They tend to attract qualified candidates through a formal recruitment process using supporting tools. Companies draft an annual plan to forecast workforce needs in order to adequately respond to staff positions due to retirement, resignation, end of contract, and lay-offs or in order to respond to expansion plans and the creation of new positions within the organization. They conduct job interviews and use diverse types of tests, originated from developed countries, to select and hire employees.

Companies that adopt a reactive HR management approach resort to more traditional techniques, with recruitment considered as a mere selection decision taken solely by line managers. These organizations invest less time and financial resources on recruitment and selection methods. They are characterized by over reliance on loyalty and family connections as a basis for determining who gets employed. Loyalty or allegiance is a crucial value in the Moroccan culture as it refers to followers who obey leaders due to the latter's integrity and honesty (Allali, 2008). This is rooted in a twofold belief according to which (1) a known employee would be more committed to work than an individual who is not familiar; and (2) a loyal employee is able to acquire new competencies, but a competent employee would not be able to learn loyalty. In this regard, it is difficult to disassociate cultural and institutional influences from managerial behaviour (Budhwar and Sparrow, 2002).

It is important to note that all respondents agree that their respective organizations resort to hiring based on 'networking', social relations and ties. None of the research organizations proceed on the basis of making predictions about future behaviours while recruiting employees. There is an absence of systematic processes of assessing the organization–individual fit to determine whether a candidate would be suitable for a given job position.

Remuneration

It is crucial to highlight the fact that institutional rules limit the latitude of Moroccan organizations in terms of remuneration. There is a level of minimum wages (Salaire Minimum Interprofessionnel Garanti – SMIG) that employers in Morocco have to abide by. In addition, collective agreements also impose a minimum level of compensation for each professional category.

Wages and other fringe benefits in Moroccan organizations are designated by collective bargaining between unions and employers or employees' associations. In private organizations, the basic wages are generally higher than those within public sector organizations. Evidence demonstrates that wage scales are not based on job analysis and appraisal to ensure equity, and salary increases are not usually based on merit or performance.

In companies that adopt a proactive HR management approach, the system of remuneration combines a set of components (fixed part, variable part and various benefits) in order to establish a balance between the financial imperatives, employees' expectations and the strategic objectives of productivity. These companies attempt to allocate bonuses based on their individual performance. The managers set the objectives and the employees try their best in order to achieve them.

In companies that adopt a reactive HR management approach, there are no standardized ratios between the basic salaries of different wage levels. There is, however, a wage bracket for every position; this serves to justify seniority of employees rather than their merit or performance. In some cases, this wage bracket is arbitrarily established; hence the overlap between various salary levels exists. Most of the organizations of the respondents contend that they generalize the bonus system regardless of the performance of their employees or any other precise criterion of attribution. Remuneration is considered to be the most sensitive aspect of the HR system.

Training and Development

Employee training in Morocco, like elsewhere, constitutes a true challenge due to requirements in areas of productivity, competitiveness and employability, and in building a knowledge-based society. These requirements continue to gain momentum due to global transformations in the environment where Moroccan organizations operate. In fact, both agreements of free trade and the dynamics of globalization have in recent years demanded that Morocco revisits the purposes of its training system (Hassi, 2012). Consequently, the importance of training and education has increased and has been established as a national priority, second to territorial integrity (Hassi, 2011).

In our current study, companies that adopt a proactive HR management approach emphasize the need to train their employees as they consider it mutually beneficial for employers and employees. Within these organizations, line managers, supervisors and HR managers, along with employees, are responsible for ensuring that workers are effectively trained. To do so, they design appropriate training activities to meet employees' needs. These organizations provide workers with subsidies for job-related training. Every employee's training and development needs are reviewed annually and plans are established to address any gaps. Conversely, in companies that adopt a reactive HR management approach, the responsibility of identifying employees' training needs rests with personnel managers rather than with line managers, supervisors or the employees themselves. Training activities are designed by senior management in house and are closely related to the position. These companies favour training that is specific to the company and which is provided through on-the-job training programmes and/or by various means of job rotation methods.

Performance Appraisal

Performance appraisal consists of evaluating the achievements and the performance of the employees. This evaluation is necessary to establish compensation and succession plans. Companies that adopt a proactive HR management approach evaluate employee performance through a system of management by objectives followed up with interviews to all categories of employees. The evaluation is conducted periodically (at least once a year), by HR managers and supervisors. The managers conduct their annual performance interviews with all their subordinates in order to verify if the target of the previous year was attained or not. Performance appraisal, which is a written appreciation, assesses the professional contribution of employees to accomplishing their tasks and achieving goals. Some of these companies use technology as they have internal software that evaluates the time it takes to accomplish a task, for example.

However, in companies that adopt a reactive HR management approach, performance appraisal is rarely carried out, and where it is, it mainly serves as a basis to give salary increases. It is about behaviours at work and punctuality. It deals with rewarding employees based on their efforts rather than their effectiveness and efficiency. Employee performance per se is not fully taken into account in other HRM spheres such as career development or employee training. These companies are not familiar with modern methods and techniques of performance appraisal. They resort to subjective performance appraisals given that the hierarchical superior evaluates appraisals, without necessarily meeting with the concerned employee. Thus, the nature of the relationship between employees and their supervisors can bias the assessment.

Succession Planning

Companies that adopt a proactive HR management approach strongly believe that succession planning is a vital dimension of the HR function. It is the most effective way to internally staff the most important positions within the company. To avoid job plateauing and to motivate employees, these companies set up regular internal mobility plans through training partnerships to provide the workers with the possibility to pursue graduate studies in higher education institutions. Many of these companies have begun to think not only in terms of hiring talent, but also in terms of developing their talent. However, although this is a good start, they still need to be more efficient in implementing new strategies and thinking about new tools and ideas regarding succession planning. On the other hand, companies that adopt a reactive HR management approach lack a formal system of succession planning. Climbing the organizational ladder is a factor of the potential loyalty to the boss in these companies.

Occupational Health and Safety

In the research organizations, occupational health and safety procedures and mechanisms aim primarily at dealing with prejudices related to workplace accidents and professional illness. Few organizations from our sample have formal and structured preventive actions that are taken (such as ergonomic-based approaches). However, some physical ambiance conditions are put in place such as sonority, visual conditions, hygiene and adequate flooring conditions. A few organizations have created 'hygiene committees' as required by the law, which include both employers and employees in managing occupational health and safety within organizations. Nonetheless, the organizations of our respondents are far from having a participative culture in regard to occupational health and safety issues. This context seems to be due to lack of involvement of workers in designing and implementing occupational health and safety-related activities and programmes as the latter appears to be exclusively led by employers. In addition, many workers in Morocco are not aware of their right to work in a safe and secure environment which must be free of occupational hazards, as well as the adequate compensation that should be rendered in cases of incidents resulting in psychological or physical implications for the employee.

Employee Labour Unions

Workers unite and organize in unions to protect and promote their interests. In Morocco, although trade unions are legally recognized, employee unionization is considerably weak, with a unionized workplace of barely 10 per cent in the private sector, one of the lowest in the world. Unions have yet to exert any substantial form of effective influence at the workplace (Hassi, 2012).

Respondents of our study contend that social relations are usually tense between employers and union representatives. Most of the employers have limited belief and trust in unionization as they argue that it enhances conflicts between employers and workers. They assume that their respective companies observe the Moroccan Labour Code, thus rejecting the need for unionization. In some companies, according to our respondents, there are union representatives of workers, but they have a symbolic role, without any means of substantial and real effect on the HR-related decisions within the organization.

It has been noted that Moroccan organizations have leaned towards a modernistic HR strategy consisting of protecting the rights of all employees while respecting the corporate culture with an open-door policy. The latter is a twofold incentive: the idea is for all workers to communicate and negotiate directly with senior management while, at the same time, creating common forums to discuss issues and identify strategies for a better working relationship.

New Labour Code

After more than three years of heated debates and tough negotiations between the government, employers and trade unions, a new Labour Code, congruent with all international conventions, was adopted in June 2004 in Morocco. This new code was established as a legal framework with the objective to promote dialogue among social partners. It aimed at addressing two major social and economic concerns: (1) employers claimed more flexibility in the area of HRM in hopes of improving their competitiveness; and (2) trade unions and workers requested better and more decent work conditions.

The new Labour Code only applies to labour relations that are formalized with a labour contract between an employer and a worker. However, some categories of employees are not covered under the code such as employees working for public companies and local communities, workers employed in the mining industry, professional journalists and domestic workers. Further, the scope of the code remains limited due to the importance of informal employment. Two main critiques can be yielded with the new Labour Code: (1) a legal vacuum in some situations such as the absence of provisions related to private life and the use of modern means of communication; and (2) interpretation issues as with provisions related to teamwork and with sanctions in cases of professional errors caused by workers.

According to our respondents, the impact of the new Labour Code has been positive, as it has assisted in establishing a balance between the freedom of association and work responsibilities; it has led to an improvement of the quality of the employer–employee relationship. It has also contributed to a more available and accessible workforce for employers. Nonetheless, there is a cost associated with the provisions of the new Labour Code, which is incurred by employers and is regarded by the latter as an additional increase in their wage bill.

CHALLENGES FACING HRM IN MOROCCO

Employee demographics have yielded a diverse and changing workforce within Moroccan organizations where women account only for 26.3 per cent of the total active working population aged 15 and above (Verme et al., 2014). In fact, studies (see for example, Badri and Alami Lâaroussi, 2013; Hassi, Foutouh and Ramid, 2015) indicate that there has been a significant increase in the number of young workers, single parents, dual-career couples and women in the workplace. Nowadays, hiring and motivating a diverse labour force constitutes a major HR challenge. Hence, Moroccan organizations need to develop and implement innovative HR programmes to address the needs of a changing workforce to successfully compete in a more intense and fiercely competitive globalized economy.

Equality between men and women is another major and pressing concern in the country. Although several Moroccan companies are aware and attempting to ensure a balance between men and women in regards to HRM aspects, much remains to be done as the process takes time and involves changes and alterations in the behaviours and attitudes of the various stakeholders involved in the process. In this regard, Safi-Eddine and Bentaleb (2010) investigated diversity management in more than 20 Moroccan organizations and consistently found in all analysed cases that assistant positions were filled with women, while every single member of the boards of directors were men. Organizations ought to implement formal HR rules with underlying policies that respect gender equity in the entire HR process.

Balancing the demands of employees' professional and private life has become a real challenge for today's Moroccan workers and their employers. Once a conflict emerges in one of these two spheres, the other one is likely to experience the effects of the impact, and as a result, end up being subjected to its negative consequences. It has been documented that work–life balance conflicts affect mainly women as they are also in charge of household activities and they favour family when they encounter conflicts between family and work (Demos Consulting, 2011).

New information technologies seem to have significantly impacted the way companies operate. This transformation is first and foremost a human and cultural one, with changes influencing both the work organization and employee behaviours, including information sharing within the organization. In this digital era, where information is easily accessed, Moroccan organizations fall short when it comes to fully taking advantage of modern sources in conducting various HRM activities. Hence, the HR function needs to embark on this perspective as there seems to be significant gains in terms of efficiency for both organizations and workers benefiting from the opportunities presented from the use of modern technological advances.

Moroccan organizations face major challenges to fill in vacant positions to ensure succession and proper functioning of the organization once an employee is promoted or transferred, particularly in specialized areas. They often fail to find the adequate talent in a timely manner (Habriche, 2011).

Employee training and development faces enormous challenges and we are still a long way from establishing employee training structures and practices within organizations, and far from developing a long-term sustainable human capital. In this regard, the current legislation, particularly the 1.6 per cent levy firms' pay for vocational training, appears to be ineffective, as it does not fund employee training but rather supports initial training programmes. In fact, as of 2007, and in virtue of the levy decree, only 30 per cent of funds have been transferred to employee training (Secrétariat d'état Chargé de la Formation Professionnelle, 2007). Further, only 20 per cent of this funding scheme is used by 3 per cent of formal sector companies, which are unequally distributed in terms of their size, industries and regions (Hassi, 2012), with the majority of them located in the industrialized Casablanca–Rabat–Tangiers axis. It has been documented that SMBs are reluctant to commit to employee training due to a lack of perceived training importance (Hassi, 2012). To tackle these challenges, we propose the adoption of an Employee Training Act, which would aim at promoting a culture of training with various actors engaged. It is noteworthy to highlight that the Act would not be an end in itself, but would rather be a means likely to support and favour the emergence of a training culture at the workplace.

Furthermore, there is no detailed information available on the exact number or qualifications of HRM services providers. It should also be mentioned that the current legislation does not propose a legal definition of these specialists. In this regard, it is important to point out that HRM specialists and consultants are not specialized and do not possess adequate experience in the subject of consultation they provide as they do not hold academic degrees in training or any related field (DIORH, 2002).

There is an important increase of contract or temporary employment resulting in a decrease in the number of full-time employees, with only 27.1 per cent of the Moroccan workforce having an indeterminate term contract. Further, 80 per cent of employees do not have any form of social protection or insurance (Agueniou, 2013), hence the importance of putting in place measures to protect employees and tackling precarious employment.

Most of the interviewees admit that factors that impede a better HRM within Moroccan organizations are (1) employers' lack of ambition and the desire to maintain status quo, (2) the resistance to change of some senior managers, (3) an absence of delegation, (4) the lack of an adequately qualified workforce, and (5) an absence of well-defined control and evaluation systems. It has been highlighted that oftentimes inattention to employees' concerns and issues on the part of general managers leads to excessive absenteeism, high turnover numbers and substandard productivity.

FUTURE OF HRM IN MOROCCO

In the light of the above presentation, an important question that emerges from the findings is: *how should organizations face and confront the various challenges regarding HRM in Morocco?*

In view of these challenges, it seems that a strong and resilient culture of HRM can pave the roadmap for Morocco to obtain a highly qualified labour force that will contribute to the development of organizations heading towards an HRM-oriented corporate culture. Thus, all concerned actors and players must be engaged with common aims and objectives in order to set in motion any future prospects of establishing a human-capital-oriented society.

As the professionalization of human resources is gaining momentum within Moroccan organizations, traditional HR approaches based on command and control will be losing ground to new and modern approaches marked by employee commitment, involvement and participation.

Academic and scientific preparation of HR professionals, along with experience and practice, has become a necessity. HR departments at present are largely a 'borderless function' as they welcome any organizational members to work as an HR specialist. However, modern-day organizations need more and more HR specialists who can critically accomplish HR tasks, draft effective HR policies and implement efficient HR methods to maximize organizational productivity, employee well-being and customer satisfaction. In corollary, the HR function will need to adapt itself to new work organizations and modes characterized by high-order thinking, constant learning and increased flexibility.

Companies must also be able to achieve the best alignment of their human resources with their strategic objectives. Having involved and motivated employees, especially given that the human dimension can transform inert economic assets to real strategic capabilities, can help to attain this. In this context, and based on our analysis, companies with a proactive HRM approach appear to adopt rigorous HR practices and seem to manage their human assets effectively; however, there are some flaws and gaps that must inevitably be overcome.

HR planning needs to be part of the overall organizational strategic planning. A HR department needs to perform the following critical roles: (1) developing and implementing HR policy; (2) offering advice; (3) providing services; and (4) managing HR programmes and procedures. The HR function will be in a continuous state of change, as traditionally it played more of a disciplinary role (HR manager: 'police officer'), then an administrative role (HR manager: 'pencil pusher'). In the future, it will play more and more of a strategic role.

Specifically, due to globalization and an increased presence of multinational companies in Morocco, HR managers are expected to adopt some of the following best practices: transparency and objectivity of the hiring process, flexibility in HR processes, strategic orientation of HRM, leveraging internal talent, enforcement of equal employment provisions, favouring of cooperation and collaboration through involving employees in decision-making processes and increased employee participation.

It is evident that the paucity of research on HRM in Morocco does not allow drawing a conclusive and comprehensive picture of the topic. Most of the academic research remains fragmented and descriptive in nature, making generalizations virtually impossible. In corollary, research revolving around theoretical depth, methodological rigour and clearer focus is much needed. In this regard, researchers need to investigate differences in HR practices across organizations operating in Morocco. Specific HR-related issues such as youth integration in the labour market, low female labour force participation and adoption of modern HR practices need to be adequately addressed.

CONCLUSION

Undoubtedly, in today's rapidly changing global marketplace, companies aiming to achieve a competitive edge and maintain it need to do so through, inter alia, an efficient management approach of their human resources.

The Moroccan workplace is exposed to a variety of different HR ideologies from international organizations operating in Morocco: French and European companies due to Morocco's strong ties to Europe in general and France in particular (Kessels, 2002) and multinational companies; hence, the lack of local and comprehensive HRM models which constitutes one of the major challenges facing HRM practices in Morocco.

Multinational companies operating in Morocco generally provide better work conditions than local companies, with more competitive compensation packages, access to training and development opportunities, and career advancement potential to name a few. Consequently, these transplanted foreign organizations attract the best profiles for their workforce. Hence, Moroccan employees with the necessary skills (i.e., required language proficiency) prefer to work for multinational companies. The public sector, which is based on seniority, provides employees with lifetime employment, guaranteed wages and 'cradle-to-grave' welfare coverage. It combines a lower base salary with various benefits.

Within Moroccan SMBs, the HRM system is far from being homogenous, with its apparent two-tier system as illustrated in the current study. In companies that adopt a reactive HRM approach, the HR function still plays a more traditional personnel role consisting of wage calculation and dealing with personnel records keeping. Moroccan companies are suffering from repetitive absences and extensive grievances from employees who do not fully understand internal rules and procedures and who do not recognize the authority of immediate supervisors. Conversely, with the advent of globalization, the opening of the markets and agreements of free exchange, and information technology, a more modern HRM system is emerging which is marked by a gradual introduction of HR strategic planning in response to operational needs and objectives. These developments, along with increasing foreign investments in Morocco, have contributed to changes in HRM practices within some companies that adopt a proactive HRM approach. Nonetheless, the gap between these two categories seems to be wide. It is noteworthy to mention that it is difficult to generalize the insights of the current study due to the small sample size (20 interviewees) and the sampling method used (convenience).

Moroccan organizations are more and more conscious about the fact that several HR-related problems and issues such as high employee turnover, absenteeism and job dissatisfaction are costly and hamper both organizational performance and employee well-being. However, HRM practice and research have not been fully developed in Morocco, where HRM is still at an embryonic stage both in terms of research and practice. Different reasons have been given for the challenges facing HRM practices in Morocco; hence the importance of resorting to the services of HR professionals, consultants and experts to assist in shaping and establishing an HR culture.

USEFUL WEBSITES

Public Administration

Agence Nationale de Promotion de l'Emploi et des Compétences: http://www.anapec.ma.
Agence Nationale des Petites et Moyennes Entreprises: http://www.anpme.ma.
Contrats Spéciaux de Formation: http://www.csf.ofppt.org.ma.
Department of Employment, Vocational Training, and Social Development and Solidarity/Secretariat of State for Vocational Training: http://www.dfp.ac.ma.
Direction de statistique: http://www.statistic.gov.ma.
OFPPT: http://www.ofppt.ma.

Employers' Organizations

Association marocaine des industries du textile et de l'habillement: http://www.amith.org.ma.
Confédération Générale des Entreprises du Maroc: http://www.cgem.ma/index.php.
Fédération des industries mécaniques, métallurgiques, électriques et électroniques: http://www.fimme.ma.

Trade Unions

Confédération Démocratique du Travail: http://www.cdt.ma.
Union Générale des Travailleurs Marocains: http://www.ugtm.ma.
Union Marocaine du Travail: http://www.usf-umt.com.

Others

Association des Gestionnaires et Formateurs de Personnel: www.agef.ma.
European Training Foundation: http://www.etf.europa.eu/web.nsf.
HRM Symposium in Morocco: http://www.grhaumaroc.com.

REFERENCES

Agénor, P.R. and El Aynaoui, K. 2003. Labor market policies and unemployment in Morocco: a quantitative analysis. The World Bank, Policy Research Working Paper No. 3091.
Agueniou, S. 2013. Les deux tiers des salariés sans contrat de travail! La VieEco. http://www.lavieeco.com/news/economie/les-deux-tiers-des-salaries-sans-contrat-de-travail--24974.html (accessed March 2013).

Allali. B. 2008. Culture et gestion au Maroc: une osmose atypique. In E. Davel, J.P. Dupuis and J.F. Chanlat (eds.), *Gestion en contexte interculturel: approches, problématiques, pratiques et plongées*. Québec: Presses de l'Université Laval, pp. 1–36.
Baayoud, M. and Zouanat, H. 2011. Evolution de la fonction ressources humaines au Maroc. In Mediterranean Federation of Human Resources. http://www.fmrh.org/observatoire-des-rh/etudesetprojets/projetagora/fonctionrhpaysmediterranee/13-agora-evolution-de-la-grh-/31-evolutionmaroc%3Fformat=pdf (accessed March 2014).
Badri, S. and Alami Lâaroussi, S. 2013. Fonction RH: quels challenges et quels défis? *Le Matin*, 24 March 2013, N 14990.
Benson, P.G. and Al Arkoubi, K. 2006. Human resource management in Morocco. In P.S. Budhwar and K. Mellahi (eds), *Managing Human Resources in the Middle East*. London: Routledge/Francis Group, pp. 203–290.
Budhwar, P.S. and Sparrow, P.R. 2002. An integrative framework for understanding cross national human resource management practices. *Human Resource Management Review*, **12**(3): 377–403.
Cox, J., Estrada, S., Lynham, S. and Motii, N. 2005. Defining human resource development in Morocco: an exploratory inquiry. *Human Resource Development International*, **8**(4): 435–447.
Demos Consulting 2011. Conciliation travail-famille des femmes et des hommes fonctionnaires au Maroc. http://www.mmsp.gov.ma/uploads/file/Rapport_Conciliation.pdf (accessed February 2014).
Denoeux, G.P. 2001, 'Morocco's economic prospects: daunting challenges ahead. *Middle East Policy*, **8**(2): 66–87.
DIORH 2002. *Enquête sur la fonction ressources humaines au Maroc*. Casablanca: DIORH.
Habriche, B. 2011. C'est une bonne solution pour remédier à la pénurie de compétences. *L'Economiste*, 11 January 2011. http://www.lavieeco.com/news/la-vie-eco-carrieres/c-est-une-bonne-solution-pour-remedier-a-la-penurie-de-competences-18558.html (accessed March 2014).
Hassi, A. 2011. International briefing 23: training and development in Morocco. *International Journal of Training and Development*, **15**(2): 169–178.
Hassi, A. 2012. *Employee Training in Morocco: Insights and Reflections*. Rabat: Rabat Net Publishing.
Hassi, A., Foutouh, N. and Ramid, R. 2015. Employee perception of diversity in Morocco: empirical insights. *Journal of Global Responsibility*, **6**(1): 4–18.
Hassi, A. and Storti, G. 2011. Organizational training across cultures: variations in practices and attitudes. *Journal of European Industrial Training*, **30**(1): 45–70.
Hassi, A. and Storti, G. 2014. Authentic leadership: the case of Miloud Chaabi, a shepherd who became a business legend. Emerald Emerging Markets Case Studies (EEMCS).
Hassi, A., Storti, G. and Azennoud, A. 2011. Corporate trainers' credibility and cultural values: evidence from Canada and Morocco. *Cross-Cultural Management: An International Journal*, **18**(4): 499–519.
Haut-commissariat au plan, Royaume du Maroc 2012. *Le Maroc en chiffres 2012*. file:///C:/Users/Walmart/Downloads/Le%20Maroc%20en%20chiffres,%202012%20(version%20arabe%20&%20fran%C3%A7aise)%20.pdf (accessed 25 June 2013).
Hofstede, G. 2001. *Culture's Consequences: Comparing Values, Behaviours, Institutions, and Organizations across Nations*. Thousand Oaks, CA: Sage Publications.
Kessels, J. 2002. HRD practice: a comparison of European and US models. The Third Conference on Human Resource Development Research and Practice across Europe: Creativity and Innovation in Learning, Edinburgh, 25–26 January 2002.
Safi-Eddine, B. and Bentaleb, C. 2010. Gestion de la diversité au Maroc et représentations: quelques résultats exploratoires. Research Unit on Organization Management, ENCG Business School, Marrakesh.
Secrétariat d'Etat chargé de la formation professionnelle, Royaume du Maroc 2007. *La formation professionnelle et le développement des compétences au Maroc*. Rabat: MEFPDSS.
Verme, P., Barry, A.G., Guennouni, J. and Taamouti, M. 2014. Labor mobility, economic shocks and jobless growth: evidence from panel data in Morocco. World Bank Policy Research Working Papers No. 6795.

PART III

EMERGING THEMES AND FUTURE OF HUMAN RESOURCE MANAGEMENT IN THE MIDDLE EAST

14. Employment relations of domestic workers in Kuwait: the employer's perspective

Khaled Essa Al-Ajmi, Manjusha Hirekhan, Pawan S. Budhwar, Sara Essa Al-Ajmi and Sneha Singh

INTRODUCTION AND BACKGROUND

The International Labour Office (ILO, 2013) defines 'domestic work' as 'work performed in or for a household or households'. Occupations involving domestic work are considered as a crucial source of employment for an estimated 52.6 million people worldwide (ILO, 2011). In the case of the Middle East, most domestic workers come from the Far East and Africa (e.g., the Philippines, Thailand, Indonesia, Nepal, Myanmar, Sri Lanka, Ethiopia, Kenya). The governments of these migrant domestic workers encourage their people to work abroad due to the lack of work opportunities in their respective countries (also see Fernandez and de Reget, 2014). According to a recent ILO (2013) report, there are over 2.2 million migrant domestic workers (who are formally registered) in the Middle East. When discussing the issue of domestic workers in the Middle East, issues of abuse, modern-day slavery, and exploitation are some of the key notions highlighted in the popular media, newspapers and reports. The Human Rights Watch (2008, 2010a, 2012, 2015), that covers domestic workers' well-being in the Middle East, frequently highlights such issues. In addition to international human rights organisations, independent researchers have also looked into the human resource (HR) related issues concerning domestic workers in the region. For example, Lina Abu-Habib (1998) investigated the abuse of female Sri Lankan domestic workers in Lebanon, whereas Attiyya Ahmad (2010) spent two years in Kuwait and South Asia examining how states govern and support migrant domestic workers. Fernandez and de Reget's (2014) edited volume covers a range of issues related to domestic workers in the Middle East, whereas Pande's (2013) research primarily focuses on the '*Kafala*' (sponsorship-letter) system. Regular media and related reports demonstrate the overreliance of many Middle Eastern countries on overseas domestic workers, their ill treatment, developments of new legislations, the ban on travel of domestic workers from their home country, registration with respective embassies and so on (see The Guardian, 2015; Kisika, 2015; Begum, 2015; Migrants' rights, 2015).

It is beyond the scope of this chapter to provide an in-depth analysis on different above-mentioned aspects of domestic migrant workers in the Middle East. The existing research highlights the significance of examining employer–employee relationships (e.g., Herriot, 2001). The existing literature also shows that very little is known about the relationship that domestic workers have with their employers (see The Guardian, 2015; Fernandez and de Reget, 2014), especially from the employer's point of view. Understanding the issue from an employer's perspective may uncover previously unknown factors that could provide solutions to present problems faced by the domestic workers in the Middle East context such as employee runaways, crimes, abuse, the dissatisfaction of both employers and employees and related matters. This chapter adds value to the field of migrant domestic workers by exploring how employers claim they treat their migrant domestic workers, what support they provide for them and how satisfied they are with the recruitment agencies that supply employers with domestic workers.

The social exchange theory (see Blau, 1964) and employment relations (Simon, 1951) perspective are useful to underpin this analysis. The focus of the empirical investigation is to explore the satisfaction of Kuwaiti employers of domestic workers with the services of recruitment agencies and the way they treat their domestic workers. Additionally, we examine the awareness of Kuwaiti employers of domestic workers about Kuwait's labour laws (regarding their employees' rights), and on the hiring process that migrant domestic workers go through via the recruitment agencies. The empirical investigation for this chapter is based on data from Kuwait. However, we feel the outcomes of this analysis should be relevant for other countries in the region. The remaining chapter is organised as following. Next, an overview regarding the scenario of domestic workers in the Middle East is presented. This is followed by information about the methodology adopted for the empirical analysis, discussion on the key results and a conclusion and recommendations.

THE MIGRATION OF DOMESTIC WORKERS IN THE MIDDLE EAST REGION

In the last three decades or so there has been a significant increase in the number of migrant domestic workers going to the Middle East region. Reports show that between 1995 and 2010, the numbers of migrant domestic workers have doubled from 1.1 million to 2.2 million (ILO, 2013). According to an ILO report entitled *Domestic Workers across the World: Global and Regional Statistics and the Extent of Legal Protection* (2013: 31), 'domestic work accounts for 5.6 per cent of total employment in the Middle Eastern region, but this share is far exceeded in some countries, such as Bahrain (12.8 per cent in 2009), the United Arabs Emirates (12.8 per cent in 2008) and Kuwait (21.9 per cent in 2005)'. Many of the migrant domestic workers in the Middle East come from countries in South and East Asia (Shah et al., 2002; Ahmed, 2010; Fernandez and de Reget, 2014).

Most domestic workers that migrate for work opportunities have generally had limited education, and were often raised in poverty. Some domestic worker applicants may be well educated but have no choice other than to work as a domestic worker abroad, and this is mainly due to the lack of employment opportunities in their home countries (Kodoth and Varghese, 2011). In most cases, every worker that decides to work abroad, sets out in the hope of earning enough money to support their families back home in order for them to have a better life. However, Parrenas (2001) raises an important point by highlighting that some domestic workers migrate to the Middle East and to various other countries in an attempt to escape abuse or family problems in their homes.

Nevertheless, most of the domestic workers coming from the South and East Asian countries mentioned above live under poor economic conditions. Therefore, governments opt to provide their citizens with foreign job opportunities by signing agreements with other countries in order to allow their people to work abroad (Ministry of Overseas Indian Affairs, 2007). This enables individuals to provide for their families and to contribute to their country's economy by remitting their income back to their home country. According to the Human Rights Watch (2012) report, the Philippines have an estimated one million Filipino domestic workers currently working in foreign countries. Collectively they inject over US$20 billion per year back into their country's economy.

DOMESTIC WORKERS IN KUWAIT: NUMBERS AND STATISTICS

In addition to the mentioned reasons, several other factors contribute to the rise in the numbers of migrant domestic workers in the Middle East region. Baldwin-Edwards (2005) highlights that one of the most evident factors for this rise is directly related to the oil boom in the 1970s. The lives of people that lived in oil-saturated countries improved significantly after the discovery of oil. With their newfound wealth, people from oil-rich countries like Kuwait were able to hire household help more than ever. The percentage of Kuwaiti households that employed domestic workers jumped from 13 per cent in the mid-1970s to 90 per cent in 2000 (Shah et al., 2002). Migrant domestic workers are simply very affordable for many Kuwaitis due to the low wages that migrant domestic workers can be hired for in comparison to their employers' incomes. Furthermore, having a domestic worker has become a necessity for most Kuwaitis, as this has become part of their way of living. Ahmed (2010) asserts that the employment of domestic workers can be used as an indicator of an employer's social status. However, for most Kuwaitis, having a domestic worker work for them is quite ordinary, thus they may often take them for granted.

According to the Human Rights Watch (2010a) report entitled *Abuse of Migrant Domestic Workers through Kuwait's Sponsorship System*, Kuwait is the country with the highest rate of domestic workers among all other countries in the Middle East when looking at it from a 'nationals–domestic workers' ratio. The State of Kuwait currently has a population of approximately 1.3 million Kuwaiti nationals (natives), and has a migrant domestic workforce that exceeds 660,000 individuals from various countries (also see Begum, 2015).

Domestic Workers Legislation

All Middle Eastern countries, with the exception of the Kingdom of Jordan, do not include domestic workers in their labour laws. Researchers such as Bajracharya and Sijapati (2012), Manseau (2007), Chammartin (2004) and Pande (2013) report that the reason why domestic workers are not included in Middle Eastern labour laws is because governments in the Middle East claim that relationships between migrant domestic workers and their employers are more like family relationships rather than formal employment relations.

According to ILO (2013), domestic workers in the State of Kuwait and the Republic of Lebanon regulate migrant domestic workers through standardised employment contracts that are enforced by the government on recruitment agencies. The Trade Arabia (2012) and Gulf News (2012) report that the Kingdom of Bahrain and the United Arab Emirates have announced that they too will adopt similar approaches to standardising domestic workers' contracts. These contracts serve to protect both domestic workers and their employers by clearly stating the expectations and responsibilities of both sides. The contracts are often used to settle disputes between domestic workers and their employers. Some of the things that these standardised contracts include are working hours, wage, food and accommodation rules.

Domestic workers are not allowed to self-sponsor themselves to be able to work in Kuwait. They may only enter Kuwait if they have a local sponsor (Kuwaiti employer). This sponsorship system is known as '*Kafala*'.[1] The *Kafala* places full legal responsibility on the employer known as the '*Kafeel*'[2] (Manseau, 2007). The *Kafala* system is discussed in detail in the following sections.

EMPLOYMENT RELATIONS

The ILO (2011) defines employment relationship as 'the legal link between employers and employees. It exists when a person performs work or services under certain conditions in return for remuneration'. Employment relationships are most obvious in professional occupations where employees have colleagues and have access to company policies and government legislations that protect their rights. However, it is quite different in the case of migrant domestic workers, as many countries in the Middle East consider domestic work as an informal occupation.

It is difficult to determine what kind of employment relationship domestic workers have with their employers, due to the isolated nature of their jobs. Most domestic workers are cut off from the outside community simply because their work is generally limited to their employer's house. The working sphere of domestic workers exists within the private sphere of their employers. Consequently, employers typically have a stronger status in the relationship because domestic workers reside in their employer's house and have limited access to seeking help if a situation arises. Abu-Habib (1998) points out that the media has reported incidents of rape, mistreatment and suicide of migrant domestic workers in Kuwait (for recent reports see Kisika, 2015; The Guardian, 2015). However, it is important to note that domestic workers' relationships vary considerably depending on the nature of their employers.

There are several additional factors that contribute to the employer holding a substantially more important say than the domestic worker in their employment relationship in the Middle East, and specifically in the Gulf Cooperation Council (GCC)[3] countries. The main reason for this is the non-existence of formal governmental legislation for domestic workers in the GCC. In addition, as emphasised by Khan and Harroff-tavel (2011), the very nature of the sponsorship system (*Kafala*) empowers the employers *(Kafeel)* to act on behalf of the migrant domestic worker, as they are fully responsible for them. For instance, an employer can refuse to transfer the migrant domestic worker's sponsorship to another potential sponsor if the migrant domestic worker wishes to transfer their sponsorship to another *Kafeel* (sponsor). Moreover, the *Kafeel* also has the power to cancel the sponsorship and deport the domestic worker from the country if they wish to do so (also see Pande, 2013). The employment relations and the non-existence of legislation regarding the occupation, and the way it ultimately impacts both employees and employers, is further discussed below.

Issues and Problems

International research efforts have been made to examine issues related to domestic workers worldwide. Many studies (see Anderson, 2000; Albin and Mantouvalou, 2012; Fernandez and de Reget, 2014) have explored issues related to wages, working conditions and labour protection of domestic workers in different countries. However, the Human Rights Watch (2010a, 2015) has intensively explored issues related to migrant workers in the Middle East due to the significant growth of migrant domestic workers in the region in the past three decades or so. As mentioned above, the major problem is related to the sponsorship system (*Kafala*) implemented in most Middle Eastern countries as it prevents migrant workers from moving freely from one job to another. A migrant worker is unable to get another job (with another sponsor) unless their current sponsor approves the transfer. If for any reason a sponsor refuses to transfer the *Kafala*, then the employee is forced to work for their current sponsor until the contract between them expires (generally two years). Consequently, many employees run away from their employers to work illegally elsewhere without a *Kafala*. When an employee runs away, their *Kafeel* immediately reports the missing employee to the authorities. Once found, the runaway employee could face deportation. Moreover, legal action is taken against any individual that shelters or employs migrant workers without a *Kafala*.

Bakan and Stasiulis (1997) claim that employers in Kuwait and in other Middle Eastern countries commonly confiscate their employees' passports, in an attempt to reduce the risk of their employees running away. Although employers have no legal right to keep hold of their employees' passports, it happens more often than not. This raises the issue of trust between employers and their employees (Pande, 2013).

A number of countries (such as Kenya, Indonesia and Thailand) and international human rights organisations (e.g., Human Rights Watch and Migrant-Rights.org) have criticised the *Kafala* system implemented in the GCC as being a mode of modern-day slavery, due to its restricting nature. These international bodies have exerted pressure on the GCC countries to reform the *Kafala* system to a more fair and effective system. As a result, countries such as Bahrain, Kuwait and the United Arab Emirates have made promises to review the *Kafala* system (also see Begum, 2015). One of the proposals suggests that the government should sponsor migrant workers rather than local employers (Harmassi, 2009; Khan and Harroff-Tavel, 2011; Murray, 2012). However, this has not been implemented as yet in any country. Apart from such efforts, countries such as the Philippines took a step further to secure the rights for a minimum wage of $400 per month for their men and women working abroad (see Arab Times, 2010).[4] However, this did not work, as workers from other nations were available to work at lower wages.

RESEARCH METHODOLOGY

Due to the complex and sensitive nature of the research topic, and to get a robust picture of the scene, the study adopts both qualitative and quantitative methods of data collection. The data were collected in 2012–2013. A survey and interviews were conducted with Kuwaiti employers in order to obtain first-hand accounts of their experiences with domestic workers and recruitment agencies. Moreover, interviews were conducted with recruitment agency owners/managers to acquire information from professionals in the field about the hiring processes of domestic workers in Kuwait. Semi-structured interviews were conducted with recruitment agency owners, and domestic worker employers. Information from secondary sources, such as books, magazines, journals, websites and reports, are also utilised for this analysis.

FINDINGS

Employers Composition

The survey gathered a total of 220 respondents (50 per cent males and 50 per cent females). All individuals surveyed in this study are Kuwaiti nationals living in the State of Kuwait. They were all responsible for at least one migrant domestic worker at the time the survey was conducted. All 220 participants were married, and most of the participants (63 per cent) were between the ages of 31 and 54. The majority of the participants (60 per cent) held a bachelor's degree. In addition, most of the participants worked in the public sector. Table 14.1 shows a breakdown of the survey participants' education levels and the sectors in which they work. Apart from the survey, the first author also conducted 15 interviews with selective employers and with 2 recruitment agencies.

Thirty per cent of the employers that participated in the survey earn over 2000 Kuwaiti Dinars (KD) per month, which is equivalent to approximately £4545.[5] While 19 per cent earn between 1500 and 1999KD, 28 per cent earn between 1000 and 1499KD, and 22 per cent earn between 500 and 900KD. The two most common types of residence in Kuwait are houses and apartments. Due to cultural traditions it is not uncommon for a married man to bring his wife and children to live in his parents' home ('shared residence'). However, only 57 out of the 220 survey participants were living in shared residence.

One of the major complaints migrant domestic workers have is directly related to the number of children their employers have and the increased workload caused by the children. According to a recruitment agency manager, many domestic workers that demand to be returned to the agency do so because they are not willing to work in homes that have many children. Therefore, the number of children participants have is highly significant when attempting to make a correlation between this and the number of times they have

Table 14.1 Details of research participants

Education level	Occupation Sector						Total
	Public sector	Private sector	Self-employed	Unemployed	Student	Other	
High School	39	8	—	3	—	8	26%
Bachelor's	83	27	7	6	—	10	61%
Master's	7	14	—	—	1	2	11%
PhD	3	—	2	—	—	—	2%
Total	60%	22%	4%	4%	1%	9%	100%

cancelled a domestic worker's *Kafala* (sponsorship), which basically means returning the domestic worker to the agency. A quarter of the participants that took part in the study have three children (25 per cent), whereas only 1 per cent has more than eight children.

The Demographics of the Migrant Domestic Workers

The sample employers are collectively responsible for 404 migrant domestic workers. These migrant domestic workers include both men and women from a range of countries including Bangladesh, the Philippines, India and Indonesia. They occupy various jobs such as cooks, drivers, gardeners, nannies, guards and servants. However, female Filipinos in particular stand out in their numbers from all other nationalities. Most of the domestic workers hired by the participants were Filipino females (119). On the other hand, male Indian domestic workers represented 67 per cent of all male domestic workers. In addition, they constituted 70 per cent of all males employed as drivers. Table 14.2 provides a breakdown of the sample migrant domestic workers (i.e., employees' gender, nationality and occupation).

Most of the migrant domestic workers that work for the research participants are Christians from the Philippines, India and Sri Lanka. The second largest religion that the domestic workers follow is Islam. Most migrant domestic workers earn between 60 and 89KD (£136 and £201) a month. Only 17 of them earned more than 120KD (£271) a month. Table 14.3 provides details of the wages of domestic workers covered by this study.

Kuwaiti Employers' Satisfaction

Sixty-nine per cent of the employers recruited their migrant domestic workers through recruitment agencies. The remaining 31 per cent hired their employees through recommendations made to them by family members, friends and other domestic workers they

Table 14.2 Details of migrant domestic workers in Kuwait

Nationality	Gender	Occupation						Natio-nality	Total
		Cook	Driver	Gardener	Nanny	Guard	Servant		
Bangladeshi	Male	—	7	—	—	2	2	11	3%
	Female	—	—	—	—	—	2	2	
Ethiopian	Male	—	—	—	—	—	—	—	15%
	Female	5	—	—	3	—	51	59	
Filipino	Male	—	—	—	—	—	—	—	29%
	Female	4	—	—	22	—	93	119	
Indian	Male	2	40	2	—	1	4	49	28%
	Female	8	—	—	8	—	47	63	
Indonesian	Male	—	—	—	—	—	—	—	3%
	Female	2	—	—	1	—	7	10	
Sri Lankan	Male	—	10	—	—	—	2	12	18%
	Female	9	—	—	14	—	38	61	
Others	Male	1	—	—	—	—	—	1	4%
	Female	—	—	—	2	—	15	17	
Occupation total		8%	14%	0%	12%	1%	65%	404 (100%)	

Table 14.3 Nationality and salary of domestic workers in Kuwait

Domestic worker nationality	Pay (KWD)								Total
	40–49	50–59	60–69	70–79	80–89	90–99	100–109	110+	
Bangladeshi	—	3	1	—	1	1	2	5	13
Ethiopian	2	25	23	8	—	1	—	—	59
Filipino	—	3	11	22	47	24	8	4	119
Indian	3	12	30	19	27	4	7	10	112
Indonesian	—	—	2	1	6	—	—	1	10
Sri Lankan	3	11	11	27	8	3	—	10	73
Other	1	4	9	3	—	—	—	1	18
Total	9	58	87	80	89	33	17	31	404

Table 14.4 Sources of employment and satisfaction of employers of domestic workers in Kuwait

Source of employment	Not at all satisfied	Slightly satisfied	Somewhat satisfied	Very satisfied	Extremely satisfied	Total
Recruitment agency	23 (8%)	53 (19%)	96 (34%)	75 (27%)	32 (12%)	279 (100%)
Other sources	3 (2%)	18 (15%)	45 (36%)	35 (28%)	24 (19%)	125 (100%)
Total of both sources	26 (6%)	71 (18%)	141 (35%)	110 (27%)	56 (14%)	404 (100%)

knew. Thirty-five per cent of the research participants reported that they are somewhat satisfied with their domestic worker, while 27 per cent are very satisfied, and 18 per cent are slightly satisfied. Only 14 per cent are extremely satisfied, whereas 6 per cent are not satisfied at all. Any employees hired through channels outside recruitment agencies will be referred to as 'other' sources from this point onwards. In order to identify if there is any association between employers' satisfaction and the source of employment, participants were asked to identify from where they recruited their employees and how satisfied they were with them. Table 14.4 demonstrates the satisfaction rate of employers that recruit through recruitment agencies in comparison to those that recruit through other sources. As can be seen, employers that hired domestic workers from other sources were generally more satisfied with their employees. For instance, 19 per cent of the participants that hired through other sources were 'extremely satisfied'. In contrast, satisfaction with recruitment agencies was only 12 per cent.

This is further confirmed by the interview data. Interviewee B hired her domestic worker through another domestic worker she knew (a nanny that works for her sister). She expressed her satisfaction with her employee by stating that, 'because the other *murabeya* [nanny] knew me well, she referred her own sister to me. I was very happy when her sister came to work for me because they are very good with the kids, they teach them English and take good care of them'. When asked why she did not approach a recruitment agency to hire a nanny, she responded by saying:

> It is always better when someone you know directs you to someone [an employee to hire], because the person that you know knows exactly what you are looking for. They will only refer you to someone that they know will work well for you. Agencies on the other hand, only want to make profit.

Sponsorship Cancellation and Probation

Employers often cancel sponsorships upon returning a domestic worker back to the recruitment agency because they are unhappy with the employee, or when the employee demands to be returned to the recruitment agency because they no longer want to work for their employer. This usually occurs during the three months probation period, where the employer is entitled to receive a refund from the recruitment agency. Employers also typically cancel sponsorships when their employee runs away. The cancellation of sponsorships is often related to employer dissatisfaction, thus it was important to ask participants how many times they cancelled sponsorships ever since they were first eligible to sponsor a migrant domestic worker (usually after marriage). Most participants (71 per cent) have cancelled a domestic worker sponsorship at least once and 18 per cent of them cancelled sponsorships five times or more. Moreover, as mentioned by recruitment agency owners, and also reported above, domestic workers are often returned to the recruitment agency due to the worker complaining about the large number of children their employers have.

All migrant domestic workers recruited via a recruitment agency are insured for three months, called the probation period. During these three months both the employer and the employee have the right to discontinue the two-year work contract. Employers are entitled to a refund when a domestic worker is returned to the recruitment agency within the probation period. Once a domestic worker is returned, the recruitment agency will often provide the employer with another employee or a refund. However, the recruitment agency is not responsible if the employer no longer wants the employee after the probation period or if the employee no longer wants to work for the employer. Many problems often arise after the probation period is over, because it is often after the probation period that domestic workers begin to show a disinterest in working for their employers. Interviewee C expresses this phenomenon by stating:

> At first [the domestic worker] is willing to work – they show you that they are committed to working for you. But as soon as the probation period is over, suddenly they tell you 'sir, take me back to maktab [the agency]. It has happened to me personally more than 3 times! . . . I've heard many times before from various friends and family members that recruitment agencies threaten the domestic workers not to return during the probation period, because the agencies do not want to give employers a refund, so the employees will wait until the probation period is over before telling their employers that they no longer want to work for them. All in fear of what the recruitment agencies might do to them.

When this issue was raised to one of the recruitment agency owners/managers, he commented:

> I will not tell you that it doesn't happen, it does. I've seen it happen in agencies on this very floor [in another agency in the complex, on the same floor], but for me, it makes no difference if the employee wants to leave his/her employer before the probation period is over. I will refund the

> employer and that's it, because I know that someone else will hire this employee. There is always a market for domestic workers in Kuwait.

Survey participants were also asked to rate how satisfied they were with the duration of the probation period allocated for domestic workers. Fifty-two per cent expressed that they were 'not at all satisfied', 24 per cent were 'slightly satisfied', 21 per cent were 'somewhat satisfied' and 3 per cent were 'very satisfied'. None of the participants were 'extremely satisfied'. This strongly suggests the need to further look into this matter (also see Human Rights Watch, 2015 regarding dissatisfaction of domestic workers with their assignments).

Applicants' Profile, Standards and Cost

In order to examine how satisfied employers are with the pool of migrant domestic worker applicants available in recruitment agencies, participants were asked to rate the current pool. Forty-one per cent of the participants are not at all satisfied with the domestic worker applicants available for hire from recruitment agencies. Whereas 33 per cent are slightly satisfied, 22 per cent are somewhat satisfied, and 3 per cent very satisfied. Only 1 per cent of all participants are extremely satisfied with the employees recruitment agencies have to offer. These results confirm the above-mentioned findings where a significant number of respondents use other (than recruitment agencies) sources to recruit their domestic workers.

The cost of hiring a domestic worker from recruitment agencies varies from one to another. Agencies often set a specific price depending on the domestic worker's nationality, because airfare, visa, training and medical fees vary from one country to another. Hiring a domestic worker from a recruitment agency can cost a potential employer anywhere from 500 to 1000KD (£1124 to £2248). Survey participants were asked how satisfied they are with the prices recruitment agencies charge employers who want to hire migrant domestic workers. Not surprisingly, a cumulative 93 per cent of participants are not at all satisfied with the prices set by the recruitment agencies.

Information Provided about Applicants

A number of survey respondents (56 per cent) are not at all satisfied with the information provided by recruitment agencies about the domestic worker applicants (specialism, prior work experience, etc). Whereas 31 per cent are slightly satisfied, and 12 per cent are somewhat satisfied. Many employers felt that the information provided to them by the recruitment agency was vague. Participant A expressed her frustration by emphasising that:

> We want to know more about the applicants, especially when they have work experience working in other homes in the Middle East. I would like to know more about their experiences, and the reasons they left their former employers. It should be compulsory for applicants to provide reference letters from former employers, even if their employers were from their native country. This is standard for any job; I don't understand why recruitment agencies don't demand these letters from them [domestic worker applicants].

It takes approximately 2–3 months for a migrant domestic worker to arrive in Kuwait, once an employer picks their application in the recruitment agency located in Kuwait.

Sixty-five per cent of employers expressed that they are not at all satisfied with the duration they have to wait in order for the domestic worker to reach Kuwait and begin work, whereas 24 per cent are slightly satisfied and 10 per cent are somewhat satisfied.

In an interview with a recruitment agency owner/manager, the time it took for a migrant domestic worker to reach Kuwait was explained from a professional perspective. The agency manager claims that the reason why the process takes so long was due to a number of factors. The most prominent reason was that the recruitment agencies generally collect a number of employer requests before processing the applications. This is done because it is the most cost efficient way of running a recruitment agency. The manager explains that:

> The domestic workers we bring to Kuwait must go through a training programme in their home country, and the training programme cannot be conducted unless the minimum number of prospective employees are present. Also, it is easier to process applications in batches; that way the domestic workers are taken to get medically checked in groups. If we processed each application individually, we would never be able to keep up with all the employer application requests we get!

On a related topic, we asked how the employers treat migrant domestic workers. The majority of the respondents (75 per cent) did not consider their domestic workers as employees, but rather as a family member. On the other hand, 25 per cent consider them as employees. This finding justifies claims made by the Kuwaiti government that Kuwaiti employers regard their domestic workers as a part of the family. Accordingly, domestic workers in Kuwait are currently not covered by the Kuwaiti labour laws that serve to protect the rights of employees. When the research participants were asked if they supported the idea of including domestic workers in Kuwait's labour laws, surprisingly, 64 per cent of the respondents were not sure what the relevant Kuwaiti labour law was, whereas 21 per cent supported the idea of including domestic workers in the labour law, and the remaining 15 per cent objected to the idea.

Working Hours and Salary

The most prominent complaints domestic workers have are often related to their working hours. Calculations made on the responses given by participants in the survey show that domestic workers work an average of 94 hours a week, approximately 13 hours a day. This finding validates the complaints made by migrant domestic workers and the reports conducted by the Human Rights Watch regarding issues of long working hours (for details see Human Rights Watch, 2015).

When the participants were asked if they gave their domestic workers time off work, most employers (70 per cent) established that they gave their employees time off on weekends and religious holidays. In contrast, 30 per cent did not grant their domestic workers time off. Interviewee D was one of the participants that did not give his domestic worker time off. He supported his action by stating that it was 'for her safety [his Sri Lankan house maid] . . . [I]f I allow her to go out alone who knows who she will meet; there are many opportunities for men to take advantage of her, and to be honest, I'm not willing to be dragged into such issues and problems'.

Interviewee A also had a similar opinion. She claimed that she gave her domestic workers time off, but time off did not necessarily mean that the employee would be allowed to leave the house on their own. 'Our maids get time off every time we leave the house, whether it was a day out on the beach, or simply walking around in the mall', she asserted.

Most employers (87 per cent) gave domestic workers their wages in cash. Fifty-one per cent of respondents did not document the transactions, whereas 49 per cent documented all transactions made to their employees. Eleven per cent of the total number of employers gave their employees salaries through a bank transfer to a foreign account. The remaining 2 per cent transferred their employees' salary to a local account.

Passport Possession and *Kafala* Transfer

As mentioned above, it is common practice for employers of migrant domestic workers in Kuwait to keep possession of the employees' passports. The vast majority of the employees that took part in the survey (93 per cent) keep their employees' passports with them. Only 7 per cent allow their employees to keep their passports. Interviewee B was one of the few employers that did not take her employee's passport away. She expressed her trust in her employee by making the statement 'we trust them [domestic workers] with our homes, our kids, and everything we own. Keeping the passport in my possession will not keep them from running away if they wanted to, so I see no point in taking away their passports'.

As reported above, the issue of the *Kafala* system is the most controversial, and one that is attacked the most by international human rights organisations. As mentioned earlier, the *Kafala* system does not allow an employee to change their *Kafala* to new *Kafeel* without the permission of their current *Kafeel*. Although many criticise the *Kafala* system, it is the only security employers have to protect them from losing the money they have paid as charges to bring the employee to Kuwait.

In this regard, when the survey participants were asked if they supported the proposal of having migrant domestic workers transfer their sponsorship to another potential employer without the approval of their current employer, most employers (92 per cent) did not support the idea, whereas only 8 per cent supported the proposal. More than 150 comments were made in the survey to give reasons for not supporting the idea of giving employees the right to change employers whenever they pleased. The common theme in most of the comments was related to the money employers spent on hiring their employees. An interviewee commented that, 'This will encourage domestic workers to continuously be on the hunt for a higher salary, which will cause distraction to their duties with their current employer'; 'this would be unfair for the employers that initially paid a big amount to the recruitment agency to hire the domestic worker'; and 'granting the right for domestic workers to transfer their sponsorship to another employer without the consent of their current employer, will cause a great shift of power from the employer to the employee'.

On the other hand, participants that supported domestic workers to have the right of transferring their sponsorship to another employer without the consent of their current employer claimed that 'this will protect the domestic workers from employers that do not treat them as members of the family'; 'Some domestic workers are being treated really badly, and providing them with this option will protect them in a way'; and 'this will be fair as it will balance domestic workers' rights to what current employers enjoy from rights'.

DISCUSSION

The Treatment of Domestic Workers

The research findings show that most of the employers in this study consider their domestic workers as members of the family rather than employees. This confirms claims made by the Kuwaiti government that domestic workers in Kuwait are regarded as family members, therefore excluding them from any labour laws in Kuwait (Bajracharya and Sijapati, 2012; Manseau, 2007; Chammartin, 2004). Results show that employers took full responsibility of their domestic workers as per domestic work contracts drafted by the recruitment agencies. In this regard, the employers provide food, clothing and accommodation for their employees.

However, employers' responses to work-hours related questions verify accusations previously put forward by various human rights and international labour organisations regarding long working hours (average of 13 hours a day – 94 hours a week). This finding confirms claims by the ILO (2013), Willoughby (2006) and Aljazeera (2013). However, it is important to note that when employers maintained that their employees work approximately 13 hours a day, they do not imply that they work non-stop. The 13 hours of work signifies the time in which employees must be alert to perform any household duties required by their employers.

Nevertheless, in order to break free from work contracts, domestic workers that no longer want to work for their employees often run away to seek refuge in their embassies (see, for example, Kisika, 2015). The *Arab Times* (2010) reports that the most common claim runaway domestic workers make when they arrive at their embassies is that their employers do not pay them. The employers of runaway domestic workers often cannot prove that they have been falsely accused because as our findings show, most employers in Kuwait pay their employees' salaries in cash, in which 51 per cent do not hold receipts or documentation that their workers received their salaries. This begs for a policy change and perhaps one being promulgated by a new law in Kuwait (see Begum, 2015).

Employers lose the most when domestic workers run away. As mentioned earlier, the fee for hiring a domestic worker from a recruitment agency can be anywhere from 500 to 1000KD (£1124 to £2248) for employers. Thus, when an employee runs away, the employer inevitably loses all that was paid to the recruitment agency in order to get that employee. Therefore, it is vital that employers document any monetary transactions made to their employees. It is preferred that employers pay their employees via bank transactions in order to prove when needed that salaries have in fact been given, and on time.

Results show that almost all the participants take away their domestic workers' passports. This finding confirms the normality of this action in Kuwait. Most employers do not return the employee's passport to domestic workers until their contract is over and they are ready to leave the country. Employers reported that the reason why so many of them take this action is directly related to the intimate nature of the employee's working space. Employers keep hold of their employees' passports for security measures, though legally they can't do this. Nevertheless, the confiscation of passports attempts to reduce the risk of theft-and-flee incidents, but raises serious issues related to principles of employment relations, ethics, trust and human rights.

There are two very contrasting views when discussing the issue of the *Kafala* system. The Human Rights Watch (2010b, 2015) and researchers (see Sleem, 2013) regard the system as a modern form of slavery, which restricts the rights of domestic workers in Kuwait. Kuwaiti employers on the other hand consider the *Kafala* as the only way that protects their rights in relation to contract breeches and financial losses. Most participants rejected the proposal of allowing employers to transfer their *Kafala* from one *Kafeel* to another, without the approval of their current *Kafeel*. In the current way that domestic workers are brought to Kuwait, if this proposal were put to effect, the employers believe and argue that it would cause great injustice to the initial *Kafeel* that has waited long periods of time and has paid large sums to bring the employee to work for them, only to be taken by another employer.

If domestic workers had the right to transfer their *Kafala*, then it would give them the freedom to move jobs if not satisfied with their current employers (it can be related to mistreatment or exploitation, etc.). Furthermore, one can expect in such circumstances that the salaries of domestic workers would increase drastically as a result of employers luring domestic workers to work for them in return for a higher salary than the one they receive from their current employers.

Employer's Satisfaction

Most of the Kuwaiti employers that took part in the study stated that they are 'somewhat satisfied'[6] with the domestic workers they currently employed. However, it is important to note that employers that hired domestic workers through 'other' sources (friends, family and other domestic workers they knew) were found to be more satisfied with their employees than those that hired domestic workers from recruitment agencies. This could be due to the fact that workers hired through networks are usually recommended to employers. In addition, workers that are hired in Kuwait through networks are usually experienced and familiar with the Kuwaiti culture. They often also have a fair command of Arabic and the English language. On the other hand, workers coming through recruitment agencies often have limited knowledge of the culture, no experience and poor English and Arabic communication.

Despite the low satisfaction rate indicated by employers in this study (regarding the costs of recruitment agencies, time it takes for a domestic worker to arrive in Kuwait, and the provision of a poor pool of candidates), recruitment agencies still succeed in operating without being significantly impacted by their low standards of services. This could be the result of Kuwaiti nationals' high dependency on domestic workers in their daily lives. Thus, whether or not clients are satisfied with the quality of service, they would still turn to recruitment agencies in order to obtain domestic workers. Nevertheless, the high cost of hiring a domestic worker through recruitment agencies, and the low quality of services they provide, could also be the reason why some potential employers chose to hire through other sources.

The Hiring Process of Migrant Domestic Workers

Most Kuwaiti employers were unsure if their migrant domestic workers had attended any sort of training before their hiring (despite the fact that the Kuwaiti government obligates agencies to train domestic workers on Kuwaiti culture and modern home appliances) and arrival in Kuwait. Instead, some recruitment agencies provide their applicants with fake training certificates in order to meet the visa criteria to come and work in Kuwait as a domestic worker. According to one of the recruitment agency managers, these false certificates are often obtained by bribing the authorised training centre. Consequently, these false documents and lack of training are possibly one of the key contributors to why most employers were less satisfied with their workers. The high cost of hiring a domestic worker via an agency further aggravates this. As a result, despite the poor quality of workers, the employers want to have clear control over them (e.g., not allowing them to change sponsors and keeping their passports). In such circumstances, if the employers allow their domestic workers to change sponsors, then it will shift the power from the employer to the employee, as they could walk out on them any time they wanted.

Employment Relations and Social Exchange

Our results (based on both primary and secondary data) provide a mixed picture regarding the satisfaction of employers with their domestic workers. This ambiguity can be addressed via the social exchange theory. Homans (1961: 13) defines the social exchange theory as 'an exchange of activity, tangible or intangible, and more or less rewarding or costly, between at least two persons'. The social exchange is built on microeconomic principles that suggest that individuals seek to maximise their rewards, while minimising their costs. In the field of sociology, Emerson (1976: 336) describes this as 'the economic analysis of non-economic social situations'. The social exchange has the power to predict the success and continuity of one's relationship through a combination of three factors.

The first factor is the cost–benefit analysis factor. This includes the process of evaluating a relationship in terms of what a person is being rewarded for what they have to put up with in the relationship. This evaluation process identifies whether the relationship is positive or negative by subtracting the cost from the rewards (Adams, 1965). For example, a domestic worker may find that their employer is too demanding, and that the house they are expected to clean is too big (cost), but in return the employer is polite, pays a high salary, offers accommodation and food, and provides sufficient rest time (reward). In this case, the domestic worker's reward outweighs the cost, thus it is most likely that the worker would want to start or continue this relationship as it is perceived to be a positive one.

The second component of this model is the comparison level. This may occur, for instance, when a domestic worker compares their current employment with a previous one. If their previous employment required less input and offered more rewards, then domestic workers would frequently expect the same with their current employer. If the domestic worker was not offered the same cost–reward level as in their previous employment, then it is predicted that the worker would reconsider working for their current employer.

The third and final factor is the comparison level of alternatives. A domestic worker with a high comparison level of alternatives is confident that they are worth more than what they are receiving from their current employer, in terms of the cost that they have to put in and the reward that they are receiving. In such cases, the domestic worker is most likely going to seek another employer. However, if the domestic worker has a low comparison level of alternatives, or has no other alternative, then they are more likely to continue in the relationship even if the cost outweighs the rewards.

Based on the literature related to current Kuwaiti labour legislations, foreign employees that are covered by the Kuwaiti labour law can legally leave their current employers if one of the three above-mentioned factors arises. They are able to terminate their employment because Kuwaiti labour laws protect them. However, migrant domestic workers are unable to terminate their employment contract due to the fact that Kuwaiti labour laws do not include them. Therefore, it is understood that migrant domestic workers do not have a legal way to exit an employment relationship. Thus, they are driven to unofficial ways of terminating their employment (e.g., by seeking refuge in their embassies and falsely accusing their employers of the non-payment of wages, or exposure to immoral or life-threatening environments). That being said, the embassy is obligated to protect their citizens due to the non-existence of laws that protects domestic workers in Kuwait. Whether the non-payment of wages claims are true or false, this is inevitably the only way domestic workers can escape an employment relationship without being subjected to the employer's mercy or tangled in financial matters.

CONCLUSION AND RECOMMENDATIONS

The above analysis indicates that migrant domestic workers are not formally recognised as employees in the State of Kuwait. Research shows that the Kuwaiti government and employers in Kuwait consider migrant domestic workers as a member of the family for which they work, thus Kuwaiti labour laws do not protect them. Consequently, the working conditions of domestic workers depend immensely on the way their employers treat them. International human rights bodies have failed to persuade Kuwait and other Middle Eastern countries to formally recognise domestic worker roles as official jobs that are protected by labour laws. International human rights organisations have claimed that the '*Kafala*' sponsorship system is the main contributor to many of the issues migrant domestic workers encounter in Middle Eastern countries, and regard it as a form of modern-day slavery that prompts bounded labour.

Due to the non-existence of protection provided by the Kuwaiti government, domestic workers are potentially exposed to some extent to undesirable work conditions, such as long working hours and no days off. Domestic workers that face intolerable working conditions and do not find aid often run away from their employers to work illegally in the country. This solution could in fact worsen their living conditions, and they may also be subject to legal fines if caught. In more severe cases, some migrant domestic workers find themselves in such hopeless situations that they commit suicide in a bid to escape. However, most migrant domestic workers that no longer want to work for their employers will often run away to seek refuge in their embassies, as they have no other option.

It is important to note that many times the migrant domestic workers will falsely accuse their employers for the non-payment of their wages or bad working conditions. One reason for such accusations could be that the migrant domestic worker feels homesick and wishes to return to their country or feels that that they are not satisfied with the employment relationship they have. However, in order to break their work contract and to return to their country, they must seek refuge in their embassies to avoid being put in the awkward situation of employers asking them to pay back the money that they have spent on hiring them. Therefore, upon their arrival to the embassy, the domestic workers often accuse their employers of neglect, abuse and/or the non-payment of wages in order to be protected and sent back to their countries.

In any case, anytime a work contract is breached by an employee results in the dissatisfaction of the employer. In addition, this creates tension between the employer and the local recruitment agency, which can potentially extend further to the foreign recruitment agencies that the domestic worker was hired through. Moreover, migrant domestic workers are often also negatively affected by their decision to leave their employers before completing the duration of their contract; this is due to the fact that most migrant domestic workers borrow money from 'shark loaners' in order to take their first steps to working abroad. Therefore, although runaways may return to their countries, they will often be unable to repay their debt.

Nevertheless, Kuwait and other Middle Eastern governments have displayed initiatives that aim to protect the conditions of migrant domestic workers by enforcing standardised work contracts (for details see Begum, 2015). These contracts set the minimum expectations for both employers and employees. Despite the initiative from these GCC countries, there seems to be a lack of measurement and observation methods to ensure that the minimum expectations are being followed thoroughly. The non-existence of observation methods may be justified by drawing on the fact that the nature of domestic worker roles is often limited to in-house private spheres. Cultural and legislation factors forbid the entrance of any official to one's private residence without their consent, or a high court warrant.

To conclude, this research shows that migrant workers frequently bypass the training required by all migrant domestic workers in Kuwait. Furthermore, it has been flagged that Kuwaiti recruitment agency licences are illegally rented and shared to a number of foreigners with the sole purpose of generating profit only. Moreover, the study offers recruitment agencies with valuable feedback from employers on areas for further improvement, such as quality of their services and the pool of their domestic worker applicants. Based on the above analysis, the key recommendations are directed to the government, recruitment agencies and the potential employers of domestic workers in Kuwait.

The Kuwaiti government should reform the current *Kafala* system implemented for domestic workers through carefully studying alternative methods for granting work permits for this occupation. It is crucial that any new system is carefully analysed in regard to the potential effects it may have on domestic workers, employers, recruitment agencies and, foremost, the country's security and economy. In addition, the government should also take into account balanced solutions for both employers and employees when implementing alternative work permit methods, or in the case of formalising the roles of domestic workers as employees that are protected by the Kuwaiti labour law.

The changes should most importantly include the formalisation of the employment relationship and the improvement of migrant domestic workers' working conditions. In addition, the government must ensure safe channels for domestic workers to seek help from the Kuwaiti government when required. Furthermore, it must be compulsory for all domestic workers to have bank accounts into which their salaries are transferred, as non-payment of wages is currently one of the main accusations domestic workers make. Additionally, the changes should also protect employers from sudden or continuous increases on domestic workers' salaries.

Moreover, since Kuwait does not currently have a set of job descriptions for domestic workers, the government should seek consultation from local and foreign recruitment agencies, employers and previous domestic workers to design a generic job description for the roles. Once designed, this uniformed job description should be adopted by all local recruitment agencies. Creating a job description would help to better understand the essential training that domestic workers need. It also provides employees and employers a guideline of what is expected from both sides. Consequently, such job descriptions would further assist in improving work contracts and related legislations.

Further, the government should also consider designing and implementing a short compulsory training workshop for employers prior to hiring a domestic worker. The workshop should include general employment relationship guidelines and expectations. Laws and regulations that protect both employers and domestic workers must also be addressed in the workshop. The aim of educating both sides on their expected roles and rights is to effectively bridge the training of both domestic workers and employers in order to achieve a more successful relationship.

The Kuwaiti government should also strictly forbid recruitment agency owners from renting their licences to foreigners that are not legally tied to the recruitment agency. Harsh fines and an effective monitoring mechanism must be implemented in order to control and prevent this state of affairs from occurring. The government also needs to ensure that the training of domestic workers is not being bypassed; certifying certain institutes in each country, and conducting regular audits can help correct this problem.

In addition, the Kuwaiti government should carry out awareness campaigns that aim to educate employers and their families on how to treat migrant domestic workers. The campaign should address cultural differences, time management and the general treatment of domestic workers.[7] This campaign would further support the compulsory training workshop recommended for employers in order to strengthen the awareness of employers in Kuwait.

Recruitment agencies need to focus on the areas that require improvement as indicated by the employers in this study. This can be achieved by understanding what potential employers expect from their migrant domestic workers. The expectations of employers are an important aspect that could significantly assist in continuously improving training programmes designed for domestic workers. Recruitment agencies should work alongside the government in the campaigns suggested earlier. They should provide potential employers with educational leaflets and booklets that highlight the responsibilities and rights of both employers and employees.

In addition, recruitment agencies need to provide more details in domestic workers' profile applications. For instance, profiles should include references for those that have work experience in their hometown or abroad. Recruitment agencies should consider initiating a standardised references form for employers to fill once their domestic worker has ended their contract. These references would benefit both the domestic workers and future employers.

Furthermore, recruitment agencies should follow up with their clients on how they are finding their newly employed workers. Moreover, recruitment agencies should promptly contact their clients before their current domestic worker contract ends, in order to arrange for new potential recruits if the current worker does not wish to renew their contract with the same employer. These steps would strengthen the relationship recruitment agencies have with their clients, and would solve the employer's dissatisfaction with the waiting period shown in this study.

There are many ethical issues that need to be addressed on the issue of recruitment agencies using websites to market their pool of applicants. It is very common for recruitment agencies to publicly upload a domestic worker's passport and documents that expose personal information. It is crucial that recruitment agencies find a more ethical way to market their domestic worker applicants without publicly exposing confidential documents. For instance, recruitment agencies may use websites to announce the applicants that they have; however, potential employers must formally contact the agency to obtain specific details about the applicant.

Employers are advised to warmly welcome newly hired domestic workers to their homes and pay their domestic workers on a specified date, and preferably through an automated bank transfer to their domestic worker's bank account. In the case of paying by cash, employers should document the transaction as proof that their domestic workers have received their wages. Employers should also make sure that their domestic worker is not being overloaded with work or working for long hours. Creating a weekly timetable of the work required by the worker, and coordinating it with all the members of the family living in the employer's residence, can help organise the domestic worker's time and duties. Finally, employers are also recommended to provide their domestic worker with a yearly increment. Annually increasing domestic workers' salaries provides a sense of appreciation, and in return maintains positive relationships.

Lastly, it is important to acknowledge that the primary investigation for this analysis was based on the employers' perspective, which is one way of seeing things. Future research should focus on other perspectives to get a comprehensive picture of the scene.

NOTES

1. The literal translation of *Kafala* is sponsorship.
2. The literal translation of *Kafeel* is sponsor.
3. The six members of the GCC include: The State of Kuwait, the State of Qatar, the Kingdom of Saudi Arabia, the Kingdom of Bahrain, the United Arab Emirates and the Sultanate of Oman.
4. Established in 1977, the *Arab Times* is the first English-language newspaper published in Kuwait, and is the most popular English newspaper in Kuwait.
5. 1 Kuwaiti Dinar is equivalent to approximately 2.54 British Pounds (August 2016).
6. From a scale of 1 to 5, rating 'somewhat satisfied' is number 3.
7. The Saudi Human Rights Organization located in the Kingdom of Saudi Arabia has already launched an awareness campaign regarding the treatment of domestic workers. Many advertisements have been made and circulated to promote this campaign; such an advert can be see via this link: http://www.youtube.com/watch?v=teo6SyFuW5M.

USEFUL WEBSITES

ILO: http://www.ilo.org/beirut/projects/WCMS_226948/lang--en/index.htm.
Gulf Talent: http://www.gulftalent.com.
Human Rights Watch: https://www.hrw.org/news/2015/06/30/kuwait-new-law-breakthrough-domestic-workers.
Migrants Rights Org: http://www.migrant-rights.org/2010/04/migrant-domestic-workers-in-the-middle-east-exploited-abused-and-ignored/.

REFERENCES

Abu-Habib, L. 1998. The use and abuse of female domestic workers from Sri Lanka in Lebanon. *Gender and Development*, **6**(1): 52–56.

Adams, J.S. 1965. Inequity in social exchange. *Advances in Experimental Social Psychology*, **2**: 267–299.

Ahmad, A. 2010. Migrant domestic workers in Kuwait: the role of state institutions. In The Middle East Institute, *Migration and the Gulf*, pp. 27–29. http://www.voltairenet.org/IMG/pdf/Migration_and_the_Gulf.pdf (accessed 4 October 2013).

Albin, E. and Mantouvalou, V. 2012. The ILO convention on domestic workers: from the shadows to the light. *Industrial Law Journal*, **41**(1): 67–78.

Aljazeera 2013. Maid to work: Gulf labourers hope for day off. http://www.aljazeera.com/indepth/features/2013/04/201342192746837551.html (accessed 4 October 2013).

Anderson, B.J. 2000. *Doing the Dirty Work: The Global Politics of Domestic Labour*. London: Zed Books.

Arab Times 2010. Some employers take advantage of weak legal protection. http://www.arabtimesonline.com/NewsDetails/tabid/96/smid/414/ArticleID/160437/reftab/69/t/Some-employers-take-advantage-of-weak-legal-protection/Default.aspx (accessed 4 October 2013).

Bajracharya, R. and Sijapati, B. 2012. The Kafala system and its implications for Nepali domestic workers. *CESLAM Policy Brief*, **1**: 1–16.

Bakan, A.B. and Stasiulis, D.K. 1997. *Not One of the Family: Foreign Domestic Workers in Canada*. Toronto: University of Toronto Press.

Baldwin-Edwards, M. 2005. *Migration in the Middle East and the Mediterranean*. Athens: Mediterranean Migration Observatory. http://www.mmo.gr/pdf/news/Migration_in_the_Middle_East_and_Mediterranean.pdf (accessed 4 September 2013).

Begum, R. 2015. *Kuwait: New Law a Breakthrough for Domestic Workers*. Human Rights Watch, 30 June. https://www.hrw.org/news/2015/06/30/kuwait-new-law-breakthrough-domestic-workers (accessed 1 September 2015).

Blau, P. 1964. *Exchange and Power in Social Life*. New York: Wiley.

Chammartin, G. 2004. Women migrant workers' protection in Arab League states. In S. Esim and M. Smith (eds), *Gender and Migration in Arab States: The Case of Domestic Workers*. Beirut: Regional Office for Arab States, pp. 8–23. http://www.ilo.org/wcmsp5/groups/public/---arabstates/---ro-beirut/documents/publication/wcms_204013.pdf (accessed 26 July 2016).

Emerson, R.M. 1976. Social exchange theory. *Annual Review of Sociology*, **2**: 335–362.

Fernandez, B. and de Regt, M. (eds) 2014. *Migrant Domestic Workers in the Middle East*. Basingstoke, UK: Palgrave Macmillan.

Gulf News 2012. Domestic workers get more protection from exploitation. http://gulfnews.com/news/gulf/uae/employment/domestic-workers-get-more-protection-from-exploitation-1.1016692 (accessed 4 October 2013).

Harmassi, M. 2009. Bahrain to end 'slavery' system. http://www.upr.bh/articles/end_sponsershp_system_6_May_2009.pdf (accessed 4 October 2013).

Herriot, P. 2001. *The Employment Relationship: A Psychological Perspective*. London: Routledge.

Homans, G. 1961. *Social Behavior: Its Elementary Forms*. New York: Harcourt Brace Jovanovich.

Human Rights Watch 2008. '*As If I Am Not Human': Abuses against Asian Domestic Workers in Saudi Arabia*. http://www.hrw.org/sites/default/files/reports/saudiarabia0708_1.pdf (accessed 4 October 2013).

Human Right Watch 2010a. *Walls at Every Turn: Abuse of Migrant Domestic Workers through Kuwait's Sponsorship System*. http://www.hrw.org/sites/default/files/reports/kuwait1010webwcover.pdf (accessed 4 October 2013).

Human Rights Watch 2010b. Dignity overdue: decent work domestic workers. http://www.huffingtonpost.com/human-rights-watch/middle-eastasia-partial-r_b_555385.html (accessed 9 March 2013).

Human Right Watch 2012. Domestic workers convention: labor right treaty to take effect. http://www.hrw.org/news/2012/08/06/domestic-workers-convention-labor-rights-treaty-take-effect (accessed 4 October 2013).

Human Rights Watch 2015. Kuwait: new law a breakthrough for domestic workers. https://www.hrw.org/news/2015/06/30/kuwait-new-law-breakthrough-domestic-workers (accessed 19 July 2016).

International Labour Office 2011. *Employment Relationship*. http://www.ilo.org/ifpdial/areas-of-work/labour-law/WCMS_CON_TXT_IFPDIAL_EMPREL_EN/lang--en/index.htm (accessed 4 October 2013).

International Labour Office 2013. National labour legislation and domestic workers. In *Domestic Workers across the World: Global and Regional Statistics and the Extent of Legal Protection*. http://www.ilo.org/wcmsp5/groups/public/---dgreports/---dcomm/---publ/documents/publication/wcms_173363.pdf (accessed 4 October 2013).

Khan, A. and Harroff-Tavel, H. 2011. Reforming the Kafala: challenges and opportunities in moving forward. *Asian and Pacific Migration Journal*, **20**(3/4): 293–313.

Kisika, S. 2015. CS wants Kenyans banned from Middle East domestic workers jobs. News24.com.

http://m.news24.com/Kenya/MyNews24/CS-wants-Kenyans-banned-from-Middle-East-domestic-workers-jobs-20150625 (accessed 1 September 2015).

Kodoth, P. and Varghese, V.J. 2011. Emigration of women domestic workers from Kerala: gender, state policy and the politics of movement. CDS Working Paper No. 445.

Manseau, G.S. 2007. Contractual solutions for migrant labourers: the case of domestic workers in the Middle East. *Human Rights Law Commentary*, **3**: 25–47.

Ministry of Overseas Indian Affairs 2007. The Kuwait covenant. Pravasi Bharatiya: connecting India with its diaspora, 2, 6. http://www.overseasindian.in/pdf/2007/may/Parvasi-English-May07.pdf (accessed 29 October 2013).

Murray, H.E. 2012. Hope for reform springs eternal: how the sponsorship system, domestic laws and traditional customs fail to protect migrant domestic workers in GCC countries. *Cornell International Law Journal*, **45**: 461–723.

Pande, A. 2013. 'The paper that you have in your hand is my freedom': migrant domestic work and the sponsorship (Kafala) system in Lebanon. *International Migration Review*, **47**(2): 414–441.

Parrenas, R.S. 2001. *Servants of Globalization: Women, Migration and Domestic Work*. Stanford, CA: Stanford University Press.

Shah, N.M., Shah, M.A., Chowdhury, R.I. and Menon, I. 2002. Foreign domestic workers in Kuwait: who employs how many. *Asian and Pacific Migration Journal*, **11**(2): 247–269.

Simon, H.A. 1951. A formal theory of the employment relationship. *Econometrica*, **19**(3): 293–305.

Sleem, A. 2013. CASES: the sponsorship system (Kafala) in GCC countries: the modern-day slavery, 23 July. http://youtu.be/4B9OUEwE5_I (accessed 4 October 2013).

The Guardian 2015. Indonesia to stop sending domestic workers to Middle East – reports. http://www.theguardian.com/world/2015/may/05/indonesia-to-stop-sending-domestic-workers-to-middle-east-reports (accessed 1 September 2015).

Trade Arabia 2012. New laws to protect migrant workers in Bahrain. http://www.tradearabia.com/news/law_218377.html (accessed 4 October 2013).

Willoughby, J. 2006. *Ambivalent Anxieties of the South Asian-Gulf Arab Labor Exchange*. http://rabida.uhu.es/dspace/bitstream/handle/10272/467/b1512574.pdf?sequence=1 (accessed 4 October 2013).

15. Labour localisation and human resource management practices in the Gulf countries

Marie F. Waxin and Rob E. Bateman

INTRODUCTION AND BACKGROUND

The states of Bahrain, Kuwait, Qatar, Oman, Saudi Arabia and the United Arab Emirates (UAE) make up the Gulf Cooperation Council (GCC). Each of these nations has enjoyed rapid economic growth, even while struggling with the social, economic and political consequences of extensive reliance on a large expatriate workforce. The need to create more employment opportunities for local citizens has gained increasing attention throughout the GCC over the past 30 years, with each member country adopting some form of politically led localisation initiative (Al-Dosary and Rahman, 2005; Looney and Hamad, 2004; Rees, Mamman and Bin Braik, 2007).

Labour localisation programmes can be described as the recruitment and development of citizens to increase their employability, thereby reducing the country's dependence on an expatriate workforce (Cave, 2004). These efforts have been formally defined as 'a multi-level process through which dependency on the expatriate labour force is reduced and nationals are prepared to take up jobs performed by expatriates' (Abdelkarim, 2001: 56). These efforts date back to at least the early 1980s in Saudi Arabia, but Oman adopted a moderately successful programme in 1995 and the UAE has become something of a policy leader in recent years.

For member states of the GCC, the development of human capabilities, especially in nationals, is recognised as a major strategic priority. The Kingdom of Saudi Arabia's (KSA) economic strategy, Bahrain's Vision 2030, Qatar's Vision 2030, Oman's five-year strategic plan, Kuwait's development plan and UAE's strategy 2011–21 share a common emphasis on human development. Each of the GCC countries invests extensively in the education and development of its people. Government policy and legislation to enhance the participation of nationals in the workforce have changed the human resources landscape in the GCC (Randeree, 2009) and made labour localisation a significant staffing consideration for international businesses operating in this particular region (Looney and Hamad, 2004; Mellahi, 2007; Rees, Mamman and Bin Braik, 2007). It has become increasingly unlikely for a large organisation to establish itself in the GCC without some plan to address the localisation of human resources (Randeree, 2009).

Human resources are the 'organizationally relevant capabilities of groups and individuals' (Scott-Jackson et al., 2014a), and strategic human resource management (HRM) is defined as 'the development of a consistent aligned collection of practices, programs and policies to facilitate the achievement of the organization's strategic objectives' (Mello, 2006: 152). According to these definitions, then, HRM has a key role to play in the economic and social achievement of national and organisational strategies in the GCC countries (Scott-Jackson et al., 2014a).

However, although anecdotal records and literature on localisation exist in most GCC countries – particularly in the UAE, KSA and Oman – there is still a lack of academic and empirical research on localisation programmes (Forstenlechner, 2010; Randeree, 2012) and the HRM practices that support them. Given the importance of these programmes for the GCC countries and the enabling role that HRM could play, it is surprising to find relatively few published articles about HRM practices that further the employment of nationals. Although several researchers have addressed particular human resource (HR) practices with respect to localisation, there has been no comprehensive study encompassing the key HR processes. The difficulty of collecting reliable statistical and empirical data as well as the challenges of conducting research in the region generally may be contributing factors to this deficit (Williams, Bhanugopan and Fish, 2011; Harry, 2007).

This chapter reviews the literature on labour localisation programmes in the GCC countries and the HRM practices that facilitate the implementation of these programmes. We searched the ABI/INFORM database for published peer-reviewed academic articles using the keywords 'human resource management, HR practices, HR policies, HR strategies, HR roles, HR planning, job analysis, recruitment, selection, training, development, performance management, rewards, compensation, talent management' in combination with 'localisation, nationalisation, Emiratisation, Qatarisation, Kuwaitisation, Bahrainisation, Saudisation and Omanisation', without limiting the time frame. Out of the 17 articles we retrieved, only a few had an empirical focus on specific HRM practices that facilitate localisation. Other academic articles examined GCC demographics, educational systems, localisation policies, general challenges related to localisation programmes, and suggested intuitive HRM practices that would facilitate the employment of nationals. The most extensive studies on labour localisation and related HRM practices have focused so far on the UAE. However, their findings are relevant to the other countries in the Gulf region due to similarities in their labour markets and development patterns. Because the selected articles were not comprehensive enough to sufficiently inform readers about HRM practices that facilitate localisation programmes, we extended our review to include other relevant empirical reports.

The chapter is organised as follows: first, we examine the literature on core issues pertinent to this theme, such as demographic and labour market characteristics in the GCC, the objectives of these localisation programmes, and the major components of localisation policies. Second, we review the literature on HRM practices that facilitate the implementation of localisation programmes. Third, we review multiple challenges related to the implementation of these programmes. Finally, we present some recommendations intended to enhance the impact of the localisation efforts.

CORE ISSUES AND FACTORS INFLUENCING HRM

Demographic and Labour Market Characteristics in the GCC

The six GCC nations share similar demographic and labour market characteristics: rapid growth in total population, extensive reliance on expatriates, high rates of unemployment among citizens, low levels of private sector employment for nationals and low participation of women in the workforce.

Table 15.1 Demographic imbalances in the GCC countries in 2010

Country	2010 population (millions)			Population %		Workforce %	
	Total	Nationals	Expatriates	Nationals	Expatriates	Nationals	Expatriates
Bahrain	1.05	0.51	0.54	48.57	51.43	36.10	63.90
Qatar	1.68	0.22	1.46	13.10	86.90	5.70	94.30
Oman	3.41	2.39	1.02	70.09	29.91	28.70	71.30
Kuwait	3.47	1.04	2.43	29.97	70.03	16.90	83.10
UAE	8.19	0.95	7.24	11.60	88.40	4.20	95.80
KSA	28.69	20.94	7.75	72.99	27.01	50.50	49.50
GCC	46.50	26.05	20.45	56.02	43.98	38.30	61.70

Source: Forstenlechner and Rutledge (2011).

Rapid growth in total population. The aggregate population in the GCC has increased more than tenfold in little over half a century, from 4 million in 1950 to 40 million by 2006 (Kapiszewski, 2006). This trend probably represents the highest population growth rate of any region in the world, reflecting both the active importation of labour and the relatively high birth rates among the local population. The Economist Intelligence Unit (2009) estimates that the GCC population will raise to 53 million by 2020.

Extensive reliance on expatriates. Sustained increases in wealth since the 1970s have allowed GCC countries to undertake aggressive programmes of investment in public infrastructure, which have in some nations paralleled a boom in private property development. Because the small local population had little interest in construction work and lacked the necessary skills, most of these relatively young states turned to the use of imported labour and developed relatively tolerant rules governing expatriate employment (Al-Waqfi and Forstenlechner, 2010; Mellahi and Al-Hinai, 2000). Heavy dependency on expatriate workers is obvious across the entire GCC: 62 per cent of the overall workforce is composed of non-nationals. In 2011, the UAE, Qatar and Kuwait had the largest percentages of foreign labour (96, 94 and 83 per cent, respectively), while in Saudi Arabia, Bahrain and Oman the percentages were 49.5, 64 and 71 respectively (Forstenlechner and Rutledge, 2011, see Table 15.1). Rees, Mamman and Bin Braik (2007: 33) suggest that dependence on an expatriate workforce has serious long-term political, economic and social consequences. Expatriates have a fundamentally different relationship with foreign employers than with those in their home countries, as manifested by lower long-term commitment abroad. Thus, having too many expatriate workers can negatively affect a country's human capital over the long term (Richardson and McKenna, 2006).

High unemployment rates among citizens. The steady demand for imported labour creates an interesting paradox as unemployment among nationals increases in all GCC countries, especially among young citizens. The GCC countries all have an age pyramid with a wide base, resulting in substantial numbers of new labour market entrants annually. Almost all reported unemployment is among nationals, as most of these countries require expatriates who lose their employment to return home if not able to find other work within 30 days. The so-called Arab Spring has highlighted the sensitive nature of high unemployment levels, particularly among young citizens, and GCC leaders

Table 15.2 GCC labour market characteristics (between 2004 and 2007)

Country	Public sector labour force %		Private sector labour force %		Unemployment among nationals %	
	Nationals	Expatriates	Nationals	Expatriates	All nationals	Aged 15–29
Bahrain	90.80	9.20	28.60	71.40	18.40	27.00
Qatar	52.80	47.20	17.00	83.00	3.20	11.00
Oman	80.50	19.50	15.50	84.50	6.30	
Kuwait	74.60	25.40	2.70	97.30	3.70	8.00
UAE	27.40	72.60	1.30	98.70	13.80	12.00
KSA	91.30	8.70	45.30	54.70	9.80	28.00
GCC	72.30	27.70	31.70	68.30	9.20	17.20

Source: Data aggregated in 2009 – Forstenlechner and Rutledge (2010).

recognise that unemployment issues must be addressed if political support is to be maintained. Forstenlechner and Rutledge (2010) reported unemployment rates in the GCC countries ranging between 8 and 28 per cent for nationals in the 15–29 age bracket (for details, see Table 15.2).

However, even as unemployment rates are rising among national citizens, their levels of participation in private sector employment remain low (see Table 15.2). This is because many GCC nationals have a strong preference for public sector positions due to higher compensation, cultural factors and easier working conditions relative to business. This public sector appeal makes it difficult for industry to attract and keep young nationals. Many would prefer to wait for a job in government rather than take a private sector position immediately.

The participation of women in the GCC labour force merits special mention. Although employment patterns for women have changed dramatically in recent years, their participation remains low relative to other Organisation for Economic Co-operation and Development (OECD) countries. In 1975, women represented between 2 and 8 per cent of the total waged workforce in the different GCC countries (Willoughby, 2008). Between 2005 and 2008, the participation rates of national women in the labour force was 17 per cent in KSA, 28 per cent in the UAE, 30 per cent in Bahrain and 35 per cent in Qatar. Participation rates of all females (nationals + expatriates) were 25 per cent in Oman, 42 per cent in the UAE and 51 per cent in Kuwait (Shehadi et al., 2011). Even though fewer than half of the women in most Gulf countries are active in the labour force, unemployment rates among those who are active remain high – even among the most educated women – and most national women work in the public sector (Shehadi et al., 2011). It is fair to say that GCC national women form an interesting, but underutilised talent pool for private sector organisations.

At least six factors should be converging to facilitate women's employment in the GCC. The first of these is the improvement in women's educational opportunities (Karoly, 2010; Williams et al., 2011). Kuwait took the lead in 1937 by instituting a scheme for women's education (Talhami, 2004). When the UAE was formed in 1971, it also established educational programmes for women (Randeree and Gaad, 2008). Oman and the UAE have introduced women's empowerment programmes (including, for example, credit counselling and business planning), reflecting the recognition and importance of entrepreneurship for women's employment (Al-Lamki, 2000; Metle, 2001). A second factor is the gradual liberalisation of social and cultural norms, with the UAE usually playing the role of leader, and with similar trends evident in the other GCC countries, notably in Qatar and Bahrain (Randeree, 2012). Traditionally in the GCC, cultural norms and practices ensured the exclusion of women from mainstream economic activities, and opportunities outside of the household were limited. However, attitudes in the region are changing, and women today increasingly have the education and desire to play a more central role in the region's labour market (Shehadi et al., 2011). Third, localisation programmes created pressure to increase nationals' participation in the workforce, which has improved the employment prospects of women (Randeree, 2009, 2012; Rutledge et al., 2011). Fourth, patterns of economic diversification towards a knowledge-based economy have led to the emergence of well-educated women in corporate leadership positions (Augsberg, Claus and Randeree, 2009) who serve as role models for the next generation (Williams et al., 2011). Fifth, growth in female employment has also been facilitated by increased political representation (Al-Lamki, 2000) and, sixth, by rapid urbanisation across the GCC (Forstenlechner and Rutledge, 2010). It is worth mentioning that in contrast to other geographic areas, the presence of extended families and live-in help with childcare are common, so women in the GCC do not necessarily face some of the same constraints that might limit their employment opportunities elsewhere.

Objectives of Localisation Programmes in the GCC Nations

Nationalisation programmes have multiple national, organisational and individual objectives that can be examined from diverse economic, social and political perspectives (Scott-Jackson, et al., 2014b). These goals depend on the viewpoint of the stakeholders and sometimes actually conflict. Economic objectives do vary across the Gulf countries and have an impact on the structure of the labour market. In some nations complementary proportions of expatriate workers are high, meaning that expatriates are doing jobs that nationals find undesirable. Nationals may actually be scarce in the labour market. In other countries, there are competing proportions of expatriates doing jobs that nationals would want, thus leading to high competition for jobs and the resulting unemployment as a major issue. UAE and Qatari nationals form a small proportion of the local workforce, for example, so it is considered imperative that they maximise their impact and take up leadership roles, wherever possible.

Organisational objectives also vary according to the size and ownership structure of the employing institution. Public sector entities may have 'national' as well as organisational obligations. Of course, when employers must address government objectives they will try to do so in ways that will work to their own advantage. Forstenlechner and Mellahi (2011) examined the process and outcomes of cultivating legitimacy through the employment of UAE nationals by UAE affiliates of multinational enterprises (MNEs). Their research used 48 semi-structured interviews with local managers of MNE subsidiaries. They found that in sectors where the employment of national citizens is almost taken for granted, such as in banking, MNEs are driven by a sense of appropriateness and social legitimacy. In contrast, in sectors where the employment of UAE nationals is almost non-existent, those MNEs engaging in localisation efforts are driven by the logic of economic efficiency and tend to employ nationals in order to reduce the risk of being disadvantaged vis-à-vis local firms and to extract rents from the government. From a policy perspective, the findings suggest that coercive pressure to force MNEs to employ UAE nationals through laws and regulations are most effective when complemented with non-legal initiatives and voluntary agreements.

For their part, national citizens want to gain education and experience, maximise their personal growth, prepare for career and economic success, and proudly contribute to their country's development (Scott-Jackson et al., 2014b).

Localisation Policies

By the mid-1990s, shrinking public sector opportunities prompted most governments to focus on more effectively integrating local workers into the private sector. In general, all GCC countries, with varying degrees of commitment, adopted three types of localisation policies: enhancing educational attainment, diversifying the economy away from the hydrocarbons sector and intervening directly in the labour market (i.e., introducing quotas and designating certain occupations to be staffed solely by nationals). According to Forstenlechner and Rutledge (2010), the next generation of localisation policies, formulated during the recent oil-price boom, covers the same areas but is perhaps better thought out and more systematic in nature.

Education reform

Many authors have commented that educational attainment levels are inadequate in the GCC and suggest that education reforms present an important challenge in the region (Al-Dosary and Rahman, 2005; Stasz et al., 2007; Budhwar and Mellahi, 2007; Lootah and Simon, 2009; Pech, 2009).

As the GCC countries increasingly came to govern their own affairs in the 1960s and 1970s, the predominant focus of the few formal schools then available in the region was Islamic studies with an emphasis on memorisation. Most occupational training was on-the-job, with boys trained by watching and working with their elders while girls learned to become wives and mothers at home (Calvert and Al-Shetaiwi, 2002). Harry (2007) notes that well into the 1980s, the study of Arabic and Islamic teachings, culture, tradition and history remained the principle focus.

The rigour of public secondary school programmes remains low, often leaving students unprepared for university studies. Instruction in quantitative skills is particularly weak, leading many students to choose tertiary degree programmes that require less mathematics. Although investments in physical infrastructure were often significant, school curricula failed to build critical thinking and analytical skills (Gallup, 2010). Lootah and Simon (2009) reported that fewer than half of executives responding to a survey in the region felt that national school leavers were equipped with the required competencies. Further, according to the *UAE Yearbook 2010*, only 10 per cent of Emirati high school graduates meet the English eligibility benchmark to enter their first year at Higher Colleges of Technology without an expensive one- to two-year academic bridge programme to rectify skill deficiencies in English, maths, computing and personal development (UAE Yearbook, 2010). Some GCC governments try to address the reform needs of their secondary education systems by collaborating with non-profit or foreign institutions to introduce up-to-date teaching methods and curricula. For example, Qatar worked with the Rand Corporation to update curricula and teaching practices in its schools, and the UAE engaged Singapore's National Institute of Education to help train its secondary-level teachers (Noland and Pack, 2008).

There is a large gap between the traditional orientation of the educational system and nationals' preferred topics on the one hand (e.g., Islamic and cultural studies) and the different, market-driven skills that are needed by employers, on the other hand. This divide is an important obstacle to localisation (Forstenlechner and Rutledge, 2010; Harry, 2007; Middle East Youth Initiative, 2009; UNDP, 2009). All GCC countries invested and continue to invest significant sums to reform their educational systems. Saudi Arabia allocated \$36.7 billion of its 2010 budget to education, or 25 per cent of planned total expenditure. The UAE committed 22.5 per cent of its total government budget, and Qatar allocated 20.5 per cent of its 2008–09 budget (Bains, 2009). Leaders in these countries have also taken an active role in encouraging well-known foreign universities to set up branch campuses, as in Qatar's 'Education City' or Dubai's 'Academic City'. Neighbouring Sharjah has emphasised building its own educational institutions and pushing them to meet international quality and accreditation standards. Abu Dhabi reportedly provided very attractive terms to bring New York University and the Sorbonne to their Emirate. Saudi Arabia opened a new graduate-level university reported to have cost \$2.6 billion (Bains, 2009).

Table 15.3 provides the Global Competitiveness indicators related to education for the GCC (Schwab, 2014). For comparison purposes, we included Switzerland, the most competitive country, and two other emerging countries, China and South Korea. The higher education and training indicators contain measures of secondary and tertiary enrolment rates, as well as the quality of education as evaluated by business leaders. The extent of staff training is also taken into consideration because of the importance of vocational and continuous on-the-job training for ensuring constant upgrading of workers' skills. Examination of these indicators shows that the UAE is the regional and even a global leader in higher education, followed by Qatar. But the table shows also that there are important differences among the GCC countries. Oman and Kuwait are still lagging behind, even in comparison to other emerging countries such as China and Korea (Schwab, 2014).

These figures raise an interesting dichotomy. The quality of public schools in the GCC is often low, but families with sufficient means generally send their children to one of the many tuition-based, English-language 'international' schools that strive to meet world standards.

Although women in the GCC tend to participate in the workforce at much lower levels than men, female students generally attain higher education levels. Women represent three-quarters of the students in post-secondary institutions in Qatar (Karoly, 2010), and about two-thirds of participants in tertiary programmes in the UAE and Bahrain (Randeree, 2009). Women's educational attainment in the GCC seems driven by an increase in the visibility of female role models and an increase in the ambition of young women, who are gaining higher levels of education in order to offset the traditional preference for men (Williams et al., 2011).

Table 15.3 The global competitiveness and education indicators, 2014–15 (rank: out of 144)

Competitiveness indicator	Switzerland	UAE	Qatar	Bahrain	KSA	Oman	Kuwait	China	Korea
Quality of primary education	4	13	9	47	69	73	104	59	44
Primary education enrolment rate	77	98	82	51	50	52	86	4	12
Higher education and training (global rank)	4	6	38	55	57	79	81	65	23
A. Quantity of education									
Secondary education enrolment rate	50	64	9	53	7	60	34	72	48
Tertiary education enrolment rate	47	N/A	107	76	55	83	67	85	2
B. Quality of education									
Quality of the education system	1	9	3	38	47	81	105	52	73
Quality of maths and science education	4	11	6	58	73	95	102	56	34
Quality of management schools	1	18	10	59	78	113	87	85	73
Internet access in schools	13	18	25	39	63	60	80	38	10
C. On-the-job training									
Local availability of specialised research and training services	1	17	19	42	73	94	100	58	36
Extent of staff training	1	11	6	29	60	49	97	46	53

Source: Schwab (2014).

Economic-diversification strategies

GCC nations were heavily reliant on Western technical expertise for the early development of their petroleum resources, but most have given high priority to employing nationals in the oil and gas industry. These efforts have met with significant success, but this is a capital-intensive business that requires few workers relative to the economic value created. Many managerial or professional positions continue to be staffed by geologists, chemical engineers and other experts from North America, Europe or Australia. Sometimes, these expatriate professionals are hired directly, but often as not they are seconded from the major oil companies with which GCC governments have joint venture projects.

Given the limited number of opportunities in oil and gas, most of the GCC nations have made attempts to diversify their economies in ways that would create more employment for nationals in the private sector. These efforts have met with mixed results. For both educational and cultural reasons, nationals in the GCC have been unable or unwilling to work in certain industries or in positions with less-than-ideal working conditions. Jobs that have traditionally been staffed with low-paid labourers from abroad are often considered inappropriate for GCC citizens. These include work in industries as diverse as manufacturing, construction, maintenance and retail. Although Dubai has been effective at attracting some production and assembly plants to its free trade zones, for example, nationals have shown limited interest and the workforce has remained overwhelmingly non-native. Likewise, in societies that have large personal services elements, nationals are conspicuous by their relative absence, at least in the non-managerial ranks. Developing tourism has been a priority in the UAE and Qatar, but here again the number of local nationals taking up positions has been relatively small.

Spiess (2010) considered attempts to nationalise various sectors of the workforce to be an incomplete success at best. Some success has been realised through state-controlled enterprises, which give priority to hiring nationals, particularly in the UAE. The Dubai government owns DP World, which operates more than 30 port facilities around the world. Its management ranks are staffed overwhelmingly by Emiratis, though foreign workers often fill lower-level positions. Generally, these businesses are well run and globally competitive. Emirates Airlines is another prime example. The management, operational and administrative ranks include many nationals. The number of pilots from the UAE is reportedly increasing, but as with other airlines from the region there are few nationals in cabin crew positions or maintenance. Some airlines are making more use of local check-in and gate agents, however. State-owned enterprises are also active in insurance, banking, telecommunications and other industries as well.

Governments in the region have tried to invest in technologies in ways that will create more employment for nationals, either directly or indirectly. An early example was the Saudi government's purchase of military aircraft and radar systems under programmes called Peace Shield and Peace Sentinal in the 1980s (see www.gobalsecurity.org/military/world/gulf/sa-peace-shield.htm). As part of their obligations under the contract, systems suppliers were committed to train Saudis to maintain the aircraft and to support other technology-based enterprises that could employ nationals. Although these efforts did not meet their localisation objectives, more recent efforts to invest in job-creating technologies may have better prospects for success. Mubadala, a government-controlled investment company in Abu Dhabi, has made a number of major investments in high-tech enterprises (Bains, 2009). Although some are based abroad and are likely to remain there, each must compete globally and make a profit on its own merits. Some of these initiatives are expected to create job opportunities for nationals in new industries that are associated with high skill levels and high wages in the UAE. For nationals these new jobs also lack the stigma of having been filled traditionally by low-wage foreigners. The most widely publicised example is Strata, a business that makes composite panels for new generation aircraft. Technical advisers report the need for extensive training in order to meet expected quality standards, but the company expects to have Emiratis making up half of its workforce and it has won some major contracts from Boeing and Airbus (Gale, 2010).

If any traditional sector can claim a degree of success with localisation, however, it may be finance and banking. Most of the GCC countries have pressured banks to meet hiring quotas for nationals, and both locally owned and international banks have felt the need to make a serious effort to comply. Although often not remotely close to meeting the quotas, many of these institutions have adopted special recruiting and selection methods for national employment candidates. Some banks complain that national employees often leave as soon as they are trained, but others, such as Standard Chartered, have been active in developing retention programmes to keep their local employees from jumping to the competition at the first offer of higher compensation.

Direct interventions in the labour market

The third pillar of localisation programmes in the GCC is direct labour market intervention with measures such as quotas and the allocation of certain job roles to be staffed solely by nationals. GCC nations have employed a variety of quota systems in attempts to stimulate the hiring of nationals in the private sector. Forstenlechner and Rutledge (2010) noted that banks in Kuwait have been given the goal of 50 per cent national employment, whereas Saudi Arabia has limited certain jobs to nationals only.

The region's latest localisation programme has come from the UAE. Historically, the government has imposed different employment goals for each sector, with banks typically facing the highest targets. In a new initiative, the UAE announced a tier-based system of targets, with financial incentives and penalties designed to encourage firms to achieve higher levels of workforce localisation (WL). Under the new rules, companies achieving higher localisation levels will be rewarded by paying lower fees to process visas for their expatriate employees (GulfTalent, 2011). In contrast, Bahrain effectively taxes the use of expatriate labour, directly raising its cost relative to the use of national employees. Although no one knows the degree to which businesses may have decided against investing in the GCC due to these requirements, the number of MNCs relocating their regional offices outside of the GCC does not seem to be high. This may suggest that the market opportunities in the region outweigh rising employment costs.

Oman stands out as an interesting case study with respect to localisation. Probably more than in any other GCC nation, Omanis have been willing to take jobs that would have been filled elsewhere by low-wage foreign workers. As Forstenlechner and Rutledge (2010) point out, this nation has limited oil reserves relative to its population, so the government may be less able than most of its neighbours to sustain an overstaffed and well-paid workforce in the public sector. World Bank (2014) statistics for 2012 suggest that per capita income in Oman is about one-quarter of that in Qatar and less than three-fifths that of the UAE. Oil production is increasingly based on enhanced recovery techniques as the country tries to maintain production at past levels. Fiscal constraints dictate that social programmes are more limited than in other parts of the GCC. More than in other GCC nations, employment quotas are actively enforced. This is accomplished primarily using a system that requires companies asking to import labour to justify each case, but certain occupational categories are off limits to foreign workers entirely.

As noted previously, some positions have been specifically reserved for national employees elsewhere as well. These include public relations officers in the UAE and procurement officials in Saudi Arabia. Perhaps due in part to the need to hire more local employees, the HR function itself is increasingly seen as a target for localisation. In the public sector, government offices will often have difficulty securing approval to hire a HRM professional who is not a national, but the private sector is also beginning to replace more departing expatriates with locally trained HRM staff. This trend makes the need for effective HRM education more urgent.

In spite of some notable successes, most localisation efforts have failed to deliver significant growth in the employment of nationals in the private sector (see Tables 15.1

and 15.2). Many local workers are simply not interested in private employment paying market rates that are below public service salaries and which offer more limited benefits than government jobs (Suliman, 2006; Harry, 2007). In Kuwait, for instance, more than 90 per cent of the national work force is on the public payroll. Dr Jassem Al-Saadoun, a leading Kuwaiti economist, suggests that half of the total could qualify as 'masked unemployment' through which the government 'distributes oil dividends' (Spiess, 2010).

HRM PRACTICES FACILITATING IMPLEMENTATION OF LOCALISATION PROGRAMMES

Although WL strategies vary from country to country, they all involve key HRM activities such as recruitment and selection, training and development, career management, performance management, compensation policy and talent management for national employees. We organised our discussion accordingly into the following sections: staffing processes to recruit and select GCC nationals, training and development practices, engagement and retention practices, gender issues and HRM in the context of localisation, and key factors of success for implementation of localisation programmes.

Development of Effective Staffing Processes to Recruit and Select GCC Nationals

Recruiting local talent is one of the most important challenges in the GCC (Scott-Jackson et al., 2014a). However, very few articles have focused specifically on recruitment and selection practices that facilitate localisation. Forstenlechner (2010) identifies three challenges related to the recruitment and selection of UAE nationals. In order of importance, these are (1) pressure to lower selection standards, (2) creation of a sufficient applicant pool, and (3) the difficulty of differentiating among many national CVs, particularly from fresh graduates without any kind of work experience. These challenges show the importance of developing strong recruitment and selection processes.

A first best practice approach to attracting more GCC nationals to private organisations is to align employers' brands and employee value propositions to the aspirations of nationals (Scott-Jackson et al., 2014c). However, these authors found that most UAE employers do not understand the key motivations and aspirations of Emirati graduates. On the one hand, young Emiratis professed to be most motivated by helping the country (41 per cent), money (38 per cent), challenge (37 per cent), development (36 per cent) and contributing to society (33 per cent). On the other hand, Emirati employers felt nationals were most motivated by money (76 per cent), challenge (48 per cent) and pride (44 per cent). Less than one in ten employers felt they were motivated by contributing to society (8 per cent), and no employers mentioned a desire to contribute to the country (0 per cent).

A second practice to attract the best local talent is for employers to promote their professional development practices and their respect for the national culture. The GulfTalent (2013) report shows that a small number of UAE graduates prefer the private sector due to perceived opportunities for greater challenge and learning in private companies, particularly multinationals. Moreover, the cultural atmosphere of the workplace also plays an important role in their job selection. Emiratis are attracted by the prospect of working with other Emiratis, and it is important for them to feel that their culture and values are respected in the workplace (GulfTalent, 2013).

A third group of best practices to increase the recruitment base of designated employees is to use multiple and specifically targeted external recruitment methods. Successful localising organisations develop strong relationships with educational institutions that have a high enrolment of nationals (Forstenlechner, 2010; Mathias, 2006). Other organisations offer them internships, summer jobs or part-time employment (Forstenlechner, 2010). Scott-Jackson et al. (2014c) recommended a version of executive research to target lower-level nationals, involving careful identification of the social communities containing the most likely candidates, then making connections through mutual contacts and approaching likely candidates personally and proactively. Shehadi et al. (2011) point to the common practice of sponsoring students, noting as an example Saudi Aramco's identification of promising high school and undergraduate students for sponsorships that commit them to work with the company upon graduation. In contrast, the use of recruiting agencies is more common for experienced professionals. Finally, employers can specifically target under-tapped talent pools such as national women, lower qualified or non-graduates, nationals living in remote areas of the country, and disabled and special needs nationals (Scott-Jackson et al., 2014c). If these nationals lack the skills necessary for specific roles, employers can create intensive training centres and be more creative in finding ways to accommodate those underutilised nationals who do want to work (Scott-Jackson et al., 2014c).

Finally, it is important for employers to carefully examine the characteristics of the local market and the preferences of the targeted candidates in order to recruit efficiently. Scott-Jackson et al. (2014c, 2014d) highlight a mismatch between national job-seekers and employers regarding preferred recruitment methods, both in the UAE and in Qatar. The three most popular ways for UAE university students to look for job opportunities were applying online (31 per cent), seeking recommendations from personal contacts in the organisation (32 per cent) and by attending recruitment fairs (32 per cent). However, employers in the UAE preferred to attend recruitment fairs (52 per cent), commission a recruitment agency (52 per cent) and seek recommendations from senior business colleagues (44 per cent). In Qatar, both employers (80 per cent) and students (71 per cent) relied heavily on recommendations from personal or professional contacts. However, 84 per cent of employers used online job adverts, whereas only 38 per cent of students looked for job opportunities online. We do not have relevant data on the preferred recruitment methods in the other GCC countries, but find it interesting to note that two countries sharing many common labour market characteristics are dissimilar with respect to preferred recruitment methods, demonstrating the importance of precisely examining the preference of targeted employees.

Regarding selection practices that facilitate localisation in the GCC, the only reported practice we found in the WL literature consists of lowering selection standards for GCC nationals (Forstenlechner, 2010). Whereas the literature on diversity management and selection of diverse employees offers some best practices, these have not yet been examined in the context of WL in the GCC. We did not find any research so far that has examined how organisations evaluate the effectiveness of their recruitment and selection practices in a context of WL in the GCC.

Training and Development Practices

Based on recognised shortcomings of the educational system and the lack of market-related skills and experience, effective training and development programmes are key for successful integration of national citizens into the workforce.

A first useful practice involves organising special recruitment and induction schemes, including special training periods for new graduates in the GCC – particularly for those who lack experience (Al-Dosary and Rahman, 2005; Randeree, 2009; Forstenlechner, 2010).

Another practice is to organise sectorial joint training or development initiatives to attain a mass effect. Development initiatives could include joint intra- or inter-sector programmes, partnerships with universities and other institutions of higher education, or cooperation with governmental organisations and agencies associated with localisation (Scott-Jackson et al., 2014b, 2014c). For example, the UAE insurance sector has developed a joint vocational training programme with one of the UAE's largest education providers (Gulf News, 2006), and a major bank has established strong ties with a government-run university (Khaleej Times, 2007).

Of course, GCC nationals must not only be hired, but they must be adequately prepared to perform to a level that warrants their retention. Scott-Jackson et al.'s (2014c) research demonstrates the need for development of leadership skills among GCC nationals. Many educated expatriates occupy roles that are strategic in that they require leadership abilities or critical knowledge areas. In order to reduce the reliance on expatriates, nationals should be developed to acquire those strategic leadership capabilities. Training future leaders may be the most effective approach for promoting the growth of long-term human capital. According to these authors, the small population of Emiratis creates a scenario in which 64 per cent of nationals should fill leadership roles, compared to approximately 10 per cent in other countries.

Successful companies at localisation do not aim to simply meet quotas, but use local talent management practices to develop nationals into skilled positions and leadership roles over time (Scott-Jackson et al., 2014b, 2014c, 2014d). They identify fast-track career paths, which utilise local strengths, and support weaknesses with training, systematise the development of locals, and deploy a wide range of interventions across the whole talent management process. The authors advise that employers should use the best talent development methods, such as regular appraisal; career development reviews; individual development plans; mentoring or coaching; and systematic monitoring of developmental actions. However, Scott-Jackson et al. (2014c, 2014d) found that most UAE organisations use the least effective development methods (e.g., classroom instruction) most often and use the most effective methods least often (e.g., structured on-the-job learning). The two main methods UAE employers used to develop nationals were management training (48 per cent) and personal development plans (20 per cent). Less than 10 per cent offered technical training (8 per cent), secondments (8 per cent), mentoring schemes (4 per cent) or communicated internal job vacancies (4 per cent). Sixteen per cent did not use any development resources at all (Scott-Jackson et al., 2014c). In Qatar, over half of employers (57 per cent) developed Qatari nationals through regular appraisals; others offered personal development plans (49 per cent), and management or technical training (37 per cent). Less than one in seven employers reported using mentoring schemes that would allow Qatari nationals to learn from more senior professionals in the organisation (14 per cent), secondments (12 per cent) or job shadowing (8 per cent) (Scott-Jackson et al., 2014d).

Engagement and Retention Practices

Employee engagement is one of the most important HRM priority areas in the GCC, cited by both HR and business leaders (Scott-Jackson et al., 2014a). Singh, Jones and Hall (2012) studied the components of engagement in the GCC and expatriate workforces. Based on a questionnaire completed by 4,599 employees from 40 companies in the UAE, Qatar and Bahrain, they found that GCC nationals were less engaged than expatriates (50.8 per cent highly engaged versus 56.9 per cent). Men were altogether more engaged at work than women (57.3 per cent versus 49.7 per cent highly engaged). Female nationals were the least engaged demographic, at 48.4 per cent highly engaged. Compared to Aon Hewitt's worldwide scores of workplace engagement on this metric, these are some of the lowest recorded scores for a major demographic. Perhaps even more interesting is the stratification of engagement across age cohorts, with a significant trough during the years between 25 and 45 when the pressures of family life may take their toll. Moreover, Singh, Jones and Hall (2012) highlight how much identity influences the approach to work and engagement in the GCC. Sixty-five per cent of nationals responded 'strongly' or 'very strongly' that their national or religious identity influences their approach to work. This reaction was nearly double that of expatriate responses to this question (35 per cent answered 'strongly' or 'very strongly'). The implication is that private foreign companies must keep identity in mind when aiming to engage their GCC workforce. Scott-Jackson et al. (2014a) explained that in order to maximise engagement, organisations must deploy both individual interventions (such as individual interviews, clear development and career plans, personal employee support) and organisation-wide general approaches (such as exit interviews, focus group surveys or engagement surveys). However, the authors found that very few organisations in the GCC use any kind of engagement survey and those that had tried them stressed the need for confidentiality and independent administration to avoid receiving unrealistically positive responses.

Retention is another crucial topic in the GCC, where a transient environment with high turnover numbers and lack of commitment-oriented corporate culture do not provide employees with training or career paths (Al-Ali, 2008). Retention rates among Emiratis in the private sector are at about 40 per cent, and one of the major reasons identified for low retention is the lack of career development plans within organisations (AMEInfo, 2007). Forstenlechner (2010) highlighted two specific challenges related to retention of national employees. First, starting in a non-managerial role is considered unappealing by many nationals, so it is important for local employees to have a clear career path from the start. Second, and particularly relevant for female staff, the need to move in order to advance within an organisation constitutes a serious constraint that undermines retention and motivation.

The broader social and psychological contract between employer and employee is often more important than financial rewards to engage and retain talent. 'Career growth' and 'learning and development' have been identified as the principal factors behind the engagement of national employees, with pay and benefits in third place

(Aon Hewitt, 2011). The implication here is that employers may be too simplistic in relying on compensation as the key motivator. The private sector may have some comparative advantages over the public sector: private sector respondents reported greater satisfaction with growth and learning opportunities (Aon Hewitt, 2011). However, Scott-Jackson et al. (2014c) found that many employers in the UAE do not actively use developmental initiatives to retain their talent. Only 8 per cent offered professional development programmes and none sponsored further academic qualifications. Employers were most likely to offer bonus entitlements (64 per cent), flexible working hours (56 per cent) and pension schemes (48 per cent) to retain Emirati nationals. Still, McDermott and Neault (2011) describe the development and implementation of an in-house coaching programme to support newly hired UAE employees in a financial services firm. The organisation arranged a partnership with a Canadian training provider to give its human resources and learning and development professionals career coaching skills. The first evaluation showed promising results in terms of employee engagement and retention.

Gender Issues and HRM in the Localisation Context

Another research stream focuses on HRM organisational policies that support local women's employment and development (Metcalfe, 2007; Scott-Jackson et al., 2014e). These authors suggest that national and organisational policies must be improved if they are to support additional participation of national women in the workforce.

Current studies of gender and HR management issues in the GCC tend to report concerns similar to those of Western critiques of women in management (Al-Lamki, 1999, 2000; Metcalfe, 2007). Al-Lamki (1999: 22) reveals how the perception of women managers in Oman is constituted in patriarchal ways, and suggests that the lack of HR policies and strategies addressing women is a major obstacle to their progress and development, without being more specific. Metcalfe (2007) examines the employment experiences of women professionals from different nationalities in Bahrain (including national citizens) in relation to diversity and equal opportunity initiatives. The author revealed that major perceived barriers to the progress of female managers were business culture (76.5 per cent), few female role models (72.5 per cent), child-related family commitments (62.7 per cent), stereotypical perceptions of women managers (60.8 per cent), limited training opportunities (56.9 per cent), and family commitments related to grandparents or other relatives (37.3 per cent). The author's qualitative analysis highlighted three key thematic areas. First, there is a lack of HR policy planning relating to women and to equal opportunity generally. Very few organisations had formal policies related to equal opportunity, mentoring programmes for women, and sexual harassment. Second, training and development opportunities for women are very limited. Job appointments and training allocation were often not based on personal qualification and competencies, but on an individual's relations and family networks. Third, this study highlights the significance of Islam in a work environment. The lack of HR policies related to equality issues and training opportunities reflect the 'equal but different' philosophy underpinning Islam. In this research the gendered formation of training structures and career paths created limitations for women.

A study by Scott-Jackson et al. (2014e) focused on the employment of women in

Saudi Arabia. The researchers found strong preferences of Saudi women for working in female-only offices (73 per cent). Part-time work options were favoured by 56 per cent of respondents, though 86 per cent of employers had no such alternatives. Although these authors reported an unemployment rate of more than 60 per cent of female graduates, most respondents were not pursuing employment with much determination. The level of preparation for the workplace, understanding of job roles and the degree of knowledge about science-related topics were judged to be inadequate in most cases. Limited advice about career options and transportation challenges were also noted as major impediments. For their part, Saudi employers pointed to a variety of complications in hiring women, though almost three-quarters indicated their willingness if these impediments could be overcome. Employers pointed specifically to lack of appropriate facilities (namely, lavatories), family obligations, cultural obstacles and social attitudes. Although most expressed willingness to hire females, an overwhelming majority (83 per cent) did not support the belief that women might be able to progress into management. Still, the report makes a number of useful suggestions for employers interested in hiring women, many of which might be relevant throughout the GCC.

Key Factors of Success for Localisation Programmes Implementation

Three key success factors for localisation programmes in the GCC include management commitment to their implementation, treating localisation as a strategic talent management issue, and closely evaluating and monitoring the localisation processes. First, as with diversity management and change management generally, the commitment of senior management to Emiratisation is essential (Rees, Mamman and Bin Braik, 2007).

Second, successful organisations see localisation as an integral part of their strategic talent management programme. Scott-Jackson et al. (2014b) found that organisations successful at localisation have a clear, business-related strategy, precise localisation policies and a plan with business outputs and objectives. They adapt their employer brand, staffing, development and retention strategies to fully exploit local talent. Successful organisations also tend to use their own tailored recruitment and development solutions, using, but not relying on, assistance provided by governmental entities. Unfortunately, many companies engage in costly one-time initiatives, rather than pursuing a step-by-step approach, to successfully roll out their Emiratisation strategy (Mellahi, 2007; Forstenlechner, 2008) and adapting their HRM strategies to localise their workforce.

Third, strategic HRM is based on facts and measures, emphasising the need to monitor and evaluate the effectiveness of any HRM practices. At the organisational level, the success of localisation should not only be measured in terms of the percentage of GCC nationals in the workforce. A national talent management process should be carefully monitored and managed, with the different aspects of the programme such as local talent strategy, acquisition, development, management, engagement and retention regularly assessed with appropriate measures (Scott-Jackson et al., 2014b). Rees, Mamman and Bin Braik (2007) stressed the importance of using both quantitative and qualitative methods for evaluating an Emiratisation programme.

KEY CHALLENGES RELATED TO LOCALISATION PROGRAMS IN GCC COUNTRIES

Based on our literature review, we identify five categories of significant challenges to the implementation of localisation programmes in the GCC.

Demographic, Educational and Motivational

The relative scarcity of qualified local candidates is related to the fact that they are a minority in the workforce (as discussed above). Educational and training gaps are related to the lack of market-driven education (discussed above). Local candidates have limited experience and lack the needed language skills in English that are typically required in the private sector (Al-Ali, 2008; Randeree, 2009) and employers do not trust their work-readiness (Al-Ali, 2008). GCC nationals' lack of vocational motivation (aptitude to work), and aversion to business-oriented risk, is found in several academic articles (Mellahi, 2007; Rees, Mamman and Bin Braik, 2007; Forstenlechner et al., 2012a). Based on a quantitative analysis involving HRM personnel from all nationalities, including UAE nationals, Forstenlechner et al. (2012a) found that the four specific factors, ordered by degree of magnitude, that most often dissuade employers from hiring more Emirati employees are lack of motivation, social status, cultural sensibilities and regulatory uncertainties. In terms of labour localisation policy direction, these suggest that the first two focus areas should be motivation and regulation, as these factors are easier to address than cultural and social issues.

Social and Cultural

Our literature review allowed us to find five social and cultural challenges. First, GCC nationals have a strong preference for the public sector due to better salaries and easier working conditions. For nationals, a government job often provides a salary several times higher than the equivalent private sector position as well as a very generous pension (Booz and Co., 2009; Abdalla et al., 2010). In part due to high wages in the public sector, GCC nationals often expect a higher level of compensation than private employers think justified by their qualifications and experience (Fasano-Filho and Goyal, 2004). Due to extensive social programmes, many nationals may have lower income needs than their counterparts elsewhere, but as is the case in many other societies, a highly paid job is considered an important contributor to status and image (Brown, 2007). It is not uncommon to meet nationals who forego the search for a private sector job in the belief that a public job will come available in the future (Achoui, 2009; Harry, 2007; Forstenlechner and Rutledge, 2010; Williams et al., 2011). Taken together, these attractions have pulled 85 per cent of working Emiratis into the public sector, according to the UAE National Bureau of Statistics (Al Ittihad Newspaper, 2010).

Second, as noted earlier, the social status of the job is important for GCC nationals. The type of work, sector of employment and related social interactions are important determinants of the social status of a person in GCC societies (Mellahi, 2007). Culturally speaking, many job categories are deemed socially unacceptable for Emiratis. The aversion to such positions is even more acute for female citizens (Baud and Mahgoub, 2001;

Adam, 2003). Perceptions play an important role in the jobs nationals are willing to accept, with some authors arguing that nationals see themselves as a natural middle class that should only accept white-collar and managerial positions (Mashood, Verhoeven and Chansarkar, 2009). National employers are reluctant to recruit a compatriot for a position that they considered to be inappropriate (Forstenlechner, 2010; Forstenlechner et al., 2012a).

Third, cultural issues, such as the fear of offending indigenous sensibilities, particularly gender-related ones (Felder and Vuollo, 2008), and the HRM issue of a non-national supervising a national peer or subordinate (Al-Ali, 2008), often reduce an employer's willingness to recruit a national (Forstenlechner et al., 2012a).

Fourth, expatriate resistance may hamper successful integration of national workers into the private sector, particularly if a successful localisation programme will ultimately lead to the replacement of the expatriates themselves. It is not unusual for expatriates to be asked to train their national replacements (Mellahi and Wood, 2002; Rees, Mamman and Bin Braik, 2007; Forstenlechner, 2010). There are also perceived inequities when nationals receive higher compensation and experience faster career progression, a reality in many private sector organisations, which may encourage resentment towards national employees (Forstenlechener, 2010).

Fifth, UAE nationals suffer from negative stereotypes. Al-Waqfi and Forstenlechner (2010) were perhaps the first to empirically examine stereotyping of national citizens in the GCC region. Using quantitative data from expatriates and national citizens in the UAE, the authors showed that both nationals and expatriates share negative stereotypes about Emiratis' lack of relevant skills, competencies and work ethics. They present UAE citizens as a minority in need of acculturation to their own country's work environment: local citizens born and raised in a traditional, conservative, tribal society become foreign in their own country and have to adapt to a culturally different work environment in order to function in the workplace. However, the authors do not explore ways to overcome these stereotypes.

Employers' Economic and Employment Rights Uncertainties

The direct salary cost of a national compared to the cost of a similarly qualified and experienced expatriate tends to be one of the first reasons cited by employers when explaining why so few nationals work in the private sector (Godwin, 2006; Mellahi, 2007). Compensation data from the UAE Banking Forum in 2011 (Aon Hewitt, 2011), with 19 participating banks, indicates there is an average premium of 17 per cent for national staff, 14 per cent for junior management, 11 per cent for middle managers and 23 per cent for senior management roles held by UAE nationals as compared to expatriates working at the same level. In addition, nationals bring with them additional costs in the form of payroll taxes, mandatory pension contributions or, in some cases, minimum wage requirements that do not apply to expatriates. Employers often complain that nationals are expensive in part because so many quit during training or leave after their training to take up better offers elsewhere (Forstenlechner, 2010) or move to an expected job in the public sector. However, Forthenlechner (2010) found that budget allocation did not necessarily have an influence on the success of Emiratisation, but his interviewees all confirmed that major investments were needed for their programmes.

Further, uncertainties surrounding differences in employment rights are likely to act as an additional deterrent to hiring national employees. Terminating the employment of unproductive nationals is not easy. A recently passed law in the UAE bans the firing of Emirati workers except under specific conditions (Hafez, 2009). For their part, employers are reluctant to hire employees with potentially unlimited job security (Forstenlechner et al., 2012a). In contrast, the legal framework gives employers more control over expatriate workers, who usually have residence permits tied to one specific employer. Although certainly unintended, these policies may tip the balance in labour appeal unfavourably against nationals (Mellahi and Wood, 2002).

Policy Level

Finally, other important policy-level challenges are associated with the difficulty of developing, communicating, enforcing and monitoring effective employment regulations that support labour localisation, while at the same time protecting the global competiveness of the whole workforce. Based on studies focused on these aspects, we conclude that localisation policy is progressing but still needs fine-tuning to be effective.

Marchon andToledo (2014) studied the impact of occupational quotas on native employment and found that its effect is ambiguous. Their model demonstrates that the demand for native and expatriate labour responds to two forces. First, a binding quota for native workers increases the share of native workers in each firm. Second, it reduces the quantity of labour the industry hires, because of increased cost of production and output price. For expatriate labour, the two effects reinforce each other thereby reducing its demand. The authors show that the quota may backfire if set at a level higher than the quota that maximises employment of native workers in the industry. However, so far, the authors note that employment quotas for native workers appear to have been set as arbitrary political targets which attempt to equate the country's economic progress with employment instead of productivity (Toledo, 2013). Another criticism of quotas is that it does little to enhance the effective utilisation of local citizens. As Scott-Jackson et al. (2014b) point out, the quota system is intended to give nationals access to a share of jobs in the private sector workforce, but it does little to ensure that these positions add real value for the organisation or contributes to the development of the employee.

Another challenge relates to the effective communication of localisation policies. Based on interviews with 180 respondents in the UAE, Baker (2013) argues that Emiratisation has made limited progress, in part because the government has not made significant efforts to promote the idea with a concerted marketing effort. His research suggests that there are many misperceptions and stereotypes that could be addressed through a campaign to make localisation more appealing with a branding exercise that positions the policy as a positive benefit to several stakeholder groups. Pointing out that the absolute numbers of Emiratis looking for employment could be easily absorbed without a major displacement of the existing expatriate workforce in the private sector, he recognises, however, that an economic environment giving employers great latitude in many aspects of their operations is not necessarily conducive to fostering policy compliance on matters of hiring and retention.

Finally, that few employers raise serious protests about these quotas is likely due to the lack of serious enforcement of the localisation policies (Forstenlechner et al., 2012).

Harry (2007) points out that most business owners are able to bypass restrictions and quotas. Because all foreign-owned businesses must have a local partner with 51 per cent ownership, there is always a well-connected individual capable of sidestepping fines and renewing business licences for enterprises not in compliance with localisation requirements. Compliance, when it occurs, may be motivated more by a desire to secure government favour in the awarding of contracts (Forstenlechner et al., 2012) or it may take the form of a token effort intended to impress an influential decision maker.

RECOMMENDATIONS AND WAY FORWARD

Our review of the literature shows that there are some common barriers to labour localisation throughout the GCC: extensive reliance on expatriates; low GCC national participation in the workforce; education systems that fail to respond to market needs; very generous public employment benefits; a cultural focus on status and prestige rather than performance; ineffectual quota systems; lack of communication and enforcement of the localisation policies; constraining cultural practices concerning women in the workforce; and HRM competencies that are still maturing. Individuals, organisations and nations in the GCC will need to invest in human capital to achieve declared strategic objectives and to sustain the growth in physical infrastructure and financial investment in the region that has emerged over the last two or three decades. Localisation in the GCC will require committed and effective participation of nationals in both the private and public sectors. In the unique context of employment markets in the Gulf region, national employees may be characterised as a distinct ethnic and cultural minority (Al-Waqfi and Forstenlechner, 2010; Forstenlechner and Rutledge, 2010; Forstenlechner et al., 2014). In this respect, localisation policies should represent an attempt to integrate HRM diversity management methods with strategic talent management and change management practices.

At the national level, we recommend a holistic approach in designing, communicating, implementing and monitoring policies that effectively promote localisation in the private sector. These include upgrading the education and training systems in qualitative and quantitative terms to enhance the skills and productivity of local citizens as well as developing additional jobs in strategic non-extractive sectors. It will also be essential to implement employment policies for the private sector that recognise and respond to both economic and cultural challenges associated with hiring national employees, though these should be adjusted to match the ambitions and goals of each individual GCC country. Statistics on the effectiveness of localisation programmes are already being collected in most GCC nations, with the methods and level of accuracy improving in each country, but we did not find any published research focusing specifically on the evaluation of localisation effectiveness.

At the organisational level, the strategic implementation of localisation programmes will require expertise in HRM, talent, diversity and change management. Organisations aiming to utilise national talent to achieve important objectives should see localisation as a form of local talent management and work to develop effective talent management processes to ensure that (1) capability gaps are identified and planned for in terms that meet the organisation's strategic intent; (2) roles are staffed using continuously maintained databases of internal and external talent; (3) nationals, once recruited, are helped to develop themselves effectively in ways that understand and leverage cultural differences; (4) regular, useful information is maintained so that retention interventions can be targeted at high-potential nationals; and (5) the local talent management process itself is monitored and audited to ensure it is achieving the required results (Scott-Jackson et al., 2014b). Inclusion of women is crucial to successful localisation, as women are a key part of the educated workforce in the Gulf States.

Moreover, implementing localisation programmes at the organisational level will require expertise in diversity management and change management strategies. Successful diversity and change management programmes both require the buy-in of all relevant stakeholders, active support from top management, a careful analysis of the organisation's situation, the definition of precise objectives and plans, the nomination of a special 'committee or taskforce' and the identification of an accountable manager. In addition, broad communication to all employees and managers, formulation and implementation of specific policies and practices, training and education of all employees and managers regarding the change, measuring and monitoring programme progress, and regularly communicating about the programme successes are also essential elements (Waxin and Panaccio, 2004; Waxin, 2009; Panaccio and Waxin, 2010). Shedhadi et al. (2011) insist that Board-level oversight and monitoring of key metrics by senior executives will help to reinforce the message within the organisation. Individual and departmental commitment to national employment goals should become an evaluation criterion in company reward programmes (Shedhadi et al., 2011).

At the individual level, both men and women in the GCC who have had access to good primary and secondary education will also have opportunities to study at the university level. Those with the motivation and capacities to become professional leaders will have unprecedented opportunities to actively contribute to development of human capital in their countries.

Research Implications

Our literature review allowed us to identify several specific research gaps. We note that too few empirical academic articles have been published on HRM practices that can facilitate effective localisation in the GCC. More quantitative and qualitative research is needed to determine what HR practices work in the WL context and suggest how they can be improved. It would be interesting to research the specific challenges and best practices used to recruit, select, train, develop, manage the performance and enhance the careers of GCC nationals. We did not find any article on recruitment and selection or on performance management in the localisation context, for example. Further, it would be interesting to examine the extent to which HRM diversity management practices apply to the WL context, and whether efficient HR localisation practices vary by industrial sector. How is localisation managed in public and semi-governmental organisations, specifically those organisations that have been created to help diversify the GCC economies? How do organisations evaluate the effectiveness of their HR practices in terms that are meaningful for localisation? Finally, it would be interesting to examine the individual, personal experiences of successful GCC nationals working in the private sector.

To sum up, we first reviewed the literature on core issues pertaining to labour localisation programmes in the GCC, on the HR processes that facilitate their implementation, and on their main implementation challenges. This literature review extends our understanding of the ways in which HRM processes can be used to strategically integrate GCC nationals into the workforce. Second, we identified some precise research gaps in the literature and avenues of future research on this topic. By doing so, we hope to attract additional attention to some unique aspects of HRM in the Gulf region which are not yet addressed in international academic journals.

USEFUL WEBSITES

The Arabian Society of Human Resource Management: http://www.ashrm.com.

The National Human Resources Development and Employment Authority, Tanmia: http://www.tanmia.ae/english/Pages/default.aspx.

REFERENCES

Abdalla, I.M., Al-Waqfi, M.A., Harb, N., Hijazi R.H. and Zoubeidi, T. 2010. Labour policy and determinants of employment and wages in a developing economy with labour shortage. *Labour*, **24**(2): 163–177.

Abdelkarim, A. 2001. *UAE Labour Market and Problems of Employment of Nationals, an Overview and Policy Agenda*. Research Report 1. Tanmia, Dubai: Centre for Labour Market Research and Information.

Achoui, M.M. 2009. Human resource development in Gulf countries: an analysis of the trends and challenges facing Saudi Arabia. *Human Resource Development International*, **12**(1): 35–46.

Adam, K. 2003. *Women's Empowerment and Leadership in Education: A Key Factor for Emiratisation in the United Arab Emirates*. Pretoria: University of South Africa. http://uir.unisa.ac.za/bitstream/handle/10500/1758/00FRONT.pdf?sequence=1 (accessed 4 January 2015).

Al-Ali, J. 2008. Emiratisation: drawing UAE nationals into their surging economy. *International Journal of Sociology and Social Policy*, **28**(9/10): 365–379.

Al-Dosary, A.S. and Rahman, S.M. 2005. Saudisation (localisation) – a critical review. *Human Resource Development International*, **8**(4): 495–502.

Al-Lamki, S.M. 1999. Paradigm shift: a perspective on Omani women in management in the Sultanate of Oman. *Advancing Women in Leadership Journal*, Spring: 1–30.

Al Ittihad Newspaper. 2010. Unemployment rate among UAE nationals is 14% in year 2009. 13 May 2010. http://www.alittihad.ae/details.php?id= 27716&y=2010 (accessed 4 January 2015).

Al-Lamki, S.M. 2000. Women in the labour force in Oman: the case of the Sultanate of Oman. *International Journal of Management*, **17**(2): 166–174.

Al-Waqfi, M. and Forstenlechner, I. 2010. Stereotyping of citizens in an expatriate-dominated labour market. *Employee Relations*, **32**(4): 364–381.

AMEInfo 2007. Nationalization taking root in Gulf region. 26 September 2007. http://www.ameinfo.com/133128.html (accessed 4 January 2015).

Aon Hewitt 2011. *Qudurat Report*. http://www.aon.com/middle-east/thought-leadership/hr/qudurat/default.jsp (accessed 4 January 2015).

Augsberg, K., Claus, I.A. and Randeree, K. 2009. *Leadership and the Emirati Woman: Breaking the Glass Ceiling in the Arabian Gulf*. Berlin: LIT-Verlag.

Bains, E. 2009. Raising standards and aspirations. *MEED: Middle East Economic Digest*, **53**(51): 38–41.

Baker, A.A. 2013. Branding employment related public policies: evidence from a non-Western context. *Employee Relations*, **35**(4): 423–440.

Baud, I. and Mahgoub, H.K. 2001. *Towards Increasing National Female Participation in the Labour Force*. Tanmia, Dubai: Centre for Labour Market Research and Information.

Booz and Co. 2009. *The Case for GCC Pension Reform from Sinking to Sustainable*.. http://www.strategyand.pwc.com/media/file/Case_for_GCC_Pension_Reform.pdf (accessed 4 January 2015).

Brown, M. 2007. UAE's drive for Emirati-run economy is thwarted by handouts. 3 October 2007. http://www.bloomberg.com/apps/news?pid=newsarchive&sid=axmdijbZMi5k (accessed 4 January 2015).

Budhwar, P. and Mellahi, K. 2007. Introduction: human resource management in the Middle East. *International Journal of Human Resource Management*, **18**(1): 2–10.

Calvert, J.R. and Al-Shetaiwi, A.S. 2002. Exploring the mismatch between skills and jobs for women in

Saudi Arabia in technical and vocational areas: the views of the Saudi Arabian private sector business managers. *International Journal of Training and Development*, **6**: 112–124.
Cave, B. 2004. Legal issues related to doing business in the United Arab Emirates. The American Business Council of Dubai and the Northern Emirate. http://www.bryancave.com/files/Publication/21ff51bc-b3ac-4b09-91aa-c6caabf8a72b/Preview/PublicationAttachment/7c560e5a-5489-47b2-ba09c8e352b14c1b/MiddleEastArticle2-04.pdf (accessed 4 January 2015).
Fasano-Filho, U. and Goyal, R. 2004. Emerging strains in GCC labor markets. International Monetary Fund, Working Paper WP/04/71.
Felder, D. and Vuollo, M. 2008. Qatari women in the workforce. RAND Corporation, Education Working Paper No. WR-612-QATAR.
Forstenlechner, I. 2008. Workforce nationalisation in the UAE: image versus integration. *Education, Business and Society: Contemporary Middle Eastern Issues*, **1**(2): 82–91.
Forstenlechner, I. 2010. Workforce localisation in emerging Gulf economies: the need to fine-tune HRM. *Personnel Review*, **39**(1): 135–152.
Forstenlechner, I., Madi, M.T., Selim, H.M. and Rutledge, E.J. 2012. Emiratisation: determining the factors that influence the recruitment decisions of employers in the UAE. *International Journal of Human Resource Management*, **23**(2): 406–421.
Forstenlechner, I. and Mellahi, K. 2011. Gaining legitimacy through hiring local workforce at a premium: the case of MNEs in the United Arab Emirates. *Journal of World Business*, **46**(4): 455–461.
Forstenlechner, I. and Rutledge, E.J. 2010. Unemployment in the Gulf: time to update the 'social contract'. *Middle East Policy*, **17**(2): 38–51.
Forstenlechner, I. and Rutledge, E.J. 2011. The GCC's demographic imbalance perceptions, realities and policy options. *Middle East Policy*, **18**(4): 25–43.
Forstenlechner, I., Selim, H.M., Baruch, Y. and Madi, M.T. 2014. Career exploration and perceived employability within an emerging economy context. *Human Resource Management*, **53**(1): 45–66.
Gale, I. 2010. Industry flies into Strata's sphere. *The National*, 11 March 2010. www.thenational.ae/business/aviation/industry-flies-into-stratas-sphere (accessed 4 January 2015).
Gallup 2010. The Silatech Index: voices of Young Arabs. http://www.somalilandtimes.net/sl/2010/422/Silatech_Report_Final.pdf (accessed 4 January 2015).
Godwin, S.M. 2006. Globalisation, education and Emiratisation: a case study of the United Arab Emirates. *Electronic Journal of Information Systems in Developing Countries*, **27**: 1–14.
Gulf News 2006. Honing the right skills. 11 April 2006. http://gulfnews.com/honing-the-right-skills-1.27043 (accessed 4 January 2015).
GulfTalent 2011. Employment and salary trends in the Gulf. http://www.gulftalent.com/home/Employment-and-Salary-Trends-in-the-Gulf-2010-2011-Report-26.html (accessed 4 January 2015).
GulfTalent 2013. Recruiting top Emirati graduates. http://www.gulftalent.com/home/Recruiting-Top-Emirati-Graduates-Report-35.html (accessed 4 January 2015).
Hafez, S. 2009. Ministry confirms ban on sacking of Emirati workers. *The National*, 17 February 2009. http://waned.blogspot.ae/2009/02/ministry-confirms-ban-on-sacking-of.html (accessed 4 January 2015).
Harry, W. 2007. Employment creation and localisation: the crucial human resource issues for the GCC. *International Journal of Human Resource Management*, **18**(1): 132–146.
Kapiszewski, A. 2006. Arab versus Asian migrant workers in the GCC countries. United Nations Expert Group Meeting on International Migration and Development in the Arab Region, Beirut, May 2006. http://www.google.ae/url?sa=t&rct=j&q=&esrc=s&source=web&cd=1&ved=0CBwQFjAA&url=http%3A%2F%2Fwww.un.org%2Fesa%2Fpopulation%2Fmeetings%2FEGM_Ittmig_Arab%2FP02_Kapiszewski.pdf&ei=x8djVM3IA8mrPL7mgPgI&usg=AFQjCNHnI32FnQn2B2wewOMGhTNMnoOidA (accessed 4 January 2015).
Karoly, L. 2010. The role of education in preparing graduates for the labor market in the GCC countries. RAND Corporation Publications Department, Working Papers 01/2010. http://www.researchgate.net/publication/46464332_The_Role_of_Education_in_Preparing_Graduates_for_the_Labor_Market_in_the_GCC_Countries (accessed 4 January 2015).
Khaleej Times 2007. Zayed University, ADNB join hands for Emiratisation. 16 September 2007. http://www.khaleejtimes.com/DisplayArticle09.asp?xfile=data/theuae/2007/September/theuae_September416.xml&section=theuae (accessed 4 January 2015).
Looney, R. and Hamad, T. 2004. Can Saudi Arabia reform its economy in time to head off disaster? *Strategic Insights*, **3**(1): 1–8.
Lootah, S. and Simon, A. 2009. Arab human capital challenge – the voice of CEOs. Mohammed Bin Rashid Al Maktoum Foundation. http://www.google.ae/url?sa=t&rct=j&q=&esrc=s&source=web&cd=1&ved=0CBwQFjAA&url=http%3A%2F%2Fwww.pwc.com%2Fm1%2Fen%2Fpublications%2Fabir%2Fahccenglishfeb172009.pdf&ei=ONVjVKrwH4XCOajJgaAO&usg=AFQjCNHgTOITC1vplj3dpy-_G-3Qa_1hrg&bvm=bv.79189006,d.ZWU (accessed 4 January 2015).

Mathias, A. 2006. Honing the right skills. *Gulf News*, Dubai, 4 November 2006.
Marchon, C. and Toledo, H. 2014. Re-thinking employment quotas in the UAE. *International Journal of Human Resource Management*, **25**(16): 2253–2274.
Mashood, N., Verhoeven, H. and Chansarkar, B. 2009. Emiratisation, Omanisation and Saudisation – common causes: common solutions? *Proceedings of the Tenth International Business Research Conference*, Crowne Plaza Hotel, Dubai, 16–17 April 2009.
McDermott, D. and Neault, R.A. 2011. In-house career coaching: an international partnership. *Journal of Employment Counseling*, **48**(3): 121–128.
Mellahi, K. 2007. The effect of regulations on HRM: private sector firms in Saudi Arabia. *International Journal of Human Resource Management*, **18**(1): 85–99.
Mellahi, K. and Al-Hinai, S.M. 2000. Local workers in Gulf co-operation countries: assets or liabilities. *Middle Eastern Studies*, **36**(3): 177–190.
Mellahi, K. and Wood, G. 2002. Desperately seeking stability: the making and remaking of the Saudi Arabian petroleum growth regime. *Competition and Change*, **6**(4): 345–362.
Mello, J.A. 2006. *Strategic Management of Human Resources*, 3rd edn. Cincinnati, OH: South Western Cengage Learning.
Metcalfe, B.D. 2007. Gender and human resource management in the Middle East. *International Journal of Human Resource Management*, **18**(1): 54–74.
Metle, M.K. 2001. Education, job satisfaction and gender in Kuwait. *International Journal of Human Resource Management*, **12**(2): 311–332.
Middle East Youth Initiative 2009. *Missed by the Boom, Hurt by the Bust, Making Markets Work for Young People in the Middle East*. Washington, DC: Wolfensohn Center for Development/Dubai School of Government. http://www.brookings.edu/research/reports/2009/05/middle-east-youth-dhillon (accessed 4 January 2015).
Noland, M. and Pack, H. 2008. Arab economies at a tipping point. *Middle East Policy*, **15**(1): 60–69.
Panaccio A.J. and Waxin, M.-F. 2010. HRM case study: diversity management: facilitating diversity through the recruitment, selection and integration of diverse employees in a Quebec bank. Pedagogical notes. *Journal of International Academy for Case Studies*, **16**(4): 27–40.
Pech, R. 2009. Emiratisation: aligning education with future needs in the United Arab Emirates. *Education, Business and Society: Contemporary Middle Eastern Issues*, **2**(1): 57–65.
Randeree, K. 2009. Strategy, policy and practice in the nationalisation of human capital: Project Emiratisation. *Research and Practice in Human Resource Management*, **17**(1): 71–91.
Randeree, K. 2012. Workforce nationalisation in the Gulf Cooperation Council states. Center for International and Regional Studies, Georgetown University, School of Foreign Service in Qatar. https://repository.library.georgetown.edu/bitstream/handle/10822/558218/CIRSOccasionalPaper9KasimRanderee2012.pdf?sequence=5 (accessed 4 January 2015).
Randeree, K. and Gaad, E. 2008. Views on the 'Knowledge Economy Project' of the Arabian Gulf: a gender perspective from the UAE in education and management. *International Journal of Diversity in Organisations, Communities and Nations*, **8**(2): 69–77.
Rees, C.J., Mamman, A. and Bin Braik, A. 2007. Emiratisation as a strategic HRM change initiative: case study evidence from a UAE petroleum company. *International Journal of Human Resource Management*, **18**(1): 33–53.
Richardson, J. and McKenna, S. 2006. Exploring relationships with home and host countries: a study of self-directed expatriates. *Cross Cultural Management: An International Journal*, **13**(1): 6–22.
Rutledge, E., Al Shamsi, F., Bassioni, Y. and Al Sheikh, H. 2011. Women, labour market nationalisation policies and human resource development in the Arab Gulf States. *Human Resource Development International*, **14**(2): 183–193.
Schwab, K. 2014. *The Global Competitiveness Report 2014–2015*. World Economic Forum. http://www3.weforum.org/docs/WEF_GlobalCompetitivenessReport_2014-15.pdf (accessed 4 January 2015).
Scott-Jackson, W., Owen. S., Whitaker, D., Owen, S., Kariem, R. and Druck, S. 2014a. HRM in the GCC: a new world HR for the new world economy. Oxford Strategic Consulting Research Series.
Scott-Jackson, W., Porteous, A., Gurel, O. and Rushent, C. 2014b. Building GCC national talent for strategic competitive advantage. Oxford Strategic Consulting Research Series.
Scott-Jackson, W., Owen, S., Whitaker, D., Cole, M., Druck, S., Kariem, R., Mogielnicki, R. and Shuaib, A. 2014c. Maximizing Emirati talent in engineering. Oxford Strategic Consulting Research Series.
Scott-Jackson, W., Owen, S., Whitaker, D., Druck, S., Kariem, R. and Mogielnicki, R. 2014d. Maximising Qatari talent. Oxford Strategic Consulting Research Series.
Scott-Jackson, W., Michie, J., Al Sharekh, A., Druck, S., Kariem R. and Albury, S. 2014e. How to maximise female employment in KSA. Oxford Strategic Consulting Research Series.
Shehadi, R., Hoteit, L., Lamaa, A. and Tarazi K. 2011. *Educated, Ambitious, Essential Women Will Drive the GCC's Future*. UAE: Booz and Co. http://www.strategyand.pwc.com/media/uploads/Strategyand-Educated-Ambitious-Essential.pdf (accessed 4 January 2015).

Singh, A., Jones D.B. and Hall, N. 2012. Talent management: a research based case study in the GCC region. *International Journal of Business and Management*, **7**(24): 94–107.

Spiess, A. 2010. Demographic transitions and imbalances in the GCC: security risks, constraints and policy challenges. Exeter Gulf Studies Conference: The 21st-Century Gulf: The Challenge of Identity. http://ndrd.org/Demographic_Transitions_and_Imbalances_in_the_ GCC.pdf (accessed 4 January 2015).

Stasz, C., Eide, E.R., Martorell, P., Salem, H., Constant, L., Goldman, C.A, Moini, J.S. and Nadareishvili, V. 2007. Identifying priorities for post-secondary education in Qatar. http://www.rand.org/pubs/research_briefs/RB9276z1.html (accessed 4 January 2015).

Suliman, A.M.T. 2006. Human resource management in the United Arab Emirates. In P.S. Budhwar and K. Mellahi (eds), *Managing Human Resources in the Middle East*. London: Routledge, pp. 59–78.

Talhami, G.H. 2004. Women, education, and development in the Arab Gulf countries. The Emirates Center for Strategic Studies and Research, The Emirates Occasional Papers, no. 53.

The Economist Intelligence Unit. 2009. The GCC in 2020: the Gulf and its people. http://graphics.eiu.com/upload/eb/Gulf2020part2.pdf (accessed 4 January 2015).

Toledo, H. 2013. The political economy of Emiratisation in the UAE. *Journal of Economic Studies*, **40**(1): 39–53.

UAE Yearbook 2010. http://www.uaeyearbook.com/yearbook2010.php (accessed 4 January 2015).

United Nations Development Programme 2009. *Arab Human Development Report*. Regional Bureau for Arab States. http://www.arab-hdr.org/publications/other/ahdr/ahdr2009e.pdf (accessed 4 January 2015).

Waxin, M.-F. 2009. Le recrutement et la sélection à l'international. In M.-F. Waxin and C. Barmeyer (eds), *Gestion des ressources Humaines Internationales*. Paris: Les Editions de Liaisons, pp. 151–204.

Waxin, M.F. and Panaccio, A.J. 2004. Le recrutement et l'intégration des minorités visibles dans les entreprises québécoises. *Proceedings of the Association francophone de Gestion des Ressources Humaines*, pp. 2369–2388.

Williams, J., Bhanugopan, R. and Fish, A. 2011. Localisation of human resources in the State of Qatar: emerging issues and research agenda. *Education, Business and Society: Contemporary Middle Eastern Issues*, **4**(3): 193–206.

Willoughby, J. 2008. Segmented feminisation and the decline of neopatriarchy in GCC countries of the Persian Gulf. *Comparative Studies of South Asia, Africa and the Middle East*, **28**(1): 184–199.

World Bank 2014. GDP per capita data. http://data.worldbank.org/indicator/NY.GDP.PCAP.CD (accessed 29 October 2014).

16. Expatriate management across the Middle East and North Africa region

Edelweiss C. Harrison and Arno Haslberger

INTRODUCTION AND BACKGROUND

The literature on human resource management (HRM) in the Middle East has grown significantly in the last decade or so (Afiouni et al., 2014). Three special editions have been published to highlight the state of HRM in the region: Budhwar and Mellahi (2007) and Afiouni et al. (2014) in the *International Journal of Human Resource Management*, and Mellahi et al. (2011) in the *Journal of World Business*. Despite this growing body of work, comprehensive coverage of the region's HRM practices has remained elusive. Afiouni et al. observe in their 2014 review that the academic literature 'remains fragmented, conceptual and descriptive in nature, making generalizations difficult' (p. 134). Nevertheless, significant advances have been made, particularly in the last decade, as researchers investigated differences in HR practices and employment policies and their implications for locals and expatriates (Rees et al., 2007; Forstenlechner, 2010a).

Within the international HRM (IHRM) field, research on expatriate management includes studies, among others, on selection (Mendenhall et al., 1987; Feitosa et al., 2014), cross-cultural training (Brewster and Pickard, 1994; Black and Mendenhall, 1990), expatriate failure (Tung, 1987; Gupta et al., 2012), repatriation (Tharenou and Caulfield, 2010), compensation (Suutari and Tornikoski, 2001) and performance evaluation (Kraimer et al., 2001), general/work/personal/family adjustment (Caligiuri et al., 1998) and expatriation through a gendered lens (Adler, 1984; Westwood and Leung, 1994). More recently, the literature on specialized topics such as self-initiated expatriates (SIEs) has grown as well (Haslberger and Vaiman, 2013). Yet the research on expatriates has historically focused on Westerners' experiences in European or Asian contexts (Altman and Shortland, 2008). Werner's (2002) study of international management articles from 20 top management journals, for example, yielded 16 articles on expatriate management of which none focused on the Middle East and North Africa (MENA). One of Werner's sample articles included a large study of 452 expatriates in which over 80 per cent of those sampled were from the United States, Britain and Australia (Shaffer and Harrison, 1998). While the host countries in that study did include three MENA countries – Bahrain, Saudi Arabia and the United Arab Emirates (UAE) – the results were not discussed at country level, which makes insights about the region's expatriate management inappropriate. Similar sample characteristics are present in a study of 268 expatriates by Bolino and Feldman (2000). Their sample was 80 per cent from the United States and none of the assignment countries were from the MENA region. Overall this indicates an underrepresentation of expatriate management literature for the MENA region.

Our purpose for this chapter is to provide scholars, students and practitioners in the field of IHRM and an interest in the MENA region with an understanding of the work developed to date on expatriate management. Given the region's diversity, our expectation is that like the fragmentation identified in broader HRM literature, expatriate management research will also lack cohesion and depth at this stage of development. To our knowledge no attempt has been made to explore the research on expatriate management across the whole MENA region. The aim of this chapter is to address that gap. The following research objectives guided our work: (1) to compile and review articles on expatriate management across the MENA region published in 24 of the top IHRM journals; (2) to identify and discuss the key themes addressed to date; and (3) to discuss gaps in the literature and suggest a research agenda for future consideration. Coupled with the country-specific HRM insights provided throughout this handbook, practitioners and researchers alike should gain a robust understanding of the current IHRM knowledge regarding the MENA region.

This chapter is organized as follows: the next section will address core issues, followed by a discussion of factors influencing expatriate management. We then present our conceptual and empirical developments and identify key challenges. We conclude with recommendations for future research in the field of expatriate management across the MENA region and the limitations of the content presented.

CORE ISSUES PERTINENT TO EXPATRIATE MANAGEMENT ACROSS THE MENA REGION

For the purposes on this handbook, the MENA region includes Arabic-speaking countries and Iran, 18 countries that share close cultural proximity (refer to earlier chapters for full analysis). The countries in this region are broadly characterized by their religious alignment to Islam and large Arab populations, but the exceptions to these characterizations have important implications for our topic, namely the presence of expatriates.

The heterogeneity of this region should not be underestimated as the term 'MENA' masks a diverse set of nuances with regard to languages, religions, ethnicities and different economic and political systems. These differences have been discussed elsewhere (for example, Budhwar and Mellahi, 2006; Budhwar and Mellahi, 2007). This chapter is restricted to questions related to expatriation: how important is the issue of expatriate management across the region? What is already known? What have we yet to understand? Before answering these questions, it is worth addressing what this chapter means by the term 'expatriate'. The CIA Factbook and United Nations data presented in Table 16.1 reflect an all-encompassing definition of expatriate. The UN Department of Economic and Social Affairs (United Nations, 2013) reports international migrant numbers based on 'official statistics on the foreign-born or the foreign population', which include both low- and high-skilled labour. This broad characterization is also consistent with the definition of an expatriate as one that works in a foreign location for more than one year (Richardson and McKenna, 2003). The expatriate population is often segmented by level of skill and type of profession. Highly skilled individuals such as those that have completed a bachelor's degree and are in professional, managerial or administrative positions are often studied separately from low-skilled individuals such as those that work as labourers on construction projects or as domestic workers (Leonard, 2005; Connell and Burgess, 2013). For the purposes of this chapter, we will use the term in its broadest sense to provide as complete a picture of the extant literature as possible.

Table 16.1 Expatriate and selected demographic figures across the Middle East and North Africa

Country	Total population	Number of expatriates	% expatriate	% unemployment	Male/female ratio	Country of origin of expatriate
Algeria	38.8M	271,600	0.7%	28.4%	1.03 male(s)/female	Arab-Berber 99%, European less than 1%
Bahrain	1.3M	711,100	54.7%	5%	1.54 male(s)/female	Asian 45.5%, other Arabs 4.7%, African 1.6%, European 1%, other 1.2% (includes GCC, North and South Americans, and Oceanians)
Egypt	86.9M	347,600	0.4%	24.8%	1.03 male(s)/female	Egyptian 99.6%, other 0.4% (2006 census)
Iran	80.8M	2,747,200	3.4%	23%	1.03 male(s)/female	Persian 61%, Azeri 16%, Kurd 10%, Lur 6%, Baloch 2%, Arab 2%, Turkmen and Turkic tribes 2%, other 1%
Iraq	32.6M	97,800	0.3%	n/a	1.03 male(s)/female	Arab 75%–80%, Kurdish 15%–20%, Turkoman, Assyrian, or other 5%
Jordan	7.9M	3,175,800	40.2%	29.3%	1.03 male(s)/female	Arab 98%, Circassian 1%, Armenian 1%
Kuwait	2.7M	1,625,400	60.2%	11.3%	1.43 male(s)/female	Kuwaiti 31.3%, other Arab 27.9%, Asian 37.8%, African 1.9%, other 0.6% (includes European, North American, South American, and Australian) (2013 est.)
Lebanon	5.9M	1,038,400	17.6%	16.8%	0.96 male(s)/female	Arab 95%, Armenian 4%, other 1%
Libya	6.2M	761,789	12.2%	n/a	1.08 male(s)/female	Berber and Arab 97%, other 3% (includes Greeks, Maltese, Italians, Egyptians, Pakistanis, Turks, Indians, and Tunisians)
Morocco	32.9M	65,800	0.2%		0.97 male(s)/female	Arab-Berber 99%, other 1%
Oman	3.2M	979,200	30.6%	n/a	1.22 male(s)/female	Arab, Baluchi, South Asian (Indian, Pakistani, Sri Lankan, Bangladeshi), African

Table 16.1 (continued)

Country	Total population	Number of expatriates	% expatriate	% unemployment	Male/female ratio	Country of origin of expatriate
Qatar	2.1M	1,549,800	73.8%	1.3%	3.29 male(s)/female	Arab 40%, Indian 18%, Pakistani 18%, Iranian 10%, other 14%
Saudi Arabia	27.3M	8,572,200	31.4%	28.3%	1.21 male(s)/female	Arab 90%, Afro-Asian 10%
Syria	17.9M	1,148,905	6.4%	19.2%	1.03 male(s)/female	Arab 90.3%, Kurds, Armenians, and other 9.7%
Tunisia	10.9M	32,700	0.3%	42.3%	0.99 male(s)/female	Arab 98%, European 1%, Jewish and other 1%
United Arab Emirates	5.6M*	4,711,310	83.7%	12.1%	2.19 male(s)/female	Emirati 19%, other Arab and Iranian 23%, South Asian 50%, other expatriates (includes Westerners and East Asians) 8% (1982)
West Bank and Gaza	4.6M	268,294	5.9%	38.8%	1.04 male(s)/female	Palestinian Arab and other 83%, Jewish 17%
Yemen	26.0M	338,689	1.3%	33.7%	1.03 male(s)/female	predominantly Arab; but also Afro-Arab, South Asians, Europeans

Note: * There is a significant discrepancy between the CIA Factbook 2014 estimates (5.6M) and those available from a 2010 census (8.3M). For the sake of consistency, we have used the former figures. Earlier studies have also noted the challenges inherent in obtaining reliable data for the region (Harry, 2007; Forstenlechner, 2008).

Source: CIA Factbook (CIA, 2014) and UN Report on Trends in International Migrant Stock (United Nations, 2013).

Now we answer the question of the relevance of expatriate management to the region by reviewing and discussing the population and expatriate figures for our cohort of 18 countries as outlined in Table 16.1. Of the 18 countries, four have expatriate populations that represent more than half of the total population, namely the UAE (83.7 per cent), Qatar (73.8 per cent), Kuwait (60.2 per cent) and Bahrain (54.7 per cent). The next three largest expatriate populations are in Jordan (40.2 per cent), Saudi Arabia (31.4 per cent) and Oman (30.6 per cent). For the remaining countries, less than a quarter of their populations are expatriates. Estimates put the total number of expatriates across this region at more than 28 million, or over 7 per cent of the total population. The aforementioned seven countries are home to 21 million expatriates or 75 per cent of the total expatriate population in the region. It is noteworthy that all six of the Gulf Cooperation Council (GCC)[1] countries make the list of those with the highest numbers of foreign residents. Expatriates represent 43 per cent of the residents in their sub-region. When GCC data is excluded from the MENA figures, expatriates represent less than 3 per cent of the total population. The data therefore suggests that expatriate management is not likely to be a key consideration when discussing HRM practices in MENA except when referring to GCC countries.

Table 16.1 shows that the concentration of expatriate populations across the MENA region is highest in the Arabian Peninsula, plus Jordan, while the countries in North Africa have low expatriate numbers. Intuitively this makes sense. The North African economies are smaller but have larger populations. Egypt's population, for example, is approximately twice the size of the combined population of Bahrain, Kuwait, Oman, Saudi Arabia and the UAE, which arguably lessens the demand for expatriates. The counterpart to the expatriate population is the national workforce. The GCC local populations are a minority in their own lands. Pressured by increasing unemployment rates, particularly among youth and women, the region's governments have attempted to reduce dependency on expatriates. In particular, they have implemented localization policies known as Emiratization (UAE) and Omanization (Oman) (Afiouni et al., 2014). Historically, GCC demand for expatriates was driven by the need to develop infrastructure; at the time the local population had neither sufficient numbers nor the experience needed (Mohamed, 2002). In recent times, cultural attitudes towards work have hindered the effectiveness of such policies. Locals now view many of the jobs available as beneath them, preferring instead positions in the public sector where there is less pressure to perform and more attractive work conditions, including 'lifelong employment, further educational opportunities, higher benefits, lower and more amenable working hours, and retirement benefits' (Al-Ali, 2008). Interest in assessing the effectiveness of these policies, particularly in the GCC, is evident from articles published in the last few years (Harry, 2007; Williams et al., 2011). A review of those studies led Forstenlechner (2010a) to conclude, 'the only empirical evidence for tangible benefits of localization is the gain of legitimacy and goodwill with legitimizing actors such as respective governments and ruling class' (p. 240).

A final issue to be addressed in this section pertains to legal work requirements. While details vary by country, expatriates in the GCC are typically given only short-term work visas, which need regular renewals. They are also discouraged from becoming citizens. These policies encourage high turnover and foster an environment focused on short-term goals rather than long-term commitment to organizations or nations (Forstenlechner, 2010a). The very real challenge facing leaders in both the public and private sector is that the demand for a sufficient number of qualified workers and professionals continues to require significant sourcing from the expatriate population. In the following section we review some of the key factors influencing expatriate management and research across the MENA region.

FACTORS INFLUENCING EXPATRIATE MANAGEMENT ACROSS THE MENA REGION

Three sets of factors influence HRM policies and practices: national factors (for example, national culture), contingent variables (organization ownership) and corporate organizational strategies (Budhwar and Debrah, 2001; Budhwar and Sparrow, 2002). The scarcity of material relevant to the MENA region suggests this is an under-researched topic. It also makes it more difficult to address all the factors that could potentially impact expatriate management in MENA.

Efforts to understand national factors that impact IHRM policies and practices have relied on a complementary body of work devoted to understanding national culture differences. In his seminal work, Hofstede called this, 'cultural distance' (Hofstede, 1980). In addition to Hofstede's work, researchers have developed four other significant cultural frameworks: (1) Trompenaars and Hampden-Turner (1998) proposed five value orientations and ranked a number of countries according to their characteristics; (2) Inglehart (2007) led the World Values Survey work; (3) the GLOBE project built on the work of these three preceding frameworks as well as other studies to understand the impact that culture has on leadership and organizations (House and Javidan, 2004), and (4) Schwartz and Bilsky have developed a cultural values model over many years with initially seven and now ten dimensions (Schwartz and Bilsky, 1987; Schwartz and Bilsky, 1990; Schwartz, 1999; Schwartz and Rubel, 2005). Research into cultural distance between Middle Eastern and Western regions using these frameworks indicates significant levels of cultural distance (Harrison, 2008), suggesting particular challenges related to cross-cultural adjustment for expatriates from and to these countries.

Middle Eastern societies have high scores for power distance and collectivism (Harrison, 2008). Power distance refers to the degree to which members of a culture expect and appreciate the separation of those who have power and those who do not, whereas the collectivism dimension reflects the extent to which individuals are group-oriented. Societies which value collectivism more highly will tend to support and expect individuals to act with the best interests of the group in mind. One of the implications of high scores for these cultural values is the impact not only on expatriate management dynamics such as work adjustment but also on the research of expatriate management in this region. There is anecdotal evidence from the region that providing insight into situations that are not working as well as might be expected could be viewed as challenging the status quo or those in power – resulting in negative professional repercussions for both the subject of the research and the researcher if they want to continue working in the region. Forstenlechner (2010a) observed that one of the authors retracted her paper because it would have been published before she left the country it covered. Researchers may favour studies that domestic leaders would view positively to enable them to both conduct such work in the first place and to ensure they could continue to work in the region. Anecdotal evidence also reflects some research project participants' efforts to maintain a positive impression in the host country with the host employer. When conducting research for an earlier project, two expatriate interviewees asked the first author to exclude all information from their interviews that might allow their employers to identify them (Harrison, 2008). Difficulty in obtaining access to research subjects may be a barrier to conducting critical analyses of actual policies and practices in the region. Afiouni et al. (2013) list as a limitation of their study that their data was collected from a single source – the HR manager in each bank covered. Given that their study aimed to examine the HR function's characteristics, including strengths and weaknesses, research subjects may not have felt free to respond with absolute honesty. If in fact a culture of fear – influenced by the cultural values of collectivism and power distance – is common in organizations across the region (Bealer and Bhanugopan, 2014), concerns regarding one's job security may be pervasive and therefore present challenges to researchers attempting to obtain reliable data.

CONCEPTUAL, THEORETICAL AND EMPIRICAL DEVELOPMENTS

Having reviewed the sections on core issues and factors impacting expatriate management and research in this field and geographic region, this section outlines the three arguments we developed in order to ground our literature review of the top 24 IHRM journals. The first argument builds on the earlier review of the expatriate population across the region. Given that approximately 64 per cent of the foreign-born population working in the MENA region is concentrated in GCC countries, we postulate that GCC countries will dominate the expatriate management articles in the published IHRM research for the region.

The composition of the expatriate population in this region indicates the region's ethnic diversity (see Table 16.1). Of the seven countries that have large expatriate populations, six of them have sizeable Iranian numbers and significant Asian populations, particularly from countries such as India, Pakistan and Bangladesh. The Indian population alone in the Arabian Peninsula represents an estimated four million expatriate workers who are engaged 'at every level of occupation and society' (Gulf Research Center, 2009). Indians have secured a prominent position in Middle Eastern society and economy, which leading publications such as *Forbes Middle East* recognized when it launched its 2013 list of Top Indian Leaders in the UAE. In 2014 the list was extended to the Top Indian Leaders in the Arab World (Forbes Middle East, 2014). The list of leaders included 120 business owners, 10 chief executive officers and 10 chief financial officers. Of the countries with high expatriate populations, Jordan is the exception: it does not have large Asian populations. Instead their ethnic diversity is largely made up of Jews and Arabs many of whom were foreign born and therefore is included in the UN figures. Indeed, the geopolitical circumstances that Jordan faces would suggest that 'expatriates' within their territories may have very different characteristics, for example with regard to their motivations, adjustment as well as the stress they face, from the expatriates working elsewhere in the region. Finally, Europeans, North Americans and Latin Americans are a minority among the region's expatriate population. An estimated 100,000 British and 20,000 American expatriates live and work in the UAE (Arlidge, 2007; Harrison and Michailova, 2012). Unofficial figures of expatriates in Saudi Arabia estimate Europeans at 150,000 and North Americans at 50,000 of the total expatriate population (Al-Husseini, 2009). These Western expatriates represent less than 3 per cent of the total expatriate population, leading to our second expectation that the literature will instead explore the particular nuances involved in managing the much larger non-Western workforce. In the IHRM literature, expatriate management has been addressed through several interrelated subjects: planning, selection (Mendenhall et al., 1987), training (Black and Mendenhall, 1990; Brewster and Pickard, 1994), mid-assignment support, performance management and repatriation (Li et al., 2009). Studies investigating expatriate 'failure' and ways to solve those problems date back to the 1970s (Hays, 1971, 1974). Female expatriates (Adler, 1993; Taylor and Napier, 1996; Altman and Shortland, 2008), family adjustment (Larson, 2006; Haslberger and Brewster, 2008; Lazarova et al., 2010) and the more recent topic of SIEs (Araujo et al., 2013; Haslberger and Vaiman, 2013) are also represented. Expatriate management literature has a long and storied body of work that researchers studying in the MENA region would presumably have relied upon as the foundation of their work. The known cultural distance between the countries in the MENA region and those of other cultures around the globe will likely have influenced researchers towards investigating expatriate adjustment. Our third expectation is therefore that research in the MENA region will follow the existing categorizations, while prioritizing studies on expatriate adjustment. Next we discuss the methods we used as well as provide a review of our findings.

METHODS

Our study is qualitative and descriptive in nature, which is appropriate for outlining a body of work that is arguably still in its infancy (Afiouni et al., 2014). Table 16.2 compiles the list of journals we reviewed. This list was first developed based on the top 21 IHRM journals as identified by Caligiuri (1999). Three more journals were then added: (1) *Personnel Review*, which has published a number of expatriate-related articles (Ozbilgin, 2004); (2) *Team Performance Management*, which published a special edition reviewing expatriate relations in the MENA region (Forstenlechner, 2010a); and (3) *Journal of Global Mobility*, which was launched in 2013 focusing exclusively on issues pertaining to expatriate management. Together these 24 journals were considered an appropriate group of publications to review for the purposes of our chapter.

Using the ProQuest academic database, the first researcher performed the searches where the only filters applied were 'scholarly journal' and 'English language'. In the interest of gathering a comprehensive initial list we did not filter by time frame. The results confirmed earlier findings that the last decade has witnessed growing academic interest in the region evident by an increased volume in publications pertaining to MENA countries (Afiouni et al., 2014). Using the broad definitions of expatriate as explained above (Richardson and McKenna, 2003; Leonard, 2005; Connell and Burgess, 2013), the initial searches included keywords such as 'expatriate' and 'migrant' and the title of each publication. This approach generated a large number of articles (1,449) addressing every region of the globe. In hindsight a more efficient approach might add country name filters at the beginning to reduce the number of abstracts for review. Abstracts were then downloaded and reviewed to ensure they focused on topics and countries that were relevant to

Table 16.2 Journals reviewed and number of relevant articles identified

Journal name	Final count of articles	Publication years
Academy of Management Executive	0	
Academy of Management Journal	0	
Academy of Management Review	0	
Administrative Science Quarterly	0	
Asia Pacific Journal of Human Resources	0	
European Management Journal	0	
Human Resource Management	1	2009
Human Resource Management Journal	0	
International Business Review	0	
International Journal of Human Resource Management	14	2003–2014
International Journal of Intercultural Relations	0	
International Journal of Selection and Assessment	0	
International Labor Review	0	
Journal of Applied Psychology	0	
Journal of Cross-Cultural Psychology	0	
*Journal of Global Mobility	1	2013
Journal of International Business Studies	0	
Journal of International Compensation	0	
Journal of International Management	0	
Journal of Management	0	
Journal of World Business	3	2005–2012
Management International Review	1	2013
*Personnel Review	5	2000–2010
*Team Performance Management	2	2010
Totals	27	

Note: * Publications that were not included in Caliguiri's (1999) list of 21 journals, all others in this table are from her list.

Source: Authors' analysis.

our study; for example, we excluded studies that examined national HRM issues such as women at work (Elamin and Omair, 2010) or departmental innovation (Mohamed, 2002), where expatriates were only mentioned as a description of the study participants rather than being an integral aspect of the study. This resulted in an abbreviated list of 36 of which a further 9 articles were removed once both authors read and discussed the full texts. A final list of 27 articles was the result of this multi-step sifting process. The full list of journals, the number of pertinent articles and years of publication are listed in Table 16.2.

The 27 articles were then reviewed using a set of topics derived from the analysis developed by McEvoy and Buller (2013) and Lin et al. (2012), with further additions detailed below. The first is a systematic review of expatriate management that identifies research questions relevant for management practice. The second is a review of 243 articles and theses from an Asian perspective. It identifies commonalities and differences between 'Western' and 'Eastern' approaches to expatriate management. By combining the two we hope to infuse our review with practical relevance and a broader perspective that allows for the differences between 'Western' and 'Middle Eastern' conceptions of expatriate management. McEvoy and Buller (2013) provide a flow chart of expatriate assignments that include steps before and after expatriation and after repatriation. Lin et al. (2012) add to this female expatriates, expatriate partners or spouses and *guanxi* in China. Some studies suggest *wasta* as a comparable concept for the MENA region (Hutchings and Weir, 2006). In response, we expanded our exploration of the literature and included a category of 'other' to capture any other topics that might have been studied, such as *wasta*. The list encompasses all items except for 'health, safety, and crisis management' (Briscoe and Schuler, 2004) that common textbooks on IHRM and expatriate management regularly cover (cf. Briscoe and Schuler, 2004; Dickmann et al., 2008). The security situation in some MENA countries, such as the rise of the violent 'Islamic State (ISIS)' group in Iraq and surrounding countries or the hostilities in the wake of the Arab Spring in countries like Libya and Egypt, warrants inclusion here. Finally, there is a developing literature on SIEs (cf. Andresen et al., 2013; Vaiman and Haslberger, 2013), which includes MENA countries (cf. Richardson, 2006). Therefore, we include expatriate status in our topic list as well. Our review also tracks the specific MENA country covered and whether the article uses a national, organizational or individual expatriate lens. The detailed list of categories used for our analysis as well as the count of the articles that addressed each topic is available in Table 16.3.

RESULTS AND DISCUSSION

The *International Journal of Human Resource Management* has published the most studies related to this topic in the MENA region with 14 articles, almost three times as many as the next journal, *Personnel Review*, which has published five. The publications are all from the last 15 years,[2] with 17 published in the last five years suggesting an evolving interest in understanding expatriation in this region. The research shows that the articles on expatriate management in the MENA region represented less than 2 per cent of the total number of articles on expatriate management for those 24 IHRM journals, making clear the subject is under-researched.

Most articles (20) conducted individual analyses; five articles provided a national analysis while the balance (two) focused on the organizational level. Of those at the national level, four studied localization policies in the UAE (Emiratization) (Rees et al., 2007; Forstenlechner, 2010b; Al-Waqfi and Forstenlechner, 2014; Marchon and Toledo, 2014) while the other (Connell and Burgess, 2013) provided a theoretical analysis of the labour market with a particular study of vulnerable workers in the UAE. The latter study was also the only article of the 27 to explore the experiences of the broader expatriate workforce specifically including those performing low-skilled work such as construction workers and domestic servants.

As outlined in our first postulation, the findings confirmed that GCC countries dominate the literature on expatriate management because expatriates represent more significant portions of their total population. The literature addresses only 9 of the 18 MENA region countries: the UAE, Saudi Arabia, Qatar, Oman, Jordan, the West Bank and Gaza, Iran and Kuwait. Bahrain was the only GCC country not represented in our sample (cf. Figure 16.1). The results show that expatriates in the UAE have been studied the most, followed by those in Saudi Arabia. The multi-country studies included results from at least one MENA country, with the UAE studied in five of the six multi-country articles. To provide some

Table 16.3 Key themes used for analysis of the 27 articles and summary of results

Key theme	Count	Other data	Count
Before Expatriation	*8*	Individual vs. Organizational Perspective	20 Ind / 2 Org / 5 National
Recruitment and selection	1	Status: AE, SIE, type of worker	3 AE / 9 SIEs / 3 AE & SIEs results combined
Decision to accept	3	Methods	
Training	4	Methodology (quant, qual, case study, other)	9 Quant / 11 Qual / 3 case / 2 mixed, 1 theoretical analysis, 1 microeconomic analysis
After Expatriation	*35*	Number of respondents	Qual 20–86 respondents Quant 174–5,459 respondents
Adjustment	13		
Performance	10		
Compensation	5		
Early returns	5		
Health, safety, and crisis management	2		
After Repatriation	*1*		
Commitment and turnover (career outcomes)	1		
Performance and knowledge transfer	0		
Special Topics	*28*		
Female expatriates	4		
Expatriate partners/spouses/family	5		
Other topics, including *wasta*, Islamic work ethic (IWE), careers	19		

Note: SIE = self-initiated expatriate, AE = assigned expatriate.

Source: Authors' analysis.

further insight we also tracked the authors' university affiliations and found, not surprisingly, that seven of the articles had author affiliations with universities in the UAE. Authors with affiliations to universities in the United Kingdom, Australia and New Zealand also had a notable presence. Country-related findings are summarized in Figure 16.1. These findings echo the results from Afiouni et al.'s (2013) review of HRM literature regarding the MENA region. This research showed a marked increase in published studies from 2007 onward, with data from the UAE figuring prominently. Further inquiry into the author data revealed 46 authors and only four individuals who authored more than one paper. This result suggests that there may be scope for specialization in this field, should a scholar so choose. Table 16.4 lists the four authors and their corresponding numbers of publications.

Table 16.4 Authors who published more than one paper reviewed in this study (4 out of 46)

Author name	Number of papers in this study	Number of papers as lead author	Number of papers as sole author
Julia Richardson	3	3	1
Ingo Forstenlechner	3	1	1
Edelweiss C. Harrison	2	1	0
Snejina Michailova	2	0	0

Source: Authors' analysis.

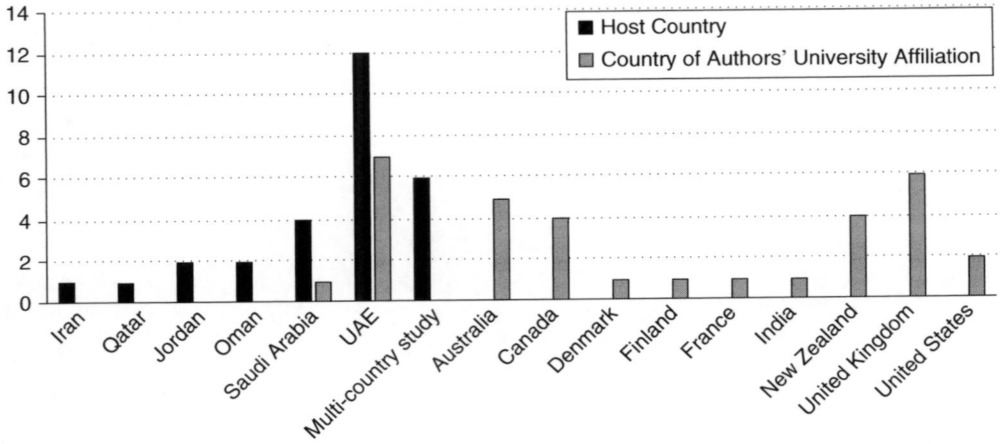

Figure 16.1 Host country and country of author's university affiliation

We also postulated that the literature would pay attention to the large non-Western workforce given that they dominate the region's expatriate landscape. This expectation was largely unsupported. While non-Western expatriates, particularly those from Asia and other Arab nations, were included in seven of the studies (for example, Al-Ahmadi, 2014; Showail et al., 2013; Bealer and Bhanugopan, 2014), the results were reported only at aggregate level and thus were not presented in such a way as to explore the experiences and challenges that those groups faced. Indeed, the more in-depth studies of individual analysis focused on Western expatriates (see Richardson and McKenna, 2003; Lauring and Selmer, 2009; Schoepp and Forstenlechner, 2010; Harrison and Michailova, 2012). Overall, 22 of the studies focused on a single host country and 5 conducted multi-country reviews. Conversely, 22 studies combined multiple expatriate nationalities in the sample while only 5 studied the experiences of individual expatriate nationalities. Figure 16.1 juxtaposes host countries and the countries of author university affiliations. The UAE was the setting for 12 single host-country studies (and 4 multi-country studies) followed by Saudi Arabia represented in 5 studies. Authors affiliated with UAE-based universities conducted 7 of the 12 UAE studies, while Saudi Arabia had one locally affiliated author.

The remaining studies were largely conducted by researchers affiliated with Western institutions, with one exception for an author affiliated with an institution in India. It appears that academic publications on expatriate issues in MENA are guided more by the authors' affiliation than by the size of the population under study. Charges of a 'Western'-bias attention, levelled by commentators on self-initiated expatriation and immigrant studies (Ariss and Özbilgin, 2010; Beitin, 2012; Cerdin et al., 2014), seem to apply to expatriate research in the MENA region as well.

Our third and final expectation was that research in the MENA region would follow the existing categorizations, while prioritizing studies on expatriate adjustment. The literature did have a significant bent towards studying adjustment after expatriation as indicated by the number of studies that addressed that issue. Performance during expatriation was also frequently explored. Of the special topics category, female expatriates and family adjustment or expatriate partners both have been well represented in the literature, relatively speaking. It was also particularly interesting to note that SIEs were addressed in nine articles, which specified expatriate types. Overall, the articles explored a broad distribution of topics using quantitative and qualitative methods with sample sizes ranging from 20 to over 5,000 persons, leaving significant gaps in the literature. We explore these further in the section below with recommendations for a future research agenda.

KEY CHALLENGES

Since 16 out of the 27 articles (60 per cent) we reviewed had studied the UAE, one should proceed with caution when generalizing the findings. While the UAE is an Arab country in the GCC, its particular socio and cultural dynamics are not identical to those of others in the MENA region or even in the GCC; therefore, expatriate management dynamics in other countries may differ significantly from the findings to date.

RECOMMENDATIONS AND WAY FORWARD

This chapter aimed at exploring the research available regarding expatriate management across the MENA region. The chapter advances the literature on expatriate management by providing a benchmark for the current state of research in this field regarding the MENA region. Specifically, our findings indicate that expatriate management literature is underdeveloped at this point. As per Afiouni et al.'s (2013) overall HRM literature in the region, it is not possible to make broad statements on expatriate management research since the existing work includes few studies that address more than one national context or industry. Furthermore, the four studies that provided more in-depth insights into a single expatriate national group studied minority groups of Western expatriates, namely Danish (Lauring and Selmer, 2009) and British expatriates (Richardson, 2006; Richardson and Mallon, 2005; Richardson and McKenna, 2003). Therefore their findings are not representative of the expatriate population for the MENA or GCC regions as a whole. Finally, the studies that included multiple nationalities tended to report their findings at an aggregate level, restricting the opportunity to develop nationality-specific insights particularly pertaining to non-Western expatriates.

The introduction to the *Team Performance Management* special issue on the subject of managing diverse teams in the Middle East (Forstenlechner, 2010a) cautions against neglecting research into the expatriate population given the fact that such a large portion of the GCC population are foreign born. We support his recommendation to encourage such research. Specifically, our study has identified the following five areas that would benefit from further scholarly research. The results of such work would benefit both researchers and practitioners in the region and local governments that are attempting to best manage their expatriate populations for the good of their own nations. First, the UAE has received the most attention to date. It would be valuable to understand whether the dynamics of expatriate management evident in the UAE also apply to the rest of the GCC. It is reasonable to expect that expatriates in Saudi Arabia would have a different set of challenges than those in the UAE while a more nuanced set of differences might be found in Oman or Qatar (cf. Lauring and Selmer, 2009; Neal, 2010). Second, the English-language IHRM journals reviewed have a significant gap with regard to the provenance of the expatriates studied. Studying non-Western expatriate populations, particularly Indians given their prominence in the region, would add relevant insight into other important groups in the region. A third and complementary area of inquiry would be research into other aspects of expatriation, particularly the categories prior to expatriation (for example, are Western or non-Western expatriates more likely to be SIEs and what are the implications from a recruitment, performance and retention perspective? Given cultural distance considerations, which nationalities seem to adjust the best to the region and which industries would benefit the most from tailoring their recruitment efforts accordingly?).

Given the countries in the MENA region follow Islam, a fourth area of future research should address the nuances of managing expatriates where an Islamic HRM model is in place (see Tayeb, 1997; Al-Hamadi et al., 2007; Ali, 2010). Despite the significant groundwork that has been laid (Afiouni et al., 2013), the presence of a de facto Islamic HRM model across the region has yet to be confirmed. Deeper queries could also investigate whether IHRM policies in Iran differ from the rest of the region given their Shia majority in contrast to the Sunni populations in the remainder of the region, particularly the GCC.

Finally, there is a need for more research at the organizational level. One possibility would be to identify which industries tend to have the highest number of expatriates. This should include a breakdown by the relative value they bring to the organizations: for example, based on high- versus low-skilled jobs. One could then begin to develop a body of work that addresses the IHRM challenges particular to them. The banking industry may be a promising option given its extensive presence across Arab countries and large workforce (Afiouni et al., 2013). Organizational research could perhaps be tied to localization research to identify to what areas in a local economy expatriates might add the most value without undermining localization efforts, maybe even supporting those policies. One thing is certain, as the MENA region and the GCC in particular continue to develop, expatriate management will continue to offer important challenges for those involved in policy making at the national level, resource managers at the organizational level and the individuals filling expatriate roles whether of their own or their company's initiative.

LIMITATIONS

This analysis suffers from some limitations. First, it includes only articles published in English. Second, it covers only a selection of management journals. And third, it excludes non-managerial journals in areas such as immigration studies, sociology, anthropology, ethnology, psychology and economics. That said it arguably captures most of the published ideas relevant for expatriate management in the MENA region because management journals are more likely to focus on applicable issues and because English is the language in which the largest portion of related research is published. Even if an important study first appears in a language other than English, the fact that English is the leading language in academia means that significant results are likely to eventually appear in an English-language journal.

NOTES

1. Gulf Cooperation Council, established in 1981 and consisted of Bahrain, Kuwait, Oman, Qatar, Saudi Arabia and the UAE.
2. We did identify and then exclude one article (Feldman and Thomas, 1992) that included expatriates in Saudi Arabia as well as three other countries and regions; however, the results were not reported by country and, given the fact that the article was 20 years old, we determined there were limited insights provided for our purposes.

USEFUL WEBSITES

American Bedu: http://americanbedu.com/.
Arabian Society of Human Resource Management ASHRM: http://www.ashrm.com/.
ASHRM LinkedIn Group: https://www.linkedin.com/groups/ASHRM-Arabian-Society-HR-Managment-2320730.
Society for Human Resource Management MEA: http://www.shrm.org/pages/mena.aspx.
GulfTalent: http://www.gulftalent.com/HRZone/.
Bayt Research: http://www.bayt.com/en/research-reports/.
HSBC Expat microsite: https://www.expat.hsbc.com/1/2/hsbc-expat/expat-experience?HBIB_dyn_lnk=hme_tab_products.
Facebook Expatriates Pages (e.g., search for 'UAE Expatriates' or 'Qatar Expat Women's Support Group').

REFERENCES

Adler, N.J. 1984. Women do not want international careers and other myths about international management. *Organizational Dynamics*, **13**: 66–79.
Adler, N.J. 1993. Competitive frontiers: women managers in the triad. *International Studies of Management and Organization*, **23**: 3–23.
Afiouni, F., Karam, C.M. and El-Hajj, H. 2013. The HR value proposition model in the Arab Middle East: identifying the contours of an Arab Middle Eastern HR model. *International Journal of Human Resource Management*, **24**: 1895–1932.
Afiouni, F., Ruël, H. and Schuler, R. 2014. HRM in the Middle East: toward a greater understanding. *International Journal of Human Resource Management*, **25**: 133–143.
Al-Ahmadi, H. 2014. Anticipated nurses' turnover in public hospitals in Saudi Arabia. *International Journal of Human Resource Management*, **25**: 412–433.
Al-Ali, J. 2008. Emiratisation: drawing UAE nationals into their surging economy. *International Journal of Sociology and Social Policy*, **28**: 365–379.

Al-Hamadi, A.B., Budhwar, P.S. and Shipton, H. 2007. Management of human resources in Oman. *International Journal of Human Resource Management*, **18**: 100–113.

Al-Husseini, H. 2009. The expatriate population in Saudi Arabia. American Bedu. http://americanbedu.com/2009/06/06/the-expatriate-population-in-saudi-arabia/ (accessed 19 July 2014).

Al-Waqfi, M.A. and Forstenlechner, I. 2014. Barriers to Emiratization: the role of policy design and institutional environment in determining the effectiveness of Emiratization. *International Journal of Human Resource Management*, **25**: 167–189.

Ali, A.J. 2010. Islamic challenges to HR in modern organizations. *Personnel Review*, **39**: 692–711.

Altman, Y. and Shortland, S. 2008. Women and international assignments: taking stock – a 25-year review. *Human Resource Management*, **47**: 199–216.

Andresen, M., Al Ariss, A. and Walther, M. 2013. *Organizations and Self-Initiated Expatriation: Individual, Organizational, and National Perspectives*. New York: Routledge.

Araujo, B.F.V.B.D., Teixeira, M.L.M., Cruz, P.B.D. and Malini, E. 2013. Understanding the adaptation of organisational and self-initiated expatriates in the context of Brazilian culture. *International Journal of Human Resource Management*, **25**: 2489–2509.

Ariss, A.A. and Özbilgin, M. 2010. Understanding self-initiated expatriates: career experiences of Lebanese self-initiated expatriates in France. *Thunderbird International Business Review*, **52**: 275–285.

Arlidge, J. 2007. Britons feel at home in Dubai. *Telegraph*, 29 October.

Bealer, D. and Bhanugopan, R. 2014. Transactional and transformational leadership behaviour of expatriate and national managers in the UAE: a cross-cultural comparative analysis. *International Journal of Human Resource Management*, **25**: 293–316.

Beitin, B.K. 2012. Syrian self-initiated expatriates: emotional connections from abroad. *International Migration*, **50**: 1–17.

Black, J.S. and Mendenhall, M. 1990. Cross-cultural training effectiveness: a review and a theoretical framework for future research. *Academy of Management Review*, **15**: 113–136.

Bolino, M.C. and Feldman, D.C. 2000. The antecedents and consequences of underemployment among expatriates. *Journal of Organizational Behaviour*, **21**: 889–911.

Brewster, C. and Pickard, J. 1994. Evaluating expatriate training. *International Studies of Management and Organization*, **24**: 18–35.

Briscoe, D.R. and Schuler, R.S. 2004. *International Human Resource Management*. New York: Prentice Hall.

Budhwar, P.S. and Debrah, Y. 2001. Rethinking comparative and cross-national human resource management research. *International Journal of Human Resource Management*, **12**: 497–515.

Budhwar, P.S. and Mellahi, K. 2006. Introduction: managing human resources in the Middle East. In P.S. Budhwar and K. Mellahi (eds), *Managing Human Resources in the Middle East*. London: Routledge, pp. 1–19.

Budhwar, P.S. and Mellahi, K. 2007. Introduction: human resource management in the Middle East. *International Journal of Human Resource Management*, **18**: 2–10.

Budhwar, P.S. and Sparrow, P.R. 2002. An integrative framework for understanding cross-national human resource management practices. *Human Resource Management Review*, **12**: 377–403.

Caligiuri, P.M. 1999. The ranking of scholarly journals in international human resource management. *International Journal of Human Resource Management*, **10**: 515–519.

Caligiuri, P.M., Hyland, M.M., Joshi, A. and Bross, A.S. 1998. Testing a theoretical model for examining the relationship between family adjustment and expatriates' work adjustment. *Journal of Applied Psychology*, **83**: 598–614.

Central Intelligence Agency (CIA) 2014. *CIA World Factbook*. Central Intelligence Agency.

Cerdin, J.-L., Diné, M.A. and Brewster, C. 2014. Qualified immigrants' success: exploring the motivation to migrate and to integrate. *Journal of International Business Studies*, **45**: 151–168.

Connell, J. and Burgess, J. 2013. Vulnerable workers in an emerging Middle Eastern economy: what are the implications for HRM? *International Journal of Human Resource Management*, **24**: 4166–4184.

Dickmann, M., Brewster, C. and Sparrow, P. 2008. *International Human Resource Management: A European Perspective*. New York: Routledge.

Elamin, A.M. and Omair, K. 2010. Males' attitudes towards working females in Saudi Arabia. *Personnel Review*, **39**: 746–766.

Feitosa, J., Kreutzer, C., Kramperth, A., Kramer, W.S. and Salas, E. 2014. Expatriate adjustment: considerations for selection and training. *Journal of Global Mobility*, **2**: 134–159.

Forbes Middle East 2014. *Top Indian Leaders in the Arab World 2014*. Dubai: Forbes Middle East.

Forstenlechner, I. 2008. Workforce nationalization in the UAE: image versus integration. *Education, Business and Society: Contemporary Middle Eastern Issues*, **1**: 82–91.

Forstenlechner, I. 2010a. Expats and citizens: managing diverse teams in the Middle East. *Team Performance Management*, **16**: 237–241.

Forstenlechner, I. 2010b. Workforce localization in emerging Gulf economies: the need to fine-tune HRM. *Personnel Psychology*, **39**: 135–152.

Gulf Research Center 2009. *India's Growing Role in the Gulf: Implications for the Region and the United States*. Gulf Research Center and The Nixon Center.

Gupta, R., Banerjeeb, P. and Gaura, J. 2012. Exploring the role of the spouse in expatriate failure: a grounded theory-based investigation of expatriate spouse adjustment issues from India. *International Journal of Human Resource Management*, **23**: 3559–3577.

Harrison, E.C. 2008. *Western female expatriates in the United Arab Emirates: an assessment of cross cultural training needs*. Auckland, New Zealand: University of Auckland.

Harrison, E.C. and Michailova, S. 2012. Working in the Middle East: Western female expatriates' experiences in the United Arab Emirates. *International Journal of Human Resource Management*, **23**: 625–644.

Harry, W. 2007. Employment creation and localization: the crucial human resources issues for the GCC. *International Journal of Human Resource Management*, **18**: 132–146.

Haslberger, A. and Brewster, C. 2008. The expatriate family: an international perspective. *Journal of Managerial Psychology*, **23**: 324–346.

Haslberger, A. and Vaiman, V. 2013. Self-initiated expatriates: a neglected source of the global talent flow. In V. Vaiman and A. Haslberger (eds), *Talent Management of Self-Initiated Expatriates*. Houndmills, Basingstoke, UK: Palgrave Macmillan, pp. 136–156.

Hays, R.D. 1971. Ascribed behavioral determinants of success–failure among U.S. expatriate managers. *Journal of International Business Studies*, **2**: 40–46.

Hays, R.D. 1974. Expatriate selection: insuring success and avoiding failure. *Journal of International Business Studies*, **5**: 25–37.

Hofstede, G. 1980. *Culture's Consequences: International Differences in Work-Related Values*. Beverly Hills, CA: Sage Publications.

House, R.J. and Javidan, M. 2004. Overview of GLOBE. In R.J. House, P.J. Hanges, M. Javidan, P.W. Dorfman and V. Gupta (eds), *Culture, Leadership, and Organizations: The GLOBE Study of 62 Societies*. Thousand Oaks, CA: Sage Publications, pp. 9–28.

Hutchings, K. and Weir, D. 2006. Guanxi and wasta: a comparison. *Thunderbird International Business Review*, **48**: 141–156.

Inglehart, R.F. 2007. The worldviews of Islamic publics in global perspective. In M. Moaddel (ed.), *Values and Perceptions of the Islamic and Middle Eastern Publics*. New York: Palgrave Macmillan, pp. 25–46.

Kraimer, M.I., Wayne, S.J. and Jaworski, R.A. 2001. Sources of support and expatriate performance: the mediating role of expatriate adjustment. *Personnel Psychology*, **54**: 71–99.

Larson, D.A. 2006. Here we go again: how a family's cross-cultural and repatriation adjustment relates to the employee's receptivity to future international assignments. *SAM Advanced Management Journal*, **71**: 46–57.

Lauring, J. and Selmer, J. 2009. Expatriate compound living: an ethnographic field study. *International Journal of Human Resource Management*, **20**: 1451–1467.

Lazarova, M., Westman, M. and Shaffer, M.A. 2010. Elucidating the positive side of the work–family interface on international assignments: a model of expatriate work and family performance. *Academy of Management Review*, **35**: 93–117.

Leonard, K. 2005. South Asians in the Indian Ocean world: language, policing, and gender practices in Kuwait and the United Arab Emirates. *Comparative Studies of South Asia, Africa and the Middle East*, **25**: 677–686.

Li, X., Troutt, M.D. and Knapp, D.E. 2009. Expatriate management: an organizing framework using phase and reliability theories. *Journal of Global Commerce Research*, **1**: 9–33.

Lin, C. Y.-Y., Lu, T.-C. and Lin, H.-W. 2012. A different perspective of expatriate management. *Human Resource Management Review*, **22**: 189–207.

Marchon, C. and Toledo, H. 2014. Re-thinking employment quotas in the UAE. *International Journal of Human Resource Management*, **25**: 2253–2274.

McEvoy, G.M. and Buller, P.F. 2013. Research for practice: the management of expatriates. *Thunderbird International Business Review*, **55**: 213–226.

Mellahi, K., Demirbag, M. and Riddle, L. 2011. Multinationals in the Middle East: challenges and opportunities. *Journal of World Business*, **46**: 406–410.

Mendenhall, M.E., Dunbar, E. and Oddou, G.R. 1987. Expatriate selection, training and career-pathing: a review and critique. *Human Resource Management*, **26**: 331–345.

Mohamed, M.A.K. 2002. Assessing determinants of departmental innovation: an exploratory multi-level approach. *Personnel Review*, **31**: 620–641.

Neal, M. 2010. When Arab-expatriate relations work well: diversity and discourse in the Gulf Arab workplace. *Team Performance Management*, **16**(5): 242–266.

Özbilgin, M. 2004. 'International' human resource management: academic parochialism in editorial boards of the 'top' 22 journals on international human resource management. *Personnel Review*, **33**: 205–221.

Rees, C.J., Mamman, A. and Braik, A.B. 2007. Emiratization as a strategic HRM change initiative: case study evidence from a UAE petroleum company. *International Journal of Human Resource Management*, **18**: 33–53.

Richardson, J. 2006. Self-directed expatriation: family matters. *Personnel Review*, **35**: 469–486.
Richardson, J. and Mallon, M. 2005. Career interrupted? The case of the self-directed expatriate. *Journal of World Business*, **40**: 409–420.
Richardson, J. and McKenna, S. 2003. International experience and academic careers: what do academics have to say? *Personnel Review*, **32**: 774–795.
Schoepp, K. and Forstenlechner, I. 2010. The role of family considerations in an expatriate majority environment. *Team Performance Management*, **16**(5): 309–323.
Schwartz, S.H. 1999. A theory of cultural values and some implications for work. *Applied Psychology: An International Review*, **48**: 23–47.
Schwartz, S.H. and Bilsky, W. 1987. Toward a universal psychological structure of human values. *Journal of Personality and Social Psychology*, **53**: 550–562.
Schwartz, S.H. and Bilsky, W. 1990. Toward a theory of the universal content and structure of values: extensions and cross-cultural replications. *Journal of Personality and Social Psychology*, **58**: 878–891.
Schwartz, S.H. and Rubel, T. 2005. Sex differences in value priorities: cross-cultural and multimethod studies. *Journal of Personality and Social Psychology*, **89**: 1010–1028.
Shaffer, M.A. and Harrison, D.A. 1998. Expatriates' psychological withdrawal from international assignments: work, nonwork and family influences. *Personnel Psychology*, **51**: 87–118.
Showail, S.J., Parks, J.M. and Smith, F.L. 2013. Foreign workers in Saudi Arabia: a field study of role ambiguity, identification, information-seeking, organizational support and performance. *International Journal of Human Resource Management*, **24**: 3957–3979.
Suutari, V. and Tornikoski, C. 2001. The challenge of expatriate compensation: the sources of satisfaction and dissatisfaction among expatriates. *International Journal of Human Resource Management*, **12**: 389–404.
Tayeb, M. 1997. Islamic revival in Asia and human resource management. *Employee Relations*, **19**: 352–364.
Taylor, S. and Napier, N. 1996. Working in Japan: lessons from women expatriates. *Sloan Management Review*, **37**: 76–84.
Tharenou, P. and Caulfield, N. 2010. Will I stay or will I go? Explaining repatriation by self-initiated expatriates. *Academy of Management Journal*, **53**: 1009–1028.
Trompenaars, F. and Hampden-Turner, C. 1998. *Riding the Waves of Culture: Understanding Diversity in Global Business*. New York: McGraw-Hill.
Tung, R.L. 1987. Expatriate assignments: enhancing success and minimizing failure. *Academy of Management Executive*, **1**: 117–126.
United Nations 2013. *Trends in International Migrant Stock: The 2013 Revision – Migrants by Age and Sex*. UN Department of Economic and Social Affairs.
Vaiman, V. and Haslberger, A. 2013. *Talent Management of Self-Initiated Expatriates: A Neglected Source of Global Talent*. Houndmills, Basingstoke, UK: Palgrave Macmillan.
Werner, S. 2002. Recent developments in international management research: a review of 20 top management journals. *Journal of Management*, **28**: 277–305.
Westwood, R.I. and Leung, S.M. 1994. The female expatriate manager experience: coping with gender and culture. *International Studies of Management and Organization*, **24**: 64–85.
Williams, J., Bhanugopan, R. and Fish, A. 2011. Localization of human resources in the State of Qatar: emerging issues and research agenda. *Education, Business and Society: Contemporary Middle Eastern Issues*, **4**: 193–206.

17. Talent management practice in Oman: the institutional perspective

Rayya Al Amri, Alison J. Glaister and David P. Spicer

INTRODUCTION

This chapter analyses talent management (TM) practice in the Sultanate of Oman and examines the relevance of institutional theory in shaping both the antecedents and the consequences of TM programmes. The chapter draws on empirical evidence from private sector organisations located in Oman. This context is valuable because it tackles an under-researched area and will help to find other factors and assumptions of TM that do not exist in the Western and US contexts.

As a phenomenon, TM is rather new and controversial in the Middle East region, including Oman. Despite the amount of research devoted to TM, there is no deep research on the nature of TM in the Omani context. Furthermore, a number of studies emphasise the importance of considering the institutional and cultural factors that influence human resources (HR) in general and TM in particular (e.g., Budhwar and Mellahi, 2007; Mellahi and Collings, 2010; Afoiuni et al., 2013) and discuss cultural challenges while implementing TM systems (Mellahi and Collings, 2010). The role of institutional and cultural factors should therefore be taken into consideration while exploring the TM for a given nation. In particular, the role of nationalisation (Omanisation) is a significant factor in this regard.

Therefore, the aim of this study is to explore and understand the nature of the TM phenomenon in the Omani private sector and examine the role of institutional factors in shaping TM systems in Omani companies. The structure of the remaining chapter is as follows: it begins with an analysis of Oman's environment and discusses the impact of nationalisation policy (Omanisation) on Oman's industrial sectors. The concept of TM is introduced in the context of Oman's institutional environment, and, thereafter, the multiple perspectives of institutional theory are examined. Each of these perspectives is then related to our empirical findings and these are used to critically evaluate the impacts of the institutional environment on TM programmes and the challenges that lay ahead.

THE STUDY CONTEXT

Responding to calls to go beyond US and Western contexts in terms of understanding and exploring the TM phenomenon in new nations (Collings and Mellahi, 2009; CIPD, 2012; Meyers et al., 2013; Thunnissen et al., 2013), we have chosen Oman as a context of our study. Afiouni et al. (2013) suggest that the current HR literature in the Middle East region needs to have further research examining the impact of the Arab Spring and the influence of nationalisation policy on TM. Although, the Middle East shares same socio-contextual factors (namely culture), which have led to similar management practices across the region, there are also some factors (e.g., legal system, governance and economics) which cause the variations across countries in the Middle East and have a significant role in shaping human resource management (HRM) (Budhwar and Mellahi, 2007). Therefore, our research explores the TM phenomenon in a non-Western nation in order to enhance our understanding of the role of institutional pressures in shaping TM in a novel context – that of Oman. Management practices in countries such as Oman are shaped by its unique social, cultural and historical environments, and a research along the same lines should help to develop theories and models that will contribute to the TM literature locally and globally.

Oman, alongside Qatar, Bahrain, Kuwait, the United Arab Emirates and Saudi Arabia, forms part of the Gulf Cooperation Council (GCC) being its fifth largest economy (Global Research, 2011). At a macro level, these are culturally similar countries that are economically dependent on oil production. However, the nature of oil production and oil exploration varies from one country to another, and Oman's oil production has moved from the primary stage to the secondary stage that requires deeper oil exploration and more sophisticated tools for oil extraction. As a result the Omani government has focused its attention on the diversification of its economy, reducing its reliance on oil and turning, instead, to services and the industrial and financial sectors.

This diversification has led to a governmental focus on the development of human capital, emphasising the need to up-skill and reskill Omanis and reduce the prevalent role that is played by expatriates in the economy. In response to this, the Omani government implemented its Vision 2020 programme, aimed at developing local human capital and upgrading Omani skills to respond to technological progress and to create a stable macroeconomic framework focused on the development of the private sector. This development was premised on the recruitment and development of the Omani workforce, ensuring their occupation of middle management and senior management positions (Global Research, 2011). As such, the Vision 2020 programme sought to ensure that Omanis filled 75 per cent of vacancies in the private sector and 95 per cent of vacancies in the public sector, thus reducing dependence on the expatriate workforce.

Table 17.1 shows the extent and success of Omanisation in different areas. It also shows that the best results have been achieved in clerical roles, with a 96 per cent overall Omani

Table 17.1 Success of Omanisation

Job area	% of Omanisation
Clerical roles	96%
Services	20%
Specialist professions	19%
Sales roles	16%
General industrial (other industries not include agriculture, construction industries	13%
Basic engineering	7%
Agriculture	7%
Technical roles	2%

Source: Times of Oman (2014).

occupation of these roles. However, Omanisation has had limited success in engineering, agriculture and technical roles (7 per cent, 7 per cent and 2 per cent, respectively).

The regulator of the private sector, the Ministry of Manpower, plans to shift a further 100,000 jobs from the expatriate workforce in Oman to the Omani workforce (Times of Oman, 2014). However, as Table 17.1 shows, Omanis are resistant to taking on particular roles, and until recently the expatriate labour market population has increased faster than the Omani population. In 2008 the expatriate population made up 31 per cent of the total working population (Global Research, 2011). Between 2005 and 2009, expatriates employed in the private sector rose from 81.2 per cent to 84.7 per cent. This grew by a further 10 per cent in the following year whereas the employment of Omanis grew by only 7.6 per cent during the same period (Global Research, 2011).

The challenges for higher education (HE) institutions in providing a suitable, competent, local workforce and the pressure from the Omanisation policy, as well as the challenges to attract the highly skilled people who prefer to work in the government sector, have led private sector organisations to place greater emphasis on their training and development strategy. Training programmes in organisations in the private sector initially focused on technical and vocational skills. However, due to the rise in the Omanisation percentage at the professional levels, these organisations have identified the importance of developing experienced local employees to occupy the strategic positions. This may result in the recognition of the importance of TM as a strategy capable of helping to meet the Omanisation policy's requirements as well as organisational growth and productivity. The success of TM in this sector relies on the proper investment in human capital in terms of having future leaders who might run the business in the long term. However, Omanisation policy might involve potential problems such as the sense of inequity between local and expatriate employees, with former in receipt of more recruitment and development opportunities despite a lower return on investment, which may affect the organisations' efficiency.

TALENT MANAGEMENT

Talent is defined 'as the collective knowledge, skills, abilities, experiences, values, habits and behaviours of all labour that is brought to bear on the organization's mission' (Schiemann, 2014: 282). The definition of TM is contested; however, such programmes tend to focus on the management of high performers or high potentials (Lewis and Heckman, 2006). TM is a process involving the attraction and recruitment of talent and continues with their identification, development and retention (Chabault et al., 2012). The Chartered Institute of Personnel and Development (CIPD, 2014: 1) defines TM as 'the systematic attraction, identification, development, engagement, retention and deployment of those individuals who are of particular value to an organisation, either in view of their "high potential" for the future or because they are fulfilling business/operation-critical roles'. TM programmes are therefore specific to the organisation and contingent upon organisational priorities (CIPD, 2011).

Cooke et al. (2014: 226) consider TM as 'the newer fashion of human resource management', including the practice of HRM planning, recruitment, selection, retention, turnover reduction, training and development, performance measurement and compensation. It is the configuration of these that can lead to 'maximum effectiveness' (Schuler et al., 2011: 510). Cerdin and Brewster (2014) emphasise the importance of HRM practices that focus on the development of skills and competencies. These practices might include coaching, mentoring, skills training, challenging assignments, leadership development, fast-track promotion and performance management (Cooke et al., 2014; Meyers et al., 2013). Indeed Cooke et al. (2014: 234) suggest that 'TM is not something different from HRM . . . it is part of HRM and good HRM practices are those that will attract and motivate employees to achieve high performance'.

While scholarly research on TM and TM practice is increasing, much of the theoretical and empirical foundations upon which an understanding of TM is premised are based on a certain (read *US centric*) way of thinking and behaving (Collings and Mellahi, 2013). This has encouraged scholars to develop and conceptualise a more nuanced and contextual understanding of TM across Europe and the Far East (Huang and Tansley, 2012; Illes et al., 2010; Skuza et al., 2013). Such contextual insight is particularly important, as institutions determine both the antecedents and the consequences of TM programmes. While talent is defined as those who are considered high performers, the Omani government's focus on Omanisation and the achievement of specific quotas will play a key role in redefining the meaning and the practice of TM within the Middle Eastern context. Based on our findings, TM refers to 'the development and retention of Omani high performers with high potential'. This suggests that the meaning of talent and TM is shaped and defined by the external (Omanisation policy) and internal (business needs) factors of an organisation.

Paauwe and Boselie (2003) argue that the differences in embeddedness and institutional settings between countries impact the nature of HRM; as such, Oman's institutional environment will shape how TM is conceived and implemented. Institutional theory has developed to offer a powerful explanation for individual and organisational action (Dacin et al., 2002). The changes in the GCC context correspond to some degree to *rational choice institutionalism*, which considers institutions to be the 'shared patterns of action that economic agents devise in order to overcome uncertainty' (Morgan and Hauptmeier, 2014: 191). Institutional change occurs through punctuated equilibrium caused by exogenous shocks – in the case of Oman, the need to reduce dependence on oil production and greater competition in the services and industrial sectors after signing a free-trade agreement with the United States in 2004 (Anon, 2005). A focus on the oil and gas industries led to a lack of integration and delayed investment in an appropriate Middle Eastern HR model (Looney, 2003). Morgan and Hauptmeier (2014) suggest that under rational choice institutionalism new institutional structures are created that might use features of the old regime in new ways. *Historical institutionalism* (Steinmo et al., 1992), on the other hand, suggests that institutions are not merely products of rational choices; instead they are path dependent, built up over time and dependent upon a country's historical roots, which shape stakeholder preferences and actions. This approach assumes that actors are passive and choice is, to some degree, predetermined. Historical institutionalism favours stasis and suggests that radical institutional change is not possible.

Sociological institutionalism (also known as neo-institutionalism or new institutionalism) views organisations as social entities that seek approval for their performance in socially constructed environments (Scott, 1995). It focuses on the normative contexts within which organisations exist. Therefore, an understanding of organisational structures and actions cannot be understood separately from their social environment. In other words, it strongly emphasises the aspects of social structure including rules, norms and routines that will guide one or influence one to embrace particular social behaviours (Scott, 2004). Scott (1995) argues that organisations should respond to the rules and systems that exist in an environment in order to grow and survive. For example, social, economic and political factors exist in specific environments that provide organisations with an advantage in engaging in particular types of activities, especially if these factors act as supportive tools for an organisation. Institutional theorists state that the institutional environment can strongly influence the development of structures in organisations (DiMaggio and Powell, 1983). Sociological institutionalism suggests that institutionalised activities are the results of interrelated processes at different levels, such as individual level (manager norms), firm level (corporate culture) and inter-organisation level (government regulations) (DiMaggio and Powell, 1983).

The main contributions to institutional theory are DiMaggio and Powell's (1983) framework and Scott's (1995) framework. DiMaggio and Powell (1983) demonstrated that in order to gain legitimacy, firms need to increase the homogeneity of organisational structures in an institutional environment. Therefore, they proposed three types of pressures: mimetic, coercive and normative. Mimetic pressures suggest that firms imitate successful practices of other firms in order to gain legitimacy, such as replicating the TM practices of the most successful organisations within the same environment for competitive advantage. Coercive pressures stem from other organisations upon which firms are dependent and from cultural expectations that encourage organisations to become similar (Boon et al., 2009). For example, the government's Omanisation programme sets sectoral targets for the employment of Omani nationals; the failure to achieve these targets may result in governmental sanctions. Finally, normative pressures within and between organisations legitimise organisational practice. Thus the nature of TM will depend upon the extent to which such practice is considered good practice amongst key occupational groups and decision makers, such as senior managers and HR directors.

Furthermore, Scott's (1995) framework outlines three types of institutional environments – regulatory, cognitive and normative, each of which is motivated by coercive, mimetic and normative types of pressure. Moreover, each of these provides a basis for legitimacy, a notion previously developed by DiMaggio and Powell (1983). A regulatory institution represents rules and laws that promote certain types of behaviour that may restrict the flexibility of an organisation's structure. Inability to conform to regulation may prevent the firm from accessing resources or from gaining support from top levels of government (Scott, 1995). Cognitive components mean shared social knowledge and shared conceptions of reality in a particular society (Scott, 1995). In other words, it is assumed that legitimacy comes from adopting a common frame of reference for the situation (Owens et al., 2013). Yiu and Makino (2002) suggested two ways in which firms can achieve cognitive legitimacy: external mimetic behaviour, which imitates successful firms in a sector through the adoption of similar systems such as HR practices; and internal mimetic behaviour, which means conforming to internal routines and habitual behaviour from past experience. The third type of environment in Scott's framework is normative, which denotes the values, beliefs and norms of human action considered acceptable behaviour from cultural perspectives.

Consequently, these three types make up the institutional profile of a specific sector or country. Kostova and Roth define institutional profile as 'the issue-specific set of regulatory, cognitive and normative institutions in a given country' (2002: 217). Arguably, if institutional pressures are country- or sector-specific, isomorphic mechanisms can lead to fewer differences in organisational strategies within the same country, thus TM strategies will be similar in the same institutional environment. Moreover, sociological institutionalism suggests the need for organisations to monitor the practice of organisations in order to ensure the articulation and dissemination of best practice (Morgan and Hauptmeier, 2014; Brunsson and Sahlin-Andersson, 2000). Oman has created various ministries to ensure that practice aligns with institutional diktat.

However, each of these institutional theories fail to consider the role of agency – the role of actors who are able to 'speak outside the institutions in which they continue to act' (Schmidt, 2008: 315) and are part of social networks that impact decision making (Campbell, 2004). While TM in Oman is considered a pressing governmental agenda, TM practice will be interpreted differently as actors act in ways that are not determined by the institutions in which they exist (Streeck and Thelen, 2005). According to Morgan and Hauptmeier (2014: 197) 'actors can . . . review the past, identify for themselves the origins of institutions . . . and decide in the present, that these conditions no longer hold'. TM systems in Oman may not be socially acceptable as they create sensitivity towards perceptions of equity and parity amongst employees. These sensitivities will impact the effectiveness of TM design and implementation. Such resistance is also possible at an organisational level, as organisations can be active in influencing and shaping their structure rather than merely depending on the institutional forces at play (Scott, 1995), and they can control institutional pressures through pro-active strategies (Owens et al., 2013).

TM strategies are subject to these institutional shapers and institutional theory can explain why and how TM strategies and practices are selected. Festing et al. (2013) examined the impact of Germany's institutional environment on the features of TM amongst small and medium-sized firms in Germany. They found that pressure within SME environments led to the adoption of typical features ascribed to the German national business system, thus providing support for the role of historical institutionalism akin to the varieties of capitalism approach suggested by Hall and Soskice (2001). Similarly, researching TM practice in Beijing, Preece et al. (2011) found that TM in these companies was influenced by the role of fashion-setters and followers in the fashion-setting process and thus lends credence to the importance of mimicry in the institutional environment. Sidani and Al Ariss (2014) highlight the problems caused by the mimetic and coercive influence in the institutional environment. In their examination of TM practices in the GCC region, they found that organisational responses to nationalisation policy were manifested through different TM policies and development initiatives between expatriate and local workers. This exacerbated the sense of inequity, with the latter in receipt of more development opportunities despite a lower return on investment. Yet each of these studies failed to explain the specific institutional pressures that influenced the decision to select a particular approach to TM.

Table 17.2 Case summary of data collection in Oman

Number of interviews	BM (Banking)	BO (Banking)	DA (Petroleum)	DO (Petroleum)	Overall
Strategic directors	(1)	(1)	(1)	(1)	17
HR managers	(1)	(1)	(1)	(1)	
TM advisers	(3)	(1)	(2)	(3)	
Line managers	(2)	(1)	(4)	(2)	9
Talented employees	(4)	(2)	(5)	(2)	13
Total	11	6	13	9	39

Note: The number of each interview participant is indicated in brackets (1, 2. . .).

METHODOLOGY

This study is exploratory in nature and adopts an interpretivist position, which believes that social practices are constructed through interactions between human beings and their languages and experiences. A case-study strategy is employed which includes two banks and two petroleum companies, both of which have formally adopted TM systems. Accordingly, primary data were collected through semi-structured interviews with Strategic Directors, HR managers and TM advisers, and with line managers and talented employees who are, and have been, experienced in the TM programmes. Details on the interview participants are presented in Table 17.2.

The four cases are coded as: BM, BO, DA and DO to ensure the anonymity and confidentiality of each organisation's identity. The interviews were based on an interview guideline reflecting our study's aim. There were two different sets of questions for two different groups: the management (decision maker, HR manager and TM adviser) and line managers and employees. All questions in both sets focused on TM, specifically on the role of institutional pressures in shaping TM. All the interviews were conducted in English as a common language in these two sectors. The interviews lasted around one hour and were recorded, transcribed and analysed by the researchers. For the thematic analysis, the data gained from the interviews on TM were coded into main themes, and these were grouped into categories. Initial themes were generated from the literature but then were removed and developed through the analyses.

FINDINGS AND DISCUSSION

Based on our research evidence, Oman's institutional environment has shaped TM provision in a number distinctive ways. These are shown in Figure 17.1.

Figure 17.1 shows the different pressures that shape TM strategy in Omani organisations. The coercive pressures in Oman derive from the government's policy of Omanisation, but also strong labour unions promote the rights of employees and shape TM practice, and their presence in organisations is increasing (Curtis et al., 2009). This has led to organisations designing TM systems that focus mainly on Omani employees.

Mimetic pressures appear to be strong, as Oman has experienced an increase in the number of local firms and inward foreign investment, suggesting an increase in the

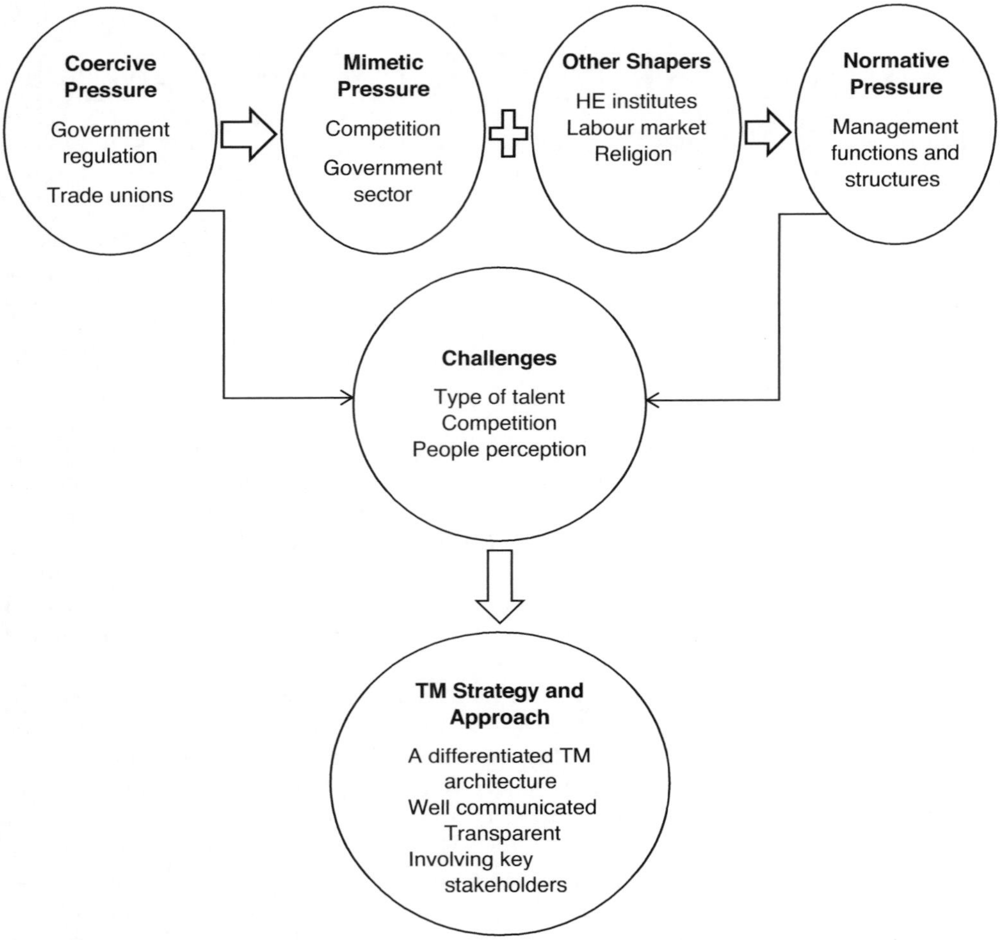

Figure 17.1 The antecedents and consequences of TM in Oman

competition for talent. While these create mimetic forces, much will be influenced by the strong government sector in Oman, which has more resources to engage in TM practice and shapes perception of a less pressured work environment. This powerful sector 'raises the bar' for organisations across different sectors. Figure 17.1 shows that coercive pressures lead to mimicry but need to be combined with other shapers before impacting norms and creating normative pressure. These shapers include HE establishments that, until now, have not created a suitable talent pipeline from which organisations can draw. While they contribute to the shape of TM, they also experience the consequences of coercive and mimetic pressure from the external environment as legislation and government initiatives force a change in the development of indigenous human capital. The banking industry struggles with the commercial aspects of its role and the country's religion – thus commercial banks struggle to attract, recruit and retain the right talent. These factors, together with the characteristics of the local labour market, lead to normative pressures and force the creation of managerial structures and systems to cope with the idiosyncratic nature of Oman's environment.

Each of these pressures and shapers are then filtered through a range of challenges, including the type of talent that organisations are seeking to develop, the nature of competition within specific sectors and the perceptions that employees have of their role in the workplace and their expectations of work. For instance, the Omani organisations in our study are challenged by the unavailability of talent within the local labour market that are specialised enough to enable the business to continue. Oil companies in Oman are not able to find those with the right skills to engage in oil exploration. The government sector competes for talent with the private sector and the former has more resources to increase remuneration and reward packages in order to attract employees. High salaries and a perception of lower work pressure in the government sector attract new recruits. While organisations in Oman have introduced graduate programmes, they are also engaging with top international universities to sustain a talent pipeline and to respond to both the mimetic and coercive forces within the environment.

Our research evidence suggests that organisations are creating robust and differentiated TM architectures that are driven by the government agenda. This differentiated TM architecture approach aims to include all Omani employees but stratify them at different levels of development need (e.g., the creation of new graduate programmes aimed at early entrants to the labour market and professional programmes for managers and longer-serving employees). This stratification is based on demographic factors, work experience, performance and perceived potential. Such measures place an emphasis on some key enablers of Oman's TM system, and this is the expectation of fairness and transparency in TM design and delivery. Performance and potential is 'measured' by clear selection criteria and open communication in an attempt to ensure the TM system remains as objective as possible. While Huselid and Becker (2011) argue that TM systems may have a negative impact on the people who are excluded from them, our research shows that the way in which the TM system is designed and implemented provides an opportunity for those who are not immediately included in the talent pool to understand the performance requirements of that talent pool and seek to improve their own performance. This perceived fairness and transparency provides a sense of distributive justice and, when combined with the involvement of key stakeholders, sustains the TM system and fosters employee commitment. Organisations manage the expectations of their employees and are, at the same time, provided with a sufficient pool of indigenous technical and leadership capability that is able to substitute the expatriate labour force.

Our findings also suggest that while sociological approaches to institutionalism (new or neo-institutionalism) explain the development of such TM systems, there is also a key role to be played by both historical institutionalism – where TM is dependent upon the country's historical roots, shaping preferences and actions, and a more actor-centred form suggested by Streeck and Thelen (2005) and Morgan and Hauptmeier (2014). This more holistic approach is central to the discussion of TM, as the nature of the institution and what it seeks to achieve has ripple effects throughout the entire system. It is not enough to consider TM in isolation, without considering the eco-system within which it resides. Our research indicates that historical, sociological and more actor-centred institutional pressures have manifested themselves in the creation of similarly structured TM programmes with only slight variations between them.

Yet, the nature of Oman, its culture and its heritage still pose particular challenges for TM – thus institutional theory provides an understanding of how and why TM is enacted, but also provides a backdrop against which the challenges for the future of TM can be analysed. For example, our data suggests that a number of challenges that might limit the effectiveness of TM could include:

1. the nationalisation policy;
2. the lack of talented workforce in the labour market;
3. local HE institutions;
4. people's perception towards working in private sector organisations.

The nationalisation policy, which forces organisations to employ Omanis, and the lack of talented workforce in the labour market as a result of poor quality graduates provided by local HE institutions, as well as people's perception, who prefer to work in the government sector than in the private sector organisations, act as the main challenges that may limit the effectiveness of TM systems in an organisation. Excluding expatriates from TM systems in Oman may also create challenges for organisations in retaining expatriates as well as create problems between Omanis and expatriates. Therefore, further research needs to analyse the views of expatriates who work in these two sectors (banking and petroleum) in terms of TM systems. Future research may also include the international companies that operate in the Omani context, comparing them with the local companies in terms of the challenges they face in operating the TM system in this context.

A number of practical implications can be drawn from this study for local and multinational companies. Our data reveals that the implementation of TM systems is driven by a combination of external and internal factors (e.g., Omanisation, competition and business needs), which have led to the inclusion of all Omani employees in TM programmes with differentiated development programmes (a differentiated TM architecture approach). For example, those who are identified as high potential and located in the top level of TM systems receive different development programmes than those who are in the middle and lower levels of TM systems.

However, companies should be aware of the disadvantages of excluding non-Omanis from the TM programmes, which may have a negative impact on the TM systems' effectiveness. Thus, decision makers, HR managers and TM advisers could revisit existing TM practices in light of the potential for ethnicity-related discrimination in TM, to improve the inclusion of a diverse workforce. In addition, companies could decrease discrimination risk by increasing the transparency of TM programmes and by having clear objectives for TM systems shared amongst all the parties in an organisation. Furthermore, multinational companies should seek to find a balance between global and local requirements in respect of their TM practices.

CONCLUSION

The aim of this study was to make an empirical contribution to the TM literature by examining the nature of the TM system under the influence of external and internal factors, based on institutional theory and by gaining in-depth primary data from four cases in the banking and petroleum sectors in the Sultanate of Oman. The study found that the TM system is driven by external and internal drivers, such as government regulations, competition and the needs of organisations, all of which have significant impacts on how TM should be operated and managed, whereby it was found that the dominant TM approach in these four organisations is characterised by differentiated TM approaches.

Exploring TM through the lens of institutional theory might be of interest to many TM academics and practitioners, particularly given the current situation in the Middle East region in particular (conflicts in Syria, nationalisation policy and lack of skilled labour) and war for talent across the globe. Further, discussion on the role of institutional pressures in shaping TM systems and its impact on organisations within the Omani context can help explain how differences in context shape the meaning of TM and its implementation. While this research is still at an explorative stage in this valuable context, the results are encouraging and call for a further development of effective TM in the Middle East region.

USEFUL WEBSITES

National Centre for Statistics and Information: http://www.ncsi.gov.om/.
Ministry of Manpower: http://www.manpower.gov.om/.
Central Bank of Oman: www.cbo-oman.org/.
Ministry of Oil and Gas: www.mog.gov.om/english.

REFERENCES

Afiouni, F., Ruël, H. and Schuler, R. 2013. HRM in the Middle East: toward a greater understanding. *International Journal of Human Resource Management*, **25**(2): 133–143.

Anon 2005. Middle East/Africa: key developments. *Country Monitor*, **13**(39): 10.

Boon, C., Paauwe, J., Boselie, P. and Hartog, D.D. 2009. Institutional pressures and HRM: developing institutional fit. *Personnel Review*, **38**(5): 492–508.

Brunsson, N. and Sahlin-Andersson, K. 2000. Constructing organizations: the example of public sector reform. *Organization Studies*, **21**(4): 721–746.

Budhwar, P. and Mellahi, K. 2007. Introduction: human resource management in the Middle East. *International Journal of Human Resource Management*, **18**(1): 2–10.

Campbell, J.L. 2004. *Institutional Change and Globalization*. Princeton, NJ: Princeton University Press.

Cerdin, J.-L. and Brewster, C. 2014. Talent management and expatriation: bridging two streams of research and practice. *Journal of World Business*, **49**(2): 245–252.

Chabault, D., Hulin, A. and Soparnot, R. 2012. Talent management in clusters. *Organizational Dynamics*, **41**(4): 327–335.

CIPD 2011. *Learning and Talent Development Annual Survey Report*. London: CIPD.

CIPD 2012. *Annual Survey Report Learning and Talent Development*. London: CIPD.

CIPD 2014. *Talent Management Factsheet: An Overview*. http://www.cipd.co.uk/hr-resources/factsheets/talent-management-overview.aspx (accessed 2 December 2014).

Collings, D.G. and Mellahi, K. 2009. Strategic talent management: a review and research agenda. *Human Resource Management Review*, **19**(4): 304–313.

Collings, D.G. and Mellahi, K. 2013. Commentary on: 'Talent – innate or acquired? Theoretical considerations and their implications for talent management'. *Human Resource Management Review*, **23**(4): 322–325.

Cooke, F.L., Saini, D.S. and Wang, J. 2014. Talent management in China and India: a comparison of management perceptions and human resource practices. *Journal of World Business*, **49**(2): 225–235.

Curtis, Mallet-Prevost, Colt & Mosle 2009. Oman law blog – focus on labor unions. http://omanlawblog.curtis.com/2009/06/focus-on-labor-unions.html (accessed 2 December 2014).

Dacin, M.T., Goodstein, J. and Scott, W.R. 2002. Institutional theory and institutional change: introduction to the special research forum. *Academy of Management Journal*, **45**(1): 45–56.
DiMaggio, P. and Powell, W. 1983. The iron cage revisited – institutional isomorphism and collective rationality in organisational fields. In W. Powell and P. Dimaggio (eds), *The New Institutionalism In Organisational Analysis*. Chicago: Chicago University Press, pp. 63–82.
Festing, M., Schäfer, L. and Scullion, H. 2013. Talent management in medium-sized German companies: an explorative study and agenda for future research. *International Journal of Human Resource Management*, **24**(9): 1872–1893.
Global Research 2011. Oman economy. Global Investment House, Safat, Kuwait.
Hall, P.A. and Soskice, D. 2001. *Varieties of Capitalism: The Institutional Foundations of Comparative Advantage*. Oxford: Oxford University Press.
Huang, J. and Tansley, C. 2012. Sneaking through the minefield of talent management: the notion of rhetorical obfuscation. *International Journal of Human Resource Management*, **23**(17): 3673–3691.
Huselid, M.A. and Becker, B.E. 2011. Bridging micro and macro domains: workforce differentiation and strategic human resource management. *Journal of Management*, **37**(2): 421–428.
Illes, P., Chuai, X. and Preece, D. 2010. Talent management and HRM in multinational companies in Beijing: definitions, differences and drivers. *Journal of Business Research*, **45**(2): 179–189.
Kostova, T. and Roth, K. 2002. Adoption of an organisational practice by subsidiaries of multinational corporations: institutional and relational effects. *Academy of Management Journal*, **45**(1): 215–233.
Lewis, R.E. and Heckman, R.J. 2006. Talent management: a critical review. *Human Resource Management Review*, **16**(2): 139–154.
Looney, R. 2003. Hawala: the terrorists' informal financial mechanism. *Middle East Policy*, **10**(1): 164–167.
Mellahi, K. and Collings, D.G. 2010. The barriers to effective global talent management: the example of corporate elites in MNEs. *Journal of World Business*, **45**(2): 143–149.
Meyers, M.C., van Woerkom, M. and Dries, N. 2013. Talent – innate or acquired? Theoretical considerations and their implications for talent management. *Human Resource Management Review*, **23**(4): 305–321.
Morgan, G. and Hauptmeier, M. 2014. Varieties of institutional theory in comparative employment relations. In A. Wilkinson, G. Wood and R. Deeg (eds), *The Oxford Handbook of Employment Relations*. Oxford: Oxford University Press, pp. 190–221.
Owens, M., Palmer, M. and Zueva-Owens, A. 2013. Institutional forces in adoption of international joint ventures: empirical evidence from British retail multinationals. *International Business Review*, **22**(5): 883–893.
Paauwe, J. and Boselie, P. 2003. Challenging 'strategic HRM' and the relevance of the institutional setting. *Human Resource Management Journal*, **13**(3): 56–70.
Preece, D., Iles, P. and Chuai, X. 2011. Talent management and management fashion in Chinese enterprises: exploring case studies in Beijing. *International Journal of Human Resource Management*, **22**(16): 3413–3428.
Scott, R. 2004. Institutional theory. In G. Ritzer (ed.), *Encyclopaedia of Social Theory*. Thousand Oaks: Sage.
Scott, W. 1995. *Introduction: Institutional Theory and Organisations: The Institutional Construction of Organisations*. London: Sage.
Schiemann, W.A. 2014. From talent management to talent optimization. *Journal of World Business*, **49**(2): 281–288.
Schmidt, V.A. 2008. Discursive institutionalism: the explanatory power of ideas and discourse. *Annual Review of Political Science*, **11**: 303–326.
Schuler, R.S., Jackson, S.E. and Tarique, I. 2011. Global talent management and global talent challenges: strategic opportunities for IHRM. *Journal of World Business*, **46**(4): 506–516.
Sidani, Y. and Al Ariss, A. 2014. Institutional and corporate drivers of global talent management: evidence from the Arab Gulf region. *Journal of World Business*, **49**(2): 215–224.
Skuza, A., Scullion, H. and McDonnell, A. 2013. An analysis of the talent management challenges in a post-communist country: the case of Poland. *International Journal of Human Resource Management*, **24**(3): 453–470.
Steinmo, S., Thelen, K.A. and Longstreth, F. 1992. *Structuring Politics: Historical Institutionalism in Comparative Analysis*. Cambridge: Cambridge University Press.
Streeck, W. and Thelen, K.A. 2005. Introduction: institutional change in advanced political economies. In W. Streeck and K.A. Thelen (eds), *Beyond Continuity:Institutional Change in Advanced Political Economies*. Oxford: Oxford University Press, pp. 1–39.
Thunnissen, M., Boselie, P. and Fruytier, B. 2013. Talent management and the relevance of context: towards a pluralistic approach. *International Journal of Human Resource Management*, **23**(4): 326–336.
Times of Oman 2014. 100,000 expats to lose jobs in Omanisation: News. February. http://www.timesofoman.com/News/ (accessed 18 November 2014).
Yiu, D. and Makino, S. 2002. The choice between joint venture and wholly owned subsidiary: an institutional perspective. *Organization Science*, **13**(6): 667–683.

18. Privatisation, investments and human resources in foreign firms operating in the Middle East

Faten Baddar AL-Husan and Fawaz Baddar ALHussan

INTRODUCTION AND BACKGROUND

Against a background of globalisation and internationalisation, the period since the mid-1980s has been characterised by changes in the world economy that led to a significant increase in foreign direct investment (FDI), mainly through multinational corporations (MNCs). This was accompanied by developments in the locations of cross-border investments and in MNCs' strategies and structures. A number of forces driving these developments have been identified (United Nations, 1993; Bartlett and Ghoshal, 1998) including the continuing integration and growth of regional trade blocs; the liberalisation of financial markets; the deregulation and privatisation of monopoly state utilities; the removal of trade barriers; the intensification of global competition; advances in information technology; and some cross-national convergence in demand patterns.

As a result of these changes, MNCs adopted fast-track expansionary strategies by spreading activities over different locations worldwide, including the high-risk developing countries (LDCs),[1] to acquire a good portfolio of locational assets and to enhance their competitiveness (United Nations, 2000; Dicken, 2003). These moves were matched by the desire of countries to attract more FDI, which was reflected by steps taken, for example, by many emerging[2]/developing countries and transition economies[3] to create more friendly business environments to achieve greater integration into the global economy, including integration into the regional or global production networks of MNCs, in order to become more prominent players in the world market and to benefit from FDI. Such steps included the reduction of sectoral restrictions on foreign entry, or the liberalisation of operations in industries, which had previously been either closed or restricted to FDI. As a result, the stock of FDI in developing countries grew from US$307 billion in 1980 to US$551 billion in 1990, and to US$2,340 billion in 2002 (United Nations, 2003).

More recent figures indicate that emerging/developing countries have been the destination of more FDI inflows than developed countries. According to a United Nations report, in 2013 the lion's share of the US$1.46 trillion global FDI went to developing economies, with FDI flows to these economies reaching US$759 billion and accounting for 52 per cent of the global total. Transition and developed economies accounted for only 9 per cent and 39 per cent of the global total, respectively (United Nations, 2013, 2014).

It must be noted, however, that privatisation in particular has been utilised as a major vehicle for attracting FDI into developing/emerging economies and for the expansion of MNCs into these economies. For example, in the 1990s approximately 40 per cent of the over US$700 billion in assets that have been privatised occurred in developing/emerging economies and over 90 per cent of FDI in developing countries[4] has come from privatisation transactions. One-third of the FDI flowing into LDCs was coming from the privatisation and deregulation of infrastructure sectors such as power, telecommunication and transportation, and water (Ramamurti, 2004; Zahra et al., 2000).

However, contrary to Western developed economies, such as Britain, in which privatisation has been to a large extent informed by ideologically inspired policy changes, the shift in LDCs from the public sector to the private sector has often occurred more as a response to economic crises and the subsequent need to obtain financial assistance (Ramamurti, 2000). Hence, against the background of such economic and financial crisis, the period from the beginning of the 1980s in particular witnessed many developing countries being forced by the World Bank and the International Monetary Fund (IMF) to adopt economic structural adjustment programmes with a focus on the privatisation of public sector enterprises and the encouragement of FDI (International Labour Organization ILO, 1995; Morris, 2004).

Consequently, in these economies privatisation has been used as a means of transplanting a pro-capitalist political ideology by liberalising the economy, promoting foreign investment, infusing new technology and practices, and increasing national standards of living. In some emerging economies, like Mexico and Brazil, privatisation has been used also as a means to upgrade infrastructure and facilitate future industrial growth, and in some as a change strategy of organisations that includes changes in organisational values, cultures, systems and strategies, as in the case of Jordan, for example (Zahra et al., 2000; AL-Husan and James, 2003, 2009; Inderst and Stewart, 2014).

Nevertheless, privatisation and the large public sector are controversial issues in the Middle East region, and much of this contention is embedded in the political, social and economic structure of these countries (Akoum, 2012). Developments in the region, in particular with the so-called Arab Spring since 2011, demonstrate that the people of the region are demanding real reform that addresses the need for higher and inclusive growth, job creation and deep-rooted structural and governance issues, and provides more tangible socioeconomic benefits and facilitates global integration through policies geared towards attracting foreign capital and investments, absorbing technological progress and upgrading human capital (Abed et al., 2011).

However, since evidence indicates that host countries can only benefit from FDI when there is sufficient absorptive capacity and a minimum threshold of human capital, and since improving public sector performance and governance is a key pillar in the World Bank's engagement strategy for the Middle East and North Africa (MENA) region (World Bank, 2003), it is important to understand how MNCs manage their human resources in their operations in the Middle East, how they transfer their innovative human resource management (HRM) practices and how they can contribute to the development policies in the region.

Accordingly, this chapter begins with an overview of FDI and privatisation in the Middle East. This is followed by a discussion of the factors that influence MNCs' transfer of HRM practices, the mechanisms used in the transfer process and the enablers and constraints of this transfer. The section to follow presents empirical evidence from three case studies to examine the transfer of HRM practices from Western MNCs to state-owned enterprises (SOEs) that were privatised under the auspices of the Jordanian government's privatisation programme. Jordan can be seen as a case study in the region, as there have been calls to build on the examples of the early reformers in the region such as Jordan and

Morocco, who enjoyed the region's most rapid growth rates over the past two decades. The chapter concludes by covering the key challenges in the region and its way forward.

FDI AND PRIVATISATION IN THE MIDDLE EAST

The MENA region is of strategic importance due to its geopolitical location and abundant natural resources.[5] It is the bastion of the world's largest oil reserves with about 57 per cent of the world's proven oil reserves and 41 per cent of proven natural gas resources and other minerals, with a fairly skilled workforce and close proximity to European markets. Nevertheless, despite this potential to attract substantial inflows of FDI, the level of FDI inflows to MENA countries has been modest over the past three decades compared to their capabilities and to other developing countries (El Sayed, 2011).

However, the MENA countries' negative attitudes towards free trade and FDI were altered by the debt crisis and the decrease of commercial bank lending to developing countries, which forced them to follow the steps of the South East Asian model that relied upon attracting FDI and implementing an export-led growth model (Soliman, 2003). Consequently, since the early 1990s a number of countries in the MENA region have been engaged in extensive reform efforts to attract foreign investment into their economies, as many countries in the region have come to realise that FDI is a key source of economic development and an important strategy to integrate into the global economy and to acquire the necessary know-how for advancement. For example, in Oman, recent economic development plans related the country's future prospect of social, economic and political development with its ability to attract more FDI (Mellahi et al., 2003).

Inward stock of FDI in the region saw a huge increase of almost 200 per cent between 1995 and 2005, and cross-border mergers and acquisitions in the region surged from US$1,018 million in 2004 to US$17,116 million in 2005. In 2008 FDI inflow to the MENA region reached its peak of US$95 billion, representing 14.4 per cent of total inflows to developing countries. The strong growth in FDI inflows to the MENA region reflected positive economic situations, mainly in the oil-rich GCC countries, the privatisation of SOEs in several countries and the effort made by a number of countries in the region to make them investor-friendly by making the business environment more open via structural and institutional reforms. Table 18.1 shows the ranking of Middle Eastern countries by the World Bank in terms of reforms done to 'ease doing business' in a country.

However, this positive trend was interrupted by the international economic crisis, with FDI flows decreasing by 25 per cent in 2009 and a further 12 per cent in 2010 (Chauvin, 2013). The situation worsened as most economies in the MENA region have suffered as a result of the regional political turmoil that erupted in 2011 with the so-called Arab Spring and the global economic slowdown. FDI flows into the region have fallen by over 50 per cent from a high of US$114 billion in 2008 to US$38 billion in 2012 (United Nations, 2009, 2013). The persistence of social and political uncertainties together with the shrinking availability of finance from the ailing banking sectors in developed countries have restricted foreign investors' propensity and capacity to invest, and has been holding back FDI recovery, despite differences between countries (United Nations, 2013).

A number of factors determine FDI inflows to the region. Accordingly, it is argued that

Table 18.1 Rankings on the ease of doing business in the Middle East in 2011

Country	Middle East rank	World rank	Country	Middle East rank	World rank
Saudi Arabia	1	11	Morocco	14	114
Bahrain	2	28	Iran*	15	129
Israel*	3	29	West Bank and Gaza	16	135
United Arab Emirates	4	40	Algeria	17	136
Qatar	5	50	Syria	18	144
Turkey*	8	65	Sudan	19	154
Kuwait	9	74	Djibouti	20	158
Egypt	10	94	Comoros	21	159
Yemen	11	105	Mauritania	22	165
Jordan	12	107	Iraq	23	166
Lebanon	13	109			

Note: Non-Arab countries.

Source: Adapted from World Bank (2011).

while the MENA region offers competitive advantages to foreign investors regarding economic growth, the lack of trade openness, the poor performance of institutional factors, lack of political stability and predictability, corruption and bureaucratic red tape that persist in many MENA countries still hamper market economies and the region's ability to attract FDI (e.g., Dunning, 1993; Onyeiwu, 2003; Demirbag et al., 2008; Mohamed and Sidiropoulos, 2010). Other researchers emphasise the importance of the institutional factors in the Middle East and consider them to be more important than the traditional macroeconomic factors such as market potential and size, economic growth rates, unit labour costs and relative natural endowment (Wky and Lal, 2010). For example, Chan and Gemayel (2004) found that the degree of political, financial and economic instability associated with investment risk is a much more critical determinant of FDI in MENA countries than it is in other developing countries. In a similar vein, Mellahi et al. (2003) found that political and economic stability are the two most important motives for investing in Oman.

The quality of institutions is very important for the MENA region. This is due to the fact that, like other developing countries, immaturity or ineffectiveness of formal institutions causes what is called institutional 'void', which raises transaction costs and risk levels for foreign investors (Khanna and Palepu, 2000; Meyer, 2004). The effect of weak institutions in the MENA region has been reflected in the entry mode of MNCs as most foreign investment in the region has taken the form of joint ventures to reduce their transaction cost (Mellahi et al., 2011; El-Said and McDonald, 2001), rather than wholly owned subsidiaries that are usually accompanied by larger benefits for both the recipient country and foreign investor.

The main source of such high transaction costs is considered to come from the formal institutional constraints stemming mostly from continued strong government intervention and state policies in the economy, and the informal institutions that still pervade the economies of the region. For example, research evidence from the survey conducted by El-Said and McDonald (2001) about FDI in Jordan revealed that all firms, regardless of their origin, preferred joint venture investment in developing countries. They also revealed that the foreign firms operating in Jordan faced problems with both formal and informal institutional constraints.

However, what was interesting is that foreign firms expressed more concern with the informal institutional system. These informal institutional constraints included '*Wasta*'/cronyism, tribal mentality, the '*Bukrah*' and '*Inshallah*' attitude, a habit of bribing officials and corruption. Such informal institutional constraints were the main reason why foreign firms preferred to have a Jordanian partner whose job was not to provide finance but rather to deal with the different business environment that exists in Jordan.

Evidence also reveals that even those countries that have been engaged in extensive reform efforts and reduced the size and role of the state in their economies, and have been among the largest recipients of foreign investment and pursued privatisation programmes, such as Egypt, Tunisia, Jordan and Morocco, could not reap the benefits because of internal obstructions such as legal frameworks, political uncertainties and the weakness of local entrepreneurial culture (Talib, 1996; Abed, 2003; Budhwar and Mellahi, 2006). Consequently, El-Said and McDonald (2001) argue that this failure stems from the fact that formal institutional reforms have not been accompanied by informal institutional reforms.

This remains a main challenge for investors in the region. Internally, at the organisational level, this has implications for the management of human resources as such informal institutions are more people-related issues. Hence, it is important for MNCs and foreign investors in general to understand the nature of informal institutions to be able to design and implement HRM strategies and policies that not only curb the effect of such informal institutions but also help in reforming them. For example, cultural change can be enhanced through training and development policies linked to a clear career path and promotions that are linked to performance rather than loyalty to certain people or connections. Similarly, in terms of recruitment and selection, for example, foreign investors may become more directly involved in recruitment due to such factors as nepotism and family relationships. A referral system may also be implemented in which employees can recommend their family members and friends only if they have the required qualifications and pass through the formal competitive process of selection.

Privatisation in the Middle East

As mentioned earlier, privatisation is the main vehicle used by MNCs to expand into developing countries. It is also used as a strategy to attract FDI and reduce state involvement in the economy. For example, Onyeiwu (2003) argues that trade liberalisation and privatisation are important preconditions for FDI flows to the MENA region. In a similar vein, Shehadi (2002) argues that the most important policy initiative that Arab governments can take to encourage foreign investments is to launch privatisation and to open infrastructure sectors to private participation. This is due to the fact that countries in the region are often and continue to be characterised by large public sectors with centralised governments, large and overstaffed civil services, and weak systems of accountability, which are seen to hinder the flow of FDI into the region (Wyk and Lal, 2010; World Bank, 2014).

The large public sector in the Middle East can be attributed to the public policy during the 1960s and 1970s that in much of the developing world was characterised by a confidence in the capacity of governments to act as the main spur of development and a related belief that such an approach was necessary in order to address the underdeveloped nature of indigenous private sectors and capital markets, and to either reduce or avoid economic dominance by foreign MNCs (George, 2000).

As a result, in most LDCs, the decades up to the 1980s saw substantial growth in public sector employment and its share of GDP as a result of the state-led and import-substitution industrialisation policies that characterised the Middle East. Turkey and Egypt were pioneers in adopting import-substitution industrialisation strategies during the global capitalist depression of the 1930s. After World War II more comprehensive versions of state-led development were adopted in Iran, Turkey, Egypt, Syria, Iraq, Tunisia and Algeria. Even countries that rejected this orientation, such as Jordan and Morocco, developed large public sectors (Beinin, 1999). The large public sector in the GCC countries can be attributed to the weak private sector.

However, in the 1980s, with the sharp drop of oil prices and financial crisis, many developing countries resorted to the World Bank and the IMF for financial assistance and as a result had to engage in structural adjustment programmes, a main ingredient of which was public sector privatisation. Turkey was one of the first countries in the Middle East to adopt privatisation in 1985, but progress was slow until December 1999 when an agreement was signed with the IMF that placed a particular emphasis on privatisation. Other countries in the MENA region have begun privatisation belatedly in the early 1990s, and, at first, reluctantly.

The primary objectives of privatisation programmes were to minimise state involvement in economic activities and increase the involvement of the private sector; promote competition; improve allocation of resources, efficiency and productivity in the public sector; facilitate wider distribution of share ownership; reduce fiscal losses of SOEs and create revenue for the government; and attract FDI and secure international financing and support for broader development programmes. However, priorities may differ across countries in the region. In Libya, for instance, the privatisation policy was driven by the need to attract private sector expertise to create jobs and diversify the economy and not by the need to attract capital, which is relatively similar to the situation in GCC oil-rich countries.

Progress has been relatively slow as the MENA region's share of the total investments in developing countries averaged 3.4 per cent in 1998 and 1999. During the period 2000 to 2008 the MENA region accounted for only 7 per cent of the total value of privatisation transactions in developing countries (Shehadi, 2002; United Nations, 2008; Akoum, 2012). The link between privatisation and unemployment has created resistance towards privatisation because of the likely increase in lay-offs, especially initially. It also led to the continued delay in privatisation in some countries, such as GCC countries, due to political and social concerns, as most of the national labour force is employed in the public sector and already there is high unemployment among the nationals in these countries (Arab Times, 2014).

This has been exacerbated by the general attitude of most people in the region who prefer to work in the public sector as it offers job security, good benefits and higher salaries. For example, a Gallup survey in 2011 showed that more than half of the unemployed young people in Egypt, Tunisia and Jordan were seeking a government job compared to only 10 per cent who were looking for a private sector job (World Bank, 2014). Therefore, it is important that privatisation is dealt with using utmost care and competency and in a way that yields tangible benefits to countries and employees in the region. Where MNCs are involved in these privatisations, the transfer of know-how and the development of human capital must be the focus of such a process, and in a way that serves the development objectives of the region.

MNCs AND THE TRANSFER OF HRM PRACTICES

Evidence indicates that the contribution of FDI to economic growth is higher when a sufficient absorptive capability is available at the host country, and that domestic firms' absorptive capacity – that is their ability to utilise spillovers from MNCs determines whether they benefit or not from FDI (Girma, 2005). For example, Borensztein et al.'s (1998) study about FDI from industrial countries to 69 developing countries suggests that FDI is an important vehicle for the transfer of technology that contributes relatively more to growth than domestic investment and that 'the higher productivity of FDI holds only when the host country has a minimum threshold of human capital' (p. 115). Countries in the Middle East have realised the importance of building their human capital to increase the absorptive capacities and competitiveness of their economies.

MNCs are the main vehicle for the transfer of know-how, capital, technology and managerial skills and hence one of the means of building this human capital with their advanced HR practices. The role of MNCs in transferring knowledge and best practices across borders is also reflected in the World Bank and the IMF imposed requirements relating to the introduction of modern Western management practices and techniques, including the adoption of 'result-driven, customer focused, and participative and accountable HRM'. These are often conditions of World Bank/IMF management-led structural adjustment programmes and privatisation deals in both the developing world and former Soviet bloc countries/transition economies (Jackson, 2004, p. 231).

It is widely acknowledged that the ability to transfer knowledge effectively across borders is a key characteristic of the successful MNC. This is particularly essential for knowledge that is believed to be critical for the company's competitive advantage, such as the knowledge embodied in strategic organisational practices (Bartlett and Ghoshal, 1998; Kostova, 1999). Consequently, learning what factors might facilitate or impede the process of transfer of HR practices is therefore of strategic importance for MNCs.

Factors Influencing the Transfer of HRM Practices

In this section, the theoretical background about the transfer of the HRM practices concept and country-level factors are first discussed. This is followed by a discussion of the factors at the industrial and organisational levels, and at the HRM-specific level.

Theoretical background and country-level factors

Theoretically, two primary perspectives can be identified concerning the transfer of HR policies and practices from one national context to another, namely the 'universalist' and 'contextual' approaches (Child, 2000; Evans et al., 2011). The 'universalistic' or 'best practice' approach effectively suggests that all organisations, regardless of size, industry or business strategy, should adopt these so-called best practices to be competitive.

The implicit assumption in this perspective is that the effects of 'best practice' are not firm specific, but rather universal and transferrable, and therefore it is desirable and feasible for a MNC to export its home country policies and practices and 'international best practices' to other national contexts and compete more effectively with local competitors (Bamberger and Meshoulam, 2000). In line with this approach, for example, Taylor et al. (1996), drawing on the resource-based theory of the firm, argued that HRM policies are transferred only when they are conceived to be a significant source of competitive advantage for the MNC and critical for the success of their subsidiaries.

In contrast, the contextual approach, such as the cultural and institutional perspectives, argues that MNCs will frequently need to take into account many contingent factors, including institutional and cultural factors, in order to establish an appropriate approach to HRM in a specific national environment. In particular, cultural and institutional variations between the host country and the home country of the parent company may prevent, or inhibit, the diffusion of desired policies and practices (Child, 2002). More specifically, the cultural perspective argues that every society has its own unique sets of deep-lying values and beliefs that reflect how nations organise, conduct and manage work. Hence, the larger the cultural distance and variations in cultural values between the host country in which the MNC operates and its home country, the more difficult it becomes to transfer parent company practices to the subsidiaries and standardise the HR practices.

Similarly, the institutional perspective argues that firms are embedded in their institutional environment. Institutions provide the 'rules of the game' in which organisations act and compete as they constrain which actions by those organisations are acceptable and supportable within the institutional framework. Hence institutions may be defined as 'the humanly devised constraints that structure human interaction' (North, 1990, p. 3), and may be categorised as formal and informal. Formal institutions include laws, political (and judicial) rules, economic rules, regulations and contracts. Informal institutions include codes of conduct, norms of behaviour, ethics and convention, which are embedded in culture and ideology. This means that the country of origin with its historical and economic institutional settings within which a MNC is embedded acts to shape its behaviour in terms of such things as work organisation and modes of control.

For example, institutionalists argue that societal institutions such as the national education and training system of a country determine the supply and quality of the workforce. This, in turn, influences the recruitment, selection, and training and development activities of organisations. The legal institutions also determine the bargaining structure and employee representation and communication systems (Tregaskis, 1998; Marginson and Sisson, 1994). As a result, it is further argued that since these institutions continue to differ across countries, so too do the strategies and practices of companies (Edwards, 1998), and the larger the institutional distance between the country of origin/home country and the host country the more difficult it becomes to transfer parent country practices to the subsidiaries and they will need to adapt their practices to gain legitimacy and societal fitness.

The latter point is particularly emphasised by the 'neo' or 'new' institutionalism perspective that has emerged over the last two decades as a leading theoretical foundation for research on the global diffusion of practices and the adoption of these by organisations. According to DiMaggio and Powell (1983), to gain legitimacy firms seek to implement socially acceptable business structures, strategies and practices to comply with three main types of institutional isomorphism:[6] coercive, mimetic and normative. Coercive isomorphism stems from informal and formal pressures. Formal pressures include such factors as political and regulatory influences.

Mimetic isomorphism results when organisations in situations of uncertainty respond by imitating and modelling themselves on other organisations in the environment; and normative isomorphism results primarily from professionalisation and professional organisations disseminating appropriate organisational practices. Both mimetic and normative isomorphism stem from the informal institutions. This implies that strategic choices and the discretion of executives are limited by the degree of institutional constraints prevailing in different societies and national business systems (Powell, 2007).

In light of the above, a number of scholars have argued that such cultural and institutional differences will make it difficult to transfer Western practices to developing countries in general and to Middle Eastern countries in particular. For example, Buckley and Casson (1991, p. 50) have suggested that the sophisticated systems thinking and strategic attitudes of MNCs are not easily transferable to developing countries because of cultural barriers. Jackson (2004), in turn, noted that the characteristics of management systems within former colonial countries, including many Middle Eastern countries, such as top-down management style with paternalistic and centralised decision making, can act as a barrier to such transfers.

A number of studies have provided support to such arguments and demonstrated the influence of cultural and institutional factors on the transfer of practices. For example, Yahiaoui (2007) found that Tunisian institutional factors have led to the rejection of some transferred practices from MNCs to Tunisian subsidiaries, such as the use of head hunters and newspaper advertisements to recruit employees, as these were considered inappropriate in the Tunisian context which relies on informal and interpersonal relations in recruitment practices – a common characteristic in Arab culture. Another example was the performance appraisal which was rejected in Tunisia due to the 'face saving' principle in Arab culture and hence the inappropriateness of criticisms and sanctions.

In a similar vein, Nakhle (2011), in his study about the transfer of HR practices from American and European MNCs to their Lebanese subsidiaries, found that several socio-cultural and institutional factors were behind the adaptation of HR practices in the Lebanese subsidiaries. These included cultural (interpersonal relations, family spirit, 'loss of face', relationship-orientation), societal (religion, political diversity) and institutional (labour law, educational system and national business system) factors.

Institutional duality

Applying the tenets of DiMaggio and Powell's (1983) work, an MNC's subsidiary located in a foreign country is subject to 'institutional dualism' arising from the competing pressures of the host-country and home-country institutions and the need to gain legitimacy with both the local environment (external legitimacy/local adaptation) and the worldwide organisation of the MNC (internal legitimacy/global integration) (Kostova and Roth, 2002).

At the macro-level, this indicates that isomorphic pressures (coercive, mimetic and normative) are forcing organisations to be consistent with their external institutional environment, suggest convergence towards a dominant model of management resulting in similarities among organisations' behaviours and practices at a given point in time. There is an expectation that the US model will be the dominant one and that all HRM practices will eventually converge on that US model (Pudelko and Harzing, 2007).

At the micro-organisational level, however, there are internal isomorphic pressures to gain internal legitimacy and hence a tendency to apply parent company practices rather than local practices. Such a tendency is driven by corporate culture, values and administrative heritage stemming from the MNCs' home institutional context (Kidger, 1991; DiMaggio and Powell, 1983).

As a result, it is argued that whether MNCs adapt their HRM practices to local contexts depends on the relative ease of diffusing and managing a standard practice across borders, and the extent to which that standard practice is important and is considered a fundamental organisational value to the MNC (Björkman and Levrik, 2007; Mellahi et al., 2013). The strength of the local cultural and institutional framework in the host country do cause a change in the practice transferred. For example, if a practice is not consistent with the host country's cognitive institutions (i.e., people's shared social knowledge and models for interpreting reality), subsidiary employees are likely to have difficulty in interpreting and judging the practice correctly, and hence the transfer will be impeded. For example, ALHussan et al. (2014) found that subsidiaries in Jordan had to adapt some of the training programmes as local staff did not understand the content and the practices were culturally different.

Mellahi et al. (2013), in their empirical study of HRM practices adopted in MNCs' subsidiaries and local firms in Turkey, found significant differences between MNC subsidiaries located in Turkey and domestic Turkish firms in relation to the following practices: competence-based performance appraisal, performance-based compensation, employee empowerment, and the strategic emphasis placed on the HRM department. These differences highlight the importance of the cultural and institutional factors as determinants of the nature of HRM practices in local firms.

However, the researchers found some evidence of convergence with regard to specific aspects of HRM practices and the emergence of an established set of best practices among MNCs as reflected in the relative similarities in the practices adopted by subsidiaries from different countries of origin. On the other hand, the results indicate that some practices were adapted to the local context as they were posited to be difficult to diffuse and required sensitivity to local institutional pressures. These practices were employee training, merit-based promotion and internal communication.

Industrial- and organisational-level factors

In addition to country-level factors expressed in terms of the institutional and cultural factors of both home and host country, a number of other factors can also potentially act to shape the HRM policies and practices in a MNC subsidiary and explain patterns of cross-national transfer within MNCs. At the industry level, Porter (1986, 1998) noted that industries vary along a spectrum of multi-domestic to global industry in their international competition.

Porter further notes that where competition is highly internationalised, MNCs attempt to 'capture the linkages across borders', through increased coordination and control and through adopting HRM practices that are more consistent with the parent company/ best practices. In contrast, where competition is largely local or national, the MNC will make little attempt to generate linkages between operations in different countries and will have a relatively greater need to gain local legitimacy. In terms of HRM, this implies a tendency to adapt HRM practices to the local practices to be more responsive to the host environment.

At the organisational level, a variety of factors have been identified. One factor is the international business strategy and structure, which are related to the industry sector. The second factor is the MNC's administrative heritage, which is shaped by the founders' or strong leaders' norms and values, the home country socio-cultural system and the internationalisation history of the firm. For example, research evidence shows that top management beliefs about the strategic role of the subsidiary and the generalisability of a firm's HRM practices have strong influences on the transfer of HRM practices across borders (e.g., AL-Husan and James, 2009).

The third factor relates to the subsidiary's nature and strategic role. Evidence suggests that in a 'greenfield' subsidiary, HR and industrial relations issues tend to be more centralised since the MNC has more scope to be innovative and to introduce country of origin practices (Ferner, 1994; Hamill, 1984). In contrast, if the subsidiary is created by taking over an already existing local firm, through an acquisition or joint venture, labour issues will be more likely to be decentralised and local management will maintain a considerable degree of autonomy, as the MNC will be more constrained by pre-existing practices and organisational culture (Hamill, 1984). Therefore, the new firm will, at least initially, continue to apply many local practices (Tayeb, 1998; Edwards, 1998).

It also appears that the location of the subsidiary tends to influence the choice of strategy. Evidence suggests that MNCs tend to exert more control in developing countries, where there is lack of qualified and experienced host country nationals (HCNs), and where subsidiaries have lower operational integration with the total MNC operations (Welch, 1994). Evidence further shows that the higher the dependence of the subsidiary on the parent for financial resources and/or the weaker its financial performance, the more likely that the parent company will be heavily involved in the subsidiaries operations. In addition, smaller, younger and less experienced subsidiaries tend to be subject to more centralised control than their older counterparts (Dunning, 1993). For example, Rosenzweig and Nohria (1994), in their study of HRM practices in 294 US affiliates, concluded that MNCs tend to decentralise the management of labour in subsidiaries which depend more on the local environment rather than on the centre for inputs, such as raw materials and intermediate parts.

Finally, the strategic role of the subsidiary, defined in terms of the amount and direction of the resource flow between the subsidiary and the rest of the corporation, has also been found to influence the HRM strategies and policies of MNCs (Tregaskis and Brewster, 2001). Gupta and Govindarajan (1991) distinguish four types of subsidiary roles based on knowledge flows: (1) global innovator, with high outflow of resources to the rest of the organisation and low inflow of resources to the subsidiary; (2) integrated player, with high outflow and high inflow; (3) implementer, with low outflow and high inflow; and (4) local innovator, with low outflow and low inflow.

It is argued that as the resource flows between the parent company and the subsidiaries increase, the resource dependence and hence the need for control will increase (Ferner, 2000; Bartlett and Ghoshal, 1989, 1998). Accordingly, global innovators and integrated players will be subject to higher levels of control from the parent company and serious attempts to transfer HRM to them. In contrast, the 'implementer' and 'local innovator' subsidiaries, with a limited role in non-strategic environments, are more likely to be subject to lower control and fewer attempts to transfer HRM practices to them.

HRM-specific level

Evidence shows that in the same subsidiary, some HRM management practices might closely resemble parent company ones, while others may more resemble those of the host country. This is due to the fact that some practices are more sensitive to the local cultural and institutional influences than others. For example, Nakhle (2011) found in his research of MNCs' subsidiaries in Lebanon that the socio-cultural impact on practices studied varied according to the specific practice as it was more evident in some practices (code of conduct, recruitment and selection, performance appraisal) than other practices (training and development, compensation and benefits). He also found that the HR practices were not adapted with the same intensity, as adaptation intensity has varied even within the same practice according to the importance of the practice strategically to the MNC and to the employee targeted by the practice.

In a similar vein, a study undertaken by Yahiaoui (2007) about the transfer of HR practices from French MNCs to their subsidiaries in Tunisia show that certain practices are strongly hybridised or unilaterally transferred such as career management. Others are neutral or insensitive and are either moderately transferred or moderately hybridised such as compensation or recruitment. Chebbi et al. (2013) note that hybridisation is not simple adaptation to the local environment, but rather an organisational practice stemming from the interaction of two or more actors in a given context, and is based on activities of successive adjustment to the initial model from headquarters and the subsidiaries and leading to the joint construction of a final hybrid practice.

In summary, engaging with the literature and research evidence indicates that the degree to which transferred practices are standardised or adapted is the result of the interplay of a number of factors, as demonstrated above, and their relative weight. For example, a study into the transferability of HRM practices in joint ventures based in Iran by Namazie (2003), found that ownership and control of critical resources, the compatibility of national culture, socio-cultural differences, mutual trust and respect between partners and the compatibility of management styles were the most important factors that influenced the transfer of HRM practices and the degree to which HRM practices were standardised or localised.

Research also indicates that not all practices are subject to the same strength of influence as some practices may be more sensitive to pressures of local adaptation, while others may be more prone to internal consistency and hence will be transferred due to their universal nature (Rosezweig and Nohria, 1994; Kostova and Zaheer, 1999; Björkman and Levrik, 2007).

Furthermore, evidence reveals that the interaction of these factors may also result in hybrid practices implemented at the subsidiaries. Hence, it is argued that it is important to allocate more resources to understand isomorphic needs through analysing the reactions of different stakeholders in the subsidiaries and through interacting with local management and involving them in co-decision making between the headquarters and the subsidiaries.

MULTINATIONAL INTEGRATION AND TRANSFER MECHANISMS

Research evidence suggests that MNCs can successfully influence the integration of individuals' specialised knowledge and transfer of intra- and inter-unit knowledge by the deployment of a range organisational coordination and control mechanisms to varying extents to achieve the desired level of global consistency and local responsiveness without sacrificing the firm's core competence (Björkman et al., 2004; Yamin and Otto, 2004; Yan and Child, 2004; Le, 2009; Smale, 2008).

Global integration, which is considered mandatory rather than discretionary for MNCs facing increased global competition (Porter, 1986; Yip, 1992), is achieved only through the use of organisational mechanisms for coordination and control across borders. Coordination involves developing linkages between dispersed units of the MNC to achieve a collective goal, while control concerns influencing the behaviour and output of these units through various means to align them with the expectations set in targets. Integration has been classified by Kim et al. (2003) and Smale (2008) into centralisation-based integration, people-based integration, formalisation-based integration and information-based integration.

As for control, using Harzing (1999) classification, control mechanisms can be divided into personal centralised control, control by socialisation and networks, bureaucratic formalised control, and output control. The first two are considered to be personal types of control while the last two are indirect and impersonal. Personal centralised control involves decision making at the MNC headquarters and the enforcement of these corporate decisions and policies by expatriates assigned, often, to key positions in the subsidiaries. This contributes to centralisation integration.

Control by socialisation and networks involves creating shared organisational vision, values and norms, building trust among members and forming networks of communication channels that supplement formal hierarchy. This type of cultural control is founded on social interaction between parent company and subsidiary personnel and, hence, is used to achieve 'people-based integration' through such means as the transfer of managers, meetings, teams, training, committees, task forces and integrators. This mode is likely to be most effective in situations where information and knowledge are best conveyed face to face, as in the Middle East which is characterised by a collectivist culture, and in which business relationships are personal and trust based (ALHussan and AL-Husan, 2013; Hofstede, 1980).

Bureaucratic formalised control refers to pre-specifying, mostly in a written form, the behaviour that is expected from the employees. This includes written policies and manuals, rules and regulations. Output control refers to specifying goals/results/outputs and monitoring them through reporting systems. Such control methods contribute to formalised integration.

Such control and integration mechanisms have been applied by MNCs operating in the Middle East. For example, Nakhle (2011) found that American MNCs operating in Lebanon used strict and various control mechanisms that included formalised, direct and indirect control mechanisms including information systems, reporting, compliance officers and standardised HR policies. In contrast, he found that European MNCs used less formalised control mechanisms and sometimes informal control mechanisms, with Swiss and British MNCs being stricter than French MNCs. Headquarters of American MNCs were also found to play a more active role in setting HR policies and interfering in their implementation in their subsidiaries than the European ones.

IMPEDIMENTS TO THE SUCCESSFUL TRANSFER OF HRM PRACTICES

It is widely acknowledged that knowledge is 'sticky', that is, difficult to transfer, and that the transfer can be very costly and time consuming. As mentioned above, a central argument in the literature is that the ability to transfer critical knowledge across borders, such as the knowledge embedded in strategic organisational practices, is a key characteristic of the successful MNC and is essential for enhancing firms' competitive advantage (Kostova, 1999; Szulanski, 1996).

The success of the transfer can be measured by the degree of the institutionalisation of the practice. According to Kostova (1999) institutionalisation is 'the process by which a practice achieves a taken-for-granted status at the recipient unit – a status of "this is how we do things here"' (p. 311), and it is achieved at two levels: *implementation* and *internalisation*. *Implementation* takes place when the practice is formally implemented and its rules strictly followed. *Internalisation* takes place when the employees develop a positive attitude towards the practice and attach value to it. A practice may be implemented but not internalised if employees are not satisfied with it or do not recognise its value, and hence, in such a situation, the practice is not successfully transferred.

As a result, three main elements appear to be pertinent for successful transfer. The first element involves developing distinct capabilities and certain organisational mechanisms to transfer knowledge efficiently and to overcome transfer barriers, as explained above (Björkman et al., 2004; Gooderham, 2007). The second element involves understanding the stages of the knowledge transfer process. Four stages have been proposed in the literature: initiation, implementation, ramp-up and integration. In the first stage, the knowledge gap and the type of knowledge to be transferred are identified, while the second stage involves the identification of knowledge transfer conduits based on the type of knowledge – explicit and tacit. Hence the first two stages comprise all events that lead to the decision to transfer and the actual flow of knowledge from the source to the recipient. The last two stages begin when the recipient starts utilising and internalising the transferred knowledge (Szulanski, 1996, 2000; Minbaeva et al., 2003).

The third element involves understanding the factors that are pertinent to the properties of particular policies and practices, and which facilitate or hinder transferability. Using Szulanski's (1996) eclectic model, these include the characteristics of knowledge transferred in terms of its 'tacitness' or causal ambiguity; characteristics of the sender in terms of motivation to transmit and share knowledge, and its perceived reliability; characteristics of the recipient in terms of motivation to accept knowledge, absorptive capacity and retentive capacity. Absorptive capacity denotes the ability to recognise the importance and value of externally created knowledge, acquire that knowledge, assimilate it, and use it to create value (Zahra and George, 2002).

CASE STUDY: MULTINATIONAL HRM IN JORDAN

The Hashemite Kingdom of Jordan is one of the main countries in the Middle East region that have been a major recipient of FDI. Jordan has been attractive to foreign investors due to its strategic geopolitical location; the hospitable environment to FDI and international trade (Ali, et al., 2001, p. 88); the major strides made in cooperation with the World Bank and the IMF in liberalising, privatising and deregulating the economy; and its success in the structural economic reforms made (IMF, cited in El-Said and McDonald, 2001, pp. 73–74).

Other reasons include the classification of Jordan as a front-runner country, as in 2004 Jordan was one of the five Arab countries (namely, Bahrain, Jordan, Lebanon, Qatar and the United Arab Emirates) classified as front-runners, with high FDI performance and high FDI potential, according to the UNCTAD index[7] (United Nations, 2006, p. 24); the joining of the World Trade Organization (WTO) in 2001 and the signing of a number of trade agreements with, for example, its largest trading partner the United States, Europe and other Arab countries to reinforce its globalisation plans (Anani, 2001, p. 163); the relatively developed infrastructure and relatively well-developed banking sector, with the second most important stock market in the Arab World after Kuwait (Wilson, 1991, p. 3); and the highly skilled and educated labour force (El-Said and McDonald, 2001; Ali et al., 2001; Wilson, 1998).

Indeed, because of its modest natural resources, Jordan has historically placed considerable attention on developing its human resources. An important consequence of this has been that, in the context of limited domestic employment opportunities, the country has, with government encouragement, long been an exporter of skilled technical and professional labour, particularly to other Middle Eastern states in the region (United Nations, 1994, p.142). By the mid-1980s, approximately 46 per cent of the Jordanian workforce worked outside the country (United Nations, 1994, p.142).

Privatisation in Jordan: Background

The Jordanian government's heavy involvement in development efforts, particularly from the mid-1970s to the mid-1980s, was accompanied by a substantial growth of the public sector to the point where it accounted for 35–37 per cent of GDP (Anani, 1997) and came to comprise 25 ministries with 20 central departments and 37 public corporations (Ministry of Planning, 1993). Many of the major enterprises were owned and controlled by the government besides the public utilities (e.g., water, electricity and telephone companies) and ports.

However, due to the economic crisis and deteriorating fiscal and social conditions, which started in 1983, and continued pressures from the World Bank and the IMF, in 1996 the Jordanian government announced its privatisation programme six years after it was first initiated in 1990. Privatisation was one major component of Jordan's economic structural reform programme, which was implemented under the auspices of the World Bank and the IMF. Prime aims of this privatisation programme included attracting external and foreign investment, generating foreign exchange and improving efficiency.

Overall, progress on implementing this privatisation programme, which was initiated in the early 1990s, was, however, initially very slow due to a number of factors, notably a lack of political consensus and strong central direction; fears about the negative impact of privatisation on prices and employment as the public sector constituted about 55 per cent of employment by the mid-1990s; concerns about loss of revenue and national wealth by the divestment of state-owned assets, especially those regarded as strategic; fears of foreign asset stripping and concerns that the World Bank and the IMF would act 'as agents for multinational corporations and banks'; and doubts as to whether the local financial market had sufficient capacity to absorb a comprehensive privatisation programme (Al-Khalidi, 1998; Anani, 1997).

With regard to the possible impact of privatisation on labour, this also reflected a number of distinct areas of concern. One of the most important of these was the threat of potential labour redundancies in a situation of high unemployment and against a background of the government bearing the main responsibility for employing nomadic Bedouins and people from East Bank origins – people who have traditionally provided the backbone of popular support for the Hashemite monarchy (World Bank, 1995; Al-Nabulsi, 1999). Another concerned the possible impact of privatisation on the pension entitlements of employees (World Bank, 1995).

Such political contingencies had important implications for the way in which the Jordanian government went about the privatisation of its public enterprises. In particular, to allay fears about foreign asset stripping and loss of control over strategic national assets, the government decided to impose conditions on foreign investors that would enable the government to keep control over broad decisions that could harm national interests and at the same time achieve its privatisation objectives. These included holding a golden share, the training of employees, restricting lay-offs at least for the first two years, transferring know-how, increasing the efficiency and productivity of the privatised firms, and introducing modern Western management techniques.

The privatisation programme was implemented in two phases: the first phase included eight major transactions which included Jordan Cement Company (Cement Co), Jordan Telecommunication Company (JTC) (Telecom Co) and Jordan Water Company (Water Co). The first breakthrough in the privatisation programme took place with the successful privatisation of Jordan Cement Company in December 1998. The success of this deal, involving, as it did, a foreign company, helped overcome fears about passing control to overseas investors and hence facilitated the subsequent progress of the privatisation programme.

Three Case Illustrations

In this section we examine evidence from three privatised companies that were taken over by three French MNCs in the first phase of privatisation, namely: Cement Co, Telecom Co, and Water Co. The evidence covers the following issues: HR structure and role, the HRM practices transferred, factors influencing the transfer of HR practices, transfer mechanisms and the nature of the transfer facilitators and impediments.

Cement Co

Cement Co was established in 1951. The government owned 58 per cent of equity shares and the company employed 2,600 people. In December 1998 the company was the first to be privatised through the sale of government shares to a French MNC. Operational control by the MNC was obtained through the purchase of a minority shareholding of initially 33 per cent, which was gradually increased to reach 50.2 per cent in 2008. The MNC also became a strategic partner through the signing up of a two-year technical agreement with the government that incorporated the transfer and sharing of know-how and the training of staff. The French MNC was founded in France in 1933 and has a high level of international experience as it began its international growth in 1914.

Telecom Co

Telecom Co was a state department holding a monopoly in the telecommunication industry, registered in 1977 as a public shareholding company owned by the Jordanian government with around 4,900 employees. In 2000, the company was privatised, and operational control was obtained by the new strategic partner through, initially, the purchase of 35.2 per cent of equity shares by a consortium led by the French MNC and a five-year management contract to transfer know-how and improve performance. In 2008, the MNC became the company's main stockholder of Telecom Co with 51 per cent of shares. This MNC has a comparatively lower level of international experience having started its internationalisation process in 1997.

Water Co

Water Co was privatised through the award of a four-year management contract to a consortium led by the French MNC, extended to a fifth year, to manage the distribution of water and wastewater treatment for the city of Amman and its outskirts. In return for a fixed annual fee and additional performance-related payments, paid from a World Bank loan, the MNC's task was to improve the company's performance and transfer of know-how, while the government retained ownership and ultimate strategic control. The French MNC is the world's leading water treatment company that began its international expansion in 1914.

HRM Policies and Practices

After privatisation, and as highlighted by AL-Husan and James (2009), the main changes introduced by the MNCs in the three Jordanian companies consisted of both major revisions to the structure and role of the HRM function and considerable reforms in a number of specific areas of HR practice.

The HR function and role

The findings obtained revealed that before privatisation the personnel function in the public sector enterprises in Jordan had mainly an administrative role that was reactive and focused on personnel matters, and with centralised bureaucratic structures and systems. However, after privatisation and the takeover by the French MNCs, significant changes were made and HRM was placed to the forefront in expressly stated 'modernisation' initiatives, including enhancing the contribution of the HR function itself.

More generally, new HR functions had been created and these given a more strategic role as a business partner and as a change agent. The process was demonstrated by the appointment of directors to head these functions who were made members of the executive committee or board responsible for the day-to-day running of the company. At the same time, action had been taken to devolve greater HR responsibilities down to line managers as part of organisational restructurings which aimed to reduce hierarchical levels, simplify management structures, and increase the responsibility and direct accountability of managers in the acquired companies. As a change agent, the HR function was involved in ensuring that the companies in Jordan had the capacity for change by introducing both structural and cultural reforms. For example, the training activities in the companies focused not only on the provision of technical skills but also on supporting the broader process of cultural reform.

Reforms of HRM policies

The findings show that the changes introduced by the three MNCs in the area of HRM policies were remarkably similar. Minor differences existed in terms of periphery details and in the implementation. The investigation included each of the specific areas of HR activity related to staffing; recruitment and election; performance appraisal, training development; rewards; and communication and employee participation. In summary, the changes introduced included the following:

- extensive use of both long-term and short-term expatriate appointments, with a number of the former being appointed to senior management positions;
- the establishment of recruitment and selection criteria which stressed the need for candidates to possess relevant qualifications and competencies, and facilitated the identification of high potentials;
- development of a new objectives-based appraisal scheme which encouraged a greater emphasis on the identification of training and development needs and was linked to an individual performance-related pay system;
- the raising of salary levels and the introduction of a variable bonus scheme based on company performance;
- promotion based on merit, and priority to internal promotions – thus, moving from seniority-based promotion and patronage promotion;
- a significant increase in training expenditure and activities that encompassed a much greater use of overseas, as well as locally based training, the training being focused on all levels but with more emphasis on high potentials and managerial levels;
- the introduction of better systems of both upward and downward internal communication.

Hence, as shown above, at the core, the policies were very similar, but there were some variations in the application of these policies in practice and in the periphery details. For example, the three companies introduced performance-related pay and appraisal of performance against set targets. Different ratings were given for different performance. Limits were also placed on the percentage of staff getting top ratings. However, the actual percentages given for each performance rating were different among the companies.

Factors shaping the transferred HRM practices

A number of interrelated factors influenced the transfer of HRM practices and the degree to which they resembled parent company practices. The most important factors that shaped the HRM practices are institutional and cultural factors, top management beliefs, industry sector, entry mode and strategic role of the subsidiary.

In terms of institutional and cultural factors, the host country played a dual role. On the one hand the Jordanian government's and the World Bank's desire to apply modern HRM practices facilitated the introduction of Western HRM practices. On the other hand, some restrictions were laid down by the government, which imposed short-term adaptations. These included, for example, the restrictions placed by the government on the pay allowances and incentives provided to employees and on the amount of maximum salaries offered to new employees at Water Co. It was a condition by the government to employ two local senior managers in the executive committee at Telecom Co. and not lay off employees for two years. Similarly, at Cement Co. employees were not to be laid off for two years. All companies were required to provide training to the employees and to develop local managers, particularly in Water Co., as local managers were to take over the positions by the end of the management contract. The trade union at Cement Co. was able to influence some of the policies, particularly those related to appraisal, pay and bonuses provided.

The industry sector and related strategy influenced the degree to which the MNCs were seeking to integrate their operations and hence the extent of similarity between the parent and subsidiary practices. Thus, in Cement Co., which was pursuing a global strategy and integration of its operations, company-wide policies were implemented. Water Co. and Telecom Co., which were pursuing more multi-domestic strategies, gave more autonomy to their subsidiaries, but kept the core policies similar. For example, all subsidiaries were supposed to apply performance-related pay, as a core policy. However, subsidiaries had more freedom in the way they applied the policy.

The subsidiary characteristics including mode of entry and strategic role were an important influence. Hence, with brownfield modes such as mergers and acquisitions, joint ventures and management contracts, there were restrictions on how the practices were applied, with some degree of resistance. However, the strategic role of the subsidiaries, on the one hand, was pushing for internal consistency to maintain worldwide standards and reputation. At the same time, a desire to maintain an amicable relationship with the government and to gain legitimacy led to some concessions and adaptations.

Transfer mechanisms

The results show that the three MNCs utilised the four methods of control mechanisms distinguished by Harzing (1999) and integration mechanisms, but they differed with regard to the emphasis placed on them. For example, in the companies that relied less on formalised control and integration mechanisms, such as Water Co, there was heavy utilisation of 'personalised central control' through the existence of a larger number of expatriates in key positions. Lack of direct involvement of the parent company and corporate HR was compensated for by the physical presence of corporate staff that personally transferred parent company practices and monitored compliance with the outcomes of 'top-level' decision making. Similarly, Telecom Co relied more on the presence of expatriates in key managerial positions and in the Board.

In contrast, Cement Co, which utilised more formalised bureaucratic control and had direct involvement of corporate HR, and was seeking to integrate its operations globally, placed more emphasis on 'informal' control via socialisation and the creation of information networks through such means as the provision of extensive training and interactions between local- and corporate-level managerial personnel. Overall, in the three companies expatriates were found to be not only the main channel to transfer HRM practices and knowledge, but also an important channel to develop local managers and talent.

HRM transfer: enablers and constraints

The findings of the case studies indicate that a number of factors influenced the extent to which the HRM practices were easy or difficult to transfer to the Jordanian context. The first factor was pertinent to each of the parent company's ability to transfer the desired HRM practices. Each of the MNCs had a motive to transfer the HRM practices in line with their agreements with the Jordanian government and their wider objectives in the region. However, they differed in terms of their ability to transfer these practices, which had implications for the success of the transfer.

The ability to transfer was linked to the international experience of the MNC, its knowledge about the Middle East region, its culture and institutional framework, the extent of support provided by corporate HR, and the presence of parent company HR specialists at the subsidiaries during the design and implementation process. Thus, for example, the presence of the expatriate British HR director at Water Co and the presence of the Middle East regional HRM director at Cement Co to oversee the design and implementation of the HRM policies made it much easier to implement the new HR policies in the two companies. These expatriate managers were available to communicate with local staff and explain issues that were difficult to understand. Their long international experience in transferring practices to different subsidiaries also facilitated the process.

The second factor was linked to causal ambiguity, subsidiary motivation and capacity to learn. It was found that an important obstacle to the transfer of HR policies and practices was the subsidiaries' lack of knowledge of HRM, as this was a new concept to be applied in the subsidiaries. However, this difficulty was overcome when the MNC was actively involved in transferring the know-how through dedicating resources and specialised personnel from the parent company to assist the subsidiary and local staff in understanding and implementing the new policies. The findings also show that the practices were successfully transferred when they were internalised by the employees, who were made to realise and feel the benefits of the new policies in terms of, for example, the implementation of fair appraisal policies and the upgrading of their skills and knowledge through training and development.

The third factor was linked to issues of trust, cultural distance and communication. The findings show that lack of trust and cultural misunderstandings between local staff and corporate staff minimised the open flow of information and reduced learning opportunities. This, in turn, affected the success of the transfer of the desired HRM practices. For example, it was difficult for some expatriate managers to understand the behaviour of local staff and how to obtain the right information in a face saving and shame culture in which it is difficult for employees to speak and express their views openly so as not to appear to be opposing seniors. Corporate staff's inability to build trust and open communication made it more difficult for local staff to share information, which affected the success of the transfer.

In conclusion, the study shows that it is feasible to transfer Western HRM practices to Middle Eastern countries. However, some practices are more difficult to transfer and hence need to be adapted to facilitate its transfer. The political will supports the transfer of Western HRM practices and gives it the legitimacy required. The findings also confirm that there is some convergence in MNCs' HRM practices on the Anglo-Saxon model (e.g., Pudelko and Harzing, 2007). The interaction between the external factors and internal factors determine the final shape of HRM practices. Lastly, due to cultural and institutional distance, it is vital that the subsidiaries appoint HR expatriates not only with appropriate knowledge and experiences, but also with appropriate coaching skills for sharing and transferring knowledge. It is equally important that the local personnel with appropriate background in HR knowledge and learning skills are selected.

KEY CHALLENGES AND FUTURE DIRECTIONS

The distinctive political, social, economic and cultural forces of the Middle East represent unique challenges and opportunities for both indigenous and foreign MNCs. The greatest challenge facing governments across the Middle East region is unemployment, particularly youth unemployment, which is becoming a main cause of political and social instability in the region as witnessed by the Arab Spring, which was spearheaded by educated young people with no job prospects in their home countries. For example, over 30 per cent of those with tertiary education were unemployed in Egypt, Tunisia and Jordan in 2011 and 2012 (World Bank, 2014).

Smaller, richer countries like Qatar, Kuwait and the United Arab Emirates used oil revenues to spend their way out and as a buffer against related unrest by increasing wages, offering public sector employment and spending to meet social demands. But for MENA's non-oil producers, spending their way out is not an option as they suffer from insecurity and falling budget revenues from tourism, remittances and exports; deteriorating fiscal balances; and increased debts. Hence, these countries have become dependent on foreign investment more than ever to help fund job creation and improve productivity.

Overall, the unprecedented opportunity for political reform in the MENA region needs to be accompanied by further transparent economic reforms to deal with the interdependent structural challenges faced by many countries in the region such as high unemployment, low levels of private sector development, pervasive corruption, cronyism, weak public and corporate governance, bloated public sectors and limited competition (O'Sullivan et al., 2011). The changes in the region are envisaged to provide great investment opportunities for MNCs and investors. However, the lesson learned from the recent experience is that FDI policies must aim at different goals, as investments must generate jobs and employment opportunities. They also need to focus on developing the human capital necessary to increase the host countries' capacity to benefit from FDI. This poses a number of challenges for host governments, foreign investors/MNCs, and HR functions.

More specifically, the main challenge faced by MNCs resides in their need to align their objectives with the host countries' wider political, social and development objectives. For oil-rich GCC countries, for example, the first challenge faced by foreign investors and MNCs is the localisation or labour nationalisation policies of these countries to replace foreign workers with nationals. They also face the challenge of keeping up with the varying quota regulations and levels of enforcement. For instance, in Qatar, firms must report their percentage of Qataris every six months and must train Qataris if they employ certain foreign technical specialists. In Saudi Arabia, the introduction of new laws, such as '*Nitaqat*', poses a limit on the number of foreign workers that companies can hire, and non-compliance can result in a number of restrictions on the companies, such as limitations on issuing or renewing visas for expatriate workers, while compliant ones benefit from an expedited hiring (United Nations, 2013).

Such policies further represent challenges in a number of ways as firms face structural and cultural issues that make it difficult for them to hire and retain local employees. First, with such localisation policies of the GCC countries, foreign firms face great challenges in hiring and retaining local employees as many locals look first to government jobs that offer higher salaries, job security, benefits and prestige, which reduces the demand for private sector jobs. Second, the types of jobs experiencing steady growth – such as those in services, construction and trade – are unappealing to nationals, while there is a dearth of suitably qualified graduates for more highly skilled jobs. Third, national labour is less attractive than expatriate labour as it is more expensive, less skilled and less flexible.

Fourth, the growth of traditional sectors, such as energy, is already causing severe talent shortages at all managerial levels. The situation is worsening with the new diversification strategies adopted by many GCC countries in the region that seek to address rising youth unemployment and social tension and to reduce dependence on the oil sector by developing non-energy industries. However, while many of these countries are creating and implementing programmes to develop the skills of local citizens in order to meet this need for talent, the relatively small number of local nationals limits the impact of these programmes. Hence, there are concerns about the lack of sufficient talent or skills within the local population to take on some highly specialised jobs. This is another challenge as foreign investors are particularly keen to ensure that they can employ immigrant labour and hire managers from around the world in order to have a workforce with the appropriate skills and experience.

Another challenge stems from the shortage of talent in the Middle East in general. More recently, this shortage has been exacerbated by the 'Arab Spring' that led to a new wave of brain drain from the Arab Spring countries like Tunisia, Egypt, Syria, Libya and Yemen as well as other neighbouring countries in the region that were also negatively affected by the events like Jordan and Lebanon. More generally, talent management is critically important to companies operating in the Middle East because of the significant opportunities and challenges these organisations face today. Due to the shortage of this talent, MNCs often compete with one another. Therefore the HR function in these companies faces the challenge of deeply understanding local practices and expectations and of working differently to attract and retain high-potential employees by offering such things as more choice in their compensation and benefits packages, career development, learning opportunities and interaction opportunities with their leaders. The focus will be on developing a cadre of high potentials who can be deployed in regional and global operations.

For localisation policies to work, fundamental changes in the capabilities and attitudes of many local citizens are needed to achieve the desired transformation in the GCC economies. HR in MNCs can play an important role in changing these attitudes by developing the local employees to have the right skills to qualify them for working in specialised jobs, and by playing a more active role in these localisation policies by taking part in the planning with the governments.

In general, as HRM is still in the early stages in many countries in the region, MNCs and other external investors may be challenged with the lack of availability of specialised HR managers. Therefore, one of the tasks of MNCs is to develop a new breed of local HR managers with the right knowledge and competencies to help in developing more efficient HRM systems to improve the performance of local companies.

The current on-going transition towards more democracy in the Middle East is expediting the dramatic transformation in the economic scene. The privatisation of SOEs is gaining momentum in the region and is expected to rise significantly in the coming years, as governments in the region are becoming increasingly aware of the societal benefits of transparency, accountability, competitive markets and independent regulation. The challenge is to make them successful privatisation programmes. This may be achieved by not focusing on head count reduction as happened in the past, but on developing human capital, transferring know-how, and taking into consideration the wider public interests. In the HR domain, where foreign investors are involved, the inflow of capital must be used to develop local talent and managerial competencies, implement modern HRM systems that treat employees as assets and preserve their rights, and transfer know-how.

For Middle Eastern governments and foreign companies eyeing the emerging opportunities in the region, they need to learn from past experience of privatisation in the region and elsewhere, but with a mindful and sensitive approach to two fundamental considerations: the country-specific drivers of privatisation; and the local context such as the country's particular political, social, economic and legal characteristics. To respond to people's needs in the region, more regulation is required, not less, to attract the right kind of investment, including performance requirements to ensure incoming investment contributes to local economies and domestic development.

Finally, one needs to consider the HRM implications of the changing trends as FDI trends indicate that the BRICS (Brazil, Russia, India, China and South Africa) are bound to become economically more important in the region in the future. As pointed out by Alessandrini (2012), there are signals in the economic agreements and bilateral contacts that the region seeks to reduce dependence on European countries and that it is interested in attracting more Gulf (in Morocco and Jordan) or Brazilian and Chinese investment (in Morocco, Egypt and Algeria).

NOTES

1. Developing Countries (Least Developed Countries): according to the World Bank classification, countries with low or middle levels of gross national income (GNI) per capita.
   For the current (at the time of writing) 2016 fiscal year, low-income economies are defined as those with a GNI per capita of US$1,045 or less in 2014; middle-income economies are those with a GNI per capita of more than US$1,045 but less than US$12,736; high-income economies are those with a GNI per capita of US$12,736 or more (http://data.worldbank.org/about/country-and-lending-groups). The World Bank also notes that the term *developing* used to denote all low- and middle-income countries in this context does not imply that all economies in the group are experiencing similar levels of development or that other economies have reached a preferred or final stage of development.

2. Emerging economies (Emerging markets): countries that are in the growth stage of their development cycle and have low to middle per capita incomes (Mobius, 2012). Although the terms developing and emerging are used interchangeably, it is noted that not all developing countries can be characterised as emerging. Only those that have started an economic reform process aimed at alleviating problems such as poor infrastructure and overpopulation, achieved a steady growth in gross national product (GNP) per capita, and increased integration in the global economy, may truly be called emerging economies (Cavusgil et al., 2012).
3. Transition economies (transition markets): countries moving from centrally planned to market-oriented economies, e.g. China, Russia.
4. Developed countries (industrial countries, industrially advanced countries): according to the World Bank are high-income countries in which most people have a high standard of living. Sometimes also defined as countries with a large stock of physical capital, in which most people undertake highly specialised activities (Soubbotina, 2004).
5. MENA countries can be grouped into three groups. First, the GCC (Gulf Cooperation Council) group is composed of natural-resource-rich, labour-importing countries: Bahrain, Kuwait, Oman, Saudi Arabia, the United Arab Emirates and Qatar. Second, the non-GCC group comprises natural-resource-rich, labour-abundant countries such as Algeria, Iraq, Libya and Syria. Third, the emerging group comprises natural-resource-poor countries such as Egypt, Jordan, Morocco and Tunisia. For additional comparison, a fourth non-Arab group is also included, namely other natural-resource-rich countries comprising Iran and Turkey.
6. Isomorphism is the extent to which organisations adopt the same structures and processes as other organisations within their environment (Zucker, 1977).
7. Comparing their inward FDI potential and performance using the UNCTAD indices, countries in the world can be divided into the following four categories: front-runners (countries with high FDI potential and performance); above potential (countries with low FDI potential but strong FDI performance); below potential (countries with high FDI potential but low FDI performance); and underperformers (countries with both low FDI potential and low FDI performance).

USEFUL WEBSITES

CIPD Resources on the Middle East: http://www.cipd.co.uk/global/middle-east/.
Middle East Review of International Affairs: http://meria.idc.ac.il.
Arab Monetary Fund: www.amf.org.ae.
The Egyptian Center for Economic Studies (ECES): http://www.eces.org.eg/.
Economic Research Forum: http://www.erf.org.eg/.
UN Conference on Trade and Development FDI Country Report: http://www.unctad.org/.
UNDP Human Development Report: http://hdr.undp.org/.
World Bank Doing Business: www.doingbusiness.org/economyrankings/.
World Bank's Website site on The Middle East and North Africa: http://www.worldbank.org/en/region/mena.
Middle East Economic Association: http://meeaweb.org/.
UN Economic and Social Commission for West Asia: http://www.escwa.un.org/.
The World Bank MENA Quarterly Economic Brief: http://www.worldbank.org/en/region/mena/publication/mena-quarterly-economic-brief.
Middle East Economic Survey (MEES): http://www.mees.com.
Middle East Economic Digest: http://www.meed.com/.
Zawya: http://www.zawya.com/.
Publication by DLA Piper: Top Employment Issues in the Middle East: http://www.dlapiper.com/en/africa/insights/publications/2014/08/top-employment-issues-in-the-middle-east/.
Topics in Middle Eastern and African Economies: http://www.luc.edu/orgs/meea/.
Transnational Corporations Journal: www.unctad.org/tnc.

REFERENCES

Abed, G.T. 2003. Unfulfilled promise: why the Middle East and North Africa region has lagged in growth and globalization. *Finance and Development*, **40**(1): 1–11.

Abed, G.T., Iradian, G., Hedley, D. and Zouk, N. 2011. *Voltairenet.* http://www.voltairenet.org/IMG/pdf/The_Arab_World_in_Transition.pdf (accessed 14 August 2014).

Akoum, I. 2012. The political economy of SOE privatization and governance reform in the MENA region. *International Scholarly Research Notices Economics*, pp. 1–9.
Alessandrini, S. 2012. Foreign direct investments (FDI) to the Middle East and North Africa region: short- and medium-term developments. Policy Brief, The German Marshall Fund of the United States.
AL-Husan, F.B. and James, P. 2003. Cultural control and multinationals: the case of privatized Jordanian companies. *International Journal of Human Resource Management*, **17**(4): 1284–1295.
AL-Husan, F.B. and James, P. 2009. Multinationals and the process of post-entry HRM reform: evidence from three Jordanian case studies. *European Management Journal*, **27**(2): 142–154.
ALHussan, F.B. and AL-Husan, F.B. 2013. The nature of Arab business environment and its implications for industrial marketing and business relationships. In G. Ogunmokun and R. Gabby (eds), *Marketing, Management and International Business Theory and Practice: Contemporary Issues and Research in Selected Countries*. Perth: Global Publishing House, pp. 41–62.
ALHussan, F.B., AL-Husan, F.B. and Fletcher-Chen, C. 2014. Environmental factors influencing the management of key accounts in an Arab Middle Eastern context. *Industrial Marketing Management*, **43**(4): 592–602.
Ali, A.J., Becker, K. and Taiani, V. 2001. Import orientations for Jordanian-based companies. In H. El-Said and K. Becker (eds), *Management and International Business Issues in Jordan*. New York: The Haworth Press, pp. 85–103.
Al-Khalidi, S. 1998. Jordan energises privatisation drive. http://www.access2arabia.com/jordantimes/Sat/economy/economy5.htm (accessed 29 October 1998).
Al-Nabulsi, M.S. 1999. Privatisation in Jordan between success and failure: the urgent need for a legal framework. *Privatization News*.
Anani, A. 1997. Windows over privatization. Amman, Institute of Banking Studies (Jordan) in cooperation with the Islamic Institute of research and training (Saudi Arabia).
Anani, J. 2001. The political sociology of Jordan: an analysis for the map of gains and pains. In H. El-Said and K. Becker (eds), *Management and International Business Issues in Jordan*. New York: The Haworth Press, pp. 163–194.
Arab Times 2014. Privatization best to cut inefficiencies GCC amidst fundamental paradigm shift in healthcare. https://www.arabtimesonline.com/Newsdetails/tabid/96/smid/414/articleid/1153490/reftab/96/t/privatization-best-to-inefficiencies/default.aspx (accessed 9 October 2014).
Bamberger, P. and Meshoulam, I. 2000. *Human Resource Strategy: Formulation, Implementation, and Impact*. London: Sage.
Bartlett, C. and Ghoshal, S. 1989. *Managing across Borders: The Transnational Solution*. Boston, MA: Harvard Business School Press.
Bartlett, C. and Ghoshal, S. 1998. *Managing across Borders: The Transnational Solution*. 2nd edn, London: Random House.
Beinin, J. 1999. *The Working Class and Peasantry in the Middle East: From Economic Nationalism to Neoliberalism*. Stanford: Middle East Report.
Björkman, I., Barner-Rasmussen, W. and Li, L. 2004. Managing knowledge transfer in MNCs: the impact of headquarters control mechanisms. *Journal of International Business Studies*, **35**(5): 443–455.
Björkman, I. and Lervik, J.E. 2007. Transferring HRM practices within multinational. *Human Resource Management Journal*, **17**(4): 320–335.
Borensztein, E., De Gregorio, J. and Lee, J.-W. 1998. How does foreign direct investment affect economic growth? *Journal of International Economics*, **45**: 115–135.
Buckley, P.J. and Casson, M. 1991. Multinational enterprises in less developed countries: cultural and economic interactions. In P. Buckley and J. Clegg (eds), *Multinational Enterprises in Less Developed Countries*. London: Palgrave Macmillan, pp. 27–55.
Budhwar, P.S. and Mellahi, K. 2006. Introduction. In P.S. Budhwar and K. Mellahi (eds), *Managing Human Resources in the Middle East*. Oxford: Routledge, pp. 1–19.
Cavusgil, T.S., Ghauri, P.N. and Akcal, A.A., 2012. *Doing Business in Emerging Markets: Entry and Negotiation Strategies*. 2nd edn. London: Sage.
Chan, K.K. and Gemayel, E.R. 2004. *Risk Instability and the Pattern of Foreign Direct Investment in the Middle East and North Africa Region*. Washington, DC: International Monetary Fund.
Chauvin, N.M. 2013. FDI flows in the MENA region: features and impacts. *IEMS Emerging Market Brief*, **13**(1): 1–24.
Chebbi, H., Yahiaoui, D., Vrontis, D. and Thrassou, A. 2013. Knowledge hybridization: an innovative business practices to overcome the limits of the top-down transfers within a multinational corporation. In D. Vrontis and A. Thrassou (eds), *Innovative Business Practices: Prevailing a Turbulent Era*. Newcastle upon Tyne, UK: Cambridge Scholars Publishing, pp. 1–16.
Child, J. 2000. Theorizing about organization cross-nationally. *Advances in International Comparative Management*, **13**: 27–75.
Child, J. 2002. A configurational analysis of international joint ventures. *Organization Studies*, **23**(5): 781–815.

Demirbag, M., Tatoglu, E. and Glaister, K.W. 2008. Factors affecting perceptions of the choice between acquisition and green field entry: the case of Western FDI in an emerging market. *Management International Review*, **48**(1): 5–38.
Dicken, P. 2003. *Global Shift: Reshaping the Global Economic Map in the 21st Century*, 4th edn. London: Sage.
DiMaggio, P. and Powell, W.W. 1983. The iron cage revisited: institutional isomorphism and collective rationality in organizational fields. *American Sociological Review*, **48**(2): 147–160.
Dunning, J.H. 1993. *The Globalization of Business: The Challenge of the 1990s*. London: Routledge.
Edwards, T. 1998. *Multinational Companies and the Diffusion of Employment Practices: A Survey of the Literature*. Coventry, UK: Coventry University.
El Sayed, L. 2011. Determinants of FDI inflows to the MENA region: macroeconomic and institutional factors. Frankfurt, Finance and Economic Conference.
El-Said, H. and McDonald, F. 2001. Institutions and joint ventures in the Middle East and North Africa: the case of Jordan. *Journal of Transnational Management Development*, **6**(1–2): 65–84.
Evans, P., Pucik, V. and Björkman, I. 2011. *The Global Challenge: International Human Resource Management*, 2nd edn. New York: McGraw-Hill/Irwin.
Ferner, A. 1994. Multinational companies and human resource management: an overview of research issues. *Human Resource Management Journal*, **43**(2): 79–102.
Ferner, A. 2000. The underpinnings of bureaucratic control systems: HRM in European multinationals. *Journal of Management Studies*, **34**(7): 521–540.
George, G. 2000. Developmental financial institutions as catalysts of entrepreneurship in emerging economies. *Academy of Management Review*, **25**: 620–629.
Girma, S. 2005. Absorptive capacity and productivity spillovers from FDI: a threshold regression analysis. *Oxford Bulletin of Economics and Statistics*, **67**(3): 281–306.
Gooderham, P.N. 2007. Enhancing knowledge transfer in multinational corporations: a dynamic capabilities driven model. *Knowledge Management Research and Practice*, **5**: 34–43.
Gupta, A.K. and Govindarajan, V. 1991. Knowledge flows and structure of control within a multinational corporations. *Academy of Management Review*, **13**(4): 768–792.
Hamill, J. 1984. Labour relations decision making within multinational corporations. *Industrial Relations Journal*, **15**(2): 30–34.
Harzing, A.W. 1999. *Managing the Multinationals: An International Study of Control Mechanisms*. Cheltenham, UK and Northampton, MA: Edward Elgar.
Hofstede, G. 1980. *Culture's Consequences: International Differences in Work Related Values*. London: Sage.
Inderst, G. and Stewart, F. 2014. *Institutional Investment in Infrastructure in Emerging Markets and Developing Economies*. Washington, DC: World Bank.
International Labour Organization (ILO) 1995. *Privatization, Employment and Social Protection*. World Labour Report VIII, Geneva: International Labour Office.
Jackson, T. 2004. HRM in developing countries. In A.W. Harzing and J.V. Ruysseveldt (eds), *International Human Resource Management*, 2nd edn. London: Sage, pp. 221–248.
Khanna, T. and Palepu, K. 2000. The future of business groups in emerging markets: long-run evidence from Chile. *Academy of Management Journal*, **43**(3): 268–285.
Kidger, P.J. 1991. The emergence of international human resource management. *International Journal of Human Resource Management*, **2**: 149–163.
Kim, K., Park, J.H. and Prescott, J.E. 2003. The global integration of business functions: a study of multinational businesses in integrated global industries. *Journal of International Business Studies*, **34**(4): 327–344.
Kostova, T. 1999. Transnational transfer of strategic organizational practices: a contextual perspective. *Academy of Management Review*, **24**(2): 308–324.
Kostova, T. and Roth, K. 2002. Adoption of an organizational practice by subsidiaries of multinational corporations: institutional and relational effects. *Academy of Management Journal*, **45**(1): 215–233.
Kostova, T. and Zaheer, S. 1999. Organizational legitimacy under conditions of complexity: the case of the multinational enterprise. *Academy of Management Review*, **24**(1): 64–81.
Le, N.H. 2009. Foreign parent firm contributions, experiences and international joint venture control and performance. *International Management Review*, **5**(1): 56–69.
Marginson, P. and Sisson, K. 1994. The structure of transnational capital in Europe: the emerging Euro-company and its implications for industrial relations. In R. Hyman and A. Ferner (eds), *New frontiers in European Industrial Relations*. London: Blackwell, pp. 15–51.
Mellahi, K., Demirbag, M., Collings, D.G., Tatoglu, E. and Hughes, M. 2013. Similarly different: a comparison of HRM practices in MNE subsidiaries and local firms in Turkey. *International Journal of Human Resource Management*, **24**(12): 2339–2368.
Mellahi, K., Demirbag, M. and Riddle, L. 2011. Multinationals in the Middle East: challenges and opportunities. *Journal of World Business*, **46**: 406–410.

Mellahi, K., Guermat, C., Frynas, J.G. and Al-Bortmani, H. 2003. Motives for foreign direct investment in Oman. *Thunderbird International Business Review*, **45**(4): 431–446.
Meyer, K.E. 2004. Perspectives on multinational enterprises in emerging economies. *Journal of International Business Studies*, **34**(4): 259–277.
Minbaeva, D., Pedersen, T., Björkman, I., Fey, C.F. and Park, H.J. 2003. MNC knowledge transfer, subsidiary absorptive capacity, and HRM. *Journal of International Business Studies*, **34**: 586–599.
Ministry of Planning 1993. *Hashemite Kingdom of Jordan: Economic and Social Development Plan 1993–1997*. Amman: Jordan Press Foundation.
Mobius, M. 2012. *The Little Book of Emerging Markets: How to Make Money in the World's Fastest Growing Markets*. Singapore: Wiley.
Mohamed, S.E. and Sidiropoulos, M.G. 2010. Another look at the determinants of foreign direct investment in MENA countries: an empirical investigation. *Journal of Economic Development*, **35**(2): 75–94.
Morris, J. 2004. The future of work: organizational and international perspectives. *International Journal of Human Resource Management*. **15**: 263–275.
Nakhle, S. 2011. *The Transfer of Human Resource Practices from American and European Multinational Companies to Their Lebanese Subsidiaries: A Study of the Host-Country Effects and of the Standardization–Adaptation Dilemma*. Fribourg: University of Fribourg.
Namazie, P. 2003. Factors affecting the transferability of HRM practices in joint ventures based in Iran. *Career Development International*, **8**(7): 357–366.
North, D. 1990. *Institutions, Institutional Change and Economic Performance*. New York: Cambridge University Press.
Onyeiwu, S. 2003. *Analysis of FDI Flows to Developing Countries: Is the MENA Region Different?* Marrakech, Economic Research Forum Conference Proceedings.
O'Sullivan, A., Rey, M.E. and Mendez, J.G. 2011. *Opportunities and Challenges in the MENA Region*. Arab World competitive report, Geneva.
Porter, M. 1986. Competition in global industries: a conceptual framework. In M. Porter (ed.), *Competition in Global Industries*. Boston, MA: Harvard Business School Press, pp. 15–60.
Porter, M. 1998. *The Competitive Advantage of Nations: with a New Introduction*. London: Palgrave Macmillan.
Powell, W. 2007. The new institutionalism. In S. Clegg and J. Bailey (eds), *The International Encyclopedia of Organization Studies*. London: Sage, pp. 975–979.
Pudelko, M. and Harzing, A.W. 2007. Country-of-origin, localization or dominance effect? An empirical investigation of HRM practices in foreign subsidiaries. *Human Resource Management*, **46**: 535–559.
Ramamurti, R. 2000. A multilevel model of privatization in emerging economies. *Academy of Management Review*, **25**(3): 525–551.
Ramamurti, R. 2004. Developing countries and MNEs: extending and enriching the research agenda. *Journal of International Business Studies*, **35**: 277–283.
Rosenzweig, P.M. and Nohria, N. 1994. Influences on human resource management practices in multinational corporations. *Journal of International Business Studies*, **25**(2): 229–251.
Shehadi, K. 2002. *Lessons in Privatization: Considerations for Arab States*. United Nations Development Programme.
Smale, A. 2008. Foreign subsidiary perspectives on the mechanisms of global HRM integration. *Human Resource Management Journal*, **18**(2): 135–153.
Soliman, M. 2003. *Foreign Direct Investment and LDCs Exports: Evidence from the MENA Region*. http://www.mafhoum.com/press6/173E14.pdf (accessed 6 September 2014).
Soubbotina, T.P. 2004. *Beyond Economic Growth: An Introduction to Sustainable Development*. Washington, DC: World Bank.
Szulanski, G. 1996. Exploring internal stickiness: impediments to the transfer of best practice within the firm. *Strategic Management Journal*, **17**(Winter Special Issue): 27–43.
Szulanski, G. 2000. The process of knowledge transfer: a diachronic analysis of stickiness. *Organizational Behavior and Human Decision Process*, **82**(1): 9–27.
Talib, Y. 1996. Privatisation: a review of policy and implementation in selected Arab countries. *International Journal of Public Sector Management*, **9**(3): 3–21.
Tayeb, M. 1998. Transfer of HRM practices across cultures: an American company in Scotland. *International Journal of Human Resource Management*, **9**(2): 332–358.
Taylor, S., Beechler, S. and Napier, N. 1996. Toward an integrative model of strategic international human resource management. *Academy of Management Review*, **21**(4): 959–985.
Tregaskis, O. 1998. HRD in foreign MNEs. *International Studies of Management and Organization*, **28**(1): 136–164.
Tregaskis, O. and Brewster, C. 2001. *International HR Capability through Local Employees: A Subsidiary Perspective*. Global Human Resources Management Conference, Barcelona.

United Nations 1993. *UNCTAD World Investment Report: Cross-Border Mergers and Acquisitions and Development*. New York: United Nations.
United Nations 1994. *UNCTAD World Investment Report: Transnational Corporations, Employment and the Workplace*. New York: United Nations.
United Nations 2000. *UNCTAD World Investment Report: Cross-Border Mergers and Acquisitions and Development*. New York: United Nations.
United Nations 2003. *World Investment Report: FDI Policies for Development: National and International Perspectives*. New York and Geneva: United Nations.
United Nations 2006. *UNCTAD World Investment Report: FDI from Developing and Developing and Transition Economies*. New York: United Nations.
United Nations 2008. *UNCTAD World Investment Report: Transnational Corporations*. New York: United Nations.
United Nations 2009. *UNCTAD World Investment Report: Transnational Corporations, Agricultural Production and Development*. New York: United Nations.
United Nations 2013. *UNCTAD World Investment Report: Global Value Chains: Investment and Trade Development*. New York: United Nations.
United Nations 2014. *UNCTAD World Investment Report: Investing in the SDGs: An Action Plan*. New York: United Nations.
Welch, D. 1994. Determinants of intemational human resource management approaches and activities: a suggested framework. *Journal of Management Studies*, **31**(2): 139–164.
Wilson, R.J. 1991. *Politics and the Economy in Jordan*. London: Routledge.
Wilson, R.J. 1998. Jordan's trade: past performance and future prospects. *International Journal of Middle East Studies*, **20**: 325–344.
World Bank 1995. *Jordan: Private Sector Assessment*. Washington, DC: The World Bank, Private Sector Development and Infrastructure Division.
World Bank 2003. *Better Governance for Development in the Middle East and North Africa: Enhancing Inclusiveness and Accountability*. Washington, DC: The World Bank.
World Bank 2011. *Doing Business in the Arab World: Making a Difference for Entrepreneurs*. Washington, DC: The World Bank.
World Bank 2014. *Predictions, Perceptions and Economic Reality: Challenges of Seven Middle East and North Africa Countries Described in 14 Charts*. Washington, DC: The World Bank.
Wyk, J.V. and Lal, A.K. 2010. FDI location drivers and risks in MENA. *Journal of Business Research*, **9**(2): 99–115.
Yahiaoui, D. 2007. *L'hybridation des pratiques de GRH dans les filiales Françaises implantées en Tunisie*. Lyon: Universite Jean Moulin Lyon 3.
Yamin, M. and Otto, J. 2004. Patterns of knowledge flows and MNE innovation performance. *Journal of International Management*, **10**: 239–258.
Yan, Y. and Child, J. 2004. Investors resources and management participation in international joint ventures: a control perspective. *Asia Pacific Journal of Management*, **21**: 287–300.
Yip, G. 1992. *Total Global Strategy: Managing for Worldwide Competitive Advantage.* London: Prentice Hall.
Zahra, S.A. and George, G. 2002. Absorptive capacity: a review, reconceptualization, and extension. *Academy of Management Review*, **27**(2): 185–203.
Zahra, S.A., Ireland, R.D., Gutierrez, I. and Hitt, M.A. 2000. Privatization and entrepreneurial transformation: emerging issues and a future research agenda. *Academy of Management Review*, **25**(3): 509–542.
Zucker, L.G. 1977. The role of institutionalization in cultural persistence. *American Sociological Review*, **42**(5): 726–743.

19. A blueprint for the role of human resource management in corporate social responsibility in the Middle East

Dima Jamali and Ali El Dirani

INTRODUCTION

As the concept of corporate social responsibility (CSR) continues to gain traction within both academic and practitioner communities, the search for practical applications and internalization for its notions and principles becomes more challenging than ever. The internal organizational dimensions of CSR are as important as its external dimensions and any strategic approach to CSR must be based on solid internal foundations. It is hard in this sense to think about a sustainable CSR initiative that is not well anchored and grounded in the internal organizational systems and institutional structures, and this is when the human resource management (HRM) role and intervention take on additional importance in the context of CSR. In this chapter, we argue that HRM could potentially play an important role in CSR, especially by way of support and facilitation. Through a CSR-HRM blueprint, which we put forward, we examine how HRM can make its contribution within a clearly defined strategic CSR approach. We support our arguments with case study examples from the Lebanese context and then conclude by recommending further attention to the internal micro foundations of CSR.

The concept of CSR continues to gain significant traction and consideration within both academic and practitioner communities. CSR succeeded to transcend geographical boundaries, cultural complexities and even contextual differences to become a mainstream issue of concern for businesses around the globe (Aguinis and Glavas, 2012). It could be claimed that CSR is no longer considered a marginal or peripheral matter or a passing fad, but rather is increasingly being viewed as a strategic priority with sustainable business impacts and results (Carroll and Shabana, 2010). At the same time, the challenge of institutionalizing CSR internally and aligning it with other organizational functions (particularly HRM) is just starting to attract the attention needed in various academic and practitioner circles (El Dirani, Jamali and Ashleigh, 2010; El Dirani, 2012; Jamali and El Dirani, 2014; Jamali, El Dirani and Harwood, 2015).

With continuing strides to mainstream CSR, there are various frameworks and tools on offer that are intended to guide organizations in this regard. Many of these tools touch on the internal dimensions of CSR, which have strong HRM affinities. For example, some HRM-specific guidelines are included in the standards of the 'global reporting initiative' (GRI), a non-profit that promotes reporting by organizations on their economic, environmental and social performance. Another example is the UN Global Compact, a strategic policy initiative introduced by Kofi Anan in 2000, whose first six principles address various human rights and labour rights issues, which have strong HRM connotations and implications. In other words, the internal dimensions of CSR are starting to attract attention, and these invariably overlap with HRM traditional domains and functions.

In this chapter, we will examine the increasing affinities between CSR and HRM, particularly within a clearly defined strategic CSR orientation. We make the case that HRM's capabilities, expertise and knowledge in executing organizational strategies can potentially help in ensuring the integration of CSR within an organization's culture and fabric and significantly advancing the CSR agenda. We compile accordingly the CSR-HRM blueprint, outlining how the CSR and HRM functions can be better integrated, and provide two successful case examples from the Middle East where companies have made significant strides in terms of enacting the necessary alignment and reaping the desired benefits from the synergies of CSR and HRM. We conclude with some implications and remarks on the way forward in relation to how organizations can create a better alignment between CSR and HRM and the expected outcome benefits resulting from this.

CSR: IMPLEMENTATION AND INTERNALIZATION CHALLENGES

The most challenging aspect of any CSR initiative remains its translation into managerial actions and tangible business inferences. Practitioners as scholars are highly committed to presenting practical CSR frameworks as guidance for businesses in their efforts to integrate CSR with core business practices beyond complex inapplicable taxonomies. By business practices we mean the external as well as the internal dimensions equally. Many CSR initiatives have a short life span if the focus is solely and primarily on the external business environment, ignoring the internal factor and failing to build tight links with organizational mission and functional practices. As we see it, the internal organizational grounding of CSR enhances the chances of its success outside. We turn attention in this chapter to precisely this sort of internal organizational alignment, how to make it happen in practice, and its implications.

The calibration between CSR notions and principles and business managerial functions, including HRM, appears to be pivotal to move CSR forward based on strong strategic orientations. We argue here that HRM could potentially play an important role in moving CSR into practical applications especially within the internal organizational aspects and helps in addressing the application challenges mentioned above. By empowering HRM to attend to the employee-related aspects of CSR in areas such as training and development, staffing, employee citizenship and employee engagement, HRM can facilitate CSR institutionalization and implementation and ensure the forging of a sustainable, effective and credible CSR initiative anchored and supported by relevant internal organizational systems and institutional processes, policies and structures.

HRM: STRATEGIC IMPORTANCE

Parallel to the development in the field of CSR, which we touched upon in the introduction, HRM continues to be highly involved in communicating systems and employee engagement practices and changing initiatives across organizations (Ulrich and Brockbank, 2005). HRM is increasingly responsible for many key organizational systems, approaches and processes in departmental and stakeholder contexts, including health and safety, recruitment, training, and effective delivery of organizational strategies and objectives (Wright and McMahan, 2011). In addition, HRM always drives social, environmental and ethical responsibilities and champions organizational initiatives within these important areas.

In fact, in today's business environment, we have growing and valid evidence and support for HRM's essential role and valuable contribution to business strategy success, competitiveness, and sustainable results and outcome values compared with traditional wisdom and practice (Ulrich and Beatty, 2001). HRM is no longer considered a purely administrative function, which is only called upon for policing or transactional purposes. In fact the essential contribution of HRM as a strategic partner has been accentuated in the context of globalization, cultural complexities, the advent of technology, and the increasing quest for equal opportunities, diversity and inclusion, with HR managers increasingly called upon to assume key leadership functions to help address the unfolding challenges of managing people in a cut-throat competitive environment.

It is precisely in this context that we see an important role for HRM in supporting CSR and helping to translate CSR into a concrete legitimate function that is well anchored within the core fabric of the organization. In fact, HRM's dedication to individual and organizational development, and increasing concerns with ethics and sustainability, imply that HRM and CSR have strong affinities and that there is room for better alignment and collaboration to ensure outcome benefits for HR and CSR managers, and organizations and their stakeholders more broadly (Jamali, El Dirani and Harwood, 2015; El Dirani, 2012). We capture the potential links and various aspects of potential collaboration between HRM and CSR in our CSR-HRM blueprint presented in the next section.

CSR-HRM BLUEPRINT: HRM CONNECTING WITH CSR

To start with, HRM's strategic direction is enacted only once the strategic direction of the whole organization is clearly defined and established. Any HRM effort and activity must be aligned with the mission, vision and strategic objectives of the organization (Mondy and Mondy, 2012). HRM prepares all needed competences, resources, expertise, processes and policies in order to assist the organization in achieving its strategic objectives, fulfilling its mission and sustaining its competitive advantage over the long term. Using the language of the resource based view (Barney, 2001), other external stakeholders or organizations consider HR practices and investments an internal source of sustainable competitive advantage as they can provide a tacit and valuable advantage to organizations that is difficult to imitate.

Our CSR-HRM blueprint must also be understood in the context of a strategic CSR framework. Strategic CSR entails formulating CSR strategies that are aligned with the strategy of the firm and can generate both short-term and long-term outcome values (Porter and Kramer, 2011). The strategic CSR approach recognizes that the economic benefits of organizations and the interests of society can be intertwined to achieve competitiveness within stakeholder and market segments (McWilliams and Siegel, 2010;

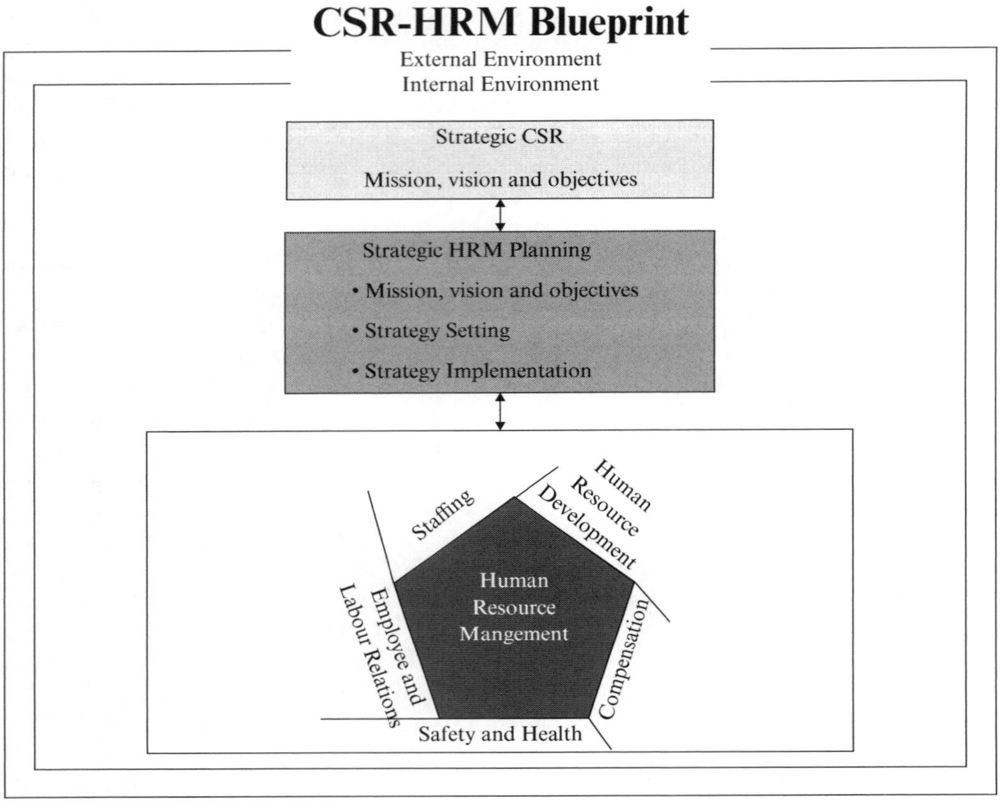

Figure 19.1 CSR-HRM blueprint: HRM contribution

Carroll and Shabana, 2011). Strategic CSR comprises CSR initiatives that are aligned with core competence and are intended to improve the welfare of those in society and also to contribute to organizations' resources and competitive positioning (Bhattacharya and Sen, 2010).

Keeping this overall strategic flair in mind, we begin the process as illustrated in Figure 19.1 by analysing the internal as well the external organizational environment to define the available opportunities, threats, weaknesses and strengths. This could be done as well within a stakeholder relationship management framework. The next step will be to define the strategic CSR framework including the CSR mission, CSR vision and CSR objectives. The outcome of such effort is a CSR framework, which represents the general umbrella and desired direction for the organization in the context of CSR. Some existing CSR frameworks such as the United Nations Global Compact and the international standard ISO26000 could be adapted and implemented. The next stage in our blueprint is to gain an understanding of how HRM within its current mission, vision and objectives can go in line with the strategic CSR direction and define the necessary HRM functions and infrastructure that will be used to achieve and maintain CSR objectives. The third step is to begin the implementation stage, whereby HRM conducts a review of its existing practices and policies within its functions to make sure they are in line with the CSR strategic framework. This process is ongoing and feeds again into the next round of formulating a new set of CSR objectives.

In order to understand the CSR-HRM blueprint more clearly, we will take an example. Let us say that a business firm decided to adapt ISO 26000 as a strategic framework for its CSR activities and practices. ISO 26000 is composed of core areas such as human rights, labour practices, the environment, and community involvement and development.

In a way, those represent broad CSR objectives or areas of strategic importance for CSR success, and HRM can take the following steps to assist in achieving CSR objectives:

- Define key HRM competencies, resources and capabilities that can assist in achieving CSR objectives.
- Review existing HRM practices and introduce necessary changes within areas such as recruitment and selection, talent management and performance management to reflect the CSR objectives of the organization.
- Elaborate or amend new or existing assessment devices such as performance management and balanced scorecard systems to include measures for CSR aspects.
- Put into action the new HRM strategy and communicate the change to employees and establish cross-functional systems to get the whole organization involved.
- Report and assess the impact and results.

In the area of recruitment and selection, HRM can review its hiring methods and sources so to select, for example, employees with personality traits that have affinity to CSR (e.g., organizational citizenship behaviour – OCB propensity) to enable them to better contribute in CSR practices. In the area of training and development, HRM can design and implement training and development programmes related to CSR such as training on sustainability greening practices in order to increase employees' effectiveness and responsiveness to CSR practices. In the area of performance management, HRM can review and introduce performance indicators related to CSR and take them into account when planning employee career development, compensation, benefits, bonuses and promotion schemes. Also, HRM can introduce training programmes on issues such as diversity, health, safety at work and anti-discrimination practices that have a strong affinity to relevant CSR components.

In this sense, HRM is expected to invest in its capabilities and core competences to ensure the effective translation of CSR strategy into HRM practices in areas such as training and development, staffing and employee relations. By doing so, HRM ensures the internalization of CSR and strengthens the CSR-HRM affinities. When properly communicated and explained to employees, the role of HRM in CSR and the solid CSR-HRM alignment are likely to have positive spillovers to increase employees' loyalty to their organizations, that is, the normative and affective satisfaction levels. In this respect, Glavas and Piderit (2009) report that employees are more engaged, develop higher-quality relationships and are more creatively involved when they perceive their company to be socially responsible (and this takes HRM buy-in and support for CSR of course). Rego, Leal, and Pina e Cunha (2010) also found that employees' perceptions in relation to the CSR orientations of their organizations predict their affective commitment. We argue that there is an important role for HRM in mediating and further facilitating the relationships between CSR and employee commitment to the organization and that both HRM and CSR converge around these common goals and outcomes within a co-creation framework. We further argue that it is precisely through these dynamics that CSR evolves into a fully-fledged and differentiated capability and sustainable competitive resource for the firm.

Other important outcomes resulting from a better integration of HRM and CSR are those relating to heightened ethical sensitivity and awareness and increased trust and loyalty to the firm. Ethics has already been recognized as a source of sustainable competitive advantage (Litz, 1996), and the affinities between ethics and CSR are well documented in the literature (Greenwood, 2013; Ehnert and Harry, 2011). Nurturing both ethical and CSR awareness provides reassurance to customers, shareholders and investors and helps in sustaining trustworthy relations with market and non-market stakeholders. Positive stakeholder relationships reduce in turn transaction costs, build reputational capital and enhance long-term sustainable competitive advantage (Fombrun, Gardberg and Barnett, 2000). There is thus a range of worthwhile outcomes that could result from a more effective integration of HRM and CSR that can in turn provide organizations with sustainable advantages over time, ranging from increasing employee commitment and motivation (Collier and Esteban, 2007; Zappalà, 2004) to bolstering trust and loyalty on the part of internal and external stakeholders (Litz, 1996). These worthwhile outcomes are valuable for HRM, CSR and the business as a whole, and are likely to help the firm gain visibility in the eyes of internal and external stakeholders while also helping it to capture or internalize the benefits of CSR programmes as suggested by Burke and Logsdon (1996).

As our suggested roadmap illustrates, there is an important role for HRM that kicks in right after the CSR strategy and general framework are designed. So after the CSR strategy is clearly defined and planned and the specific and measurable CSR objectives are carefully determined, HRM completes the CSR life cycle and gets involved in the CSR strategy implementation and internalization. By doing so, HRM starts playing a pivotal role in addressing the challenges that are commonly encountered with an excessive external focus in CSR while completely overlooking important internal underpinnings. What HRM does is that it finds the action dimension and detailed practical applications for CSR through HRM systems and practices. We see that this role with what it requires from designing new or changing existing HRM policies, processes and practices as channelled and aligned towards achieving CSR objectives is of high added value. Embedding CSR within the internal organizational practices and culture makes CSR a part of the organizational DNA, values and principles and makes an uncontested difference in forging a legitimate CSR strategic orientation and value proposition.

HRM/CSR ISSUES AND CHALLENGES IN THE MIDDLE EAST

The CSR movement in Europe and the US has gained rapid momentum since the late 1970s and has moved beyond the narrow and pure altruistic CSR orientations to broader strategic and sustainability considerations. There are in fact consistent strides to moving beyond CSR as pure philanthropy to new CSR practices which are more institutionalized and more systematic, with mixed progress reported across different parts of the world

(Jamali, Karam and Blowfield, 2015; Jamali and Lanteri, 2015; Jamali and Sidani, 2012). A general, good piece of advice for organizations is to stick to the knitting, or in other words to stick to what they do best. The same applies in the domain of CSR, in the sense that the firm should maintain a link between its CSR and its core business, which will help it to reap the benefits over time.

In the Middle East, CSR progress remains sketchy, and only a handful of organizations have taken active steps towards integrating CSR into the fabric of the business in a systematic way. Today, what prevails in the Middle East are hybrid versions of CSR and Social Entrepreneurship that combine elements of philanthropy with more systematic forms of capacity building and value creation (Jamali, Karam and Blowfield, 2015; Jamali and Lanteri, 2015; Jamali and Sidani, 2012). Yet despite some pockets of best practice, as with the Jordanian government that is seeking to mandate CSR, progress remains uneven at best, whether at the level of local organizational practice, governments, non-governmental organizations (NGOs) and/or universities, and there is more that can be done to lead CSR towards greater maturation and institutionalization (Jamali and Sidani, 2012).

The importance of the role of HRM in CSR, especially the integration between CSR and HRM systems and practices, remains affected by this general, sketchy progress in the domain of CSR. In the absence of real CSR champions within organizations and a clear strategy for CSR deployment, HRM support becomes difficult to leverage. So we have to work on two parallel fronts, namely moving CSR into the strategic realm and enhancing the CSR-HRM interfaces and commonalities (Jamali, El Dirani and Harwood, 2015). Some organizations have taken this transition and put forward a strategic roadmap for how CSR is to be practised in a proactive and strategic manner to become a source of competitive advantage. The below selected case studies from the Middle East context reflect this evolving transitional state of CSR and show growing investments in the role of HRM in CSR.

CASE STUDIES FROM THE MIDDLE EAST

This section draws on specific and practical examples of organizations in the Middle East that have made significant strides in aligning their CSR and HRM functions. The section provides a good practical illustration of the role of HRM in CSR as portrayed within the CSR-HRM blueprint above, and within an overall strategic framework.

The first example to illustrate CSR-HRM affinities and the potential application of our CSR-HRM blueprint is Bank Audi, a leading regional bank headquartered in Lebanon. Over the past few years, Bank Audi has been able to sustain a solid growth, building a legacy of excellence in banking. Bank Audi has set a clear CSR strategy revolving around five distinct pillars including Corporate Governance, Economic Development, Community Development, Human Development and Environmental Protection. This CSR strategy is clearly defined and planned with specific and measurable CSR objectives that are carefully determined. We can also notice that HRM completes Bank Audi's CSR life cycle from the internal angle and is instrumental in various aspects of CSR strategy implementation and proper internalization.

Bank Audi was one of the first organizations in Lebanon to pilot ISO 26000 and is also a recent signatory of the UN Global Compact. Its strategic CSR vision is to be the leading bank in Lebanon on issues pertaining to CSR and sustainability. In pursuing this vision, the CSR and HR managers of the bank have forged a close collaboration or partnership, revolving around aligning various HRM functions to support the goals of both CSR and HRM. For example Bank Audi is keen on nurturing its internal human capital and accords high priority to developing the skills and competencies of its employees, which the bank considers as its most vital asset. The bank also fosters a culture of continuous improvement and development. The bank has developed a three-tiered approach to employee development founded around training and development, continuous assessment, and coaching and mentoring. These various employee-centred functions are intended to support the overall business strategy but also the CSR goals and vision of the company particularly in the domain of labour rights, human rights and progressive employment.

Following is a summary of Bank Audi's human development efforts:

- *Training and Development*: The bank deployed more than 79,000 training hours in 2013, covering a range of 2,080 employees of the bank which are almost equally split in terms of gender representation, and target all levels of employment.
- *Learning Programmes*: The bank assists employees in upgrading their competence and abilities in areas related to technical skills such as banking, finance and economy, human resources, information technology, languages, legal, regulations, Anti Money Laundering (AML) and fraud, retail and risk management, and languages; and various soft skills such as managerial and organizational behaviour, leadership, negotiation, among others. The ratio of successfully trained employees to total employees is around 81 per cent.
- *Performance Appraisal*: The assessment of performance of employees at the bank revolves around providing feedback to employees about their communication style, skills, behaviour and performance and involves a prerequisite information collection stage about the employees from their peers, managers and customers. This process is applicable to all Bank Audi employees, staff, middle managers and top managers, who have a yearly performance and career development review. In addition, the bank has a formal grievance procedure that is at the core of its employee handbook, where employees are encouraged to file complaints regarding work, working conditions and relationships with colleagues when deemed necessary.
- *Talent Management*: The bank established the Talent Assessment Center (TAC) in 2013, an advanced assessment methodology that seeks to select qualified candidates based on performance inputs from multiple exercises and assessors.
- *Diversity and Equal Opportunity*: The bank also strives to ensure diversity and inclusion in all aspects of employment. The bank tries to maintain a reasonable balance with respect to the gender composition of its workforce and gender representation at multiple levels. In terms of women empowerment, the bank works on breaking the glass ceiling and helping women achieve their full potential by reaching the highest organizational echelons.
- *Human Resource Planning (HRP)*: HRP is also a main driver for the bank's functional HR activities. The bank participates in appropriate aggregate planning of supply and demand of employees and succession planning which stem out of the HRP cycle and serves as a buffer to changing external and internal requirements.

The bank, accordingly, makes visible efforts to be present in job fairs hosted in various universities across Lebanon and offers internships to university students, which in turn feeds into the HRP cycle, by helping in spotting the most outstanding interns as potential future recruits.

- *Compensation and Benefits*: The bank strives to become an employer of choice that offers both attractive career opportunities coupled with fair and competitive pay rates. The bank also awards its employees' children for their outstanding school performance.
- *Rewards System*: The bank continuously rewards its employees for their hard work, commitment and loyalty and acknowledges their top performers and best employees in each quarter of the year.
- *Occupational Health and Safety*: Safeguarding employees' safety is crucial at Bank Audi, where the bank takes specific measures against threats and violence and places specific coping measures and detection systems to attend to vibration, fire, hold-up or intrusion situations (Bank Audi, 2013).

DELOITTE ME – A CLEAR CSR STRATEGY WITH AN INTERNAL HUMAN DEVELOPMENT PILLAR

The second example we introduce to illustrate CSR-HRM affinities and the potential application of our CSR-HRM blueprint is Deloitte & Touche Middle East (ME), which is a member firm of Deloitte Touche Tohmatsu Limited (DTTL) and is the first Arab professional services firm established in the Middle East region, with a presence spanning over 85 years. With a globally connected network of member firms in more than 150 countries, DTTL member firms bring world-class capabilities and high-quality service to clients, delivering the insights they need to address their most complex business challenges.

Deloitte ME is a firm believer that a comprehensive Corporate Responsibility (CR) policy is an asset both to the firm and its stakeholders, whether employees, clients, suppliers, or the community at large. Embedding CR in the core of the business helps in stimulating greater employee engagement, drive and productivity, ultimately leading to better quality of work. Accordingly, Deloitte's stance on sustainability and CR is incorporated in the firm's core values, mission and vision, rooted in its culture, and translated into initiatives and activities that directly support societal impact while preserving the interest of the company.

CR at DTTL focuses on three main themes, namely '*responsible business*', '*investing in people*' and '*environmental sustainability*'. Deloitte strives to ensure that its operations across all member firms maintain high levels of responsibility, responsibility towards communities, clients, suppliers, and employees alike.

As a strategic partner, HR has been able to select CR schemes that do not only capitalize on those milestones but also enhance its resource base. Through adopting an employee-oriented CR strategy that focuses on educating Deloitte's staff and fostering their skills, Deloitte is automatically developing its human capital base, improving performance and gaining a strong competitive edge. Simultaneously, it is also forging a culture of integrity that enhances the firm's reputation among all stakeholder groups.

The first step towards embedding a CR culture within Deloitte ME was steering and mainstreaming internal CR efforts. The latter comprised setting a clear and transparent HR system and procedures that attract and retain the most qualified candidates in the region, and setting a comprehensive CR strategy that focuses on educating Deloitte's staff and fostering their skills through easily accessible and measurable CR initiatives. HRM at Deloitte ME is positioned as a strategic business partner and empowered to be highly involved in articulating the action plan of Deloitte's CR strategy at the regional level, and to take part and deliberate on CR initiatives across Deloitte globally. Deloitte has identified its people as the most valuable asset to the organization, recognizing that the success of the firm lies in the performance of its human capital and the patterns through which they work and coordinate. As such, HRM at Deloitte plays the role of a strategic partner that is highly involved in articulating the action plan of Deloitte's CR strategy in the region (Deloitte ME website: http://www2.deloitte.com/be/en/pages/about-deloitte/topics/corporate-responsibility-sustainability.html).

CONCLUDING REMARKS

In conclusion, the surge of interest in the notion of CSR coupled with an explosion in the number of articles, books and chapters written on the topic have led to the theoretical advancement of the field of CSR. This significant progression in CSR theory supports practitioners with practical and dynamic frameworks for strategic CSR. With this increased development in CSR comes the challenge to strategize it and mainstream it internally to achieve the intended objectives in terms of both social and economic outcomes (McWilliams and Siegel, 2010; Morgeson et al., 2013). To this end, our suggested roadmap highlights the role that HRM can play after the setting of a clear CSR strategy. In fact, HRM completes the CSR life cycle and is deeply involved in the internal CSR strategy implementation and institutionalization. At the same time, CSR complements HRM in its ability to give room for HRM to demonstrate a strategic focus and act as a business partner and operationalize what might be perceived as complex, fuzzy or distant CSR objectives. Consequently, the relationship between CSR and HRM is a symbiotic and mutually beneficial one in which the strategic value of either one is measured by its ability to generate valuable and unique core competences and capabilities or benefits/outcomes that enhance the competitiveness of the organization (Barney, 2001), and this is more likely to happen when CSR and HRM work together collaboratively and in close alignment.

The case studies we have presented from the Lebanese context represent clear examples as to how such a CSR-HRM blueprint could be deployed and enacted in practice. Bank Audi and Deloitte ME reflected their commitment to internalizing CSR through elaborating socially responsible HRM practices. Both organizations value the internal dimensions of CSR and emphasize the human development pillar within their wider CSR strategy, which takes into account the external environment analysis and stakeholders' views. Bank Audi and Deloitte ME reflect such orientation through their HRM expenditure in areas such training and development, staffing, career development and talent management. Such progressive HRM understanding portrays a genuine commitment to CSR and a clear understanding for the strategic foundations of any CSR initiative. The

Bank Audi and Deloitte ME examples from the Lebanese context therefore provide clear support for the main thesis of this chapter, namely that there is room for better alignment of CSR and HRM and that the outcomes are likely to be positive for CSR, HRM and the firm overall. We hope this chapter has also provided some initial evidence in relation to the importance of further exploring the micro foundations of CSR and hope that this topic continues to attract the attention it deserves in both academic and practitioner communities.

USEFUL WEBSITES

http://deloittemiddleeastmatters.com/tag/csr/.
http://www.bankaudigroup.com/group/publications?section=2601#2601.
http://www.csrlevant.com/.
http://www.holcim.com/sustainable/social/csr-projects-and-community-engagement.html.
http://www.dubaichamber.com/en/about-us/initiatives/crb-new.

REFERENCES

Aguinis, H. and Glavas, A. 2012. What we know and don't know about corporate social responsibility: a review and research agenda. *Journal of Management*, **38**(4): 932–968.

Bank Audi 2013. *CSR Report*. http://www.banqueaudi.com/GroupWebsite/openAudiFile.aspx?id=2374 (accessed 27 July 2016).

Barney, J. 2001. Resource-based theories of competitive advantage: a ten-year retrospective on the resource-based view. *Journal of Management*, **6**: 643–650.

Bhattacharya, C.B. and Sen, S. 2010. Maximizing business returns to corporate social responsibility (CSR): the role of CSR communication. *International Journal of Management Reviews*, **12**: 8–19.

Burke, L. and Logsdon, J.M. 1996. How corporate social responsibility pays off. *Long Range Planning*, **29**(4): 495–502.

Carroll, A.B. and Shabana, K.M. 2010. The business case for corporate social responsibility: a review of concepts, research and practice. *International Journal of Management Reviews*, **12**: 85–105.

Collier, J. and Esteban, R. 2007. Corporate social responsibility and employee commitment. *Business Ethics: A European Review*, **16**(1): 19–33.

Ehnert, I. and Harry, W. 2011. Recent developments and future prospects on sustainable human resource management: introduction to the special issue. *Management Revue*, **23**(3): 221–238.

El Dirani, A. 2012. Uncovering the role of human resources in corporate social responsibility: case evidence from Lebanon. Doctoral dissertation, University of Southampton, Southampton, UK.

El Dirani, A., Jamali, D.R. and Ashleigh, M. 2010. Corporate social responsibility: what role for human resource? *Hummingbird, University of Southampton's Doctoral Research Journal*, **1**: 12–14.

Fombrun, C., Gardberg, N. and Barnett, M. 2000. Opportunity platforms and safety nets: corporate citizenship and reputational risk. *Business and Society Review*, **105**(1): 85–106.

Glavas, A. and Piderit, S.K. 2009. How does doing good matter? Effects of corporate citizenship on employees. *Journal of Corporate Citizenship*, **36**: 51–70.

Greenwood, M. 2013. Ethical analyses of HRM: a review and research agenda. *Journal of Business Ethics*, **114**(2): 355–366.

Jamali, D. and El Dirani, A. 2014. Synergies of CSR and diversity management: a converging agenda. In M. Karataş-Özkan, K. Nicolopoulou and M.F. Özbilgin (eds), *Corporate Social Responsibility and Human Resource Management: A Diversity Perspective*. Cheltenham, UK and Northampton, MA: Edward Elgar, pp. 51–65.

Jamali, D., El Dirani, A. and Harwood, I. 2015. Exploring HRM roles in CSR: the CSR-HRM co-creation model. *Business Ethics: A European Review*, **24**(2): 125–143.

Jamali, D., Karam, C. and Blowfield, M. 2015. *Development Oriented CSR*. London: Greenleaf Publishing.

Jamali, D. and Lanteri, A. (2015) *Social Entrepreneurship in the Middle East*. London: Palgrave Macmillan.

Jamali, D. and Sidani, Y. 2012. *CSR in the Middle East: Fresh Perspectives*. London: Palgrave Macmillan.

Litz, R. 1996. A resource-based-view of the socially responsible firm: stakeholder interdependence, ethical awareness, and issue responsiveness as strategic assets. *Journal of Business Ethics*, **15**(12): 1355–1363.
McWilliams, A. and Siegel, D. 2010. Creating and capturing value: strategic corporate social responsibility. *Journal of Management*, **26**: 117–127.
Mondy, R.W. and Mondy, J.B. 2012. *Human Resource Management*. Edinburgh: Pearson Education Limited.
Morgeson, F.P., Aguinis, H., Waldman, D.A. and Siegel, D.S. 2013. Extending corporate social responsibility research to the human resource management and organizational behavior domains: a look to the future. *Personnel Psychology*, **66**: 805–824.
Porter, M. and Kramer, M. 2011. Creating shared value. *Harvard Business Review*, **1**: 62–77.
Rego, A., Leal, S. and Pina e Cunha, M. 2010. How the perception of five dimensions of corporate citizenship and their inter-inconsistencies predict affective commitment. *Journal of Business Ethics*, **94**: 107–127.
Ulrich, D. and Beatty, D. 2001. From partners to players: extending the HR playing field. *Human Resource Management*, **40**: 293–307.
Ulrich, D. and Brockbank, W. 2005. *The HR Value Proposition*. Boston, MA: Harvard Business Press.
Wright, P.M. and McMahan, G.C. 2011. Exploring human capital: putting human back into strategic human resource management. *Human Resource Management Journal*, **21**(2): 93–104.
Zappalà, G. 2004. Corporate citizenship and human resource management: a new tool or a missed opportunity? *Asia Pacific Journal of Human Resources*, **42**: 185–201.

20. Human resource management in the public sector in the Middle East

Nelarine Cornelius, Eric Pezet, Ramin Mahmoudi and Dima Ramez Murtada

INTRODUCTION

Human resource management (HRM) policy and practices in the public sector in the Middle East are affected by many contextual factors, particularly politicisation; social, cultural and institutional pressures; and family, clan and religious values, as well as the pervasive presence of androcentrism with its inevitable influence on gender equality issues. Additionally, international influences, including international businesses and supra-governmental organisations (the latter also fund public sector development projects), have and continue to influence how public sector HRM (PSHRM) is understood and practised in the Middle East and in particular in Bahrain, Egypt, Iran, Jordan, Kuwait, Libya, Morocco, Oman, Saudi Arabia and the United Arab Emirates (UAE).

A range of hybrid forms of policy and practice prevail in the Middle East, drawing on pre-colonial, postcolonial, local, national and international, and public and private sector ideas and practices. Further, there are also many sources of pressure for change from international policy and funding agencies such as the United Nations (UN), World Bank, International Monetary Fund (IMF) and European Union, in most Organisation for Economic Co-operation and Development (OECD) countries (Kulshreshtha, 2008). All are seeking improvements in efficiency, effectiveness, transparency and service delivery, with HRM an important locus for change. However, a number of distinctive local and contextual factors can be a source of resistance to change.

Many of the changes proposed and implemented are based on the principles of new public management (NPM) (Hammami et al., 2006; Pollitt and Bouckaert, 2004; Manning, 2001; Van der Wal et al., 2006): an ideological position, which asserts and promotes the need for a more 'business-like' approach to public administration. The focal points for NPM-based reforms are downsizing, managerialism, decentralisation, de-bureaucratisation and privatisation of some support and front-line services, primary industries owned by the state, and public–private partnerships. In practice, the outcomes of NPM implementation were mixed, especially in developing and emerging economies (Haque, 2001; Manning, 2001).

All of these changes have implications for HRM policy and practice. Further, the implicit rationale that guides HRM choice or *meta-logic* – the series of factors that operate at the national level, setting the overall climate (Budhwar and Sparrow, 2002) and the contextual factors that influence meta-logic – along with shifts over time in meta-logic, are especially visible in the public sector.

In this chapter, first we review briefly public sector policy development across the Middle East; second, we present a summary of the characteristics of HRM in the public sector (PSHRM); and finally, we consider the challenges for practice and implications for future research.

HRM IN THE PUBLIC SECTOR IN THE MIDDLE EAST – CONTEXTUAL FACTORS

Public Sector Policies

A UN survey of public administration policies in the Middle East suggests that its role, and what is regarded as the best focus for change, differs greatly across the region (United Nations, 2008). For example, in Egypt in 2004, the UN research established that the public sector employed one-third of the country's workforce and a series of reforms were implemented with the aim of reducing the number of civil servants. In Jordan, the civil sector was poorly organised and not regarded as a good employment prospect. A reform initiated in 2004 aimed to implement administrative cultural change, with the changes part of a programme of reform aimed to give citizens better access to public services. Religion is a major contextual factor in Middle East countries and the civil service reflects the religious composition of the population. For example, in Lebanon, in accordance with the Ta'if agreement of 1989, specific religious communities are assured representation and employment in specific government posts and ministries. Across the region the UN researchers noted a drive to simplify administrative procedures and implement e-government. The private sector and its management practices were viewed positively in Jordan, Lebanon and Syria and thus were more likely to be seen as a source of knowledge transfer for the public sector.

Other examples of modernisation efforts include efforts to decentralise agencies in the Saudi Arabian public sector organisations with a more participatory structure (Al-Yahya, 2009). More broadly, across the Middle East there are certain trends, such as the adoption of more quasi-governmental agency forms, and delegation of operational management and recruitment to individual agencies (Al-Yahya, 2009). In all these cases, HRM is central to the implementation of change, through operational practices including recruitment, training and development, job classification and promotion policies, as well as more strategic action. These and similar administrative reforms aimed to reduce the weight of central administration: an evolution of public administration giving more autonomy to local government through modernisation activities.

PSHRM – HISTORICAL AND CONVENTIONAL INFLUENCES

Contextual Issues

There are a number of themes that appear commonly in the literature on HRM policy and practice in the Middle East, influencing the private, public and third sectors to varying degrees. These include the central importance of the family and Islam and tribal influence, all of which underline the importance of traditional values in management policy and practice development (Afiouni et al., 2014; Iles et al., 2012; Metcalfe, 2006, 2008; Budhwar and Debrah, 2003). In their review and editorial, Afiouni et al. (2014) note that there has been growing interest in research on HRM in the Middle East in terms of theoretical depth and methodological rigour, and that more recently, certain topics have characterised the direction taken in the development of the field. These include employment nationalisation policies, self-initiated expatriation, local employee's view on expatriate managers, female talent retention, HRM knowledge transfer from multinational companies (MNCs) to local subsidiaries, high performance work systems, and employee and leader behaviour.

Overall, research suggests that management and HRM styles are conflicted, characterised by, for example, nepotism alongside attempts to develop transparency and more professional practice (e.g., Iles et al., 2012). Leaders are often those who have secured their position based on age rather than qualifications (Iles et al., 2012). Iles and colleagues also note that across the Middle East, politicisation of the civil service affects recruitment, selection and promotion practices (e.g., favouritism, political loyalty) and also reduces the link between performance and reward, the latter often characterised by political interference. Most of the countries in the region are postcolonial, with their national public policy structures and laws built on this original colonial administrative heritage, and vary considerably also with regard to social, cultural and institutional status and norms, business environment and income levels. Other differences include stage of economic development, the degree of politicisation of the civil service, foreign ownership and organisational-level variables such as organisational size, age, strategies (Iles et al., 2012; Metcalfe, 2006) and HR orientation towards preferential recruitment of locals especially in Gulf State countries characterised by low population and high wages (Rutledge et al., 2011; Rees et al., 2007; Achoui, 2009). Further, some of these influences are found most strongly in specific national clusters. For example, the influence of membership of tribe or family is common in Iran (Yeganeh and Su, 2007), Oman (Aycan et al., 2007) and Saudi Arabia (Mellahi and Wood, 2001). The influence of the oil industry (including state-owned enterprises, SOEs) and its practices is strongest in Iran (Namazie and Frame, 2007), Oman (Aycan et al., 2007; Budhwar and Debrah, 2003) and Saudi Arabia (Mellahi and Wood, 2001; Budhwar and Debrah, 2003).

We now highlight in more depth general characteristics of PSHRM that are found commonly across the Middle East, specifically legal issues and national initiatives; paternalism and androcentrism; culture, religion and gender; authority and performance evaluation; Western influence and local/ foreign worker issues; recruitment and selection; training and development; and career planning and dynamics.

CHARACTERISTICS OF PSHRM IN THE MIDDLE EAST

Legal Issues and National Initiatives

The public sector is often a major employer and especially so in the Middle East. In addition to an array of national government policies to ensure financial and political stability, there are many laws in place to regulate the content of employment contracts (Leat and

El-Kot, 2007). Across the region, HRM policy in the public sector is usually built on extensive legal foundations, emphasising centralised decision-making and detailed regulations (Iles et al., 2012), and a desire to avoid mistakes (Leat and El-Kot, 2007), a proxy for risk aversion. The politicisation of the public sector has affected, and continues to affect, recruitment, selection and promotion practices (Iles et al., 2012).

Changes are often mediated through an array of government initiatives often focused on very specific aspects of PSHRM. For example, there have been a number of nationalisation policies aimed to develop the role of women (Metcalfe, 2006) and initiatives to create job opportunities for women, as well as a review of maternity provision in Saudi Arabia (Metcalfe, 2011). In the Gulf in particular, there have been many initiatives to increase the number of nationals in the public and private sector (Al-Hamadi et al., 2007; Rees et al., 2007). However, in some countries such as Morocco, there have been more root and branch efforts to reform and improve HRM in the public sector, much of it through the adoption of more Western practices (Al-Arkoubi and McCourt, 2004).

Paternalism Androcentrism

In Iran, employment is largely paternalistic (Yeganeh and Su, 2007; Tayeb, 2001), and it is strictly controlled in the public sector (Namazie and Frame, 2007). In much of the Gulf, HRM practices are not only paternalistic but also oriented towards elites (Aycan et al., 2007; Rutledge et al., 2011). Generally, relationships are characterised by subordinate obedience, an avoidance of conflicts (Aycan et al., 2007) and a high level of hierarchical authority at work, as boundaries are clearly drawn between levels of management and other employees (Al-Hamadi et al., 2007). In addition, it is oriented towards localism or preferred employment status for locals in order to contain the dominance of expatriates (Rutledge et al., 2011). Broadly, the culture of much of the Middle East could be described as paternalistic, which has obvious implications for gender and work.

Culture, Religion and Gender

Islam is the predominant religion in the Middle East. Its influence is felt not only as part of the cultural norms of most Middle Eastern societies, but also in the workplace. Yeganeh and Su (2007) have suggested that Islamic principles are oriented towards good conduct, self-control, kindness, obedience, loyalty and discipline, and a participative but paternalistic management style (Yeganeh and Su, 2007); conflict avoidance (Bakhtiari, 1995; Soltani, 2010); marked respect for elders and seniors (Yeganeh and Su, 2007); and responsibility to obtain perfection -'*ehsan*' (Ali, 2010, cited by Mellahi and Budhwar, 2010). These principles play important roles in all aspects of life, including HRM in semi-private and public sector organisations (Al-Hamadi et al., 2007). Many authors have indicated what they believe to be the main characteristics of Islam as it manifests itself in social settings.

Research on public sector organisations suggests that although officially there is often parity between women and men regarding access to employee development opportunities in Iran, Oman, Bahrain, Jordan and parts of the UAE (Metcalfe, 2008), women have restricted access to employment in Saudi Arabia (Mellahi and Wood, 2001; Rutledge et al., 2011; Rees et al., 2007; Metcalfe, 2008). In Saudi Arabia, women have limited chances to obtain work because of the very high degree of professional segregation. Although the percentage of women participating in the Saudi workforce saw an increase between 1992 and 2007, from 5.4 per cent to 14.4 per cent (Welsh et al., 2014), it remains modest, with a concentration of working women in the public sector in primary school education (Welsh et al., 2014; Le Renard, 2014). On the other hand, although they cannot become judges, Saudi women can become lawyers (since 2012) and practise other law-related professions within businesses; they also have access to computer-based professions (Le Renard, 2014), and their participation in trade and commerce is displaying remarkable progress. In this regard, women owned 30 per cent of the businesses in Saudi Arabia in 2005 (Qureshi, 2014).

As in all countries, the work environment is gendered, but in the Middle East, culture and religion combine to create a highly androcentric environment. In practice, women's access to jobs, training and development in the public sector differs greatly, and scholars such as Tlaiss and Mendelson (2014) have expressed caution in research, arguing that a more diverse picture emerges. For example, in the Emirates, the challenges facing working women are similar to those in the West (Lirio et al., 2007; Hutchings et al., 2012) but social pressures to raise a large family and not overshadow their partners' contributions remain strong, and in the public sector in particular, continuing education, role redefinition and seeking employment options that allow a better work–life balance are ways that these issues are addressed by many women (Marmenout and Lirio, 2014). However, Vidyasagar and Rea (2004) note that constitutional restrictions exist that prevent gender equality, while across the region, many women do not enjoy equal rights as regards employment (Sidani, 2005; Omair, 2008). A number of women in the Arab Middle East have successful career experiences, like Farha Alshamsi, who holds a senior position in a government agency and runs her own communications and advisory company on the side in UAE (Redvers, 2015). Notwithstanding, women in the Middle East continue to suffer from a lack of decent work opportunities as they are more than three times as likely as men to be unemployed in Saudi Arabia or Qatar (Zukowska, 2015). Women are widely employed in Oman but remain underrepresented in senior roles and the workplace more generally, though they are well represented in the departmental management position in HRM, marketing, public relations, project management, transport and finance (Linzi and Madsen, 2014). In Lebanon, although women expressed dissatisfaction with pay levels, pensions and promotions, which may reflect the pay gap common across the region (Al-Lamki, 1998, 2000), they did express high levels of satisfaction with their work, although women managers are rare (Tlaiss and Mendelson, 2014). In Lebanon, women managers in private organisations are facing gender discrimination in accessing career development and training and learning opportunities. Hence, they use an adaptive approach to secure learning opportunities, such as personally funded external training (Tlaiss and Dirani, 2015). It is possible that women in the public sector might also seek training and education opportunities privately if they are unavailable from the government.

Barriers to gender equality of opportunity include social cultural norms, family commitments and stereotypical views of women managers (Metcalfe, 2006). In many Gulf countries women are discouraged from certain professions, for example architecture and fields in medicine and engineering (Moghadam, 2005; Metcalfe, 2007, cited by Metcalfe, 2011). However, in countries like Bahrain, the UAE, Qatar and Saudi Arabia, women have expanded into previously limited professional areas; for example, 40 per cent of all doctors in Saudi Arabia are now female (Freedom House, 2010, cited by Metcalfe, 2011).

In the Gulf Cooperation Council (GCC) countries, there is less *aib* (shame) for women in working for the government than in working for the private sector, so women seeking employment prefer public sector jobs (Harry, 2007). Additionally, a policy of women acceptation is being implemented in the public sector, insofar as public sector employment offers Emirati women a guarantee of employment even in cases of long absences due to sickness of immediate family members and paid maternity leave (Abdulla, 2006). For Hodgson (2014), UAE women account for 66 per cent of the government workforce and hold 30 per cent of senior jobs at the decision-making level. In Qatar, women, such as the ambassador and permanent representative to the United Nations, Alya Bint Ahmed Bin Saif Al Thani, pursue a diplomatic career.

In the Gulf countries, the majority of women work in restricted areas such as education, social care and health (Mellahi and Wood, 2001; Metcalfe, 2011). Fields like foreign languages, architecture and political sciences are not officially forbidden but are inaccessible for Saudi female students (Le Renard, 2014). The public sector in the Arab Gulf countries provides gender-segregated employment opportunities, especially in Saudi Arabia, where law, that will negatively influence the female-to-male ratio in the national workforce in Saudi Arabia compared to the UAE, prohibits mixed-gender environments (Rutledge et al., 2011). In Saudi Arabia, prohibition of mixing of the sexes leads to low levels of female participation in the labour market (Rees et al., 2007; Metcalfe, 2011). Access to training and development opportunities is also limited (Metcalfe, 2006, 2011; Soltani, 2010). However, in Oman, the UAE and Iran, governments see the training and recruitment of women as of increasing importance in order to 'modernise' the public sector (Soltani, 2010; Rees et al., 2007).

Authority and Performance Evaluation

Authority is largely a personal, individual affair (Leat and El-Kot, 2007) with an expectation of obedience on the part of subordinates (Aycan et al., 2007; Mellahi and Wood, 2001), although others have suggested that there is a high level of hierarchical authority at work (Al-Hamadi et al., 2007). For example, in Oman, HRM practices are paternalistic, adapted to expatriates rather than locals and oriented towards elites (Aycan et al., 2007; Rutledge et al., 2011). They are also characterised by subordinate obedience, an avoidance of conflicts (Aycan et al., 2007) and a high level of hierarchical authority at work as boundaries are clearly drawn between levels of management and other employees (Al-Hamadi et al., 2007). In addition, they are oriented towards localism, 'Omanisation', to avoid the potential dominance of expatriates who are the overwhelming majority of the working population (Rutledge et al., 2011). Leadership opportunities are related to age, rather than qualifications (Abu-Doleh and Weir, 2007; Al-Arkoubi and McCourt, 2004; Yeganeh and Su, 2007). In the public sector, decision-making remains highly centralised, with consequences for the manner in which performance appraisal, training programme design, wage determination and HR development policy and practice are constructed and implemented (Budhwar et al., 2002; Iles et al., 2012).

The degree of authoritarianism and centralisation in most public sector organisations in the Middle East means that performance appraisal is often undertaken in order to meet legal requirements fitting with the rhetoric of modernisation of policy, but falls short in practice. Tradition appraisal approaches, methods and sources may remain strong in specific country contexts (Khoury and Analoui, 2004) even where modernisation, at the policy level, is viewed as desirable. Moreover, there is often a lack of a significant relationship between performance appraisal results and the setting of personal development goals, as well as a likelihood of a failure to apply appraisal results to key HR decisions such as layoffs, identification of training and development needs, and employee transfers and assignments (Abu-Doleh and Weir, 2007). There is often little relationship between performance, reward and, indeed, the overall strategy of the organisation (Al-Arkoubi and McCourt, 2004; Iles et al., 2012). Reward is often based on culturally and socially desirable behaviour rather than on work outcomes (Yeganeh and Su, 2007; Namazie and Frame, 2007). This performance context often results in a lack of a significant relationship between performance and overall job satisfaction (Ibrahim et al., 2004).

Western Influence and Local/Foreign Worker Issues

Metaphorically, much of Middle East management practice is at a crossroads between the 'East' and 'West'. In the private sector in particular, Western practices have had an important influence (Iles et al., 2012; Siddique, 2004). However, the public sector is paradoxical, often viewed as important not only for the maintenance of customs and values, but as a designated source of employment for locals and the sector where locals must be in control. It is also viewed as a key target for modernisation. This is especially of note in countries with low numbers of locals and high numbers of foreigners. Consequently, a number of countries have positive discrimination policies and quotas in favour of locals, as exemplified by Emiratisation, Omanisation and Saudisation initiatives (Al-Waqfi and Forstenlechner, 2014; Aycan et al., 2007; Mellahi and Wood, 2001). This nationalistic focus prevails even when local applicants lack the necessary skills, competence and work ethic.

Nonetheless, the notion that Western practices can improve competency is long established (Siddique, 2004), and in the public sector, Western education of locals (Iles et al., 2012), the presence of MNCs (Khilji, 2001; Siddique, 2004) and the influence of supranational organisations has influenced PSHRM. Specifically, there has been a drive in many countries to improve efficiency through the practice of outcome-based appraisal (Mellahi and Wood, 2001), and some governments (e.g., Iran) have established partnerships with foreign countries, in part for know-how transfer (Namazie and Frame, 2007; Tayeb, 2001). It has been argued that such actions might move public organisations towards a more strategic approach to HRM (Iles et al., 2012). Research by Syed et al. (2014) also suggests that many HR managers in the Middle East may assist expatriates and local employees to develop mutual cross-cultural understanding, especially around sensitivity to local customs and work environment norms, and that in spite of nationalisation policies, there is general positivity towards expatriates, with competence, rather than nationality, the main consideration. However, the desire to adopt Western practice is often subject to local cultural, religious and political restrictions. To Khoury and Analoui (2004), in Arabic Middle Eastern countries, high power distance, strong uncertainty avoidance and mechanistic or bureaucratic organisations limit the implementation of Western practices in these countries. For example, a performance appraisal system based on Western contexts, which encourages two-way communication between superiors and subordinates and requires feedback about faculty members' performance from several sources that are familiar with their performance, has limitations when applied to the Arabic Middle Eastern countries. Hence, many Middle Eastern organisations that have implemented Western HR models and practices have maintained paternalistic relationships, allowing employees to get privileges from their managers regardless of their performance (Dirani, 2006, cited by Giangreco et al., 2010).

Recruitment and Selection

For recruitment, practices in Gulf countries and socially desirable behavioural criteria are deemed to be important. In conjunction with these values, the notion of *wasta*, or contacts, is widespread, with influence on advancement of individuals in business and social life strong, although it is perceived as an unfair practice by many (Tlaiss and Kauser, 2011). Consequently, there is an expectation that individuals in positions of influence and power will help those related to them as well as those well-connected politically (Iles et al., 2012). There is also a preference for filling vacancies from within (Leat and El-Kot, 2007; Namazie and Frame, 2007; Mellahi and Wood, 2001; Mellahi, 2007; Rees et al., 2007; Rutledge et al., 2011). This form of nepotism, often based on clan, village, political or family connections, can limit opportunities for merit-based recruitment.

The Emiratisation process (the UAE's labour nationalisation programme) has an objective to give preference to the recruitment of national job-seekers in the private sector. However, the national unemployment rate remains high, 12 per cent in the UAE in 2009, showing an internal resistance to Emiratisation (Forstenlechner et al., 2012). The policy of preference for recruitment of national job-seekers in the private sector is applied in other countries of the GCC (Bahrain, Kuwait, Oman, Qatar and Saudi Arabia). Forstenlechner et al. (2012) found that there is a resistance from the private sector to supporting Emiratisation due to a number of factors (see also Forstenlechner and Mellahi, 2011):

- *Social*: Hiring an Emirati for a manual or unskilled position would be socially unacceptable.
- *Cultural*: If the position offered to a local requires direct supervision by a non-national peer or offends traditional gender sensibilities and customs.
- *Regulatory*: Non-nationals are easier to control. In other words, they are easier to hire, manage and fire.
- *Motivational*: Nationals have little motivation to seek employment outside of the public sector, and HRM personnel refuse to hire a less motivated national candidate.

Training and Development

Across the Middle East, great importance is placed on education, training and qualifications (Yeganeh and Su, 2007; Namazie and Frame, 2007). Education and training tend not to be generic, with the specific skills and qualifications tightly prescribed for specific jobs across all sectors (Leat and El-Kot, 2007; Mellahi and Wood, 2001). In the public sector, there is a strong focus on systematic identification of training and development needs and programmes for nationals, in line with broader nationalisation policies (Rajasekar and

Khan, 2013). In Jordan, training policies are decentralised, devolved to individual ministries (Yaghi et al., 2008), and in the Gulf States, there is an incremental and systematic allocation of resources for education and technical and vocational training (Al-Yahya, 2010).

Career Planning and Dynamics

There are a number of factors that impact career and career dynamics. Many employees do not have clear job descriptions and defined career paths, and there is little recognition of the importance of linking HR development (HRD) to business objectives or, indeed, implementing HRD effectively (Al-Hamadi et al., 2007; Budhwar et al., 2002), which can lead to limited interest in career planning (Leat and El-Kot, 2007). A study conducted on 40 state-owned enterprises (SOEs) in Oman showed that more than 50 per cent of the sample units do not have clear career paths for their employees (Al-Hamadi et al., 2007; Budhwar et al., 2002). HRD doesn't contribute to the organisation's high-level strategy building, as it was found that only 28 per cent of HR managers are involved in the development of corporate strategy in the Omani case and managers resist organisational change efforts regarding the implementation of a career path (Al-Hamadi et al., 2007).

In many parts of the public sector, employees have a job for life, irrespective of performance, which may constrain job motivation. Besides, training and development programmes in Arab countries are influenced by low individualism. In this sense, there is a focus on supporting a team rather than an individual when it comes to any training and development that is undertaken (Leat and El-Kot, 2007).

FINAL COMMENTS

There are many pressures to change PSHRM from more traditional practices at both the regional and international levels, but many contextual factors limit the nature and pace of change. Pragmatically, it may be more realistic to encourage incremental change in areas that are deemed 'politically neutral'. However, some of the restrictive practices within the public sector regionally may not only be a potential source of inefficiency but also of tension and dissatisfaction, given the desirability of relatively stable and reliable jobs, especially where unemployment levels are high. Moreover, the slowness of change may frustrate many employees who would welcome a more forward-looking and dynamic approach. Al-Yahya (2009) has noted that the changes seen as important for progressing the public sector include organisational culture change, but that this will be difficult because of top-level resistance to formal power sharing practices, political and official leadership norms, and the attitude of public officials who may be concerned about employees using power for personal gain. These difficult issues are among some of the challenges facing PSHRM in the Middle East. A selection of challenges is now considered.

PSHRM Policy and Practice Effectiveness

In Oman, many employees do not have job descriptions or career paths (Al-Hamadi et al., 2007). The HRD function is facing restrictions in the areas of financial support and commitment (Al-Hamadi et al., 2007). The implementation of HRD programmes is often poor, with an absence of clear career paths for employees and with decision-making concentrated in the hand of managers within the HRD departments (Budhwar et al., 2002). Although there is a strong emphasis on training and development in the public sector, there is a lack of carefully targeted and aligned policies and strategies, budgetary constraints and many poorly qualified training managers, and the effective use of information and communications technology (ICT) in training methods is limited (Rajasekar and Khan, 2013). Yaghi et al. (2008) observed that training is often not aligned with organisational development and planning, or with validated and reliable evaluation methods, especially in relation to economic outputs and organisational-level performance. Indeed, these authors argue that these shortcomings have resulted in underutilisation of employee skills and, ultimately, increased employee turnover.

In their study of Morocco, Al-Arkoubi and McCourt (2004) also found that there is no strategic integration of HRM in the civil service, with an absence of HR strategy and of a conscious attempt to link individual HR activities such as recruitment and selection to an overall strategic plan. In addition, there are constraints on delegation to lower levels within ministries and on recruitment and promotion by ministers and senior officials in the absence of the required qualifications. Also, performance management is not linked to any overall strategy. Finally, placing reform in the hands of the Civil Service Ministry (CSM) was also found to be a factor that impedes effective HRD as this unit lacked the expertise to adequately develop and progress HRM changes.

Therefore, overall, new policies may struggle to take root due to a lack of local expertise and political interference in the routine elements of HRM operations and administration, thus impeding effective policy implementation.

Job Satisfaction and Choice of Employment

Across the region, employment in the public sector is regarded as desirable. Reasons to reject a private sector job are longer hours, job insecurity and less annual leave entitlement, while the most important reason for rejecting a job in the public sector is the job field or specialisation (Al-Ajmi and Elhagrasey, 2010). For example, Al-Ajmi and Elhagrasey found that the most important criteria that affect the choice of employment in the Kuwaiti public and private sector is salary and job security, with the least important the field of the job. Satisfaction is found to be positively correlated to occupational commitment behaviour (OCB), except in cases in which distributive and procedural justice holds constant (Alotaibi, 2001), as well as high performance HR planning (Mostafa and Gould-Williams, 2014). However, Kuwaiti culture and tradition negatively affect Kuwaiti women employees' feeling of satisfaction towards their co-workers, advancement opportunities, level of payment and supervision techniques (Metle, 2002).

About the UAE, Abdulla et al. (2011) have noted that salary and incentives are the most powerful determinants of job satisfaction in the public sectors. They also observe that other environmental factors, such as the skills variety required to carry out the job, task significance, autonomy, interaction with co-workers, and public perception, are strong predictors of job satisfaction. Other organisational factors such as organisational policy and strategies, promotion and equity in appraising employees' performance have also a positive impact on job satisfaction. Further, in the UAE, Ibrahim et al. (2004) found a significant effect of performance, nationality and position on some facets of job satisfaction (e.g., satisfaction with pay and benefits, professional development and work environment). Ibrahim and colleagues also found that satisfaction is also related to an employee's position, since employees in higher-level positions are more satisfied with their work environment than employees in lower-level management. Therefore, extrinsic rather than intrinsic factors may provide greater sources of motivation, and irrespective of modernisation efforts, improvements in work performance and service levels may be compromised.

An Evolving Situation

Karam and Afiouni's (2014) observation that women's work opportunities are dynamic and subject to change, could be applied more generally to PSHRM in the Middle East. Policies and practices are evolving and there are different rates of improvement across the region. Contextual factors remain a strong influence, but the impact of Western, private sector practices, directly through public sector modernisation initiatives, or indirectly through the diffusion of practices from international companies in the region, have and will continue to mould PSHRM.

The legacy of modernisation initiatives, cross-sector learning and development, the changing roles and opportunities for women, the impact of technology adoption through parallel modernisation policies, specifically internet and communication technology for development (ICT4D), and changes in the aftermath of the Arab Spring, will also help to better assess our understanding of how PSHRM is changing across the region. Increasingly, the 'safe bet' of a job in the public sector may be at risk where local employment opportunities are strong, or international recruitment is buoyant, especially in areas where there is intensified political instability.

USEFUL WEBSITES

Jordanian Vocational Training Corporation: http://vtc.gov.jo/vtcen/.

The Directorate of Human Resources and Finance in Bahrain: http://www.cio.gov.bh/CIO_ENG/SubDetailed.aspx?subcatid=48.

Egyptian labour law: http://www.egypt.gov.eg/english/laws/pdf/Preface.pdf.

Iranian Ministry of Cooperatives, Labour, and Social Welfare: http://www.mcls.gov.ir/en/home.

Moroccan Ministry of Employment and Vocational Training: http://www.emploi.gov.ma/index.php/en/.

Ministry of Manpower in Oman: http://www.manpower.gov.om/Portal/en/VocationalTrainingCenter.aspx.

Ministry of Labor and Social Affairs in Qatar: http://portal.www.gov.qa/wps/portal/directory/agency/ministryoflaborandsocialaffairs.

The GCC countries: http://www.sheikhmohammed.com/vgn-ext-templating/v/index.jsp?vgnextoid=b10a4c8631cb4110VgnVCM100000b0140a0aRCRD.

Challenges women face in GCCs: http://www.forbes.com/sites#/sites/ashoka/2014/01/29/how-does-sheryl-sandbergs-message-apply-to-the-middle-east/; http://www.bbc.com/capital/story/20150422-which-women-get-ahead-in-dubai; http://www.ilo.org/beirut/media-centre/news/WCMS_370188/lang--en/index.htm.

REFERENCES

Abdulla, F. 2006. Education and employment among women in the UAE. *International Higher Education*, **45**(4): 9–10.

Abdulla, J., Djebarni, R. and Mellahi, K. 2011. Determinants of job satisfaction in the UAE: a case study of the Dubai police. *Personnel Review*, **40**(1): 126–146.
Abu-Doleh, J. and Weir, D. 2007. Dimensions of performance appraisal systems in Jordanian private and public organizations. *International Journal of Human Resource Management*, **18**(1): 75–84.
Achoui, M.M. 2009. Human resource development in Gulf countries: an analysis of the trends and challenges facing Saudi Arabia. *Human Resource Development International*, **12**(1): 35–46.
Afiouni, F., Huub, R. and Schuler, R. 2014. HRM in the Middle East: toward a greater understanding. *International Journal of Human Resource Management*, **25**(2): 133–143.
Al-Ajmi, S.R. and Elhagrasey, M.G. 2010. Factors and policies affecting employment choice in Kuwaiti public and private sectors: the role of demographic variables. *International Journal of Business and Public Administration*, **7**(2): 151–162.
Al-Arkoubi, K. and McCourt, W. 2004. The politics of HRM: waiting for Godot in the Moroccan civil service. *International Journal of Human Resource Management*, **15**(6): 978–995.
Al-Hamadi, A., Budhwar, P.S. and Shipton, H. 2007. Management of human resources in Oman. *International Journal of Human Resource Management*, **18**(1): 100–113.
Al-Lamki, M.S. 1998. Barriers to Omanization in the private sector: the perceptions of Omani graduates. *International Journal of Human Resource Management*, **9**(2): 377–400.
Al-Lamki, M.S. 2000. Omanization: a three tier strategic framework for human resource management and training in the Sultanate of Oman. *Journal of Comparative International Management*, **3**(1): 37–55.
Al-Waqfi, M.A. and Forstenlechner, I. 2014. Barriers to Emiratization: the role of policy design and institutional environment in determining the effectiveness of Emiratization. *International Journal of Human Resource Management*, **25**(2): 167–189.
Al-Yahya, O.K. 2009. Power-influence in decision making, competence utilization, and organizational culture in public organizations: the Arab world in comparative perspective. *Journal of Public Administration Research and Theory*, **19**(2): 385–407.
Al-Yahya, K.O. 2010. The over-educated, under-utilized public professionals: evidence from Oman and Saudi Arabia. *Journal of Management and Public Policy*, **1**(2): 28–47.
Alotaibi, A.G. 2001. Antecedents of organizational citizenship behavior: a study of public personnel in Kuwait. *Public Personnel Management*, **30**(3): 363–376.
Aycan, Z., Al-Hamadi, A., Davis, A. and Budhwar, P. 2007. Cultural orientations and preferences for HRM policies and practices: the case of Oman. *International Journal of Human Resource Management*, **18**(1): 11–32.
Bakhtiari, H. 1995. Cultural effects on management style: a comparative study of American and Middle Eastern management styles. *International Studies of Management and Organization*, **25**(3): 97–118.
Budhwar, P.S., Al-Yahmadi, S. and Debrah, Y. 2002. Human resource development in the Sultanate of Oman. *International Journal of Training and Development*, **6**(3): 198–215.
Budhwar, P.S. and Debrah, Y.A. 2003. *Human Resource Management in Developing Countries*. London: Routledge.
Budhwar, P.S. and Sparrow, P.R. 2002. An integrative framework for understanding cross-national human resource management practices. *Human Resource Management Review*, **12**(3): 377–403.
Forstenlechner, I., Madi, M.T., Selim, H.M. and Rutledge, E.J. 2012. Emiratisation: determining the factors that influence the recruitment decisions of employers in the UAE. *International Journal of Human Resource Management*, **23**(2): 406–421.
Forstenlechner, I. and Mellahi, K. 2011. Gaining legitimacy through hiring local workforce at a premium: the case of MNEs in the United Arab Emirates. *Journal of World Business*, **46**(4): 455–461.
Giangreco, A., Carugati, A., Pilati, M. and Sebastiano, A. 2010. Performance appraisal systems in the Middle East: moving beyond Western logics. *European Management Review*, **7**: 155–168.
Haque, S.M. 2001. The diminishing publicness of public service under the current mode of governance. *Public Administration Review*, **61**(1): 65–82.
Hammami, M., Ruhashyankiko, J.-F. and Yehoue, E. 2006. Determinants of public–private partnerships in infrastructure. IMF Working Paper, no. 06/99.
Harry, W. 2007. Employment creation and localization: the crucial human resource issues for the GCC. *International Journal of Human Resource Management*, **18**(1): 132–146.
Hodgson, S. 2014. Women's status in the labor market: Canada versus the UAE. *Middle East Journal of Business*, **9**(1): 18–23.
Hutchings, K., Lirio, P. and Metcalfe, D.B. 2012. Gender, globalisation and development: a re-evaluation of the nature of women's global work. *International Journal of Human Resource Management*, **23**(9): 1763–1787.
Ibrahim, E.M., Al Sejini, S. and Al Qassimi, O.A.A. 2004. Job satisfaction and performance of government employees in UAE. *Journal of Management Research*, **4**(1): 1–12.
Iles, P., Almhedie, A. and Baruch, Y. 2012. Managing HR in the Middle East: challenges in the public sector. *Public Personnel Management*, **41**(3): 465–492.

Karam, C.M. and Afiouni, F. 2014. Localizing women's experiences in academia: multilevel factors at play in the Arab Middle East and North Africa. *International Journal of Human Resource Management*, **25**(4): 500–530.
Khilji, S.E. 2001. Human resource management in Pakistan. In P.S. Budhwar and Y.A. Debrah (eds), *Human Resource Management in Developing Countries*. London: Sage, pp. 102–120.
Khoury, G.C. and Analoui, F. 2004. Innovative management model for performance appraisal: the case of the Palestinian public universities. *Management Research News*, **27**(1/2): 56–73.
Kulshreshtha, P. 2008. Public sector governance reform: the World Bank's framework. *International Journal of Public Sector Management*, **21**(5): 556–567.
Le Renard, A. 2014. *A Society of Young Women: Opportunities of Place, Power and Reform in Saudi Arabia*. Stanford, CA: Stanford University Press.
Leat, M. and El-Kot, G. 2007. HRM practices in Egypt: the influence of national context? *International Journal of Human Resource Management*, **18**(1): 147–158.
Linzi, K.J. and Madsen, R.S. 2014. Oman's labour force: an analysis of gender in management. *Equality, Diversity and Inclusion*, **33**(8): 789–805.
Lirio, P., Lituchy, T.R., Monserrat, S.I., Olivas-Lijan, M.R., Duffy, J.A., Fox, S., Gregory, A., Punnett, B.J. and Santos, N. 2007. Exploring career-life success and family social support of successful women in Canada, Argentina and Mexico. *Career Development International*, **12**(1): 28–50.
Manning, N. 2001. The legacy of new public management in developing countries. *International Review of Administrative Sciences*, **67**(2): 297–312.
Marmenout, K. and Lirio, P. 2014. Local female talent retention in the Gulf: Emirati women bending with the wind. *International Journal of Human Resource Management*, **25**(2): 144–166.
Mellahi, K. 2007. The effect of regulations on HRM: private sector firms in Saudi Arabia. *International Journal of Human Resource Management*, **18**(1): 85–99.
Mellahi, K. and Budhwar, P.S. 2010. Introduction: Islam and human resource management. *Personnel Review*, **39**(6): 685–691.
Mellahi, K. and Wood, G.T. 2001. Human resource management in Saudi Arabia. In P.S. Budhwar and Y.A. Debrah (eds), *Human Resource Management in Developing Countries*. London: Routledge, pp. 135–152.
Metcalfe, D.B. 2006. Exploring cultural dimensions of gender and management in the Middle East. *Thunderbird International Business Review*, **48**(1): 93–107.
Metcalfe, D.B. 2008. Women, management and globalization in the Middle East. *Journal of Business Ethics*, **83**(1): 85–100.
Metcalfe, D.B. 2011. Women, work organization, and social change: human resource development in Arab Gulf States. *Human Resource Development International*, **14**(2): 123–129.
Metle, M. 2002. The influence of traditional culture on attitudes towards work among Kuwaiti women employees in the public sector. *Women in Management Review*, **17**(6): 245–261.
Moghadam, V.M. 2005. Women's economic participation in the Middle East: what difference has the neoliberal policy turn made? *Journal of Middle East Women's Studies*, **1**(1): 110–146.
Mostafa, A.M.S. and Gould-Williams, J.S. 2014. Testing the mediation effect of person–organization fit on the relationship between high performance HR practices and employee outcomes in the Egyptian public sector. *International Journal of Human Resource Management*, **25**(2): 276–292.
Namazie, P. and Frame, P. 2007. Developments in human resource management in Iran. *International Journal of Human Resource Management*, **18**(1): 159–171.
Omair, K. 2008. Women in management in the Arab context. *Education, Business and Society: Contemporary Middle Eastern*, **1**(2): 107–123.
Pollitt, C. and Bouckaert, G. 2004. *Public Management Reform: A Comparative Analysis – New Public Management, Governance, and the Neo-Weberian State*. Oxford: Oxford University Press.
Qureshi, R. 2014. Human resource development and the status of women in the labor force in Saudi Arabia: a critical analysis. *International Journal of Current Research and Academic Review*, **2**(4): 144–155.
Rajasekar, J. and Khan, S.A. 2013. Training and development function in Omani public sector organizations: a critical evaluation. *Journal of Applied Business and Economics*, **14**(2): 37–52.
Redvers, Louise 2015. BBC – Capital – Is Dubai the best place for women in the Middle East? 23 April. http://www.bbc.com/capital/story/20150422-which-women-get-ahead-in-dubai (accessed 27 July 2016).
Rees, C.J., Mamman, A. and Braik, B.A. 2007. Emiratization as a strategic HRM change initiative: case study evidence from a UAE petroleum company. *International Journal of Human Resource Management*, **18**(1): 33–53.
Rutledge, E., Al Shamsi, F., Bassioni, Y. and Al Sheikh, H. 2011. Women, labour market nationalization policies and human resource development in the Arab Gulf states. *Human Resource Development International*, **14**(2): 183–198.
Sidani, Y. 2005. Women, work, and Islam in Arab societies. *Women in Management Review*, **20**(7): 498–512.
Siddique, M.C. 2004. Job analysis: a strategic human resource management practice. *International Journal of Human Resource Management*, **15**(1): 219–244.

Soltani, E. 2010. The overlooked variable in managing human resources of Iranian organizations: workforce diversity – some evidence. *International Journal of Human Resource Management*, **21**(1): 84–108.
Syed, J., Hazboun, N.G. and Murray, P.A. 2014. What locals want: Jordanian employees' views on expatriate managers. *International Journal of Human Resource Management*, **25**(2): 212–223.
Tayeb, M. 2001. Human resource management in Iran. In P.S, Budhwar and A.Y. Debrah (eds), *Human Resource Management in Developing Countries*. London: Sage, pp. 121–134.
Tlaiss, H.A. and Dirani, K.M. 2015. Women and training: an empirical investigation in the Arab Middle East. *Human Resource Development International*, **18**(4): 366–386.
Tlaiss, H. and Kauser, S. 2011. The importance of wasta in the career success of Middle Eastern managers. *Journal of European Industrial Training*, **35**(5): 467–486.
Tlaiss, H.A. and Mendelson, M.B. 2014. Predicting women's job satisfaction with personal demographics: evidence from a Middle Eastern country. *International Journal of Human Resource Management*, **25**(3): 434–445.
United Nations 2008. *Governance in the Middle East, North Africa and Western Balkans: Challenges and Priorities in Reforming Public Administration in the Mediterranean Region*. New York: United Nations, Department of Economic and Social Affairs.
Van der Wal, Z., Huberts, L., Van Den Heuvel, H. and Kolthoff, E. 2006. Central values of government and business: differences, similarities and conflicts. *Public Administration Quarterly*, **30**(3/4): 314–364.
Vidyasagar, G. and Rea, D.M. 2004. Saudi women doctors: gender and careers within Wahhabic Islam and a 'Westernised' work culture. *Women's Studies International Forum*, **27**(3): 261–280.
Welsh, D.H.B., Memili, E., Kaciak, E. and Al Sadoon, A. 2014. Saudi women entrepreneurs: a growing economic segment. *Journal of Business Research*, **67**(5): 758–762.
Yaghi, A., Goodman, D., Holton, E.F. and Bates R.A. 2008. Validation of the learning transfer system inventory: a study of supervisors in the public sector in Jordan. *Human Resource Development Quarterly*, **19**(3): 241–262.
Yeganeh, H. and Su, Z. 2007. Pratiques de gestion des ressources humaines en Iran: caractéristiques et déterminants sociaux. *Gestion 2000*, **24**(4): 71–94.
Zukowska, M. 2015. An uphill battle: too few women in the boardroom. *Solutions*, **5**(3). http://www.thesolutionsjournal.com/node/237251 (accessed 27 July 2016).

21. *Wasta* in the Jordanian context

Mohammad Ta'Amnha, Susan Sayce and Olga Tregaskis

INTRODUCTION

'*Wasta*' is a powerful and pervasive social mechanism underpinning the employment relationship in Arabic societies. It is a specific form of social capital that influences several aspects of people's lives and the way in which business is conducted (Sabri, 2011). Therefore, '[o]ne of the greatest challenges to managers and researchers in the Arab world has been in understanding the social networks or "*Wasta*" that pervade business activities' (Iles et al., 2012, p. 4). Nevertheless, there is a huge gap in the literature on several aspects of *Wasta*, including its meanings, influences, downsides and usage, and how it is perceived by people and organizations (Aldossari and Robertson, 2016; Barnett et al., 2011; Loewe et al., 2008). The relational dynamic connecting individual, work environments and societal norms makes *Wasta* a mechanism of particular relevance to the study of human resource management (HRM) issues, and one that has been recognized as lacking attention (Aladwan et al., 2014; Budhwar and Mellahi, 2007; Altarawneh and Aldehayyat, 2011). The significance of *Wasta* has arguably taken on new meaning arising from the current transitions taking place in the Arab region that offer an unprecedented 'quasi-experimental setting' in which to examine theories and frameworks (Zahra, 2011, p. 2). For instance, Sidani and Showail (2013) claimed that the Arab Spring revolutions that started in mid-2011 have revealed that the young generation is less attached to many traditional values, and they have therefore developed new understandings and perceptions of their lives. In contrast, 25 years ago Faisal (1990) found that 79.4 per cent of respondents in an Arabic context indicated that both old and young people used *Wasta*; and just prior to the rise of political tensions in Jordan, the Arab Archives Institute (2000) found that 78 per cent of the Jordanian people believed that *Wasta* would remain strong in Jordanian society and that the need for its intervention was increasing.

This chapter is devoted to beginning to address the void in our understanding of the meaning and impact of *Wasta* in contemporary Jordanian society. This chapter will draw on available literature and empirical research to clarify the realities of *Wasta* as experienced by those working in a Jordanian context, and to identify the cultural and institutional factors shaping the meaning of *Wasta* and its impact.

THE JORDANIAN CONTEXT

Jordan was established in 1921 under the name of the Emirate of Trans-Jordan during the British mandate, which ended in 1946. In 1950 the state was renamed The Hashemite Kingdom of Jordan, and the special defence treaty with the United Kingdom was rescinded in 1957. Arabic is the official language of Jordan, but people speak it in different dialects (north, south, city, village, etc.); in addition, English is widely spoken, especially among the educated working in the Jordanian government, and private business.

Jordan is a small country of about 81,328 square kilometres, located in an unstable area in the Middle East. It borders Syria to the north, Israel, the Dead Sea and the West Bank to the west, Saudi Arabia to the south, and Iraq to the east. Jordan is a lower-middle income country with a population of around 6,388,000, 80 per cent of whom are located in urban areas. It is a young society, with more than a third of its population under the age of 15 and about 60 per cent between 15 and 64 years of age (Department of Statistics, 2012a). Ninety-two per cent of the Jordanian population are Sunni Muslims while about 2 per cent are Shia Muslims and Druze, and 6 per cent are Christians.

Since the 2000s, Jordan has experienced visible improvements in several areas, including healthcare, literacy, democracy, politics, the economy and human resources. However, Jordan is still facing many challenges such as high rates of unemployment, lack of natural resources, political instability in the region, inconsistency in financial aid, and huge numbers of refugees particularly from Palestine, Iraq and, recently, from Syria, which puts more pressure on the infrastructure, the limited resources and job opportunities (see Chapters 1 and 3 in this volume).

THEORETICAL BACKGROUND: *WASTA* AND SOCIAL CAPITAL

Social capital is a popular concept in the social sciences, resulting from its significant impact on social actors and their societies at macro and micro levels (Lin, 2001). Analysis at the macro level has examined the effect of social capital on wellbeing, public health, democracy, politics, economies, innovation adoption and diffusion, and development of markets (Weaver and Habibov, 2012; Putnam, 2000; Sampson et al., 2002; De Silva et al., 2005; Szreter and Woolcock, 2004; Aarikka-Stenroos et al., 2014). At the micro level, evidence has demonstrated the impact of social capital on the development and management of human resources, particularly in relation to people's career experiences, employability, development opportunities and career success (Cappellen and Janssens, 2008; Petersen et al., 2000; Boxman et al., 1991; Ibarra and Deshpamde, 2008; Nabi, 1999; Seidel et al., 2000; Forret and Dougherty, 2004).

Social capital refers to the resources that are generated through relationships with other social actors in a given context. Social capital is often identified in the literature as a positive form of capital that facilitates the generation of new knowledge, the flow of knowledge between actors, and the diffusion and uptake of innovations (Sanchez-Famoso et al., 2014; Dess and Sauerwald, 2014). Many organizations will create support structures to help their employees develop social capital internally and externally because of the knowledge creation, diffusion and learning benefits it creates (Tregaskis et al., 2010).

However, social capital can also be generated through institutional norms or conventions that govern relations and responsibilities between social actors and define the boundaries between members and non-members. For instance, social capital exists as Guanxi in China (Chen and Chen, 2004), Jeitinho in Brazil, Svyazi in Russia, and Pulling Strings in the United Kingdom (Smith et al., 2011), Tropil in Turkey (Özbay, 2008), Nepotism in Latin American and Africa (Wated and Sanchez, 2015; Bekker, 1991), Family Tree in Zambia, and *Wasta* in the Arabic world (Cunningham and Sarayrah, 1993). The one element common to all these mechanisms for developing social capital is how they are perceived to be biased by offering unfair advantages to those who are members. Thus, in the business world such mechanisms for social capital development are not seen as progressive and commensurate with 'good practice'. Despite these negative connotations, these practices have endured. In Jordan, the institutionally embedded mechanism for developing social capital is *Wasta*, which is the phenomenon of interest here.

WASTA: MEANING AND CHARACTERISTICS

Wasta can be seen as 'the intervention of a patron in favour of a client to obtain benefits and/or resources from a third party' (Mohammad and Hamdy, 2008, p. 1). This definition indicates the parties involved including (1) the *Wasta* person (intercessor) who does the *Wasta* (verb) and (2) the Wastee (supplicant) who receives benefits (called objects), sometimes from (3) a third party. These three elements form the key components of *Wasta* (Cunningham and Sarayrah, 1993).

There are two facets of *Wasta*: mediation and intercession (Cunningham and Sarayrah, 1993). The former refers to mediating activities between disputing parties to resolve a conflict between them, or to facilitate a social rapprochement such as in the case of marriage. Mediating *Wasta* aims to promote cooperation and security among society members; thus, it receives more societal approval and less criticism. The latter involves bypassing the law and obtaining favours and benefits at the expense of other people; therefore, it is widely opposed by Arabic people.

Wasta consists of multifunctional 'social networks of interpersonal connections . . . implicating the exercise of power, influence, and information sharing through social and politico-business networks. It is intrinsic to the operation of many valuable social processes, central to the transmission of knowledge and the creation of opportunity' (Hutchings and Weir, 2006, p. 143). This means that the scope of *Wasta* is not confined to support and favouritism provided to family members, such as nepotism. *Wasta* involves several other relationships such as cronyism, kinship, colleagueship, friendships and business relationships.

Wasta is also perceived as an unwritten social contract comprising cooperation and obligation among certain social groups' memberships including families. However, it does not always imply direct reciprocity in the relationship. Sometimes the intercessors or those providing benefits to the supplicant do not expect to receive support in return or from the same beneficiaries directly. However, people sometimes expand their networks and offer their help and support in order to receive reciprocal benefits in the future (Adler and Kwon, 2002). Therefore, *Wasta* is deemed a 'hidden force' (Cunningham and Sarayrah, 1993; see also Cuervo-Cazurra, 2016) or 'invisible hand' that is not always apparent during the benefits exchange process (Barnett et al., 2011). In this way, *Wasta* sets out the governance rules or expectations of the participants.

Prevalence of *Wasta*

Wasta is prevalent and historically is integrated deeply into the social fabric of Arabic societies (Barnett et al., 2011). It is part of day-to-day Arabic language and activities, and represents 'a way of life' (Tlaiss and Kauser, 2011b, p. 479). For example, Ezzedeen and Swiercz (2001) found that 65 per cent of the Lebanon Mobile Company's employees obtained their jobs through *Wasta*. The Arab Archives Institute (2000) found that more than 90 per cent of respondents expected to use it and 75 per cent had used it to facilitate procedures. Faisal (1990) found that 79.4 per cent of respondents from a Saudi university indicated that both older and younger people use *Wasta*. Tlaiss and Kauser (2011b) conducted their research in five Arabic countries (Lebanon, Syria, Kuwait, the United Arab Emirates (UAE) and Saudi Arabia) and studied the opinions of managers from different managerial levels. They found that 89 per cent of respondents had used *Wasta*, 80 per cent use it regularly and 86 per cent believe that *Wasta* improves all sorts of interactions.

WHY DOES *WASTA* PREVAIL DESPITE ATTEMPTS TO ERADICATE IT?

It is clear from the evidence base that *Wasta* prevails despite the unease associated with such forms of social capital. Therefore we turn our attention to a consideration of some of the factors that may explain its endurance. In doing so our explanation is anchored within the institutionalist frame of reference, which helps explain the embedding of mechanisms, such as *Wasta*, within the fabric of social relations. This section therefore is divided into four parts: Rules and Regulations, Professionalism and Education, Economic Challenges, and Cultural Factors.

Rule and Regulations

Wasta is a punishable crime by the Jordanian Anti-Corruption Commission. In law No. 62 for the year 2006, Article 5, point (f) states that 'Acceptance of nepotism and favouritism, which nullifies a right or validates what is void.' However, such regulations and rules are not effective in eliminating *Wasta* from the society for several reasons.

First, Jordan's administrative and governmental system lacks transparency and accountability on all levels (Loewe et al., 2008).The absence of trust between people and the government encourages people to turn to informal institutions to attain what they believe to be their right or to access resources from the labour market (Rothstein, 2004). People in Jordan therefore tend to rely on *Wasta*, which is an informal institution (El-Said and Harrigan, 2009), to achieve outcomes swiftly and with less effort (Faisal, 1990)

Second, *Wasta* stems from the state's desire to maintain influence and grip on authority to govern (Mohammad and Hamdy, 2008). Examining the development of *Wasta* in Jordan helps explain the significance of this point. Historically, *Wasta* was employed to ensure security in societies. It was used, particularly in its mediation function, by the sheikhs to resolve conflict between tribes or tribe members (Ronsin, 2010) to prevent people taking revenge should disputes be unresolved (Cunningham and Sarayrah, 1994). Later, *Wasta* witnessed a transition with the establishment of Jordan at the beginning of the twentieth century. In 1921, the emerging central Jordanian government used tribal sheikhs to act as intermediaries between their tribesmen and the administrative institutions to impose and promote the state law to gain legitimacy for the new institutional structures of political and economic governance. Meanwhile, sheikhs intervened on behalf of their tribesmen in the government to create jobs and collect economic benefits (Ronsin, 2010). As a result, more key positions were filled by the close confidants of the political regime regardless of their competences (Mohammad and Hamdy, 2008). Such practices are believed to still play a key role in Jordan's public administration. *Wasta* also has become a more institutionalized practice in Jordan; for instance, it is a common practice for sons of security officers to be given preference in the admission at universities and given scholarships to cover fees and living expenses through being on the Honoured Military list or '*Makromah Eskareha*'. On graduation they are given preference in filling vacancies in the military institutions. This process maintains homogeneity and stasis within the administration system across several generations.

The third reason that explains the difficulties in using regulation to change *Wasta* behaviour concerns the people who draw up the laws and monitor compliance. These responsibilities lie with members of parliament (MPs), who themselves are under pressure to exercise *Wasta* to increase their status and influence. MPs in Jordan are to some degree expected by the Jordanian people to undertake *Wasta* to help them find jobs, achieve transfers to other workplaces, gain promotions or obtain medical exemptions. Therefore, MPs are under continuous pressure from people in their electoral strongholds to provide them with various benefits, including benefits in the workplace. This means that the MPs, instead of working to draw up strong regulations to fight *Wasta* and monitor the government's application of rules, may through their actions promote *Wasta*. Further, it might be argued that they are under government pressure to allow *Wasta* to continue in order for the government to meet its *Wasta* obligations to its supporters.

Wasta is also used by the Jordanian central government as a mechanism to resolve numerous societal problems. For instance, after the results of the 2013 election were published, riots and tribal clashes erupted in several districts in Jordan. People who were dissatisfied with the results publicly protested, causing some injuries and damage to property; therefore, the district governors used tribal mechanisms to resolve the disputes. Such activities add significant value to, and strengthen, *Wasta* in Jordan.

Fourth, *Wasta* prevails in the private sector due the sheer volume of family-run businesses in Jordan. For example, a few highly influential companies and families mainly govern the insurance sector. Given that the monitoring of the governance in these family-run companies is weak, it is not surprising to see *Wasta* still operating in Jordan. The strong bonds among the Jordanian people can weaken the authorities' effort to fight *Wasta*.

Fifth, the lack of employee protection afforded by the labour law in Jordan is believed to have an impact on *Wasta*. It represents another challenge in the Jordanian labour market. This law suffers from many deficiencies, such as in the articles related to unfair dismissal and ending employees' contracts. For instance, during 2009/10 many employers took advantage of labour law gaps and used articles, particularly 25, 26, 28 and 31, to terminate thousands of employees' contracts. These articles allow organizations that restructure themselves to terminate unspecified numbers of employees' contracts simply by informing the Labour Ministry (Phenix Center, 2011). The violations of employees' rights also take the form of low compensation received as a result of unfair dismissal. At best, they receive only half a month's salary for each year of service. The gap in the social protection of workers is also exacerbated by the small number of trade union representatives and the weak role played by the existing ones in protecting their members' rights (Phenix Center, 2011). So people tend to use *Wasta* because it offers some protection from redundancy whereas less well-connected employees have weaker job security.

Finally, the large number of migrant workers in Jordan and competition for jobs may also explain, in part, the persistence of *Wasta*. Around 17 per cent of the workforce is migrant workers, the majority from Egypt, Palestine, Syria and East Asia. A huge number of those migrant workers are working without work permits, while others are working in sectors other than those for which they obtained permission to work, particularly the agricultural sector (Phenix Center, 2011). This situation increases competition for jobs and therefore the Jordanian people try to use *Wasta* to improve their chances.

Professionalism and Education

The educational system has also affected the *Wasta* footprint primarily because of its disconnect from the needs of businesses and an expanding economy. Thus, *Wasta* has played an important role in transitioning people from the educational system into employment. The educational system in Jordan is advanced compared with its counterparts elsewhere in the Middle East.

The formal education system in Jordan is organized into three levels: a compulsory level for children aged 6 to 15 consisting of primary schools, preparatory schools, a comprehensive secondary education (academic and vocational) and applied secondary education; and higher education consisting of either two-year intermediate-level courses offered by community colleges or courses of four years or more provided by public and private universities. Acceptance at the universities and colleges, particularly the state-owned ones, is determined mainly by the results of the General Secondary Education Certificate Examination (*Al-Tawjihi*).

The educational system in Jordan has undergone dramatic changes since 1921 when there were only four primary schools. Today, Jordanian society is commonly described as a students' society (Branine and Analoui, 2006) with over 1.5 million young people involved in schooling. There are also 372,120 undergraduate students and 14,390 postgraduate students studying in about 30 Jordanian universities and 11,173 students studying abroad. In addition, there are more than 14,344 students taking intermediate diplomas in 54 community colleges. Given that the population of Jordan is just over 6 million, these figures demonstrate a serious commitment to education (Department of Statistics, 2012a). The advanced nature of the Jordanian educational system also makes it attractive to 28,000 foreign students (Alghad, 2013).

In 1961 the illiteracy rate was 67.6 per cent, in 2012 it was 6.7 per cent (Department of Statistics, 2012b). This figure shows the huge advancement and spread of education in Jordan. Jordan showed progress in the Human Development Index (HDI) from .715 to .752 on a scale of 0–1 between 1997 and 2005 (European Neighbourhood and Partnership Instrument, 2007). This is linked to how Jordan is one of the better-performing countries in the Middle East region in terms of life expectancy at birth (72 years old), adult literacy (97.7 per cent), and access to basic services and education (enrolment has reached, respectively, 91 per cent, 80 per cent and 31 per cent at primary, secondary and tertiary levels).

The great attention paid to education in Jordan is largely a result of the lack of natural resources. The government has invested significantly to develop the human resources in Jordan. However, the educational system in Jordan suffers from a lack of coordination between its outputs and the needs of the labour market (European Neighbourhood and Partnership Instrument, 2007). Therefore, the Jordanian people try to diminish this weakness through using *Wasta* to compensate for the lack of professionally originated skills or experience. This therefore increases the usage of *Wasta* in the Jordanian labour market and indeed strengthens its existence.

Economic Challenges

One of the key factors driving the use of *Wasta* in Jordan has been the harsh economic conditions. Indeed, people tend to use *Wasta* to meet their needs, though they understand its negative impact on their society and organizations.

Jordan suffers from a lack of natural resources such as energy resources (e.g., oil, coal), water resources (in which it is one of the five poorest countries in the world) and fertile land (only 10 per cent of its land is arable). Jordan's economy depends mainly on phosphates, potash and natural gas, which meets only 10 per cent of the country's energy needs. The service-producing sector in Jordan accounted for 65.8 per cent of gross domestic product (GDP) compared with 34.2 per cent provided by the commodity-producing sectors in 2009.

The performance of the Jordanian economy is still affected by the repercussions of the unstable regional and global circumstances and challenges. According to figures released by the Central Bank of Jordan (2012), the economic and political pressures on Jordan have been escalating since the Arab Spring erupted in 2011. The fiscal deficit increased significantly to 8.2 per cent of GDP in 2012 from 6.8 per cent in 2011. In addition, the current account deficit increased to 18.1 per cent of GDP, from 12.0 per cent in 2011. Furthermore, the foreign currency reserves in the Central Bank of Jordan slumped by 37.0 per cent at the end of 2012 and the outstanding balance of extended credit facilities increased by 12.5 per cent compared with the preceding year, with the private sector representing 50 per cent of the expansion.

The high levels of unemployment (see Table 21.1) force job-seekers to use *Wasta* in the competition of getting jobs (Mohammad and Hamdy, 2008). It is argued that *Wasta* is used in job competition because people see no other way to meet their objectives (Loewe et al., 2008).

Furthermore, Jordan has a high number of refugees, which creates challenges. The

Table 21.1 Unemployment rate in Jordan

Unemployment rate	Total (%)	Female (%)	Male (%)
2009	12.9	24.1	10.3
2010	12.5	21.7	10.4
2011	12.9	21.2	11.0
2012	12.2	19.9	10.4

Source: Department of Statistics (2012a).

high number of refugees is caused mainly by wars and conflicts. The majority of refugees are Palestinians (1,952,000), Syrians (1,300,000), Iraqis (500,000) and Circassians (80,000), in addition to those from other nations such as Armenians and Chechens. This places huge pressure on the country's infrastructure as well as on the limited natural resources. These refugees are also competing significantly with the Jordanian workforce in the labour market. This means that Jordanian employees have tended to turn to *Wasta* more to find good jobs in this highly competitive Jordanian labour market.

The global financial crisis has also impacted on Jordan. The Jordanian market is strongly integrated into global markets. Companies in Jordan, particularly those in the financial sector, are dealing with many challenges that affect their operations and thus their survival. This can mean that in some instances firms may undertake *Wasta* involving supporting job opportunities for family members of clients in order to retain a lucrative contract with a customer (Ta'Amnha, 2014). Thus, *Wasta* has important trade-offs, which can make a difference to the survival of a firm and the job security of that firm's workforce in tough economic markets.

Cultural Factors

Cultural aspects are key sources of influence in Arabic societies. In particular, the strong family relationships have a key impact on the economic, political and social life in these societies (Ali, 1992; Hutchings and Weir, 2006; Rice, 1999).

Wasta is a social construct that is a key dimension in the Jordanian culture by which the tribal values of solidarity, loyalty and cooperation are achieved. *Wasta* is promoted and sustained in Jordanian society through several embedded informal mechanisms. For instance, any person who occupies an influential position is expected to exercise *Wasta* to their relatives. People do *Wasta* to meet their obligations to their tribes and families so that they can show their loyalty and solidarity (Loewe et al., 2008). Otherwise, people who refuse to exercise *Wasta* for their relatives will become outcasts and lose support, protection and status provided by their groups (Ronsin, 2010; Cunningham and Sarayrah, 1994). *Wasta* therefore has the ability of survive in society by shaming and shunning those who refuse to exercise *Wasta* for their relatives. Indeed, the Arab Archives Institute (2000) found that around 60 per cent of Jordanian respondents said that they are subjected to social pressure to exercise *Wasta*.

Wasta is also deep-seated in the Jordanian society because it enhances people's social status and success. Whiteoak et al. (2006) introduced the concept of 'utility of *Wasta*', which explains that people's successes are sometimes evaluated based on their connections with other influential people. Undeniably, *Wasta* is a source of pride, prestige and influence for both the intercessors and those who provide the support and for the supplicants who have influential *Wasta* connections. This clearly explains the motivation for various parties to be involved in *Wasta* and its promotion.

CHALLENGES TO *WASTA*

Undoubtedly, *Wasta* is widespread in Arabic societies, a characteristic of the lack of democracy in the region (Touzani et al., 2015). Others perceive it as inequitable, a form of corruption that implies breaching the laws and regulations enacted to ensure justice and equal opportunities among the societies' members. Obviously, the influence of *Wasta* in decision-making processes in the workplace results in available resources and benefits being given to some people at the expense of others who may be more qualified or experienced.

Certainly, the intervention of *Wasta* in hiring decisions sometimes results in unqualified employees gaining roles who are then unable to meet their job responsibilities due to a lack of knowledge or skill. Re-qualifying these employees and solving the problems they often create requires considerable resources, affecting the productivity and competitiveness of their organizations detrimentally (Warren et al., 2004).

The detrimental effects of *Wasta* are seen not only in the lack of 'know-how' competence in the professional profiles of *Wasta* employees (supplicants). Unprofessional behaviour, for example absence and habitual tardiness, can have destructive consequences for the organization's performance, and its existence (Samuel and Justina, 2006; Chirasha and Mahapa, 2012). The use of *Wasta* also impacts on the perception of justice in organizations, affecting the satisfaction, commitment and citizenship behaviours of unsupported employees or those who refuse to use *Wasta* in their jobs. *Wasta* affects the job satisfaction and motivation of employees negatively and leads to a reduction in their work involvement and organizational commitment, low morale and high levels of stress and frustration, according to an analysis of 511 human resources managers' responses from Jordan and Egypt (Hayajenh et al., 1994). *Wasta* can render these organizations more vulnerable to the risk of resentment and retaliation from dissatisfied employees who may feel discriminated against or marginalized (Skarlicki and Folger, 1997). *Wasta* has a destructive impact on the companies' abilities to increase their 'know-how' competence or intellectual capital, which are needed to maintain competitive advantage (Edvinsson et al., 1997). This happens when key employees find themselves unable to hone their practical skills by performing tasks associated with HRM or undertake their managerial responsibilities through practice and learning from experience (Davies and Easterby-Smith, 1984; Kolb et al., 2001). In addition, many of the principles of equity and fair treatment underpinning effective HRM can be compromised by the use of nepotism (Arasli et al., 2006). Tlaiss and Kauser (2011b) indicated that *Wasta* destroys equality in the workplace. They found that 83 per cent of the participants in their study perceived *Wasta* as an unfair practice because it leads to unqualified people being assigned to significant positions, resulting in poor performance in the organization.

The opportunity to leverage the level of knowledge in the organization is also lost when employees hesitate to invest their resources by enrolling in university or training institutions because they consider their status will be unchanged as they do not have powerful *Wasta* (Tlaiss and Kauser, 2011b). Certainly, organizations where favouritism is practised are undesirable places in which to work, particularly for ambitious professional managers (Rhoades and Eisenberger, 2002; Arasli et al., 2006). Metcalfe (2006), after analysing research from Jordan, Bahrain and Oman, found that employees who are not connected with intercessors do not receive certain work-related benefits such as job appointments or training opportunities because such resources are allocated according to personal relationships and family networks rather than individuals' qualifications and merits. As a result, talented and qualified people were not given the chance to improve their careers and enhance their life conditions (Metcalfe, 2006). In the longer term the use of *Wasta* can discourage a generation of well-educated employees to stay in Jordan, opting instead to take their human capital elsewhere to pursue opportunities in the global workplace.

Research suggests that the use of *Wasta* also reflects poorly on those who benefit. For instance, Mohammad and Hamdy (2008) found that those employees who used *Wasta* were rated lower in terms of their perceived competence than those who did not use it; furthermore, in terms of perceived morality, their study revealed that job incumbents who used *Wasta* were rated lower with regard to morality than those who did not use it.

Wasta affects human resources management practices because it impacts on employees' careers in Arab organizations. Hutchings and Weir (2006) explained that hiring and selecting decisions are subjective processes that are influenced largely by personal contacts, nepotism, regionalism and family name. Managers usually do *Wasta* to fulfil their duties to these groups, and their exercising of *Wasta* is not usually based on the beneficiaries' qualifications and abilities to meet organizational goals and objectives. Similarly, Altarawneh (2009) argues that managers' relatives and friends in the Jordanian banking sector receive extra benefits through participating in the organizations' training and development programmes. Tlaiss and Kauser (2011a) found similar results when analysing qualitative data with 32 managers who work in service and manufacturing industries. They found that the respondents believe that *Wasta* influences decisions on recruitment, promotion and career advancement opportunities.

PRESSURE FOR CHANGE: THE FUTURE OF *WASTA*

Social Pressures

Social pressure stems mainly from Islamic values and ethical codes that are highly dignified in Jordanian society, significantly affecting its members' attitudes and activities (Hashim, 2010). One of these principles is justice (Rice, 1999), and therefore any practices or activities that deprives some people of equal access to society's welfare are strongly condemned (Al Jallad, 2008).

The Islamic teachings encourage people to treat each other and allocate the societies' resources according to the principles of fairness and worthiness. Islam urges the decision makers to select honest people who are able to perform their jobs' responsibilities well. For instance, the Holy Qur'an, the major source of the Islam teachings, stated that 'The best you can hire is the strong and the trustworthy' 28:26. Also, the behaviours and practices of Omar Bin Alkhatab, the companion of Prophet Mohammad and Muslim Khalifa (successor), are considered a source of legalization and preferable examples and guidelines in administration. For instance, he rebuffed requests for hires in exchange for personal gain and influence and opposed hiring relatives; he said 'one betrays the God and his messenger if he hires a man based on their intimacy or kinship.' Accordingly, the religious community considers the intercessor who exercises *Wasta* for others as a devious and dishonest person (Cunningham and Sarayrah, 1993).

Therefore, the religious view discourages *Wasta* in society. But this is in contrast to the tribal mindset. Indeed, there is a degree of contradiction and tension between Islamic values and the tribal values, though both of them try to promote similar values. For example, the Islamic values aim to promote cooperation and solidarity among all of society members whereas at the tribal level there is a focus on promotion of values among the tribe members. Thus Islam condemns *Wasta* whereas it is highly encouraged in a tribal setting.

Pressure on *Wasta* also stems from face norms in Jordan. The face norm seems to have a strong effect on people's behaviours. Engaging in certain activities that are encouraged by members of society produces a positive image or white face. *Wasta*, for instance, was found to be a positive mechanism encouraging *Wasta* employees to do their jobs satisfactorily in order to give their intercessors a positive image or white face for those who provide benefits to the *Wasta* employees based on the intercessors' recommendations. However, this informal mechanism also works in an adverse way. People are now increasingly avoiding any potential embarrassment that might be caused by taking an interest in the actions of their recommended employees as negative feedback could affect their social standing. So face norms are resulting in intercessors continuing to monitor the performance of the *Wasta* employees in order to encourage them to perform properly and resolve any problems that may occur (Cunningham and Sarayrah, 1993).

Politics and Arab Spring

The heated political conditions currently present in Jordan are having a considerable impact on many issues and practices in Jordanian society and its organizations. The continuing call for economic, political and social reforms by the Jordanian people places many pressures on *Wasta* and the people who exercise it. The momentum of these pressures has increased dramatically since the Arab Spring uprisings challenged long-standing custom and practice in the Arabic world.

The Arabic people see *Wasta* as a major cause of poverty and backwardness in their society, and they are therefore eager to eliminate it. For instance, Hassan (2013, p. 69) explained that *Wasta* was one of the main factors that ignited the revolution in Tunisia since the 'market liberalization was very much tied to cronyism' and the privatization of state-owned businesses was confined to 'a context in which special connections (*Wasta*) prevailed rather than a Weberian "rational" bureaucracy'. In addition, Kilcullen and Rosenblatt (2014) explained that the revolution in Syria was started by people who do not have links to the regime and no *Wasta* to get jobs or bribe money to buy them. Similarly, in Morocco, *Wasta* causes tensions, particularly for unemployed graduates who do not have *Wasta* to go to higher-rated education institutions and graduate automatically to jobs that are allocated or created for the elite. This situation leaves the deprived job-seekers dissatisfied that they belong to an inferior social category (Badimon, 2013). Jamali et al. (2013, p. 159) outline how *Wasta* reduces the effectiveness of societies' economies, thus negatively affecting people's living standards and security leading to political tension and unrest; how *Wasta* 'permits the avoidance of costs or taxes, thereby reducing state revenues; the acquisition of positions of power without having the required experience and skills, thereby weakening institutions; or the acquisition of monopolies over rent-generating assets'.

Noticeably, the Arab Spring has affected the spread and usage of *Wasta* adversely. For instance, in Tunisia, Touzani et al. (2015) found that even though *Wasta* is a key obstacle for the Tunisian entrepreneurs, post-revolution it has become more feasible for *Wasta* outsiders to gain prestige and initiate entrepreneurial activities.

In Jordan, because of continuing demands for reform, the government has focused increasingly on the role of the Anti-Corruption Commission, which is responsible for monitoring the performance of government institutions and to some extent the private sector. A major role for this institution is the investigation of any *Wasta* activities. Many Jordanian people find that *Wasta* plays a negative role in the development and advancement of the country, with negative consequences for their standards of living. This has been the result of favouritism and dominance of subjective criteria in hiring and promotion decisions, which has meant that performance levels have become less important requirements, in turn affecting organizational efficiency and effectiveness. Thus, as the quality of the services provided to the citizens has deteriorated, so their voices have become louder.

Globalization

The other factor driving change on *Wasta* comes from the external pressures on Jordan. Certainly, the Jordanian workplace has witnessed many changes arising from the country's desire for modernization, and in response to globalization pressures. In fact, the Jordanian market has become more liberal and open. For instance, Jordan, the 136th member of the World Trade Organization (World Trade Organization, 2000), in 2000 signed a free trade agreement with the United States. It participated in the European Free Trade Association in 2001, and promotes free economic, industrial zones and privatization (Al-Shammari and Hussein, 2008). During this period (1999–2010) foreign direct investment increased by 600 per cent.

These indicators and events have stimulated deregulation of national economies and integration into a single market (Lane and Maeland, 2010). They are also increasing the competition for recruiting, developing talented human resource, and adopting Western management approaches (Fagenson, 1994), mainly Anglo-Saxon approaches (Sultana and Watts, 2008). The international companies that enter tend to work under high-level governance from headquarters that places pressure on *Wasta*. Typically, these companies rely on objective criteria when it comes to making decisions pertaining to HRM. These companies are perceived as very successful in the Jordanian market, and therefore the Jordanian companies tend to imitate these companies' practices in order to be perceived as legitimate to high potential candidates, giving them access to global labour markets and business markets. Certainly, the institutional isomorphic mechanisms effectively lead to substantial changes in societies and their organizations. For instance, Abu-Doleh (2000) indicated that the focus on modern HRM has increased recently in some Jordanian companies because it has significantly improved their productivity and enhanced their position in the market. Therefore, Jordanian organizations are realizing that the intervention of *Wasta* in their businesses can affect negatively their competitiveness, and as a result they begin to show signs of rejection of *Wasta* in their organization.

Islamic Business Ethics

Attention to Islamic Work Ethics (IWEs) has increased recently in the social science literature and is potentially an important driver in changing the use of *Wasta* practice. The importance of these ethics stems from their key influence on the sense-making processes of Muslims, shaping their beliefs and logics and thus determining their taken-for-grantedness.

Islamic ethics are easier to define given that there is otherwise a big debate on what is ethical and unethical. Muslims are more likely to accept ethics and values if they are rooted in Islam compared with their high sensitivity to other cultures' values such as the Western Protestant Work Ethics (PWEs), although they are similar in promoting 'hard work, commitment and dedication to work, work creativity, avoidance of unethical methods of wealth accumulation, cooperation and competitiveness at the work place' (Yousef, 2001, p. 154).

However, the IWEs are different from the PWEs in that the former place considerable emphasis on the intention rather than the results or profit, and they also give great consideration to the welfare of society and its organizations, such as justice and generosity in the workplace and duties to society, believing that participation in economic activities is an obligation (Yousef, 2001). Furthermore, IWEs consider both the spiritual and material aspects of people's lives and distinguish Islamic management from other approaches (Sabri, 2011).

Islamic ethics are derived mainly from two sources: the Qur'an – the holy book believed to have been sent to Prophet Mohammad by God; and the Sunnah – the written guidelines of Prophet Mohammad's sayings and practices. These ethics promote moral codes to organize and manage people's personal and professional lives. Rice (1999, p. 346) indicated that 'Islam is generally misunderstood and it is often surprising to some that it contains an entire socio-economic system'.

Indeed, Islam is a comprehensive system involving guidelines and rules for 'a complete way of life' (Sabri, 2011, p. 217). This system influences families' normal lived lives and their relationships to others; the guidelines explain the mission of individuals and groups within society and dictate the conduct required in economic activities, and educational, economic and judicial systems (Sabri, 2011, p. 217). For instance, the system intervenes in business and government activities, individuals' enterprises, and rewards, wages and relationships with employees (Iles et al., 2012). Another example is the expansion in Islamic insurance and banking businesses such as Takaful NasionalSdnBhd and Syarikkat Takaful Malaysia Bhd in Malaysia, Syarkat Takaful Singapura (Agencies) Pte Ltd in Singapore and Qatar Islamic Insurance Company in Qatar. It can also be seen in the way that Islam influences the businesses of some of the more conventional financial institutions such as Citibank, ANZ Bank and UBS Warburg, which have established Islamic banking systems to meet Islamic customers' needs (Ahmad and Petrick, 2003).

Islamic ethics have proved to be a positive influence in the workplace. For instance, Yousef (2001) surveyed 425 Muslim employees working for various organizations in the UAE and found that the IWEs affect both organizational commitment and job satisfaction and moderate the relationship between them. Similarly, Yousef (2000) analysed the responses of 474 employees from 30 organizations in the UAE and found that IWEs positively affected attitudes to organizational changes and organizational commitment. Ali and Al-Kazemi (2007) found that IWEs lead to increased loyalty of Kuwaiti managers to their companies, and they thus work hard to improve the performance and the positions of their companies compared to competitors. Mousavi et al. (2013), analysing 133 questionnaires completed by employees working in ten Iranian manufacturing companies discovered that IWEs have a significant positive influence on employees' job satisfaction.

Sadozai et al. (2013), analysing the responses of 460 full-time federal and provincial government employees, found that IWEs were positively related to organizational commitment, thus leading to a decrease in the turnover rate. Rokhman (2010), studying the responses of 49 employees from ten Islamic microfinance institutions in Indonesia, found that IWEs positively affect both job satisfaction and organizational commitment. Kumar and Rose (2010), studying 472 responses from employees in the Malaysian public sector, found that IWEs were pervasive in this sector and positively connected with innovation capabilities.

Rice (1999) explained four interrelated guidelines that stem from Islamic ethics, developing a framework that could be used to promote acceptable practices in Islamic societies and their organizations:

1. *Unity*: this principle has two faces – the first one reflects the belief that God is the only creator of the universe, while the other proposes that all Muslims are equal and are brothers and sisters; thus they have to cooperate and promote equal opportunities between them. Certainly, the ontology of humanity in the Qur'an's approach implies that all human beings are *umma wahida* (one community), come from a single origin, and have a common purpose (Hashmi, 1993).
2. *Justice*: this principle explains that one of the main messages of Islam is the need to eliminate all forms of inequity, injustice, exploitation and oppression from society. For instance, employment under the umbrella of Islam is governed by the Islamic laws of fairness and justice, with rewards matching performance (Possumah et al., 2013; Mellahi and Budhwar, 2010). The Qur'an mentioned that rewards and punishments should be based on the individual's merit or guilt and not on favouritism: '. . . no bearer of burdens can bear the burdens of another; . . . man can have nothing but what he strives for . . .' (Qur'an 53:38–39). The Islamic teachings encourage people to treat each other and allocate society's resources according to the principles of fairness and worthiness
3. *Trusteeship*: this principle implies that people are the trustees of the earth on behalf of God. This means that all people are encouraged to exploit the available opportunities to improve their living conditions. It is presumed that everyone has the right to access the available resources and benefit equally without depriving other people of what they deserve or have worked for. This principle also supposes that the available resources should be used properly and efficiently.
4. *The Need for Balance*: this principle implies that Muslims are encouraged to be moderate in all aspects of their lives, as Prophet Mohammad described Islam as a 'middle way', meaning that achieving social wellbeing and continued advancement in life requires a balance. IWEs, for instance, refer to attitudes to work, assuming that work is the most effective way of establishing a balance in one's personal, social and professional lives (Ali, 1992).

These ethics can be promoted when the different institutions in society share this responsibility, such as the Ministries of Education, Schools and Universities, religious institutions, and legislators (AL-Shaikh, 2003). Other international or regional institutions can also take part. Rokhman (2010) suggested that organizations' managers can work to ensure that employees understand IWEs by taking part in training and educational programmes that focus on applying Islamic morals and values in the workplace.

CONCLUSIONS

Overall, this chapter aimed to provide an understanding of the significance and use of *Wasta* in the workplace, but then to move beyond this by considering the societal factors that have embedded *Wasta* and the societal changes that may eventually influence its evolution.

Certainly, *Wasta* is a big dilemma in Jordan. On the one hand, *Wasta* is widely practised in Jordanian society and its institutions due to many reasons, including weaknesses in the rules and regulations, disconnect between the educational system and the needs of businesses and a growing economy, harsh economic conditions, and strong cultural tribal values of solidarity, loyalty and cooperation.

On the other hand, however, *Wasta* faces several challenges resulting from the negative effects of *Wasta* on Arabic societies and their organizations. As a result, *Wasta* is under incremental pressures comprising social disapproval, politics and Arab Spring, globalization, and application of IWEs.

This situation therefore indicates the presence of a significant tension occurring within the institution of *Wasta*. Some factors sustain and spread *Wasta* and some other factors operate in an adverse way. *Wasta* provides an example of institutionalizing and/or deinstitutionalizing processes in action, and how it will evolve remains to be seen. *Wasta* therefore provides fertile ground for research from several perspectives given that it intervenes in the economic, political, social and, recently, security issues in Arabic societies.

This work calls for paying more attention to the IWEs such as unity, justice, trusteeship, cooperation, solidarity and balance; and understanding how IWEs may play out in the workplace. Based on the evidence, we might suggest that as IWEs rise in the workplace the role of *Wasta* may decline, as the former acts to replace or substitute for the latter.

However, the evidence currently suggests that *Wasta* is widely used in Jordan (Arab Archives Institute, 2000; El-Said and Harrigan, 2009) even though it is perceived to be corrupt and against the notion of justice and equal opportunities in society. It is not compatible with principles of corporate governance and professionalism, and therefore there is a continuous demand by the Jordanian people for its eradication from Jordanian society and its organizations. However, by considering the historical context of *Wasta* we hope to have demonstrated that regulation alone is unlikely to create change. Globalization has opened the economic marketplace in Jordan, and the expansion of foreign direct investment and tight competition for talent is forcing firms to look at how social capital is created and utilized in the workplace.

Reacting to the negative effects of *Wasta*, organizations can create healthy working environments that give stronger consideration to the qualifications, education and experience of their employees than to any other factors in making career-related decisions. This can lead to increased levels of employee satisfaction and motivation towards their work. Thus, employees become more willing to invest their resources to develop their human capital while enriching their knowledge and skills. This situation would improve the organization's performance. Indeed, employees may consider the importance of investing in their human capital when they find that their organizations are applying fair systems that reward them according to the contributions they make to their organizations, rather than according to personal relationships such as *Wasta*. Human resource departments can play a major role in establishing such an organizational system that reduces the usage of traditional *Wasta*. They can draw clearer objective criteria that improve the assessment processes in career-related decisions such as recruiting, selecting, promoting and offering developmental opportunities.

The evidence suggests that many employees resort to *Wasta* because they feel it is the only option available to them. Therefore, there is scope for organizations to do more to provide access to opportunities for all. By introducing mentoring or transparent networking systems, organizations could give all employees an equal chance to receive advice and training from expert employees. The benefits gained from such exposure would enable employees to build their networks 'within' and beyond the organizations' boundaries, thus reducing the need for *Wasta*.

USEFUL WEBSITES

Transparency International: http://action.transparency.org.

Arabian Business.com: http://www.arabianbusiness.com/qatar-seeks-end-*Wasta*-culture-court-boss-474912.html#.Vre8h0v8FZh.

Corruption Research Network: http://corruptionresearchnetwork.org/workspace/mena/research/the-impact-of-favouritism-on-the-business-climate-a-study-on-*Wasta*-in-jordan.

Business-Anti-Corruption.com: http://www.business-anti-corruption.com/country-profiles/middle-east-north-africa.aspx.

REFERENCES

Aarikka-Stenroos, L., Sandberg, B. and Lehtimäki, T. 2014. Networks for the commercialization of innovations: a review of how divergent network actors contribute. *Industrial Marketing Management*, **43**: 365–381.

Abu-Doleh, J. 2000. The Jordanian financial and manufacturing human resource managers: a profile. *Al-Manarah*, **6**: 57–76.

Adler, P.S. and Kwon, S.-W. 2002. Social capital: prospects for a new concept. *Academy of Management Review*, **27**: 17–40.

Ahmad, K. and Petrick, J.A. 2003. The challenge and opportunity of Islamic insurance. *Risk Management*, **50**(3): 28.

Al Jallad, N. 2008. The concepts of al-halal and al-haram in the Arab-Muslim culture: a translational and lexicographical study. *Language Design: Journal of Theoretical and Experimental Linguistics*, **10**: 77–86.

Al-Shaikh, F.N. 2003. The practical reality theory and business ethics in non-Western context: evidence from Jordan. *Journal of Management Development*, **22**: 679–693.

Al-Shammari, H.A. and Hussein, R.T. 2008. Strategic planning in emergent market organizitions: empirical investigation. *International Journal of Commerce and Management*, **18**: 47–59.

Aladwan, K., Bhanugopan, R. and Fish, A. 2014. Managing human resources in Jordanian organizations: challenges and prospects. *International Journal of Islamic and Middle Eastern Finance and Management*, **7**: 126–138.

Aldossari, M. and Robertson, M. 2016. The role of *Wasta* in repatriates' perceptions of a breach to the psychological contract: a Saudi Arabian case study. *International Journal of Human Resource Management*, **27**(16): 1854–1873.

Alghad 2013. The increasing number of Arab and foreign students studying in the University of Jordan. http://www.Alghad.com/index. php/article,663423.html (accessed 16 November 2013).

Ali, A.J. 1992. The Islamic work ethic in Arabia. *Journal of Psychology*, **126**: 507–519.

Ali, A.J. and Al-Kazemi, A.A. 2007. Islamic work ethic in Kuwait. *Cross Cultural Management: An International Journal*, **14**: 93–104.

Altarawneh, I.I. 2009. Training and development evaluation in Jordanian banking organizations. *Research and Practice in Human Resource Management*, **17**: 1–23.

Altarawneh, I.I. and Aldehayyat, J.S. 2011. Strategic human resources management in Jordanian hotels. *International Journal of Business and Management*, **6**: 242–255.

Arab Archives Institute 2000. A survey on *Wasta* in Jordan. Towards Transparency in Jordan Conference in Cooperation with Transparency International held in Amman-Jordan on 22 May 2000.

Arasli, H., Bavik, A. v Ekiz, E.H. 2006. The effects of nepotism on human resource management: the case of three, four and five star hotels in northern Cyprus. *International Journal of Sociology and Social Policy*, **26**: 295–308.

Badimon, M.E. 2013. Does unemployment spark collective contentious action? Evidence from a Moroccan social movement. *Journal of Contemporary African Studies*, **31**: 194–212.

Barnett, A.H., Yandle, B. and Naufal, G. 2011. *Regulation, Trust, and Cronyism in Middle Eastern Societies: The Simple Economics of 'Wasta'*. http://www.pearlinitiative.org/tl_files/pearl/data/*Wasta*-2011.pdf (accessed 21 October 2012).

Bekker, J.C. 1991. Nepotism, corruption and discrimination: a predicament for a post-apartheid South African public service. *Politikon: South African Journal of Political Studies*, **18**: 55–73.

Boxman, E.A.W., De Graaf, P.M. and Flap, H.D. 1991. The impact of social and human capital on the income attainment of Dutch managers. *Social Networks*, **13**: 51–73.

Branine, M. and Analoui, F. 2006. Human resource management in Jordan. In P.S. Budhwar and K. Mellahi (eds), *Managing Human Resources in the Middle East*. London: Routledge, pp. 145–160.

Budhwar, P. and Mellahi, K. 2007. Introduction: human resource management in the Middle East. *International Journal of Human Resource Management*, **18**: 2–10.

Cappellen, T. and Janssens, M. 2008. Global managers' career competencies. *Career Development International*, **13**: 514–537.

Central Bank of Jordan 2012. Jordanian Central Bank annual report. Amman, Jordan: Central Bank of Jordan.

Chen, X.-P. and Chen, C. 2004. On the intricacies of the Chinese Guanxi: a process model of Guanxi development. *Asia Pacific Journal of Management*, **21**: 305–324.

Chirasha, V. and Mahapa, M. 2012. An analysis of the causes and impact of deviant behaviour in the workplace: the case of secretaries in state universities. *Journal of Emerging Trends in Economics and Management Sciences*, **3**: 415–421.

Cuervo-Cazurra, A. 2016. Corruption in international business. *Journal of World Business*, **51**(1): 35–49.

Cunningham, R.B. and Sarayrah, Y.K. 1993. *Wasta: The Hidden Force in Middle Eastern Society*. Westport, CN: Praeger.

Cunningham, B.R. and Sarayrah, K.Y. 1994. Taming *Wasta* to achieve development. *Arab Studies Quarterly*, **16**: 29–39.

Davies, J. and Easterby-Smith, M. 1984. Learning and developing from managerial work experiences. *Journal of Management Studies*, **21**: 169–182.

De Silva, M.J., McKenzie, K., Harpham, T. and Huttly, S.R. 2005. Social capital and mental illness: a systematic review. *Journal of Epidemiology and Community Health*, **59**: 619–627.

Department of Statistics 2012a. *Jordan Statistical Yearbook 2012*. Amman, Jordan: Department of Statistics.

Department of Statistics 2012b. Percentage distribution of Jordanians age (15+) years by educational level and sex, 2012. Amman, Jordan. http://web.dos.gov.jo/?lang=ar (accessed 27 March 2014).

Dess, G.G. and Sauerwald, S. 2014. Creating value in organizations: the vital role of social capital. *Organizational Dynamics*, **43**: 1–8.

Edvinsson, L., Roos, J., Roos, G. and Dragonetti, N.C. 1997. *Intellectual Capital: Navigating in the New Business Landscape*. London: Macmillan.

El-Said, H. and Harrigan, J. 2009. 'You reap what you plant': social networks in the Arab World – the Hashemite Kingdom of Jordan. *World Development*, **37**: 1235–1249.

European Neighbourhood and Partnership Instrument 2007. Jordan Strategy Paper 2007–2003 and National Indicative Programme 2007–2010.

Ezzedeen, S.R. and Swiercz, P.M. 2001. HR system effectiveness in the transformative organization: lessons from Libancell of Lebanon. *Competitiveness Review: An International Business Journal incorporating Journal of Global Competitiveness*, **11**: 25–39.

Fagenson, E.A. 1994. Perceptions of proteges' vs nonproteges' relationships with their peers, superiors, and departments. *Journal of Vocational Behavior*, **45**: 55–78.

Faisal, A.A. 1990. Favouritism (*Wasta*): an exploratory study of university students. *Journal of King Saud University*, **2**: 693–711.

Forret, M.L. and Dougherty, T.W. 2004. Networking behaviors and career outcomes: differences for men and women? *Journal of Organizational Behavior*, **25**: 419–437.

Hashim, J. 2010. Human resource management practices on organisational commitment: the Islamic perspective. *Personnel Review*, **39**: 785–799.

Hashmi, S.H. 1993. Is there an Islamic ethic of humanitarian intervention? *Ethics and International Affairs*, **7**: 55–73.

Hassan, N. 2013. Reviving revolution: the role of market-driven transnationalism, democracy, and agents. *The Mellon Mays Undergraduate Fellowship Journal: A Collection of Scholarly Research by Fellows of the Mellon Mays Undergraduate Fellowship Program*, 69–72.
Hayajenh, A.F., Maghrabi, A.S. and Al-Dabbagh, T.H. 1994. Research note: assessing the effect of nepotism on human resource managers. *International Journal of Manpower*, **15**: 60–67.
Hutchings, K. and Weir, D. 2006. Guanxi and *Wasta*: a comparison. *Thunderbird International Business Review*, **48**: 141–156.
Ibarra, H. and Deshpamde, P.H. 2008. Networks and identities: reciprocal influences on career processes and outcomes. In H. Gunz and M. Peiperl (eds), *Handbook of Career Studies*.Thousand Oaks, CA: Sage Publications, pp. 262–282.
Iles, P., Almhedie, A. and Baruch, Y. 2012. Managing HR in the Middle East: challenges in the public sector. *Public Personnel Management*, **41**: 1–15.
Jamali, D., Lanteri, A. and Walburn, A. 2013. Corruption and economic security in the Arab countries: the role of business schools. *International Journal of Sustainable Human Security*, **1**: 156–177.
Kilcullen, D. and Rosenblatt, N. 2014. The rise of Syria's urban poor: why the war for Syria's future will be fought over the country's new urban villages. PRISM Syria Supplemental Center, pp. 33–41.
Kolb, D.A., Boyatzis, R.E. and Mainemelis, C. 2001. Experiential learning theory: previous research and new directions. *Perspectives on Thinking, Learning, and Cognitive Styles*, **1**: 227–247.
Kumar, N. and Rose, R.C. 2010. Examining the link between Islamic work ethic and innovation capability. *Journal of Management Development*, **29**: 79–93.
Lane, J.-E. and Maeland, R. 2010. Global financial crisis and international institutions: challenges, opportunities and change. *Public Organization Review*, **11**(1): 29–43.
Lin, N. 2001. Building a network theory of social capital. In N. Lin, K. Cook and R.S. Burt (eds), *Social Capital: Theory and Research*. Piscataway, NJ: AldineTransaction, pp. 3–30.
Loewe, M., Blume, J. and Speer, J. 2008. How favoritism affects the business climate: empirical evidence from Jordan. *Middle East Journal*, **62**: 259–276.
Mellahi, K. and Budhwar, P. 2010. Introduction: Islam and human resource management. *Personnel Review*, **39**(6): 685–691.
Metcalfe, B.D. 2006. Exploring cultural dimensions of gender and management in the Middle East. *Thunderbird International Business Review*, **48**: 93–107.
Mohammad, A.A. and Hamdy, H. 2008. The stigma of *Wasta*: the effect of *Wasta* on perceived competence and morality. German University in Cairo, Working Paper Series No. 5.
Mousavi, D.S.M., Keyfarzandi, A.A. and Allah, Z.A. 2013. A study of the relationship between Islamic work ethics and work satisfaction of Iranian employees. *Asian Journal of Research in Social Sciences and Humanities*, **3**: 236–247.
Nabi, G.R. 1999. An investigation into the differential profile of predictors of objective and subjective career success. *Career Development International*, **4**: 212–224.
Özbay, Ö. 2008. Does social capital deter youth from cheating, alcohol use, and violence in Turkey?: Bringing torpil in. *Journal of Criminal Justice*, **36**: 403–415.
Petersen, T., Saporta, I. and Seidel, M.-D. L. 2000. Offering a job: meritocracy and social networks. *American Journal of Sociology*, **106**: 763–816.
Phenix Center. 2011. *Challenges Facing the Jordanian Labor Market*. Amman, Jordan: Jordan Labor Watch.
Possumah, B., Ismail, A. and Shahimi, S. 2013. Bringing work back in Islamic ethics. *Journal of Business Ethics*, **112**: 257–270.
Putnam, R.D. 2000. *Bowling Alone: The Collapse and Revival of the American Community*. New York: Simon & Schuster.
Rhoades, L. and Eisenberger, R. 2002. Perceived organizational support: a review of the literature. *Journal of Applied Psychology*, **87**: 698–714.
Rice, G. 1999. Islamic ethics and the implications for business. *Journal of Busniess Ethics*, **18**: 345–358.
Rokhman, W. 2010. The effect of Islamic work ethics on work outcomes. *Electronic Journal of Business Ethics and Organization Studies*, **15**: 21–27.
Ronsin, C. 2010. *Wasta* and state–society relations: the case of Jordan. *Revue Averroes*, **3**: 1–7.
Rothstein, B. 2004. Social capital and institutional legitimacy: the corleone connection. In S. Prakash and P. Selle (eds), *Investigating Social Capital*. India: Sage Publications India Pvt Ltd, p. 113.
Sabri, H.A. 2011. Beyond Arab Spring: societal context and prospects for a new paradigm of Arab management. *Journal of Social and Development Sciences*, **2**: 214–222.
Sadozai, A.M., Marri, M.Y.K., Zaman, H.M.F., Yousufzai, M.I. and Nas, Z. 2013. Moderating role of Islamic work ethics between the relationship of organizational commitment and turnover intentions: a study of public sector of Pakistan. *Mediterranean Journal of Social Sciences*, **4**: 767–775.
Sampson, R.J., Morenoff, J.D. and Gannon-Rowley, T. 2002. Assessing 'neighborhood effects': social processes and new directions in research. *Annual Review of Sociology*, **28**: 443–478.

Samuel, I. and Justina, O. 2006. Deviant behaviours in the workplace: causes, impact and effective discipline. *Inter-World Journal of Management and Development Studies*, **2**: 78–87.

Sanchez-Famoso, V., Maseda, A. and Iturralde, T. 2014. The role of internal social capital in organisational innovation: an empirical study of family firms. *European Management Journal*, **32**: 950–962.

Seidel, M.-D. L., Polzer, J.T. and Stewart, K.J. 2000. Friends in high places: the effects of social networks on discrimination in salary negotiations. *Administrative Science Quarterly*, **45**: 1–24.

Sidani, Y. and Showail, S. 2013. Religious discourse and organizational change: legitimizing the stakeholder perspective at a Saudi conglomerate. *Journal of Organizational Change Management*, **26**: 931–947.

Skarlicki, D.P. and Folger, R. 1997. Retaliation in the workplace: the roles of distributive, procedural, and interactional justice. *Journal of Applied Psychology*, **82**: 434–443.

Smith, P.B., Torres, C., Leong, C.-H., Budhwar, P., Achoui, M. and Lebedeva, N. 2011. Are indigenous approaches to achieving influence in business organizations distinctive? A comparative study of guanxi, *Wasta*, jeitinho, svyazi and pulling strings. *International Journal of Human Resource Management*, **23**: 333–348.

Sultana, R.G. and Watts, A.G. 2008. Career guidance in the Middle East and North Africa. *International Journal for Educational and Vocational Guidance*, **8**: 19–34.

Szreter, S. and Woolcock, M. 2004. Health by association? Social capital, social theory, and the political economy of public health. *International Journal of Epidemiology*, **33**: 650–667.

Ta'amnha, M. 2014. An investigation of *Wasta* and the effects of human and social capital on Jordanian insurance employees' career experiences and success. PhD thesis, University of East Anglia.

Tlaiss, H. and Kauser, S. 2011a. The impact of gender, family, and work on the career advancement of Lebanese women managers. *Gender in Management: An International Journal*, 26: 8–36.

Tlaiss, H. and Kauser, S. 2011b. The importance of *Wasta* in the career success of Middle Eastern managers. *Jouranl of Eurpean Industrial Training*, **35**: 467–486.

Touzani, M., Jlassi, F., Maalaoui, A., Bel Haj Hassine, R. and Matlay, H. 2015. Contextual and cultural determinants of entrepreneurship in pre-and post-revolutionary Tunisia: analysing the discourse of young potential and actual entrepreneurs. *Journal of Small Business and Enterprise Development*, **22**: 1–29.

Tregaskis, O., Edwards, T., Edwards, P., Ferner, A. and Marginson, P. 2010. Transnational learning structures in multinational firms: organizational context and national embeddedness. *Human Relations*, **63**: 471–499.

Warren, D.E., Dunfee, T.W. and Li, N. 2004. Social exchange in China: the double-edged sword of guanxi. *Journal of Business Ethics*, **55**: 353–370.

Wated, G. and Sanchez, J. 2015. Managerial tolerance of nepotism: the effects of individualism–collectivism in a Latin American context. *Journal of Business Ethics*,**130**(1): 45–57.

Weaver, R.D. and Habibov, N. 2012. Social capital, human capital, and economic well-being in the knowledge economy: results from Canada's General Social Survey. *Journal of Sociology and Social Welfare*, **39**: 31–53.

Whiteoak, J.W., Crawford, N.G. and Mapstone, R.H. 2006. Impact of gender and generational differences in work values and attitudes in an Arab culture. *Thunderbird International Business Review*, **48**(1): 77–91.

World Trade Organization. 2000. Jordan becomes 136th member of the WTO. WOT press release, press/174, 11 April.

Yousef, D.A. 2000. Organizational commitment as a mediator of the relationship between Islamic work ethic and attitudes toward organizational change. *Human Relations*, **53**(4): 513–537.

Yousef, D.A. 2001. Islamic work ethic – a moderator between organizational commitment and job satisfaction in a cross cultural context. *Personnel Review*, **30**: 152–169.

Zahra, S.A. 2011. Doing research in the (New) Middle East: sailing with the wind. *Academy of Management Perspectives*, **25**: 6–21.

22. Towards a framework for the analysis of labour localisation practices in Saudi Arabia and the Gulf Cooperation Council countries

Yassir Abdulaziz Nasief

The literature on the localisation of labour in the countries of the Gulf Cooperation Council (GCC) has been developing since the 1990s. However, this literature has been criticised for being rather scattered and not easily available to human resource management (HRM) professionals and academics. This is in part because there is no single framework that categorises this research according to the relevant theory. Most of the work in this area is either descriptive or only lightly connected to established theories or frameworks. The purpose of this chapter is therefore to suggest a framework for the analysis of human resource (HR) localisation practices in the GCC countries. In order to achieve this aim, the chapter first covers the background of, and recent literature on, localisation within the GCC, mainly in Saudi Arabia. Second, it introduces work on institutional HRM and the main developments in this area of research. Third, it presents a suggested framework for labour localisation, focusing in particular on a case study conducted by the researcher as a way of examining the framework. It is important to note that while this framework was applied to a case study in Saudi Arabia, the chapter will argue that the framework can be applied in other GCC countries with little if any adaptation. Finally, the chapter will propose ways in which to employ and develop the framework further.

THE LOCALISATION OF LABOUR IN SAUDI ARABIA AND THE GCC COUNTRIES

The GCC countries, like many other nations, are facing particular economic challenges. Among the labour market challenges in the GCC is high unemployment among nationals and demographic imbalances between locals and non-locals. Unemployment in 2008 was at 13 per cent, 14 per cent and 15 per cent in Saudi Arabia, Kuwait and the United Arab Emirates (UAE), respectively, while it stood at 15 per cent in both Oman and Bahrain, and 3.2 per cent in Qatar (US Department of State, 2008). More recently, a 2013 study by the Cooperation Council of the Arab States of the Gulf on unemployment rates suggests rates of 14 per cent and 11 per cent in UAE and Saudi, respectively, 8 per cent in both Bahrain and Oman, and 6 per cent and 3 per cent in Kuwait and Qatar, respectively (IMF, 2014). Moreover, foreign workers represent more than 30 per cent of the entire GCC population (Center for International and Regional Studies, 2012). According to the International Monetary Fund (IMF) report, foreign workers filled 88 per cent of jobs created in the GCC private sector between 2006 and 2013 (IMF, 2014).

The general approach used by all the members of the GCC to counter these problems is localisation of labour (i.e., nationalisation). The term '*alsa'wada*', commonly translated to 'Saudisation', and denoting the localisation of the workforce, was coined by the Saudi Arabian government in its third five-year development plan (1980–1985). As a consequence, the trend of intervention to promote labour localisation spread across the rest of the GCC countries (Al-Humaid, 2003). These attempts at localisation are known as Emirisation in the UAE, Bahrainisation in Bahrain, Omanisation in Oman, Qatarisation in Qatar and Kuwaitisation in Kuwait.

However, despite their different labels, these localising policies share common features. For instance, all the GCC states employed the quota system for locals in one way or another. These systems take various approaches to force the private sector to be pro-active in this area, and employ locals in positions typically filled by non-locals. In addition to the quota system, the members of the GCC created national fund agencies to subsidise the wages of nationals to encourage nationalisation. Training funds also exemplify the programmes and bodies introduced to tackle the skills shortage among locals. These similarities do not imply, however, that localisation activities were identical throughout the GCC. However, to keep it to a reasonable length, this chapter will describe in detail only cases from Saudi Arabia.

The Saudi government responded to the challenge of unemployment among Saudi nationals by taking several bold measures, including the nationalisation policy. These initial nationalisation measures developed into what is now known as the *National Saudisation Policy* (NSP). The Saudi–US Relations Information Service (2003) defines Saudisation as: 'the development strategy that seeks to train Saudi workers and replace foreign workers in Saudi Arabia. . . . [T]he government looks at Saudisation as an ultimate goal for development at the cost of short-term transitional disruption' (Saudi–US Relations Information Service, 2003).

According to Al-Humaid (2003), the underlying rationale of the first Saudisation policy was to encourage the private sector to provide more opportunities for Saudis, sustain an intensive policy of work permits and residency regulations, promote labour-oriented work among nationals through the public media, engage Saudi women in the labour force, and identify appropriate mechanisms to follow up the implementation progress based on pre-set priorities.

Over time, the idea of Saudisation gained momentum, and its general aims began to appear in official policies and reflected in practical actions on the ground. For instance, the fourth and fifth Saudi development plans (1985–1990 and 1990–1995 respectively) indicated that 75 per cent of the workforce of each company had to comprise Saudi nationals. It was stated in the previous labour law issued in 1979, specifically in Articles 45 and 48, that Saudi workers should receive at least 51 per cent of the overall company wage, and that employers must attempt to fill all vacancies with Saudis before they could be offered to workers of other nationalities (Alzalabani, 2004). Nevertheless, the Council of Manpower proposed the first practical measure towards Saudisation. This resulted in Decree no.50, which compelled private firms with 20 employees or more to fill all their employment vacancies with Saudis. In addition, firms are obliged to increase their proportion of Saudi employees by 5 per cent annually or face penalties (Mellahi and Wood, 2002).

The main aim of this decree was to force private sector firms to engage Saudis in their workforce. At the same time, the government sought to improve the overall employability of Saudi nationals, in particular through gradual changes in education, making it more compatible with the needs of the private sector (Al-Humaid, 2003). The government also

Table 22.1 Four key events around Saudisation

Date	Event
27 September 1994	Ministerial Decree no.50 which enforced Saudisation
6 August 2000	The establishment of the Human Resources Development Fund (HRDF)
Spring 2004	The introduction of the '*Nitakat*' programme, which classified companies according to their Saudisation percentage as platinum, green, yellow or red, where premium and green zones include companies with acceptable Saudisation rates, while yellow and red zones include the ones with low rates
15 November 2012	Continuous restrictions on working visas for foreign workers by increasing their work permit fees from SAR200 (£35) to SAR2400 (£400) per annum

started to offer incentives to firms to encourage Saudisation (see Table 22.1). For instance, the Human Resources Development Fund (HRDF) was established in 2000 in order to subsidise, to a significant level, the training and employment of Saudis in the private sector.

Since the concept of Saudisation was first proposed, government agencies and academics have conducted substantial research into it from various perspectives such as policy making, private sector challenges, young Saudis and their readiness for the job market and others. However, most of the literature and research in the area has been either descriptive (Mellahi and Al-Hinai, 2000) or unpublished (e.g., Bosbait, 2003; Al-Thobyany, 2007; Al-Shammari, 2009). Table 22.2 summarises the extant literature on Saudisation based on topic of research and main outcome.

As shown in Table 22.2, the descriptive stream of research focused on examining Saudisation as a whole phenomenon (cf. Mellahi and Al-Hinai, 2000; Mellahi and Wood, 2001; Al-Dosary and Rahaman, 2005; and Fakeeh, 2009). Other descriptive work looked into matters related to Saudisation such as HRM in Saudi Arabia and the Saudi labour market (e.g., Alzalabani, 2004). While these studies contributed to understanding the area of Saudisation through various findings, they fell short of building a comprehensive approach in understanding the phenomenon.

The other set of research used a theory-based approach in tackling Saudisation and Saudisation-related issues. Various theories were used by researchers including human capital theory (e.g., Bosbait, 2003; Al-Shammari, 2009), the theory of reasoned action (e.g., Al-Taweel, 2004) and institutional theory (e.g., Mellahi, 2007; Alanezi, 2012). This stream of research, moreover, tackled the issue of Saudisation using a different approach. Part of these researches looked into Saudisation through studying issues related to young Saudis (e.g., Al-Taweel, 2004), while others investigated the education system and its output to the job market (e.g., Bosbait, 2003; Al-Thobyani, 2007; Al-Shammari, 2009). More relevantly, researchers started studying the impact of the regulative and institutional changes in shaping HRM and Saudisation practice (e.g., Mellahi, 2007; Alanezi, 2012).

The above discussion suggests that the literature on Saudisation has developed in various directions. Some literature is merely descriptive, while other literature is theory-based. Part of literature looked into the phenomenon of Saudisation as a whole, while other parts focused on Saudisation elements such as young Saudis and education outcomes in the country, among others. This development has contributed by increasing

Table 22.2 Selected literature on Saudisation

Nature	Research	Topic of research	Outcome
Descriptive	Mellahi and Al-Hinai (2000)	The general localising phenomenon in Saudi Arabia and Oman	Five factors were hindering localisation in the two countries
	Mellahi and Wood (2001)	HRM in Saudi Arabia	Lists the factors impacting HRM in the country and future challenges
	Alzalabani (2004)	Saudi Arabia HRM, industrial relations and labour market	Discusses the relationship between three notions as an institutional environment
	Al-Dosary and Rahaman (2005)	The definition and rationale of Saudisation	Highlights governmental initiatives in the domain and private sectors approaches in tackling Saudisation requirements
	Fakeeh (2009)	Understanding Saudisation through studying the root of the labour market situation and its prospect	Examines the root of the problem, the initiative to rectify the problem, and level of success in solving the problem
Theory- based	Bosbait (2003)	Young Saudis' transition from school to work and the demographic factors impacting their activity level. The study applied human capital theory	Reports that young Saudis' level of activity in the job market is related to family economical background, education level, gender and awareness of market opportunities
	Al-Taweel (2004)	The negative attitude of private sector managers towards Saudi candidates by using the theory of reasoned action	Advocates that managers do not have negative attitudes towards Saudis' education, experience, level of English or level of discipline. However, financial demand caused some negative attitudes
	Al-Thobyani (2007)	Investigates the perceptions of teachers, staff, employers and students about the level of mismatch between the output of university Arts & Humanities faculties and the needs of the private sector labour market by applying grounded theory	Reports a high level of mismatch between the output of university Arts & Humanities students and the private sector, as a result of weaknesses in communication and sharing of information between the two
	Mellahi (2007)	Explores how regulations impact on Saudi private sector HRM by applying some aspects of institutional theory	Highlights the main legal changes related to the labour market and its impact on HRM and Saudisation

Table 22.2 (continued)

Nature	Research	Topic of research	Outcome
Theory-based	Al-Shammari (2009)	National skills formation system and its effect on Saudisation, focusing on the General Organisation for Technical Education and Vocational Training by employing human capital theory and HRM models	Discusses that the shortcomings of the Saudi skills formation system comprise the main factors hindering Saudisation strategies. That includes high government engagement and unfocused planning, regulation, financing and implementation
	Alanezi (2012)	The impact of the institutional field on the success of Saudisation in multinational enterprises (MNEs)	Reports that recruitment, training and the role of the HR director are significant determinants of the success of localisation

our understanding of the phenomenon of Saudisation. However, the lack of a comprehensive theoretical framework remains a key limitation in the literature. Nonetheless, while much recent work touched base on institutional theory, it remains limited in stipulating a framework for studying labour localisation in Saudi Arabia or in the GCC.

THE INSTITUTIONAL HRM PERSPECTIVE

As noted in the previous section, the work on the localisation of labour and, in particular, Saudisation has been attempting to move from a descriptive to a theory-based approach. This positive development in the literature makes it timely to move towards a framework for localisation in Saudi Arabia and in the GCC. This section presents in detail the HR literature, mainly concerning institutional HRM, which could be a useful basis for constructing such a framework.

Institutional theory perspectives on HRM have existed since the 1980s. For instance, the work of Eisenhardt (1988) is an example of an empirical study which uses the premises of institutional theory (and agency theory) to explain variations in compensation practice in retail outlets. Wright and McMahan (1999: 66) state cautiously that: 'One theory that has recently evolved in organisational theory is the institutional perspective . . . Although this theory is currently not well developed and consists of a variety of approaches, the idea of institutionalism may help in understanding the determinants of HRM practices.'

An extensive body of research on institutional HRM has recently taken place within the Dutch HR Network (DHRN).[1] A sample of their work includes Paauwe and Boselie (2003), who made four propositions about the relationship between the institutional setting and the homogeneity of HR practice. Boxenbaum (2006) investigated the ways in which Danish businesses adapted American diversity management practices from an institutional perspective. And, finally, Boon et al. (2009) discussed the concept of *institutional fit*, the alignment between HRM goals and the institutional context (including government agencies, professional bodies and employees). The contextually

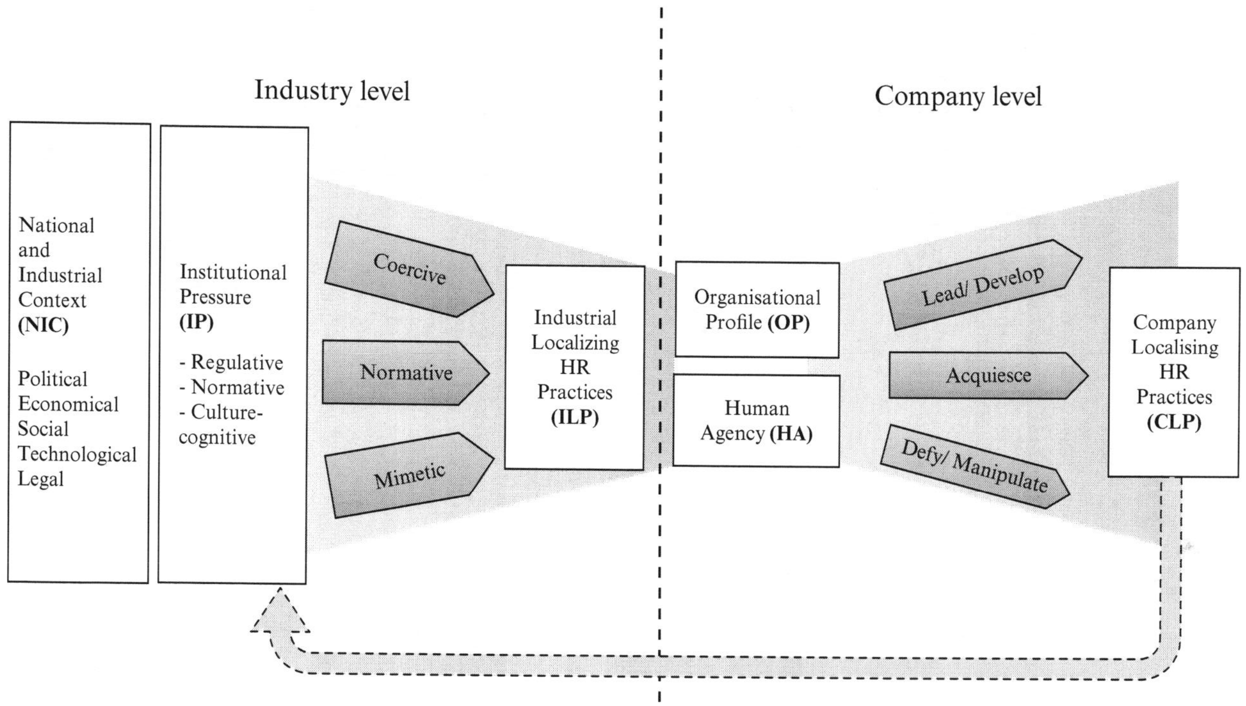

Figure 22.1 Labour localisation framework

based human resources theory (CBHRT) (Paauwe, 2004) came to represent the theoretical development of contextual/institutional HRM in one single theory. These developments are essential in understanding the proposed framework in this chapter.

A PROPOSED FRAMEWORK FOR THE ANALYSIS OF LABOUR LOCALISATION

This section describes the suggested framework (Figure 22.1) to analyse labour localisation (and, in particular, Saudisation) and its associated measures. The main aim of this framework is to analyse the impact of the institutional environment on the localisation practices of HR. As mentioned earlier, one stream of research has examined HR practices from an institutional perspective. Paauwe's (2004) theory and framework of CBHRT consolidate most of the research into this topic. Deriving from the literature on this topic, this theoretical framework borrows some premises of institutional theory and CBHRT, in order to construct a framework for the context of labour localisation.

According to the above framework, localising practices are primarily established at the industry level because of two main forces. The first is the national and industrial context (NIC), including political, economic, social, technological and legal factors. The second is the institutional profile, which is shaped by three forms of institutional pressure (IP): regulative/coercive, normative and culture-cognitive. These two sets of forces shape the localisation practices of HR at industry level.

According to institutional theory, while organisations pursue their business objectives, they seek legitimacy by adhering to institutional forces in the environment. This legitimacy-attaining motive leads firms to enact certain norms (e.g., Scott, 1987; Zucker, 1987). More precisely, firms tend to become isomorphic in their practices through the three institutional isomorphic mechanisms: coercive, normative and mimetic (DiMaggio and Powell, 1983). Hence, according to Meyer and Rowan (1977) and DiMaggio and Powell (1983), organisational practices become socially constructed, due to time and pressure, as proper, adequate, rational and necessary practices within the institutional field, or as 'rationalised myths'. Hence, the overall rationale of this part of the framework suggests that the adoption of Saudisation practices results from institutional isomorphic mechanisms in the environment.

The other domain affecting the adoption of localising HR practices occurs at the company level. The framework considers two of the main internal forces that impact localising practices in organisations. The first force is the 'organisation profile' (OP). This consists of some organisational features such as company size, level of political connections (Edelman, 1990; Sutton et al., 1994); company age (Edelman, 1990; Sutton et al., 1994; Goodstein, 1994); company's stance on the practice (Boxenbaum, 2006; van Gestel and Nyberg, 2009); and the organisation's administrative heritage (Paauwe, 2004).

The second force affecting the choice of Saudisation practices is 'human agency' (HA). According to CBHRT, human agency is primarily represented by the dominant coalition, which consists of senior management, middle management, HR managers and others (Paauwe, 2004). In addition to this general perspective on human agency, one needs to draw on upper echelons theory (see Hambrick and Mason, 1984) to gain insights into the demography of the dominant coalition inside the organisation.

The framework here applies the concept of decoupling established in the literature of institutional theory. This concept suggests that while most organisations adopt some common practices, others might diverge from them. According to Greenwood, decoupling occurs when 'organisations abide only superficially by institutional pressure and adopt new structures without necessarily implementing the related practices' (Greenwood, 2008: 81). As Meyer and Rowan (1977) claim, organisations tend to decouple from institutionalised organisational practices under two conditions. The first occurs when the rationalised myth does not make sense to the organisations, while the second occurs when the rationalised institutional myth contradicts internal myths within the organisation. Organisations can therefore solve these conflicts by decoupling from the institutional practices they espouse.

The framework, moreover, applies the work of Oliver (1991) in predicting the strategic responses of companies to institutional pressures. According to Oliver (1991), organisational response is determined by several internal factors including the characteristics of the firm, the ownership setting and the autonomy of its HR department. The framework also employed Paauwe's (2004) three directions of adopted practices: (1) lead/develop (constructive approach); (2) acquiesce (conforming approach); and (3) defy/manipulate (resisting approach). These directions are reached through organisational attempts to find the right institutional fit (CLP). This indirectly alters institutional pressure at the industry level.

To summarise, in the proposed theoretical framework for the analysis of Saudisation (GCC-isation) practices, the external environment (NIC and IP) plays a critical role in the shaping of localising HR practices at the industry level. These localising practices (ILP) are generally followed by organisations in the industry. However, this industry adoption does not imply a full homogeneity of practice. Organisations, which focus on their internal environment, choose the best fit for their individual organisation (CLP).

The localising framework suggested above is accompanied by a set of suggested measures intended to assist in the collection of empirical evidence. Table 22.3 shows the measures derived from the theoretical framework and the literature with a brief description of each measure. The following section presents a case study conducted by the researcher in which this framework was used in the analysis of Saudisation practices in Saudi Arabia.

EMPIRICAL EXAMPLE: SUPERMARKET CHAINS IN SAUDI ARABIA

The empirical work involved studying HR localising practices in Saudi Arabia, specifically in the supermarket industry. The researcher used the above framework to collect data from five supermarket chains operating in Saudi Arabia. The data included all the required measures (see Table 22.1) for the period from 2003 to 2007. Using a multi-case-study approach, the researcher aimed to examine the validity of the framework in the analysis and interpretation of the development of Saudisation practices.

Initially, the researcher established 'Saudisation practices' as an institutional field. The field has prime actors such as the Ministry of Labour, leading supermarket chains and young Saudis. These primary actors and other secondary actors apply regulative, normative and culture-cognitive pressures. The result of these pressures is the isomorphism of Saudisation practices, in which practices are diffused in the industry. The study confirms that Saudisation IP has three forms: regulative, normative and culture-cognitive.

Table 22.3 Measures used in the theoretical framework to study Saudisation

Stage	Element	Description
National and industrial context (NIC)	PESTL	The political, economic, social, technological and legal (PESTL) aspects surrounding the nation and the industry
	Supermarket industry context	The industry-specific context of Saudi supermarket chains
Institutional pressures (IP)	Regulative factors	Regulatory and legal changes in the environment related to Saudisation and Saudisation practices in firms
	Normative factors	The set of norms required (i.e., how things should be done professionally) to achieve Saudisation targets and avoid industry sanctions
	Culture-cognitive factors	The social perceptions and conceptions related to Saudisation and how they should be approached
Institutional localisation practices (ILP)	Compensation and benefits	The financial incentives used by firms to attract, retain and capitalise on Saudis
	Training	The training provision practised in firms
	Obtaining HRDF support	Agreements between firms and HRDF to receive subsidies for the recruitment and training of Saudis
	Employing women	Using women in the workforce as a way of increasing Saudisation
	Subcontracting jobs	Using subcontracted workers to increase the aggregated Saudisation percentage
	Employing part-timers	Using part-time contracts to increase the number of Saudis in a firm
	Targeting new labour segments	Approaching new segments of the labour market to bring more committed Saudis into the firm
	Meeting Saudisation percentage	The degree to which the firm meets the Saudisation percentage required by the Ministry of Labour
	Compliance with restricted jobs	The degree to which the firm complies with the Ministry of Labour's list of jobs restricted to Saudi nationals, such as cashier, security guard etc.
	Career choice and development	The use of career choice and development as a means of attracting, retaining and capitalising on Saudis
Organisational profile (OP)	Age	The age of the firm from its establishment
	Origin	The firm's city of origin
	Size (number of employees)	The size of the firm in terms of the number of employees
	Size (number of stores)	The size of the firm in terms of the number of stores
	Geographical presence	The geographical presence of the firm's supermarket branches (provinces)
	Expansion strategy	Expansions in the number of branches between 2003 and 2007
	Strategic focus	The firm's strategic focus, based on available secondary sources

Table 22.3 (continued)

Stage	Element	Description
Human agency (HA)	Ownership setting	The ownership setting, based on legal and actual governance
	HR department autonomy	The level of autonomy given to HR to determine its functions
	Upper echelons demography	Characteristics related to senior management, such as age, tenure and length of experience
Company localisation practices (CLP)	The firm's position on specific Saudisation practices	The position of the firm on Saudisation practices. The positions are namely lead/develop, acquiesce or defy/manipulate

The main regulative pressure is Decree no. 50 of 1994, which stipulated the policy of Saudisation and the required percentages for private sector firms. Other regulative pressures included restricting certain jobs to Saudis, penalising violators with work permit suspensions, the Saudisation calculations for females and disabled individuals, training as a requirement for the HRDF fund, legislation on working women, the sex segregation law, the decree concerning work visas for non-Saudis and sponsorship.

The core normative pressures applied in institutional fields include the pioneering Saudisation programmes of leading firms, the employment of Saudisation managers, the deployment of training to attract Saudis and to improve public relations, mass recruitment events, and the popularity of employing orphans.

Finally, the culture-cognitive pressures consisting of taken-for-granted beliefs. They included the ideas that Saudis would not accept low-level jobs, that Saudis see training as having great added value, that Saudis are attracted by financial rewards, and that employing women harms society. These pressures combined shape the ILP of the framework.

The study empirically focused on nine Saudisation practices in order to closely examine six different propositions. According to the localising framework, the first three propositions (see below) were related to ILP conversion, while the other three are related to CLP divergence. The propositions were as follows:

P1*. Extensive institutional pressure leads to similar Saudisation HR practices in the industry.*

P2a*. Limited institutional pressure with a good business case leads to similar Saudisation practices in the industry.*

P2b*. Limited institutional pressure with a poor business case leads to decoupling in Saudisation practices in the industry.*

P3*. Contradictory institutional pressure leads to decoupling in Saudisation practices in the industry.*

P4*. Organisations characterised by age, a larger operation, wider geographical presence and/or expansions are likely to lead the development of Saudisation practices.*

P5*. Firms with a higher percentage of Saudis in senior management and decentralised decision-making, including HR autonomy and less engagement from owners, are likely to lead the development of Saudisation practices.*

***P6**. Organisations with highly educated, younger and/or less experienced upper echelons are likely to lead the development of Saudisation practices.*

To examine these propositions, the researcher applied the pattern matching technique in analysing the data collected to construct testable scenarios. The scenarios where divided to tackle both convergence and divergence practices. Table 22.4 summarises the scenarios through practices, related institutional pressure and related propositions.

The analysis reveals that practices made under extensive pressure and those made under limited pressure but with a strong business case were diffused in the industry so that every firm was employing those practices in order to achieve their Saudisation objectives. However, Saudisation practices made under limited pressure, without a strong business case, or under contradictory pressure were not diffused in the industry. This applies to practices such as subcontracting basic jobs, employing part-timers, targeting new labour segments and suggesting career development choices.

Further analysis was made to investigate the factors determining which firms lead/develop, acquiesce, or defy/manipulate in the industry (CLP). It was found that (OP) factors such as age, larger operations, wider geographical presence, a higher percentage of Saudis in senior management and decentralised decision-making (involving HR autonomy and less engagement from owners) were related to some extent to a firm's leadership position in the institutional field. However, there was no evidence that the demography of senior management (HA) affects either the decisions made about Saudisation practices or the positions of firms. The lack of evidence for this could be partly the result of the small number of cases in the study. A larger-scale study might find otherwise. The investigation of leading firms in the industry therefore validated Propositions 4 and 5. However, Proposition 6 was not validated in the study.

This empirical work is a primary step towards validating the localisation framework in the GCC countries. The case study shows both the possibility of employing the framework and the validity of its core premises. Further cases in Saudi Arabia or other GCC countries and in other industries, together with comparative studies, are needed to confirm the soundness of the localisation framework.

In conclusion, research on localisation has been developing for several years. However, this chapter has suggested a new framework with which to analyse localisation in the GCC, together with an empirical example demonstrating how the framework could be applied. Further work in this direction could examine different GCC states with similar or other industries. Moreover, the framework presents a structured way of conducting studies comparing different GCC countries at many levels.

NOTE

1. The literature covered in this section does not derive exclusively from the DHRN, but they are the main advocates of this new trend in HR studies.

Table 22.4 Saudisation practices and related propositions

Practice	Related institutional pressures	Institutional pressures and status of practice	Related hypothesis
Compensation and benefits	National minimum wage. Saudis do not accept low-level jobs. Saudisation as a national obligation. A compensation and benefits system is the only effective way of attracting Saudis.	Pressure is pushing the industry to pay high salaries to Saudis and to deal with their high turnover. Compensation and benefits are generally employed in the industry with variations in strategies.	**P1**. Extensive institutional pressure leads to similar Saudisation HR practices in the industry.
Training	Training required by HRDF. Leading supermarkets encouraging Saudisation programmes. Training presented as a professional way to achieve Saudisation. Promotion of training by professional associations. Saudis have fewer skills and less experience and discipline.	Pressure encourages the industry to employ training as a strategic investment in Saudis. Training generally employed in the industry with variations in the setting of training in firms (in-house vs outsourced).	
Obtaining HRDF support	Providing financial support.	Support for the practice comes not from the institutional pressure but rather from the strong business case that firms can earn financial support while fulfilling their Saudisation requirement. Obtaining HRDF support is a generally adopted practice because of its clear added value to business.	**P2a**. Limited institutional pressure with a good business case leads to similar Saudisation practices in the industry.
Employment of women	One woman has the same value as two men in the Saudisation calculation. Laws empowering women. Men forbidden from working in women's clothes shops.	The institutional pressures surrounding the employment of women are contradictory. While some actors in the institutional field, such as the Ministry of Labour, advocate the practice, other actors, such as the religious	**P3**. Contradictory institutional pressures lead to decoupling in Saudisation practices in the industry.

Table 22.4 (continued)

Practice	Related institutional pressures	Institutional pressures and status of practice	Related hypothesis
Employment of women	Sex-segregation law and other restrictions. Suspension of Decree no.120 concerning women's clothes shops. Inspections by religious police. Social and political classifications based on views about the employment of women, and sex segregation.	establishment, object to it in most of its forms. Employing women is still a reversely adopted practice with clear variation in the industry.	
Subcontracting	Saudis do not accept low-level jobs.	Limited pressure supports the practice, but there is a possible business case for firms to limit their Saudisation requirements by decreasing the number of non-Saudis they employ. The practice is adopted with some variations in the nature of subcontracted jobs.	**P2b**. Limited institutional pressure with a poor business case leads to decoupling in Saudisation practices in the industry.
Employing part-timers	Saudis do not accept low-level jobs.	Limited pressure supports the practice, and the business case is also limited. The practice is only adopted in a minor way by some firms.	**P2b**. Limited institutional pressure with a poor business case leads to decoupling in Saudisation practices in the industry.
Targeting of new labour segments	A disabled person has the same value as three men in the Saudisation calculation. Non-governmental organisations (NGOs) related to orphans, the disabled and the empowerment of women have established links with the private sector.	Limited pressure supports the practice, and there is a reasonable business case if firms can employ Saudis they can retain. The practice is not widely adopted, although some firms have made unstructured attempts to use it.	**P2b**. Limited institutional pressure with a poor business case leads to decoupling in Saudisation practices in the industry.

Table 22.4 (continued)

Practice	Related institutional pressures	Institutional pressures and status of practice	Related hypothesis
Targeting of new labour segments	Recruiting the disadvantaged ensures their welfare and is seen as virtuous.		
Career choice and development	Saudis do not accept low-level jobs.	Limited pressure supports the practice, with a reasonable business case, as the working environment can be improved through a wider choice of career options. The practice has not been adopted in the industry.	**P2b**. Limited institutional pressure with a poor business case leads to decoupling in Saudisation practices in the industry.
Mass recruitment	Decree no.50, concerning Saudisation. Decree no.50 concerning restricted jobs. NGOs lead mass recruitment events as part of corporate social responsibility (CSR) programmes.	The institutional pressures surrounding mass recruitment support the adoption of the practice but are limited and indirect. Some actors encourage the practice by offering logistical support to firms to recruit Saudis. Mass recruitment is widely adopted in the industry.	**P2a**. Limited institutional pressure with a good business case leads to similar Saudisation practices in the industry.

USEFUL WEBSITES

Ministry of Labour, Saudi Arabia: https://www.mol.gov.sa/.
Ministry of Labour and Social Affairs, Qatar: http://www.molsa.gov.qa/.
Ministry of Labour, United Arab Emirates: https://www.mol.gov.ae.
Ministry of Social Affairs and Labour, Kuwait: http://www.mosal.gov.kw.
Ministry of Labour, Kingdom of Bahrain: http://www.mol.gov.bh/.
Ministry of Manpower, Oman: http://www.manpower.gov.om.
Dutch HR Network http://www.hrm-network.nl/about/mission.

REFERENCES

Alanezi, A. 2012. Workforce localisation policies in Saudi Arabia: the determinants of successful implementation in multinational enterprises. Proceedings of *Management Knowledge and Learning, International Conference 2012, pp.957–968*. http://issbs.si/press/ISBN/978-961-6813-10-5/papers/ML12_201.pdf (accessed on 20 August 2016).

Al-Dosary, A.S. and Rahman, S.M. 2005. Saudisation (localization) – a critical review. *Human Resource Development International*, **8**(4): 495–502.

Al-Humaid, M.I.A. 2003. The factors affecting the process of Saudisation in the private sector in the Kingdom of Saudi Arabia: a case study of Riyadh city. PhD thesis, University of Essex.

Al-Shammari, S. 2009. Saudization and skill formation for employment in the private sector. PhD thesis, University of Stirling.
Al-Taweel, I. 2004. Managers' attitude towards employment localisation in the Saudi private sector. PhD thesis, University of Cardiff.
Al-Thobyany, H. 2007. The university and the labour market in Saudi Arabia: an exploration of structural mismatches in Jeddah City. PhD thesis, University of Essex.
Alzalabani, A.H. 2004. Industrial relations and the labour market in Saudi Arabia. The Conference of International Industrial Relations Associations (IIRA), Seoul, Korea. 23:26.
Boon, C., Paauwe, J., Boselie, P. and Den Hartog, D. 2009. Institutional pressures and HRM: developing institutional fit. *Personnel Review*, **38**(5): 492–508.
Bosbait, M. 2003. The school-to-work transition and youth unemployment in Saudi Arabia: the case of Al-Hasa Province. PhD thesis, University of Durham.
Boxenbaum, E. 2006. Lost in translation: the making of Danish diversity management. *American Behavioral Scientist*, **49**(7): 939–948.
Center for International and Regional Studies 2012. Workforce nationalization in the Gulf Cooperation Council states. Georgetown University School of Foreign Service in Qatar, Occasional Paper No. 9.
Dimaggio, P.J. and Powell, W.W. 1983. The iron cage revisited: institutional isomorphism and collective rationality in organisational fields. *American Sociological Review*, **48**: 147–160.
Edelman, L.B. 1990. Legal environments and organisational governance: the expansion of due process in the American workplace. *American Journal of Sociology*, **95**(6): 1401–1440.
Eisenhardt, K.M. 1988. Agency-theory and institutional-theory explanations: the case of retail sales compensation. *Academy of Management Journal*, **31**(3): 488–511.
Fakeeh, M.S. 2009. Saudization as a solution for unemployment. PhD dissertation, University of Glasgow.
Goodstein, J.D. 1994. Institutional pressures and strategic responsiveness: employer involvement in work family issues. *Academy of Management Journal*, **37**(2): 350–382.
Greenwood, R. (ed.) 2008. *Sage Handbook of Organisational Institutionalism*. Los Angeles, CA and London: Sage.
Hambrick, D.C. and Mason, P.A. 1984. Upper echelons: the organisation as a reflection of its top managers. *Academy of Management Review*, **9**(2): 193–206.
International Monetary Fund 2014. Labor market reforms to boost employment and productivity in the GCC – an update. Annual Meeting of Ministers of Finance and Central Bank Governors.
Mellahi, K. 2007. The effect of regulations on HRM: private sector firms in Saudi Arabia. *International Journal of Human Resource Management*, **18**(1): 85–99.
Mellahi, K. and Al-Hinai, S.M. 2000. Local workers in Gulf co-operation countries: assets or liabilities? *Middle Eastern Studies*, **36**(3): 177–190.
Mellahi, K. and Wood, G.T. 2001. Human resource management in Saudi Arabia. In P.S. Budhwar and Y.A. Debrah (eds). *Human Resource Management in Developing Countries*. London: Routledge, pp. 222–237.
Mellahi, K. and Wood, G. 2002. Desperately seeking stability: the making and remaking of the Saudi Arabian petroleum growth regime. *Competition and Change*, **6**(4): 345–362.
Meyer, J.W. and Rowan, B. 1977. Institutionalized organisations: formal structure as myth and ceremony. *American Journal of Sociology*, **83**(2): 340–363.
Oliver, C. 1991. Strategic responses to institutional processes. *Academy of Management Review*, **16**(1): 145–179.
Paauwe, J. 2004. *HRM and Performance: Achieving Long-Term Viability*. Oxford: Oxford University Press.
Paauwe, J. and Boselie, P. 2003. Challenging strategic HRM and the relevance of the institutional setting. *Human Resource Management Journal*, **13**(3): 56–70.
Saudi–US Relations Information Service 2003. Saudization: development and expectations management, 31 October. http://susris.com/2003/10/31/saudization-development-and-expectations-management/ (accessed 26 July 2016).
Scott, W.R. 1987. The adolescence of institutional theory. *Administrative Science Quarterly*, **32**(4): 493–511.
Scott, W.R. 2008. *Institutions and Organisations: Ideas and Interests*. London: Sage.
Sutton, J.R., Dobbin, F., Meyer, J.W. and Scott, W.R. 1994. The legalization of the workplace. *American Journal of Sociology*, **99**(4): 944–971.
US Department of State 2008. *Labor Force Survey 2008*. UAE Ministry of Economy, Central Department of Statistics. http://www.state.gov/r/pa/ei/bgn/ (accessed 21 May 2009).
Van Gestel, N. and Nyberg, D. 2009. Translating national policy changes into local HRM Practices. *Personnel Review*, **38**: 544–559.
Wright, P.M. and McMahan, G.C. 1999. Theoretical perspectives for strategic human resource management. In R. Schuler and S. Jackson (eds), *Strategic Human Resource Management*. Oxford: Blackwell, pp. 49–72.
Zucker, L.G. 1987. Institutional theories of organisation. *Annual Review of Sociology*, **13**(4): 443–464.

23. Human resource management in the Middle East: state of the field and directions for future research

Kamel Mellahi and Pawan S. Budhwar

As the chapters in this volume demonstrate, there is an emerging, vibrant scholarship in the field of human resource management (HRM) in the Middle East. Research on HRM in the region is burgeoning at a rapid and unprecedented rate. Encouragingly, while old themes continue to dominate the literature, new interesting themes are emerging. The topic of localisation and management of expatriates has been and continues to be of particular interest to scholars and practitioners in GCC (Gulf Cooperation Council) countries (see Waxin and Bateman; Harrison and Haslberger, Chapters 15 and 16 in this volume, respectively). Similarly, the issue of gender remains intensively discussed but largely absent from the majority of empirical research on HRM in the region. The third persistent issue is that of the role of national culture (Namazie and Venegas, Chapter 2 in this volume), and the pervasiveness of distinctive practices such as *wasta* (Ta'Amnha, Sayce and Tregaskis, Chapter 21 this volume; see also Tlaiss and Kauser, 2011; Sidani and Thornberry, 2013; Hutchings and Weir, 2006; Smith et al., 2012). In addition to traditional themes, this volume highlights a number of emerging themes including talent management (Raheem; Al Amri, Glaister and Spicer, Chapters 5 and 17 this volume, respectively; see also Sidani and Al Ariss, 2014; Ali, 2011; Biygautane and Al Yahya, 2014), corporate social responsibility (CSR) and HRM (Jamali and El Dirani, Chapter 19 this volume), HRM in multinational enterprises (MNEs) (AL-Husan and ALHussan, Chapter 18 this volume), performance management (Giangreco and Vakkayil, Chapter 4 this volume), and HR practices and organizational performance (see also Moideenkutty et al., 2011; Suliman and Iles, 2000; Afiouni et al., 2013; Ramdani et al., 2014; Mansour et al., 2014). Below we discuss the current state of research in HRM in the Middle East and highlight the emerging challenges and present directions for future research.

CURRENT STATE OF RESEARCH

Dominance of Country-Specific Research

A notable feature of the HRM field in the Middle East is the persistent focus on country-specific issues and particularities. While this literature provides valuable insights about the practice of HRM within a particular country, the findings are not necessarily comparable across Middle Eastern countries. We observed that country-specific chapters rarely build on and/or cite research on other Middle Eastern countries. The lack of cross-citations reflects the paucity of cross-fertilization of ideas and perspectives between HRM scholars in the region. The fractured nature of HRM literature in the Middle East is partially understandable because of the diverse contexts in which HRM is practised.

As highlighted in this volume (in particular in the introductory chapter), the Middle East is not a homogeneous region, due to varying economic and political systems, significant differences in levels of income and a diversity of social and managerial values. We tried in the book to capture this heterogeneity/plurality in HRM practices by deliberately commissioning a large number of country-specific chapters. We hope the country-specific chapters have captured the idiosyncratic nature of HRM practices in the Middle East. But we also believe that the lack of cross-citations between scholars interested in HRM in the Middle East is a reflection of the low level of interaction between them. Our review of the literature suggests that scholars based in the Middle East rarely collaborate across national boundaries. This is reflected in the absence of cross-comparison studies of HRM practices in the region. This is an area of research that needs serious attention.

Common Denominators

After reading the chapters in the volume and a significant portion of the vast literature on HRM in the Middle East, we have attempted to identify some of the common denominators or similarities in how HRM is studied and practised in the region. We identified a core set of themes where societal and demographic factors have shaped how people are managed in the region. They include youth employment and localization, management of expatriates and gender.

Youth employment and localization – current knowledge and future research agenda

The issue of localization and guest (foreigners with low skills working at lower levels) workers' rights continue to dominate the HRM literature in the Middle East, especially in GCCs countries. The issue of employment of locals, particularly the youth, is of great importance in the Middle East. Indeed, youth employment has always been the centrepiece of national development policies in the Middle East. It is widely believed that youth unemployment is one of the key contributors to the Arab Spring. At the macro-level, public policies towards employment of youth in the Middle East have been dominated by two policies – education and vocational training to facilitate access to the labour market, and incentive schemes (such as apprenticeships) to entice firms to employ young people. At the organizational and individual levels, anecdotal evidence suggests that there are considerable differences between the work values and work-related expectations of previous and new generations. Research on the management of the young generation and its potential implications for HRM policies is sorely needed. In particular, more research is needed to better understand the new generations' attitudes towards work, career expectations, and perceptions of work–life balance. Managers may need to learn new skills to successfully attract, motivate, train and retain young individuals to achieve their organizational goals.

In the GCC countries, youth unemployment has been tackled through comprehensive localization policies. Over the past few decades, scholars have struggled with the meaning, practice and performance of the various localization initiatives. At first glance, the concept is straightforward – it simply means substitution of foreign workers with qualified locals. In practice, however, localization is very complex. For decades, societies in GCC countries have prescribed separate employment roles for locals and lower-skilled guest workers. Traditionally, locals were allocated jobs in the public sector, while vocational and manual work was the domain of lower-skilled guest workers. Although, we have witnessed a shift in social acceptability of lower-skilled jobs in private sector firms, which have led locals to enter the private sector labour market, social stereotypes of lower-skilled jobs in the private sector remain. Also, even though a record number of locals are entering the private sector, they are still concentrated in non-manual jobs that are seen to be suitable for them (Al-Waqfi and Forstenlechner, 2014). Further, locals taking lower-skilled jobs have to contend with the negative stereotype of being perceived as undisciplined and lacking in work ethics, which often results in prejudiced attitudes and discriminatory actions towards them (Al-Waqfi and Forstenlechner, 2010; Al-Waqfi and Forstenlechner, 2012; Budhwar and Mellahi, 2007).

As the chapters in this volume demonstrate, the emphasis of localization research has changed over the years. Scholars have started looking for theoretical explanations for the practice of localization as well as its implications on performance. For example, Nasief (Chapter 22 in this volume) drew on institutional theory to develop a framework for the study of localization in Saudi Arabia. Similarly, Ryan (2016) drew on insights from Adams's (1963) equity theory to study localization in the United Arab Emirates (UAE). This is highly welcomed. In the past, research on localization was dominated by descriptive accounts of the concept and challenges associated with its implementation (cf. Budhwar and Mellahi, 2007). Although this line of research has been very informative, we believe it has reached a point of diminishing returns. We do not expect novel contributions to emerge from this saturated, dead-end research area. Thus, we encourage scholars to focus on how, why and the extent to which localization practices impact organizational and social outcomes. Localization proponents argue that the initiatives not only reduce unemployment and provide locals with a chance to participate in the economic development of their society, but localization is also good for business (see Forstenlechner and Mellahi, 2011). On the other hand, opponents of localization argue that localization initiatives have a negative impact on firms' competitiveness because of the unnecessary costs associated with it. Empirical findings have not been consistent, and therefore the nature of the relationship between localization and firm performance remains uncertain. This is partly because, in our judgement, available empirical studies have lacked the rigour and sophistication needed to establish such a relationship. There is a need for more sophisticated research that considers the multiple factors that influence the various localization strategies on organizational performance. Studies that seek to examine the long-term effects and/or seek to identify the causal processes, pathways and mechanisms that underlie the relationship between localization and performance are highly warranted.

Guest workers and self-initiated expatriates

The literature on guest workers and self-initiated expatriates focuses on two key themes – lower-skilled guest workers' rights and self-initiated expatriates. Although law now protects expatriates' rights, job security and respectable treatment at work and outside work of lower-skilled foreign labour remain contentious issues in GCC countries (AlMazrouei and Pech, 2015; Connell and Burgess, 2013; Ryan, 2016). Qatar winning the rights to host the FIFA World Cup in 2022 and Dubai expecting to be the host of World Expo 2020 have brought guest workers' labour rights in the region into focus. The Western media has recently intensified its reporting on alleged mistreatment of guest workers in the region, especially in Qatar and the UAE. A stronger pressure for change is being created. Over the years, the major challenge to employee rights in the region has been the sponsorship system known as *kafala* (also see Al-Ajmi, Hirekhan, Budhwar, Al-Ajmi and Singh, Chapter 14 in this volume). The system is currently under consideration in a number of GCC countries. We are also seeing a sea change in the legal framework governing employment of foreign labour in the region ranging from tightening the employment of unskilled foreign labour, particularly in Saudi Arabia, to protecting their rights. It would be interesting to see how the emerging legislations are implemented in practice. Will they be evaded and ineffectively implemented as with previous legislations? Or will the glare of the media spotlight, because of the hosting of global events such as the FIFA World Cup, force GCC countries' governments to intervene more strongly this time?

There is a growing research on self-initiated expatriates in the Middle East. This line of research has examined career development (Harrison and Haslberger, Chapter 16 in this volume; Harvey and Groutsis, 2012; Rodriguez and Scurry, 2014; Al Ariss and Özbilgin, 2010; Bozionelos, 2009) and adjustment (Isakovic and Whitman, 2013) of self-initiated expatriates, as well issues related to their identity (Scurry et al., 2013) and gender (Stalker and Mavin, 2011). Surprisingly, there is little research on the interaction between locals and self-initiated expatriates. Research on knowledge transfer from self-initiated expatriates to locals is highly warranted. Self-initiated expatriates are widely regarded as knowledge transfer agents. Knowledge transfer from self-initiated expatriates to locals is believed to be vital to localization success. Scholars may examine self-initiated expatriates ability, willingness and motivation to share knowledge with locals.

Gender and labour market in the Middle East

Literature on HRM and gender has flourished over the past few decades (Karam and Afiouni, 2014; Kargwell, 2008; Kattara, 2005; Kauser and Tlaiss, 2011; Kemp and Madsen, 2014; Marmenout and Lirio, 2014; Mehdizadeh, 2011; Metcalfe, 2006, 2007, 2008; Moghadam, 2003, 2004; Omair, 2008; Tlaiss, 2013, 2015; Tlaiss and Mendelson, 2014; Tlaiss and Kauser, 2010). Interestingly, the literature has moved on from an early preoccupation with religion and cultural values to focus on practical concerns facing women in the workplace. According to Moghadam (2003: 2–3), the vast literature on gender and religion is often misplaced. She argues that the debate on gender issues in the labour market has been often viewed through narrow and very limited and distorted socio-cultural and religious lenses, as she puts it:

> Since the 1980s, the subject of women and gender in the Middle East has been tied to the larger issue of Islamic revival and, particularly, the emergence of fundamentalist or politicized Islamist movements . . . The Islamic revival has generated polemics and debates as well as numerous scholarly works, with critics and advocates holding divergent views . . . [T]he position of women in the Middle East cannot be attributed to the presumed intrinsic properties of Islam.

Despite the extensive debate about gender issues in the labour market, there is remarkably little empirical research on gender differences in leadership styles, attitudes towards women as managers and co-workers, and work–life balance in the Middle East. There is even less research on the occupational roles of female employees in organizations (Farrell, 2008). Although the nature and magnitude of male/female participation in the labour market have changed in recent years, the gender differentials in the labour market have persisted. Also, while there is anecdotal evidence that the male/female wage gap has narrowed in recent years, there remains a substantial gap in our knowledge about the role of women in organizations. We hope future empirical research on gender in the Middle East remedies this gap in our knowledge.

The issue of 'sameness and difference' in understanding women's status within organizations in the Middle East has also emerged as an important issue of debate. So far, the literature is guided by the principle of justice, gender empowerment and removal of prejudices. However, there is little engagement with the strategic value of gender diversity. So far the link between gender diversity and organizational outcomes has been largely overlooked in the Middle Eastern context. While the intrinsic goal of workplace diversity is an important goal, and is of value in itself, we argue that more work on the instrumental value of gender diversity is required. Understanding the effects of gender diversity on the bottom line is even more important in the Middle East than other parts of the world given the expected increase in women's participation in the labour market and the cultural context influencing interactions between male and female employees at the workplace. Equality is important, and there is a strong need to understand the contextual conditions under which there are positive or negative effects of gender diversity on performance. We expect the relationship between gender diversity and performance to vary significantly under different types of environmental conditions and across Middle Eastern countries. The extant literature holds conflicting views on the effects of gender diversity on performance. On the one hand, it is advocated that gender diversity results in higher performance because it brings multiple perspectives to the firm's strategy and facilitates the generation of novel ideas. On the other hand, it is also argued that such demographic heterogeneity may result in a lack of group cohesion and subsequently lower organizational performance. Therefore, we posit that gender segregation, which is common practice in some Middle Eastern countries, is likely to influence the link between gender diversity and organizational outcomes.

FACTORS SHAPING THE FUTURE OF HRM IN THE MIDDLE EAST

A number of trends are shaping the practice of HRM in the region. They include (1) increased presence and influence of MNEs (Mellahi, Demirbag and Riddle, 2011; Forstenlechner and Mellahi, 2011), (2) the ditching of traditional practices by local players with global ambitions, (3) the rapid growth of global business schools to the Middle East, (4) reliance on management consultants and 'gurus', and (5) dominance of Western textbooks and best-sellers (among other trends highlighted in this volume). The increased presence of MNEs through international joint ventures (IJVs) and wholly foreign-owned enterprises has led to a stream of literature on the effectiveness of imported management ideas in the Middle Eastern context (Ramdani et al., 2014). Although the jury is still out on the effectiveness of MNEs' practices in the Middle Eastern context, there is evidence that they are shaping HRM practices in the region as they have done for other regions such as south-east Asia (Thite et al., 2012). However, our knowledge of the extent to which and the manner and speed with which MNEs' practices are diffused locally is very limited. More research is needed, especially research examining local firms' absorptive capacity to identify, absorb and apply MNEs' HRM practices.

Similarly, emerging global players from the Middle East are understandably keen to emulate what they perceive to be efficient and superior global practices used by global firms. In their scramble for global competitiveness they often discard what is commonly perceived as ineffective local practices (Ramdani et al., 2014). It would be interesting for scholars to examine the impact of heavy borrowing by aspiring global players from the Middle East on traditional HRM practices.

In addition to the role of Western MNEs and local players with global aspiration, the increased presence of Western business schools is prompting the adoption of global practices by Middle Eastern firms. The flood of Western universities to the Middle East is changing the landscape of business education and practice in the region. For instance, the Dubai Knowledge Village, which was established in 2003 with a purpose-built education facility, has become a hub for many world-leading business schools. Leading business schools, such as the London Business School with a campus in Dubai and INSEAD with a campus in Abu Dhabi, are no doubt substituting traditional Middle East management practices with standard global practices. Interestingly, and perhaps understandably, we have observed that local business schools have been imitating global business schools as the model for business education in the region.

The fourth agent in the diffusion of Western practices in the region is management consultants and 'gurus'. The latter are at the forefront of the diffusion of global HRM practices pushing for the consumption of imported faddish management practices. The fifth agent is professional business magazines and textbooks. With the increase in the education level of managers in the Middle East, professional magazines, whether in English or translated into Arabic, such as *Harvard Business Review Arabic* (https://hbrarabic.com/), play a crucial role in diffusing the latest global management fads and fashions. Similarly, nearly all HRM textbooks adopted by universities are translated best-sellers. Future research examining the impact of the demand for global best practices by organizations and supply by global management magazines, textbooks, and popular books on HRM practices in the Middle East is highly warranted.

EMERGING THEMES

Several exciting research themes are emerging. Researchers in talent management are paying increasing attention to the role of HRM in attracting and retaining high-performing employees. Also, a growing literature has homed in on the effectiveness of HRM practices, investigating the link between HRM systems and individual practices and organizational outcomes. Below we provide a short outline of these burgeoning areas of research and highlight some of the key themes for future research.

Talent management is one of the key challenges facing firms operating in the Middle East (Sidani and Al Ariss, 2014; Ali, 2011; Biygautane and Al Yahya, 2014 – see Collings and Mellahi, 2009 for a review of talent management research). There is a huge demand–supply gap in talent. There are two key drivers for this. The education system is failing to produce an adequate supply of talent. This is largley due to the lack of relevance and quality of education provided by education institutions which are often considered as the bottleneck of economic development in the region (Heyneman, 1997; Chapman and Miric, 2009). The second driver is the brain drain of local talent through imigration of home-grown talent particularly from North African countries to Europe. Moreover, political instability in several Middle Eastern countries has accelerated the outflux of talent from the region. In addition to the supply side, organizations lack the required managerial skills to attract, retain and obtain the best out of highly talented individuals. Current recruitment, compensation and retention practices are not suitable for the management of high-performing employees, leading to what is called in the region 'brain waste'. Effective talent management requires a change in mindset and an appreciation of the valuable and unique contribution high-performing individuals contribute to their organizations. Overall, talent management is a promising and fertile area of future research.

The relationship between HRM practices and organizational outcomes has been the subject of increased research attention (Moideenkutty et al., 2011; Suliman, and Iles, 2000; Afiouni et al., 2013; Ramdani et al., 2014). Most of the studies have concentrated on HRM systems, such as high performance work practices (HPWP) (Ramdani et al., 2014), with little research focusing on single HR practices such as selection, promotion and compensation. For instance, merit-based compensation systems are widely perceived to have a positive impact on performance but this presumption has not yet been verified empirically. Research on the link between HR practices and the bottom line is long overdue. Scholars and practitioners need to understand how HRM systems and individual HR practices add value. In so doing, research will not only demonstrate the strategic significance of HR practices, but will also contribute to a better understanding of their role in creating and improving organizational performance.

Overall, we believe that the emerging literature in the area of HRM in the Middle East, including the chapters appearing in this book, are not only filling important gaps in our knowledge but are also highlighting important new themes for future research. We hope that the chapters in this book inspire future scholars to take up the challenge of engaging with these themes using the highest methodological standards. Given the immense usefulness of context-specific HRM research, it is high time that researchers test, validate and develop constructs, which are relevant for the Middle East set-up. To some extent, such initiatives have been recently pursued (e.g., Smith et al., 2012), but this needs urgent priority, as it will help to develop context-relevant theory and practice.

USEFUL WEBSITES

The Society for Human Resource Management MEA: http://www.shrm.org/pages/mena.aspx
OLI in the Arab States: http://www.ilo.org/beirut/lang--en/index.htm

REFERENCES

Adams, J.S. 1963. Towards an understanding of inequity. *Journal of Abnormal and Social Psychology*, **67**(5): 422–436.

Afiouni, F., Karam, C.M. and El-Hajj, H. 2013. The HR value proposition model in the Arab Middle East: identifying the contours of an Arab Middle Eastern HR model. *International Journal of Human Resource Management*, **24**(10): 1895–1932.

Al Ariss, A. and Özbilgin, M. 2010. Understanding self-initiated expatriates: career experiences of Lebanese self-initiated expatriates in France. *Thunderbird International Business Review*, **52**(4): 275–285.

Al-Waqfi, M. and Forstenlechner, I. 2010. Stereotyping of citizens in an expatriate-dominated labour market: implications for workforce localisation policy. *Employee Relations*, **32**(4): 364–381.

Al-Waqfi, M.A. and Forstenlechner, I. 2012. Of private sector fear and prejudice: the case of young citizens in an oil-rich Arabian Gulf economy. *Personnel Review*, **41**(5); 609–629.
Al-Waqfi, M.A. and Forstenlechner, I. 2014. Barriers to Emiratization: the role of policy design and institutional environment in determining the effectiveness of Emiratization. *International Journal of Human Resource Management*, **25**(2): 167–189.
Ali, A. 2011. Talent management in the Middle East. In H. Scullion and D.G. Collings (eds), *Global Talent Management*. New York: Routledge, pp. 155–178.
AlMazrouei, H. and Pech, R.J. 2015. Working in the UAE: expatriate management experiences. *Journal of Islamic Accounting and Business Research*, **6**(1): 73–93.
Biygautane, M. and Al Yahya, K.O. 2014. Talent management in the MENA and GCC regions: challenges and opportunities. In A. Al Ariss (ed.), *Global Talent Management: Challenges, Strategies, and Opportunities*. Switzerland: Springer International Publishing, pp. 197–215.
Bozionelos, N. 2009. Expatriation outside the boundaries of the multinational corporation: a study with expatriate nurses in Saudi Arabia. *Human Resource Management*, **48**(1): 111–134.
Budhwar, P. and Mellahi, K. 2007. Introduction: human resource management in the Middle East. *International Journal of Human Resource Management*, **18**(1): 2–10.
Chapman, D.W. and Miric, S.L. 2009. Education quality in the Middle East. *International Review of Education*, **55**(4): 311–344.
Collings, D.G. and Mellahi, K. 2009. Strategic talent management: a review and research agenda. *Human Resource Management Review*, **19**(4): 304–313.
Connell, J. and Burgess, J. 2013. Vulnerable workers in an emerging Middle Eastern economy: what are the implications for HRM? *International Journal of Human Resource Management*, **24**(22): 4166–4184.
Farrell, F. 2008. Voices on Emiratization: the impact of Emirati culture on the workforce participation of national women in the UAE private banking. *Journal of Islamic Law and Culture*, **10**(2): 107–168.
Forstenlechner, I. and Mellahi, K. 2011. Gaining legitimacy through hiring local workforce at a premium: the case of MNEs in the United Arab Emirates. *Journal of World Business*, **46**(4): 455–461.
Harvey, W. and Groutsis, D. 2012. Skilled migrants in the Middle East: definitions, mobility and integration. *International Journal of Business and Globalisation*, **8**(4): 438–453.
Heyneman, S.P. 1997. The quality of education in the Middle East and North Africa (MENA). *International Journal of Educational Development*, **17**(4): 449–466.
Hutchings, K. and Weir, D. 2006. Guanxi and wasta: a comparison. *Thunderbird International Business Review*, **48**(1): 141–156.
Isakovic, A. and Forseth Whitman, M. 2013. Self-initiated expatriate adjustment in the United Arab Emirates: a study of academics. *Journal of Global Mobility*, **1**(2): 161–186.
Jain, H.C., Lawler, J.J. and Morishima, M. 1998. Multinational corporations, human resource management and host-country nationals. *International Journal of Human Resource Management*, **9**(4): 553–566.
Karam, C.M. and Afiouni, F. 2014. Localizing women's experiences in academia: multilevel factors at play in the Arab Middle East and North Africa. *International Journal of Human Resource Management*, **25**(4): 500–538.
Kargwell, S. 2008. Is the glass ceiling kept in place in Sudan? Gendered dilemma of the work–life balance. *Gender in Management: An International Journal*, **23**(3): 209–224.
Kattara, H. 2005. Career challenges for female managers in Egyptian hotels. *International Journal of Contemporary Hospitality Management*, **17**(3): 238–251.
Kauser, S. and Tlaiss, H. 2011. The Arab women manager: participation, barriers, and future prospects. *Journal of International Business and Economy*, **12**(1): 35–56.
Kemp, L.J. and Madsen, S.R. 2014. Oman's labour force: an analysis of gender in management. *Equality, Diversity and Inclusion: An International Journal*, **33**(8): 789–805.
Mansour, N., Gara, E. and Gaha, C. 2014. Getting inside the black box: HR practices and firm performance within the Tunisian financial services industry. *Personnel Review*, **43**(4): 490–514.
Marmenout, K. and Lirio, P. 2014. Local female talent retention in the Gulf: Emirati women bending with the wind. *International Journal of Human Resource Management*, **25**(2): 144–166.
Mehdizadeh, N. 2011. Gender and reconciliation of work and family in Iran. *International Labour Review*, **150**(3–4): 405–417.
Mellahi, K., Demirbag, M. and Riddle, L. 2011. Multinationals in the Middle East: challenges and opportunities. *Journal of World Business*, **46**(4): 406–410.
Metcalfe, B.D. 2006. Exploring cultural dimensions of gender and management in the Middle East. *Thunderbird International Business Review*, **48**(1): 93–107.
Metcalfe, B.D. 2007. Gender and human resource management in the Middle East. *International Journal of Human Resource Management*, **18**(1): 54–74.
Metcalfe, B.D. 2008. Women, management and globalization in the Middle East. *Journal of Business Ethics*, **83**(1): 85–100.

Moghadam, V.M. 2003. *Modernizing Women: Gender and Social Change in the Middle East*. Boulder, CO: Lynne Rienner Publishers.

Moghadam, V.M. 2004. Patriarchy in transition: women and the changing family in the Middle East. *Journal of Comparative Family Studies*, **35**: 137–162.

Moideenkutty, U., Al-Lamki, A. and Sree Rama Murthy, Y. 2011. HRM practices and organizational performance in Oman. *Personnel Review*, **40**(2): 239–251.

Omair, K. 2008. Women in management in the Arab context. *Education, Business and Society: Contemporary Middle Eastern Issues*, **1**(2): 107–123.

Ramdani, B., Mellahi, K., Guermat, C. and Kechad, R. 2014. The efficacy of high performance work practices in the Middle East: evidence from Algerian firms. *International Journal of Human Resource Management*, **25**(2): 252–275.

Rodriguez, J.K. and Scurry, T. 2014. Career capital development of self-initiated expatriates in Qatar: cosmopolitan globetrotters, experts and outsiders. *International Journal of Human Resource Management*, **25**(7): 1046–1067.

Ryan, J.C. (2016). Old knowledge for new impacts: equity theory and workforce nationalization. *Journal of Business Research*, **69**(5): 1587–1592.

Scurry, T., Rodriguez, J.K. and Bailouni, S. 2013. Narratives of identity of self-initiated expatriates in Qatar. *Career Development International*, **18**(1): 12–33.

Sidani, Y. and Al Ariss, A. 2014. Institutional and corporate drivers of global talent management: evidence from the Arab Gulf region. *Journal of World Business*, **49**(2): 215–224.

Sidani, Y.M. and Thornberry, J. 2013. Nepotism in the Arab world: an institutional theory perspective. *Business Ethics Quarterly*, **23**(01), 69–96.

Smith, P.B., Torres, C., Leong, C.-H., Budhwar, P., Achoui, M. and Lebedeva, N. 2012. Are indigenous approaches to achieving influence in business organizations distinctive? A comparative study of Guanxi, Wasta, Jeitinho, Svyazi, and Pulling Strings. *International Journal of Human Resource Management*, **23**(2): 333–348.

Stalker, B. and Mavin, S. 2011. Learning and development experiences of self-initiated expatriate women in the United Arab Emirates. *Human Resource Development International*, **14**(3): 273–290.

Suliman, A. and Iles, P. 2000. Is continuance commitment beneficial to organizations? Commitment–performance relationship: a new look. *Journal of Managerial Psychology*, **15**(5): 407–422.

Thite, M., Wilkinson, A. and Shah, D. 2012. Internationalization and HRM strategies across subsidiaries in multinational corporations from emerging economies – a conceptual framework. *Journal of World Business*, **47**(2): 251–258.

Tlaiss, H. 2013. Women managers in the United Arab Emirates: successful careers or what? *Equality, Diversity and Inclusion: An International Journal*, **32**(8): 756–776.

Tlaiss, H. 2015. Neither-nor: career success of women in an Arab Middle Eastern context. *Employee Relations*, **37**(5): 525–546.

Tlaiss, H. and Kauser, S. 2010. Perceived organizational barriers to women's career advancement in Lebanon. *Gender in Management: An International Journal*, **25**(6): 462–496.

Tlaiss, H. and Kauser, S. 2011. The importance of wasta in the career success of Middle Eastern managers. *Journal of European Industrial Training*, **35**(5): 467–486.

Tlaiss, H.A. and Mendelson, M.B. 2014. Predicting women's job satisfaction with personal demographics: evidence from a Middle Eastern country. *International Journal of Human Resource Management*, **25**(3): 434–458.

Index

NOTE: page references in **bold** indicate authored chapters